Overreach

Overreach

How China Derailed Its Peaceful Rise

Susan L. Shirk

OXFORD
UNIVERSITY PRESS

OXFORD
UNIVERSITY PRESS

Oxford University Press is a department of the University of Oxford. It furthers
the University's objective of excellence in research, scholarship, and education
by publishing worldwide. Oxford is a registered trade mark of Oxford University
Press in the UK and certain other countries.

Published in the United States of America by Oxford University Press
198 Madison Avenue, New York, NY 10016, United States of America.

CIP data is on file at the Library of Congress

ISBN 978–0–19–006851–6

DOI: 10.1093/oso/9780190068516.001.0001

1 3 5 7 9 8 6 4 2

Printed by Sheridan Books, Inc., United States of America

To my Chinese friends and colleagues
who helped me understand their country.

Contents

Acknowledgments

.

I BEGAN THIS BOOK IN 2008 as an investigation into puzzling changes in Chinese foreign policy. I originally planned to update *China: Fragile Superpower*, but *Fragile Superpower* morphed into *Overreach*.

Conversations with my wonderful colleagues in the UC San Diego School of Global Policy and Strategy and the Political Science Department—Stephan Haggard, Weiyi Shi, Barry Naughton, Peter Cowhey, Victor Shih, Tai Ming Cheung, Ruixue Jia, Molly Roberts, Yiqing Yu, Eddy Malesky, and David Lake—helped stimulate my thinking.

I am especially grateful to Lei Guang, the executive director of the UC San Diego 21st Century China Center, whose partnership has been invaluable at every step of the way both with the book and the center's development.

I learned as much from the talented hard-working graduate students who were my research assistants on this book project, Adam Wu, Yin Yuan, Jiying Jiang, Jason Wu, and Yuanhao Liu as they did from me.

The participants in the 21st Century China Center's 2016 conference on the Evolution of Communist Political Institutions contributed greatly to the evolution of my ideas. Alice Lyman Miller was a patient collaborator as we worked together on the PRC's political institutionalization, and Jack Snyder's writings and personal encouragement provided valuable guidance.

Orville Schell has been a great partner as co-chair of the UC San Diego – Asia Society Task Force on US Policy Toward China since 2015. The thoughtful and well-informed debates among the Task Force members have shaped my views on American policy toward China.

Thank you to the individuals and foundations (Carnegie Corporation and Luce) who by generously contributing to the 21st Century China Center have thereby helped me write this book.

The clarity and style of the writing were greatly improved by the time and skill that my Oxford University Press editor Timothy Bent devoted to it. Also at Oxford, Gabriel Kachuck did a great job of publicizing the book, and Erin Cox of marketing it. Ginny Faber was the copy editor and Jayne Rising the indexer. I'm also very grateful to my literary agent Jill Marsal, for her patience, confidence, and wise judgment.

My thanks to Lei Guang, Jack Snyder, Peter Gourevitch, and Barry Naughton for reading the manuscript and providing helpful suggestions for revision. Of course, any mistakes remain my own responsibility.

My husband, Sam Popkin, to whom I have been married for fifty happy years, provided loving encouragement, intellectual questioning, and delicious home-made bread. Fortunately, my children Lucy Shirk Popkin and David Shirk Popkin have always been tolerant and proud of their working mother. They chose wonderful spouses, Seth Demain and Paige Fitzgerald, and gave me the role I love the most, grandmother of Sadie Demain, Henry Demain, and Rowan Popkin.

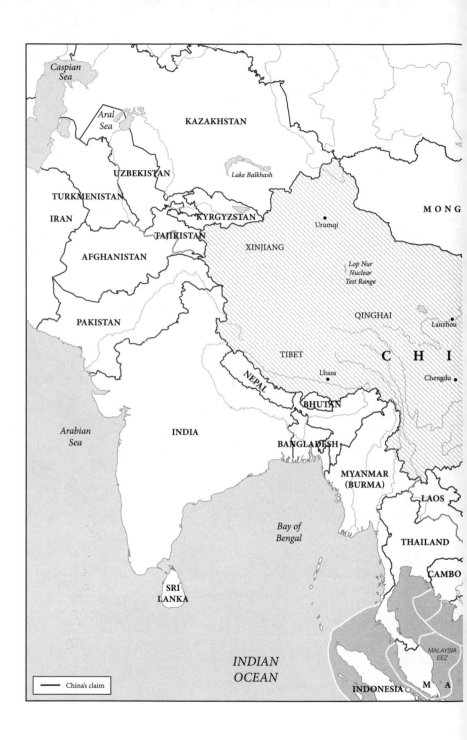

Caspian
Sea

Aral
Sea

KAZAKHSTAN

Lake Balkhash

UZBEKISTAN

TURKMENISTAN

IRAN

KYRGYZSTAN

TAJIKISTAN

XINJIANG

Urumqi

M O N G

AFGHANISTAN

Lop Nur
Nuclear
Test Range

PAKISTAN

QINGHAI

Lanzhou

TIBET

C H I

Lhasa

Chengdu

NEPAL

BHUTAN

Arabian
Sea

INDIA

BANGLADESH

MYANMAR
(BURMA)

LAOS

Bay of
Bengal

THAILAND

CAMBO

SRI
LANKA

MALAYSIA
EEZ

INDIAN
OCEAN

INDONESIA

M   A

China's claim

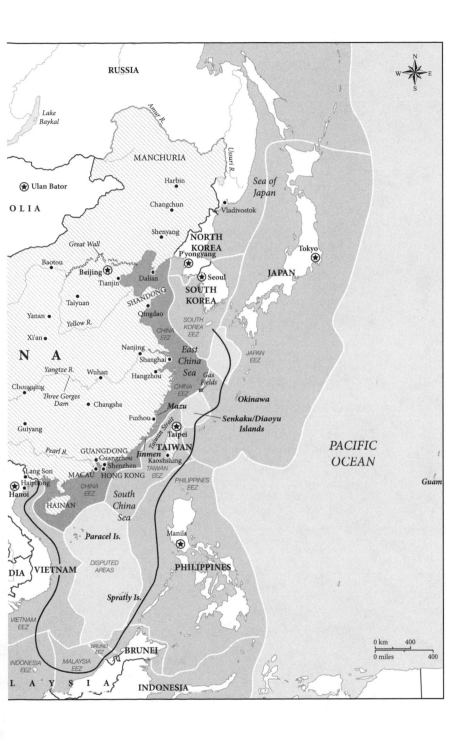

Prologue

How China Lost the West

A NEW COLD WAR HAS already begun. It will be very different from the first cold war, which pitted the United States against the Soviet Union until it dissolved in 1991. In this cold war, the United States faces China, which is both a rival and a partner. With the former Soviet Union, the lines of separation were clear. With China they are not. China and the United States are economically and socially interdependent, more so than the Soviet Union and the United States ever were. Yet the interconnections haven't prevented them from hurtling into hostility. Paradoxically, their interdependence could make the new cold war more dangerous than the old one.

How did things end up in this way? Over the past forty years China and the United States had gotten along remarkably well, despite the vast differences between their political systems and China's rapid rise as an economic and military rival. They wove a dense fabric of trade, investment, technology, education, and personal ties that benefited people in both countries. China's transformation into a manufacturing dynamo with a huge appetite for oil, iron, copper, and other raw materials from Africa, Latin America, Asia, and the Middle East helped narrow the global inequalities between wealthy and developing nations. International production chains based on economic advantage rather than on ideology created an incentive for all countries to get along with one another, creating the foundation for this long era of peace. Scientists and engineers born in China, America, and other countries worked side by side in US research labs, making breakthrough discoveries. Students, tourists, and businesspeople flowed back and forth across the Pacific.

Today China and America have become so fearful of one another that they are weaponizing their interdependence. Not even the common threat of the COVID-19 pandemic in 2020 could convince the two governments to coordinate their efforts. Indeed, the virus revealed just how hostile the relationship had become, particularly compared with how they cooperated to combat health threats such as SARS (2004–5), the swine H1N1 flu (2009–10), and Ebola (2014–16). During the first cold war, the Soviet Union and America overcame their mutual suspicion to lead the global effort to eradicate the scourge of smallpox. But when COVID-19 broke out, Xi Jinping and Donald Trump first underestimated the threat and hid it from the public, and then, to deflect criticism, sacrificed any remaining shred of amity in the relationship by blaming each other for starting the disease and allowing it to spread. US senator Tom Cotton and Trump administration officials claimed that the virus may have originated from a leak in a Wuhan biological warfare laboratory and Trump started calling it the "Chinese virus." Chinese Foreign Ministry spokesperson Zhao Lijian accused US Army athletes who participated in the October 2019 Military World Games of bringing the virus to Wuhan. When the Trump administration refused to lift tariffs on masks, gowns, and other medical protective devices imported from China, relations hit a low point.[1]

Hostilities became even more enflamed when Xi Jinping embraced Russian leader Vladimir Putin in a lengthy statement pledging their "friendship without limit" in February 2022, on the eve of the Beijing Winter Olympics and just weeks before Putin invaded Ukraine. When faced with a stark choice of whether to align China with Russia or the West, Xi acted out of autocratic affinity. Relations with America and Europe may never recover from China's backing of Russia's unprovoked war against the Ukrainian people.

The more that China and America exploit their economic and technological leverage to pressure each other, the more each feels the need to reduce its vulnerability by decoupling their economies and technologies. Washington and Beijing have been punishing the other's companies as proxies for the governments, trading sanctions in a tit-for-tat battle that pummels both economies. Meanwhile, the governments are investing heavily to bring their production chains safely home or move them to a reliably friendly country.

The consequences of decoupling would be costly. The Chinese and American economies constitute a very large share—40 percent—of the world's economy. As the two countries accelerate their drives for economic and technological self-reliance, they are pressing other countries to join their bloc, forcing an either-or choice that most nations wish to avoid. China is now the top trading partner of most of the world's countries, many more than the United States.[2] Decoupling has already begun to disrupt the global economy. Even before the onset of the COVID-19 pandemic, global growth in 2019 was the lowest in a decade.

Detaching the Chinese and American innovation ecosystems could imperil humanity's scientific advances. Many of the discoveries that improve and save lives are the work of teams of scientists and engineers from both countries. American life scientists have more collaborations with China than with any other country.[3] China and the United States are at the center of the global network of coronavirus research; as COVID-19 broke out, they increased their bilateral research partnerships.

The new cold war is being waged in economic, technological, political, and informational spheres, not on the battlefield. China hasn't engaged in outright military aggression since its brief war with Vietnam in 1979. Still, as the relationship between China and the US deteriorates, the risk that an accident or misunderstanding could escalate into a shooting war also grows. China's growing military might undergird its ambitions.

During the first cold war, Berlin, divided by an "iron curtain" between the democratic West and the communist East, was the regional flashpoint, one that had symbolic value to the legitimacy of both sides and where the contest of wills between the two nuclear powers played out. Asia has even more flashpoints, places where Chinese and US forces might find themselves in direct confrontation: the Taiwan Strait, the South China Sea, the East China Sea between China and Japan, and the Korean Peninsula.

First, the Taiwan Strait. An attack by the People's Republic of China (PRC) on Taiwan, the island democracy that the Chinese Communist Party (CCP) has always claimed as part of China, would be viewed by the United States as a "threat to the peace and security" of the region and legally require the president to consult with Congress on its response. China's military has grown stronger, and its government has cut off dialogue with Taiwan. As a result, the possibility of an attack has increased. So has congressional support for Taiwan. The 2021 Congress introduced thirty-eight bills to support Taiwan.[4] The United States has approximately 100,000 soldiers deployed in the Asia Pacific to defend our allies and deter aggression. If the United States didn't defend Taiwan against an unprovoked attack, American credibility and its support for democracy would be seriously damaged.

The South China Sea has also turned into a potential flashpoint between the two powers. Since 2006, China has been using force to press its expansive claims over the South China Sea and the tiny Spratly and Paracel Islands within it. These claims are contested by Vietnam, the Philippines, Malaysia, and Brunei. Taiwan makes the same claims as China. China accelerated its effort to establish its control over the area when it built more than 3,000 acres of artificial islands on seven reefs and islets during 2014 and 2015. At a summit meeting in 2015, Xi publicly assured President Obama that China had no intention of militarizing the artificial islands, but the People's Liberation Army continued to build up installations on the outposts nevertheless. At the same time, China expanded its so-called grey zone harassment of other claimants by the coast guard and fishing boat militia. An international law tribunal rejected China's historic claims over almost the entire Sea in 2016 in a ruling that China ignores and flouts; meanwhile the navies of the United States and other countries, treating the Sea as international waters, conduct military exercises and transits through them. Tanker traffic through the South China Sea, most of it transporting oil and gas from the Middle East to Northeast Asia, constitutes more than half the global transport of these vital resources. A collision or altercation in the Sea could escalate into a naval battle that draws in the United States.

In the East China Sea, antagonism between China and Japan could embroil the United States in a clash. China and Japan both claim five tiny uninhabited islands and three rocks—called Senkaku in Japan and Diaoyu in China—that are located between the two countries in an area with undersea oil and gas reserves. The waters surrounding the islands have become crowded with coast guard patrol vessels and fishing boats from both sides. China has sent its aircraft carrier and other navy ships into the Western Pacific through the East China Sea, and Chinese Air Force jets increasingly scramble over it. Although Washington doesn't officially take sides on the territorial claim, it has committed to come to Japan's defense if the islands are attacked by China.[5] Should Chinese and Japanese politicians, pushed by public opinion, allow the next maritime incident to spin out of control, US naval vessels could be ordered in.

Finally, China's unpredictable neighbor and ally North Korea could force it into a war with the United States. Decades-long negotiations and international sanctions have failed to convince the North Korean regime to abandon its nuclear weapons program, and it has accelerated its missile testing program to the point where it will soon be able to reach the continental United States with an intercontinental ballistic missile. If North Korea collapses or the United States attacks a North Korean missile launch pad or its nuclear facilities in order to pre-empt an attack on Japan, South

Korea, or the United States itself, China and the United States could find themselves fighting in a second Korean War.

When histories of this new cold war are written, some may ignore China's actions and argue that it was started by Donald Trump. Trump campaigned for president on the claim that China was robbing America by selling more products to the US than it was buying. When I joined a few China experts to meet with Trump campaign aide Steve Bannon in 2017, he took credit for getting Trump to blame China for the loss of manufacturing jobs in states like Wisconsin, Ohio, and Pennsylvania, sealing Trump's victory in these swing states. After he took office, Trump sought to deliver on his campaign promise to eliminate America's trade deficit with China by imposing unilateral tariffs on imports from China. He ignored the fact that the tariffs hurt American firms manufacturing in China because he wanted them to bring their factories back home; the tariffs also raised costs for businesses and consumers based in the US.

Other officials in the Trump administration knew that bilateral trade deficits have little real consequence and that American firms are more likely to move their plants to Vietnam, Mexico, or Bangladesh than to Ohio. But their national security concerns made them embrace Trump's tough approach. While Trump was fixating on the bilateral trade deficit and tariffs, his administration declared China the country's greatest national security threat and mobilized a government-wide campaign to counter it. Strategic competition with China and Russia was the keystone of the Trump administration's foreign policy. For the first time, the American National Security Strategy openly called out China as a "revisionist power," meaning a country that seeks to undermine the existing international order and eventually supplant the United States as the leading world power.[6] In a speech he gave in October 2018, Trump's vice president, Mike Pence, used the most hostile language toward Beijing of any American leader since President Nixon's historic state visit in 1972. Pence framed his speech as a wake-up call to the American people — a full-throated declaration of a global contest of values with a China that persecutes its own people and subverts the global order.[7]

The mobilization against China extended beyond the Trump administration. A bipartisan American consensus has formed around the idea that China is an adversary determined to supplant United States leadership and harm democracies. President Biden is reinforcing this consensus by declaring that Xi firmly believes that within a decade or so China "is going to own America because autocracies can make quick decisions." Biden has been framing much of his domestic as well as his foreign policy agenda as a "battle between democracies and autocracies."[8] In Congress, practically the only thing Democrats and Republicans can agree on is legislation to condemn China's actions and restrict its access to American technology. Democratic senator Mark Warner and Republican senator Marco Rubio—ideological antagonists—teamed up to convene sessions for counterespionage briefing teams from the FBI and other intelligence and law-enforcement agencies, their purpose being to warn universities, businesses, and state and local governments about the Chinese spies and agents operating in their midst.[9] The National Institutes of Health, which provides the lion's share (46 percent) of all federal science funding, caused the firing of a number of Chinese American scientists when it sent letters to their universities warning about individual scientists who hadn't disclosed their research activities in China.[10] The Department of Energy and the National Science Foundation have also forbidden their grantees from participating in the PRC's Thousand Talents program, which recruits overseas scientists and engineers to train Chinese students and undertake China-based research.[11] Chinese graduate students and visiting scholars in robotics, aviation, and advanced manufacturing now are only granted one-year visas. And the Commerce Department has prepared new export controls that restrict Chinese students from doing research in university and corporate laboratories that are working on emerging technologies.

As this extensive campaign by the FBI, Justice Department, Department of Homeland Security, and other government agencies to track down and limit the access of Chinese researchers spread through American universities and research labs, ethnic Chinese scientists and engineers— American, as well as Chinese or Taiwanese—came under a cloud of suspicion. Chinese Americans feel that they are being targeted by a version of the Red Scare that swept the country during the 1950s. Blaming China for COVID-19 further inflamed public anger toward China, causing a rise in violent hate crimes against anyone who looks Asian. Many have become afraid to go out to public places for fear of being attacked. Chinese students are thinking twice about applying to American universities. As a result, the United States may be losing one of its greatest competitive advantages—namely, its ability to attract and retain scientific and technological talent from China and around the world.

The American government argues that China's rapid advances in such emerging dual-use technologies as artificial intelligence, digital communications, robotics, quantum computing, and biotechnology pose a grave threat to American national security. When I briefed a group of US admirals the subject they most wanted to discuss was "Made in China

2025," Xi Jinping's ambitious plan to seize command of the high-tech commanding heights. The most senior admiral in the room argued for technological containment of China: "We have to slow down their rise."

In the past, whenever the Pentagon and the other security agencies sought to limit technology transfer to China, business groups lobbied for unrestricted commerce, and the White House struck a happy medium. Today, the business community is no longer standing up for engagement with China. Companies are fed up with Chinese regulatory shakedowns and pressures to transfer technology as the price of gaining access to China's huge market. This bargain has become less and less appealing as China's leaders have been open about their game plan to build up their own national champions to replace foreign firms. It is the rare American business executive who dares to speak out about any unfair treatment for fear of retaliation. Most of them, however, are ready to go along with a tougher US government approach.

Without corporate support to provide the ballast, the security and defense agencies' perspective dominates America's response. Senator Mark Warner has stated his belief that "the Chinese government's effort to outmaneuver the United States technologically [is] one of the most alarming threats we face."[12] He is not alone. When President Trump equivocated on a proposal to ban sales of American technology to Huawei, China's leading telecom firm, which is in the vanguard with 5G digital infrastructure, Democrats and Republicans in the Senate and the House of Representatives introduced a bill that would tie Trump's hands and prevent him from making any deal that included concessions to Huawei. George Soros, a human rights philanthropist and one of the largest donors to Democratic Party candidates, called the Trump administration's tough China policy its greatest foreign policy achievement. Soros also favors restricting American investments in China.

Until recently, the American public was more sanguine than the politicians about our relations with a rising China. Year after year, public-opinion polls showed that roughly half of all Americans had a favorable attitude toward China and saw China as equally a rival and a partner.[13] Pew surveys showed that American views on China turned somewhat more negative after 2013 but improved again in 2017 and 2018.[14] But in 2019, all the major opinion surveys showed a sharp increase in negative views. By 2020, according to Pew, two-thirds of Americans were unfavorable to China, a historic high and a big increase from two years before (47 percent in 2018).[15] As of 2022, 82 percent of Americans are unfavorable toward China.[16] The coronavirus pandemic that originated in Wuhan and spread internationally during an information cover-up by Chinese government officials further damaged the country's image in the eyes of Americans.[17] The gap between public and elite opinion is therefore closing. Both are turning more hostile toward China.[18]

Americans' perspective may be colored by worries about a loss of dominance, but other countries also are growing more suspicious of China, suggesting that its own actions are the source of the problem. A broad international backlash is snowballing. Many European Union countries are increasing scrutiny of Chinese investments to restrict access to European technology. They also are banning Huawei's 5G networks mainly because they don't trust the Chinese government not to interfere. European public opinion is becoming more unfavorable toward China, with countries in Western and Northern Europe, such as Sweden, Germany, France, and the United Kingdom being the most critical;[19] their positive views declined precipitously after 2018.[20] European attitudes toward China now are hardening even more because of China's failure to distance itself from the Russian invasion of Ukraine.

Europeans are particularly critical of China's human rights violations. In an unprecedented move, the European Union joined Canada and the United States in March 2021 to impose sanctions on four Chinese officials and one organization responsible for abuses against Uighur Muslims in Xinjiang, their placement in what are being called "re-education" camps. After Beijing imposed retaliatory sanctions that extended to European think tanks and scholars, the European Parliament killed the comprehensive trade and investment agreement that it had recently concluded with China.

Even in developing countries, where China has made large loans to fund the building of dams, ports, railroads, and other infrastructure projects — many of them part of Xi Jinping's signature Belt and Road Initiative — politicians and citizens are debating whether the benefits of these projects outweigh the risks of dependency on China. Public opinion in Africa, where China has concentrated its investments, is the most positive in the world, though there has been a moderate decline in some countries.[21] In Latin America, sizable minorities in Brazil, Mexico, and Argentina have unfavorable views of China.[22] In every country that holds elections, ties with China have become politically controversial. Challengers go after incumbents for cozying up to China.

China's Asian neighbors have experienced the sharpest decline in friendly feelings toward it, expressing the greatest worries about military aggression from China.[23] Pew found that opinion in the Asian countries had fallen to historic lows. In South Korea, positive views fell 42 percent in 2022 compared with 2015.[24] A survey of Southeast Asian elites found that they considered China the least trustworthy country in the region when compared to Japan, the European Union, the United States, and India.[25] The percentage of elite respondents having little or no confidence in China to "do the right thing" when it comes to contributing to global peace, security, prosperity, and governance rose from 51.5 percent in 2019 to 63 percent in 2021.[26] Elite distrust is particularly (and understandably) high among countries with sovereignty disputes with China—82.1 percent in the Philippines and 75.4 percent in Vietnam. As an analyst looking at Pew results put it, almost half of all surveyed elites view China as "a revisionist power with an intent to turn Southeast Asia into its sphere of influence."[27] Australians' views also have turned much colder. When asked by the Lowy Institute whether China could be trusted to act responsibly in the world, only 23 percent of Australians polled in 2020 said it could, less than half the 52 percent who said it could in 2018.[28] Eighty-one percent of Australians now see China negatively.[29]

This is more than a popularity contest. Chinese leaders since Mao have boosted their domestic standing by touting on their billboards, "We have friends all over the world." Xi Jinping clearly relishes playing host to leaders of developing countries at lavish extravaganzas showcasing the Belt and Road Initiative, China-Africa friendship, and other diplomatic occasions. One Chinese scholar observed that Xi stands in the center of the group photographs at Belt and Road summits, whereas the American president never stands in the center at meetings of APEC (the Asia Pacific Economic Cooperation), an organization founded by the United States.

The growing global perception is that friendship with China is no longer unconditional. Beijing rewards countries that endorse its stance on sensitive domestic issues, such as Taiwan, Xinjiang, Tibet, and Hong Kong, by providing them with access to its huge market and generous investments; and it punishes countries who don't by withholding its economic favors. Malaysian prime minister Mahathir Mohamad explained in an interview in 2019 why Beijing was able to persuade thirty-seven countries, half of them Muslim, including his own, to defend China's camps in Xinjiang at the United Nations. "You don't just try and do something which would anyway fail," as he put it, "so it is better to find some other less violent ways not to antagonize China too much, because China is beneficial for us."[30]

Some domestic international relations experts acknowledge that China lacks genuine friends or allies even among its neighbors, and that despite its being the most important economic partner of every Asian country, these countries increasingly fear China.[31]

Much as American politicians and officials in the past have periodically recriminated one another for mishandling relations with China, Chinese policy elites are asking themselves, How did China lose the West? and casting about for whom to blame. Privately, many Chinese experts blame Xi Jinping for provoking the animosity toward China. Obviously, they don't do it to the degree that foreign critics do, some of whom vilify Xi as an evil dictator bent on destroying universal values and global order. Nonetheless President Trump had fans in China who welcomed his pressure as a check on Xi's imprudent policies.

The CCP, however, has a simple explanation for why the West has turned against China—it's the inevitable outcome of the shifting balance of power, they argue, and was bound to occur as soon as the power gap between China and the US narrowed. Some claim that America always turns against a country once it reaches 60 percent of US GDP, as the Soviet Union did during the Cold War and Japan did in the 1980s.[32] Now it's China's turn. As China's economic, technological, and military power grows, America protects its superpower status by going all out to impede it. This mechanistic view resembles the ideas of realist international relations scholars, who argue that the rise and fall of nations always causes the reigning power to exaggerate the threat, a misperception that can lead to war between it and the rising power. This pattern has been called the Thucydides Trap, named for the Greek historian who chronicled Sparta's overreaction to Athens' rise, which led to the Peloponnesian War.[33] For decades, Chinese leaders have recognized the risk that other countries will view their country as a threat just because of its rapid rise. In a 2015 speech in Seattle, Xi Jinping argued that there was "no such thing as the so-called Thucydides trap in the world." But he went on to say that "should major countries time and again make the mistakes of strategic miscalculation, they might create such traps for themselves."[34]

According to China's official media, the escalating tensions between the two countries are entirely due to America's containment policy, which is itself a strategic miscalculation. Official commentaries in *People's Daily*, the most authoritative source for government policy, refute "erroneous views and pessimistic arguments" being circulated that say that China provoked the United States by taking high-profile postures. "No matter what China does, China's development endangers American primacy" and leads America to re-emphasize its policy of containment, the newspaper asserts.[35] "The trade war has become a way to mobilize society for containment of China," explains the influential Chinese nationalist tabloid *Global Times*.[36]

Some commentators in other countries share the Chinese view that the American backlash is an inside-the-Beltway phenomenon caused by Americans' anxieties about their decline, and completely unrelated to any actions on China's part. But ignoring the role of China's own behavior makes the explanation of US-China enmity incomplete.

I would argue that China's leaders have brought the backlash on themselves, and they have done it, as this book will show, by overreaching. "Overreach" means "to defeat oneself by seeking to do or gain too much," or according to another definition, "going to excess in a way that is costly to oneself." After decades of restraint, the Chinese government started confronting other countries and tightening controls over domestic social and economic life. Then the policy choices of China's leadership boomeranged, provoking a defensive counterreaction from other countries by harming and alarming them.

Conventional wisdom traces the break-down in US-China relations to Xi and Trump, both disruptive leaders who grabbed more power (or attempted to) than did previous leaders. This is shortsighted. Signs of China's overreach could be seen a decade earlier, in the mid-2000s, under Xi's predecessor, Hu Jintao (2002–2012). And though there may be many reasons for China's new assertiveness—including the global financial crisis and the perceived narrowing of the relative power gap between China and the United States—it is puzzling that it started under Hu, a colorless, mild-mannered leader, who was only first among equals in the collective leadership of the CCP. To understand this paradox, we must look into what I call the "black box" of high-level Chinese politics.

We'll find that ever since Mao's time, the CCP has swung between two patterns of rule: personalistic dictatorship and collective leadership. After Mao Zedong died in 1976, Deng Xiaoping established what we thought were permanent institutions of collective leadership that reached their apex under Hu Jintao. But then in 2012, Chinese politics made a U-turn, as Xi Jinping turned back to personalistic dictatorship. The institutional limits on the power of the leader turned out to be weaker than anyone had thought.

We'll also discover that surprisingly, collective leadership as well as personalistic dictatorship can lead to overreach, even though the dynamic that causes it is very different when authority is shared by a group of leaders than when it is concentrated in the hands of one leader. Theoretically, when officials make decisions by consensus in a collective leadership, their ability to check one another should produce restraint, or even inertia, not overreach. Yet collective leadership didn't operate that way under Hu. Instead, the Party oligarchs in the Politburo and its Standing Committee sought bigger budgets and influence for the interest groups they represented by exaggerating the foreign and domestic threats confronting the country; and they swapped favors among themselves by backing one another's programs. This dynamic drove foreign policies to become more truculent and domestic policies to become more autocratic.

When Hu retired, in 2012, Xi Jinping rapidly reversed the collective model, consolidating more power than any leader since Mao. He capitalized on the shortcomings of oligarchic rule under Hu, shortcomings that were obvious to both political elites and the public. The most conspicuous failure of the Hu era was widespread corruption. High-ranking politicians and military officers raked in huge amounts of money under the system of dispersed power. The public therefore welcomed Xi's determination to end the dishonest dealings of high-level politicians, the "tigers," as well as of petty officials, the "flies."

Divisions among Party leaders also emerged despite the efforts to prevent them. As we will see, a rivalry between Chongqing Party secretary Bo Xilai and Xi broke into the open on the eve of Xi's ascension to power. The open split dramatized the centrifugal forces that had taken hold under collective leadership and made the case for a stronger leader to enforce Party unity. During Xi's first term, he imprisoned six other senior politicians for plotting to seize power, motivated by what he described as "burning personal ambition," and punished more than a million-and-a-half officials for corruption.

Since taking power in 2012, Xi has centralized power by creating an ambitious, integrated program that combines much of what each bureaucratic interest group wants and also plays well to the nationalist public. Building on the fables about domestic and foreign threats that the interest groups spun during the Hu era, Xi's one-man rule is taking China even further in the direction of overreach. He believes his own myths. No one dares question him or give him bad news. Other politicians, officials, mass media editors, and corporate executives "bandwagon" behind Xi's line, competing with one another to gain his favor and protect themselves from his wrath. When they carry out his policies, they "overcomply," going to extremes to stand out as the most loyal. The result is foreign and domestic policy hubris.

Now nearly a decade into his administration, Xi's personalistic dictatorship looks to be much less interested in restraining overreach than

Hu's collective leadership ever was. Instead of modeling his diplomacy on the prudent approach used, for example, by German chancellor Otto von Bismarck in the late nineteenth century to head off a coalition of European countries that resisted Germany's rise, Xi is acting more like Emperor Wilhelm II, who took over after Bismarck and whose military buildup and expansion frightened Germany's neighbors.[37] By exercising its growing economic and military power to coerce other countries, China has harmed its reputation as a responsible power and is triggering a negative international reaction. In short, China's political system itself—both in its collective leadership and personalistic leadership forms—impedes the exercise of self-restraint necessary for a peaceful rise.

China's actions have aroused a bipartisan political consensus in America that China is its greatest threat and must be confronted on every continent and in every domain—from economic policy and technology to human rights and foreign policy. Some of the US responses are, however, overreactions to overreach, and could hinder America's ability to compete successfully with China. America's open society and economy have always been its greatest assets. It risks losing them if it engages in a race to the bottom with an autocratic China.

There has never been a more important time to open that black box of Chinese politics—to discover what is driving these troubling changes in China's behavior both at home and on the world stage and to figure out what Americans, Chinese, and people in other countries can do about them. Is there a way of bringing this new cold war to an end? And to begin to answer that question we need to look for the origins of the overreach.

1

The Origins of Overreach

OVERREACH BEGAN ON THREE fronts: The economy, social control, and foreign policy. Beginning in 2006, the government launched new industrial policies that would ultimately grow into a lavishly funded state-directed policy to build China into a high-tech superpower. From the beginning, lessening dependence on foreigners was a central, stated objective of the policies.[1] Second, on the eve of the 2008 Beijing Olympics, the Chinese Communist Party ramped up its control over the media, Internet, and society, and to this day, it has not relented. And third, China started to act more belligerently in world affairs. Strikingly, all three major shifts in foreign and domestic policy started at roughly the same time, under Hu Jintao. Up to that point, China's strategy to develop its economy and rise peacefully had been a historic success. Then, between 2006 and 2009, it started overreaching.

Much of it began with events that unfolded before the 2008 Beijing Olympics, an event that inspired great national pride and should have been the high point of China's peaceful rise. But violent protests by Tibetans against religious repression in the Tibet Autonomous Region and the Tibetan areas of other Western provinces broke out and embarrassed the central government. Demonstrators supporting Tibetan autonomy also heckled and roughed up Chinese Olympic torchbearers in foreign cities. Infuriated, Party leaders rallied the public and stirred up a surge of popular nationalism against the Dalai Lama and the Western media that had reported sympathetically on the protests.

The Tibet issue, which previously had not received much attention from the Chinese media or the public, suddenly emerged as a priority in Chinese foreign policy and diplomacy. The government injected Tibet into every encounter with its Western counterparts; canceled important meetings, such as the China–European Union summit, after President Sarkozy of France said he planned to meet with the Dalai Lama; and started to include Tibet in its category of "core interests," meaning an interest so crucial to the nation that it would use force to defend it. The category of core interests previously had been limited to Taiwan, referring to the imperative to keep the island from declaring its formal independence.

In March 2009, less than a year after the Olympics, violent conflict with the Muslim Uighurs in the Xinjiang region produced a similarly strong reaction from the government, including a further redefinition of its "core interests," to now include Xinjiang. Instead of re-evaluating the effectiveness of their own policies toward ethnic minorities, Party leaders blamed foreign interference for the unrest, creating a "we-they" nationalist narrative to bolster their popularity with the Han Chinese majority.

But perhaps the most alarming change in China's redefinition of its "core interests" was its forcibly enforcing its ownership of the waters and small islands in the South China Sea—as noted, one of the most heavily trafficked maritime transport waters in the world.[2] Beginning in 2006, having formally declared to the United Nations its claim to almost the entire South China Sea as delineated by the so-called nine-dash line inherited from pre-communist China in the 1940s, Beijing started to use law-enforcement ships for sovereignty "rights protection" (*weiquan*) in disputed waters, including by shouldering and ramming Vietnamese and Philippines ships. It also formally withdrew from the dispute-resolution procedures in the UN Convention on the Law of the Sea.[3]

The South China Sea *weiquan* transformed the international narrative about what kind of rising power China was—a responsible power or an aggressive risk-taker, the latter starting to predominate. All the claimants, not just China, had ramped up their maritime activities as advanced technologies for extracting undersea oil and gas opened new possibilities for energy prospecting and depleted fish stocks forced fishermen further offshore. But only China, openly and without apology, was using large fleets of fishing boats and maritime law-enforcement vessels to press its claims, intruding into waters that according to the United Nations Convention on the Law of the Sea (UNCLOS) legally belonged to Vietnam and the Philippines. Maritime standoffs between the countries' fleets became more frequent and difficult to de-escalate.

Chinese ships even dared to confront the American navy. In March 2009, two Chinese fishing trawlers, a fishery patrol ship, and a State Oceanographic Administration patrol ship (with a Chinese navy ship nearby) harassed the USNS *Impeccable*, an American surveillance ship that was collecting underwater intelligence on Chinese submarines and the contours of the ocean floor 75 miles off Hainan Island. The Chinese vessels used poles to try to snag the acoustic array sonars the ship was towing as they dangled underneath. Chinese fishing boats attempted the same maneuver against another American surveillance ship a few months later, in May 2009. The Americans believe that collecting military-related undersea information is within their rights in the "international waters" that begin 12 nautical miles off the Chinese coast. But the Chinese government asserts its right to exclude foreign military activities from the maritime and air space for up to 200 nautical miles offshore (their exclusive economic zone under UNCLOS).

The Hu government gave an unexpectedly cold reception to the newly elected president Barack Obama when he visited the PRC for the first time in November 2009. Instead of trying to charm him through gracious Chinese hospitality, the government sought to limit the publicity about his visit. It refused to allow his speech to Shanghai college students to be televised nationally, though it had broadcast the speeches of Presidents Clinton and Bush. According to the American diplomats who negotiated the matter, the Chinese officials were afraid that Obama's rhetoric might stir up the public. They believed that Obama's speech to students at Cairo University on June 4, 2009, had mobilized the Egyptians to revolt against their government. Photographic images of President Obama walking alone on the Great Wall, with no Chinese official at his side, and Hu and Obama's short, stiff press conference made clear that the Chinese hosts had decided to emphasize China's differences instead of affinities with the United States.

Chinese testiness toward the new administration was evident at the December 2009 United Nations Climate Change Conference in Copenhagen as Chinese officials critiqued the United States in public; and Chinese security guards attempted to physically block Obama as he tried to join a meeting in which Chinese premier Wen Jiabao was participating. The incident shocked international observers.

From 2009 onward, three decades of restrained and effective diplomacy were left behind. China's efforts to cultivate friendship with South Korea went down the drain when Beijing refused to condemn acts of North Korean aggression against South Korea. In March 2010, the *Cheonan*, a South Korean corvette, was sunk, and forty-six sailors lost their lives. China declined to send a team to Seoul to review the findings of an international investigation that had concluded a North Korean torpedo was responsible. And it didn't censure the North Korean attack. Months later, the Chinese again refused to condemn an unprovoked artillery attack by North Korea on Yeonpyeong Island that killed two civilians and two South Korean marines. China's only criticism was of the United States–Republic of Korea (ROK) joint exercises, which involved an American aircraft carrier, held shortly after the artillery attack in the waters between the Korean Peninsula and China.

China's loss of restraint was on display at the 2010 Association of Southeast Asian Nations (ASEAN) Regional Forum meeting in Hanoi. Chinese foreign minister Yang Jiechi lost his diplomatic cool and angrily insulted the twelve Southeast Asian countries that had spoken in favor of taking a collective approach to managing the conflicting territorial and maritime claims in the South China Sea. Staring down the Singaporean foreign minister, Yang said, "China is a big country and other countries are small countries, and that's just a fact." He scolded secretary of state Hillary Clinton for conniving with the Asian countries against China on the issue.[4]

In 2012, before Xi Jinping took power, the Chinese government established a prefectural administration based in the city of Sansha on Woody Island (Yongxing Island). It is charged to rule over the 130 tiny islands and waters of the Paracel Islands in the northern half of the South China Sea, which are also claimed by Vietnam. The People's Liberation Army (PLA) announced its intention to garrison a military unit there. The Chinese military also started planning to build out the rocks it controlled in the Spratly Islands in the southern half of the sea into large artificial islands with runways, hangars, and other military installations, but then put the plans on the shelf, according to PLA officers. In 2014, under Xi Jinping, the government carried out the plans. Other South China Sea claimants had previously reclaimed land and constructed installations, but the Chinese effort was unprecedented in its speed and scale. China laid thousands of tons of concrete to create completely new islands on reefs that had only been above water at low tide. In contrast to its earlier efforts to reassure Southeast Asians of its desire to cooperate to manage tensions in the South China Sea, Beijing resorted to bullying tactics. Its assertive defense of its maritime and territorial sovereignty heightened perceptions of a China threat.

Loss of Restraint

A number of foreign experts had always predicted that once China was no longer a poor, developing country it would start flexing its muscles to

push the United States out of Asia and restore China's traditional dominance of the region.[5] But there also was a domestic dynamic in Hu's rule
launching the country into its more aggressive trajectory: the dispersed
power in the top echelons of the Chinese Communist Party (CCP)
spurred the bureaucracies under them to hype threats and overdo their
actions—ostensibly to defend China, but additionally to boost their own
power and funding. Hu recognized the need for better coordination—
he called for "coordinated planning of the domestic and international
overall situations" in a major foreign affairs speech in 2006—but he never
achieved it.[6]

Two years after Hu's speech, the collective leadership lost all remaining ability to restrain itself when it was jolted by the external shock
of the global financial crisis. The crisis degraded respect for the United
States among many Chinese. The global consensus concluded that the
poor regulation of American financial institutions was responsible for
the crisis. The Western open economies also suffered the most from it;
the impact on China was milder because of its relatively closed financial
system. The Chinese system further won new respect because it recovered from the crisis first; its central government decisively commanded
its banks and local governments to inject a massive stimulus—over $4 tril-
lion of investment—into the economy. Chinese proponents of domestic
economic and political reforms had always held up American practices
as their ideal. As Western market democracies lost their luster and people
gained a new appreciation for the Chinese model of a hybrid economy
heavily controlled by the state, it became harder for Chinese liberal
reformers to make the case for emulating Western market capitalism and
continuing to accommodate the US.

It is not surprising that the 2008 financial crisis stimulated the demand
by Chinese officials and the public alike for a more ambitious foreign
policy. The Chinese government had for years calculated a measure it
calls "comprehensive national power" for ranking itself in comparison to
other countries. After the crisis, the leadership believed that because the
country's power relative to the US had dramatically increased, it could
seize new opportunities for international influence.[7] According to public
opinion surveys, ordinary people also started to view the United States as a
superpower in decline; and China as a rising power that was well on its way
to supplanting America, a perception that has grown stronger since then.
In one poll, the proportion of Chinese who viewed their country as the
world's leading economic power jumped from 21 percent in 2008 to 41 percent in 2009.[8] This belief that China's time had arrived inspired both its

political elites and the public, to demand their government stop deferring to the United States and claim greater leadership for itself.

Strategic Prudence

Until 2008, the Chinese acted toward other countries in a mostly restrained and accommodating manner even as China's economy grew at double-digit rates and its military was turned into a modern fighting force. China and the United States managed to get along remarkably well despite the differences in their political systems. After China opened its markets to join the World Trade Organization in 2001, it became the largest trading partner of all its Asian neighbors, who came to view the country as more of an economic opportunity than a threat. Foreign investment flowed to China as it became the manufacturing factory of the world and the hub of regional supply chains. American corporations enthusiastically endorsed Washington's friendly engagement with Beijing. Ties between the two societies flourished.

International relations scholars have found that although it is not an ironclad guarantee of peace, economic interdependence generally motivates countries to pursue cooperation and avoid conflict (particularly with their trading partners). Chinese foreign policy looked like a textbook case. The country's growth relied on trade and foreign investment much more than in most large continental countries. China's leaders, moreover, were more preoccupied with domestic threats to their rule than with threats from abroad. Maintaining popular support and keeping the Party in power depended on delivering the goods—growing the economy and improving living standards. That is why for three decades Chinese leaders after Mao—Deng Xiaoping, Jiang Zemin, and Hu Jintao—adopted a cautious, low-key foreign policy. They sought to avoid provoking any international conflict that could disrupt growth and stir up political unrest at home.

Underlying this strategic prudence was the CCP leaders' deep sense of political insecurity. Their legitimacy as leaders is tenuous because they are self-appointed. Unlike the revolutionaries who founded the PRC, Jiang Zemin and Hu Jintao were Communist Party organization men who had climbed the ladder without notable accomplishments or a national following. And despite Xi Jinping's red pedigree—his father had been a comrade-in-arms of Deng Xiaoping—he also feels insecure because he rose to power on his father's coattails.

As China's leaders look out from their headquarters in Zhongnanhai in the center of Beijing, they see a society that is dramatically different from the one that Mao Zedong ruled. They must wonder how long they can remain in control of a society that is more mobile, open to the world, and better informed than Mao's China. Between 1985 and 2018, over 220 million farmers moved from the countryside to work in the cities;[9] by the end of 2018, the middle class had grown to 400 million;[10] university enrollments increased from 27,000 in 1977 to 7.9 million in 2018;[11] and Chinese travelers abroad increased from 20.22 million person-times in 2003 to nearly 150 million in 2018.[12] There is no precedent or recipe for how a communist regime can effectively govern a modern market economy that is open to the world.[13]

In the minds of the leaders, domestic threats loom much larger than threats from abroad. Their fears about the fragility of Chinese Communist Party rule were heightened by the Tiananmen Square crisis. For several spring months in 1989, as the world knows, millions of students demonstrated against corruption and for democracy in Beijing's Tiananmen Square and in 132 other cities throughout the country. The Party leadership was split over how to handle the demonstrators, and only because the military followed Deng Xiaoping's orders to forcibly disperse the demonstrators on the night of June 4 did the communist regime survive. Shortly afterward, communist governments in the Soviet Union and Eastern Europe did collapse. China's leaders worry constantly that they could be next. They see threats to their survival lurking around every corner. Three lessons from Tiananmen Square and the collapse of Soviet communism are embroidered across the psyches of China's leaders like a sampler: prevent large-scale social unrest; avoid splits in the leadership; and keep the military on the side of the Party.[14]

With these domestic risks in mind, Deng and his successors took a cautious approach to foreign policy. They managed the country's international reputation based on the assumption that a large and formidable power on the rise could cause other countries to fear it and join forces to contain it. The Chinese elite studied the histories of other rising powers, and this topic was a focus of academic projects and a popular twelve-episode China Central Television series that aired in 2006: *The Rise of the Great Powers*.[15] At November 2003 and February 2004 study sessions Politburo members heard from academic experts about the rise and fall of nations since the fifteenth century, including the examples of twentieth-century Germany and Japan, and what factors had led to war. One lesson they drew from the fall of the Soviet Union was that if you try to challenge the United States militarily, you will bankrupt yourself and collapse from internal problems.[16] The Chinese leaders opted instead to reassure their Asian neighbors and the United States that they were not a threat by showing that their intentions were friendly, even as their capabilities drastically improved.

After the fall of the Soviet Union, Deng advised his staff that China should lie low internationally and avoid conflicts. His words, "Hide our capabilities and bide our time, but also get some things done," sounded like a form of deception to the ears of some American policymakers—who began calling Deng's policy "hide and bide"—but it set the direction of strategic restraint for Chinese foreign policy for more than a decade.[17] Putting a priority on domestic development and stability, Jiang Zemin and Hu Jintao followed Deng's guidance and avoided provoking fights that could cause other countries to restrict the foreign trade and investment that were vital to China's growth.

In reassuring rhetoric, Chinese policymakers and analysts between 1989 and 2008 depicted their country as a "responsible power," appropriating this term, along with other soothing notions like "win-win relationship," from the speeches of US officials.[18] In 2003, Zheng Bijian, Hu's adviser, proposed the slogan "peaceful rise"—frankly acknowledging that China was a growing power but emphasizing that it intended to ascend peacefully. The slogan was subsequently changed to "peaceful development" to sound even more acceptable to American ears.[19] To make these phrases credible, Beijing offered concessions agreeing to settle almost all of its land border disputes with adjacent countries (except for the one with India) and offering them free trade agreements; negotiating an agreement on a South China Sea code of conduct with ASEAN that committed all claimants to the exercise of self-restraint; and joining every Asian regional multilateral grouping and nearly every global agreement on nonproliferation, arms control, and trade. In 2003 it stepped forward to mediate the dangerous standoff between the United States and North Korea over North Korea's nuclear weapons program by organizing the Six Party Talks in Beijing. All this cooperative behavior boosted China's international prestige and dispelled what the Chinese government then called the "China threat theory." The message was that China's intentions were benign and that it would behave cooperatively even as it grew stronger. The strategy was motivated by the leaders' interest in preserving a peaceful international environment for sustaining economic growth and preventing domestic unrest.

China's strategy of restraint and reassurance succeeded in elevating it to regional and global leadership status. For its part, the United States reciprocated China's conciliatory moves by welcoming China to a seat at the head table in every forum of international cooperation. American foreign policymakers, starting with Richard Nixon, had made a strategic decision to bring China into the international system. In fact, no country has done more to promote China's rise as a global leader than the United States. In 1999, US secretary of the treasury Lawrence Summers and Canadian prime minister Paul Martin created the G-20 forum in large part to incorporate China into the management of international economic crises. The bipartisan US strategy was to encourage Beijing to step up to global leadership as a "constructive strategic stakeholder" in the international system, in former deputy secretary of state Robert Zoellick's oft-repeated 2005 words.[20]

China's cautious diplomacy showed some blind spots, particularly toward Japan and Taiwan, which were the hot-button issues of domestic politics. Even during the "peaceful rise" years, China did not handle its policies toward Japan and Taiwan as deftly as other policies. Its leaders bolstered their standing with the public by stirring up nationalist emotions about Japan's occupation of China during the 1930s and 1940s and taking tough public stands against contemporary Japanese politicians for being inadequately apologetic for this history. Japan's honoring of its war dead at the Yasukuni Shrine in Tokyo, which includes memorial plaques for fourteen war criminals convicted by an international tribunal, was the symbolic focal point of China's anti-Japanese nationalism.

The separate democratic governance of the island of Taiwan from the mainland is an open wound of nationalist irredenta that the CCP leadership can exploit whenever it seems politically expedient. But except for Japan and Taiwan, China's international behavior until 2008 gave its neighbors and the world reason to believe that its leaders had the motivation and the skill to guide the country to rise peacefully.

Reform Undergirds Restraint

Reinforcing international confidence in China's peaceful intentions were the bold reforms to China's economic system launched by Deng Xiaoping—from Stalinist-style central planning to market competition—and to a lesser extent, to its political system. Today, many critics lambast as hopelessly naive the strategy of engaging with China adopted by the nine presidents who followed Richard Nixon's opening to Beijing in 1972. To argue that engaging China was a mistake because of current retrograde trends, however, is to distort history. Reviewing the entire record of post-Mao China leads to a different conclusion: The welcoming international environment enabled Chinese leaders to modernize the country in a manner that expanded freedoms and the welfare of its people. The reform path zigged and zagged between relaxation (*fang*) and tightening (*shou*) in cycles related to economic oscillations and divisions among rival Communist Party politicians.[21] The overall trend, however, was toward lightening the hand of the state over economic and social life and making governance more predictable and rule-bound. The domestic reforms enhanced the trust of policymakers in other countries, who could see that their engagement was nudging China "in the right direction."

I saw this effect firsthand as a State Department official accompanying President Bill Clinton on his 1998 state visit to China. In advance of the visit, we had spent months negotiating a long list of "deliverables"—making specific agreements to cease targeting nuclear missiles at one another; pressing India and Pakistan to halt nuclear tests; and cooperating on drug enforcement, environmental health, clean energy, and other issues. But none of these accomplishments had the profound impact of the freewheeling ninety-minute press conference between President Jiang Zemin and Clinton in that, for the first time, the Chinese government allowed it to be televised live.[22] The leaders' dialogue on human rights, the Tiananmen crackdown, Tibet, and other previously taboo topics stunned the American visitors, as well as Chinese viewers. Clinton's candid speech to students at Beijing University was also broadcast live nationwide.[23] American officials were thrilled. Their China strategy seemed to be giving Chinese leaders the self-confidence to relax some political controls over their society.

China's post-Mao economic reforms also boosted the country's international image. Deng Xiaoping was *Time* magazine's man of the year twice, in 1978 and 1985, for China's "sweeping economic reforms that have challenged Marxist orthodoxy." He had sparked a gradual process of improvised local experimentation that allowed market competition to grow up alongside and gradually replace Soviet-style central planning.[24] Simultaneously, he welcomed foreign trade and investment to break down the walls Mao had erected to isolate China from the world economy. Deng gave a green light to family farming to replace collective agriculture and allowed factory managers to produce for the market and keep some of the profits. China's economic miracle—double-digit growth for thirty years that lifted hundreds of millions of people out of poverty—was a tribute to how market competition can unleash the energies of a great people once they are freed from the top-down design of its central government, often mischaracterized as the "China model."

China progressed on the political front as well, albeit more haltingly. Before Tiananmen, drastic change in Chinese politics looked possible, even likely. In 1980, popularly nominated candidates for city district People's Congresses openly campaigned for office. Victims of Mao-era political campaigns going back to the 1950s and through the 1966–1976 Cultural Revolution, including leaders like Deng and Xi Jinping's father, Xi Zhongxun, were rehabilitated. Deng allowed the open discussion of democratic ideals in student wall posters on Beijing's Democracy Wall in 1979. The Party's collective bodies and People's Congresses began meeting regularly.

At the Thirteenth Party Congress in 1987, limited competition (there were ten more nominees than seats) was introduced into the elections of the CCP Central Committee. Hu Yaobang, the liberal-leaning leader who had been fired as general secretary by the Politburo a few months earlier, won re-election to the Central Committee and the Politburo, and Deng Liqun, one of the main leaders of the conservative forces who had brought down Hu, lost the election to the Central Committee.[25] A Chinese official told me he anticipated that the Communist Party would soon give up its power to appoint and promote government and military officials. This so-called *nomenklatura power* (the term comes from Soviet politics) has always been the linchpin of Party rule. A small group organized by Premier Zhao Ziyang in the late 1980s had proposed a modern civil service system that would recruit officials through competitive examinations and evaluate officials based on their job performance. The measure met resistance from Party authorities, however, and was only introduced for low-level positions.[26]

At Deng's urging, the Communist Party stepped back and delegated greater authority over economic policy to government agencies whose staffs were better educated and more competent. The 1987 revision of the state constitution mandated separating Party and state by dismantling Party leading groups within government ministries.

Reforms Survive the Tiananmen Crisis and the Fall of the Soviet Union

After Mao had passed from the scene in 1976, China appeared to confirm the prediction of a number of social scientists[27] that regimes that begin as revolutions must transform themselves to achieve economic development.

Modernization replaces utopianism. Instead of charismatic leaders, they will be led by technocrats. Bureaucratic interest groups will emerge. And social forces will play a more decisive role. Little wonder that when these trends persisted in China even after the shocks of the Tiananmen crisis and the sudden fall of communism in the Soviet Union, most experts expected them to last.

In the aftermath of Tiananmen, Party conservatives, convinced that loss of Communist Party control had been responsible for the social upheaval, tried to roll back the economic and political reforms. They had some success. Party leading groups in government ministries were restored. The authority of the nation's top leader was reinforced. And Deng fired his main reform-minded lieutenant, CCP general secretary Zhao Ziyang. But Deng, though physically frail at age eighty-eight, took a highly publicized month-long trip to South China in 1992 to salvage the market reforms. The resilience of the reform effort in China even after the cataclysm of Tiananmen seemed to offer convincing proof that the economic reforms, at least, had passed the point of no return.[28]

After Deng's death in 1997, Jiang Zemin and Hu Jintao gave further impetus to political reforms. In the 1990s, China built something resembling a real legal system. Citizens started challenging state actions and suing one another in courts staffed by professional judges and lawyers. "Rule according to law" became a CCP slogan in 1997 and was incorporated in the constitution in 1999. When I met Xiao Yang, the justice minister and then Supreme People's Court Chief Justice twice during that period, he expressed a personal commitment to making the rule of law a reality. And indeed, he achieved some of his ambitious agenda. He opened trials to the public and reduced the number of executions by giving the Supreme Court the authority to review death penalty cases. But Xiao wasn't able to make much headway on achieving true judicial independence from Party interference.

Jiang sought to coopt private entrepreneurs into the Party by means of his "Three Represents" initiative. Overcoming resistance from traditionalists who objected to inviting capitalist exploiters into the Party, Jiang changed the Party constitution to allow private businesspeople to join. Private property rights were declared inviolable by an amendment to the state constitution in 2004. Yet today, only one private businessperson is an alternate member of the CCP Central Committee,[29] and private businesses still have no formal voice in the policy process.

Seeking to root out corruption and other abuses by local officials before they could spark public outrage and domestic strife, Jiang and Hu empowered the commercial media and Internet, placed under only light censorship, to act as watchdogs. The later 1990s and early 2000s were a high point of media and Internet freedom in China that hasn't been equaled since.[30]

Jiang also encouraged elections to check local abuses. Farmers throughout the countryside started electing village heads. The elections included open nominations and secret ballots. The Carter Center, the International Republican Institute, and international scholars advised and validated the elections. Although many Chinese participants hoped that direct elections would spread level by level from the bottom to the top—much as had happened in Taiwan—after a few experiments with township-level elections, the leaders lost their nerve. Today village elections have withered away, and Party secretaries have reclaimed power over the villages.[31] Hu promoted intraparty elections with the clear expectation that they might offer a path to the direct popular election of government leaders at different levels.

Jiang's and Hu's most remarkable political-reform accomplishment was that they both retired from office, more or less voluntarily, after serving two five-year terms. Political succession has always been the greatest vulnerability of authoritarian regimes. Mao and the leaders of other communist countries had clung to power until they were dragged out feet first, either dead or defeated in an internecine power struggle. No other communist regime had ever achieved a regular pre-mortem rotation of power at the top. Solving the succession problem was a major accomplishment and a clear indication that the Chinese political system was becoming more institutionalized and stable.

The fall of communist rule in the Soviet Union and Eastern Europe in 1991, coming on the heels of the Tiananmen crisis, shocked the Chinese leaders. How could China avoid meeting the same fate? Jiang and Hu concluded that for CCP to maintain public support, the political system had to adapt to the dramatic changes underway in the economy and society. They loosened the Party's grip on the media, the Internet, and social life and reformed governance to make it more responsive to popular concerns.[32] Nowadays, many foreigners are unaware of these earlier liberalizations in China.

Looking back from the vantage point of China under Xi Jinping, the attempt by Deng Xiaoping, Jiang Zemin, and Hu Jintao to adapt a Leninist autocracy to an open market economy and a modern society seems brave, ambitious—and a tragic failure. The leaders' gradual approach succeeded in building the support of local officials, entrepreneurs, and the public at large for market reforms, even if, unsurprisingly, it met stiffer opposition from Party power holders in the political domain. Although the pace of political reform was halting, the direction toward more responsive governance was clear. Practically everyone I interviewed in China during the years preceding Xi, including businesspeople and government officials, as well as students and academics, said that based on current trends, they expected China to gradually progress toward a democracy that resembled those in Japan, Korea, or Western countries. It was just a matter of time. History was on the side of the reformers—until it wasn't.

Policymaking under Collective Leadership

After Mao died, Deng deliberately crafted a system of institutionalized collective leadership to prevent the rise of another dictator who could turn against other leaders and put the nation at risk through his poor judgment. Deng, Mao's former comrade-in-arms whom Mao had purged twice, did not target Mao personally for the two tragic blunders as China's leader: the Great Leap Forward (1958–1962), the forced collectivization of agriculture that led to a devastating famine; and the Cultural Revolution (1966–1976), the mobilization of student Red Guards against Party and government authorities that threw the country into violent chaos. Instead, Deng identified the systemic source of Mao's bad decisions: "Over-concentration of power," he said, "is liable to give rise to arbitrary rule by individuals at the expense of collective leadership."[33] Deng and his colleagues introduced fixed terms of office, term limits, and a mandatory retirement age; delegated authority from the CCP to government agencies under the State Council; and started holding regular meetings of Party bodies such as the Central Committee, Politburo, and Standing Committee. All these moves were meant to decentralize authority, regularize political life, and check dictatorial power.

As noted, the centerpiece of the effort to prevent an entrenched dictatorship was to adopt a practice of peaceful leadership succession. When Jiang, who had become number one in 1992 when Deng became ill (he died in 1997), voluntarily retired as general secretary of the CCP, state president, and chairman of the Military Commission in 2002–2004, it was the first time that a leader in any communist country had left office without dying or being deposed in a coup.

Jiang's successor, Hu, was, as we'll see, initially committed to improving governance under collective leadership. He instituted a system of promotions based on job performance, experimented with intra-Party

democracy, and divided the highest posts among different leaders instead
of having one person do it all. Each of the nine members of the Politburo
Standing Committee had authority over their own policy domain. The design was purposeful. The 2007 Party Congress communique prescribed "a
system with a division of responsibilities among individual leaders in an effort to prevent arbitrary decision-making by a single top leader."[34] Because
of his self-effacing personality, Hu was content to be primus inter pares,
first among equals, but he acquired an image as an ineffectual leader. It
was widely known that retired leader Jiang still meddled in high-level personnel appointments, and Hu never established personal authority over
the People's Liberation Army.

The problem with policymaking in the Hu collective leadership was
not so much indecisiveness as a failure to rein in the parochial interest
groups within the Party, the government, and the military. Hu and the
other leaders were reluctant to second-guess one another's decisions for
fear of opening up splits in the Party oligarchy. Leaders of communist
parties always worry about open splits in the leadership. If politicians
disagree openly with one another and start to reach beyond the inner
circle to build a public following, Party rule can unravel. To preserve
the facade of unity, the barons in the top leadership bodies—the twenty-
five-member Politburo and the then nine-member Politburo Standing
Committee—instead of achieving consensus through mutual vetoes—
tended to go along with one another. Each bureaucracy, protected by
powerful representatives at the apex of Party power, sought to feather its
own nest—obtain bigger budgets, more staff, and bigger bribes—by exaggerating international and domestic threats. No one stopped them—not
Hu or any of the other leaders. Civil and military coordination conspic-
uously frayed because Hu allowed the People's Liberation Army to go its
own way. The arrangement amounted to a form of logrolling, in which
each group got what it wanted most in return for tolerating the adverse
effects of the policies the other groups wanted.[35]

Hu also allowed certain bureaucratic interest groups—I call them the
"control coalition"—to dramatically extend their sway over Chinese society by exploiting the leaders' fears of social upheaval. The control coalition includes the public security and propaganda bureaucracies as well
as the military and the paramilitary forces. These organizations beefed up
their already considerable power by exaggerating the threats to domestic
stability. No one dared question these bureaucracies when in the lead-
up to the 2008 Olympics they tightened restrictions on the media, the
Internet, and civil society organizations. At the time, many of us assumed
that the controls were temporary measures like those the Party had used in

the past to avoid embarrassing protests during major national events. But after the Olympic Games, the controls were never relaxed. The security and propaganda bureaucracies pursued a drive for "stability maintenance" (*weiwen*) that year after year has intruded more into people's lives. The control coalition also pushed through hard-line foreign policies, including military and paramilitary adventurism. Domestic overreaching went hand in hand with international overreaching after 2008, both driven by the dynamics of collective leadership. As a result, China's international actions, described in the prologue—particularly those involving the South China Sea—damaged its reputation as a responsible power, and an international coalition started to form to defend against it. Inside China, collective leadership led to a huge increase in corruption and, despite efforts to prevent them, open splits in the leadership.

Notably, the signs of a loss of restraint were there even before the global financial crisis of 2008. Beginning in 2006, white-hull ships belonging to civilian maritime agencies started harassing other countries' ships in the South China Sea, as I noted earlier. The same year, a policy to build state-owned companies into national champions that could compete with and win against international companies was instituted. Government bureaucracies poured money into upgrading the technological capacity of state-owned enterprises. As a result, private firms were squeezed out of access to credit and subsidies, and international firms were forced to transfer their technology if they wanted to do business in China. After decades of convergence with global norms of market competition, China veered off onto a state-dominated path that was economically inefficient and estranged the international businesses that had been China's biggest fans.

During his first term (2002–2007), Hu Jintao could have tried to mobilize a "reform coalition" consisting of private businesspeople, intellectuals and professionals, and the urban middle class to sustain the agenda—rule of law, media and internet opening, and civil society—that he had initially pursued and to create institutions to implement it. Two senior leaders in the Hu oligarchy—Premier Wen Jiabao and Standing Committee politician Wang Yang—were taking positions that appealed to these groups, which tells us that this potential constituency existed even though it was less well represented in the bureaucracy than the security, propaganda, and military interest groups in the control coalition. But under Hu, liberal reform remained the path not taken.

Deng Xiaoping could not have predicted the twists and turns of the economic and political transformations he initiated beginning in 1979 that now have made China more powerful but also more threatening to other countries as well as to itself. As the hero of China's post-Mao reform drive, Deng's ghost today is the focal point of the internal critique of Xi Jinping's dictatorial rule. But the shortcomings of his version of collective leadership as they appeared under Hu Jintao not only started China's derailment from a "peaceful rise" but also sent the pendulum swinging back to Xi's Mao-style overconcentration of power.

2

Deng's Ghost

IN ALMOST FIFTY YEARS of studying China, I have never heard sharper criticism of a leader than I heard about Xi Jinping when he changed the Constitution in 2018, enabling him to remain as president—just one of the titles he holds as the leader of China—for as long as he wants. The criticism came from academics, private businesspeople, journalists, military experts, and government officials, all of whom complained about his autocratic style of rule and his policy failures. All of this was in private conversation. No one dares question the leader's actions publicly or in writing. They bemoan the return to Mao Zedong–style dictatorship, the Communist Party's tightened grip over the media and social life, the excessive state intervention in the economy, and the aggressive foreign policies. In one encounter, a group of retired Chinese Communist Party historians sat down with me for what I thought was going to be a discussion of earlier political eras; instead, I got an earful about the damage Xi was inflicting on the Party and the country.

After Mao Zedong's death in 1976, Deng Xiaoping, his revolutionary comrade-in-arms and CCP general secretary, whom Mao had purged twice, in 1966 and 1976, returned to power. Deng dismantled Soviet-style central planning, gradually replacing it with market competition, and opened the economy to foreign trade and investment. Deng also modernized the way the Party governed China and loosened its totalitarian controls over people's lives. Those I met with were upset that Xi was destroying Deng's legacy, which they defined as consisting of three main elements: first, collective political leadership, with the regular turnover of power at the top; second, a market economy that is open to the world; and third, a foreign policy of restraint.

"Xi has abandoned all of them," the Party historians lamented. "He is taking China backward."

Deng, whose stature once nearly equaled Mao's, has now almost disappeared from the official histories. His speeches and writings are no longer studied or referenced in official doctrine. It's almost as if he is being purged for a third time. In 2018, Deng Pufang, his son, who has been in a wheelchair ever since Red Guards threw him out a window during the Cultural Revolution, felt compelled to speak out to remind people about the continuing relevance of his father's ideas to China's current situation. His speech implied criticism of Xi's overly ambitious approach to foreign policy: "We must keep the attitude of seeking truth from facts, keep a clear head, and know our place. We should be neither hubristic nor unduly humble."[1] An economist told me, "Reformers try to praise Deng online, but the messages are blocked. All we have is Deng's ghost."

The former leader's image was hard to find in the huge exhibition in December 2018 at the National Museum commemorating the fortieth anniversary of the Communist Party meeting at which Deng had launched China's "reform and opening" (*gaige kaifang*) agenda. More ubiquitous were images of Xi and his father, Xi Zhongxun, who was a contemporary of Deng's. China's state press noted that when Xi visited the exhibition, he stopped to look at a 1984 photo of Deng writing inscriptions for the special economic zones that he, Deng, had created to attract foreign business in Xiamen, Shenzhen, and Zhuhai. Xi used the photo as an occasion to talk, not about Deng's achievements, but about his own role when he served as deputy mayor in Xiamen in 1985.[2] As one Chinese academic interpreted the message of the exhibition, "The symbolic significance of the exhibition is that Deng Xiaoping's era has come to an end, and China is moving forward and has entered a new world: the era of Xi."[3]

When making bets about the country's future, people in China pay close attention to such signs as the Party's treatment of Deng. An executive of a Chinese hedge fund told me that his fund had divested much of its market holdings and gone liquid during 2018 because he viewed Xi's silence on Deng as a harbinger of heightened political risk, particularly for private companies. The displays at the fortieth anniversary exhibition were noticeably light on the role of private firms and heavy on the achievements of state-owned enterprises since Xi came to power: "Since the 18th Party Congress, the size of the state-owned economy and the profit margin of state firms [have] stabilized and improved," read the caption of a chart highlighting the total value of state firms' assets, which more than doubled after 2013 to reach a record high of 183.5 trillion yuan (US$26.4 trillion) in 2017.[4]

Deng has become the symbolic figurehead of the inchoate underground opposition to Xi. No living politician has dared to step up to organize an open opposition. This very fact reveals just how difficult it is for political elites in a communist state to prevent a leader from concentrating power in his own hands and stripping them of power and security.

As we seek to understand why Chinese leaders Hu Jintao and Xi started overreaching, PRC history offers key clues. Mao's totalitarian dictatorship produced disastrous consequences for the Chinese people, and his successor Deng tried to set up institutions to prevent future leaders from emulating Mao. But Deng's vision of a socialist country with a well-institutionalized collective leadership, an open market economy, and a foreign policy of restraint was a vision only partially and temporarily fulfilled. Deng was reluctant to bury Mao entirely. And he stopped short of establishing the independent courts, legislature, business firms, media, or civil society that could have checked the overwhelming power of CCP leaders.

Without such checks, the Hu system of collective leadership that followed Deng degenerated into a corrupt Party oligarchy in which bureaucratic and economic interests feathered their own nests. As I noted in chapter 1, the elite and the public, disgusted with the graft and inefficiency, started to yearn for stronger leadership. When Xi, an ambitious communist politician with a revolutionary pedigree, came into power, it was surprisingly easy for him to rehabilitate Mao's policies and imitate his personalistic rule. Some in the older generation, including the Party historians I interviewed, who had suffered through Mao's dictatorship, are horrified to see elements of it repeating today. Younger Chinese people, however, never having experienced or been taught that painful history, seem more amenable to the return to strongman rule. One "princeling" (*taizi dang*), the term used to describe the children of senior officials, who was a senior executive at a state-owned enterprise, observed that even though young people think of Mao as a hero, the fact that Mao's history has been buried makes the current Party leadership feel insecure. "They don't know when the past will be blamed on them. No one has taken responsibility. Mao did bad things even back in Yan'an, but the worst began in the 1950s. Mao thought of himself as the Qin Dynasty emperor or the Qin emperor plus Stalin."

China under Mao

From October 1, 1949, when he ascended the platform in Beijing's Tiananmen to proclaim the founding of the People's Republic, until his death in 1976, Chairman Mao, as he was known, reigned as China's dominant leader, ruling in a style that managed to combine the roles of Lenin and Stalin, the founder and the dictator, as well as the despotic Qin emperor. Mao's power derived from the Red Army's miraculous victory in the civil war, combined with a charisma constructed from a cult of personality and an official ideology summed up as "Mao Zedong Thought."[5] A cohort of revolutionary leaders had fought alongside him, but only Mao was elevated to almost godlike status.

To suppress all possible opposition to him from within the Party, Mao turned to the Stalinist *History of the Communist Party of the Soviet Union (Bolsheviks): Short Course*, which became his blueprint for dominating potential rivals.[6] Beginning from the days when the communist revolutionary movement was based in the dusty hills of Yan'an in North Central China, Mao had relied on purges and rectification campaigns to instill "discipline and unity" among Party members. Like Stalin, he framed policy disagreements in terms of who had the more correct ideological line, calling for continuing class struggle against capitalist conspirators who had snuck into the Party. In 1954, a plot by two influential regional leaders, Gao Gang and Rao Shushi, to supplant Party leaders number two (Liu Shaoqi) and three (Zhou Enlai) failed when two other senior leaders, Deng and Chen Yun, loyally tattled to Mao.[7]

The political and economic framework the PRC set up under Mao in the 1950s was also modeled on Stalin's template. Parallel Communist Party and state hierarchies extended from Beijing down to localities and work units, with the Party holding ultimate authority and controlling the selection and promotion of state officials (the so-called *nomenklatura power*). Soviet-style central planning and state ownership channeled investment to heavy industry. Private ownership and market activities were prohibited. All jobs were administratively assigned. After land reform expropriated land from landlords and rich peasants by force and gave it to peasants, Mao herded the peasants into collective farms even more rapidly than Stalin himself had advised.[8] Mandatory residence permits (*hukou*) doomed them to a lifetime of toiling in the countryside and even made it virtually impossible for city dwellers to move to another city.

China under Mao was more totalitarian than the Soviet Union under Stalin. Mao's vision for how to transform human nature was far more radical than what the Soviet leaders or many of his Chinese comrades envisioned. He wasn't satisfied with mere political conformity and compliance; he demanded the people's wholehearted commitment, selflessness, and activism. And he sought to inculcate this embrace of the cause through ideological education, mutual criticism sessions in small peer groups, manual labor, and mass campaigns targeting "bad elements" — who, according to Mao's formula, were required to constitute at least 5 percent of any group. The Soviets motivated workers to work hard by using piece rates, bonuses, and other material incentives, but Mao abjured them as morally corrupting.

I once coined the term "virtuocracy" to describe a system like Mao's in China, one in which school admissions and career promotion were based more on ideological loyalty than on academic or professional merit.[9] The official formula required being both "red and expert," but in truth, redness mattered more than expertise. Intellectuals, always politically suspect in Mao's eyes, bore the brunt of his frequent campaigns.

People lived in constant fear of making a slip of the tongue that could ruin their careers; they dared confide only in family members or, perhaps, one close friend. Mao's frequently quoted essay "Combat Liberalism" warned of the dangers of putting personal friendship ahead of political loyalty. A person's commitment to the values of the regime was measured by their willingness to criticize a friend's political mistakes. The high school students I interviewed for my research told me that you had to keep your distance from activist classmates in the Communist Youth League because they would criticize you to make themselves look good.[10]

In Mao's eyes, this interpersonal tension was desirable for sustaining the passionate intensity and unpredictability of revolutionary struggle. For Mao, China's future lay in mobilizing the energy of the people through mass campaigns that drew inspiration from the idealism of revolutionary egalitarianism and the spontaneity of collective mass action. In the mega campaigns of the Great Leap Forward (1958–1962 and the Cultural Revolution (1966–1976), Mao risked famine and chaos to achieve his personal revolutionary vision.

The Chinese people paid a heavy price for Mao's megalomania. Living standards stagnated between 1958 and 1978 at the level of $250 per capita GDP; the reason, as Deng said after Mao's death, was that Mao's methods defied "the laws governing socio-economic development."[11] During the Great Leap Forward, which was designed to overtake British steel production within fifteen years and catch up with the United States in fifty years, Mao introduced high-pressure techniques to get peasants to move to collective farms, where they would work "faster and better" and turn over most of their grain to the cities to fuel industrial expansion. Mao "cast economic policy in terms of political loyalty," turning the Great Leap into a "politically charged pledge campaign" in which party secretaries at every level vied with one another to promise large increases in output.[12] The

Great Leap resulted in a mass famine, during which per capita income dropped 35 percent, and an estimated 30 to 45 million people died.[13]

Mao's second transformative campaign was the Cultural Revolution, when he mobilized a mass insurgency of student Red Guards against teachers, intellectuals, and Party and government officials whom he believed were insufficiently loyal to him and his ideology. Among the victims were senior CCP leaders, including Liu Shaoqi, once Mao's chosen successor, and, of course, Deng, general secretary of the Party. Party and government organizations were decimated; schools and universities were shuttered for years; and almost every family was affected in some way. When I visited China for the first time in 1971, the Cultural Revolution was still underway. I found a dilapidated country where university students devoted their time to manual labor and military drills; absenteeism was rampant in the factories; housewives were picking shards of metal out of rags to reuse them in neighborhood workshops; and children were living on their own or with relatives because their parents had been sent to labor re-education camps. The Cultural Revolution death toll may have reached as high as 1.5 million and left a similar number permanently disabled, along with millions more who suffered political persecution.[14]

Overconcentration of Power

The Mao era illuminates the dangers of overconcentration of power in a communist political system, a central issue in today's China. When no one dares question the decisions of the leader, the leader is prone to make mistakes, not just small mistakes but the kind that endanger the entire society.

The Russians learned this lesson under Stalin. Three years after Stalin's death in 1953, Deng, by then the CCP general secretary, led the Chinese delegation to Moscow for the 20th Soviet Party Congress, where the Communist Party first secretary Nikita Khrushchev surprised everyone by denouncing the deceased leader for his cult of personality and for purging large numbers of Party officials. Deng wasn't in the room for what was called the "secret speech," but he received the text the next day and, after having it translated, returned to Beijing to report to Mao.[15]

De-Stalinization in the USSR sent shock waves through the political elite in China and other communist countries. With Stalin discredited, Mao had a better chance to claim leadership of the entire international communist movement. But within China, his own dictatorial style of rule was implicated in the Khrushchev critique of Stalin. Chinese Party officials, including Deng himself, tried to defend Mao by emphasizing all the ways he was different from Stalin. They referenced a 1943 decision by the CCP Central Committee, written by Mao, to oppose the "cult of the individual leader." Stalin's greatest sin in the eyes of Khrushchev was "to replace the leadership of the party by his personal dictatorship, executing or imprisoning thousands of loyal party cadres in the process." Mao's comrades insisted that Mao was different because, they claimed, he had always sought to unite with former opponents.[16] But they also piled on the criticism of Stalin for "erroneously" inflating his own role and counterposing "his individual authority to the collective leadership." He had lost touch with the people, violated intra-Party democracy, and "indulged in arbitrary individual actions."[17]

At the same time, Deng, Liu, and other senior leaders took steps to strengthen the Party's collective institutions to function as a check, preventing Mao or any future leader from repeating Stalin's errors. The Party elite established mechanisms to protect themselves from the whims of a dictatorial leader who could destroy their careers, as well as make disastrous policy mistakes.

The 8th National Congress of the CCP, in 1956, was the highpoint of efforts to institutionalize collective leadership while Mao remained the top leader. The Politburo Standing Committee, made up of seven leaders, including Deng, constituted the topmost collective leadership group. Below the Standing Committee came the Politburo (twenty members) and the Central Committee (one hundred members at the time). These bodies included key figures from the regime's various bureaucratic hierarchies, those responsible for the economy in particular. In a move signaling a promise of career security for the Party elite, all surviving members of 7th CCP Central Committee (1945) were re-elected in 1956 into the expanded Central Committee. The Congress took free nominations for Central Committee membership from the floor, and then held two rounds of voting—a form of intra-Party democracy that was never again repeated. The 1956 Congress also shifted the Party's primary goal from class struggle to economic development.

Mao appeared to go along with the changes. After the Congress, the now sixty-three-year-old leader began transitioning to eventual retirement by stepping back from day-to-day responsibilities and preparing his heir apparent, Liu Shaoqi, to take over. A significant symbolic action by the Congress was dropping any reference to the *Thought of Mao Zedong* from the Party constitution. Inwardly, however, Mao seethed with resentment at his colleagues' eagerness to seize upon Khrushchev's attack on Stalin and then use the criticism to diminish his own power and prestige.[18] His grudges against Liu, Deng, and other veteran leaders motivated him to launch the Cultural Revolution against them ten years later.

The system of collective leadership established at the 1956 Party Congress proved inadequate to check Mao's impetuousness. The Central Committee met only irregularly, and the next Party Congress was not held for more than a decade. When Mao resumed intervening in decision-making, promoting his idiosyncratic ideas, other politicians, instead of questioning them, joined in, competing with one another to prove their loyalty to the leader.[19] One of Mao's projects in 1956 was the Hundred Flowers Campaign, in which he invited the public, intellectuals in particular, to express their opinions about Party rule. The de-Stalinization in the Soviet Union and revolts in Poland and Hungary may have motivated Mao to gauge his popularity with the masses. But he didn't like the criticism he heard and reversed himself, suddenly halting the Hundred Flowers and launching a persecution campaign against about a half million regime critics, who were labeled Rightists for having dared to speak out.[20]

In 1958, Mao impatiently rejected the economic plans of the central bureaucrats as too timid. He laid out goals that he believed could be achieved if the peasants were corralled to work on collective farms, where they would work harder and send the so-called surplus to the cities to spur rapid industrialization. He fired up provincial officials to get them behind the Great Leap Forward campaign, during which, as noted, as many as 45 million people died from violence and famine.[21]

The defense minister, Peng Dehuai, who had recently returned from a visit to the USSR and Eastern Europe, was the only senior official to directly criticize the Great Leap. He wrote a letter to Chairman Mao, apparently believing it would be kept private. Instead, Mao had it printed and circulated among the participants at the Lushan Plenum, a high-level Party meeting in 1959, where he attacked Peng with a vitriol that had never before been heard in such meetings.[22] Mao purged Peng, removed his associates, and attacked the USSR for backing him. More economic disaster ensued as the Great Leap continued for two more years. At the Seven Thousand Cadres Meeting, in January 1962, Liu Shaoqi presented a report he and Deng had been asked to draft on current economic problems. The report called on the Party center (implicitly including Mao) to acknowledge the shortcomings and errors that had led to the problems caused by the Great Leap and to introduce flexible economic measures such as private plots of land or even household farming to help the economy recover. But the other cadres at the meeting leapt to their feet to defend the Leap and pledge loyalty to Mao. Following the meeting, Mao gave speeches defending himself against the criticism, objecting to the "Wind of Gloom" of talking too much about policy mistakes.[23]

After the Great Leap, it was a high-risk proposition for any politician to stand up to Mao. The Party elite no longer viewed Mao as infallible—they blamed him personally for the Great Leap Forward—yet their fear of his wrath grew. At the same time, their distrust of one another inhibited them from organizing any collective resistance. Meanwhile, Mao suspected that even though no Party members were openly opposing him, they were harboring silent doubts about his leadership and preparing to repudiate his legacy after his death.

During the 1960s, Mao constantly fretted about what he saw as the revolutionary degeneration of the Party and the possible disloyalty of its other leaders. He turned to the People's Liberation Army, led by defense minister Lin Biao, as a more reliable source of support. The PLA proselytized his ideological gospel in the "Little Red Book" of Mao's quotations, the political bible that everyone was expected to carry with them. In 1966, Mao rewarded Lin Biao by naming him as his successor, displacing Liu Shaoqi.

The Cultural Revolution, which began that year, was the political fallout of Mao's loss of confidence in the loyalty of his colleagues since the Great Leap Forward.[24] The Politburo leaders, acquiescing to Mao's will, followed their charismatic leader off a cliff. The student Red Guards destroyed them one by one, accusing them of being "capitalist-roaders" despite their decades of service to the Communist Party. The Politburo, its Standing Committee, and the central departments of the Party ceased operations as an ad hoc group of lower-level propaganda and security cadres took over the direction of the insurgency.[25] Even Lin Biao started to feel insecure about whether he was still in favor with Mao. With the help of his son, an air force officer, Lin may have started to plan for a military coup. In September 1971, he and his family were killed in a mysterious plane crash in the Soviet Union.[26]

As long as Mao was alive, Party leaders were too intimidated by him and mistrustful of one another to collectively resist him. But within a month of his death, in 1976, the Politburo moved in to arrest his wife, Jiang Qiang, and the other members of the palace clique known as the Gang of Four to stop them from claiming power.

Mao's Ghost

The Chinese Communist Party faced a crisis of legitimacy after the end of the Cultural Revolution and Mao's death. Party and government officials, as well as the general public, were disillusioned after a decade of violent power struggles and social chaos. As Chinese officials began to take study tours abroad to Japan, Singapore, Europe, and the United States, they saw with their own eyes just how poor Chinese living conditions were compared to those in other countries. As Deng Xiaoping put it in 1978, "The more we see, the more we realize how backward we are."[27]

Hua Guofeng, the successor Mao had chosen in his last months, was an unimpressive factotum who tried unsuccessfully to capitalize on Mao's charisma. He had billboards depicting Mao telling him, "With you in charge, I am at ease," plastered all over Beijing. Hua grew out his crew cut to resemble Mao and tried to sell the notion of "whateverism," which translated to "uphold whatever policy decisions Chairman Mao made and follow whatever instructions he gave." Deng countered with a more practical formulation based on what had originally been Mao's concept, "Seek truth from facts."[28] Hua had no real authority or following of his own. Deng, the highly capable survivor from the pre–Cultural Revolution leadership group, was respected by officials and the public. Deng outmaneuvered Hua and, by the end of 1978, had established himself as the country's de facto top leader.

That was when Deng set about restoring regularity and predictability to political life, to counter the traumatic upheavals of the Mao era. He made a critical strategic choice: instead of casting personal blame on Mao for the tragic mistakes of the Great Leap and Cultural Revolution, he identified the systemic source of the problem: "Over-concentration of power is liable to give rise to arbitrary rule by individuals at the expense of collective leadership." Over the course of sixteen months in 1980–1981, Deng called for a thorough assessment of the history of the Mao era and solicited hundreds of opinions as part of the process. Every Chinese dynasty has written an authoritative history for future generations. The resolution on the history of the Mao period aimed to digest the lessons of past mistakes and at the same time unify the older cadres who had been the victims of the Cultural Revolution with younger ones who had hoped to benefit from it. Formulating a credible narrative was necessary to restore the good name of those whose lives (and whose children's lives) had been ruined by accusations of being Rightists, counter-revolutionaries, or capitalist roaders during Mao-era ideological campaigns. The historical judgment was harsh: "The 'Cultural Revolution,' which lasted from May 1966 to October 1976, was responsible for the most severe setback and the heaviest losses suffered by the Party, the state, and the people since the founding of the People's Republic. It was initiated and led by Comrade Mao Zedong."[29] The resolution openly criticizes Mao for his arrogance and arbitrariness, and for putting himself above the Central Committee.[30]

Both the history resolution and Deng's commentaries during the drafting process make clear, however, that Deng sought to preserve Mao's image as the founder of the country and Mao Zedong Thought as its unifying ideology. He complained that the drafts were "too depressing" and called for a more positive rendering of Mao's contributions.[31] Even as he pivoted China toward an open market economy and regularized political processes, he was loath to renounce Mao's entire record. He believed that wholesale de-Maoization would further destabilize the Party and make it impossible to restore confidence in its rule. An influential princeling observed that Deng needed to render the Mao era in a manner that would enable him to "get the support of a broad range of people for the economic reform." Deng commented, "When we write about his mistakes, we should not exaggerate, for otherwise we shall be discrediting Comrade Mao Zedong, and this would mean discrediting our Party and state."[32] In an interview, he told the Italian journalist Oriana Fallaci that Mao's portrait would remain above the Tiananmen Gate forever and said, "We will not do to Chairman Mao what Khrushchev did to Stalin."[33]

Deng asked the drafters to add a long section on the twenty-eight years before the 1949 victory to give them more positive things to say about Mao.[34] By adding this section, the resolution was able to conclude, "If we judge his activities as a whole, his contributions to the Chinese revolution far outweigh his mistakes. His merits are primary and his errors secondary." The final assessment put Mao's contributions at 70 percent and his errors at 30 percent. Deng also tried to salvage Mao Zedong Thought as the guiding ideology by noting that it reflected the "collective wisdom" of the Party, not the ideas of one individual leader.[35] To emphasize this point, the document established that some of the notions that Mao himself promulgated during the Cultural Revolution were "inconsistent with Mao Zedong Thought."[36] Yet Deng himself "really hated ideology," a point that the influential princeling I mentioned above said he had confirmed with Deng's daughter Maomao. Pragmatism was the essence of Deng's thought: "It doesn't matter if a cat is black or white; as long as it catches mice, it's a good cat."

Deng further urged the drafters not to put all the blame for past mistakes on Mao alone. When Comrade Mao "got carried away" with the Great Leap, the rest of the Party's leaders, including Deng himself, went along with him. He said that although the chief responsibility for mistakes lay with Comrade Mao, part of the responsibility "should be borne collectively" and "it does us no harm to accept our share of the blame."[37]

By preserving Mao's image, Deng made it possible for Xi Jinping, when he became China's leader thirty years later, to further rehabilitate Mao's record and consolidate his own power by emulating features of Mao's rule. There was little resistance from the younger generation, who, as one economist told me, "don't know how bad it was." A senior finance official observed that young people have come to see Mao's ideas about central planning as prescient. "When I speak to students about the history of market reforms some of them (more than once) ask why they thought it was necessary to transition from a centrally planned economy because after all, Jack Ma [former CEO of Chinese Internet firm Alibaba] says that thanks to big data the center can plan the economy."

Because Xi's father and entire family had been prominent victims of Mao's Cultural Revolution, no one ever expected Xi to embrace the legacy of Maoism. But just weeks after ascending to power, in late 2012, Xi surprised everyone by reversing the negative verdict on the Mao era. He proclaimed in a speech that the thirty years of Mao's rule were just as positive as the thirty years of post-Mao reforms and that neither period should be used to negate the other.[38] In a speech in December 2013, celebrating Mao's 120th birthday, Xi offered a new defense of Mao's actions. "Revolutionary leaders are not gods," he said, "but human beings," and therefore, "evaluations of historical figures should be placed in the historical circumstances of their time and society."[39] Xi may not credit Deng with being the father of China's reforms, but he likes to remind others what Deng had to say about Party history to bolster his arguments against what he calls "historical nihilism" that "smears and vilifies" the Mao era.[40]

Despite his scars from the Cultural Revolution, Xi models himself on Mao. His style of rule is not identical—he puts a premium on order and stability, instead of revolutionary tension, and on centralization, instead of decentralization—but he has revived a number of Maoist practices: the cult of personality and micromanagement in every sphere; the absence of fixed terms or regular succession; policymaking by Party instead of government officials; promotion based more on ideological virtue than job performance; constant propaganda and education; folksy appeals to the public; and the requirement that Party officials must be attentive to the public according to the "mass line."

Deng's Legacy

Deng's remedy for the overconcentration of power was to institutionalize collective leadership and the orderly retirement of the leaders, an effort that was initiated at the 1956 8th Party Congress but undone by Mao in the 1960s.[41] Political scientist Samuel Huntington defined "institutional- ization" as "the process by which organizations and procedures acquire value and stability."[42] There are a multitude of definitions of "institutions," but they all involve rules or norms that regulate human behavior. Deng's institution-building aimed to provide the kind of stable, predictable gov- ernance suitable to the vibrant market economy open to the world that he hoped to create to replace central planning and autarky. In a 1980 speech to the Politburo, "On the Reform of the System of Party and State Leadership,"[43] he proposed eight key structural changes, many of which were then codified in the 1982 and 1987 revisions to the state constitution and the CCP constitution.[44]

The first was separating the responsibilities of the Party and the gov- ernment. In the Mao era, Party officials at all levels, from the factories to the provinces to the Party center in Beijing, had decided everything. The Party opted to trade off a degree of control by delegating more authority to government officials who had technical knowledge and specialized information about economic matters—to improve economic efficiency and speed up modernization. The CCP remained the ultimate authority (the "principal," in the language of Western institutional economics), but it delegated to the government (the "agent") much of the actual work of managing the economy and administering the country. The premier, as head of the State Council, the government cabinet, was delegated au- thority over economic policy, and the CCP general secretary took charge of ideology, education, and Party politics.

Second, Deng's reforms ended the policy of lifetime tenure in office, easing elderly leaders into retirement and recruiting younger leaders. Term limits (two five-year terms) and retirement ages (68) were estab- lished formally for leading posts in the government and military and estab- lished as an unwritten norm for Party Politburo and Standing Committee leaders. Third, he instituted regular meetings of Party and government bodies. CCP national congresses started meeting every five years; and the CCP Central Committee, at least once and usually twice a year. The National People's Congress, China's national legislature, meets annually and has a new slate of representatives every five years. The Politburo meets monthly and the Politburo Standing Committee meets weekly. These regular cycles, combined with the term limits and retirement ages, made the competition for power more orderly and predictable, instead of the constant and unpredictable struggle it was during the Mao era.

Fourth, he decentralized decision-making power among leaders and to lower-level and regional officials. Within Party committees (including the Politburo and Standing Committee), a system of collective leadership was established that divided policy-portfolio responsibilities among the leaders. Open deliberation within these bodies was encouraged. Provincial and local officials also were delegated greater authority, especially over economic matters. Fifth, Deng strengthened the authority of the Central Committee as the "selectorate" empowered to choose Party leaders. I adopted the term "selectorate" from British parliamentary politics to define the group within a political party that has the effective power to choose leaders.[45] The provincial officials, central Party and government officials, and military officers who constitute the approximately two hundred full members and two hundred alternate members of the Central Committee are all appointed by the top leaders, but they also have the authority to elect the top leaders, creating a relationship of "reciprocal accountability" similar to that between the pope and the College of Cardinals in the Catholic Vatican.[46]

Sixth, Deng's reforms established a system of recruitment and promotion of officials that is more meritocratic and predictable. Appointment and promotion moved toward objective performance standards even though the new system stopped short of establishing a fully professional civil service, and the CCP retained the politically valuable authority to make personnel appointments within the government and state-owned enterprises and organizations.

Seventh, the reforms professionalized the PLA and established civilian control under the CCP Central Military Commission.[47] The Red Army and the Communist Party were merged during the revolutionary struggle and after winning power. Under Mao the PLA became enmeshed in leadership competition and was called in to restore order in the civil chaos of the Cultural Revolution. Reversing this pattern, Deng professionalized the military by engineering the separation of civilian and military elites, a watershed in the institutionalization of China's civil–military relations.

Eighth, he created a nascent legal system. The National People's Congress wrote the PRC's first civil and criminal legal codes and established a system of courts. But even as dispute resolution moved into the courts, the legal system remained under Party direction as judges were appointed by the Party.

As Deng's reforms advanced under his successors, Jiang Zemin and Hu Jintao, China's politics became more stable and predictable. Party governance largely adapted to the modernizing economy and society instead of resisting it as it had done under Mao. The Party openly embraced universal values such as human rights and rule of law. As one Chinese businessman put it, Deng's reforms "were merging China with the mainstream of global civilization." Three decades of post-Mao institutionalization transformed how China's political system operates and the rules of the game for leadership competition. Many Chinese and foreign observers, including myself, believed that the institutionalization of China's politics was permanent, and that the country would never again experience strongman rule.

That prediction, of course, was wrong. Deng had played a heroic role in reforming China's political and economic system, but he left a shaky foundation for later reformers, and enabled an ambitious leader like Xi Jinping to revive many features of Mao's rule. As a Chinese tech entrepreneur put it, "Deng Xiaoping unplugged the Party's Leninist machine but Xi just put in the plug and it started up right away."

One of the most striking contradictions in Deng's rule was that while he insisted that other politicians govern through their formal institutional roles, he himself ruled entirely on the basis of informal power. His formal title was vice-premier, and though he served on the Politburo Standing Committee until 1987, someone else was the head of the Party. He did, however, retain power over the military as chairman of the Central Military Commission. His authority derived mainly from an extensive network of officials whose careers he had promoted over the years, and from his prestige as a revolutionary founder and political survivor. He pushed other revolutionary elders into retirement, but, believing that his own leadership was essential to the success of China's reforms, chose to hang on until he was physically too infirm to continue. At Politburo meetings, the CCP general secretary (first, Hu Yaobang, and then Zhao Ziyang) would preface a point by saying, "I have already talked to Comrade Xiaoping about this issue." The other retired elders, taking their lead from Deng, kept intervening in critical policy decisions and retained more de facto authority than the members of the Standing Committee. Several of the elders, including Chen Yun and Peng Zhen, had more political seniority than Deng.[48] When the general secretary briefed Deng and the elders he sat on a low stool, like an adviser addressing the Qing Dynasty emperor.[49] According to some accounts, during the 1989 Tiananmen crisis when the Politburo Standing Committee was split on whether to impose martial law on the student demonstrators, the elders, meeting in Deng's living room, overruled them and made the ultimate call to impose martial law.[50]

Although Deng embraced the economic logic of the market, he was no political liberal. He stuck to Marxist fundamentals and often warned against political reforms modeled on Western democracy. Deng believed that the American-style division of powers between the legislature, executive, and judiciary led to, as he put it in 1987, "repetitive discussion and consultation, with one branch of government holding up another and decisions being made but not carried out." The socialist system was more efficient, he thought, because "when the central leadership makes a decision it is promptly implemented without interference from any other quarters."[51] This perspective set limits on how far the political reforms could go; they fell short of establishing independent courts or legislature.

Deng also frequently tacked to the Left, paying obeisance to traditional ideological precepts even though he was not a fan of ideology. During the gradual process of market reform, the hybrid economy—part plan, part market—swung wildly between boom-and-bust phases of expansion (*fang*) and contraction (*shou*), which intensified the factional conflict between the market reformers and those who favored more state control. Whenever that happened Deng would make an ideological gesture toward the Left to mollify conservative party elders led by the powerful economic chief Chen Yun and ease the buildup of anti-reform pressures. Each fresh surge of economic reform was followed by an ideological swing back in the direction of Leninist orthodoxy.[52] In a speech he gave soon after assuming power called "Uphold the Four Cardinal Principles," Deng called for a readjustment of the overheated economy and then went on to stress the importance of adhering to the fundamentals of Chinese communism—namely, stick to the socialist road, uphold the dictatorship of the proletariat, support the leadership of the Communist Party, and maintain Marxism-Leninism and Mao Zedong Thought.[53] Tilting Left was a tactical necessity because Chen Yun and the other conservative elders held an effective veto over reform policies. But it was also in line with Deng's unwavering belief in socialist values and communist rule.

Deng also had an inveterate fear of social unrest that could topple the regime, student protests in particular. He may have suffered from a form of post-traumatic stress caused by Red Guard violence against him and his family during the Cultural Revolution. In his eyes, every student demonstrator looked like a Red Guard. In 1979, when students began posting criticisms of Mao's rule in "big character posters" on a wall near Tiananmen Square, which became known as "Democracy Wall," Deng initially encouraged them as a way they could let off steam and to bolster support for his own leadership comeback. He had already favored allowing the expression of critical views: "Even if a few malcontents take advantage of democracy to make trouble . . . the thing to be feared most is silence."[54] But as the crowds at Democracy Wall grew large and the content of the posters exhibited what Deng saw as a dangerous trend toward "liberalization," he shut it down and had some of the students arrested. Citizens' right to "speak out freely, air their views fully, hold great debates and put up big-character posters," a phrase that had been added to the Constitution in 1978, was expunged in 1980. Confronted by student demonstrations again in 1985 and 1986, Deng ordered officials to suppress them and throw the ringleaders in jail.[55] He warned of the dangers of an uprising that might be similar to what had occurred in Poland during the rise of Solidarity.

Then came Tiananmen. From April 15 to June 4, 1989, millions of students demonstrated against corruption and for democracy in Beijing and 132 other cities in every province. The Party leadership split over how to deal with the demonstrations. Deng rejected the advice of Zhao Ziyang and other leaders to accommodate the student demands, and as commander in chief, issued the order for the PLA to use lethal force against the young civilians. Deng's personal responsibility for what became known abroad as the "Tiananmen Massacre"—the number of people who were killed is unknown, but it is thought to run as high as several thousand—tarnished his historical image internationally, as well as among many Chinese.

Conservative leaders blamed the Tiananmen protests on the political and economic reforms, which they claimed had weakened Party control and polluted the atmosphere with subversive Western ideas. In a direct challenge to Deng, Chen Yun and his allies attacked the reforms in an ideological campaign against "peaceful evolution" from socialism to capitalism. The abortive Soviet coup in August 1991 and the subsequent disintegration of the Soviet Union, following on the heels of Tiananmen, intensified the debate between Deng and Chen about which was more crucial to communist party survival—economic development or upholding Marxism against peaceful evolution.[56] (Xi Jinping's views today are strikingly reminiscent of Chen Yun's following Tiananmen.)

Deng fought back against the conservatives by mobilizing public opinion behind the reforms. The retired leader, then eighty-six years old, took that well-publicized "Southern Tour" to the special economic zones in Guangdong to make the case that foreign investment and trade were essential for China to modernize its economy and improve living standards. But while Deng managed to salvage the economic reforms, he had agreed to certain political concessions that had long-term consequences. He'd fired, one after the other, the two reformist younger leaders, Hu Yaobang (in 1987, before Tiananmen) and Zhao Ziyang (after Tiananmen), who had been his chosen successors. Then in a hurry to find a replacement successor, he selected Jiang Zemin, the Party secretary of Shanghai, who was acceptable to both wings of the Party leadership.

Having barely survived the Tiananmen crisis, Deng concluded that splits within the leadership could be just as dangerous as dictatorial rule. To prevent destructive cleavages among the leaders, Jiang Zemin, who arrived in Beijing without a broad base of support, was put in the top position of all three hierarchies: general secretary of the Communist Party; chairman of the Central Military Commission (the commander of the armed forces); and president of the People's Republic of China (the head of state). This was the first time this model of fused leadership had occurred in the PRC. Before 1989, "State President" had been a mere title, and Deng Xiaoping had run the Military Commission without being CCP General Secretary. The rules reducing the Party's sway over government agencies that had been introduced in 1987 also were retracted by Deng and the other Party leaders. As a result, there was less standing in Xi Jinping's way when he decided to let the Party swallow the government and directly manage the economy.

Despite Deng's political compromises, he was able to sustain the market-reform drive. Deng deserves a memorial shrine in every farm household and private business in China. Without his replacing collective agriculture with family farming and Soviet-style central planning with a market economy open to the world, China's "economic miracle" would never have occurred. Still, while giving Deng credit, let's recognize that the Chinese reforms were not planned out in advance and did not proceed in a top-down manner. Deng and his lieutenants Zhao Ziyang and Hu Yaobang had to carry them out through a political system that had been rebuilt after the chaos of the Cultural Revolution. That meant they had to maneuver around the powerful central bureaucracies and heavy industry that had vested interests in the planned economy and to create counterweight constituencies for the market reforms.[57]

Given the political roadblocks that stood in the way, the approach taken by Deng, Zhao, and Hu was experimental and piecemeal instead of a big-bang transformation. Agricultural reform commenced first because it faced less bureaucratic resistance and created a new source of demand for the state industries. Deng and his lieutenants expanded the market sector gradually, maintaining central planning rather than replacing it with the market in one fell swoop.[58] They allowed small private businesses to sprout up but did not privatize state-owned enterprises. And because provincial officials made up the largest voting bloc in the Central Committee, they became the main constituency for market reforms. The strategy of "playing to the provinces" involved a fiscal decentralization that allowed lower-level governments to keep the profits earned by local industries.[59]

Reform "experiments" offered the freedom to offer favorable treatment to foreign investors. The experiments were granted first to particular provinces, cities, ministries, or enterprises. This special treatment helped the coastal provinces with port facilities and better infrastructure to "get rich faster," in Deng's words, before the benefits could trickle down to the backward inland regions. Other reform experiments permitted the freedom to sell to the market at higher prices and keep a larger share of the earnings. None of the experiments were scientifically designed to test the effects of the reform. The selected units received preferential treatment in taxes, bank loans, electricity rates, and so on that guaranteed successful results and could then be publicized as a model to emulate. As other units clamored to gain the privilege of being an "experimental site," political support for the reforms snowballed.[60]

Deng's decision to open China's economy to foreign investment and trade more widely than other East Asian economies had done, including Japan, South Korea, and Taiwan, which were his developmental benchmarks, also elicited enthusiasm among international businesses to engage with China. Multinational corporations became allies, encouraging their governments to improve relations with China and to bring China into the World Trade Organization.

China's piecemeal approach to reform proved remarkably successful at building a political coalition behind reforming the market, stimulating growth, and raising living standards. But in retrospect, did Deng and his lieutenants do China a favor by preserving the central economic bureaucracies and state-owned enterprises instead of more fundamentally transforming the economic system on which they were based?

Even after several decades of decentralizing market-oriented reforms, those interest groups remained closely tied to CCP elites and retained their influence; they were able to revive a more statist approach to development in the years after Deng. The State Planning Commission has taken on many new names over the years, the most recent being the National Development and Reform Commission (NDRC), but its penchant for top-down industrial policy has stayed strong. As one Chinese economist said, "There's bureaucratic continuity. It carries the same gene." Although mandatory plan targets have disappeared, the NDRC still allocates massive amounts of state investment to domestic projects, as well as to overseas ones such as the Belt and Road. Nowadays, even though the state-owned enterprises contribute only between 23 percent and 28 percent of China's GDP (as of 2018), and between 5 percent and 16 percent of employment (as of 2017),[61] they still dominate bank loans and government subsidies, squeezing out the private sector. In 2016, for example, state-owned enterprises received 83 percent of bank credit loaned to the nonfinancial sectors.[62]

Some Chinese economists bemoan that Deng's reforms did not go far enough to privatize firms and legally guarantee their independence from the state. In their view, the state remained too strong, which in turn has led it to overreach internationally. In 2019, the late Hungarian economist Janos Kornai expressed a similar view in an article in the *Financial Times*. Years earlier, Kornai had advocated privatization for Hungary because he believed that "a half-way house"—a socialist market economy without legally protected private property and democratic rights—would be a disaster. But he recalled that when he visited China in the 1980s, he modified his stance because he didn't want to put a damper on the gradualist ideas of the Chinese economists, a choice that he later regretted.[63] In his article, Kornai wrote that he and the other Western intellectuals who had advised the Chinese on the reforms should acknowledge their moral responsibility as "Frankensteins" who had created a "fearsome monster" in today's China.[64]

Deng's Charm Offensive

At the time, however, Deng proved a remarkably successful diplomatic representative for a China that was shifting away from supporting revolutionary insurgencies and toward improving relations with the governments of its Asian neighbors, the United States, and other countries. Deng hadn't spent any time out of China since the 1920s, when he lived for five years as a student–factory worker and communist organizer in France and a student in Russia. He nonetheless knew how to charm foreigners. His refreshing candor, pragmatic attitude, and sense of humor helped to build trust. And his clear priority on civilian economic growth and keeping military expenditures down lent credence to his reassuring words about China's friendly intentions.

When Mao sent him to speak to the United Nations General Assembly in 1974, Deng pledged that China would never be a superpower or seek global hegemony, and that if it did, the people of the world should "expose it, oppose it, and work together with the Chinese people to overthrow it." Although the speech had been approved by Mao, this wry suggestion that China might need help from foreigners in restraining itself sounds like typical Deng.[65] In another example of his humorous hyperbole, when President Jimmy Carter pressed him about allowing free emigration to the United States, in 1979, Deng replied, "How many would you like? Ten million?"[66]

Deng was especially revealing in private conversations with foreigners. After stepping down as national security advisor in the Carter administration, Zbigniew Brzezinski took his family on a vacation that retraced the route of the Long March, the Red Army's famous retreat to Ya'nan in Northwest China, where it spent most of the Japanese occupation. After completing the rugged journey, Brzezinski met with Deng in Beijing. He mentioned how impressed he had been with the Luding Bridge, the site of a much-celebrated battle during which the communist soldiers crossed the river over a chain bridge under hostile fire. The bridge is so iconic that many children's playgrounds have a climbing structure that is a replica. According to Brzezinski, Deng smiled and said, "That's the way it's presented in our propaganda. In fact, it was a very easy military operation. There wasn't really much to it . . . but we felt we had to dramatize it."[67] At a Beijing dinner party in 1979, actress Shirley MacLaine told Deng that a Chinese scientist had told her he was grateful to Mao Zedong for removing him from his college campus and sending him, and many other intellectuals, to toil on a farm. Deng replied, "He was lying."[68]

As he launched the reform drive in 1978, Deng traveled for the first time to Southeast Asian countries, marveling at their economic progress and listening to their somewhat negative views of China. After hearing officials' concerns about China's broadcasts encouraging revolution among ethnic Chinese in Thailand, Malaysia, and Singapore, he stopped the broadcasts. To improve relations with Southeast Asian governments, he also encouraged ethnic Chinese to be loyal to the country where they lived, and not to Beijing. In January 1979, I was one of the guests at a reception in the East

Wing of the National Gallery in Washington, DC, welcoming Deng on his historic state visit that followed on the heels of the restoration of normal diplomatic relations between the two countries. Although he spoke with such a heavy Sichuanese accent that his remarks were incomprehensible to most of us, his main message was clear: China and America should find common cause in countering the threat of Russia. As Deng traveled throughout the country, he behaved like an American politician by in-gratiating himself with the public, showing his gusto for local food and customs and being photographed at a rodeo in Texas wearing a ten-gallon cowboy hat.[69]

Equally pathbreaking was Deng's visit to Japan the year before, in 1978. Deng was the first Chinese leader to set foot in Japan in more than two thousand years.[70] Japan's brutal wartime occupation of China had left bitter feelings among the Chinese public, but Deng viewed Japan as China's best source of technological and managerial know-how and a potential ally in its contest against Russia and Vietnam. During the visit, Deng joked about how the traditional student-teacher relationship be-tween China and Japan had been reversed, and now China was seeking to learn how to modernize from Japan.[71] Deng held his first press confer-ence ever in Japan, and his answers to questions reassured the Japanese public. When a reporter asked about the islands in the East China Sea that both countries claim, Deng proposed a pragmatic solution: to put the issue aside until later generations, who might prove be wiser than the present one and solve the problem. Deng put the diplomatic and eco-nomic value of easing relations with Japan ahead of China's sovereignty claims.

As China was improving its relations with its Southeast Asian neighbors in the 1980s Deng took the same pragmatic stance of "setting aside differences and pursuing joint development" on the unresolved issue of which country had sovereignty over the South China Sea. Deng never deviated from the Chinese consensus view that China owns the South China Sea and the islands and rocks in it. In 1974, he had shared command responsibility with the PLA general Ye Jianying of the naval operation that seized control of the Paracel Islands from Vietnam.[72] But after Tiananmen and the collapse of the Soviet Union, events that had left China vulner-able to international isolation, Deng promoted diplomatic efforts for the joint development of the Spratly Islands in the southern area of the South China Sea, in an effort to preserve good relations with Southeast Asia.

Deng's legacy regarding Taiwan and Hong Kong, the irredenta territo-ries that are the focal point of Chinese nationalism, is the formula "one country, two systems": the Mainland will always be socialist, but Taiwan and Hong Kong could be capitalist. Deng was as determined as any Chinese leader to bring these lost territories back into the fold, yet he was willing to compromise to achieve broader goals. In 1979, after six years of tortuous negotiations with the United States over how Washington would treat Taiwan after switching diplomatic relations from Taipei to Beijing, Deng made the agonizing decision to normalize relations with the United States even though the US would not agree to halt its arms sales to Taiwan. "One country, two systems" was the shorthand for what Deng hoped would be an attractive offer to the people of Taiwan and Hong Kong—that is, that after reunification they could keep their own socioeconomic and legal systems and, in the case of Taiwan, even their own armed forces. He also could be patient; if complete reunification could not be accomplished in one hundred years, then it would be in one thousand years, he said.[73]

Deng approached foreign policy as a vehicle for creating an auspicious international environment for China's economic development.[74] By exercising restraint and showing a willingness to make compromises, he reassured his neighbors, the United States, and other countries that a rising China would not be a threat. After his crackdown on the demonstrators in Tiananmen Square and many other cities in 1989, Deng faced, as noted, strong international condemnation and sanctions, especially from the United States and other democracies. A few months later, after the Berlin Wall fell, and thereafter the Soviet Union, Deng urged Chinese officials to remain calm and resist calls to "take the lead."[75] It was amid this fraught situation that Deng spoke to his staff in April 1992: "Only when we keep hiding strength and biding time for a few more years can we really form a larger political force, and the weight of China's speech on the international stage will be different."[76]

Even according to Deng's own words, this low-key approach was likely to have an expiration date, as China acquired more weight domestically and internationally. By 2008, when the global financial crisis had created a sense of nationalist triumphalism in China, it was difficult for Hu Jintao and the CCP's collective leadership to sustain Deng's legacy of restraint. A leader like Xi Jinping has an even harder time disciplining his international ambitions, despite the consequences.

The ghosts of the founders of the People's Republic, Mao and Deng, are still warily circling each other in China's political life. The younger generation knows only the bare outlines of their deeds. Textbooks are devoid of detailed accounts of post-1949 China, and historical journals have been shut down for publishing critical analyses of the past, now banned as "historical nihilism." But even in their silhouettes, Mao and Deng stand in marked contrast with each other's style of leadership—Mao concentrated power and Deng began to disperse it. They also managed relations with the world and with their own society very differently—Mao through struggle and Deng though accommodation. One doesn't hear much about the Deng option today. Hu Jintao gave up his chance to lock in Deng's legacy by codifying his first-term reforms and building a coalition behind them. Peering into the black box of Chinese politics will help us understand why it was so easy for Xi Jinping to undo Deng's legacy and return China to strongman rule.

3

Inside the Black Box

C HINA'S POLITICAL SYSTEM IS almost as opaque as North Korea's, though it is far more open to the world. All governments keep some matters secret, especially when it comes to national security issues. But the secrecy in high-level Chinese politics is extreme. Chinese citizens and foreigners alike must try to figure it out by piecing together snippets of information and rumor. The mystery is how the leaders of a country with such a globalized economy and vibrant society have managed to keep its politics so contained within a black box.[1]

As we will see, though its leaders believe that giving up that level of secrecy could be politically risky, China pays a price for the secrecy of its policymaking process. Secrecy is a drag on the economy. It's almost impossible for the officials in one government agency to get information from those in another agency. Outside the government, businesses make inefficient choices because they are confused about which of multiple overlapping regulatory bodies will decide their fate, and they cannot predict how policies might change in the future. Secrecy also breeds mistrust by foreign governments and publics. China's central government and the Wuhan local government stifled information about the COVID-19 virus when it first appeared in January 2020. Who decided what to say about the virus and when remains murky. Xi Jinping quickly disappeared from public view for weeks but later gave a speech claiming that he had been in charge the whole time. By impeding the experts at the World Health Organization (WHO) from undertaking a thorough investigation of the origin of the virus China created suspicions that it must be hiding some malfeasance. When the Australian government called for a full international inquiry of the origins of the virus, the Chinese leaders punished it by cutting imports of Australian coal, wine, barley, lobsters, beef, and cotton.

Inside the black box, it's impossible to tell who actually makes decisions—the Politburo, the Politburo Standing Committee, or the leader himself. Beyond the announcement of a few of the topics that were discussed in the meetings, information about internal deliberations is minimal. Leaks are extremely rare; when they do occur, the leakers are punished by long prison terms. A Beijing journalist explained to me that he doesn't waste time trying to figure out what's going on in high-level politics because he knows he can never report it. The occasional hints about discord at the top always are directed to foreign journalists because they are the only ones who can publish them.

The lack of transparency about China's civil-military chain of command can create dangerous misperceptions in international relations. Foreigners don't know whom to hold responsible when, for example, Chinese troops cross the disputed boundary with India, or a giant deep-sea rig suddenly starts drilling off the coast of Vietnam in the contested waters of the South China Sea. Preventing crises from escalating depends on knowing enough about how the other side makes decisions that you can correctly interpret its signals. Confusion about other aspects of China's foreign policy can exacerbate the mistrust. When a magazine publishes a broadside against America, the question becomes whether to attribute it to the Propaganda Department, top leadership, or simply the magazine's commercial interest in attracting more readers.

China's relationship with the United States is unbalanced partly for just this reason: whereas the American policy process is practically an open book, the Chinese policy process is closed. The leaders in China resist American calls for greater transparency in the belief that keeping Washington guessing about its capabilities and intentions makes China look stronger. Yet by refusing to share information, Beijing endangers itself because its signals may be misread. Countries can only cooperate when they are able to make well-informed predictions about whether the other side will keep its commitments.

During Hu Jintao's first term in office, policymakers started to recognize that excessive secrecy breeds corruption—officials may extort bribes for promising to take administrative actions that are in fact automatic or the responsibility of some other department. After the SARS epidemic, in 2003, the Hu government embraced transparency (*touming*), along with the rule of law and other aspirational ideals. Local government websites started to provide information about the regulations and responsibilities of specific offices. The People's Liberation Army also made a nod to transparency by publishing defense white papers.

For years, some senior legislative experts have called for opening information about the government's budget, which China's national legislature, the National People's Congress, formally approves. Nevertheless, China remains near the bottom in international rankings of budget transparency, falling into the group that releases "minimal or scant budget information" to the public.[2] In September 2018, as the country struggled with mounting debt, slowing growth, and a trade war with Washington, Chinese censors directed journalists not to report any economic information for fear that it could harm confidence.[3] Yet businesses and investors need accurate information about market conditions to make rational decisions.

The Party's reflexive secrecy became more extreme under Xi Jinping. Yu Keping, a former adviser to Hu Jintao and a well-known advocate for governance reforms, has pointed out that it is not just businesses or foreign governments that need to know how policies get made. "Every citizen," he argues, "is entitled to political information related to his or her personal interests, such as selection of government officials, legislation, making of state policy, administration process and public budget."[4] The right to information could someday become a rallying cry for a middle-class movement in China, although most people don't realize their need for it.

Hanging Together

The Chinese Communist Party's obsession with secrecy stems from its origins as a Leninist revolutionary organization and a belief that only by presenting a facade of unanimity at the top can it prevent bottom-up opposition. As one Chinese international relations scholar explained, "Information is tightly controlled in an effort not to give the public the impression that the Party is divided on any issue."[5] A Central Committee member echoed this idea: "Chinese policymaking insists on secrecy to make sure they show unity at the top."

Two countervailing tendencies threaten to undermine all authoritarian regimes: splits in leadership and the rise of an individual who takes unchecked control. In the decade after Mao, Deng Xiaoping, as we've seen, concentrated on preventing the rise of another dictator. But ever since Tiananmen Square and the Soviet collapse, the specter of leadership splits has loomed larger. Western conventional wisdom assumes that most dictatorial rulers are overthrown by popular uprisings of the masses. In fact, most authoritarian regimes fall from the top down, not from the bottom up. More than two-thirds of the 303 authoritarian leaders who lost power by nonconstitutional means between 1946 and 2008 were forced out in coups staged by other members of the political elite.[6] Another count, dating from 1946 to 2010, which used different coding, had 35 percent of leaders falling to coups, more than to any other cause.[7] Though it happens relatively rarely, the possibility of mass uprisings against the regime also haunts authoritarian leaders. Chinese leaders are obsessed with what they call "social stability" (*shehui wending*). The term is a euphemism for the goal of achieving a quiescent society living under Communist Party rule. The Party employs a combination of economic prosperity, social control, and nationalist appeals to maintain mass support and squelch any potential opposition.

The dangers of elite splits and mass opposition are very much interconnected. Visible leadership divisions create a "political opportunity structure" that may embolden people to protest.[8] If the leadership group remains cohesive despite the inevitable internal competition, the Communist Party and the security police can keep social unrest from spreading before it threatens the regime. Without some sign of permission from the top, people will be too afraid to expose themselves, hence protests will fizzle out or never occur in the first place. Chinese leaders handle thousands of relatively small local protests every year by employing a consistent methodology: they express sympathy for the protestors, partially satisfy their demands, blame the local authorities for causing the problem, and throw the protest ringleaders in jail. When the national leaders are obviously at odds, however, protests can metastasize and the regime can unravel very fast. In the lead-up to the Tiananmen protests, Deng and Chen Yun were openly disagreeing about reform strategies. Meanwhile CCP secretary Hu Yaobang had been pushed out of power before his term ended, and his position as general secretary was handed over to Zhao Ziyang, who had been the premier. Zhao's position was also shaky, however, because he was under fire from Chen and the conservatives in the Party. Still, the students had reason to believe that some of the top leaders might be receptive to their complaints about corruption and aspirations for greater democracy or, at least, might treat them gently instead of sending them to jail.

Social unrest like the 1989 protests can create or deepen schisms at the top by forcing leaders to take a position on the protests and showing a leader who might be considering mounting a challenge that a following is already in place. After the student protestors began a dramatic hunger strike, Zhao made an unsuccessful attempt to salvage his career by aligning himself with them. He went to Tiananmen Square and apologized to the students, saying, "Sorry, we came too late," acknowledging the legitimacy of their demands. He implored them to end the hunger strike and called for a negotiated resolution to the crisis.[9] But his last-ditch effort failed. Having lost the support of Deng and the Party elders, Zhao was purged and put under house arrest until he died in 2005.

Party leaders try to keep normal policy differences secret because they can turn into politically divisive struggles. "China can have a serious political crisis only if there is a conflict within the center, among the leaders," one policy adviser told me. The tension among the leaders reflects policy differences as well as the clash of ambitions, he said. "They have different ideas about causes and remedies for the social changes that the economic changes have produced, namely inequality and corruption." Some, he added, "blame private business, foreigners, and the market economy, while others blame official corruption and the lack of reform."

Keeping elite differences concealed is considered even more crucial in the Xi administration, where the Party has reclaimed the job of policymaking that was once delegated to the government State Council. Therefore, as the Chinese scholar quoted above observed, "Issues of administration, which belong to the realm of government, and issues of ideology, which are the domain of political parties have begun to overlap." The result has infused politics into policy debates, leading to "intensely ideological disputes over the 'Party line.'" An open debate about policy can devolve into revelations of "internal Party disputes."[10] In the Mao era, Pekinologists, and Mao himself, used to talk about the "struggle between the two lines"—a battle between the leaders who supported Mao's revolutionary vision and those who favored a more practical approach to governing. Today, in the Xi era, observers are wondering whether a similar dispute over the party line between the pro- and anti-Xi politicians may exist but remain hidden.

In fact, elite unity is always hard to sustain in the face of the inevitable competition among individual politicians. As a group, the Chinese leaders want the Party's regime to survive; as the saying goes, if they don't hang together, they will hang separately. But at the same time, each politician strives to improve their standing in the inner circle or to maintain their position against the lower-ranked officials striving to replace them. What's more, each expects their fair share of the spoils of power, including patronage the job promotions and special policy treatments they can extend to their loyal subordinates. For some, the spoils of office include kickbacks for themselves and their families. CCP politicians also value career security. They live in fear of an attack from a rival or the top leader on charges of ideological deviation or corruption. As the authors of one prominent book on dictatorships put it, "Members of dictatorial elites live in grim, dog-eat-dog worlds."[11]

Although Party politics today are somewhat more predictable than they were during the Mao era, the rules of the power game remain unwritten and manipulatable. Party leaders can redesign institutional arrangements to enhance their own power. Deng was motivated to introduce retirement rules, for example, because he wanted to reduce the power of the other elders. Jiang Zemin got rid of his rival Qiao Shi in 1997 by proposing the retirement-at-seventy rule for Politburo-level officials; he then exempted himself as the core leader at age seventy-one. Hu Jintao lowered the retirement age to sixty-eight in 2002 to force Li Ruihuan, a popular rival, off the Standing Committee. Since then, the norm requiring Party leaders to retire at age sixty-eight has been consistently observed but never codified. Xi Jinping could very well make another change in retirement age rules to eliminate potential challengers and bolster his own faction at the 20th CCP National Congress in fall 2022.

The contest for power within the Party operates in a constitutional vacuum.[12] The nation's most powerful position, CCP general secretary, is not mentioned in the Constitution. Nor are the size of the Party's top bodies—the Central Committee, Politburo, and Standing Committee—fixed. The reach and decision-making authority of Party offices are not regulated by law. Party leadership is written into the Constitution, but the delegation of powers from the Party to the government remains unspecified. The CCP rules (but not the state constitution) authorize the Central Committee to elect the Politburo, Standing Committee, and general secretary, but the nomination and election process has not been standardized. As a result, leadership competition is fluid, and elite cohesion is constantly under stress.

In this amorphous environment, the CCP elite tries to coup-proof itself by doing everything it can to prevent individual leaders from plotting together. Politburo Standing Committee members are not allowed to socialize with one another or visit one another's offices; they communicate only through their secretaries. The leaders police one another, as well as the wider society, using surveillance technologies and Internet censorship. To guard against internecine power struggles, the entire Politburo must approve all corruption or Party discipline charges against officials at the vice-minister rank or above.

Despite the internal guardrails, ambitious Chinese politicians are sometimes tempted to reach out beyond the inner circle to mobilize a popular following. Mao himself did it to stop the bureaucracy from blocking his initiatives—that's what the Cultural Revolution was about. Party leaders are therefore understandably wary of politicians who seek popularity with the masses. Politics in China is supposed to be an inside game.[13] CCP norms outlaw self-promotion because it can mobilize an opposition movement. Any opposition that does take root is more likely to be led by a political insider than a complete outsider. Insiders have the organizational skills and political networks that could equip them to lead a successful break-out.

The Rise and Fall of Bo Xilai

As access to the Internet ballooned from less than 5 percent of the population in 2000 to 42 percent in 2012 to more than 70 percent in 2020, the possibilities for politicians to cultivate a popular following also grew. Although professional journalists in China observed the taboo against reporting on leadership politics and high-level decision-making, the media nonetheless turned some politicians into celebrities.

Wen Jiabao emerged as a media personality during his premiership (2002–2012), when he shared power with Hu Jintao. He appeared regularly on television, frequently with his arm around a poor peasant, tearing up like a Chinese Bill Clinton to show sympathy for the suffering from a natural or man-made disaster. He became the human face of the compassionate communism for which the Hu administration wanted to be known; his popularity was consistent with the goals of the regime. However, Wen also expressed sympathy for political reform and democracy in interviews and press conferences, which hinted at a gap between his views and those of other Standing Committee members.[14] Reports about corruption in his family rendered him a less serious challenge to the regime.[15] And in the end, his populist persona enhanced public support for the regime.

The Bo Xilai example, on the other hand, shows how a power-hungry CCP politician with a populist policy agenda can threaten the regime by exploiting new media to mobilize a public following. The rise and fall of Bo, the CCP secretary of Chongqing who was fired from the Politburo, tried for corruption, and imprisoned for life in 2012, is the most dramatic case of an ambitious politician who openly campaigned for power. A handsome, self-confident princeling—the son of Bo Yibo, one of the "Eight Immortals," the elderly revolutionary luminaries of the Long March generation who advised Deng Xiaoping in the 1980s—Bo had a master's degree in journalism and was adept at playing to the crowd. Throughout his political career, he cultivated the press and continually remade his image to adapt to the changing political terrain. When I first met Bo, in the mid-1990s, he was the mayor of Dalian, the biggest port in the northeastern province of Liaoning, pitching his reform-minded city to potential foreign investors. He then moved up to be the governor of Liaoning province, and after that, became commerce minister, a platform he used to transition from booster of international cooperation to staunch defender of China's economic interests.

Bo's open campaigning for power started ringing alarm bells among the CCP elite early in his career. In 1997, when he was both mayor and deputy party secretary of Dalian, he failed to win a seat on the Liaoning provincial delegation to the CCP National Congress—a slap in the face. With his father's help, he got to the Congress anyway, as a representative of another province, and made it onto the official slate for the new Central Committee. The Party Congress rejected him, however; he received one of the lowest vote tallies in the election of the new Central Committee. As commerce minister he became a Central Committee member in 2002, but when a new leadership team was selected in 2007, Bo received a lateral transfer to Chongqing instead of a promotion to a leading national post. The Party secretary position in Chongqing, one of China's four provincial-level cities and the only one located inland, automatically gave him a place in the Politburo. It also kept him far away from Beijing.

Considering his ambiguous political track record and apparent lack of popularity within CCP officialdom, Bo's best hope of being promoted to the Standing Committee was to ignore the traditional CCP playbook and reach outside the inner circle for mass support. Bo's populist policy innovations in Chongqing—building low-income housing, establishing a target for reducing inequality in the city, and granting urban citizenship rights for suburban farmers—appealed to the public and did not perturb the leaders in Beijing. After all, many of China's reforms were introduced first by local politicians. And his spending spree on local roads, power plants, and beautification—financed by massive debt backed up by land deals—was just an extreme form of what other local officials did to boost their hometown economies. By inviting the television cameras into his personal negotiations with the city's taxi drivers to end their strike in 2008, he won plaudits from all quarters—even the Western media—for transparency. Ordering Walmart to close stores because it had mislabeled some meat as "organic" may have been grandstanding, but it was consistent with the economic nationalism that was spreading throughout the country after 2008. Bo and his nationally known police chief, Wang Lijun, made a TV series celebrating their "strike black" crackdown against corruption and organized crime; and netizens started calling for Bo to lead a nationwide law-and-order campaign based on the "Chongqing Model." (The crackdown, not coincidentally, cast Bo's rival Wang Yang, the previous Party secretary in Chongqing and Party secretary of Guangdong, at the time, in the worst possible light.)

None of that really worried the Party leaders. What did worry them was the way Bo had mobilized a following by creating a cult of personality, much as Mao had done.[16] The popular blogger, novelist, and race-car driver Han Han compared Bo to Mao, who had also "skipped over the party organization and talked directly to the people.[17] Bo capitalized on popular nostalgia for Maoist values and culture by sending text messages of Mao's quotations to Chongqing citizens and holding huge sing-alongs of revolutionary songs in Chongqing stadiums. The revival of Cultural Revolution themes horrified many people in China, though they may have been a minority. One military officer I interviewed said that he, like other people, appreciated the positive side of the Cultural Revolution: "It was Mao's effort to attack high-level corruption, it liberated people's thinking, it enabled them to criticize their leaders for the first time, and it gave people ideals to make themselves more noble."

The last thing in the world Chinese leaders want, however, is another Mao, someone who turns the public against the CCP establishment. Neither Hu Jintao nor the Standing Committee had the gumption to stop Bo's bid for power. Any action they took to rein him in would have shattered the facade of unity. A consensus on how to deal with the Bo challenge may have been blocked by one or two individual leaders who secretly encouraged Bo's campaign or even conspired with him; the dominant theory is that retired leader Jiang Zemin and security boss Zhou Yongkang were Bo supporters. Still, as Bo's mass popularity grew, the odds against his being promoted to the Standing Committee also increased. Bo also was a threat to the other leaders; he allegedly ordered his security police to wiretap their conversations when they visited Dalian and Chongqing. To hedge against some unexpected event that might make it hard to deny Bo a Standing Committee seat, and so as not to alienate his following, sixteen of the twenty-five Politburo members, including eight of the then-nine Standing Committee members, visited Chongqing and praised Bo's achievements.[18] At the same time, the Party leaders initiated an internal investigation of possible corruption by Bo and his family and associates.

On February 6, 2012, Bo's police chief, Wang Lijun, who had fallen out with his patron and now feared for his personal safety, disguised himself and drove to the American Consulate in Chengdu with information about the role Bo's wife, Gu Kailai, had played in the murder of British businessman Neil Heywood in Chongqing. After spending thirty-six hours with the American diplomats, Wang decided to turn himself in to the central-level security agency. Secretary of state Hillary Clinton later revealed that the police chief "kept saying that he wanted to get the truth to Beijing."[19] To not embarrass China's leaders just a week before Xi Jinping's first official visit to the United States, the American diplomats were tight-lipped about what the police chief had told them. All my former colleagues would tell me when I asked at the time was that they had learned more in those thirty-six hours than they had from many years of reading intelligence reports about Chinese leadership politics. Still, once the Americans and the British were involved in the case, it became impossible for the central leaders to bury it, so they used it to bring Bo down; they charged his wife with murder and put Bo under Party disciplinary detention.

Yet even then, there were signs of differing views about how to manage the situation. Six days before he was fired, Bo was allowed to hold a press conference at the annual meeting of the National People's Congress, at which he attempted to defend himself.[20] Premier Wen Jiabao, in his own press conference, framed the situation as a fight between democratic reforms and "such historical tragedies as the Cultural Revolution," and admitted that the leadership system of the state and the Party required fixing.[21] The open splits in the top leadership unsettled the Party elite and sparked rumors of a coup. To restore cohesion, the CCP launched a massive propaganda campaign, vilifying the corruption of the Bo family and praising the Party's unity, purity, and commitment to the rule of law. At every stage of the Bo case—from his initial detention through his trial and conviction—all media were required to run the official Xinhua news service reporting and nothing more. Some leaders, nonetheless, chose to speak for themselves. Security czar Zhou Yongkang emphasized that the courts must defer to the Party.[22] In contrast, Premier Wen stressed the need for greater transparency in how the Party disciplines itself.[23] When Party propaganda insists that something is not about Party unity, everyone knows that it is entirely about Party unity.

Despite the shock of the Bo Xilai affair, Party leaders managed to navigate the 2012 leadership succession. They papered over the Bo case, mainly by trying and convicting him for relatively lesser acts of corruption and avoiding mention of his controversial practices in Chongqing. So things stood until Xi Jinping established his authority at the Party congress. Xi then accused Bo of "engaging in political conspiracy" to "wreck and divide the party." He associated Bo with several other high-level figures he accused of anti-Party plots: Zhou Yongkang, General Xu Caihou, Ling Jihua (Hu's office director), and Su Rong (former CCP secretary of Jiangxi province and China People's Consultative Congress vice chair), leaving it unclear whether they were members of one cabal or were plotting separately.[24]

In a society undergoing explosive change, political outcomes are unpredictable because the political game is evolving too. New opportunities and challenges continually present themselves to ambitious politicians in China. For one thing, the media landscape is constantly changing as commercial print and Internet publications compete for audiences by pushing the limits of what they can report. As a result, keeping competition among the leadership under wraps—as was barely the case with Bo Xilai—becomes increasingly difficult.

From Meritocracy to Virtuocracy

Because political success depends so heavily on personal connections, some think of China as a communist aristocracy more than as the meritocracy that the official media (and many foreign analysts) speak of in admiring tones. Despite all the attention the government has given since the Mao years to designing a system of official promotion based on objective measures of job performance, there are signs that the ruling elite simply replicates itself from one generation to the next.

Those within the Party who have dedicated their careers to bureaucratic reform would perhaps say that the meritocratic system makes it possible for China's political aspirants to climb the career ladder in the first place. Li Yuanchao, the head of the Organization Department during Hu Jintao's second term, was one such reformer, who had studied in an executive education program at Harvard Kennedy School in 2002. I met him in 2013. Unlike most other CCP officials, who typically greet visitors while sitting in the center of a semicircle of overstuffed chairs with lace antimacassars on the arms, Li sat on the long side of an ordinary conference table of a kind that could be found in an office anywhere in the world. He explained how he was applying the modern management methods he had learned at Harvard to improve the cadre personnel system in China. Building on the efforts of Zeng Qinghong, who had served as head of the Organization Department under Jiang Zemin and was then head of the Central Party School during the first Hu term, Li expanded the cadre evaluation targets to include environmental protection and other quality-of-life measures, encouraged 360-degree evaluation by coworkers and subordinates, and introduced open selection to fill positions by public nomination and voting. The goal, at least for reformers like Li, was to promote officials who were able professionals and well regarded by the masses, as well as having moral integrity.

The question is whether that blueprint for transforming China into a meritocracy had been faithfully implemented. For years, researchers have studied the patterns of official promotion, looking for evidence that officials are promoted based on their job performance as measured by hard quantitative targets of economic growth rate, tax revenue, social stability (number of protests), and some "softer" targets, such as environmental quality. China's dramatic economic success—and the popular support for the Party that flows from it—is often attributed to this system that ties political promotion to economic performance. But research findings have been inconsistent: some studies find that local officials compete with one another in a kind of tournament based on their economic performance scores;[25] other research finds that the personal connections between officials and those higher up count for more than job performance when it comes to promotion;[26] and still other research concludes that it is a mixture of the two.[27] The economic-growth targets are often blamed for incentivizing officials to put all their effort into growth, neglecting health, education, pensions, and clean air and water. They are also blamed for China's notoriously unreliable economic growth and environmental-quality statistics; local officials inflate their numbers to meet the targets they need to be promoted. Nevertheless, some credit this system of performance metrics for enabling the central government to drive the efforts of regional officials toward growth and other high-priority goals.

Some of the latest research on official promotion finds that the higher up you go, the more political connections matter. Performance (fiscal revenue and economic growth, but mostly revenue) matters most at the county level, less at the city level, and not at all at the provincial-ministerial level.[28] The general secretary and Standing Committee members have an interest in hand-picking officials who are loyal to them as province and ministry heads because these politicians also sit in the Central Committee that serves as the "selectorate" with the power to choose—and depose— top leaders.[29] "Performance scores are used only at lower levels," a retired Organization Department official informed me. "Evaluating provincial-level officials is too complex to measure by a single scorecard." Once you reach the peak of power, your personal relationships determine your fate.

Nonetheless, despite the limited conditions under which it is applicable, the performance-based meritocratic evaluation system still plays a role, particularly in those fleeting moments when the reformers have the upper hand. China is not in one of those moments. When he took over, Xi Jinping scrapped these methods of human-resource management, believing that they have weakened loyalty and discipline within the Party. His single-minded priority is absolute loyalty to the CCP.[30] Some in the Organization Department appear to welcome the change because it gives the agency more power by allowing them greater discretion in the process. When they were looking only at performance metrics, test scores, and recommendation ballots, the Organization Department was merely a "scoring staff."[31]

In short, under Xi, virtuocracy has returned to China after decades of effort to turn China into a meritocracy. Just as the word implies, virtuocracy promotes people according to assessments of their political virtue.[32] Communist systems are not alone in taking this approach. In religious states like Iran, individuals are promoted based entirely, or in large part, on assessments of their moral-political qualities. Mao sought to remake human nature in line with his revolutionary vision by rewarding political activists ahead of the educational and professional achievers. Xi has revised language of the Party charter to read that official promotions should "treat virtue as the first priority." The 2019 Regulations on Selecting and Appointing Leading Party and Government Cadres confirms that political standards must come first. In a related move, the performance targets for local officials now put "party building" (recruiting members, heightening their commitment, and strengthening party organizations in all units) as the primary criterion, ahead of economic growth and tax revenue.

Political virtue has also become a must in many other sectors. Affecting China's millions of public servants, whether they are Party members or not, the civil service law has been amended to require that all civil servants must have a "firm commitment to socialism with Chinese characteristics."[33] University admissions, professional advancement (including of university professors), and official promotion once again factor in political loyalty. Because definitions of virtue are always vague and subjective, officials can use it to promote their loyal followers and demote those to whom they have taken a dislike; virtuocracy fosters factionalism as ambitious politicians cultivate ties with higher-ups who will certify their loyalty.

In China, as in other virtuocratic regimes, people are expected to watch over others and to report politically deviant behavior or speech. CCP members are instructed not only to abjure criticism of the Party but also to defend the Party if they hear anyone uttering a negative word. Mutual surveillance (what the Puritans once called "holy watching") and mutual criticism are central to the life of virtuocratic institutions.[34] People start to avoid activists for reasons of self-protection, and everyone is hypercautious about voicing critical thoughts to anyone beyond one or two close friends or family. One lesson of the Mao era, an enduring one as it turns out, is that virtuocratic competition alienates people from one another as well as from the Party-state.

Nobles and Commoners

According to many people I have interviewed, the sharpest cleavage within the Communist Party today is between the *nobles*, the sons and daughters of senior officials, and the *commoners*, those from ordinary backgrounds, who typically advance through the Communist Youth League. The children of officials have a lot of advantages. "In principle, we treat everyone equally, but in reality, cadres' children have more chance to be promoted," a retired Organization Department official told me. They have been trained within the family—including learning the esoteric language political insiders use to communicate with one another—and attend good schools with the offspring of other officials, who constitute their political network; their parents can also make introductions and open doors for them, including to get a post as secretary to a senior official, which starts them one rung up the ladder. The children of officials have an edge in the virtue contest because they were "born red," and have been raised to be politically loyal since they were in diapers. They are considered a safe bet to fill positions of power because they are more invested than commoners in the survival of the Party—they and their families would lose everything if it were to fall.

The princelings known as "second-generation reds" (*hong er dai*), who are the children of the leaders of the Chinese revolution, are now in their political prime, having matured to the age when they can inherit the CCP patrimony from their fathers. Xi Jinping was the youngest of the second-generation reds eligible by rank and age to be promoted to the top when he was chosen to be the general-secretary-in-training in 2007. The second-generation reds are not a monolithic group. One group of neo-Maoists who call themselves the Children of Yan'an has called for the direct election of the National People's Congress and of 20 percent of the Central Committee, as well as for their own representation as a loyal opposition in the Politburo.[35] Others lean in the direction of the universal liberal values of a market economy and the rule of law.[36] But they all socialize together on the golf course and at historical anniversaries and memorials. They and their children and grandchildren marry one another, cementing their family alliances and collective identity. Many of Xi Jinping's most trusted advisers and senior generals are second-generation reds, notably Wang Qishan, Yu Zhengsheng, Li Zhanshu, Zhang Youxia, Liu He, Liu Yuan, Liu Xiaojiang, and Liu Weiping. Xi has sheltered members of this special class from the crackdown on corruption and violations of Party discipline—except for Bo Xilai, who directly challenged him.

Later generations of princelings do not have the prestige of the second-generation reds. Nevertheless, they have some of the same advantages, particularly if they opt for a political career instead of going abroad to school and becoming an investment banker or real estate developer. A number of executives in China's large state-owned enterprises have princeling backgrounds, which helps explain why the Party leaders protect these enterprises even though most are not profitable. Family connections through politics and business have produced a lot of millionaires.[37] Princelings perpetuate a style of politics based on informal relationships (called *guanxi* in China) rather than bureaucratic authority. During the 1980s, a transitional period when informal and institutional authority were mixed, one foreign China scholar predicted that institutionalized patterns would take over fully once all the CCP revolutionary founders had passed away. He didn't reckon on the return to power of the founders' progeny.[38]

Most of the political elites, however, are not princelings but self-made politicians who have climbed the ladder through their own efforts and talent. Because many commoners begin as university Communist Youth League (CYL) officers and go on to work in the national CYL organization, this group is often called the Youth League faction (*tuan pai*). Members of this faction, like Hu Jintao, who climbed to the top by serving as general secretary of the CYL in the 1980s, help one another get ahead just as the princelings do. Not surprisingly, these commoners favor a more merito-cratic system of promotion based on job performance over the virtuocracy that gives the "nobles" an edge. They also are more enthusiastic about institutionalizing the rules of the political game to make the competition fairer.

"Nobles" and "commoners" are loose affinity groups rather than well-structured patron-client factions. Nonetheless, the schism between them has the potential to aggravate a leadership rupture, especially now that a second-generation red "emperor" is on the throne indefinitely. According to one scholar who is a Party member, "Xi Jinping looks like he cares only about the other royalty within the Party, not ordinary members. At least that's how the ordinary members feel." With more than a tinge of resentment, some ordinary members describe the princelings as the "shareowners" of the Communist Party. They warn that conflict between the "owners" and the "mere managers" is growing. Party commoners have expressed their resentment of the favoritism accorded to the nobles by voting them down for Central Committee membership. Xi Jinping, Bo Xilai, and Chen Yuan, all second-generation reds, were on the ballot in 1992; none was elected. In 1997, Xi received the lowest number of votes of the 151 alternates elected.[39] Neither does the public have a positive image of princelings, seeing them as pampered, arrogant, and corrupt.

Playing to the Selectorate

Party leaders like Hu Jintao and Xi Jinping don't have to stand for popular election, of course, but they do have to win the support of the "selectorate," as I've called them, the group of people within the Party that has effective power to choose the leaders.[40] According to the Party charter, that group consists of the approximately two hundred full members of the CCP Central Committee (alternates don't get to vote on personnel matters) that is in turn elected by the two-thousand-member Party Congress.

The membership of the Central Committee consists of central government officials, central Party officials, provincial officials, and military officers. All of them were appointed to their jobs by the top leaders. One striking feature of China's political institutionalization is that the shares of the major blocs within the Central Committee have remained consistent since 1997 even as the size of the Central Committee has varied slightly over time. Provincial leaders constitute the largest bloc at 45 percent; the central government officials make up 25 percent; central Party officials, 10 percent; and PLA officers, 18 percent.[41] Almost all of the thirty-one provinces have two representatives in the Central Committee.[42]

The Central Committee, in turn, elects the top leaders—namely, the Politburo, the Politburo Standing Committee, and the General Secretary.[43] The election is by secret ballot. The slate of nominees—the same number of names as positions—is decided by a handful of leaders whose names are kept secret. In the case of the 2012 Party Congress, for example, most believe the nominating group included the incumbent general secretary (Hu Jintao), the presumptive incoming general secretary (Xi Jinping), the current head of the Party Organization Department (Li Yuanchao), and the previous retired top leader (Jiang Zemin). According to one party official, the list of nominees is further vetted by the Politburo and Secretariat members, and by retired Politburo Standing Committee members. Together, these leaders constitute the Standing Committee of the Presidium of the Party Congress. In 2012, this group consisted of forty-one people in total. The slate of nominees is then ratified by the entire Presidium, which has 237 members, who include Politburo members, retired Party veterans, leading ministry and provincial officials, military officers, and grassroots Party members (in 2007, the Presidium included China's Olympic champion tennis player, first astronaut, a female judge, and a so-called national model worker).[44]

The lines of authority between the top leaders and the Central Committee are what I call "reciprocal accountability."[45] The officials who are members of the Central Committee are accountable to the Party leaders who appointed them to their day jobs. At the same time, the topmost Party leaders are accountable to the officials in the Central Committee who elected them. Although top-down power is stronger than bottom-up power, the power flows in both directions, in an arrangement that is much like the relationship between the pope and the College of Cardinals in the Catholic Church. The key difference is that the cardinals have tenure and serve until they reach retirement age, whereas the officials in the Central Committee serve at the pleasure of the top leadership.

Normally, the central committees of communist regimes, and not just in China, have rubber-stamped the list of nominees handed down to them from on high. There have been some exceptions, however. In the Soviet Union, the Central Committee rejected the official slate twice.[46] The Central Committee of the Communist Party of Vietnam holds a multicandidate competitive election for the top leadership jobs: The top vote-getter becomes general secretary, the first runner-up becomes pre-mier, and the second runner-up becomes president.[47] Well-aware that one day the Central Committee members may just say no to the nominations they are handed, the top leaders have to craft a slate of nominees that anticipates the preferences of the selectorate (in the words of one offi-cial: "The Central Committee members are very powerful. If they are not satisfied, you will have problems").

Holding straw-poll primary elections is one way to prevent nasty surprises when the Central Committee makes its formal choice.[48] It also is a baby step in the direction of the "intraparty democracy" that Party reformers seek.[49] This system of gauging the popularity of candidates among the selectorate was tried out in 1956 at the 8th Party Congress, and then revived during the Hu Jintao administration at the 17th (2007) and

18th (2012) CCP Congresses.[50] One party official told me that he believed the primary election enhanced the legitimacy of the elected leader among the party elite.

However, fearing a loss of actual control, the leaders kept the primary vote totals secret and nonbinding. Because of that, rumors circulate about the process and the outcome. In both 2007 and 2012, the Xinhua News Agency openly reported accounts of the primaries, which took place before the Party Congress, only after the Congress ended. In the 2007 primary more than 400 electors (197 Central Committee members, 158 alternate members, and 50 retired leaders) picked the proposed members of the new Politburo from a list of almost 200 candidates (who had to be officials of at least minister rank and age 63 or younger).[51] A Party official contrasted the 2007 and 2012 straw polls. The 2007 primary "was the first time, it happened rather suddenly, and was conducted in a clear-cut, clean way." But in 2012, "the whole process was tainted because contenders anticipated it and tried to campaign." According to several interviewees, when Ling Jihua, the head of the CCP Central Office and Hu Jintao's right-hand man, who was also in charge of running the 2012 primary, turned out to be one of the biggest vote-getters, the leaders concluded that he had manipulated the vote count and fired him. In reports about the firing, the media[52] focused on the scandal and attempted cover-up related to an automobile accident involving Ling's son, who had died while driving a Ferrari with two partially dressed young women. However, some people believe that the real reason was the tainting of the straw poll.

It is widely believed that Xi Jinping became China's number-one leader in 2012 because he was the top vote-getter in the 2007 primary, defeating Li Keqiang, who had been Hu Jintao's first choice, and who ended up with the premiership. It would therefore be logical to assume that Xi would be a fan of intraparty elections as a method of leadership selection. Instead, after becoming general secretary, he ordered that voting no longer be used to select leaders at the national level or in provinces and cities. He scrapped the primary before the 19th CCP Congress in 2017 and substituted a nomination process that he completely controlled. Xi personally conducted fifty-seven interviews with senior officials, who likely told him what they thought he wanted to hear. Other leaders interviewed 258 ministers and 32 military officers. Xinhua praised the interview process as more democratic, free, and fair than the previous straw polls in which, it said, people voted haphazardly, voted for people with whom they had some personal connection, canvassed for votes, or even bribed to get votes.[53] (All of these behaviors, except bribery, are considered legitimate practices in democratic countries.) Xi equates open political competition with loss of control. He has lost a number of Party elections in the past, as we've seen. But he also had some experience winning an election that Party officials robbed from him: In 1986, the city of Xiamen experimented with allowing its local legislature to elect the mayor. The city People's Congress elected Xi, but the CCP Organization Department objected and nullified the outcome. Now that he's in charge, Xi has made it clear that elections have no place in leadership selection.

Provincial Clout

Since the Mao era, Party leaders have played to the provinces as a way to build support for themselves.[54] This helps to explain why policy implementation problems are endemic; provincial officials feel they can drag their feet in carrying out central directives they see as detrimental to them. Leaders in Beijing are reluctant to penalize the provincial officials because they need their backing as the largest bloc in the Central Committee (45 percent, as noted earlier). Provincial interests also are well represented on the Politburo: as of 2020, six of its twenty-five members are provincial Party secretaries, and an additional thirteen are former provincial leaders.

The leverage provincial politicians have explains why it was so hard to get China to raise the value of its currency and shift to consumption-led growth. As one economist told me, whenever the head of China's central bank suggested letting the RMB float in currency exchanges, he was accused by some of using the US government to press his view. "But the opposition comes from provincial officials who are worried about exports dropping. And most of the Politburo officials are former provincial officials." Central leaders sometimes complain, at least among themselves, about feeling powerless to command provincial officials. In 2010, I was told by a policy adviser that Wang Qishan (then vice premier and Politburo member) had made a joke at a Politburo meeting: "The central government is the opposition party and the local governments are the party in power."

But provinces also compete among themselves for investment funding and advantageous policies. As Shanghai politicians, general secretary Jiang Zemin and Zhu Rongji, his premier, were naturally sympathetic to the interests of the more advanced coastal provinces, whereas Hu Jintao and Wen Jiabao, who made their careers in inland provinces, advocated for the have-nots in the West.

In the early decades of China's economic reforms, the 1980s onward, foreign businesses could count on provincial officials to back them up in policy disputes with the central government. Although China is not formally a federalist state, the provinces checked the power of the central government by means of a quasi-federalism.[55] What some private and international business executives found particularly alarming about Xi Jinping's revising the state constitution in 2018 to scrap the two-term limit for his tenure as president, according to one private businessman, was that the provinces didn't stop him. In their minds, that meant that there was no longer any force that could prevent Xi Jinping from taking actions to squeeze or even expropriate private businesses in the future. The government's sudden cancellation of the IPO for Ant Financial (part of Alibaba) in 2020 after its founder and chairman Jack Ma dared to criticize financial regulators, as well as the penalties it charged Ant and other private Internet companies that followed, appear to confirm the businessman's belief that Xi has free rein to clip the wings of private tycoons who have become, in his view, too powerful.

Succession

It's a safe assumption that all leaders, including in democracies, view themselves as indispensable to the nation and would like to remain in office unless they are forced to step down. Many elected leaders have engineered constitutional changes or defied tradition to obtain an additional term for themselves, typically with poor results for governance. Giving up power peacefully is hard, and even harder in a nondemocracy, particularly one without any popular elections or clear rules about who gets a say in the choice. No written document fixes the retirement age or term limits for the general secretary or other top Party posts. Some of Hu Jintao's advisers I interviewed had hoped that Hu would write the two-term limit for the general secretary into the Party charter—matching that for the president in the state constitution, but he never did. If the Party elites can't agree on a successor, or if the incumbent stubbornly clings to power, the contest can turn into a power struggle that endangers the regime. The unwritten rules for how to choose leaders have been evolving in the post-Mao era, following the lines of what best protects the interests of the current powerholders and prevents public splits in their ranks. As magazine editor

Wu Si said in the lead-up to the Party Congress in 2012, "The old rules don't apply and the new ones are a work in progress."[56]

Still, two peaceful successions of leadership constituted a major achievement, one that established a valuable precedent to guide the Party's politically fraught transfer of power. When Jiang Zemin, having reached the age of seventy-seven, retired as CCP general secretary (2002) and president (2003), it was the first time a leader of a large communist country had ever handed power to a successor without dying or being violently deposed. The CCP's ability to enforce retirement rules and engineer a peaceful succession spoke well of its institutional resilience.[57]

The first peaceful handover, in 2002, was made easier because, a decade before, Deng Xiaoping had anointed Hu Jintao to follow Jiang, so the CCP elite did not have to deal with choosing a successor at the same time it was engineering Jiang's retirement. Hu leapfrogged over others who had more seniority to become a member of the Politburo Standing Committee in 1992, and then vice president and vice chairman of the Central Military Commission in 1998.

Jiang managed to hang on to his job as head of the Central Military Commission in 2002 because it did not have a formal retirement age of seventy, and the face-saving concession helped ease him out of the CCP general secretary position and the state presidency. But once he no longer carried the authority of the top Party post, Jiang's influence began to wane, and two years later, in September 2004, he retired completely. During the two years Jiang and Hu shared authority, subordinate officials were uneasy. When, on a visit to the United States, foreign minister Li Zhaoxing was asked a question about "China after Jiang," he quipped, "Not yet." And the last time two different voices were coming from China's leadership (General Secretary Zhao Ziyang and Premier Li Peng) it had caused the near disaster of the 1989 demonstrations. Now, anxious to avoid any threats to stability, senior and retired leaders reportedly convinced Jiang that the best way to preserve his legacy was to retire completely.[58] Hu, not taking anything for granted, praised Jiang's "noble character, sterling integrity, and broad-mindedness."[59] Hu had Jiang's selected works published, just as Jiang had published Deng's. Showing the previous leader respect by publishing his works is a traditional CCP form of deference.

The actual influence retired leaders have over personnel and policy decisions stands as one of the mysteries of China's politics today. Jiang, who had used his ten years in power to appoint a large flock of friends and associates to high-level positions, still held sway after his 2003 retirement, although how much is not clear. Almost everyone I interviewed insisted that he continued to have enormous power. But when I asked them to give me concrete examples of Jiang's interventions in decision-making, they couldn't provide any, other than to point to the high-level officials in Hu's administration whom Jiang had appointed, and who, they assumed, were still doing his bidding.

Hu did more than Jiang by voluntarily retiring from all his leadership positions in 2012–2013, including as head of the military. Although Hu had promoted some of the officials who had served with him when he was the head of the Communist Youth League, he lacked Jiang Zemin's appetite or aptitude for using his appointments to build a large personal faction. And he showed little desire to keep his hand in the game after retirement.

China's political elite has, on the whole, been unwilling to grant the incumbent leader the power to choose his successor; that choice requires a consensus decision by the small nominating committee of current and retired leaders and approval by the Central Committee. The first time the Party elite had to choose a successor to the current general secretary completely on its own—at the Party Congress in 2007—it opted to further restrict the incumbent Hu Jintao's authority with the informal straw poll described earlier.[60]

In the lead-up to Xi's midterm 19th Party Congress in 2017, a number of us made some predictions about what the outcome might be.[61] According to precedent, a midterm Congress prepares the way for an orderly leadership succession five years later by selecting at least one successor-in-training. If the 2017 Congress operated normally, one or two so-called sixth-generation leaders—born after 1960 (meaning they were under the age of 57)—would be promoted to the Politburo Standing Committee, to be prepared to become general secretary and premier. On the eve of the Congress, we were shocked when one of the most likely youngsters, Sun Zhengcai, was suddenly hauled away for violating Party discipline. And there was no sign of a straw-poll primary. Nevertheless, I still expected that Xi would follow precedent and appoint two young successors to the Standing Committee. Failure to do so would put a target on his back, unnecessarily exposing him to a backlash from other leaders.

Stability at the top depends on some form of power-sharing that commits the leaders to respect the interests of other politicians in the Communist Party.[62] That's why Party institutions are so important: regular meetings of the Central Committee, Politburo, and Standing Committee reveal the leader's intentions; retirement rules create opportunities for politicians to advance their careers; and the expectation of an orderly leadership succession process builds confidence between the leader and other Party politicians. But Xi revealed himself to be a risk-taker in intra-Party politics by flaunting precedent and not promoting a successor-in-training. No young leaders walked out on the stage when the new Standing Committee was presented to the 19th Party Congress. What's more, at the 2018 session of the National People's Congress, Xi pushed through the revision of the state constitution eliminating the two-term limit for the presidency, which until then constituted the only written limitation on his serving as pre-eminent leader for life.

Defying the institutionalized process of leadership succession may help Xi keep everyone off balance and dependent on him. For China, the tension and uncertainty that have ensued from his break from precedent heighten the risk of political instability and could veer China further off its course of peaceful rise.

Returning to Personalistic Rule: Why Was It So Easy?

Why, after more than thirty years of institutionalization, has China headed back to personalistic rule? That question haunts this book. Moreover, what does the apparent ease with which Xi Jinping engineered the reversal tell us about the nature of the Chinese political system—the black box with which I started this chapter?

It may be useful to sum up: First, the rules governing the transfer of leadership at the apex of Party power are unwritten. There are written rules that specify retirement ages for government, military, and Party officials at various levels and mandate universal term limits: a term is five years, and no official can serve in the same position for more than two terms, or in the same leadership rank for more than three terms.[63] However, neither the CCP constitution nor any other document fixes retirement ages or sets term limits for members of the Central Committee, Politburo, and Politburo Standing Committee, or the general secretary himself.[64] The retirement age for Party leaders has been lowered over time as a convenient tactic for eliminating rivals.

Second, the informal influence that retired leaders retain helps to check the dictatorial power of the formal leader—until it doesn't. Even though Deng Xiaoping had strengthened CCP institutions and regularized the processes of leadership turnover, after he relinquished his official posts, he remained the de facto leader until shortly before his death in 1997, at the age of ninety-two. The influence of retired general secretaries, though diminished since Deng's time, remained formidable—until recently. During the Hu Jintao era, Jiang Zemin was blamed for interfering in personnel matters and protecting corrupt officials. Yet retired leaders can also have a beneficial effect. Under term limits, the informal dynamics between the retired and current top leaders, as well as between the current leader and his heir apparent, can help to check dictatorial tendencies and ease power-sharing and patronage within the elite. As Beijing University political scientist Xiao Ma puts it, "This evolving bargain over allocation of political power among multiple generations of leaders further keeps any one faction from dominating the others."[65] But today, Jiang Zemin is ninety-four years old, and Hu Jintao, who is not yet eighty, stays out of Xi Jinping's way. And again, there is no pre-appointed successor with whom Xi must share the loyalty of the elite. The constellation of forces in elite politics skews drastically in Xi's favor.

Third, the effect of Tiananmen continues to linger. After the crackdown, influential CCP figures blamed the widespread unrest and open divisions at the top that had driven the political system to the brink of collapse on the Party's having given up too much authority by ill-advisedly delegating to the government. After the Tiananmen crisis, the Party revised the constitution, putting state officials on a shorter leash by restoring Party groups within government ministries. This reversal smoothed the way for the CCP under Xi to reclaim policymaking authority from the State Council. China's model of fused leadership in which a single person serves as general secretary of the CCP, president of the PRC, and chairman of the Central Military Commission is another product of Tiananmen. After the crisis, when Deng picked Shanghai CCP boss Jiang Zemin to succeed Zhao Ziyang, who was put under house arrest, Deng gave Jiang the title of "core leader" plus the three top jobs. The idea was to bolster Jiang's position in the face of political foes who might try to subvert him. Contrasting China's fused leadership with Vietnam's collective leadership, which divides authority among the Communist Party general secretary, the premier, and the president, highlights the long-lasting centralizing effects of the Tiananmen crisis.

Fourth, there are no institutional checks and balances outside the Chinese Communist Party. Even as he worked to make CCP rule more institutional, there was a line Deng Xiaoping would not cross, decreeing: "No Western-style separation of powers." This aversion to giving the legislature or courts the authority to check the power of the CCP or its leader meant that from the outset the institutionalization project had a built-in limitation. Today, the National People's Congress passes more legislation—and its lawmakers take their responsibilities more seriously—than before. But it remains under CCP domination, and its members are chosen by lower-level legislatures, not directly elected by voters. The courts, though they offer channels for redress of citizen grievances and commercial disputes, also still operate under the thumb of Party authorities. The Party center appoints the members of the National People's Congress Standing Committee and the judges of the Supreme People's Court. Neither institution has exercised authority over the actions of Party officials.

Finally, communist parties have an "ambiguity of authority" problem. With no institution outside the CCP able to check the behavior of Party leaders, this duty falls to the collective institutions of the Party itself, the Central Committee in particular. Over time, the Central Committee's composition has become more stable, settling at about 375 members — 203 full members and 172 alternates. The body has come to have a rough "job-slot representation," in which certain jobs, such as provincial Party secretary and provincial governor, include a Central Committee membership. Since 1997, the relative shares of the main blocs have remained, as I've said, steady.[66] The plurality that provincial politicians enjoy in the Central Committee means they are not mere agents of the Party center.

But the locus of authority within communist parties is difficult to pin down because of the relationship between the top leaders and the Central Committee — that "reciprocal accountability," as I've called it. The lines of authority and accountability flow in both directions, top down and bottom up. China's political system is a hierarchy in which the top CCP leaders name the subordinate officials of the CCP, the government, and the military. Yet the CCP constitution gives the Central Committee the formal authority to elect the Politburo and the Standing Committee members and the general secretary, making the top leaders accountable to a broader political elite. All Central Committee members, however, hold concurrent jobs in the Party, government, or military and can be dismissed or purged by the top leaders at any time.

Additionally, the Central Committee's ability to stop a leader like Xi Jinping from ruling dictatorially or making policy misjudgments is limited by how infrequently it meets (just seven sessions during each five-year period) and unwieldy processes (it lacks a committee structure). It operates in secret and is not accountable to the public. It is therefore hardly surprising that the Central Committee rarely asserts its authority. Instead, small groups of leaders at the top make all decisions.

As Deng Xiaoping noted in 1980, there is a "tradition of a high degree of concentration of power in the hands of individual leaders of communist parties in various countries."[67] Deng tried to overcome this dictatorial tradition by institutionalizing a system of collective leadership that would regularize succession from one leader to the next, govern the country responsively, and earn it international respect. But the arrangements he put in place were inadequate to prevent China's politics from reverting to strongman rule beginning in 2012.

The failure of the experiment with collective leadership began even earlier, however, in the mid-2000s, despite the good intentions of Hu Jintao. Party oligarchs and the bureaucratic interest groups under them ignored their self-effacing leader and declined to check one another. Instead, they enabled one another to pursue their own interests no matter how much they damaged the Party or the nation. As experts in American politics might put it, no one was looking out for the "party label." They overdid their actions, overreaching both internationally and domestically. The perverse consequences of collective rule—especially, the uninhibited corruption that flourished under it—became a strong argument for Xi Jinping's rejection of institutional niceties and his restoration of personalistic leadership.

4

The Rise and Fall
of Collective Leadership

Hu Jintao, the Communist Party organization man who was waiting in the wings after getting the nod as heir apparent from Deng Xiaoping in 1992, could not have anticipated the crisis that confronted him immediately after he assumed power in 2002. In November, just as the 16th Party Congress was elevating him to CCP general secretary, the first cases of the SARS (severe acute respiratory syndrome) virus appeared in the southern province of Guangdong. To prevent any disruption of the political succession, the government reacted reflexively by keeping the outbreak secret. As a result, the millions of people who traveled during the 2003 Chinese New Year winter holiday spread the disease to Beijing, other parts of China, and abroad.

In this pre-social-media era, the anxious public circulated short messages on their cellphones about the deadly flu. Then the police investigated over a hundred cases of people they claimed were "spreading rumors" by communicating SARS-related information to others. The news blackout continued into February 2003, when the independent business magazine *Caijing* broke the silence, and the Guangdong government finally acknowledged that there were more than three hundred cases. Yet Guangdong continued to claim to have the disease under control. The news blackout was reimposed in the lead-up to the March 2003 meeting of the National People's Congress, at which Hu added the position of state president to his titles. As the epidemic spread to Beijing, Ministry of Health and other officials kept insisting the situation was under control. A frustrated doctor at a military hospital who knew this was false sent emails to TV stations, but they failed to report on the story; finally, on

April 9, the US magazine *Time* exposed the epidemic and "triggered a political earthquake in Beijing."[1]

Once they were in charge, CCP general secretary Hu, the topmost leader, and Premier Wen Jiabao, the head of the government, who under Hu's collective leadership played a prominent role, tackled the crisis with novel candor and decisiveness. As newcomers who would not be blamed for the disaster, they took advantage of the opportunity to craft a fresh image for their leadership. They admitted honestly that the situation remained grave, lifted the news blackout, encouraged the public to report what was going on, imposed quarantines and health inspections, and punished officials for their failure to report cases and prevent the spread of the disease. They fired the minister of health and the mayor of Beijing and penalized nearly a thousand government officials.[2] According to one Party official, it was the first time in PRC history that government officials had been held accountable and punished for what he called "nonpolitical reasons,"[3] meaning caused by poor job performance instead of power struggles.

Western media had compared the initial information blackout in China to the cover-up of the 1986 Chernobyl nuclear plant disaster, which Mikhail Gorbachev later blamed for the fall of the Soviet regime.[4] Hu apparently concluded that he could govern more effectively if he allowed some opening of the media and Internet instead of squelching all bad news. Looking back to the SARS crisis from the vantage point of Xi Jinping's handling of the COVID-19 crisis, what's striking is that Hu called for more transparency while Xi used the public-health crisis to reinforce secrecy. Xi has strictly controlled the media and the Internet and vehemently resisted calls from the international community to provide information about the virus's origins. And his criticism of the initial cover-up by local authorities in Wuhan and Hebei province was muted in comparison with Hu's.

Under Hu the Party started applying a lighter hand to censorship. Studies of Chinese Internet censorship revealed a tolerance for political criticism—provided it didn't stir up collective action.[5] In May 2003, the media reported a submarine accident in which seventy sailors had died, and Hu and Wen were seen on television consoling the families and visiting the submarine, an unprecedented occurrence. The central government started relying on commercial journalism and the Internet to expose local corruption and other malfeasance, so it could fix problems before they aroused mass protests.[6] Watchdog journalism began to flourish.[7] Even the official media, competing for audiences, started to break important stories, such as the 2008 melamine-tainted baby formula scandal. In 2008 the Party went so far as to give the Xinhua News Agency a green light to report on mass protests. During the massive 2008 earthquake in Sichuan, *People's Daily* reported casualty statistics and received praise from Hu for doing so.[8] The trend toward government transparency got a boost from new rules—the Regulations on Open Government Information—which went into effect in 2008. Environmental departments and other government agencies started holding public hearings and using the Internet to solicit the public's views on proposed projects and regulations.

Beginning with the SARS crisis, Hu and Wen crafted their images as leaders who were in touch with the people and devoted to their best interests.[9] When Hu visited SARS-afflicted Guangdong, he invoked a formulation, "scientific outlook on development," which effectively became the bumper sticker slogan for his new administration. The concept, which *China Daily* defined as "putting people first and aiming at comprehensive, coordinated and sustainable development,"[10] entailed making a populist adjustment to the economic development strategy that had been pursued by Deng and Jiang Zemin, which concentrated on rapid growth and tolerated the inequalities that resulted from it. Deng had encouraged the coastal regions to "get rich first." The new leaders started to talk openly about the growing gap between the rich and the poor. They shifted attention and government funds to the inland and rural regions, which had gained less than the coastal areas from the market economy and foreign trade and investment. Premier Wen said that the SARS epidemic had taught them that the "uneven development" between regions could cause the country to "stumble and fall."[11] Instead of single-mindedly pursuing high growth, they began paying more attention to economic redistribution to the have-nots and the quality-of-life issues that Chinese people care deeply about, including air and water pollution, health, and education. They increased resources for public health, especially in rural areas and in central and western China. They also broke new ground by openly addressing the AIDS epidemic, a topic no Chinese leader had ever spoken about before. In December 2003, Premier Wen appeared on television shaking hands with AIDS patients and urging the country to treat them with "care and love."[12] (A few weeks earlier, former president Bill Clinton had hugged a Chinese AIDS patient at a Beijing conference on SARS and AIDS.)

Hu was an authoritarian modernizer who sought to strengthen the legitimacy of Communist Party rule by adapting it to China's increasingly mobile, urban, and affluent society. By 2008, China's middle class, which had been just 1 percent of the population in the early 1990s, had ballooned to

35 percent.[13] Hu recognized, as he noted in a Party resolution, in 2004, that the "CCP's ruling position is neither inherent nor permanent."[14] To retain public support he would have to satisfy citizen demands and, at the same time, keep the political elite cohesive. Together with other reform-minded leaders, including Wen, vice president Zeng Qinghong, Organization Department head Li Yuanchao, and Guangdong Party secretary Wang Yang, Hu tried to make CCP rule more responsive to the public's quality-of-life concerns, transparent, and welcoming of citizen participation and civil society—without going all the way to a full-fledged electoral democracy. In his first public remarks, in December 2002, Hu paid tribute to the 1982 state constitution and stressed that the Party must operate under the law.[15] Human rights and the protection of private property were incorporated into the PRC Constitution in 2004. In almost every village and in five hundred rural townships, mayors were chosen in popular elections.

Hu's style of governing reflected his modest temperament as well as his commitment to Deng's goal of preventing the overconcentration of authority. He was merely first among equals in the Politburo Standing Committee, now expanded to nine members. Each committee member took charge of a particular sector or function; the twenty-five Politburo members also had their own responsibilities.

Despite his achievements, however, by the time Hu left office in 2012, many Chinese disdained him as a weak leader who had presided over a "lost decade." Market reforms had stalled, and the government now favored state-owned "national champion" firms over private and foreign ones. To maintain stability in an increasingly restive society, the police had started beefing up grid-based surveillance and control; the propaganda agencies had tightened censorship in the lead-up to the 2008 Olympics and never relaxed it afterward. Official corruption had reached epic proportions, and splits among Party leaders broke out into the open. Internationally, China's bullying behavior in the South China Sea estranged its neighbors and alarmed the United States.

One academic disparaged the Hu decade as a period in which there was "no center" and "no real authority." Corruption thrived, and ordinary people sensed a "loss of direction." In Xi Jinping's mind the public's disappointment in Hu is behind his own popularity. "Collective leadership is just a name," he has said. "Everyone needs a final decision."

So, when we look back at the decade between 2002 and 2012, we see that China's overreaching began long before Xi Jinping took power. Paradoxically, it began under a mild-mannered leader who wanted to realize Deng's vision for stable collective leadership. We need to understand why Hu's model of collective leadership turned out to be such a failure and ended up diverting China's peaceful rise.

2008: Watershed Year

The 2008 global financial crisis shocked the Chinese system. It was universally agreed, even in the United States, that it had been caused by the failure of Western countries to properly regulate their complex financial institutions. China, protected by a financial system that was still mostly closed from the world, suffered less than Western countries from the global crash. Demand for its exports dropped, but the rest of its economy was comparatively unscathed. What's more, China recovered from the crisis much faster than other countries because the central government orchestrated and funded a massive stimulus. Beijing commanded banks and local governments to grant more than $4 trillion in loans to be used for infrastructure and industrial construction projects. Austerity was not in the program, as it was elsewhere in the world.

After 2008, the world gained a new appreciation of just how crucial China was to the global economy. Americans lost confidence in their own system and despaired that they were being surpassed by a more capable China. And many Chinese gained a newfound pride in the "China model," which meant looking at government influence in the market not as a "flaw" but as a "magic weapon" for stability and growth.[16]

The contrast between China's impressive recovery and the West's apparent decline aroused a surge of Chinese triumphalism and a craving for a higher-profile foreign policy. Liberal reformers watched the models of capitalist democracy that they once had hoped China would emulate being discredited. Zhou Xiaochuan, the governor of China's central bank, known for advocating the importation of Western systems of financial regulation, had to acknowledge that China should "not blindly believe in the financial systems of developed countries" because the financial crisis had "exposed all kinds of fatal injuries" in their systems.[17]

The year 2008 was a watershed for the CCP. Conservative Party members openly celebrated the superiority of the Chinese model and took advantage of its success to push back against the liberal "universal values" that were becoming popular among China's white-collar urbanites. A new, vibrant civil society had seemed to be emerging as people rushed to volunteer aid to the victims of a devastating magnitude 6 Sichuan earthquake in May. Charter 08, a political manifesto by activist and writer Liu Xiaobo (who later died in jail after being awarded the 2010 Nobel Peace Prize) that called for rule of law and democracy, had attacked the legitimacy of the CCP at the theoretical level. The Ministry of Propaganda and several Party-affiliated institutes pushed back at a seminar at which Standing Committee propaganda boss Li Changchun defended Chinese political concepts and criticized Western ones. The *People's Daily* followed up with six commentaries addressing questions concerning the legitimacy of CCP rule such as, Why should we maintain the guiding position of Marxism instead of diversifying the guiding ideology? and Why should we insist on socialism with Chinese characteristics instead of capitalism?[18]

In his report to the 2009 annual session, Wu Bangguo, the Standing Committee member who chaired the National People's Congress, China's legislature, pushed back against the liberalization trends, insisting that copying Western political institutions such as multiparty rotation, separation of powers, and a bicameral legislature should never be an option for China.[19] Legislators at the session boosted the Party's ruling legitimacy by reviewing what it had managed to accomplish in 2008—earthquake relief, the Beijing Olympics, and, of course, recovery from the global financial crisis.[20] The official media celebrated the country's achievements as proof "that the political path of socialism with Chinese characteristics is the only correct choice by the history and the people."[21]

Despite China's domestic successes, the official media described China's international circumstances as "grim," mainly because of the West's aggression and "hostile forces." "Our struggle against infiltration and subversion will be long-term, complicated and sometimes even fierce."[22] The more successful China was, the more Western countries would want to weaken it.

In the triumphalist atmosphere of 2008, some Chinese leaders started to take a more combative tone in their public remarks. Today, this style of rhetoric, which is associated with Xi Jinping–era foreign policy, is called "wolf warrior diplomacy," taking its name from the Rambo-style Chinese movie *Wolf Warrior II*. Xi himself had tried out this tone more than a decade earlier on a visit to Mexico. He had spoken to the staff of the Chinese Embassy and representatives of Chinese enterprises, telling them on camera: "Some well-fed foreigners with nothing better to do point fingers at us," he said, even though "China, first, doesn't export revolution; second, doesn't export starvation and poverty; and third, doesn't mess around with you."[23]

The 2008 global financial crisis may have provided the external shock that jolted China into overreach, but Hu laid the groundwork when he established a collective leadership in the Politburo Standing Committee that was more truly an oligarchy than what his more take-charge predecessors Deng and Jiang had created. The specialization of the nine Standing Committee members into separate sectors was intended to facilitate balanced decision-making; instead, it led the members "simply to defer to the authority and judgment of the leader in charge of the policy sector under debate."[24] The Standing Committee, instead of deliberating collectively, allowed each member a free hand over their own domain. The leaders achieved agreement by swapping support for one another's programs in a form of log-rolling that, like its counterpart in democratic legislatures like the United States Congress, leads to an oversupply of government programs. As a result of log-rolling in Hu Jintao's collective leadership, Chinese policymaking lost restraint and started overreaching.

A Self-Made Politician

Hu Jintao could claim no "natural redness" or political connections. One Chinese Internet entrepreneur noted that he came from a "normal family background and had no sense of entitlement," in contrast with Xi Jinping and other children of high-level CCP leaders. A Beijing law professor observed that the Hu administration was "transitional" and compared him to a volleyball player who sets up the ball for someone else to spike. His was an interim era. "The founding fathers had left the scene and their princeling children hadn't grown up yet," noted the law professor. "Hu and Wen were temporary agents, proxies, not the real owners of the Party."

The Hu family was descended from Qing dynasty teashop merchants who fell into poverty and political disfavor, and the communists confiscated their teashops and homes in the 1950s. His great-grandfather had moved to Taizhou city in Jiangsu province from Jixi county in Anhui province over 150 years before. Hu was born in Taizhou in 1942 and raised mostly by an aunt in her tiny home. Years later, his aunt described how Hu's childhood had shaped his character and made him upright. After graduating from college, he sent a substantial amount of money back home to his family every month, although he didn't earn much.[25] Years later, when his daughter went to Columbia University in New York City under an assumed name, she had to work in a bar because her father, to set an example for others, wouldn't fund her education.[26]

As a student at Tsinghua University, China's most prestigious science and engineering school, Hu not only earned top grades but also, according to one of his teachers, always tried to maintain solidarity within the group.[27] His classmates recalled that he wasn't just a bookworm; he also excelled at singing and dancing. He once performed a female role when singing in an opera at school, and he conducted the class choir;[28] he also was a student instructor for the university dance team.[29]

After graduating at the top of his class in 1965 as a hydroelectric engineer, Hu remained on campus as a Communist Youth League (CYL) officer until 1968. He was assigned to Gansu province, where he began a career as an engineer and political apparatchik. Whereas there are abundant propaganda accounts of Xi Jinping's Cultural Revolution experiences, little is known about Hu's experiences during that tumultuous time. The general assumption was that he was too old to become a Red Guard. Moreover, it is possible that his father was killed by Red Guard rebels. In an interview, one of his college classmates said that Hu had been sent down for hard labor and loathed radical politics because of it.[30]

Hu attracted the notice of mentors with diverse political leanings. His career took off when he gave a briefing that impressed Song Ping, the Gansu CCP secretary and political conservative, who, fortuitously for Hu, moved to Beijing in 1982 as head of the CCP's powerful Organization Department (see chapter 3).[31] Song promoted Hu to be Gansu provincial CYL secretary and recommended to Deng Xiaoping that Hu join the cohort of thirty-nine young future leaders who had been picked to enter the Central Committee in 1982.[32] After a stint at the Central Party School in 1982, Hu Jintao was promoted to be a secretary at the national organization of the CYL, and then was made head of the league in 1984. While working at the league's headquarters for three years, Hu formed a relationship with liberal-minded CCP general secretary Hu Yaobang, who had once headed up the Youth League himself. The two of them traveled together on an inspection tour in 1984.[33] The elder Hu's endorsement helped propel the swift rise of the younger Hu.

After Hu was appointed a secretary of the Youth League, Deng and the other Party elders tested his mettle by assigning him to poor, inland areas with ethnic minority populations like Gansu, which were notoriously difficult to govern. When he was appointed Party secretary of Guizhou, China's poorest province, in 1985, he was the youngest provincial secretary in CCP history. In 1988 he was sent to serve as CCP secretary in Tibet after the previous Party secretary had been sacked for losing control of the pro-independence activists. Deng approved of Hu's imposing martial law and suppressing the demonstrations in 1989, just when Deng himself was taking the same approach to the demonstrations in Beijing and elsewhere.

After Hu was allowed to return to Beijing and govern Tibet remotely because of his altitude sickness, his mentor Song Ping recruited him to help manage the Organization Department. Deng Xiaoping also entrusted him with preparing for the 1992 National Party Congress. At that meeting Hu was nominated as the youngest member of the Politburo Standing Committee, revealing that he was Deng's clear choice to succeed Jiang Zemin ten years hence. To Deng, the relatively young fifty-year-old with an excellent Tsinghua education, who also had earned the approval of both the conservative Song Ping and the liberal Hu Yaobang, must have looked like a good bet to unify the Party elite and lead the country into the twenty-first century.

Hu was picked out of the crowd because he was an attractive and talented young cadre who also was deferential to his elders.[34] By the time he became general secretary of the Party in 2002, however, whatever charisma he once might have had seems to have evaporated. In meetings with foreign leaders, he read the talking points prepared by his staff instead of expressing any individual views. During his time in office, everyone I interviewed described him as bland and unremarkable, virtually interchangeable with any other CCP leader in his cohort. Academics and journalists privately denigrated his ability. As one professor put it, "In China's leadership now, the number-one person is not the most able but the person most acceptable to everyone."

One explanation for Hu's rise to power was that the CCP elite protects itself by selecting leaders who are organization men, who lack the daring or personal following to challenge the status quo—or their fellow leaders. Deng saw Hu as malleable, according to one academic. An economist noted that Jiang Zemin agreed to Hu's succeeding him because he felt that Hu was weak and wouldn't resist Jiang's efforts to retain influence after retirement. Hu had worked smoothly under Jiang between 1992 and 2002, assisting him with several of his pet projects, such as the "Three Represents" campaign to bring private business executives and other social elites into the Party[35] and the closing of all the businesses of the People's Liberation Army. Hu had also supported the firing of Beijing mayor and Politburo member Chen Xitong for corruption.[36] The economist wryly noted that the fact that Hu had managed to serve as Party leader for ten years was a "sign of progress" in the Chinese political system; despite his "weak personality," the institutional norm of two five-year terms was followed.

Stepping back, we can see that China's top leaders became progressively weaker over time—from Mao to Deng to Jiang Zemin to Hu Jintao—as the political system evolved from personalistic dictatorship to more institutionalized collective leadership. "Deng could ignore his advisers. And Mao could ignore the entire Politburo Standing Committee. But now there is no strong man," observed one professor of Party history during the Hu era.

The general secretary's ability to make personnel appointments during the Hu era was limited by rules about term limits and retirement age, and the norms governing the representation of important bureaucratic groups in Party bodies such as the Central Committee, the Politburo, and the Standing Committee. Hu Jintao's low-key personality and collaborative style were well suited to this system of institutionalized oligarchy. A self-made politician like Hu naturally benefits more from a rule-bound system than from one that is based on informal relationships. For politicians without family connections, institutional authority is their most important source of power.

Intraparty Democracy

Hu Jintao envisioned what he called a "Socialist Harmonious Society" that put "democracy" up front: "The socialist harmonious society we want to build should be a society featuring democracy, the rule of law, fairness, justice, sincerity, trustworthiness, amity, full vitality, stability, orderliness, and harmony between mankind and nature," Hu said in a speech in 2005.[37] "Democracy" for Hu was a nod to Mao's concept of "mass line," but it also meant intraparty democracy—the right of Party members to express their own views, discuss them freely, and make decisions collectively—a norm Mao Zedong had propounded as early as 1938 in the CCP base in Yan'an.[38] Hu pioneered quasi-competitive elections for leaders, from the grassroots all the way up to the general secretary and Politburo. Intraparty elections could help check the monopolistic power of the "number one leader" (*yi ba shou*), manage leadership succession without destructive power struggles, and select leaders who would promote social harmony with the people at a time when social discontent, especially in the countryside, was brewing.

Hu and his advisers envisioned an incremental approach whereby intraparty democracy eventually might extend to popular elections that would be open to all citizens. Although Hu covered his political flank by emphasizing that China would never copy Western democracy,[39] when he talked about "promoting the development of people's democracy through the development of intraparty democracy" at a symposium in 2003 commemorating Mao Zedong's 110th birthday,[40] he was signaling permission for others to explore how this transition might take place.

Hu was advised by a Communist Party think-tank called the Compilation and Translation Bureau. Once a stodgy enclave of translators of Marxist texts and foreign communist party manifestos, in the 2000s, the bureau became a lively hub of political scientists doing research on foreign political systems. Two of its main conclusions were that "adaptability is key" for the survival of both communist and capitalist parties and that transparency is the international best practice to combat corruption.[41] Yu Keping, the deputy director of the bureau, wrote an influential article entitled *Democracy Is a Good Thing*, which was later turned into a book.[42] He became a popular speaker at conferences at American universities and at think-tanks like the Brookings Institution. (When the bureau was downsized and its political-science research shut down in 2015, Yu moved to Beijing University as dean of the School of Government.) Lai Hairong, another bureau researcher, collaborated with American social scientists to collect data to analyze the effectiveness of local experiments in transparency and participation in reducing corruption.[43] Lai also conducted a study of township elections in Sichuan that found that elections were a useful way to manage farmers' discontent with local officials over excessive fees and taxes.[44]

China's neighbor Vietnam had already begun to elect its communist party head in a multicandidate election by the Central Committee, and its national legislature, unlike China's, was directly elected. Chinese Party researchers and liberal intellectuals were intrigued by Vietnam as a possible model. Zhou Ruijin, a former editor of *People's Daily*, wrote that whereas Vietnam had historically learned from China, now "the student has surpassed the teacher" in intraparty democracy.[45] But the CCP Propaganda Ministry banned all media discussion of the Vietnam model, and neither Hu Jintao nor Wen Jiabao dared to openly defend it.[46]

Hu did, however, encourage provinces, cities, and townships to experiment with multicandidate elections of party secretaries and mayors. (Xi Jinping, who at the time was in charge of the Party apparatus, was at the forefront of the election drive; once he became general secretary himself, he banned such elections.) Pilot projects introduced the open primary in which a broad group of officials and notables nominated candidates, voted on a short list and handed it over to the upper-level Party committee to choose the winner.[47] Some ministries, including the Ministry of Public Security, also used this election method to choose bureau chiefs. By 2011, more than ten provinces and municipalities, including Beijing, Zhejiang,

Hunan, Jiangsu, Jiangxi, and Shenzhen, were also using it, which the official media presented as a good way to prevent the purchase of official posts
and other forms of corruption in cadre appointments, as well as to identify
new talent.

As Hu's first five-year term drew to a close, in 2007, he sparked a flurry
of open discussion among liberal Party officials and intellectuals when
he stressed intraparty democracy and the long-term goal of achieving a
people's democracy in his report to the 17th Party Congress; in his speech
he mentioned the word "democracy" more than sixty times.[48] A few
months earlier, the Central Committee had held the first-ever primary
election to select the short list for top leadership positions. Some officials at
the Party School predicted that the country was on the verge of democratic
reform.[49] Xie Tao, the former vice president of Renmin University, wrote
an essay praising the virtues of Swedish-style social democracy and said,
"We must not only catch up with other economies, we must also catch up
with the political trends overseas as well. Not everything can be decided by
one party or one person."[50] In US-China academic seminars at the time,
I engaged in lively conversations with Chinese academics who said they
anticipated that intraparty democracy would pave the way for broader democratization. But the rush of enthusiasm for intraparty democracy was
not shared by everyone in the CCP. The propaganda authorities, who generally resist unorthodox ideas, did their best to sow skepticism and tamp it
down. A *People's Daily* front-page article that appeared to be a response to
Xie Tao's comment defended China's political system, saying it was the
best suited to its national condition and warning that in undertaking political reform it was better "to make regular adjustments rather than change
with one stroke."[51]

Wen Jiabao was a forthright advocate of democracy, even more outspoken than the cautious Hu. The premier of China always holds a press
conference during the annual session of the legislature; something the
general secretary never does. At the March 2007 press conference, Wen
"set himself apart," Chinese newspaper editor Li Datong wrote in his
account of the press meeting, when he said that "science, democracy,
rule of law, freedom and human rights are not solely the domain of capitalism." Instead, Li wrote, "they are shared values pursued by humanity
over the long course of history, the products of a common civilization."[52]
On visits to Seoul and Tokyo, Wen had openly called for political reform
in the presence of foreign journalists, saying that the key to pursuing
social justice was to "let people be masters of their houses and make
every cadre understand that power is invested in them by the people."[53]

A small group of prominent elderly retired officials and intellectuals sent a memo to the Standing Committee in January 2009 to support Premier Wen and second his call for democracy, open media, and civil society to cure corruption, income gaps, and other social ills.[54] But a few years later, in 2012, rumors that Wen family's fortune was based on corruption were confirmed by David Barboza's Pulitzer Prize–winning investigative reporting in the *New York Times*. The consequence, a Chinese journalist told me, was that Wen Jiabao "gave democracy and political reform a bad name."

Hu's Oligarchy

Under Hu Jintao, Chinese politics gradually modernized—becoming more stable, predictable, and responsive to public concerns. Deng Xiaoping's goal of creating an institutional framework that would put collective decision-making in the hands of a stable oligarchy seemed within reach. With the Party now better able to manage the competition for power among the ruling elite, the dual risks of dictatorial rule and public splits appeared to recede.

The elements of that modernization meant that leadership competition was no longer a constant and unpredictable struggle. The competitive rhythm was regularized according to the five-year cycles of CCP national congresses and National People's Congresses. Term limits and retirement norms were rigorously observed. The orderly, routinized succession of the top leader was now established by precedent, if not by written rules. The incoming successor was selected two years ahead of time and prepared to assume power by serving as vice president, head of the Party School, and deputy head of the Central Military Commission. The Central Committee's authority as a "selectorate" that chooses Party leaders was reinforced by its holding of a straw vote in the primary nominating election. The Politburo's accountability to the Central Committee was reflected in the requirement that the general secretary regularly report to the committee about the Politburo's work.

The Politburo Standing Committee established itself as the decision-making and operational core of the leadership. Each member was assigned their own specialized policy portfolio.[55] Moreover, beginning in 2002, the Standing Committee was expanded from seven to nine members with the addition of the heads of the internal security and propaganda bureaucracies who constitute China's control coalition; the division of labor among the first seven members remained the same as when the system was introduced in 1997.

There were two other key elements in Hu's reorganization. First, the twenty-five-person Politburo now had consistent balanced representation from all major institutional constituencies: the party apparatus (6), government bodies (6), provincial representatives (6), and the military (2).[56] And second, the general secretary was just first among equals in the senior leadership, reversing the traditional domination by the top leader as the "core" of the leadership. When Jiang Zemin was general secretary, he was designated "the core of the Party center." Hu Jintao was never called the "core," and Party authority was described simply as "the party center with Comrade Hu Jintao as general secretary." A Party historian noted that the general secretary has only two formal powers—to call Politburo and Standing Committee meetings and to organize the work of the Secretariat. And "that's the way Hu actually ruled."

The Hu-era oligarchic rule seemed to be well suited to the national conditions in China and to fulfill Deng Xiaoping's goal of preventing bad decisions by a dictatorial leader.[57] Hu explained the main aim of the design in his mid-term report to the Party Congress in 2007: The new system was, he said outright, "an effort to prevent arbitrary decision-making by a single top leader."[58] It was to be implemented at all levels, from the center to the grassroots.[59]

The Tsinghua University scholar Hu Angang wrote a book at the time in which he praised Chinese-style collective leadership. It produced, he wrote, an innovative "collective presidency" that was far superior to the American-style presidency and the separation of powers between the executive, Congress, and the courts.[60] (After Xi Jinping came to power, Hu Angang scrambled to stay in sync with the new line; his latest writings make the case that the superiority of the Chinese system is based on its strong leadership core.[61])

Still, Hu Angang was not alone in praising Hu's collective leadership. In his book *The Politics of Authoritarian Rule*, American political scientist Milan Svolik assessed the institutionalization of collective rule in China as a positive example of stable authoritarian power-sharing.[62] Term limits and regular meetings of formal institutions, such as the Standing Committee, Politburo, and Central Committee, allowed politicians to head off any attempts by the top leader to usurp power. (Xi Jinping's subsequent concentration of power, however, revealed that the Chinese institutions of collective leadership were not as "self-enforcing" as Svolik thought they were.) Collective leadership had won China admiration from other foreigners too. In a 2012 survey, American CEOs ranked the Chinese Communist Party system as the third most competent and credible institution in the world, right behind multinational corporations and central banks, and way ahead of the US president or Congress.[63]

But, then as now, many Chinese I interviewed disagreed; they believed that under Hu Jintao, the Chinese policy process, domestic policy as well as foreign policy, was broken. Hu was too timid to make executive decisions and thus allowed the clash of interest groups, represented in government ministries, Party bodies, and provinces, to go off in different and sometime contradictory directions and stall progress on many fronts.

One Chinese academic compared the very positive "outside view" of Hu Jintao with the equally negative "inside view." The outside view was that Hu promoted intraparty democracy and allowed Weibo—China's equivalent of Twitter—to develop. The "inside view" was that there was chaos. Factional splits threatened Party control and, in turn, led to corruption, even in the PLA.

It is undeniable that coordination problems worsened under Hu as more interest groups entered the policy game. The leaders in the Standing Committee were unwilling to disagree with one another for fear of opening up splits in the oligarchy; economic policymaking in the State Council bogged down from clashes among various interest groups; and there was no clear direction coming from the Party leadership. Starting as early as 2004, Chinese scholars and journalists began to write about departmental interest groups that were pursuing their narrow self-interests through regulation and legislation.[64] Xinhua dubbed the phenomenon "legislative Balkanization";[65] other state media talked about "kidnapping legislation."[66] In industries like petroleum, coal, and electric power, which were dominated by state-owned monopolies, government agencies were the most prone to bending the rules for their own benefit. The lack of third-party monitors abetted the government's collusion with economic interest groups. Government departments exploited their authority to approve projects to solicit bribes and kickbacks.[67]

According to many people within China, the problems originated with the top leader. Hu could never fully establish his authority because he was always looking over his shoulder at retired leader Jiang Zemin. Some of the people I interviewed joked uneasily about calling this period the "Hu-Jiang era," not the "Hu era." The Jiang overhang was obvious in 2002 and 2004, the first two years of Hu's term, when Jiang clung to power as commander in chief and chairman of the Central Military Commission. Officials, particularly military officers, expressed discomfort at having two bosses. Many believed that even after Jiang had completely retired, in September 2004, he continued to meddle in decisions. Numerous Politburo, Standing Committee, and senior military leaders had served under Jiang and were believed still to be guided by their patron.

Hu's inability to establish himself as the commander in chief was one of the most conspicuous examples of how Jiang undercut his authority. Jiang's longtime secretary Jia Tingan, who had served as the deputy director of the Central Military Commission general office from 1994 to 2003, remained entrenched as director of that crucial office until 2008, four years after Jiang had retired and Hu formally taken charge.

The example of Zeng Qinghong, Jiang's closest and most powerful right-hand man, however, shows that some of the politicians affiliated with Jiang operated independently and were not just their former leader's puppets. During Hu's first term, Zeng, who had led the Secretariat and Organization Department under Jiang, joined the Standing Committee under Hu and served as vice president and head of the Party School. At the time, he worked well with his new boss, and had oversight of an important program to improve the Party's ruling capacity and related political reform initiatives. According to foreign journalists, Zeng had even helped Hu engineer Jiang Zemin's retirement.[68] Hu succeeded in co-opting Zeng and other putative Jiang loyalists to bring them into his populist program to reduce regional inequality, promote a harmonious society, and provide greater transparency and institutionalization.[69] The general secretary entrusted Zeng with drafting and expressing the Party's views on the lessons of the collapse of the Soviet Union in 2004—a highly sensitive political task.[70] Cheng Li, a Brookings China scholar, described the Hu administration as "bipartisan," an alliance between the "populist coalition" led by Hu Jintao and Wen Jiabao, who represented the interests of the inland regions (China's "red states"), more traditional economic sectors, and less-privileged groups such as farmers and migrant workers, and the "elitist coalition" of Zeng and a few others led by Jiang Zemin, which included people from Shanghai and the children of former officials and represented the interests of the coastal regions (China's "blue states"), new economic sectors, entrepreneurs, the emerging middle class, and foreign educated returnees.[71]

Nine Dragons

Another problem facing collective leadership involved the expansion, discussed earlier, of the Standing Committee to nine members in 2002, from seven members in the 1990s, and five in the 1980s. Each of the nine oligarchs was a powerful politician who defended the interests of his own organization or sector.

Singapore-based political scientist Zheng Yongnian has observed that the nine-person Standing Committee was "too big to operate." The size had mattered less when China had strongman leaders like Mao or Deng, who could bang the gavel and force agreement. But without strong leadership, wrote Zheng, the division of labor among the nine members stymied consensus-building. Debunking Hu Angang's praise of China's "collective presidency," Zheng observed that "the final outcome of the collective presidency is inevitably that there is no president, and the collective responsibility within the ruling party often turns into a situation of de facto collective irresponsibility."[72]

Why, then, was the Standing Committee expanded? As with so many decisions in the black box of Chinese politics, we don't know the backstory. Two possible explanations relate to the challenge of navigating a smooth transition between Jiang Zemin and Hu Jintao in 2002. One is that by creating more Standing Committee seats, the Party was able to promote all six of the incumbent Politburo members of eligible age to the Standing Committee, thereby avoiding the risk of disappointed losers fighting back. The other is that these six politicians had all been promoted by Jiang and that he might have insisted on elevating them as the price of agreeing to retire as general secretary. With his close associates constituting a majority inside the Standing Committee Jiang could continue to steer the Party from backstage.

What made the expansion of the Standing Committee particularly unwieldly and therefore, as I would argue, prone to overreaching was, as noted, that the two new slots were awarded to internal security and propaganda, the organizations in the "control coalition" in charge of maintaining the Party's firm grip over society, and both were led by Jiang holdovers.[73] Bureaucratic self-interest inclines internal security and propaganda agencies to hype the threat of social unrest and make overly strenuous efforts to preserve stability (*weiwen*). In the past, the heads of the internal security and propaganda departments were no higher than Politburo rank. Elevating their rank made them unstoppable unless the other Standing Committee members or the general secretary vetoed their demands, something that rarely happened. This institutional arrangement appeared to be purposeful, reflecting the growing clout of the police and propaganda censors as the Party struggled to contain the multiplying social protests, both on the Internet and in the streets. In provinces and cities, the heads of the various police and propaganda departments also were elevated from ordinary members of the Party committees to vice secretaries.

Bureaucratic Fiefdoms

Bureaucratic interest groups in China are stovepiped—meaning separate organizations that reach down from Beijing to the provinces and cities and essentially go their own way with little oversight, although the local Party committees do have some say over personnel appointments. Still, each bureaucracy pushes for policies that enhance its budgets, staffing, and influence, with little regard for the ramifications for the CCP as a whole. The businesses that get contracts from these bureaucracies and depend on them for regulatory protection become part of their teams. Old industries like oil, coal, and steel, along with new ones like electronics and telecommunications, "capture" bureaucracies, which advocate on their behalf. The Chinese bureaucratic system has a "highly competitive culture," as one journalist described it. The heads of the bureaucracies pursue self-interest "camouflaged in grand goals." They propose their own budgets and make most of the laws, he added. And their authority to approve projects or grant special policy preferences gives them ample opportunities for bribery.

Most officials spend their entire careers in one of these stovepiped bureaucracies (in Chinese: xitong, or "systems")—public security, propaganda, foreign affairs, finance, or working in various industries like electronics, steel, coal, or railroads. Only the most successful politicians rotate through regional leadership roles and different vertical bureaucracies as they rise to the top ranks of the Communist Party. But—and this is critically important—once these high-flyers rise to the pinnacle of power in the Politburo or the Standing Committee, they are assigned responsibility for a particular portfolio that requires them to oversee—and represent the interests of—a cluster of related bureaucracies. The top politicians also chair the "leading small group" (lingdao xiaozu; some relabeled "commissions," weiyuanhui, under Xi Jinping), which is supposed to coordinate the agencies within the cluster. The four vice premiers and five state councilors in the State Council also are assigned their own portfolios of agencies. This portfolio system, which was used in the Soviet Union under Brezhnev, is designed to keep the leaders from stepping on one another's toes and to maintain a proper balance among the key constituencies within the communist party-state.

Many people I spoke to described the Standing Committee under Hu as a set of feudal lords. "There are nine kingdoms and only the Emperor has very limited access to these domains," said one journalist. A law professor described the Hu system as a spoils system in which there was "a division of power and division of booty among sub-emperors." These "sub-emperors" controlled their own patronage and had the authority to select and promote the officials in the bureaucracies for which they were responsible. A recent paper by Beijing University economists confirms that the authority to make high-level appointments was dispersed among Standing Committee members under Hu and is centralized under the general secretary under Xi.[74]

"The base of the system is the appointment of personnel," one financial official told me. "Those who are appointed by you listen to you. Each official has people he promoted, which leads to factional politics." For example, Zhou Yongkang, the internal security boss under Hu, had an especially powerful faction consisting of senior officials from the energy sector, where he had spent most of his career, as well as high-level appointees in all the internal security ministries, and judicial bodies under the powerful Communist Party organization called the Political Legal Commission, which he headed. The vice chairmen of the Central Military Commission, the Communist Party organization that directs the PLA, appointed the generals. One measure of an agency's power is the number of ministerial-level positions it contains, one scholar told me, pointing to the large numbers of ministers and vice ministers under two of the most influential departments within the Party, the CCP Propaganda Department and CCP Organization Department.

Oligarchy and Overreach

The Chinese government and the Chinese Communist Party typically make decisions by consensus.[75] In the Hu-era oligarchy, however, consensus became an elusive goal. As noted, more interest groups entered the policy game, which made the leaders less willing to exert their authority or disagree with one another—as always, for fear of opening up splits among the top leaders. The specialization of each Standing Committee member in distinct policy sectors, as described earlier, led to what one scholar has called "undercoordinated and imbalanced decision-making" because the members deferred to whoever was in charge of the policy sector under debate.[76]

The question then became how to manage competition within the closed politics of the CCP. Preserving solidarity in a closed authoritarian oligarchy that has an open economy and commercialized media is extraordinarily difficult. The Party barons maintained a fragile unity by carefully respecting their division of responsibilities instead of deliberating collectively. Each of them stayed in their own lane and went along with whatever the others wanted to do in their lanes. The shortcoming of this arrangement, according to a professor of Marxism, was the lack of any mutual supervision among the barons, nothing stopping them from overdoing their own preferred policies. Neither was there any external mechanism—such as popular elections or nongovernmental organizations—to moderate the actions of the powerholders. That is why authoritarian oligarchies are more prone to overreach than democratic systems, in which the public can vote out politicians who damage the public interest in pursuit of their narrow concerns.

To paper over cracks in the oligarchy that could widen and bring the regime down, and to ensure that each leader could protect himself from the others ganging up on him, the leaders made decisions by a form of "logrolling," a term that originated in American politics meaning the "trading of votes by legislators to secure favorable action on projects of interest to each one." Vote trading often results in more total spending on government programs. The CCP Standing Committee is obviously quite different from the US Congress. Still, we find the politicians in the CCP leadership reciprocally endorsing one another's policies and funding proposals,[77] following the informal rule: "I'll go along with what you want to do in your domain if you let me call the shots in my domain."[78]

Several high-level policy advisers who have briefed the leadership tell me that, as a rule, unless it is a crisis, issues are left to the relevant agency instead of being deliberated in the group setting. If the group does discuss the issue, the politician in charge of the area dominates the process. He alone speaks on it; the others simply nod in assent. "Some agencies speak louder and others listen, even the top leader . . . the policies that result are often contradictory," said one economist. Pin Ho, a Hong Kong observer, reports: "In Politburo Standing Committee meetings, each member has his own axe to grind. They usually don't oppose one another's policy proposals and personnel appointments because they know others will repay them in kind in the future."[79]

The oligarchs functioned as an alliance of parochial interests instead of a unified executive looking after the long-term interests of the nation or the

Party as a whole. Under Hu, China was a collection of leaders, not a collective leadership. The danger of logrolling in a communist oligarchy is that well-organized parochial interest groups can hijack national policy, taking it in directions that benefit themselves but are destructive of the national good. Each group gets what it most wants and the costs are diffused — both financial costs such as state taxes and international costs imposed by foreign countries. The groups most capable of running away with national policy are those with well-structured organizations, and that can exploit the emotional resonance of national myths related to foreign and domestic threats. The whole process becomes hostage to special interests; once a powerful sector, for example, the oil industry, captures one or more Standing Committee or Politburo members, none of the other members or the top leader himself will stand in its way.

Jack Snyder's classic study of logrolling and overexpansion in pre–World War II Germany and Japan, *Myths of Empire: Domestic Politics and International Ambition*, offers insight into why Chinese foreign and domestic policy shifted toward overreach during Hu Jintao's oligarchic rule. In China, as in Germany and Japan, power assets became concentrated in parochial groups with narrow interests and advantages. The military and the control coalition benefited from overexpansion, and the costs were borne by the public at large. The groups in the coalition created myths about the existence of international threats that resonated with the people. Even those who invented the myths came to believe them. The state was unable to pull back when costs rose because the leadership was not a "unitary rational actor," but rather "the manager of a heterogeneous coalition that constrain[ed] the leadership's ability to adjust policy."[80] During the Hu era, a handful of people started to warn that China was following the catastrophic path taken by prewar Germany and Japan.[81] But Hu Jintao never was able to get the various foreign policy and security agencies to pull back.

Another path that Hu Jintao didn't take was the creation of a "reform coalition" to provide a counterweight to the control coalition and prevent his first term reforms from degenerating during his second term. Imagine if Hu had mobilized the growing middle class, private businesspeople, and intellectuals and professionals behind his efforts to strengthen rule of law, media and internet openness, and civil society. Wen Jiabao and Wang Yang, along with other Standing Committee politicians Zeng Qinghong and Li Yuanchao, were appealing to this potential constituency so we know that it existed in an inchoate form. But Hu Jintao lacked the vision or the drive to risk party unity.

China's unelected leaders are even more nervous about their lack of legitimacy than the leaders of prewar Germany and Japan were. Their insecurity means that the risk of overreaching is greater and extends to the domestic, as well as international front. The mythmakers hype the threat of both domestic chaos and encirclement by foreign powers.

Rights Defense (*Weiquan*)

As early as 2006, as I noted in the prologue, Beijing began to clash with its neighbors and the United States in the South China Sea. China expanded the category of "core interests" that it would fight to defend, previously limited to Taiwan, to include Tibet and Xinjiang; and when North Korea made unprovoked attacks on a South Korean naval vessel and a South Korean island populated by civilians as well as the military, China sided with the North. Until then Beijing's restrained diplomacy had been successful in enhancing its regional influence in a nonthreatening way. It was hard to understand what was driving the shift toward assertiveness.

Like others, my first hunch was that the global financial crisis was responsible. As noted, China recovered first, while the United States, having created the crisis by its own systemic failures, was still struggling. Misperceptions about American decline and Chinese power had stirred up nationalist demands for a more muscular foreign policy. But why Beijing had chosen the South China Sea as an arena for confrontation was a mystery. Before 2009 the South China Sea issue never got much ink in the media or attention from nationalist youth. The public dwelled much more on Japan and Taiwan than the South China Sea.

From interviews I learned that Foreign Ministry diplomats had begun to lose their monopoly over Asian regional issues. The policy arena had become crowded with Party, regional, maritime, military, and industry groups promoting their own agendas and diluting the power of the Foreign Ministry. The Propaganda Ministry, the big state energy companies, and the CCP Liaison Department, which handles party-to-party relations with other countries, such as North Korea, were among the powerful new players in the foreign policy arena. The Foreign Ministry competes with these other organizations, and it "does not always have the upper hand," according to one study.[82] One ambassador lamented, "The Foreign Ministry is now just the secretariat and the embassies are protocol offices."

Some of these groups were pursuing bigger budgets and more ships, planes, and bureaucratic influence in the guise of defending Chinese sovereignty in the South China Sea. Each of these relatively narrow interest groups had an overlord who represented it in the Politburo or on the Standing Committee, someone whom no one dared deny, not even general secretary Hu. Some of these organized interests—such as the fisheries bureau or the oceanographic bureau—were not known as bureaucratic heavy hitters. But in a logroll with the Chinese Navy, state oil companies, Hainan island (China's southernmost province), and a number of other agencies, they had an unobstructed path to overreach.

The CCP Propaganda Department and its affiliated organizations joined in the logroll. Muscle flexing is easier to sell than self-restraint in a country that is experiencing double-digit rates of economic growth. The overconfidence that followed China's rapid recovery from the 2008 crisis made the ground for territorial claims more fertile. The propagandists concocted a history in which the entire South China Sea, not just its atolls and islands, belonged to China because its "historical rights" had been established in 1948 by a line drawn on a map by the Kuomintang government.[83] The media coverage of the ships and planes operating in the South China Sea under the banner of "rights defense" (*weiquan*) soon turned the South China Sea into a popular cause. Elites started to believe their own propaganda—a phenomenon known as "blowback."[84]

Although China was using the white-hull vessels of civilian agencies in the South China Sea rather than the People's Liberation Navy and Air Force, the military and the military industries joined in the logroll and lent it greater heft. The PLA Navy had been waiting for years to extend its mission to the defense of the South China Sea. The navy's shipbuilding, training exercises, and public rhetoric powered the actions of the civilian interest groups. China's state-owned shipbuilding industry, the largest in the world, which produces both commercial and military vessels, started churning out naval ships, including aircraft carriers, at a rapid pace. In his report to the Party Congress in 2012, Hu Jintao declared that China's objective was to become a maritime great power. Between 2015 and 2020 it crossed a threshold by fielding more battle force ships (360) than the US Navy (297). Adding in the Coast Guard and Maritime Militia, China's three naval fleets total over seven hundred ships, making it the biggest maritime force in the world. Their quality is also improving, as is their sophistication. According to Andrew Erickson, a leading expert on the Chinese Navy, China is "modern history's sole example of a 'land' power successfully becoming a 'sea' power."[85]

As these groups logrolled their interests, in combination they generated more aggressive outcomes than any of them may have desired individually.[86] As I noted in the prologue, China's overreaching in the South China Sea sullied its reputation as a benign power. Chinese coast guard cutters and fishing militia clashed with the fishing boats and drilling vessels of their neighbors. They went so far as to challenge US Navy research and surveillance ships. Their aggressiveness radically revised the international narrative about the kind of rising power China was. Hu-era maritime overreach sparked a recoil that over time would build an international coalition to contain it—the costly self-encirclement that Deng Xiaoping and Jiang Zemin's more accommodating strategy had sought to avoid.

Stability Maintenance (*Weiwen*)

At roughly the same time as the Hu regime started overreaching internationally during his second term (2007 to 2012), it also started overreaching domestically by intensifying its social control. Logrolling by the control coalition, consisting of the propaganda and Party disciplinary agencies as well as intelligence, internal security, and the military, produced a gargantuan machine for what was called "stability maintenance" (*weiwen*) that brought the country closer to being a police state. The 2002 expansion of the Politburo Standing Committee to include the propaganda and internal security heads had increased the control coalition's clout. When the ambitious Zhou Yongkang replaced Luo Gan as security boss in 2007, the *weiwen* juggernaut was unstoppable.

The interest groups didn't have to invent the threats to the Party's rule. By the middle of Hu's second term, everyone could see that China's transformation toward a market-based, internationally integrated economy was making Chinese society more restive. Multiplying local protests raised the specter of a bottom-up revolution against Party rule. The dramatic increase in the number of people getting their information on the Internet also caused alarm. Social media postings revealed the extent of discontent to the leaders and to other netizens. Seeing safety in numbers, these netizens could use social media to organize collective action that might spill over onto the streets.

During his first term, Hu Jintao had tried to head off potential unrest by seeking to improve governance and opening up channels for public feedback. At the 2006 Party Congress he stated that "strengthening social management and maintaining social stability are the necessary demands of constructing a socialist harmonious society." He aimed to pre-empt unrest by gauging public opinion and satisfying it as best he could.[87] Indeed, both Hu and Wen had sought to make government more responsive to public concerns. They allowed investigative journalism and citizen criticism of local officials on the Internet. The censors and police used a relatively light hand when dealing with political dissent. To shore up the government's credibility, Hu allowed the official media, including the Xinhua News Agency, to start reporting negative news, and in 2008 lifted the ban on reporting on protests. People were permitted to petition the upper-level officials to complain about misdeeds by lower-level officials, although group petitioning was discouraged and counted against local officials. Party leaders, including Hu himself, talked frequently with netizens in online chat forums to take questions and respond to criticisms of public policies. Environmental NGOs, charities, and other forms of civil society sprouted up. When protests did break out, the central government stood on the side of the protestors and blamed local officials for causing the problems. This strategy succeeded. The Chinese public focused their negative feelings on local powerholders and lent positive support to the central government and Party.[88]

Another strategy Hu and Wen used to forestall social discontent was to make a populist swerve to move the priorities in development policy away from growth and toward redistribution and quality of life. This required more state intervention in the economy. The central government transferred fiscal revenues to the poorer inland regions and rural areas; ordered local governments to increase expenditures on social needs like health, education, and welfare; and set hard environmental targets for local leaders to meet.

But the protests grew larger and more determined, nevertheless. Outside China, popular uprisings in the former Soviet states of Georgia (2003), Ukraine (2004), and Kyrgyzstan (2005), which had come to be known as the "color revolutions," heightened the political paranoia of CCP leaders, who believed that the Americans had instigated them and that they could extend to China. As the control coalition highjacked leadership's fears, they steered the strategy toward a more authoritarian form of *weiwen*, necessitating tighter controls over the media, Internet, and civil society.[89] The 2008 Beijing Olympics were supposed to showcase a vibrant, open China; the International Olympic Committee had required Beijing to commit to journalistic freedom and allow peaceful demonstrations during the games. But these promises were not fulfilled. Petitioners were waylaid by police before they arrived in Beijing; as a result, the small spaces allocated for protests stood almost empty. The Ministry of Public Security had spent an entire year perfecting its methods of monitoring and control to guarantee that there would be no demonstrations in Beijing during the Olympic events. Although foreign journalists were treated respectfully, censorship tightened for Chinese reporters and has not loosened ever since. Large-scale eruptions of discontent convinced the leadership that it had to clamp down harder on all protest activities. The Tibetan demonstrations on the eve of the Olympics and the harassment of Chinese Olympic torchbearers by pro-Tibet demonstrators in Paris and other cities were followed in 2009 by violent clashes between Uighurs and Han Chinese in Xinjiang province.

Then China's cybersphere expanded with a big bang following the creation of Weibo, Sina's hugely popular microblogging platform that is similar to Twitter. By 2011, Weibo had become the primary source of public information,[90] and it metamorphosed from a simple communication tool into a channel possessing "social power and even political attributes," according to *Caijing* magazine.[91] Celebrities and other opinion leaders—called "Big V's"—with tens and hundreds of thousands of followers shared complaints about official corruption, air pollution, and other social ills. As a Beijing professor observed, "Weibo created a real public sphere, so by 2011 it was 'show-down time.'"

President Bill Clinton famously said that China's effort to control the Internet was "like trying to nail Jell-O to the wall."[92] Hu's collective leadership compounded the problem. As of 2011, China had at least fourteen agencies with administrative power over Internet regulation.[93] Bureaucratic competition and the dispersion of authority frustrated the drive for *weiwen* by creating niches where protestors and whistle-blowers could escape scrutiny; bureaucratic competition also was conducive to corruption by the officials who were gate-keepers and censors.

The control coalition pressed for more investments in "social management" to nip sources of instability in the bud at the local level. In 2010, the spending on public security exceeded the defense budget.[94] Grid-based management tracked the population. Those charged with ensuring *weiwen* at every level hired more personnel, enlisted volunteers, and subcontracted with security companies in what became a lucrative and corrupt business. Special off-budget "maintaining stability funds" (*weiwen jijin*) were set aside to buy off the demonstrators.[95] *Weiwen* became one of the most important indicators in local cadre evaluations. Officials lost their chance for promotion, or (more rarely) were demoted, if just one incident occurred on their watch. Predictably, such stringent criteria bred overcompliance by local officials, who went all-out to suppress group petitioning and other forms of protest activity.

Weiwen took on a life of its own, increasing social conflicts instead of reducing them. Tsinghua sociologist Sun Liping wrote in 2010 that China had succumbed to a vicious cycle, where "the more *weiwen*, the less stability *(yue weiwen yue buwen)*."[96] As one netizen wrote, "*Weiwen* has become an industry. 'Relevant departments' have used this excuse to increase budget, expand staff and equipment, and go to banquets and spend lavishly. Only exaggerating dangers and prolonging imprisonment [of dissidents] can maximize their interests."

The State Advances and the Private Sector Retreats (*Guo jin min tui*)

Simultaneously with the mid-2000s transformations in foreign and domestic policy, the country's economic development model also changed significantly. The economic miracle that had lifted more than 400 million people out of poverty during the 1980s and 1990s was achieved by what might be called the "Decentralized China Model." The economy was liberated from Soviet-style central planning and economic autarky, and the responsibility for managerial decision-making and creating incentives devolved to local governments, firms, and family farms. Today, when people talk about the "China Model," they mean something quite different from the decentralized market-oriented economy. Instead, they mean a "Centralized China Model": a strong central state that directs resources and policies toward ambitious economic, technological, and political goals.

The shift from Decentralized China Model to Centralized China Model began around 2003, a year into Hu's leadership. Central Party and state agencies and state-owned enterprises (SOEs) reclaimed their dominant role in the economy after twenty-five years of market-oriented decentralization. When China gained admission to the World Trade Organization in 2001, the bureaucratic and industrial interest groups with ties to the central government and the Party made the case that having foreign multinational firms flocking into the country might present a dangerous competitive and national security threat. *People's Daily* wrote that multinational firms would "control our country's major industries, hoping to become the overlords of some sectors, and only strong state-owned enterprises have the ability to contend with them."[97] Another rationale for strengthening the central-state interest groups was the aforementioned populist shift initiated by Hu and Wen from market-driven growth to the redistribution of the benefits of growth from the coastal cities to poorer inland regions and rural areas. Party leaders also can command SOEs to contribute to pet state projects, such as building infrastructure in inland regions and the Belt and Road Initiative.

Zhu Rongji, the premier who served under Jiang Zemin, spearheaded a reorganization of SOEs in 1997 that spun off smaller firms to restructure, close, or privatize but kept 196 large central SOEs, a number that shrank to 153 in 2006; the number as of 2020 is 97.[98] The central SOEs, some of which originated as industrial ministries or bureaus during the era of central planning, never completely disappeared during the period of market decentralization. Now their privileges as "the eldest sons of the republic" were restored.[99] SOE executives could join the CCP Central Committee and had entrée to the private offices of Party and government leaders.

In contrast, private firms have never gained a voice into the policy-making process. Even during the heyday of market reforms in the 1980s and 1990s, state banks favored the SOEs in their lending while private firms struggled to raise capital. Until 2014, private entrepreneurs could be executed for "illegal fundraising," defined vaguely. The business capital and personal safety of private entrepreneurs remain, to this day, vulnerable to the Party-state. Private businesspeople must spend a lot of their time and money cultivating ties with officials who can offer them and their companies informal protection from government predation.

China opted to keep the central state-owned enterprises under the Party leaders instead of ceding control to insider oligarchs, as the Soviet Union had. In 2003, a new body, the State-Owned Assets Supervision and Administration Commission (SASAC) was established to hold the state's shares in the central SOEs and serve as their secretariat. The CCP leaders also successfully resisted Zhu Rongji's effort to professionalize the personnel control of SOE executives by moving it under the government State Council, retaining this significant source of patronage for the Party instead. Powerful families in the Party aristocracy populate the C-suites and boards of directors of the large SOEs and use the SOEs to "harvest wealth from the system," as journalist-businessman James McGregor has put it.[100]

In 2006 the Hu-Wen administration issued a number of directives that protected strategic and pillar sectors such as telecom, power generation, automobiles, and aerospace for SOE monopolies or oligopolies.[101] Party leaders favored the central SOEs as "national champions," as they called them—a team of corporations that they hoped would make China victorious in the contest for global economic leadership. But by coddling them with special treatment—by providing them rent-free land, access to low-interest bank loans, and lower taxes—they failed to create efficient or productive companies. Once the state's subsidies were subtracted, corporate profits pretty much evaporated. Whatever profits the firms did earn, moreover, were shunted into speculative real estate or retained by SASAC as the SOE holding company. The government said in 2013 that it wanted 30 percent of the after-tax profits of the central SOEs to go into the state coffers for public goods like education, health, and welfare, but as of 2019, only 2.4 percent actually did.[102]

Beijing also ramped up a state-led campaign to make China into a global technology superpower. Wen Jiabao, as head of the CCP Leading Group on Science, Technology and Education, initiated a centrally planned and funded drive focused on megaprojects (sixteen in all) called the National Medium- and Long-Term Plan for Science and Technology Development, which was launched in 2006 and ended in 2020. Drafting of the plan took three years and involved thousands of scientists, engineers, economists, and military experts in a manner similar to earlier cold war central planning. The techno-nationalist drive was aimed at nurturing indigenous innovation as well as the absorption and repurposing of foreign technologies. The megaprojects meant big research and development budgets for a broad swath of government ministries. The leadership lavished special attention on projects with military applications and strategic objectives, such as manned space flight and lunar exploration, which progressed faster than those related to purely civilian applications, such as environmental pollution and healthcare.[103] In 2009 Wen launched another ambitious drive to identify "strategic emerging industries," where China could take the lead in cutting-edge technologies. These state-led initiatives were the progenitors of the Xi Jinping–era Made in China 2025 drive that set ambitious goals for China to overtake foreign competitors and dominate global high-tech sectors.

Enthusiastically backing these statist industrial policies were powerful central agencies that logrolled to protect the SOEs. Leading the coalition was the National Development and Reform Commission (NDRC), the giant super-ministry formed in 2003 that steers the economy in a way similar to Japan's Ministry of Industrial Trade and Industry, which directed that country's industrial policy in the 1970s and 1980s. The DNA of the commission derives from the State Planning Commission (SPC) that issued mandatory plan targets in the Soviet-style command economy from the

1950s until the 1980s. Many of today's National Development and Reform Commission bureaus originated in the old State Planning Commission; the Ministry of Industry and Information Technology, created in 2008 from the merger of a number of previous military-affiliated ministries, was also a key player in the logroll benefiting from the techno-nationalist priorities of the central government. The SASAC became a powerful holding company for the central SOEs. The political clout of the state energy companies surpassed that of many government agencies, in large part because of their patron-client ties to leading Party politicians.[104] Party politicians like to send their children to work in SOEs, where they learn business skills and, as James McGregor says, "gather assets for the family."[105]

The stimulus funds that followed the 2008 global financial crisis, estimated to be $586 billion, poured into the state sector through state banks and government funds, accelerating the return to a state-led economic model after decades of decentralizing reforms. The state sector is capital intensive; job creation depends mostly on private firms. Favoring state-owned firms reflects a political choice by Party leaders, not a strategy forced on the government to reduce unemployment.

Collective Corruption

As Hu Jintao's second term drew to a close, the Party oligarchs' greed and ambition actively threatened the future of Party rule. Corruption had metastasized throughout officialdom. And despite the leaders' efforts to preserve the facade of unity, splits within the Party started to become public.

As China grew into the second largest economy in the world, the controls on abuse of power for personal financial gain became so weak that the Party's ability to govern was undermined. Political commentator Pin Ho observed, "A collective leadership in which members only seek personal gain is not sustainable."[106] Collective leadership was conducive to "close cooperation between political power and business," one Chinese academic noted. He pointed out that everyone was aware that Ling Jihua, the head of Hu Jintao's office in the Party center, held meetings every couple of weeks in which high-ranking officials met with businessmen. "This was because the CCP controls business."

The barons failed to police corruption within their own ranks. In an effort to prevent their rivalries from spilling out beyond the inner circle the Politburo members had passed a rule that required the groups' approval for any high-level corruption investigation. Standing Committee members also declared themselves immune from prosecution even after retirement.

Hu's efforts to tackle corruption, half-hearted as they were, were thwarted by other powerful players. He did manage to charge a few high-level figures, such as Chen Liangyu, the CCP secretary of Shanghai who was considered part of former leader Jiang Zemin's "Shanghai Gang," and Wang Shouye, the deputy commander of the Chinese Navy. Yet as the Hu administration drew to a close in 2012, Australian journalist John Garnaut estimated that the children of at least six of the nine Standing Committee members had "profited handsomely" from their status. "Since the tragedy of Tiananmen," he wrote, "leaders have collectively failed to find a way of limiting each other's family privileges without fracturing the solidarity between them."[107]

The buying and selling of offices pervaded all levels of the Chinese hierarchy. Party secretaries and the Party officials in charge of personnel appointments built corrupt networks of loyalists who paid bribes—often funded by business cronies—to purchase positions with bribe-generating potential. Regulatory agencies, the police and judiciary, propaganda departments, drug approval and land management agencies, as well as local governments became hotbeds of corruption. Regional party secretaries coordinated the collusion. The bosses discouraged defections or whistle blowing by organizing their machines along *guanxi* lines, such as common hometown, clan, school, and workplace.[108] Another way of enforcing silence was to engage in deviant practices together, for example, bringing their mistresses to dinners or visiting brothels or gambling together.[109] The mistresses, as well as the children and siblings of officials, benefited from crony networks.[110] By the time Politburo member and rising star Sun Zhengcai was purged for corruption in 2018, his mistress Liu Fengzhou had built a business empire consisting of seventeen companies in localities that Sun used to run. She had nurtured his grand ambitions, giving him a tailor-made emperor's dragon robe after he was promoted to party secretary of Chongqing in 2012.[111]

When Xi Jinping succeeded Hu, he launched an anti-corruption campaign that was far more aggressive than anything his predecessor had ever attempted. Xi was motivated by both a puritanical zeal to cleanse the Party and revive its ethos of revolutionary self-sacrifice, and a ruthless determination to purge all his political rivals. Demonstrating his resolve and flaunting his power, he targeted more high-level politicians than ever before. Of course, their corrupt behavior had begun much earlier in their careers, during the Hu or Jiang eras.[112] About fifty "tigers" (vice minister– or vice governor–level and above) were investigated by the Central

Discipline Commission every year under Xi, more than twice Hu's rate. The total number of officials targeted sky-rocketed from 100,000 to 170,000 per year under Jiang and Hu to more than 300,000 per year under Xi.

Most dramatically, Xi shattered the elite norms of mutual protection by going after retired Standing Committee member and internal security boss Zhou Yongkang, the highest-level official ever charged with corruption since the nation's founding. The tentacles of Zhou's corrupt networks extended through the oil industry, where he had spent 32 years, to Sichuan province, where he served as CCP secretary for three years, and to the national police and the judiciary, where he had dominated as Minister of Public Security and then as head of the CCP Politics and Law Commission. In the months before the Party investigators arrested Zhou in 2014, they reportedly detained more than 300 of Zhou's family members and associates and seized $14.5 billion in villas, cars, art, and other assets.[113] The loot included about 300 apartments, liquor, antiques, silver, gold, cash, and stocks and bonds.[114] According to the *New York Times*, Zhou Yongkang family's business holdings amounted to $160 million, not including real estate or overseas assets.[115]

Ordinary Chinese were familiar with petty corruption in everyday life, but only after Xi's crackdown did most of them learn just how much their senior leaders and their families were stealing. Media accounts of the piles of money that had passed to senior politicians and the wealth of art, real estate, and jewelry they had acquired titillated and infuriated the public, and raised their approval of Xi. General Xu Caihou, the vice-chairman of the Central Military Commission who had been in charge of military personnel appointments for thirteen years, had reportedly been paid 20 million yuan — over $3 million — by one officer in exchange for a high-ranking position.[116] When the investigators opened the basement of Xu's lavish villa, they found over a ton of cash, literally, including US dollars, Euros, and Chinese currency. His warehouses contained over 100 kilograms of nephrite jade, 200 kilograms of precious wood and jade objects, and antiques and calligraphy dating back to the Tang dynasty. It took over a dozen military trucks to transport Xu's stash.[117]

New York Times journalist David Barboza documented the corrupt business activities of Wen Jiabao's family, which controlled investments worth $2.7 billion.[118] Bloomberg's exposé of the business investments of Xi Jinping's older sister, her husband, their daughter, and other family members showed hundreds of millions of dollars of assets, including a villa in Repulse Bay, Hong Kong.[119] Xi himself was not implicated and reportedly ordered his family members to withdraw from all their businesses as soon as he was named as China's heir-apparent in 2007.

Particularly shocking was the revelation of widespread corruption in the People's Liberation Army, which included the buying and selling of military ranks. In the waning days of the Hu era, General Liu Yuan, the princeling son of Liu Shaoqi, Mao's chosen successor before the Cultural Revolution, who was the powerful political commissar of the PLA's logistics department, which handles land, housing, food, finance, and services for the military, started calling out the rampant corruption in the PLA. Liu Yuan described the fight against corruption in the PLA as a "life or death struggle." "If there really was a war," he asked officers, "who would listen to your commands or risk their life for you?"[120]

Liu urged Hu to investigate Gu Junshan, his comrade and the deputy director of the logistics department, who ran his division "like a mafia fiefdom," as John Garnaut put it, distributing hundreds of PLA-built villas as gifts to friends and family and flying around the country in chartered planes.[121] Twice Hu's orders to dismiss Gu were blocked when there was resistance within the PLA, revealing the leader's ongoing impotence in the military hierarchy, though he had served seven years as commander in chief. Only by bypassing the PLA's discipline inspection body to enlist the help of the Party's discipline commission were Hu and Liu Yuan finally able to lock Gu Junshan up.

Once he took over as commander in chief in 2012, Xi wasted no time in cleaning up the military. He went after the PLA officers appointed by Jiang Zemin and Hu, starting at the very top with Xu Caihou and Guo Boxiong, the two Central Military Commission vice chairmen and Politburo members with whom he previously had served. Cai died before he could stand trial, and Guo received a life sentence. By charging them with the rampant selling of military ranks, Xi tainted the entire generation of military officers Xu and Guo had promoted during their decade serving as numbers one and two at the Military Commission. In Xi's first two years in power, over 4,000 officers with the rank of lieutenant colonel or higher, including 82 generals, were investigated, and 160 of them were punished.[122] In all, during Xi's first five-year term, a total of 13,000 people in the PLA were disciplined.[123] Most (90 percent) of those investigated came from the departments responsible for personnel promotions; finances, construction, fuels, health and real estate; and arms procurement.[124]

Leadership Splits

Even more alarming to the Party elite than the endemic corruption under Hu were the visible splits in the leadership. In 2012, the Party seemed to be going off the rails. A Chinese political scientist compared the "turmoil at the top" to the Tiananmen crisis in 1989.

The schisms had started appearing during Hu's second term, which was when Chongqing Party secretary Bo Xilai and Guangdong Party secretary Wang Yang were competing openly for a Standing Committee seat. Instead of playing the CCP's usual inside game, they campaigned to build public followings. They adopted very different approaches to governing and created an open rivalry between the Chongqing and Guangdong models.[125] Bo combined a patriotic revival of Mao-era culture—organizing concerts of red songs and sending out text messages of Mao's slogans—with populist redistributive policies and a fierce "strike black" police crackdown on corruption. He recruited a brain trust of New Left academics from Beijing to advise him and publicize his model, and most of the Standing Committee members made pilgrimages to Chongqing. As noted earlier, neither Hu nor the Standing Committee as a whole had the courage to stop Bo's open campaigning for power. Even Henry Kissinger visited, expressing admiration for Bo's accomplishments, remarking he had been "shaken by the vitality of the city."[126]

At the other end of the political spectrum, Wang Yang campaigned as a proponent of liberal political reform under the banner of "emancipation of thought." Wang, who had served as Party secretary of Chongqing immediately before Bo, seemed more at home in Guangdong, a province with a southern frontier tradition of being one step ahead in political, media, and economic reform.[127] Under Wang, Guangdong led the way in government transparency; Guangzhou became the first city to make budget data public.[128] He was more tolerant of civil society, simplifying the registration process for NGOs and encouraging the official union to better represent workers; he even supported a strike by Honda workers that won them a pay raise through collective bargaining. He promoted a humane alternative to police-state approaches to maintaining political stability, explaining that "People's democratic awareness is increasing significantly in this changing society, and when their appeals for rights aren't getting enough attention, that's when mass incidents happen."[129] In 2011, when the twenty thousand villagers of Wukan threw out their leaders for making illegal land sales, Wang punished the corrupt officials and allowed the rebel leaders to hold new elections.

Wang was not the blatant self-promoter Bo was. But his academic advisers promoted the Guangdong model as a superior alternative to the Chongqing model. Taking a slap at Bo's Leftist version of populism, Wang said in a speech, "We must eradicate the misconception that people's happiness is a gift from the party and the government."[130] The savvy Wang invited the writer and *New York Times* columnist Tom Friedman to visit him in Guangdong, so that Friedman could write about his environmental achievements in promoting green industries and a low-carbon economy.[131] Wang Yang also cultivated a positive image with the local domestic media, a Guangdong journalist said, and was admired as "cool (*wangshuai*), youthful, and good looking." He invited web influencers (*waming*) to join him in a round-table discussion talk about the development of the province.

There were other obvious signs of conflict at the top. Whenever Wen Jiabao called for democracy, it inspired a spate of essays by liberal journalists and academics who hoped that the time for political reform had finally arrived.[132] Other, more orthodox leaders, however, made clear that the premier was only speaking for himself. National People's Congress chairman Wu Bangguo, as noted earlier, bluntly laid down what came to be called the "six no's": no multiple-party system, no diversity in ideology, no checks and balances, no two-chamber parliament, no federal republic and no privatization."[133] In the interview with CNN's Fareed Zakaria, Wen defended free speech and constitutional rule and vowed to pursue "political restructuring" despite the formidable resistance: "I will not fall in spite of a strong wind and harsh rain and I will not yield till the last day of my life."[134] Wen's interview was censored, so that Chinese audiences could not read or hear his passionate words, a remarkable demonstration of the propaganda bureaucracy's power over even the premier.[135] One Chinese journalist observed that during the Hu Jintao decade, the general secretary's consolidation of power was "never finished" because "individual leaders went their own way." In his view, three leaders deviated from the standard Party line — Wen Jiabao, Wang Yang, and Bo Xilai. Even though two of the three were political liberalizers, Hu Jintao was never able to enlist them in a coalition to check the control coalition and sustain the reformist agenda of his first term.

A series of events related to the ideological divisions and jockeying for power almost wrecked the handover from Hu to Xi Jinping at the 18th CCP Congress in October 2012. As related earlier, in February, Bo Xilai's police chief, Wang Lijun, had fled to the US Consulate in Chengdu, seeking asylum because of his involvement in Bo's wife's murder of a British businessman, a revelation that eventually led to Bo's downfall. Remarkably, Bo was allowed to attend the March National People's Congress but was arrested the day after it had ended. In his annual press conference at the Congress, Wen distanced himself from Bo, citing the crisis in Chongqing as an example of the danger of repeating the tragedy of the Cultural Revolution if the Party failed to carry out political structural reform.[136]

Less than a week later, the son of Ling Jihua, Hu Jintao's chief of staff, who was widely expected to be promoted to the Politburo at the 18th Congress, crashed his Ferrari on the Fourth Ring Road in Beijing, killing himself and severely injuring two young, half-naked female passengers. As Hu's powerful right-hand man and the organizer of the informal primary election prior to the Party Congress, Ling sought help from security boss Zhou Yongkang in covering up the scandal and in return might have offered to join an anti-Xi plot with Zhou and Bo. He succeeded in suppressing the news of the accident until September. The collusion between the two politicians, one from the Jiang Zemin camp (Zhou) and one from the Hu Jintao camp (Ling), was revealed at Ling's trial in 2016, when he was sentenced to life imprisonment.

After Xi Jinping came to power he accused the high-level Politburo politicians whom he had sent to prison for the rest of their lives—Bo Xilai, Zhou Yongkang, Ling Jihua, Su Rong, Xu Caihou, Guo Boxiong, and Sun Zhangcai, a rising star and successor-in-waiting—not just of corruption, but also of engaging in "political conspiracies (*zhengzhi yinmou*) to immorally (*goudang*) violate and split the party."[137] He framed their crimes broadly as a warning to other politicians who might dare to challenge him. But who was conspiring with whom? These politicians came from different networks, so it's unlikely they were all part of one coordinated plot against Xi. In 2017, I asked an official from the CCP Central Discipline Commission why it informed the public about the plots but didn't provide reliable details about them, forcing people to get them from rumors instead. He replied that the higher-ranked Party officials were briefed.

In the tense atmosphere after Bo Xilai was detained in March 2012, there were unsubstantiated reports of gunfire in Beijing. On the eve of the Party Congress, the rumors started flying when Xi Jinping suddenly disappeared for most of September 2012. He missed several scheduled meetings, sparking speculation of coup and assassination attempts. He reappeared at the end of the month, but the mystery of his absence remains.

At the same time, a foreign policy crisis was unfolding after the Japanese government took ownership of three of the Senkaku/Diaoyu Islands to prevent Shintaro Ishihara, the nationalist mayor of Tokyo, from buying them himself. The Chinese official press reported that Hu had warned Prime Minister Noda, when he met him at the sidelines of the APEC (Asia-Pacific Economic Cooperation) summit in Vladivostok on September 9, not to buy the islands. Two days later the Japanese government signed the purchase contract, causing China and Hu to lose face. China reacted by sending marine surveillance ships into the territorial waters around the islands for the first time and allowing anti-Japanese demonstrations in two hundred Chinese cities. On September 17, Beijing called for all government units to uphold social stability until the end of the National Party Congress, allowing the protests but making sure that they remained peaceful.[138] The demonstrations diverted attention from the messy leadership politics that were threatening the smooth leadership transition and provided an outlet for discontent over widening inequality or other domestic issues. Some of the protestors carried portraits of Mao and appeared to be taking the opportunity to show their support for Bo Xilai. But the police only allowed slogans concerning the islands.[139]

Despite the unpredictable disruptions, the turnover of power to Xi Jinping was achieved. Yet many members of the elite had concluded from the 2012 political meltdown, coming on top of the paralysis created by the ten years under Hu Jintao, that the system was in crisis. Hu himself appeared apologetic for the failures of his leadership; he retired from all three of his positions—CCP general secretary, Central Military Commission chairman, and state president—the first PRC leader to have done so. *People's Daily* celebrated Hu's "glorious decade" by publishing a long list of achievements and yet another article by Hu Angang on the advantages of the collective presidency.[140]

But behind the scenes, politicians and intellectuals were grumbling that collective rule had been a failure, and that China needed bolder leadership to address the mounting problems of corruption, inequality, debt and slowing growth, and dangerous leadership splits.[141] Articles in the official media started discussing the shortcomings of collective leadership and the division of work and advocated for better coordination at the top.[142] "China 2030," a February 2012 blueprint for reviving stalled economic reform written by Liu He at the State Council Development Research Center with the World Bank, called for a high-powered commission to advance reforms.[143] Singapore political scientist Zheng Yongnian published an article in a PRC official journal in which he said, "Over the past several years, China has been suffering from weak political leadership. The ruling party is seeing a great number of vested interests inside itself, which aim to divide the existing pie instead of making the pie bigger."[144]

The growing consensus about the need for stronger, more centralized leadership was openly expressed in the 18th Party Congress political work report, delivered by Hu but drafted by a broad set of Party elites.[145] The report jettisoned collective leadership and the system of dividing responsibilities among the top leaders that had been written into previous reports from the 15th Congress (1997) to the 17th Congress (2007). It also called for improving the "mechanism of coordinating structural reforms" and conducting reforms "in a holistic way according to the overall plan."

The drafters of the work report didn't seem worried that Xi would misuse the enhanced powers of his office they were granting him. Deng Xiaoping's warning about the dangers of overconcentration of authority wasn't on their minds. Coups and corruption were. Xi did not have a reputation as a domineering leader. His colleagues believed that his sympathies lay with the reform camp; that was the image he had cultivated for himself. He was believed to have inherited a commitment to market reform and opening to the world from his father, Xi Zhongxun, who in 1978 had put Guangdong province in the vanguard of post-Mao reform. And he had been friendly to private and international investors during his stints as provincial leader in coastal provinces Fujian, Zhejiang, and Shanghai, places other politicians frequently visited. As Party secretary in Zhejiang, he had pitched a Zhejiang Model consisting of a "two hands" approach to economic reform—promarket but not antistate.[146] During the lead-up to the 2012 Party Congress, he prudently kept a low profile, but just weeks before the Congress, he visited Hu Deping, the son of the late iconic reform leader Hu Yaobang, and promised to "hold high the banner of reform, including political system reform."[147]

In other words, Xi Jinping didn't steal power in a coup; power was willingly bestowed on him by China's political elite that was fed up with Hu's corrupt oligarchy. But the elite got a much more dictatorial leader than they had reckoned for.

5

Loss of Restraint

As I have tried to show, many of Xi Jinping's confrontational foreign policies, such as bullying other countries in maritime sovereignty disputes and pressuring foreigners to endorse CCP positions on domestic "core interests," as well as his repressive approach to social and media control and divergence from market norms in economic management, began earlier under his self-effacing, power-sharing predecessor.[1] The dispersion of power among the top leaders gave free rein to various interest groups to pursue their own agendas without considering the consequences for China's peaceful rise. Relations with Asian neighbors and the United States took a sharp downturn as a result.

"Something went very wrong last year," a Beijing foreign policy expert told me over tea in 2010, toward the end of the Hu Jintao era. The gist of the problem was that there was too much competition between politicians representing different interest groups. "China is a top-down system. If there is consensus at the top, they can get things done. But if there are different voices, then they can't get things done. Now you hear very different voices."

Shortly after President Obama's inauguration in 2009, Chinese ships and planes from various agencies started harassing US Navy ships in the seas surrounding China. The Pentagon described these actions as "reckless and dangerous" maneuvers and the most aggressive they had seen in some time.[2] Even Chinese official media acknowledged this, calling the clash with the USNS *Impeccable*, an unarmed, civilian-operated surveillance ship conducting surveys of the ocean floor 75 miles south of the People's Liberation Army submarine base on Hainan Island, "the most serious episode between the two nations since 2001 when a US spy plane collided midair with a Chinese fighter jet near the same area in the South China Sea."[3]

China insists that foreign navies should get its permission before passing through its 200-nautical-mile exclusive economic zone (EEZ). The United States argues that the UN Convention on the Law of the Sea gives coastal states the right to limit only economic activities in the EEZ. In March 2009, the *Impeccable* was surrounded by five Chinese ships— a Fisheries Law Enforcement Command patrol vessel, a China Marine surveillance cutter, a Chinese Navy intelligence collection ship, and two small fishing trawlers. The Chinese ships approached within 50 feet of the *Impeccable*, waving Chinese flags and demanding that the vessel leave the area or "suffer the consequences." When the *Impeccable* defended it-self by spraying water from high-pressure fire hoses, one of the Chinese crews stripped to their underwear and powered to within 25 feet of the American ship. The Chinese crew used long poles to try to grab a listening device that the *Impeccable* was towing. When the American captain asked for a safe exit from the area, two of the Chinese ships stopped in front of the *Impeccable* and dropped large pieces of wood in its path, forcing it to conduct an emergency "all stop" to avoid a collision. Meanwhile, in the Yellow Sea between China and Korea, a sister ship, the USNS *Victorious*, was also hassled several times in dangerous maneuvers by Chinese patrol vessels from the Fisheries Bureau and aircraft from Marine Surveillance.

Evan Medeiros, the US National Security Council (NSC) official re-sponsible for China policy at the time, said that the NSC staff had debated whether the point of China's interference was to test the new American administration.[4] The involvement of multiple civilian agencies plus the Navy confused the signal. According to a WikiLeaked cable from the US Embassy Beijing, a diplomat from the Chinese Ministry of Foreign Affairs formally complained to the US government about the American presence, but the diplomat also sought to play down the incidents and was distressed that Washington had reported them to the media.[5] The US Navy gave no-tice that it would start sending armed warships to escort some of its ships operating in the region. It was the beginning of an era of confrontation.

Many people at the time were mystified by Hu's sharp departure from the cautious foreign policy of his predecessors and his own first term. China's diplomacy had earned it global influence and economic benefits by convincing its Asian neighbors and the United States that though its power was growing, its intentions were friendly. Beijing took tough stances toward Japan and Taiwan, the hot-button issues of Chinese nationalism. But it dealt flexibly with other foreign-policy issues, including its rela-tions with the United States.[6] Most China experts, myself included, had anticipated that Hu's prudent approach would continue. During his first term, as we've seen, he had led study sessions in the Politburo and the Standing Committee on the historical lessons to be learned from other rising powers, precisely, how to improve its status without provoking war. As I noted in chapter 1, Hu's close associate Zheng Bijian, who had been Hu's number two when he ran the Central Party School, gave a speech about China's "peaceful rise" at the Boao Forum in 2003, and the notion, intended to reassure foreigners about China's intentions, was embraced by both Hu and Premier Wen Jiabao.[7]

As we have seen, under Hu's collective leadership decisions were supposed to be made by consensus. Theoretically, everyone had a veto. Consensus rule is usually a recipe for standstill, not action, and Hu was criticized within China for being weak. But instead of producing policy inertia, as one might expect, Hu's collective leadership drove foreign policy into an aggressive mode, veering this way and that, overreacting to international slights, putting symbolic domestic issues ahead of diplomatic goals, daring to confront American power, and pronouncing ultimatums even if they had little prospect of being met. The 2008 global financial crisis provided the external impetus for the shift because it had changed assessments of relative power between China and the United States in both countries and stimulated a Chinese demand for a more muscular foreign policy.

But the root cause of the metamorphosis in China's behavior was that its policy process had become more fragmented. There were, as noted, "too many voices." As Chinese society became more engaged in the world, the foreign-policy process expanded to include different agencies, military services, and state corporations that were promoting their own agendas and diluting the power of the Ministry of Foreign Affairs. The Propaganda Department, the big state energy companies, and the CCP International Department, as well as the PLA Navy, were among the powerful new players in the foreign policy arena. The Foreign Ministry was sidelined by these other organizations, according to Chinese analyses of the process.[8] One ambassador lamented, "The Foreign Ministry is now just the secretariat, and the ambassadors are protocol officers. The real foreign policy decisions are being made elsewhere."

Domestic policies also were inconsistent because of the rivalries among the leaders at the top and the bureaucratic fragmentation below. The powerhouse Party departments that were part of the "control coalition" hijacked social management, and the government agencies tied to state-owned enterprises hijacked economic policies. China's domestic trajectory, as well as its foreign policy, began to diverge from its past pattern and global norms in a worrisome manner.

Too Many Chefs

After 2002, no member of the Politburo Standing Committee or Politburo other than Hu Jintao himself was a foreign policy official. Each of the CCP barons held a portfolio for domestic affairs, and none were well versed in foreign policy. One rung down, senior foreign policy figures, all members of the Central Committee, competed fiercely with one another. The political downgrading of China's foreign ministers over time is unmistakable.[9] Hu's foreign minister, Yang Jiechi, an experienced diplomat and America hand, was lower in rank than Dai Bingguo, head of the Party's Foreign Affairs Office and a state councilor, who had made a career mainly as a Party apparatchik—he had served as Party secretary of the Foreign Ministry and then director of the CCP International Department. The third and junior-most figure was Wang Yi, the head of the Taiwan Affairs Office, a highly respected diplomat and Japan expert.

Dai enjoyed the closest relationship with Hu, and as office director for the Foreign Affairs leading small group, he managed the interagency foreign-policy process. Yet even he often couldn't contrive to get the multiple bureaucracies to agree on policy, much less to implement it. He complained that no one listened to him when he tried to coordinate the nine civilian maritime agencies, the state energy corporations, and the PLA Navy, all of which were clamoring for bigger budgets to enforce China's sovereignty claims in the South China Sea. As a mere Central Committee member and the lowest of the state councilors, Dai lacked the political clout to tell the PLA what to do.[10] A diplomat said in 2010, "Dai isn't strong enough to coordinate policies. Dai and Yang try to figure out what the leaders want and then implement."

The balkanization of foreign policy also drove assertiveness in other foreign policy domains. China's protective stance toward North Korea, for example, was driven more by Party departments and the PLA than by the Foreign Ministry; and the internal security agencies were important players in deciding Beijing's policies toward Central Asia. When the Propaganda Department sent out instructions to say that US policy in Asia was aimed at "containment" of China, no one told it to stop. Li Changchun, an ally of the retired leader Jiang Zemin, was in charge of ideology and propaganda for the entire Hu decade, which meant that Hu never established full control of that powerful bureaucracy. The Party's United Front Work Department, responsible for relations with non-Party members inside China, cultivated support for Beijing from overseas Chinese, people of Chinese descent living in other countries. Overseas propaganda aimed at enhancing what the Party started calling its "discourse power" was a new space, one competed for by multiple agencies, including the Cyberspace Administration and the PLA's Political Work Department. The Ministry of State Security advocated for high-tech intelligence gathering and surveillance; its influence and budget were increased when it had to prepare for the 2008 Beijing Olympics and to respond to the riots in Tibet in 2008 and Xinjiang in 2009.[11]

Civil-military relations were also plagued by poor coordination, verging on outright insubordination. PLA officers and retired officers spoke belligerently about other countries in the media without being disciplined. When a Defense Ministry spokesperson took a tougher stand than their Foreign Ministry counterpart on an issue like United States–Republic of Korea joint exercises, the Foreign Ministry modified its position to conform with the military. The PLA embarrassed civilian leaders by failing to coordinate with them on the timing of an anti-satellite test (2007) and a test of a new stealth fighter (2010).

Officials from other countries complained that dealing with China had become much more complicated, and that it was difficult to determine who was calling the shots.[12] Again, China's disjointed foreign policy reflected the way Hu's oligarchy achieved consensus—through logrolling. Party leaders were reluctant to challenge one another over policy differences for fear that any leadership splits might spill out into the public and mobilize popular opposition. To keep the peace, they allowed one another to call the shots in their own domains.

Little surprise, therefore, that the high-level coordination of foreign policy broke down. The Politburo Standing Committee rarely deliberated on foreign policy as a group; it spent most of its time on domestic issues. When foreign policy was discussed, the Foreign Ministry took notes, but there were no other minutes of the Standing Committee meetings. The Foreign Affairs leading small group met only for one session, to prepare for Hu's January 2011 state visit to Washington. Unless there was a crisis, issues were left to the relevant agencies and not deliberated in a group setting. And if the group did discuss the issue, only the individual leader spoke to it, while the others simply nodded assent.

Foreign Policy under Logrolling

As Jack Snyder observes, the interest groups most capable of hijacking foreign policy are the ones that have the greatest ability to feed national fears—such as about China's encirclement by foreign powers or the risk of domestic chaos—that resonate with popular concerns.[13] Without a strong leader in charge, no one at the center dared to say no to the military, the internal security police, and the propaganda apparatus, or even to the relative bureaucratic weaklings, such as the Fisheries Bureau or the State Oceanic Administration, which had successfully got support to expand their fleets of patrol ships by stirring up popular nationalism and regional tensions. Under China's collective leadership each bureaucracy pursued its parochial interests, more or less unimpeded by the others.

The maritime domain became particularly unruly and difficult to manage from Beijing. Advanced oil- and gas-exploration technologies opened new opportunities for drilling deep beneath the sea, and overfishing motivated fishermen to venture farther away from shore for their catches. Civilian maritime law enforcement agencies, local governments, fisheries, state energy companies, and the PLA Navy dispatched boats and planes into the South China Sea and the East China Sea under the banner of defending Chinese sovereignty (*weiquan*). In 2008, during Premier Wen Jiabao's official visit to Japan, the Maritime Surveillance Administration, led by the internal security bureaucracy and its leader, Zhou Yongkang, even had the nerve to send its cutters 12 nautical miles into the territorial waters of the Diaoyu/Senkaku Islands, according to a Chinese expert who happened to be in Tokyo at the time.

As they competed for bigger budgets and influence, the maritime agencies also logrolled with one another to boost the nation's total effort on maritime sovereignty defense. The retired officials and think-tank experts connected to these interest groups took advantage of the burgeoning commercialized media and the Internet to drum up public enthusiasm for their causes. The maritime agencies often asked television crews to come along to film their defense patrols. Meanwhile, the media grew their audiences by reporting exciting stories of maritime clashes and other confrontations. After a few years of this publicity, the South China Sea started to join Japan and Taiwan as a focus of Chinese nationalism.

Unable to restrain the various organized interests, Hu was dragged into a more assertive foreign policy. In his first term, Hu's foreign policy speeches had advocated "mutual understanding and mutual accommodation" on most issues, and not "speaking too much" or "leading"; by 2009, he was calling for the country to "strive for greater action in international affairs."[14]

The shift undercut China's image as a responsible rising power, formed by decades of self-restraint (*ziwo yueshu*).[15] The South China Sea, as I've noted, was the main locus. During Hu's second term, military and government officials started treating the waters of the South China Sea as quasi-sovereign territory, planting a PRC flag on the sea floor and creating a new city government on Sansha to administer the territory. The government also refused to remove a chain it had installed to keep Philippine fishermen away from the Scarborough Reef, as it had promised to do during the negotiations for a de-escalation of the standoff with Manila. When the Southeast Asian countries backed an American initiative to discuss the maritime tensions in a regional forum, the foreign ministry rejected the collective approach and blamed the US for interfering.

As we have seen, China's new attitude also showed in its expansion of the nation's "core interests" from preventing the independence of Taiwan and to include reinforcing Chinese sovereignty over Tibet and Xinjiang. Some officials now added the South China Sea.

In short, the signs of China's assertiveness were everywhere. According to Nirupama Rao, the former Indian ambassador to China, China concluded an agreement with India in 2005 not to let the two countries' border dispute interfere with other bilateral engagements. Two years later, however, China hardened its position by reopening the agreement as if it had never been signed and there was nothing on the table. Beijing also failed to condemn the 2010 unprovoked attacks of its traditional ally North Korea on South Korea, and thereby damaged its valuable friendship with the South.

The Chinese government started directing foreign trade for political ends, a new tactic that made other countries wary. To pressure Japan to release a Chinese fishing boat captain who had rammed two Japanese Coast Guard vessels in the East China Sea in 2010, China cut off exports to Japan of rare earth metals, of which it has a near-monopoly supply, and which are necessary to produce many technology products. Its action was ruled illegal under World Trade Organization rules in 2017. When democracy activist Liu Xiaobo received the 2010 Nobel Peace Prize, the Chinese government not only strong-armed foreign governments to get them to boycott the award ceremony (though only nineteen complied) but stopped buying Norwegian salmon and froze relations with Norway until 2016, even though the Nobel committee is independent of the Norwegian government.

Beijing harmed its relations with Washington by giving a chilly welcome to President Barack Obama on his first visit to China, in November 2009, refusing to televise his speech or the leaders' press conference. And at the December 2009 UN climate meeting in Copenhagen, Chinese security guards shoved President Obama to try to block him from entering the room where Premier Wen Jiabao and officials of other countries were meeting.

China's Asian neighbors reacted to all these disturbing signs by moving closer to the United States, asking Washington to stand with them militarily and politically—even as China remained their largest trading partner. The Obama administration had come into office with a plan to step up its presence in Asia across the board, diplomatically and economically, as well as militarily, and moved expeditiously to engage in joint exercises and training programs, and construct fueling and repair facilities for US forces in Australia and Southeast Asia. During 2010, the United States and Korea held large joint exercises; the US resumed relations with Indonesia's special forces; the Indian military visited ASEAN nations; Japan announced plans to build more submarines and other mobile forces to defend its southernmost islands; Korea and Japan discussed military cooperation; and the US started stationing Marines in Australia.

China's actions may have been aimed at keeping the United States out of its surrounding seas and air space, but they had the opposite effect. They motivated the US and other countries to balance against China, countering the PRC in what came to be called the Obama "pivot to Asia."

Division and Reassurance

CCP national security adviser Dai Bingguo may have been acting on Hu Jintao's behalf when he tried to head off the coalition that was forming against China by recalibrating foreign policy to be more reassuring about China's intentions. In advance of Hu Jintao's state visit to the United States, in January 2011, Dai wrote an essay (followed by an official white paper) that re-emphasized China's peaceful development strategy. Dai's essay called for "harmonious coexistence" within the "big international family" and stated that "in order for us to be safe, it is necessary to enable others to be safe too."[16]

Weeks earlier, however, China's foreign minister Yang Jiechi had given a speech at the annual foreign affairs conference blaming the US "return to Asia" for the tense regional environment. Although he didn't explicitly use the word "containment," according to one foreign policy expert who was in the room at the time, containment was what he thought the United States was doing. Dai countered with extemporaneous remarks, which later appeared in his essay.

Dai's effort to moderate China's foreign policy line didn't succeed, though as noted, he technically outranked Yang. According to foreign policy experts and diplomats, Dai did a poor job of coordination, and he and Yang didn't speak to each other. Both men were politically insecure. Yang had lost all of his lieutenants in the America Department when Dai reassigned them, leaving China's US foreign policy in the hands of non-US experts. Moreover, as ordinary Central Committee members, both Dai and Yang were outranked by Politburo member Wang Huning, the former Fudan University political scientist who headed the Party Center's policy and speech writing office, accompanied Hu on his travels, and was probably his most influential foreign policy adviser. A Foreign Ministry official told me that Wang had drafted and polished the talking points and speeches for Hu's meetings with President George W. Bush. The entire foreign policy bureaucracy, including both the Foreign Ministry and Dai Bingguo's CCP foreign affairs office, had been marginalized relative to other domestically oriented bureaucracies.

In the lead-up to the leadership transition at the 18th CCP Congress in 2012, Dai's effort to improve foreign policy coordination and soften the message was obstructed by the interest groups in the control coalition, specifically the internal security and propaganda bureaucracies, civilian maritime agencies, and the military. Hu had even had to get the approval of the other Standing Committee members for the specific stops on the itinerary of his 2011 visit to the United States. China's shift to putting maritime sovereignty claims ahead of good relations with its neighbors was instigated by the Propaganda Department, I was told by foreign policy experts. What's more, the impending leadership transition was motivating politicians to sound nationalist themes. As one Central Committee member put it, "The campaign for 2012 started too early. Hawkish views are too popular."

Hu's indecisiveness compounded the problem. According to an adviser, "It took him one month to decide how to respond to American military exercises in the West Sea (the waters in between Korea and China) and even longer to stop the generals from making tough public statements and interviews. Even then he didn't punish the generals." The Hu administration did not tone down its approach to the South China Sea, and it failed to stabilize relations with Washington.

Nine Dragons Stirring Up the Sea

As I hope is now abundantly clear, the South China Sea presents one of the most complicated and contentious sets of conflicting sovereignty claims in the world. Six parties—Brunei, China, Malaysia, the Philippines, Taiwan, and Vietnam—assert overlapping claims to the waters and tiny land features of the sea.

The Chinese government has, of course, long wanted to establish its authority over the South China Sea. It consolidated control over the Paracel Islands in the northern part of the sea in the 1970s, and then extended it southward to the Spratly Islands, surveying energy prospects and building facilities to occupy the small islets. China and Vietnam clashed, with the loss of life, over ownership of the islands in 1974 and in 1988. At the UN Commission on the Law of the Sea negotiations in 1973, Chinese officials advocated for allowing coastal nations to claim a 200-nautical-mile exclusive economic zone, a move motivated by Cultural Revolution radicalism that ended up bolstering the jurisdictions of other coastal states against China's expansive historical claims.[17]

Following the 1989 Tiananmen crisis, however, China's leaders, worried about becoming internationally isolated, restrained themselves in the South China Sea to reassure their neighbors that China wasn't a threat. Premier Li Peng and the Chinese Foreign Ministry proposed that all the countries set aside their sovereignty claims to pursue peaceful joint development of the seabed and marine resources for mutual economic benefit, an initiative that Indonesia's Prime Minister Alatas then sought to realize through a series of dialogues.

One Chinese expert who was an architect of the post-Tiananmen "good neighbor policy" explained its logic as an attempt to prevent a "counterbalancing alliance of China's neighbors and the United States."[18] Jiang Zemin also believed that to dispel the "inevitable doubts about us" from the many smaller countries surrounding China, the government should project a friendly image.[19] China did interrupt this almost two-decade-long period of self-restraint by seizing Mischief Reef from the Philippines in 1994, and the PLA, spearheaded by Admiral Liu Huaqing from his powerful position on the Military Commission and the CCP Politburo Standing Committee, pushed to develop a modern navy to safeguard China's maritime rights.[20] Liu lobbied hard for China to build an aircraft carrier, saying, "Defending the South China Sea, peacefully reuniting Taiwan, safeguarding maritime rights and interests—all require aircraft carriers." But the Politburo Standing Committee turned down Liu's proposal in 1995 and didn't show interest in the carrier program again until the mid-2000s.[21] In 2002, Beijing signed an agreement with ASEAN to draft a South China Sea Code of Conduct, and overall, the Chinese pattern in the South China Sea from 1990 until 2007 was one of avoiding confrontation with neighbors.[22]

During Hu Jintao's second term, however, the collective leadership lost control over the interest groups promoting China's maritime rights claims (*weiquan*), a phenomenon that people in China call "nine dragons stirring up the sea," taking the image from Chinese mythology. Hu and the Standing Committee prevented maritime conflicts from escalating to war by deploying grey-hull civilian fleets and fishing militia instead of the PLA Navy to enforce China's claims. But there was little central direction of these civilian agencies, and no overall coordination of sovereignty rights defense (*weiquan*). Instead, ministerial competition broke out between the civilian maritime agencies, as each of them sought to augment their budgets and paramilitary forces by harassing the other Southeast Asian claimants to show what staunch defenders of sovereignty they were. The Fishery Law Enforcement Bureau was surprisingly influential thanks in part to its ties with the PLA Navy; it had been created by a PLA Navy ex-admiral in the 1950s and used hand-me-down PLA Navy ships. Inside the Foreign Ministry the Department of Boundary and Ocean Affairs was created in 2008 and rivaled with the Asia Department. The provinces of Hainan, Guangdong, and Guangxi also got into the paramilitary game, and state-owned energy enterprises also joined in. The former head of the State Oceanic Administration became the vice governor of Hainan. In 2010 four Hainan state enterprise groups—Nanhai fishery group, Sinopec Hainan, Hainan transportation group, and Hainan construction group—formed a strategic partnership to integrate their business interests with sovereignty protection. The fishery group came up with a snappy slogan: "Fish the political fish and spread the sovereignty net." Finally, the PLA Navy, with the South China Sea fleet growing rapidly, lobbied for the need to catch up to other claimants in rights defense.

Beginning in 2006—again, before the global financial crisis—PRC maritime law enforcement fleets had begun patrolling across the entire South China Sea, harassing foreign oil and gas projects and the fishing activities of other claimants.[23] In 2009, after Vietnam and Malaysia submitted to the United Nations a formal declaration of their extended continental shelves (and the Philippines passed its own baseline law), China submitted an objection based on a 1947 map, inherited from the former Kuomintang government, showing a nine-dash line surrounding the South China Sea. This map claims China's historic right to the entire sea or, as some moderate Chinese experts would advise, to the land features in the sea and their adjacent waters; China has not yet clarified the ambiguity in its claim.

Up until that time, the Chinese public hadn't paid much attention to the South China Sea; it wasn't a hot-button issue like Japan or Taiwan, and the media rarely discussed it. Popular interest in the South China Sea, measured by search engine activity, began increasing only in 2009, and by mid-2011, it had become a leading issue in the online nationalist agenda.[24] Even then, according to surveys, there was no evidence that the increase in China's coercive diplomacy in maritime disputes was caused by rising nationalism.[25]

Hence the impetus for China's confrontations with its neighbors came not from the pressure of popular nationalism but from the parochial interest groups that benefited from roiling the maritime disputes in the South China Sea. Local governments offered fishermen fuel subsidies and escorts to encourage them to fish all the way to the Southern Spratleys and to join the Fishing Militia. Hainan province ordered the building of eighty-four large militia fishing vessels.[26] State-owned energy companies, such as the China National Petroleum Corporation, had a symbiotic relationship with the political leadership; some of their executives held ministerial or vice ministerial rank. The oil industry focused its lobbying efforts on Zhou Yongkang, a Standing Committee member who had worked in the oil industry for over thirty years and was now the internal security boss.[27] They complained that other claimants, "thieves stealing China's energy," had drilled more than a thousand wells. ("I'm sure that number is made up," said one international relations expert.) As these well-organized interest groups highjacked maritime policy from the Foreign Ministry, their aggressive actions against other claimants and the United States aroused suspicions about China's imperialist intentions. By 2011, there was speculation in the lower ranks of the Chinese government that China might scale back its claim in the South China Sea, from the entire sea to the land features and the waters around them to salvage its positive image.

But as one expert observed succinctly at the time, "No one has the courage to say the dotted line claim is too big." Instead of scaling back, China continued to look like a dangerous risk-taker pursuing its own self-interest at the expense of other countries. Irridentist claims for territory are inherently selfish and, by nature, bound to provoke conflicts with neighbors. Putting a priority on reclaiming territory necessitates trading off some national security. That became clear in 2010 when the American secretary of state Hillary Clinton spoke out on the problem of China's claims in the South China Sea at the meeting of the ASEAN Regional Forum, a multilateral grouping of twenty-seven countries. Clinton's statement injected America into the middle of the controversy to a degree it had never done before. Without ever mentioning China, she asserted that "vital American interests" were at stake in the South China Sea, and she offered the United States to act as a mediator in negotiations for a binding code of conduct for the area. A dozen other countries, consulted in advance by US diplomats, also spoke on the issue. Chinese foreign minister Yang Jiechi lost his cool and launched into a tirade in which he warned ASEAN countries not to side with the interfering outside power. "China is a big country. Bigger than any other countries here."[28] Though he created a diplomatic fiasco, Yang's career didn't suffer. The young female diplomat responsible for preparations for the meeting, however, was fired.

Core Interests Multiply

In the past, China's notion of a "core interest," which I have been defining as an interest so crucial to the fate of the nation that it would use military force to defend it—had been limited to Taiwan. Beijing used the term to threaten that it would go to war to prevent the formal independence of Taiwan, a humiliation that could trigger a mass revolt against Party rule.[29] The use of the term was intended to deter Taipei from taking steps toward independence and Washington from endorsing them.

But beginning in the mid-2000s, China's core interests proliferated, as its domestic politics increasingly intruded into foreign policy. "Color revolutions" by democratic oppositions in the former communist states of Georgia, Ukraine, Kyrgyzstan, Belarus, and Moldova had deposed their autocratic leaders. China's autocrats believed that the Americans had engineered the revolts and feared that the same doom could befall them. The propaganda and internal security bureaucracies exploited the leaders' fears to inflate the importance of their own roles. They stretched the notion of core interests to include other issues that if mishandled could spark domestic opposition to the regime. This minefield of nonnegotiable demands on other countries hampered the Foreign Ministry's normal diplomacy. Neither Foreign Minister Yang Jiechi nor CCP foreign policy adviser Dai Bingguo had the political standing to overrule Li Changchun and Zhou Yongkang, the Standing Committee members in charge of propaganda and internal security.

The first new additions to core interests were, as noted earlier, Tibet and Xinjiang, regions on China's Western periphery with restive ethnic groups that the central government feared might become hotbeds of separatism and terrorism. In March 2008, a few months before the Olympic Games, large peaceful protests by Tibetans in more than a hundred places across the Tibetan plateau escalated into mob violence. Olympic torch carriers were roughed up by pro-Tibet activists in Paris and other foreign cities at the same time. The Chinese government blamed the "Dalai clique" and dispatched thousands of security forces to squelch the demonstrations. The Chinese public—which is 90 percent Han Chinese—were outraged by the online videos and photographs of violence by Tibetan demonstrators (carefully curated by government censors), and by the reporting by CNN and other foreign media that seemed to highlight the violence by police instead of the demonstrators. Less than a year later, in July 2009, the largest civil uprising in the PRC's history broke out in Urumqi, the capital of Xinjiang. A large protest of the killings of Uighur migrant workers in a Guangdong province brawl turned into a riot in which almost two hundred people were killed, most of them Han Chinese. Live coverage by China Central Television of the violent clashes between Uighurs and Han Chinese angered Han Chinese living in other parts of China, who blamed the central government for failing to protect its own people.

Violent ethnic conflict terrified the leaders in Beijing and enabled the police and propaganda agencies to hype the threat to hijack foreign policy as well as domestic policy. Chinese leaders started canceling high-level meetings with Europeans and Americans over their meetings with the Dalai Lama. In an unprecedented gesture, the Chinese government canceled the 2008 China–Europe Union Summit because France's president Nicolas Sarkozy, who was the EU president at the time, said he planned to meet with the Dalai Lama. Beijing also froze diplomatic relations with the United Kingdom for over a year after Prime Minister David Cameron met the Dalai Lama in 2012. It took a public kowtow, including a promise from the British government never to do it again, for Beijing to agree to restore ties.

After the University of California, San Diego, where I teach, invited the Dalai Lama to deliver the commencement address in 2017, the Ministry of Education banned academic exchanges with the university. Some Chinese officials would have liked the university chancellor to write an apology pledging to never to do it again. After all, the British government had done just that. Having forced a sovereign government to cave in, the officials may have assumed that they could make a mere university do so. But UC San Diego, insisting on the principle of academic freedom, refused to apologize or make any promises, and waited out the punishment, which lasted over two years.

By this point, however, China's redefinition of core interests was starting to dominate its foreign relations. President Obama's advisers took a lot of flak from commentators when, after being warned by the Chinese side, they delayed a proposed meeting with the Dalai Lama until after the new president's first visit to China, in 2009; the administration had wanted to avoid starting off on the wrong foot with Beijing.[30] At the insistence of the Chinese side, the Obama advisers also agreed to a "painfully negotiated" joint statement for the president's November 2009 state visit to China that committed the two countries to "respecting each other's core interests."[31] The US deputy secretary of state James Steinberg believed that these words would help provide what he called "strategic reassurance" to China, an approach that other senior figures in the administration did not embrace.[32] (The joint statement drafted for Hu Jintao's state visit to the United States in January 2011 notably excluded the core interest language.[33])

In 2009 China complicated its diplomacy even more by authoritatively redefining its core interests to include for the first time China's political system and its economic and social development. Dai Bingguo may have hoped to manage the bureaucratic free-for-all by laying down a unifying line on what constituted a core interest. At the Strategic and Economic Dialogue with the United States, Dai Bingguo stated that China's number-one core interest was regime security: "to maintain its fundamental system and state security." Next was "state sovereignty and territorial integrity," and third was "stable development of the economy and society."[34] This formulation was incorporated in Dai's essay, mentioned above, "Adhere to the Path of Peaceful Development," and the White Paper on Peaceful Development published the following year.[35]

In 2010, Chinese diplomats started to talk about the country's maritime sovereignty claims as a core interest, an escalation of its ultimatums that rang alarm bells in Washington and Asian capitals.[36] Dai Bingguo reportedly told Secretary Clinton in a meeting that the South China Sea was a core interest, and military and working-level officials made the same assertion to their counterparts.[37] A Chinese official news service article reiterated this.[38] Not everyone agreed. Those who didn't may have dissuaded the leadership from formalizing the position because it would unsettle the Southeast Asian states.[39] A few weeks later, the government must have concluded that taking an absolutist position would be too costly, so it put out word that it had not definitively declared the South China Sea a core interest. The Foreign Ministry never confirmed nor denied from the podium, however, whether it was an official "core interest."

Bureaucratic confusion over what is and isn't a core interest persisted into the Xi Jinping administration. In 2013 the Foreign Ministry spokesperson stated from the podium that since the dispute with Japan over the Diaoyu (Senkaku) Islands in the East China Sea was "about sovereignty and territorial integrity, of course, it's China's core interest." Significantly, however, when the transcript was published, these words were softened to say that the Diaoyu issue "touches on 'core interests.'"[40] And indeed, the boundary between "core interests" and other "major interests" has become vague under Xi, as Chinese scholar Zhu Feng observed.[41] According to a Chinese legislative staff member, "core interests" are defined in article 2 of the 2015 National Security Law as "the political regime; the sovereignty, unity and territorial integrity of the nation; and people's livelihoods, sustainable economic development of society and other major interests."[42]

In 2021, as I noted earlier, China banned Australian exports, except for iron ore, as punishment for the Australian government's calling for an international scientific investigation of the origins of COVID-19. Apparently, the issue of the origins of the coronavirus had turned into a "core interest" for the Xi leadership. "We will not allow any country to reap benefits from doing business with China," Foreign Ministry spokesman Zhao Lijian said, "while groundlessly accusing and smearing China and undermining China's core interests based on ideology."[43] The "core interests" language had evolved from a diplomatic signal of intent to defend a top-priority national objective—preventing Taiwan independence—to one encompassing a more expansive set of nonnegotiable issues, meant to prove to the Chinese public that the Party and the government stand up for China.

Accusations that other countries are violating China's core interests might sometimes be perceived as empty threats, which, if not acted upon, can make a government look weak to other countries and to its own domestic audience. Nonetheless, social scientists have found that bluster can increase public approval for the government if the threat is vague enough.[44]

Standing Up to the United States

For a rising China, the riskiest move is to confront the United States, and if it decides to do so, when. Making the global superpower an enemy too soon could hobble China's economic development and jeopardize its political stability. Getting along with the hegemon was a safer bet. Hu Jintao, his three top advisers, and the Foreign Ministry grasped this fundamental point. Their challenge was to get the control coalition, particularly the propaganda bureaucracies and the military, to go along with accommodating Washington, especially after the global financial crisis had tarnished America's image and created an overly confident mood in China.

Hu managed relations with the United States smoothly during his first term. In his meetings with President Bush, he emphasized that maintaining good relations with the United States was a matter of Chinese self-interest. As one Chinese participant in the meetings said, "This was the same point of Zheng Bijian's message about 'peaceful rise.'" At the time, the Bush administration was focused on the war on terrorism, and Bush himself had made clear that he was frustrated with Taiwan's pro-independence president Chen Shui-bian and favored cooperation with China to counter terrorism.[45] The United States was at war in Iraq and didn't want to have to deal with a cross-Strait conflict. Hu was also extremely grateful when Bush made the politically controversial decision to attend the opening ceremonies of the 2008 Beijing Olympics, though the leaders of Britain and Germany had decided to skip it to protest China's violent crackdown after the riots in Tibet.[46] Bush had met with the Dalai Lama at the White House in 2001, and though the Chinese government objected to the "rude interference" in domestic affairs, it did not cancel any meetings.[47]

During his second term, Hu appeared to lose his grip over China's US foreign policy. During Obama's visit to the PRC in November 2009, the Chinese government refused to allow his town hall speech to college students to be televised nationally, though in the past it had broadcast the speeches of Presidents Clinton and Bush. According to the American officials who negotiated the issue of broadcasting the speech, Hu's advisers and propaganda officials seemed worried that Obama's stirring words might arouse viewers to turn against the government, which they believed had happened with his speech to students at Cairo University, on June 4, 2009. Comparisons between the charismatic American president and a bland Hu would not be favorable to the Chinese leader.

The Propaganda Department interfered with the one press interview the president gave, to *Southern Weekend,* an unorthodox newspaper published in Guangdong province, telling journalists what questions they could and couldn't ask. What's more, the propaganda authorities censored the published interview, ripping out the pages of the newspaper in some of the issues.[48]

At the United Nations Climate Change Conference in Copenhagen held the following month, some unusually sharp vocal criticisms of the

US by Chinese officials and the aforementioned tussle between Chinese security guards and Obama as he was trying to enter a conference sent the same message. According to National Security Council official Jeffrey Bader's first-hand account, after Obama finally did manage to enter the conference room for the meeting with Wen Jiabao and the other heads of state, he took charge of trying to hammer out an agreement.[49] But a disagreement between Xie Zhenhua, the senior climate negotiator from the National Development and Reform Commission, and Premier Wen erupted. When Xie loudly exclaimed in Chinese that Obama was wrong on a point, Wen instructed the translator not to translate Xie's rebuke.[50] The background for Xie's outburst, according to a Chinese member of the delegation, was that he had acted out of pique. He thought that he would be negotiating, but at the last minute, Wen Jiabao directed the Foreign Ministry to do it instead.

During 2010, Hu Jintao and Dai Bingguo tried, as noted earlier, to stabilize relations with the United States in advance of an anticipated state visit to the US. Leaders' meetings always stimulate the bureaucracy to negotiate "deliverables" that will show the success of its diplomatic strategy. Behind the scenes, China had in fact been cooperating quite effectively with Washington to induce Iran and North Korea to abandon their nuclear weapons programs and to work through the United Nations to end the civil war in Southern Sudan. This is, of course, when Dai Bingguo's reassuring essay about "peaceful development" was published. In bilateral meetings to prepare the visit, senior Chinese officials kept repeating the mantra of cooperation.[51]

But inside China, the priority on internal stability that the control coalition was promoting kept threatening to disrupt foreign relations. When Liu Xiaobo, in prison for his writings, was awarded the Nobel Peace Prize, the Chinese government, including the Foreign Ministry, had what Jeffrey Bader called a "fit of self-induced paranoia." Having convinced themselves that Secretary Clinton had called the Nobel Committee and told it to award the prize to Liu and that she or President Obama would attend the ceremony in Oslo, Chinese officials considered delaying or canceling Hu's visit.[52] Meeting with an old friend from the Foreign Ministry, I was shaken by his uncharacteristically angry accusations against me as an American for insulting China in this way. Liu Xiaobo was not a household name in China; the censors had long since banned reporting on his activities. Most people learned his name only when the Foreign Ministry denounced his Peace Prize; it was unlikely that he could become the rallying point of a Chinese protest movement. Nonetheless, Beijing still felt compelled to punish the Norwegian government until after Liu died, in 2017.

The propaganda authorities often made policy by making the message, putting it's sharp rhetoric in conflict with the Foreign Ministry over its stance toward the United States. As noted earlier, the propaganda system was led by Li Changchun, a crony of Hu's predecessor Jiang Zemin, who felt entitled to operate independently. In 2010, the official media hammered away in protest of American containment of China, stoking the popular suspicion that the United States was seeking to exploit its military might and alliances to prevent China from becoming a major power. Diplomats told me that when the Foreign Ministry asked the editor of the *Global Times* to tone down its attacks on the US, Hu Xijin replied, "Who is your boss?" Propaganda Department head Liu Yunsan, a Politburo member, and Li Changchun, a Standing Committee member, protected the *Global Times*. "You have only Foreign Minister Yang Jiechi, just a Central Committee member behind you," the editor retorted. No one can do anything to the *Global Times* with Li Changchun at its back.

The propaganda censors orchestrated public opinion to stimulate bottom-up nationalist pressure on the government. In January 2010, Google announced that it would no longer allow the censorship of search results in China and would therefore be moving its search engine off the mainland to Hong Kong, where it still operates. The day after Google made its public announcement, the Propaganda Department saw the vast majority of the online reactions siding with Google, according to several accounts. Chinese netizens, grieving the loss of the search engine that was their door to world knowledge, left flowers outside the company's headquarters in Beijing. The Propaganda Department fought back, and the very next day, "the tide changed," as the censors put it, having orchestrated online opinion so that it overwhelmingly sided with the government in arguing that the Google action was an American political conspiracy. An article supposedly authored by Jin Canrong, a prominent nationalist academic, "What Does Google Think It Is Doing?," was commissioned in a meeting of three vice ministers of propaganda, according to someone who knew the ghostwriter.

After Hu Jintao's amicable state visit to the United States in January 2011, the Foreign Ministry debriefed a group of foreign policy experts about the outcomes of the visit. According to several participants, the briefer reported that Hu, upon his return from Washington, had ordered the Propaganda Department to ease off on the containment theme. The foreign policy experts were pleased to hear this news. However, the

Propaganda Department ignored Hu's instructions because of events that followed just days after the briefing. A small group of Chinese protestors, responding to a tweet originating from overseas activists, demonstrated outside the McDonald's on Wangfujing in central Beijing in support of the so-called Jasmine Revolutions in Tunisia and Egypt. The government had anticipated that domestic democratic activists might try to launch their own Jasmine Revolution and was prepared to "put out all the sparks so they don't ignite a fire," as one scholar put it. The entire Standing Committee summoned the heads of provinces, government departments and military organs, state-owned enterprises, banks, and universities to an emergency session, where Hu Jintao for the first time called for the creation of a national database of information about the population.[53] Any mention of the Arab revolutions or of "Jasmine" was banned from the Internet, and political activists, including the artist Ai Weiwei, were arrested. When Ambassador Jon Huntsman, wearing a jacket with an American flag on the shoulder, appeared on the scene of the small protest with his wife and two daughters (the Embassy said he had coincidentally passed by while on a family outing), it gave the appearance that the US government was behind the demonstration. After a video of Huntsman had spread over the Internet and lent credence to anti-American conspiratorial thinking, the Propaganda Department refused to drop its line about containment, and Hu acquiesced.[54]

Differences inside the Hu administration also frustrated China's handling of relations with North and South Korea, which affects its standing with the United States. China had worked hard for years to cement friendships with both South Korea and North Korea. But if one friend attacks another, choosing a side becomes inevitable. In 2010, Beijing estranged the South Korean public and perturbed Americans when it followed its Mao-era loyalties and favored the North in response to two acts of North Korean aggression. First was the attack that sank the *Cheonan*, the South Korean corvette. China was invited to send a team to Seoul to review the findings of an international investigation that had concluded that a North Korean torpedo was responsible, but it declined and never censured the North Korean attack. It took almost a month for the Chinese government to issue a statement on its position because of internal disagreement. The Foreign Ministry, protective of the relationship with Seoul, had lost control over Korea policy to the Party's international office led by Dai Bingguo, who, despite his attempts to stabilize relations with the United States, had formed personal ties with North Korean figures over the years. And though Premier Wen Jiabao had visited Seoul and promised that China would condemn whoever was found to be responsible, it never did.

The PLA was biased toward its former comrades-in-arms in Pyongyang, who had fought with the Chinese army during the Korean War, and who now claimed that they were innocent of the attack on the *Cheonan*. When the PLA offers its professional analysis of an incident—as it did when it blamed the accidental bombing of the PRC Embassy in Belgrade (1999) and a Chinese fighter jet's collision with an American EP-3 surveillance plane (2001) on the United States—it is almost impossible for its political overlords to second-guess them. A few months later, Beijing also refused to condemn an unprovoked artillery attack by North Korea on Yeonpyeong Island that killed two civilians and two South Korean marines.

Hu and the Generals

As we saw in chapter 4 on collective leadership, Hu Jintao had to wait two years to become commander in chief after he had become general secretary, and he never fully established his authority over the military during his years in power. Jiang Zemin had been allowed to hold on to his position as chairman of the Central Military Commission until 2004 as a face-saving way to ease him into retirement. Even after Jiang departed, people appointed by and loyal to him remained in the commission. "The problem is that Hu doesn't know enough people in the PLA to replace them with," one general explained at the time, noting that Hu's connections to the PLA were "very thin."

Keeping the military loyal to the incumbent leader is essential for the survival of Communist Party rule.[55] Winning the support of the PLA would therefore present a major hurdle for any rival leader hoping to claim power. The People's Armed Police, a large paramilitary force jointly commanded by the PLA and the Public Security Ministry (until, as noted in chapter 4, Xi Jinping placed it entirely under military command in 2018), and backed up by PLA regulars, would put down any large-scale protests. Of the "new historic missions" Hu enumerated in his 2004 inaugural speech to the Military Commission, number one was to ensure the military's defense of Party rule.[56]

Despite the thinness of his connections with the PLA, Hu needed to keep it on his side, which he did by funding it generously and allowing it a high degree of autonomy. Chinese military spending (according to both official PRC data and Stockholm International Peace Research Institute estimates) increased annually at double-digit rates after the 1989 Tiananmen crisis. The budget increases were particularly high during

Hu's second term. According to the January 2009 official report on the defense budget, a huge chunk of Hu's increased spending went to improving officers' and soldiers' living conditions, a move that presumably made him more popular with them but also fostered corruption.[57]

Significant as it was, this infusion of funds into the military did not match the all-out military buildups that occurred in early twentieth-century Germany and Japan and led them into war. The 12.1 percent average annual inflation-adjusted increase of military spending between 2000 and 2010 is only somewhat more than the 10.2 percent economic growth rate over that period, and in the Pentagon's view, contributed to only a "negligible" change in the defense burden on China's economy.[58] We might compare the 10.7 percent increase in the 2013 defense budget with the 18.8 percent increase on energy efficiency and environmental protection and the 27.1 percent increase on medical care—and the mere 9.3 percent increase on education.[59] In an attempt to reassure the world, Chinese officials noted that in 2017 the share of defense spending in China's GDP was only about 1.3 percent, compared to 3.3 percent in the United States.[60] Even if China's actual military spending, including items off the official budget, was $226 billion as of 2016, as the Stockholm Institute for Peace Research (SIPRI) believes, it was dwarfed by the US military budget of $598 billion.[61]

In any case, during Hu's administration the PLA enhanced its capabilities in line with the country's expanding overseas interests. Safeguarding foreign trade and energy imports joined the PLA's traditional missions of keeping Taiwan in the fold and preserving domestic peace. Today's PLA has cruise missiles, submarines, stealth fighters, drones, and guided missile destroyers. The military no longer has to rely on arms sales from Russia because its own research institutes and industries can produce their own—with a little help from Russian or Western technologies acquired through various methods, ranging from legitimate purchase to stealing and copying. Thanks to major investments in defense and dual-use technologies, China has acquired high-tech cyberwarfare and counterspace capabilities and conventional precision strike capabilities (including ballistic and cruise missiles capable of hitting ships that are as far as 1,200 miles offshore).[62] It has three conventional aircraft carriers and is in the process of building a nuclear one, and is developing its own ballistic missile defense system.[63] As of 2022 the PLA is a professional and well-equipped military force of two million soldiers and possesses the largest navy in the world (355 ships and submarines as compared with the US Navy's 293).[64]

Changes in military organization that tracked the new missions and acquisitions complicated Hu's job of overseeing the military establishment and getting accurate information from it. Before Hu's time, the Army had dominated the PLA. Now the commanders of the other services—the Navy, Air Force, and 2nd Artillery (missiles and nuclear forces)—have been given seats in the expanded eleven-member Central Military Commission. Guo Boxiong and Xu Caihou, both vice chairmen and both allies of Jiang Zemin and the heads of the four General Departments also operated very independently. The military figures I interviewed about the Hu years weren't able to tell me whether there was logrolling among the services and departments that was similar to the logrolling in the civilian Party oligarchy. But they described Hu as a figurehead, largely ignored by military leaders. And the rank-buying and other corruption scandals revealed by the Xi Jinping anti-corruption campaign speak for themselves about poor civilian oversight of the PLA under Hu.

Protecting China's Overseas Interests

Until recently, China's primary rationale for increasing the military budget was that it needed to be prepared to solve the Taiwan "problem" militarily if it had to.[65] The emergence of democratically elected presidents in Taiwan who appeared to be moving the island toward formal independence provided the impetus for the mainland's rapid military modernization. When the Clinton administration permitted President Lee Teng-hui to visit America to make a speech at his college reunion at Cornell, in 1995, China's leaders were shocked into the realization that if they didn't make China's threat to use force to prevent Taiwan independence more credible, they might be confronted with a fait accompli. Some senior PLA officers were vocal in urging a strong show of force against Taiwan.[66] After the United States responded to China's large-scale exercises and missile launches in 1995 and 1996 by deploying two aircraft-carrier battle groups, China's leaders de-escalated the crisis with a new appreciation of the country's military weakness. An article in the Chinese press in 2006 stated the connection explicitly. "The double-digit increase [in military spending] did not take place until very recent years when tension escalated across the Taiwan Straits."[67]

Starting under Hu and continuing under Xi, however, the Chinese military's mission has extended in two new directions. First, the PLA is increasingly targeting US forces operating in the Western Pacific. Deterring the United States from intervening in a Taiwan contingency has come to be viewed as even more important than deterring Taiwan's own moves toward independence. China wants to raise the cost to the US of sending its sailors and soldiers into a Taiwan crisis or another regional dispute. They want to make clear to the American military that involvement is no longer risk-free. The Chinese call them defensive "counter intervention" operations. The US calls them "anti-access, area denial" operations, a terminological difference that highlights the two countries' different views on the legitimacy of America's military role in the region. The current scope of China's maritime defense perimeter is the area formed by what Chinese strategists call the "first island chain," stretching from the Aleutians south to the Kuriles, Japan's archipelago, the Ryukyus, Taiwan, the Philippines, and Borneo; it includes the Yellow Sea between the Korean Peninsula and China, the East China Sea between Japan and China, and the entire South China Sea. Some foreign military experts anticipate that China will soon try to extend its no-go zone out to the second island chain that reaches to Guam.[68]

If China succeeds in achieving "anti-access, area denial" capability, it will challenge America's long-held peacekeeping role in the Asia-Pacific. The United States would effectively be locked out of a region that has been declared "a vital security interest by every administration in the last sixty years," according to American military experts.[69] Japan, South Korea, Taiwan, and Southeast Asian countries would no longer be able to count on the US military to help defend them. To preserve freedom of action for US forces, the Navy and Air Force have been developing a counterstrategy called the Joint Operational Access Concept, which encompasses an "Air-Sea Battle Concept." The idea is to achieve "cross-domain synergy" with flexible and lower-level integration of air, sea, space, and cyberspace operations.[70] As Chinese and American military planners plot these new strategies and counterstrategies, their generals, politicians, and publics are increasingly viewing one another as potential enemies.

According to some, the turning point that shifted China's attention to developing advanced anti-access, area-denial capabilities against the American military came in May 1999, after the accidental bombing of the Chinese Embassy in Belgrade by an American jet flying as part of a NATO mission in Yugoslavia. Even though the Americans apologized for the erroneous targeting of the embassy and paid compensation, Jiang Zemin, who was in power at the time, was seriously shaken by the incident. Dubious about the official explanation I helped to prepare as a State Department official during the Clinton administration, the Chinese public was, and continues to be, convinced that the attack was intentional, a false belief that helps explain its anti-NATO stance in the 2022 Ukraine War.[71] In meetings with military chiefs after the attack, Jiang argued that the Americans could have undertaken the same kind of long-range precision strike against the leadership compound in Zhongnanhai had the Chinese not possessed a nuclear and strategic missile deterrent. Consequently, China should develop a twenty-first-century strategic defense, including antisatellite and other asymmetric capabilities to target the vulnerabilities of the otherwise superior US forces. This shift in strategy was accompanied by large investments in military and dual-use technology projects, known as the "995 Plan" (a reference to the May 1999 Belgrade embassy bombing).[72]

Second, outside the Asia-Pacific, as China has expanded its global economic reach to Africa, Latin America, and the Middle East, the PLA has been assigned the mission of protecting energy trade routes and projecting a national presence. This new objective, involving mostly noncombat operations, has been a boon to the PLA Navy. Since Hu Jintao's 2004 speech on the PLA's "new historic missions," which included counter-piracy, counterterrorism, human assistance, and disaster relief, Chinese sailors have been sailing far beyond Asian waters.[73] Just a decade or so earlier, Chinese sailors had suffered severe seasickness when their vessels made their first oceanic voyages to San Diego and other far-off ports. Today, sailors regularly sail thousands of miles to participate in out-of-area operations, a first for China. Since 2008, PLA Navy ships have been engaged in the international counter-piracy operations in the Gulf of Aden off the coast of Somalia. A Chinese frigate operating in the Gulf of Aden and Chinese military transport jets helped evacuate 36,000 Chinese nationals from Libya during the civil war in March 2011. A Chinese hospital ship is paying port calls and treating patients in the Caribbean. That China has these global responsibilities makes a good argument for the Navy to claim more resources for modernizing its fleet.

PLA Autonomy

The People's Liberation Army is a far more professional organization than it was during the revolution, when the PLA and the Chinese Communist Party were practically merged, or during the Mao era, when military officers were politicians on the Politburo Standing Committee.[74] The PLA and the CCP remain intertwined to this day. Every PLA unit includes

a political commissar, who is a CCP cadre responsible for the ideological rectitude of the soldiers. Military representatives constitute 11 percent of the Central Committee and two of the twenty-five members on
the Politburo. Nine percent of China's legislature, the National People's
Congress, is in uniform.[75]

The Central Military Commission remains ostensibly both a CCP and
a government organ, but in fact, it is dominated by the Party. Nonetheless,
civilian control hangs by a thin thread tied to one individual, the CCP
general secretary. The only civilians on the Military Commission are the
general secretary and his successor-in-training, when there is one.[76] The
government's Ministry of National Defense lacks any real authority over
the military. A politically powerful and independent military in a rising
power could lead to war, as the historical examples of Germany and
Japan show.

For years, proposals to strengthen civilian authority over the military by
putting the PLA under the government instead of the Party (the shorthand
phrase for this is "statification," *guojiahua*) have been publicly rejected by
the PLA establishment. The *PLA Daily*, one of its official organs, charged
that there was a "conspiracy" to spread the "false ideas" of the "non-party,
non-political military," and that *guojiahua* had to be resisted.[77] The PLA
commanders clearly prefer a system that gives them direct access to the
nation's top leader and minimal government oversight of their decisions.
And the political commissars naturally oppose it because it could eliminate their positions. Some military experts believe, however, that the only
way to have a genuinely professional military is to put it squarely under
government authority. "It will never change," one of them told me. "If it
does change, it means that an even bigger change has occurred in China.
We'd like to see the change, but not change it, if you know what I mean,"
he said. The Party's top politicians also are suspicious of anything that
would attenuate their control over the military. China was initially reluctant to accept the Pentagon's offer, in 2003, to set up a military hotline
between the high-level armed forces of the two countries because it would
have delegated too much authority to the senior commanders.[78]

In any case, as the country's top military decision-making organ, the
Central Military Commission has wide-ranging autonomy in defense
matters. On military issues with major political, economic, and diplomatic
ramifications, such as over Taiwan or military-to-military activities with the
United States, the Military Commission and the PLA are supposed to consult closely with the Politburo Standing Committee and leadership small
groups. If these civilian coordinating bodies are not operating effectively,

however, the military has more latitude to act on its own. Coordination between the PLA and civilian authorities have shown signs of strain, starting under Hu Jintao.

One of the first instances of a disconnect between the military and the government occurred in 2007, when the military shot down one of its own old weather satellites in a test of an antisatellite weapon, spewing a huge amount of debris into space and endangering the satellites of the United States and other countries. When it was questioned by the US government, the Foreign Ministry didn't seem to know anything about the test. A Defense Ministry official denied the foreign news reports about the test. The Foreign Ministry spokesman didn't publicly acknowledge what had happened until two weeks later.[79]

Later in 2007, another sign of disarray in civil-military relations embarrassed China again. The US aircraft carrier *Kitty Hawk* was just hours away from mooring in Hong Kong for a long-scheduled Thanksgiving reunion for the sailors and their families, when it was suddenly informed that the PRC authorities would not allow it to enter the harbor. The port call, which had been approved through normal Foreign Ministry channels, was revoked in a last-minute decision, most likely by the Central Military Commission, as revenge for an arms sale to Taiwan announced by the Pentagon a few days earlier. (At about the same time, China also refused two US minesweepers entry to Hong Kong to escape bad weather, in a violation of standard naval etiquette.) The carrier group turned around and headed to Japan in the hopes of salvaging the family reunions. To save time in the poor weather conditions — or to pay back the Chinese for the sudden reversal — it passed through the Taiwan Strait, which the United States defines as international waters but China claims as its own. But before the ships reached Japan, Beijing informed them that they would be welcomed in Hong Kong after all. The Foreign Ministry, well aware of what a public relations disaster it was for China to deny the sailors and their families their Thanksgiving celebration, must have persuaded Hu Jintao, who at the time was the only person with the authority to overrule the military, which by now was seething over the Taiwan Strait transit. Foreign Minister Yang Jiechi, who happened to be visiting Washington, DC, tried to smooth over the situation by explaining to US officials that the "misunderstanding" was a result of "poor communications." To add to the confusion, the Foreign Ministry spokesman then denied Minister Yang's statements, and claimed that the decision to disallow the port call was due not to "miscommunication" but to China's anger over the Dalai Lama's meeting with President Bush and the Congress in Washington the previous month. The ministry's statement looked like an attempt to cover up Hu's vacillation and poor coordination and make it look as if a unified government was taking a tough principled stand.[80]

In 2011, Hu met with strong PLA resistance when he ordered the resumption of military exchanges with the United States. Preparing for his first state visit to the US, Hu had wanted to warm the atmosphere by reviving the military exchanges the Chinese had frozen in January 2010 to protest the Obama administration's $6 billion arms sale to Taiwan. China routinely protests US arms sales to Taiwan, but it had on this occasion retaliated more vigorously than in the past. The military tried to convince the Party leaders that with the United States in decline after the global financial crisis, China could reasonably demand that these arms sales end. Hu telephoned General Guo Boxiong, the vice chairman of the Central Military Commission, and ordered the resumption of military contacts, telling him that the hiatus had lasted long enough. When Guo orally communicated the order to his subordinates, the officers came back to him shortly thereafter to say that the officers would not carry out the order unless they received it in writing.[81]

At roughly the same time, defense secretary Robert Gates, traveling to China in preparation for Hu's visit to Washington, ran head-on into a problem created by the cross purposes at which the PLA and civilians operate. In the weeks before Gates's visit, the PLA had rolled out its new stealth fighter on the runway. The existence of the jet was no secret; photographs of it were the front-page news in popular newspapers and on blogs. But the Chinese Air Force chose the day of Gates's visit to give the radar-evading fighter its first test flight. Photographs of the flight were posted on military websites a few hours before Gates was scheduled to meet with Hu. Gates was furious and came close to canceling the rest of his program to protest what appeared to be a hostile gesture targeted at the US or him personally. Ambassador Jon Huntsman convinced him not to do that, reminding him that after the meeting with Hu, he was scheduled to visit the headquarters of the Second Artillery, the unit in charge of China's nuclear, missile, and space assets, which had rarely been opened to American officials in the past. (The only prior visit had been by defense secretary Donald Rumsfeld in 2005.)

Huntsman and Gates agreed that they would gently broach the topic of the test flight at the end of the meeting with Hu. According to the account of a meeting participant, Gates asked, "President Hu, I have to meet the press after our meeting. Can you please give me some advice about what I should say when they ask me about the first flight of your new jet fighter yesterday and whether I think it was aimed at me or my country?" Hu appeared startled by the question. He turned to his defense minister, Liang Guanglie, seated on his right, and asked, "Is it true?" The question was passed down the command chain of PLA officers sitting next to one another in the room. After scrambling to consult with one another, they handed Hu his talking point: "It was a 'scientific research experiment' and had absolutely nothing to do with your visit." Gates later told journalists that the civilian leadership had seemed surprised by the test. Even if we assume that Hu had approved the J-20 program and was aware of its development, the military leadership had humiliated their chairman by not prepping him for an obvious question.

Military Hawks Go Public

The stance of the Chinese military toward Japan, Taiwan, and the United States is generally more hawkish than that of civilian officials, and this nudged China's policies in a more confrontational direction during Hu Jintao's leadership. Hu appeared unable or unwilling to stop the military from going public with its views. Stoking public anger against United States' joint exercises with its allies in the region or against the territorial claims of Japan and other neighbors bolstered the PLA's influence over foreign policy, and its claims that it needed bigger budgets.

The PLA press, including the *PLA Daily*, helps to create publicity that builds popular demand for a stronger military—without actually forcing it into a war. The PLA press typically takes a tougher line on Japan, Taiwan, and the United States than does the civilian press. Many of the commercial magazines that appeal to male audiences by highlighting the technological advances of the US, European, and other Asian militaries, thereby creating public support for China's own military spending, are actually published by defense industrial firms.[82] The most outspoken military commentators are PLA scholars based at defense research and educational institutions or retired officers. It's hard to know how mainstream their views are, but their publication in the *PLA Daily* and other official journals and consistent presence on online media indicates official endorsement.

Major General Luo Yuan of the Academy of Military Science was one military expert who often called for China to stiffen its spine against foreign threats. In 2010, just two days before Premier Wen Jiabao was due to arrive on a state visit to India, where the border dispute with China remains festering, Major General Luo wrote that China could not call itself "a strong nation" unless it "recovered the land looted by neighbors." The joint communiqué issued during the visit, for the first time in recent

years, made no mention of military-to-military activities, suggesting that
the PLA may have vetoed them over the territorial dispute; Luo's point of
view was representative of the hardliners in the PLA.[83] One of Luo's favorite themes was "containment"—how the US is "laying out forces across
the Asia-Pacific region in advance to contain the rise of China."[84] He also
frequently threatened the use of force to defend China's territorial integrity in the South China Sea. "If other claimants continued to insult China
beyond its limits, the Chinese people would have no choice but to 'wield
their swords,'" he said in a 2011 Xinhua interview.[85] When in 2012 the
Chinese government de-escalated a confrontation with the Philippines in
Scarborough Shoal by promising to withdraw, the Chinese defense minister General Liang Guanglie said that the military would defer to the
diplomats in handling the situation. Major General Luo, however, told
the *Global Times* that it was a mistake to withdraw.[86]

Even in retirement, Luo continued to speak his mind, for example,
calling for an Air Defense Identification Zone in the South China Sea.[87]
Other PLA hawks gave speeches with provocative titles like "2030: America
Dismembers China," wrote books such as *C-Shaped Encirclement* about
the encirclement of China by America and its allies, and called for the "ex-
termination of troublemakers in South China Sea." When Washington
announced arms sales to Taiwan, these hawks gave interviews calling for
China to retaliate economically, even proposing that China dump US government bonds.[88]

The PLA pundits don't disguise their role in the PLA's external propaganda operations and or that they follow its internal rules. For example,
all PLA staff were banned from engaging in Internet blogging in 2010;
but in 2012, military scholars in frequent contact with foreigners and the
media were allowed to open blog accounts on Weibo.[89] One non-Chinese
PLA expert describes the public statements of PLA hawks as "propaganda
masquerading as PLA thought."[90]

Taiwan Policy

Beijing's confrontational attitude with regard to Taiwan, which exists
to this day—and grows more tense with every passing day—is one dynamic that can't be traced back to Hu Jintao's tenure. Hu's approach to
Taiwan was "very flexible," according to an international relations expert close to the Foreign Ministry. "Hu protected the policy because he
was personally committed to it. He views it as his main achievement."

Hu sought to win the hearts and minds of the Taiwan people and draw them closer to the mainland. Preventing the island democracy from declaring its formal independence remains a crucial goal for any mainland leader; achieving its eventual reunification would guarantee the leader's legacy in the history books. Hu and Xi shared the same goal, but Xi's strategy relies on intimidation instead of the ingratiation that Hu attempted.

Hu's agent in his accommodationist campaign toward Taiwan was Wang Yi, who, as noted, was the architect of the Foreign Ministry's successful Asia diplomacy and who as China's ambassador in Tokyo had negotiated with Japan's prime minister Shinto Abe a pledge not to visit the Yasukuni Shrine where a few Japanese war criminals are honored. Hu selected Wang Yi to head the government Taiwan Affairs Office ("Taiban," for short) in the expectation that as a good diplomatic deal-maker, he would unfreeze cross-Strait ties just as he had done earlier with Japan.

When Hu entered office in 2002, Beijing's cross-Strait policy appeared to be failing. Taiwan's president Chen Shui-bian was gesturing toward independence and threatening to hold a referendum to revise the constitution. Chen's re-election victory in 2004 showed that Taiwan voters supported the right to decide Taiwan's future on their own. A win for Chen's Democratic Progressive Party in the December 2004 legislative elections would make a referendum to change the constitution more likely. The Chinese policy elite was starting to talk anxiously about the possibility of war. Wang Zaixi, a former major general who was vice-head of the mainland Taiwan Affairs Office, declared threateningly that "a referendum equals independence and independence means war."[91]

To help China's leaders head-off a Taiwan referendum without resorting to military force, the Chinese government, in 2005, legislated its own "Anti-Secession Law." The law authorized use of "nonpeaceful means" if Taiwan were to secede, if "major incidents entailing Taiwan's secession from China should occur," or if "possibilities for a peaceful reunification" were "completely exhausted." Some foreigners feared that this expansive set of contingencies might corner Hu into attacking Taiwan, but, according to Chinese experts, the intention of enacting the law was in fact to provide an alternative to war. Fortunately, the surprising win by Taiwan's opposition parties in the legislative elections in December 2004 staved off a referendum, and the popular law gave Hu the domestic approval he needed to undertake friendly overtures toward the Taiwan people.

The strategic logic behind these overtures was to isolate Chen Shui-bian and build a united front with Taiwan's opposition parties and economic interest groups. In 2005 Hu hosted two leading Taiwan politicians, Lian Chan, the head of the KMT (Guomindang) Party, and James Soong, head of the People's First Party, to pay homecoming visits to the mainland; both had left as children in 1949. Invited to give live televised speeches, the politicians impressed the mainland audience, who found them to be more eloquent and genuine than the CCP politicians who were hosting them. Other benevolent gestures followed: establishing low-tariff imports of Taiwan fruit; extending a welcome to Taiwan tourists; allowing direct cargo flights across the Strait; making university tuition fees for Taiwan students equal to those paid by mainland students; recognizing Taiwan college degrees; and allowing Taiwan medical doctors to be licensed on the mainland.[92] Hu was magnanimous toward Taiwan society despite Chen Shui-bian's moves toward independence, adopting a disciplined long-term strategy that picked up steam during his second term when Taiwan was led by new KMT president, Ma Ying-jeou, who was more amenable to improving relations with the mainland.

Another benefit of Hu's nonconfrontational strategy was getting Washington on his side. The more reasonable China's approach, the more likely the US administration would be to pressure Chen Shui-bian not to risk war by holding a referendum. As noted, President Bush had criticized Chen for proposing a referendum back in 2003. Shortly before Taiwan's 2008 election, when there were two referendums on the ballot along with the presidential choice, the PLA, according to a Pentagon official, "frantically asked the Defense Department's help in reducing our mutual risk by discouraging the referendum." Tom Christensen, the deputy assistant secretary of state, helped by saying publicly that the US government didn't support the referendum. But then, just a day or so after Secretary Gates had visited China, the Bush administration announced the big Taiwan arms sales package, which led to the Thanksgiving port call incident.

At the time, Taiban officials often reminded me that "peace in the strait is good for US-China relations." They asked me to pass messages to Washington requesting a public statement praising the current cross-Strait rapprochement and saying the US hoped it would continue. Such a statement would help them sustain domestic support for their engagement of Taiwan and constrain future Taiwan leaders from trying to alter the status quo. The Taiban officials also complained that the Foreign Ministry kept sticking its nose into Taiwan policy. The foreign minister, Yang Jiechi, and Wang Yi had long been bureaucratic rivals; and the Foreign Ministry typically took tough positions on issues like Taiwan and Tibet. For example, the Foreign Ministry had endorsed canceling the EU-China summit over French prime minister Sarkozy's meeting with the Dalai Lama in 2008, and it made strong statements about the awarding of the Nobel Peace Prize to Liu Xiaobo. The Foreign Ministry "wants to demonstrate that they are tough on these nationalist issues because they are always vulnerable to being criticized as too pro-foreign," one expert explained. Another one noted that Foreign Ministry senior officials in their late fifties "have their own ambitions," so they have to appear very tough. But with Hu so obviously siding with Wang Yi and the Taiban, the views of the Foreign Ministry found a deaf ear in Zhongnanhai.

Hu accelerated his engagement of Taiwan after Ma Ying-jeou was elected president in 2008. Unlike Chen Shui-bian, Ma endorsed what was known as the "1992 Consensus," an informal agreement between the two sides that there is only "one China" even if they don't agree on exactly what "one China" means. Until 2001, PRC leaders had insisted that Taiwan acknowledge the "one China principle" as a precondition for cross-Strait dialogue; the "1992 Consensus" was a compromise to finesse doctrinal differences and facilitate the talks that both Hu and Ma desired.[93]

Both sides were eager to pick up the pace of engagement to make as much progress as possible while Ma and Hu were in office; they agreed to direct air, mail, and shipping links in 2008 and signed an economic cooperation agreement called the Economic Cooperation Framework Agreement in 2010. Both sides also went to great lengths to prevent any disruptions in the rapidly improving relationship. They enforced a tacit "diplomatic truce" in their competition for diplomatic recognition by other countries. The Foreign Ministry had objected to the diplomatic truce because it wanted to create more slots for ambassadors and show the ministry's achievements.[94] In 2009, when journalists questioned Wang Yi about a Taiwan film festival's invitation to Ribiya Kadeer, a well-known émigré leader of the Uighur movement in Xinjiang, he played it down to avoid having to criticize the Taiwan government. After the two leaders left office, however, rapprochement stalled and then reversed. Cross-Strait relations today are as tense and dangerous as they have ever been. A leader like Xi Jinping has all the authority he needs to revive cross-strait dialogue and reduce the risk of having to use military force to prevent a formal declaration of independence by Taiwan if he were willing to compromise on the "1992 consensus" and show some goodwill to the Taiwanese public. But so far there is no indication that he is headed in that direction.

Japan

Besides extending an olive branch toward Taiwan, another hallmark of Hu Jintao's foreign policy was his attempt to stabilize China's relations with Japan—a policy that stood in contrast to the overall more confrontational approach of his administration and certainly to the situation today. In fact, Hu's efforts to protect China's relations with both Japan and Taiwan were acts of political bravery. These two issues always are the focal points of popular nationalism and easily exploited by the military and the security and propaganda bureaucracies. Yet despite his unwieldy oligarchy, Hu, assisted by Dai Bingguo and Wang Yi, succeeded in managing (or ignoring) public opinion and interest-group lobbying to generate some positive momentum in both relationships.

In the early 1980s, as I noted earlier, Hu had formed a positive impression of Japan as a member of various delegations organized by one of his mentors, Hu Yaobang, and had helped organize a return visit by three thousand Japanese students.[95] When Hu rose to leadership in 2002, however, relations with Japan were fraught. In the 1990s, Jiang Zemin had stoked the younger generation's anti-Japanese emotions by means of his Patriotic Education Campaign. The history of Japanese aggression against China during World War II became the focal point of a campaign led by the Propaganda Department and the Education Ministry to nurture a nationalist attachment to the Party. Schools organized reading contests featuring books on wartime history and arranged class visits to historical shrines from the Japanese occupation, including the one commemorating the Nanjing Massacre. During the annual anniversary of China's victory against Japan in 1945, cinemas and television were saturated with anti-Japanese propaganda. Jiang visited Japan in 1998 and demanded a written apology like the one Tokyo had presented the South Korean president the month before, but he came home empty-handed and humiliated. The Japanese public resented, and resents still, China's harping on historical issues related to its occupation of China during World War II and were beginning to view China as a growing threat. Prime Minister Junichiro Koizumi was contemplating revising Japan's postwar "peace constitution" to allow the government to beef up Japan's military defenses.

In 2004, Hu agreed to Japan's proposal to start negotiations to divide up the undersea oil and gas reserves around the Senkaku/Diaoyu Islands, claimed by both countries but under the longtime control of Japan. Because the East China Sea separating China and Japan is only 360 nautical miles across, the two countries' 200-nautical-mile exclusive economic zones overlap, and so reaching any kind of agreement was going to require bilateral compromise. Yet any deal that involved sharing oil and gas fields was likely to be resisted by the military and energy companies in both countries.

In April 2005, a wave of violent, large-scale anti-Japan protests, calling for a boycott of Japanese products, swept across China.[96] Japan, together with India, Germany, and Brazil, had made a bid for a permanent seat on the United Nations Security Council and its efforts were gathering steam. Chinese anti-Japanese sentiment had already been aroused by Prime Minister Koizumi's insistence on paying annual visits to the Yasukuni Shrine and on revisions of Japanese textbooks that were viewed in China as downplaying Japan's wartime atrocities. A grassroots petition among mainland and overseas Chinese opposing Japan's Security Council bid was publicized on official Chinese media, indicating the government's tacit support, and thus encouraging demonstrators to believe they could protest on the street with impunity. Demonstrators threw stones at the Japanese embassy, the ambassador's residence, and Japanese stores and restaurants and smashed cars as the police stood by.

The protests bolstered Beijing's leverage in opposing Japanese Security Council membership and resulted in Koizumi's declaring the most public apology for Japanese wartime atrocities in a decade.[97] Had the protests been allowed to get out of hand, they could have turned against the Hu government or permanently damaged relations with China's most important trade partner and neighbor. It took high-level meetings involving no fewer than 3,500 senior officials from the central government, the military, and the Party to urge students to express their patriotism in a more rational manner, to stifle the protests. Academics and experts were dispatched to local gatherings throughout the country to persuade the angry students to calm down. Most politicians, including Bo Xilai, then commerce minister, fell into line, aligning themselves with the indignation of the Chinese people but also arguing against a boycott of Japanese products that would harm the interests of both countries.[98] There were some, however, who still insisted on grandstanding as staunch patriots: When China's vice premier, Wu Yi, reluctantly visited Tokyo in June 2005, she made a show of refusing to meet with Prime Minister Koizumi because of remarks he had made about the Yasukuni Shrine.

This was the context for Hu's efforts to orchestrate a detente with Japan. Koizumi's departure from office in 2006 meant that visits to Yasukuni were no longer an obstacle. Despite the perception that Hu was a weak leader, the Party had ample tools with which to modulate public opinion and prevent policy from being hijacked by popular nationalism. Media censors allowed some expression of anti-Japanese emotion but kept it within bounds; and the policing of anti-Japanese activists kept the movement small and under control.[99]

Wen Jiabao and Hu each visited Japan in 2007 and 2008 to lay the groundwork for an agreement on divvying up the energy resources in the East China Sea. Dai Bingguo and Wang Yi negotiated terms that would have allowed Japan to join with China in drilling in a gas field that China had been developing for over a year, which was located west of the Japanese-claimed median line, and to codevelop a new field that straddled the median line. Hu may have granted Japan these rights in return for the Japanese prime minister's pledge to attend the opening of the 2008 Beijing Olympics.[100] But the deal fell apart after the Japanese media reported that the two sides had agreed to "jointly develop" the oil and gas fields, which implied that China was giving up some sovereignty. The Chinese leaders were skittish about revealing their concessions to the public. The agreement was never implemented, and the Chinese resumed drilling in contested areas of the sea in 2009.[101]

Although the East China Sea energy negotiations collapsed, the China-Japan detente held until 2010, when the drunk captain of a Chinese fishing boat rammed a Japanese Coast Guard cutter, and instead of releasing him as had happened in past incidents, the Japanese government arrested him. The Democratic Party of Japan was now in control of the government but lacked experience. Asserting that Japan's territorial sovereignty over the Diaoyu/Senkaku Islands was not in dispute, it wanted to indict the captain under Japanese domestic law, a position that China couldn't tolerate.

Despite Japan's escalation of the crisis caused by the collision, the Chinese government discouraged anti-Japanese protests and employed other pressure tactics instead. It locked up some foreign nationals and imposed trade sanctions—the first use of the "strategic economy tools" it has been deploying more frequently since 2010. Beijing arrested four Japanese employees of Fujita, the Japanese construction company, on charges of illegally photographing military sites and halted exports to Japan of rare earths—minerals essential for manufacturing some electronic equipment, which are produced naturally in only a few countries, including China. The Chinese government publicly denied that it was punishing Japan by withholding rare earth supplies but told US counterparts that they were.[102]

After the Japanese released the captain without charge, the Politburo Standing Committee, rather than declare victory, demanded that Japan apologize for the incident and provide compensation to China for his detention, an idea Japan rejected out of hand. According to one expert, when the Standing Committee met, it asked Dai Bingguo what had been done about the 2001 collision with the US spy plane. "Demand an apology and compensation," he replied. That formula then became the focus of the leaders' discussion about the fishing-boat collision. "Everyone wanted to show the public what a strong, principled position they took; no one thought about the consequences for China's international reputation," the expert observed.[103]

A Lonely Rising Power

As the Hu Jintao decade drew to a close in 2012, China was "one of the loneliest rising powers in world history," according to an American China scholar.[104] That growing isolation was the consequence of domestic and foreign policy overreach. It would later undergird Xi Jinping's motivation to strengthen China's relations with Russia despite the checkered history of the relations between the two large neighbors. Hu's efforts to improve relations with Taiwan and Japan had unraveled because each had its own domestic qualms about getting too close to China, as well as Hu's own domestic complications. Southeast Asians, though dependent on trade with China, grew increasingly suspicious of its intentions to dominate the South China Sea and resentful of its lack of respect for their own rights under international law. South Koreans became more wary after Beijing expressed no sympathy for them after the North Korean attacks on the *Cheonan* and Yeonpyeong Island. Western governments were flummoxed by a country that would sacrifice valuable foreign policy relationships with other countries, rather than tolerate their different viewpoints on its own domestic issues regarding Taiwan, Tibet, Xinjiang, and Hong Kong. International mistrust of China, especially in Western democracies, also was heightening because of what was going on inside the country at the time, as we'll see next.

6

Stability Maintenance

EVEN AS THE CHINESE government started asserting itself internationally in the mid-2000s, it was tightening controls over society in the name of "stability maintenance" (*weiwen*), which had become Hu Jintao's priority. Demonstrations by laid-off workers, dissatisfied farmers, urban migrants—even retired Army veterans—were becoming an everyday occurrence. Chinese students, who staged successive protests in the 1980s, were relatively quiet after 1989, but even they lodged protests in 1999, 2005, and 2012. These "mass incidents," as Chinese authorities call protests, had definitely increased, but it is impossible to determine definitively how much they increased over time because we don't have any reliable statistics based on the same definitions. Once a "mass incident" was defined as one involving a crowd of more than one hundred people, but later, public petitioning by five or more people met the definition.[1] Most of the protests were small-scale local events; nonetheless, officials tracked them anxiously. Logrolling between the control coalition and the bureaucracies linked to state-owned enterprises drove security measures far beyond what might have been enough to restore social peace.

The *People's Daily* had rarely used the term "social stability" (*shehui wending*) before 1989, but after the Tiananmen protests, it started appearing with increasing frequency. "The one issue that trumps all," Deng Xiaoping declaimed in 1989, "is stability." So, too, with "maintain stability" (*weihu wending*, shortened as *weiwen*). Beginning in 2008, when Zhou Yongkang was in charge, usage in the *People's Daily* (figure overleaf), for example, showed a big jump in the number of times *weiwen* was mentioned.[2] Mentions of *weiwen* also spiked when Xi took over but then declined.

Number of Articles Mentioning *Weiwen* in *People's Daily:* 2001–2021

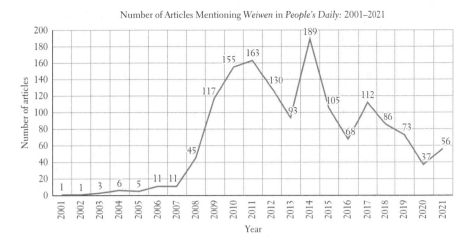

At Communist Party headquarters in Zhongnanhai, the internal threats looked more menacing than foreign ones to the Hu-era oligarchs. More people were crowding into cities; the urban population had grown from 36 percent in 2000 to 47 percent in 2008, 53 percent in 2012, and 63.9 percent in 2020. And more people started using the Internet—from 59.1 million in 2000 to 298 million in 2008 to 565 million in 2012 and 1.01 billion in 2021. Society was changing so fast that the leaders couldn't be sure which groups were solidly in their camp and which might form the base of an opposition. New social forces unleashed by domestic reforms and an opening up to the outside world brought in elements of environmentalism, religion, and feminism that challenged the regime.

Party politicians treated accidents and natural disasters as political emergencies. A snowstorm in southern China at the start of the Chinese New Year holiday in January 2008 stranded hundreds of thousands of disappointed migrants in the Guangzhou Railroad Station, unable to depart for family visits. Premier Wen Jiabao suddenly appeared on the scene with TV cameras and a large police presence to apologize and defuse what he feared would become an antigovernment mob. A Chinese commentator interpreted the apology as "fear of the people getting out of control, a lack of confidence in the huge state machinery."[3] Wen also appeared on the scene of the massive earthquake in the mountains of Western Sichuan in May 2008 and at the high-speed rail crash in Wenzhou, Zhejiang province, in 2011.

The color revolutions also instilled fear in Hu that foreigners were trying to destabilize China.[4] Vladimir Putin had reportedly warned Hu during one of their four meetings in 2005 that the philanthropist George Soros and his foundations were behind those democratic upheavals. In an internal speech that year, titled "Fight a Smokeless People's War," Hu talked about how to counter the plots by the United States by controlling the media, monitoring dissidents, and clamping down on the publishing industry.[5] He commissioned a documentary, *Think of Danger in Times of Safety - Historical Lessons of the Demise of the Communist Party of Soviet Union*, that became required viewing for all officials.[6]

The Control Coalition

The "control coalition," consisting of the internal security agencies under the CCP Political Legal Commission and the media and Internet agencies under the CCP Propaganda Department, along with the intelligence agencies, the military, and the paramilitary forces,[7] exploited the the fears of unrest by Hu Jintao and other leaders. By exaggerating the threat and arguing for the need to strengthen the social and media controls, they were able to boost their budgets, staffs, and policy influence in a logroll with the economic agencies linked to the state sector that were also making a comeback.[8]

According to several Chinese experts, the extreme nature of this social control was the outcome of expanding the Politburo Standing Committee to nine members, which elevated the power of the internal security and propaganda chiefs. It was at this point that the major figures tied to domestic security came to power. During Hu Jintao's first term, Luo Gan sat on the Standing Committee and headed the CCP Political Legal Affairs Commission (*zheng fa wei*), and Zhou Yongkang served as the Minister of Public Security and was a Politburo member. In 2007 Zhou Yongkang moved up to the Standing Committee and took charge of the entire internal security system. Li Changchun was the propaganda chief in the Standing Committee for the full ten years under Hu. Jiang Zemin's patronage connections with the internal security and propaganda heads made it more difficult for Hu to control these "systems" (*xitong*), and hence why, as one Chinese political scientist put it, "*weiwen* overreached."

Zhou Yongkang was considered perhaps the most powerful public security minister in PRC history. A formidable political operator, Zhou had built a large faction during a career in the oil industry followed by a stint in Sichuan as Party secretary before moving to the internal security system, where he rose to become its head. When he was the head of internal security, he put *weiwen* at the center of everything. He merged the police, the courts, and the security apparatus into one entity, according to a bank official. "Previous heads of the Political and Legal Commission had respected its three separate parts [police, courts, and procuratorate], but Zhou Yongkang merged them together."

Xi Jinping purged Zhou soon after the latter retired in 2012 and rounded up many of his associates—even his son. In addition to corruption, Zhou was accused of plotting with Bo Xilai against Xi and "disclosing Party and state secrets." The last allegation likely refers to Zhou's warning Bo about his impending arrest with information he had gained by tapping the communications of other leaders, including Xi Jinping himself.[9]

But the system was in place by that point. Zhou's elevation of the police chief to the leadership team was practiced at the provincial level too. The motivation for bureaucratically empowering the police and giving them perks, such as first-class air travel, special pensions and health care, and higher salaries, was to ensure their loyalty.[10] Once the police gained bargaining power by joining the provincial standing committee, they obtained more funding.[11]

As the domestic security apparatus grew more powerful, it eclipsed the courts. Neither the courts nor the procuratorate had a representative in the provincial leading groups. By 2005, Party leaders had concluded that the rule-of-law reforms introduced under Jiang Zemin "were inconsistent with the expanded domestic stability apparatus and its aims."[12] Instead of neutrally adjudicating disputes, they said, the courts would be tasked to help the Party preserve social stability. In 2008, the chief justice of the Supreme Judicial Court, a respected reformer named Xiao Yang, was purged, ostensibly for corruption, and replaced with a police official without a law degree. Law professors who advocated constitutionalism and civil rights lawyers were marginalized or arrested.

The Olympics

As noted before, the leaders' anxieties about social unrest intensified during the year before the August 2008 Olympic Games, when the eyes of the world would be on China. (The 2022 Winter Olympics, too, was a nerve-wracking challenge for the current leaders, particularly because it occurred during the COVID epidemic.) On a visit to Australia in 2007, Hu Jintao was asked (in a private conversation) what kept him up at night. "The Olympics," he replied. The internal security apparatus led by Zhou Yongkang beefed up its monitoring and policing capabilities to prevent political disturbances and guarantee stability during the games. The measures were considered a great success: not only did they prevent disturbances, but they also were tolerated by the foreigners who experienced their inconvenience first-hand. The internal security bureaucracy never loosened up again after 2008. According one Chinese sociologist, "The Olympics marked the beginning, it can be said, of the ascendance of the stability preservation regime in China." "Looking back now," he added ruefully, "it might be that the Olympics were something we did that we ought not to have done."[13]

The group in charge of preparation for the games was headed by none other than Xi Jinping, by 2007 the heir apparent to Hu. His two deputies were Zhou Yongkang and the Party secretary of Beijing. Their objective was to prevent "disturbances and sabotage organized by hostile forces," large-scale protests, and terrorism. In advance of the games, Beijing surveyed its entire population of rural-urban migrants and rental houses.[14] Zhou also teleconferenced with central and local officials, directing them to comb through the lists of their frequent petitioners and guarantee that none of them could cause a mass incident in Beijing.[15]

A half million Chinese, including police, commandos, SWAT units, and volunteer monitors, were mobilized to report suspicious actors. Visas were difficult for foreign visitors to get and denied to anyone who had been politically active.[16] At the Winter Olympics in Salt Lake City, Utah, held a few months after the September 11 terrorist attacks, security for getting in or out of the sports facilities was extra tight. Beijing went further by locking up tight the entire city of Beijing.

The International Olympics Committee, cognizant of the human rights problems in China, had insisted that the authorities set aside a few areas for demonstrations. Those spaces remained empty, however, because no group received permission to demonstrate, although seventy-seven had filed applications. The police apprehended potential protestors headed for Beijing and either arrested them or shipped them back to their hometowns.[17] After the Olympics, Zhou Yongkang announced he was entirely satisfied with the success of the "unprecedented" security methods used during the event, and he continued to employ them afterward.[18]

The *Weiwen* Leviathan

Totalitarian states create powerful internal police forces to repress enemies of the state. The Soviet Union under Stalin is the classic example. In Mao's time, China had internal security police, too, but it also relied heavily on people monitoring one another. Mutual criticism sessions in schools, work units, and neighborhoods pressured political laggards to fall into line — outright dissent was rare. When Mao died and Deng Xiaoping introduced market reforms, people began to enjoy greater freedom as the Party relaxed its controls over society. After 1989, however, the Party leaders reversed themselves and started rebuilding a *weiwen* machinery that operated at every level. The challenge of identifying and silencing potential opponents of the state had become much more difficult, of course, with people moving from one part of the country to another to find jobs, many of them in private or foreign businesses and not under the thumb of the Party.

In 1990, as a reaction to the Tiananmen crisis, the CCP Political-Legal Affairs Commission, as noted, the Party organ in charge of the internal security agencies, founded in 1980 and shuttered in 1988, was revived and strengthened. From a modest-sized coordinating bureaucracy it was made into a superorganization and put in charge of the Ministry of Public Security (which had over two million police as of 2021),[19] the Ministry of State Security (in charge of international intelligence gathering and internal security), the Ministry of State Secrets, and the State Bureau for Letters and Petitions. The Commission also has authority over the courts, the Ministry of Justice (which also runs the prisons), and Procuratorate; and until 2018, it shared the command of the paramilitary People's Armed Police (1.5 million police) with the PLA. Note that the courts are not just under the Communist Party but also under the Party's internal security organ, which appoints all the judges and reviews the verdicts.[20] The local apparatus corresponds closely to the central level set-up.[21] With so many different agencies with overlapping authority competing with one another and hoarding information from one another "coordinating China's

numerous stability maintenance organizations has long been a thorny bureaucratic problem."[22]

Under Hu, the *weiwen* operation begun earlier grew increasingly granular, permeating virtually every unit of the society. Responsibility for
maintaining stability was transferred downward to lower-level officials.[23]
Stability maintenance offices mushroomed across China, in villages,
universities, and neighborhoods. *Caijing* magazine reported on one
Guangdong county with a population of 330,000 that had 1,800 officials
involved in *weiwen* at the county, township, and village levels.[24] Local
officials were incentivized by the Party for promotion that put social stability as a top priority. Petitioning is citizens' legal right but *weiwen* requires
blocking them from practicing it.

Following the Jasmine Revolution in 2011, cities across the entire
country were ordered to deploy a high-tech, grid-management system,
one that had been first tried out in a district of Beijing and some other
cities in 2004.[25] Grid management utilizes video cameras, facial recognition, big data analytics, high-speed internet, high-capacity computers,
large databases, sensors, and remote equipment to monitor residents,
respond to unexpected contingencies, and deliver social services.[26]
Chinese political engineers value its use for surveillance. But one
Chinese political scientist warned that the continued development of
grid management would "lead to a model of a contemporary police
state."[27]

Behind the technologies, *weiwen* still to this day relies heavily on
human volunteers as ideological and behavioral monitors. Many but
not all of them are Communist Party members. Although the monitors
might have annoyed people in an apartment block with their intrusions
during normal times, during the COVID shutdowns they were appreciated for helping people stay healthy and well-fed. More and more
citizen volunteers have become involved in *weiwen*, especially in supervision of the "targeted population," who, in addition to ex-cons
or suspects out on bail, includes anyone who might cause trouble.
Duihua, an American human rights organization, estimates that approximately 1.2 million people live under such supervision—a form of
house arrest that is completely illegal, but practiced openly throughout
the country. All this started under Hu. In 2010 the newspaper *Southern
Weekend* did a report on Suqian City, a small city in Jiangsu province, which had 38,000 *weiwen* volunteers, one for every 148 people.
The local public security office pays these volunteers, some of whom

operate undercover, based on a point system that measures their contribution to stability.[28] One teacher who had been targeted because he had campaigned for decades to be elected as an independent local legislator estimates that up to fifty volunteers—many of them gym teachers at his school who have no other source of outside income— are paid to conduct round-the-clock surveillance on him ($8 for the day shift, and twice that for the night shift).[29] Private security companies also feed from the trough of security maintenance. The company An Yuan Ding was exposed in September 2010 for keeping "black jails" in Beijing. The company contracted with local governments and held villagers who came to Beijing to express their legal right to petition the central government until the local police could arrive to take them into custody. In 2011 there were more than 300,000 private security personnel in Beijing.[30] Nationally, there were more than 4 million in 2011; they grew to 5.22 million by 2020.[31]

As I've noted, stability maintenance dominated CCP and National People's Congress sessions during Hu's second term. And *weiwen* became one of the most important criteria for the evaluation and promotion of local officials. It is a "single-vote veto" measure: a local official will be fired or passed for promotion for allowing just one incident, and there is no room for negotiation or second chances. In February 2012, the Tibetan Autonomous Regional Government removed four officials for failing to fulfill *weiwen* duties during Chinese New Year.[32] Such a stringent evaluation system naturally breeds overcompliance on the part of local agents. Central leaders urge local officials to manage social conflicts with a smile and an open hand, as well as a fist. Local officials, however, whose careers are on the line, pull out all the stops to squelch incidents. They create small fiefdoms, complete with Mao-style spying on your neighbors, the hiring of plainclothes thugs to intimidate political activists, and extralegal detention of potential "troublemakers." Local governments pay off the ringleaders.[33] Central security officials plead ignorance of what their local subordinates are doing. They give local units enough autonomy so that if something goes wrong the blame can be put on them.

In April 2012, the escape of the blind legal activist Chen Guangcheng from illegal house arrest in his hometown in Shangdong province brought into sharp focus the question of whether central security officials were responsible for local abuses. Chen sent a video petition to Premier Wen Jiabao detailing the remarkable scale and corruption of the local stability-maintenance operation and asked Wen to investigate the abuses by the local machine. (Chen said that his detention cost the local government $4.3 million in 2008 and that this amount had doubled by 2011; the farmers who guarded him had to kick back 10 percent of the $16 per day they were paid to the local security officials.)[34] The central-level security officials also were put on the spot because of their failure to apprehend Chen during his remarkable flight from Shandong to Beijing and to prevent his interactions with other well-known political activists in Beijing in the days before he sought refuge in the US Embassy. Chen's negotiated departure from the embassy and, two weeks later, from China to study law at New York University included the central government's commitment to investigate the violations of Chinese law by the security operation in Chen's hometown, but it is not known if it actually did that.

A Blank Check

A sign of just how anxious China's leaders had become is the blank check they gave to the *weiwen* bureaucracies to expand their budgets and staffs, allocating amounts that were out of proportion with the actual dangers.[35] With so much money sloshing through the public security bureaucracy, it's no surprise that corruption became endemic in the sector, from Zhou Yongkang on down to grassroots officials. Local governments shoulder about 70 percent of their *weiwen* budgets, and the remaining 30 percent comes from the central government. According to a *Caijing* magazine article, the public-security expenditures of local governments in 2011 were more than three times those of the central government. In fact, when China's 2011 budget was made public, it was revealed that public security was allocated 624.4 billion yuan ($95 billion). That exceeded China's defense budget ($92 billion), which was also experiencing stunning growth.[36] The growth in public-security spending has been higher than the growth of defense expenditures in almost every year under Hu and Xi (see figure overleaf).[37] The spike in growth in 2007 shown in the figure may reflect a panicked buildup of *weiwen* capabilities in advance of the Olympics.

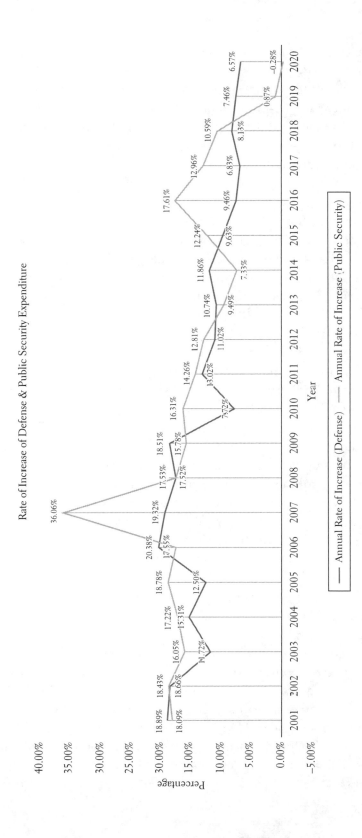

Rate of Increase of Defense & Public Security Expenditure

— Annual Rate of Increase (Defense)   — Annual Rate of Increase (Public Security)

Year

Percentage

40.00%
35.00%
30.00%
25.00%
20.00%
15.00%
10.00%
5.00%
0.00%
-5.00%

2001 2002 2003 2004 2005 2006 2007 2008 2009 2010 2011 2012 2013 2014 2015 2016 2017 2018 2019 2020

18.89%
18.09%
18.43%
18.66%
16.05%
11.72%
17.22%
15.31%
18.78%
12.50%
20.38%
17.55%
36.06%
19.32%
17.53%
17.52%
18.51%
15.78%
16.31%
7.72%
14.26%
13.02%
12.81%
11.02%
10.74%
9.49%
11.86%
9.63%
7.33%
12.24%
17.61%
9.46%
12.96%
6.83%
10.59%
8.13%
7.46%
6.57%
0.87%
-0.28%

Some argued that China had succumbed to a vicious cycle in which "the more *weiwen*, the less stability (*yue weiwen yue buwen*)." Not only does *weiwen* not reduce social conflicts, argues one Chinese sociologist, it increases them. Local officials will go to any lengths to jump on a sign of instability. They use money to buy off interest groups and employ "expedient-based governance," but ignore the rule of law. Local governments are put in an adversarial position against the public and too quickly resort to using police and paramilitary forces. Meanwhile, the public has become "trained," and people now know that, unless they stir up trouble, their grievances will never be addressed.[38]

Another Chinese scholar Yu Jianrong called the system "totalitarian." He warned that top-down pressure would only backfire against the CCP central authorities: "The central party pressures the local governments, the local governments pressure the people, and the people pressure the central party."[39]

Weiwen Along the Borders

The most violent threats to stability facing the Hu regime were the protests that began shortly before the 2008 Olympics by discontented ethnic and religious minorities in Western China. Although less than 10 percent of China's population are ethnic minorities, these groups live in strategically important border regions—Tibet, Xinjiang, and Mongolia. The CCP leadership's domestic and international insecurities feed on one another and trigger hardline reactions whenever the leadership feels threatened by a revolt by one of these groups that have external support.

A large peaceful protest by Tibetans in Lhasa, in March 2008, in the lead-up to the Olympics turned into a violent riot in which, as noted above in the discussion of "core interests," both Tibetans and Han shopkeepers, bystanders, and police were killed and injured. The protests spread far beyond the Tibetan Autonomous Region to Tibetan communities in other provinces, thanks to cellphones and possible coordination by émigré Tibetan activists.

Hu Jintao may have felt responsible for the policy failures that had led to the protests, a journalist observed. When Hu served as Party secretary of Tibet between 1988 and 1992, he took a hard line on worship of the Dalai Lama by temples and monasteries and forcibly put down the Tibetan demonstrations in 1989. "During the 2008 uprising, because of his experience with Tibet the other leaders turned to him," an official said. The propaganda bureaucracies crafted a narrative blaming the Dalai Lama for the protests that was designed to inspire popular support for the government without sabotaging international participation in the Olympic games in August. They allowed a handful of foreign media outlets to report on Tibet "because they think they have a good story on their side." The uncensored videos that were shown of burning shops and cars in the Lhasa riot aroused an angry response from Han viewers, who stood with the central government in condemning the protests.

On July 5, 2009, a little more than a year after the Tibet protests, the largest and most violent civil uprising in PRC history occurred in Xinjiang. Spontaneous street battles erupted between Uighur Muslims and local Han Chinese in Urumqi and resulted in almost 200 deaths and more than 1,700 injuries; some of the fighting was broadcast on live Chinese Central TV, which covered the event.[40] Due to a policy of government-sponsored settlement by Han Chinese, including the 2.7 million members of the Xinjiang Production and Construction Corps, a quasi-military organization of farms, factories, and prisons, Uighurs constitute only 45 percent of Xinjiang's 25 million population.[41]

The uprising began as a peaceful protest by Xinjiang University students angered by reports of Han Chinese killing Uighur migrant workers in Guangdong. That evening, wandering groups of Uighur youth in Urumqi beat some Han bystanders to death and destroyed Han-owned businesses and property; according to observers on the scene, the police had seemed unprepared. A counter-riot broke out the next day when Han vigilantes wielding clubs and knives attacked innocent Uighurs. Hu rushed back from a G-8 meeting in Italy to hold a Standing Committee meeting, and Zhou Yongkang, who spent five days investigating the scene in several Xinjiang cities, blamed the instability on "hostile forces" at home and abroad.[42]

To regain control, the Xinjiang authorities cut Internet service, international phone calls, and most text messaging for ten months, only gradually restoring access to some government sites. As a result, rumors reigned supreme. In September 2009, a mysterious panic set off by a rumor that Uighurs were stabbing Hans with hypodermic needles sparked more Han violence against Uighurs. The government had sent a text message to Urumqi residents saying that Uighur assailants had attacked passersby with hypodermic syringes and urged them not to panic. But panic they did. Hundreds of people reported being jabbed to the police in a case of mass hysteria. On September 3, thousands of Han Chinese demonstrated to demand the ouster of Wang Lequan, the Xinjiang Party secretary, for failing to protect them during the July riots and from the syringe attacks.[43] Two senior Urumqi officials were dismissed, and Wang, who had run Xinjiang for fifteen years, was transferred to Beijing. In the rest of the country, the violent upheavals in Xinjiang, like those in Tibet, evoked little sympathy for the ethnic minority group and strengthened popular identification with the central government.

Retreat from Information Freedom

One of the most important facets of *weiwen* during Hu's second term, and the one with clear relevance to the situation today under Xi Jinping, was the tightening of access to information that might arouse popular opposition to the regime after Hu's more tolerant approach during his first term.

Hu's first term was a period of peak freedom of information in the People's Republic that has never been equaled since. It was an exciting time to be a Chinese journalist. Commercial magazines and newspapers investigated regulatory failures, such as the ones that led to baby formula being tainted by melamine and chemical spills that were poisoning rivers; once the publications learned that a case was under investigation by the authorities, they also reported on high-level corruption. After the massive earthquake in Sichuan in 2008, Chinese reporters rushed to the scene and reported what they were seeing. Foreign news was widely accessible in China, despite the Great Firewall. Dramatic human-interest stories about violent attacks on Chinese copper and coal miners in Zambia or gold prospectors in Ghana created public pressure on the government to better defend its citizens abroad.[44]

In a visit to *People's Daily* in June 2008, Hu called for the timelier release of information and greater transparency in the news reports of suddenly breaking events to improve the credibility of the Party's public voice. He praised the quick release of information about the earthquake disaster, which had received "high praise from officials and the people, and also earned the esteem of the international community."[45]

Once the online reporting of ordinary people began spreading breaking news about events, official news was forced to improve the timeliness of its reporting if it didn't want to be a laughingstock. When the state-owned Chinese Central Television (CCTV) building, ignited by New Year's fireworks, burst into an inferno, bystanders posted their videos and made snide remarks accusing the much-disparaged network of burying the news at the bottom of its broadcast. A passenger sent the first microblog about a fatal collision, in July 2011, on the Shanghai–Beijing line of China's much-vaunted high-speed railroad. The official news service Xinhua reported the accident about forty minutes later.

Hu also lifted the ban against media reporting of mass protests, a bold move considering how anxious Party leaders were about contagious unrest. When the violent protests broke out in Tibet, Beijing tried unsuccessfully to squelch news about the events, and the international press stepped into the vacuum with reporting that damaged China's international reputation. As one China media analyst noted, "In the CCP's postgame analysis, Tibet was regarded as a failure of media policy."[46] Just a week after Hu's remarks at *People's Daily*, in Weng'an county, a remote region of Guizhou province in China's southwest, tens of thousands of people violently demonstrated over the police cover-up of the drowning death of a young woman they believed had been raped and murdered by well-connected local youths. The Xinhua News Service, for the first time, was authorized to report on the demonstration; readers were amazed to see photographs of the burning police station spread across the Internet.

Hu and other central leaders, moreover, made a conspicuous show of their receptiveness to online public opinion, publicizing their chats with netizens and sometimes apologizing for failures that were exposed online.[47] In some instances, online public opinion led to a reversal of unpopular policies. They also valued how journalists and citizen bloggers were able to preempt social protest by acting as watchdogs over local officials. A freer information environment was creating a vibrant public sphere and a more responsive government.[48]

No single entity represented the Hu Jintao era of transparency more than Weibo, a Chinese version of Twitter that became a craze among young urbanites and had 503 million registered users by the end of 2012. Censorship was relatively light and too slow to stop a tweet from being instantaneously circulated to millions of people before being deleted. Journalists used their personal Weibo accounts to leak juicy details from their exposés of individual officials and allegations against named high-level officials that couldn't get past the newspaper censors. Many officials' careers were ruined by photographs of them wearing a fancy watch or with a sexy young babe on their arm that went viral. Government agencies invited citizens to give feedback on policies and report problems. By the end of 2012, government agencies had opened 176,700 Weibo accounts.[49]

It was through Weibo that many people for the first time learned that millions of other people shared their doubts about the current political system. Such knowledge creates what social scientists have called an "information cascade" that reinforces disaffection and heightens the potential for collective anti-regime action. Weibo also heightened the insecurity of politicians when they read online what millions of people really think of them.

As the Weibo craze gathered steam, the propaganda authorities called a meeting of provincial and ministerial officials with Sina.com, Tencent, and other large Internet companies to discuss how to manage the new social medium. One participant described the encounter to me. "Just shut it down!!" demanded the local officials, who bore the brunt of attacks by bloggers. Before Weibo, local officials could protect themselves from online criticism by censoring the content of local platforms. But the server of the biggest Weibo platform, Sina.com, was in Beijing, under the hand of the central Internet Bureau of the State Council Information Office and its Beijing counterpart.[50] The local authorities felt helpless to defend themselves from Weibo attacks. The central authorities, however, valued the ability to monitor poorly performing local officials that Weibo affords them. At the meeting, the Internet Bureau told the local officials that shutting down the platform was impossible: "Can you imagine the public reaction if we tried to shut down Weibo with its hundreds of millions of users?" The only option, they explained, was for the Internet companies to work with them to manage Weibo to eliminate irresponsible "rumors" and correctly channel online opinion.

At the US-China Internet Industry meeting in late 2011, I heard a senior official from the Internet Bureau spell out the kinds of criticism it would tolerate: "We draw a clear line," he said. "We accept online supervision only on local leaders, not central leaders. People can comment on central policy, but not on the top leaders." The CCP secretary of Beijing, in a 2013 speech to municipal propaganda officials, proudly claimed that 90 percent of the nation's major websites and 70 percent of its total Internet traffic was in Beijing. "Let's overcome the wrong belief that the internet is impossible to regulate," he said.[51]

During Hu's second term, that's just what the officials did. The propaganda authorities joined forces with the security agencies to strengthen the control of online information for the purpose of stability maintenance. As a Beijing academic put it, "By 2010, Weibo created a real public sphere, so it was showdown time."

Competitive Censorship

The Internet control effort, however, was complicated by the reality that the propaganda bureaucracies were just as fragmented as the internal security ones. Editors and Internet platform managers could take advantage of regulatory gaps and the unclear division of responsibilities between the various agencies. The Propaganda Department, as a high-level Party organ, outranks all the other agencies and dominates media censorship. The State Council Information Office, created in 1990 to improve China's overseas image, acquired the responsibility of managing Internet news because its head, Zhao Qizheng, a Shanghai nuclear physicist brought to Beijing by Jiang Zemin, was an early enthusiast, who established a website and internal network for his organization. The Internet Information Office was later spun off as a separate department—the Cyberspace Administration of China—which was also the office for the leading group that became the Central Cyberspace Affairs Commission. The Internet Information Office was both a defender of the Internet and its censor. Its approach was more nuanced than that of the Propaganda Department, and more in line with Hu's ideas about guiding public opinion. Television was governed by the State Administration of Radio, Film and Television; and books, newspapers, and other publications, by the General Administration for Press and Publication. The agencies fought turf battles whenever oversight of a new medium, such as online video or video games, was up for grabs.

Within a few years, the censors at the Internet Information Office had developed techniques for managing Weibo to reduce the risk of collective action while preserving the appearance of openness and the value of the information they themselves can glean from Weibo communication. First, automated filtering by key words blocks certain postings and searches and puts others in a category that requires human review. According to a Chinese estimate, in 2013 there were more than two million "public opinion analysts" working at propaganda bureaus, web portals, and commercial enterprises throughout China, and more were being trained. These online analysts screen microblogs, report their viewpoints to policymakers, and get rid of those that could stir up trouble.[52] Studies of online censorship patterns in China indicate that the propaganda censors (reflecting the priorities of the Party leaders) allow criticism of the government (except, as noted, of high-level leaders and of censorship per se), but delete blogs related to group collective action even if the activity is not explicitly antigovernment.[53]

Censorship consists of more than filtering and excising dangerous information, however. One method of manipulating the information environment is to employ undercover online operatives to post pro-government viewpoints and create the impression that those who are critical of the government are an isolated minority. The presence of these commentators, some paid—those whom netizens disparagingly call the "Fifty Cent Party"—and some volunteers, has the perverse effect of discrediting any genuine pro-government postings. It also distorts the feedback loop when officials try to assess public opinion based on what they read online.

The Internet Information Office also tailored censorship to different types of netizens, treating ordinary users one way and opinion leaders another. They used various forms of *friction* to discourage ordinary users from trying to access politically sensitive information—for example, making it difficult to acquire a Virtual Private Network (VPN) to jump over the Great Firewall and access foreign news, instead of angering the users by blocking the information completely. They also *distract* ordinary users from politically sensitive information by flooding the Internet with photos and articles about movie star divorces and other entertaining stories. Propaganda coordinated across various media platforms and orchestrated pro-government cheerleading by paid and unpaid political activists *flood* the information environment and distract people from more inflammatory information.[54]

But the censors also confronted influential public opinion leaders, such as journalists and those known as "Big V celebrities," with more coercive fear-based methods. Some 210 Big V celebrities (so called because their Weibo registrations are verified under their actual names) had more than ten million followers, making them the information hubs of huge social networks. The widespread influence of public intellectuals with large followings alarmed Party leaders, who felt that their own influence was slipping. Because these influential individuals could potentially rally people behind revolutionary action, the propaganda cops started cracking down on Big V personalities, beginning by targeting wealthy private businessmen with liberal ideas.

For example, in November 2011, real estate developer Pan Shiyi dropped an information bombshell when he alerted his more than 8.6 million followers to the little-known fact that the air-pollution measurements put out by the US Embassy were more accurate than the ones provided by the Beijing government. The embassy posts its measurements of the 2.5-micron particulates that pollute Beijing's air on Twitter, which is inaccessible in China without a VPN. The public's response to Pan's Weibo revelation embarrassed the government and forced it to start measuring and reporting on the levels of 2.5-micron particulates in the air. Pan was summoned to a command performance on CCTV, where he was required to say that as a well-known online commentator, he, and others like him, "should have more discipline."[55]

In 2011, a new method targeting public opinion influencers was real-name registration, which enabled the authorities to hold Internet users accountable and arrest them for blog posts that "spread rumors." The chilling effect drove hundreds of millions of netizens to desert Weibo and move to Weixin (WeChat) on the Tencent platform. WeChat networks, limited to the circle of friends you select for yourself, appeared to be safer from the eyes of the propaganda cops. In recent years, however, even WeChat, once considered private communication, has been penetrated by official censors.

As propaganda censors sought to tighten supervision at the end of the Hu era, a disheartened journalist bemoaned that the control of information for people like him had become like North Korea's. He blamed the reversal on the propaganda bureaucracy and "separate fiefdoms" operating on their own within the Standing Committee. Another journalist observed that there existed no interagency leading group for propaganda and that the Standing Committee rarely deliberated on propaganda-related issues. Officials reacted in an ad hoc matter depending on circumstances. And these changed. Li Changchun, the propaganda chief for the entire Hu decade, had originally favored openness when he came up from Guangdong in 2002, much as Hu himself did, but later changed his views.

Along with the other controls, the decoupling of the Chinese and international Internet accelerated during Hu's second term. Facebook representatives explored joint ventures with the Chinese Internet companies Baidu, Tencent, and Alibaba, and offered to leave a copy of all its data on Chinese users inside China. The data would also be stored on Facebook's servers outside China. But because the Chinese government insisted on localizing online communication data entirely inside China to prevent any foreign access to it, it turned Facebook down. According to a Chinese Internet executive, the leaders were deeply worried about the possibility that a foreign government, organization, or group of individuals "might simultaneously send messages to 300 million Chinese users and mobilize them to action."

The propaganda bureaucracy's monopoly on information management also afforded it rich opportunities for graft. In 2013, *Caixin* magazine investigated the large public relations industry that for a fee can arrange to have the propaganda censors scrub negative publicity about companies, or about local governments.[56] As a former securities regulator told me, "Of course the Propaganda Department is working to protect particular businessmen—how could it be otherwise?" He also expressed disgust with the media people at the China Securities Regulation Commission, who arranged for the Propaganda Department to squelch news about the splitting of specific stocks to keep stock prices up. Li Dongsheng, who began as a crusading television journalist, became head of the news section of the Propaganda Department, was promoted to the position of vice minister of public security in 2009, and then was sentenced to fifteen years in jail for corruption in 2016. When I interviewed Li at the unmarked office of the Propaganda Department in 2009, he came across as an unusually reform-minded official committed to media openness. There is simply no way to know whether he was purged because he was truly corrupt, too liberal in his views, or too close to Zhou Yongkang. Or all three.

The State Advances

The disjointed policy process during Hu's collective leadership also facilitated the restoration of the state's management of the economy, as the central government, reversing three decades of marketization, started to steer the economy once again. China had built a remarkably successful market-oriented economy in which state enterprises accounted for just 27 percent of industrial output, 20 percent of industrial employment, and less than 15 percent of exports.[57] But after China joined the World Trade Organization in 2001, some of the country's leaders worried that the state-owned firms might not be able to withstand global competition and decided that the state might need to give them a cushion. The bureaucracy developed industrial policies that favored Chinese "national champions" and, as I noted earlier, required foreign-invested enterprises to share their latest technology to gain access to the China market. Private and foreign firms were disadvantaged as "the state advanced, and the private sector retreated (*guojin mintui*)," to use a catchphrase that was common at the time.[58] This change in policy generated a backlash from international business and governments; it also reduced private investment and drove many private businesspeople to move their families and wealth out of the country.

The return of state management of the economy was justified by Hu and Wen Jiabao's populist objective to build a "harmonious society" by narrowing rural-urban and regional disparities in income, health, education, and other public goods. The two leaders reoriented the economy, away from what I've called the "performance coalition," meaning the financial, industrial, and commercial bureaucracies promoting economic growth, and toward more of a "welfare coalition" that prioritized wealth redistribution and technological innovation. This worked as long as those in control saw progressive policies as strengthening their control and *weiwen.*[59] This alignment of interests made it easier for the control coalition and the economic bureaucracies to logroll together in the collective leadership.

The central ministries closely tied with state-owned enterprises dominated policymaking in the government, just as the control coalition dominated policymaking in the Party. The most powerful was the National Development Reform Commission, a comprehensive economic bureaucracy resembling the Ministry of Industrial Trade and Industry during the heyday of Japanese industrial policy, that oversaw industrial policy and macroeconomic management. The mega-agency had the power to issue commands to ministries and provinces and functioned much like the Mao-era State Planning Commission, where its bureaucratic history originated. The Ministry of Industry and Information Technology, created in 2008, allocated resources to various industries much as South Korea's Planning Board did. The State-Owned Assets Supervision and Administration Commission (SASAC) was founded in 2003 to take ownership of the 117 national-level state-owned companies; its mission was to strengthen their management but also to protect them as a precious part of the PRC patrimony. The SASAC tried to "make SOEs [state-owned enterprises] as strong and as big as possible," said a leading economist. The Ministry of Science and Technology also became an important player.

Wen and Hu's drive to accelerate China's scientific progress was also captured by state interest groups. Wen, who was head of the Party's Leading Group on Science, Technology, and Education, convened two thousand scientists and officials, organized into twenty working groups, to plan an initiative. But the bureaucrats in the National Development Reform Commission took over from the scientists and in 2006 produced a centrally planned, government-funded system focused on sixteen megaprojects, known as the Medium- and Long-Term Development Program for Science and Technology Development. A market-reform package had been prepared by government economists but was "buried by the bureaucracy immediately after being unveiled in February 2005."[60] Instead, the bureaucracy pivoted to a nationalist strategy of indigenous innovation. Although China and the United States were getting along moderately well at the time, the government bureaucrats played the national security card to get support for state investments in research and development, arguing, "Experience shows us that we cannot buy true core technologies in the key fields that affect the lifeblood of the national economy and national security."[61]

The state-led effort was well suited to the oligarchic rule in Hu's administration. The technology pork barrel was divvied up among the various industrial interests and their bureaucratic godfathers, the more
the better. The 2006 Medium- and Long-Term Plan designated sixteen
megaprojects, nine civilian and seven military/dual use, each of which
had a supervisory ministry in the central government and a high-level political patron as well.[62] The Ministry of Science and Technology was the
overall coordinator.

As we've seen, the 2008 global financial crisis convinced many Chinese
policymakers to give up modeling policies on the American market
economy and boosted their confidence in the advantages of socialism,
which Wen Jiabao described as "efficient decision-making, a powerful organization, and the concentrated power to accomplish big things."[63] Wen
observed that all through history, "major crises like the global financial
crisis were followed by major technological breakthroughs," and the successful economies were those that mastered the revolutionary technologies.[64] In 2010, he launched a second wave of industrial policy, the "strategic
emerging industries" that identified seven industrial sectors comprising
thirty-five subsectors. The massive stimulus that helped China's economy
recover in record time flowed both to these emerging industries and the
traditional state factories producing the steel, aluminum, and concrete for
infrastructure construction. A leading reform economist criticized what
he saw as the misallocation of investment: "All the talk about jobs is really
lip service. Heavy industry creates fewer jobs than light industry and services in the private sector."

Meanwhile, "state-owned enterprises grew more politically influential
and difficult to monitor."[65] The CCP Organization Department and the
Politburo claimed the power to select the chairman, CEO, and Party secretary of the central state companies (no one seriously considered giving
that authority to the board of directors, even in the joint stock companies
listed on international stock markets). Many of the executives had close
connections with the families of leading Party politicians. "The central
SOEs are the eldest sons of the People's Republic," a Beijing economist
said, quoting the first head of SASAC.[66] A banking official saw SASAC
becoming an obstacle to market reforms: "SASAC turned into a special
interest group that was the owner, operator, regulator, and beneficiary of
the state sector."

Stepping back to look at the history of the Hu Jintao era, 2002 to 2012,
we must conclude that CCP collective leadership was not just a failure
but inevitably set China on the course it is on today. Despite its original

intention to modernize governance to keep pace with Chinese society and economy, the diffusion of power at the top ended up allowing bureaucratic interest groups to drive foreign and domestic policy toward self-defeating overreach. Hu never constructed a reform coalition to help sustain the legal, media, and civil society progress he began in his first term that could have checked that overreach. By 2012, as Hu retired and handed the reins to Xi Jinping, the future of China's peaceful rise looked uncertain, though I would argue that it had not yet been fatally undermined.

7

Strongman Rule

ACCORDING TO SOMEONE WHO knows him, Xi Jinping started his reign "feeling weak and illegitimate." He worried that he had been chosen only because he was a "red princeling of the suitable age." He no doubt suspected that his peers had selected him to be Hu Jintao's successor in a straw poll in 2007 in large part because his father, Xi Zhongxun, had been a revered Long March revolutionary, Cultural Revolution martyr, and economic reformer. After all, Xi had lost Party elections in the past because other officials believed he was riding on his father's coattails instead of his own abilities.

Xi Jinping had enjoyed a privileged childhood, living in the leadership compound of Zhongnanhai when his father was serving as vice-premier and Premier Zhou Enlai's right-hand man. As noted earlier, Xi's life got much harder after Mao purged his father in 1962 and sent him to manage a tractor factory in Luoyang. But after the Cultural Revolution when Deng Xiaoping rehabilitated Xi Zhongxun and assigned him to leadership positions in the southern province of Guangdong, he re-emerged as an economic reformer, founding the Special Economic Zones and transforming Guangdong into a globalized economic powerhouse.

According to Joseph Torigian, who is writing a biography of Xi Zhongxun, Xi senior was a brutal disciplinarian and depressive, who endured repeated purges without ever losing faith in the Party.[1] The Xi family suffered severely during the Cultural Revolution. Xi's stepsister committed suicide, and Jinping's education was cut short when he was sent down to work in the poor countryside of Shaanxi province for seven years, an experience that he describes as transformative, forming his ideological consciousness and strengthening his identification with the masses.

Indeed, the story of Xi's life in the village of Liangjiahe constitutes the core of his political image as a child of the Party and a man of the people. Xi was admitted to Tsinghua University in 1975 when selection was based on political recommendation instead of entrance examination scores and students spent more time in military drills, manual labor, and political instruction than in academic courses. Xi, like other so-called worker-peasant-soldier students of that period, is disparaged, thought to be intellectually inferior to those who were admitted after the resumption of college entrance exams in 1977.

Being Xi Zhongxun's son undoubtedly helped Xi land his first job as secretary to General Geng Biao, vice chairman of the Central Military Commission, a position that enabled him to build valuable ties with PLA officers. Xi climbed the political ladder by serving as a party official in four different coastal provinces—Hebei, Fujian, Zhejiang, and Shanghai—where the key to economic development was attracting investment from private and foreign businesses.

When he was US vice president, Joseph Biden spent two weeks traveling with then–vice president Xi Jinping in 2011 and 2013, one week in China and one in the States. Biden described Xi as having "the look of a man who is about to take on a job he's not at all sure is going to end well."[2] Xi's single-minded focus on the survival of CCP rule was palpable in his probing questions about how the Obama administration controlled the military and government.

His family's history of victimhood during the Cultural Revolution had created expectations about the kind of ruler Xi Jinping would be, but when he took over in 2012, it was clear that he had also deliberately deceived people about his intentions. He had presented himself as an open-minded market reformer and a CCP organization man who would weave interest groups into a Hu-style collective leadership. "He fooled us," admitted an economist. "We thought he was a reformer, but he turned out to be a Leftist." Xi surprised everyone by coming out of the blocks acting like a Mao-style strongman determined to establish dominance over the Party elite, the military, and Chinese society. His speeches were notably devoid of respectful verbal bows to his predecessors Hu Jintao and Jiang Zemin. In fact, Hu and Jiang have pretty much disappeared from the official historical narrative. On the tenth anniversary of the devastating Sichuan earthquake of May 2008, the official praise for the government's recovery efforts mentioned Xi thirty times and Hu Jintao and Premier Wen Jiabao, who had led the relief efforts, not even once.[3] Official media extol Xi's virtues and elevate him to the level of Mao and Deng. Often repeated is the saying, "Under Mao the Chinese people stood up (*zhanqilai*); under Deng the Chinese people got rich (*fuqilai*); and under Xi the Chinese people are becoming stronger (*qiangqilai*)."

Despite this worshipful cult of personality, Xi's insecurity, just as Biden had noted in 2013, is glaring. Because of his fear that Communist Party rule in China could collapse suddenly the way it did in the Soviet Union, Xi sees the greatest risk as coming from the ranks of the elite, not the masses. He required CCP members to watch a documentary about the party's fall in Russia. According to the film, the Soviet public overwhelmingly supported the Communist Party of the Soviet Union (CPSU), but it was destroyed top-down by "corrupt and ideologically confused" Party leaders like Mikhail Gorbachev and Boris Yeltsin. Neither the CPSU members nor soldiers in the military had stepped up to defend it.[4]

The Soviet collapse explains why Xi is so fixated on shoring up the loyalty of Communist Party officials, demanding that they remain devoted to the Party "at any time, and under any circumstance," as the Xinhua News Agency reported.[5] Taking a page from Mao's playbook, Xi requires all Party officials, from provincial leaders to the Politburo, to engage in criticism and self-criticism and to pledge loyalty (*biaotai*) to the Party's central apparatus and to Xi as core leader.[6] Li Zhanshu, one of Xi's closest allies and the head of his central office, summarized a speech that Xi had given to the office staff in 2014 as being all about loyalty, and the requirement for "absolute loyalty . . . infinite loyalty . . . ready to sacrifice everything for the interests of the party and the people."[7]

Xi's signature campaign against official corruption, unprecedented in its scale and reach, was both a purge and a cleanup. It aimed to both eliminate potential rivals and restore the Party's integrity. To ensure the loyalty of everyone left standing after the campaign, he intensified the Party's requirements for discipline and ideological indoctrination. Any "improper discussion" (*wangyi*) that questions central policies is banned,[8] and Party membership standards are more stringent. So-called naked officials (*luoguan*), whose wives or children have moved abroad, are barred from promotion because they are presumed to be potentially disloyal as well as corrupt.[9] Because of his focus on—some would say paranoia about—disloyalty Xi relies on a small circle of trusted followers, almost all of whom he knew before becoming the heir apparent in 2007.

Bandwagoning

The irony is that the more forcefully Xi Jinping pressures his subordinates to pledge fealty to him, the more reason he has to suspect their sincerity. The intense pressure he puts on officials to prove their loyalty motivates ambitious politicians to jump on the bandwagon behind the leader's policy preferences as soon as he indicates what they are. They need to stay attentive to his cues. As international relations scholar Avery Goldstein's analysis of bandwagoning during the Mao era explains, a tight concentration of power at the top and the combination of positive rewards for compliance and negative sanctions for deviance creates incentives for subordinates to become "valued supporters by contributing support early enough to make a difference."[10] The result is "mechanical overcompliance" with the leader's directives, going beyond what even the leader himself may have wanted. This is the mechanism that produces overreach in a personalistic dictatorship. Lower-level politicians' attempts to demonstrate their zeal transforms policy "into a caricature of itself." Some less ambitious officials may opt to play it safe by just keeping their heads down and doing as little as possible. Still, even they don't dare to disagree with the leader or give him honest information about the consequences of his decisions. For over a decade, Xi has lived in an echo chamber of head-nodding agreement.

Some bandwagoning is wasteful but otherwise relatively harmless. Chinese tycoons seeking to ingratiate themselves with Xi, an enthusiastic soccer fan eager to build China into a world soccer power, lost a lot of money by purchasing European soccer clubs at inflated prices.[11] But other forms of bandwagoning have had global consequences. America's mismanagement during the early days of the COVID pandemic created an opening for China to step into the international leadership vacuum. But Chinese diplomats and propagandists botched their chance to win more friends by overdoing their "wolf warrior diplomacy," demanding that other countries praise China and endorse its political line in exchange for medical aid. After Australia called for an international scientific investigation of the origins of the COVID-19 virus, the Chinese Ministry of Commerce banned all Australian imports except iron ore, which China needs and can't replace, a draconian punishment that drove the Australians into a tighter military embrace with the Americans including the purchase of nuclear-powered submarines that will thwart China's expansion in the Asia Pacific. As diplomats Kurt Campbell and Mira Rapp-Hooper wrote in *Foreign Affairs* in 2020, "By leaving a power vacuum in the world's darkest hour, the United States has bequeathed China ample room to overreach—and to demonstrate that it is unqualified for a position of sole global leadership."[12]

Critics usually attribute China's combative foreign policies and its police-state repression in Xinjiang and Hong Kong to Xi's own traits, such as his upbringing during the winner-take-all politics of the Mao era and a poor education that was interrupted by the Cultural Revolution. Xi, indeed, has a typical strongman personality. As individuals, personalistic leaders like Xi are prone to having grandiose ambitions and overestimating the likelihood of achieving them.[13]

Yet character is only part of it. The centralized structure and bandwagoning dynamic of Chinese politics under the personalistic leader add impetus. The sycophants surrounding the leader are unwilling to dispel the leader's false beliefs and have incentives to encourage them.[14] Because of the secrecy shrouding Chinese high-level decision-making, it is impossible to discern just how much of its diplomacy, triumphalist propaganda, or repressive tactics are dictated by Xi personally or by officials who want to please him by acting on his preferences. For example, some blamed the regulatory crackdown on Internet-based private businesses in 2021, not on Xi Jinping himself but on the regulators, who were afraid to show moderation.

Theoretically, it should be easier for an autocrat to restrain his policies once he recognizes their costs to the nation than it would be for the leader of an oligarchy. A well-connected private businessman described Xi as "an ambitious leader who is sensitive to costs." The international backlash to China's post-COVID overreaching is testing that proposition. So far, there is no evidence that Xi is sufficiently aware of the costs to moderate his policies. No one has dared tell the emperor the truth about how the world is reacting to his hubris.

When Joe Biden replaced Donald Trump in the White House, in 2021, Xi showed little inclination to modify China's behavior to reassure the new administration about its intentions. Instead, Xi began acting assertively on many fronts at the same time.[15] Rather than taking advantage of the opening to stabilize relations with Washington, China keeps overreaching and is being encircled by a growing anti-China coalition. As the political scientist Joseph Nye noted some years ago, "If a rising China throws its weight around, it drives neighbors to seek to balance its power. In that sense, only China can contain China."[16]

After decades of collective leadership, Xi Jinping has returned China to a personalistic dictatorship. He shattered precedent by not promoting a successor-in-training at what should have been his midterm transition, the 19th Party Congress in October 2017. And by engineering the revision of the state constitution to abolish the two-term limit for the presidency, he signaled that he plans to remain in power after he completes his two terms in 2022.

China is a vibrant modern nation open to the world, with more than 400 million people in its well-educated urban middle class. As I've noted, many people — inside and outside the country — had expected its political system to follow the example of other authoritarian regimes that modernized by gradually institutionalizing governance to make it more accountable, responsive, and bound by laws. Until 2012, China was trending in that direction, although — as we have seen — collective leadership had its own drawbacks.[17] In institutionalizing collective leadership after Mao's death, the CCP had followed the path of communist parties in the Soviet Union and Eastern Europe,[18] which adapted to the needs of economic and social modernization. But those regimes lost control and collapsed.

Determined not to follow the Soviet "road of an overturned cart,"[19] Xi made a U-turn. Inspired by his admiration of Mao and his aversion to the centrifugal forces generated by collective leadership, he restored strongman rule. Xi's vision is not identical to Mao's, however; he seeks political stability under the Communist Party's iron hand rather than by trying to keep society in a state of revolutionary tension, as Mao did. Still, Xi has modeled his leadership style on Mao's, from centralized decision-making to personality cult, stress on ideological purity, and reliance on a small circle of advisers. His turn away from institutionalized collective leadership to strongman rule suggests that these two types of authoritarian regimes may alternate in a cyclical manner in China.

Xi Jinping's Agenda

The speed with which Xi Jinping reversed course amazed everyone. Just two weeks after becoming general secretary, on November 15, 2012, he led the Politburo Standing Committee to the National History Museum, where he staged his debut against the backdrop of the Road to Rejuvenation exhibition, which depicted the nationalist narrative of past humiliations by foreign aggressors. Xi launched the nationalist motto of his new reign, the "China Dream," which connected the personal dream of every Chinese individual to the collectivist patriotic dream of reviving China's wealth and power under the leadership of the Chinese Communist Party.

A week later, Xi traveled south to Shenzhen, where he portrayed himself as a direct descendent of the Party's reform tradition established by his father and by Deng Xiaoping. He declared his determination to break through the vested interests blocking market reform. During the tour, Xi also gave a speech to local officials, which was circulated inside the Party but never published, in which he expressed his fears about the fragility of CCP rule. Hu Jintao had blamed the Soviet collapse on the failures of

Soviet governance and Gorbachev's misjudgments. For Xi, however, it all came down to the wavering commitment of the Party members and the military.[20] The "ideals and beliefs" of CPSU members had been shaken; the military had become depoliticized, and, in the end, "nobody was man enough to stand up and resist."[21]

Xi's speech before the entire Central Committee on January 5, 2013, stunned the Party elite by rehabilitating Mao Zedong. (Only a brief version of the speech was published at the time.) The thirty years when Mao ruled, it proclaimed, were as positive for China as the thirty years after the reforms were introduced in 1978. The two historical periods "are by no means separated from each other, let alone fundamentally opposed. We can't use the historical period after the reform and opening up to deny the historical period before the reform," or vice versa.[22] For all that Xi and his family had suffered under Mao's totalitarianism, he was now praising Mao. In Xi's view, the fall of Soviet communism had started back in 1956, when the CPSU repudiated Stalinism; China must avoid a similar "historical nihilism" toward Maoism that would "confuse the hearts of the people" and destroy their support for the CCP.

When the full version of the speech was published in the Party's ideological journal six years later,[23] it became apparent that Xi also was casting the relationship with the West as a cold-war-type ideological contest between socialism and capitalism. Socialism with Chinese characteristics would triumph over capitalism and have increasingly greater influence in the world. The boastful message of this speech, along with Xi's gloating after China successfully controlled the COVID-19 pandemic in 2020, have caused American politicians to react with mirror imaging: officials in both the Trump and Biden administrations framed the relationship as a contest between the two systems, Chinese communist autocracy versus Western market democracy.

Initially, I wondered whether Xi's tack toward the Left was a political tactic. Deng Xiaoping had emphasized ideological orthodoxy in the 1980s and 1990s whenever he needed to keep Party elder Chen Yun, whose personal authority was barely less than Deng's own, behind his market reforms. But there was now no contemporary political figure as ideologically orthodox and powerful as Chen Yun was during the Deng period. A senior government official suggested an another reason why Xi may have chosen to embrace Leftist views, because they are more prevalent in the Party than people realize. "Bo Xilai and Zhou Yongkang are in jail, but their followers remain," he told me.

Still, many were made uneasy by Xi's rhetoric and nervously awaited the meeting of the Central Committee in the fall of 2013, when Xi would unveil his economic plans and priorities.[24] The sixty-point reform blueprint exceeded their expectations. It described the relationship between the state and the market in terms that might have been lifted from an American economics textbook by Paul Samuelson, and beyond the economy, proposed significant changes to the courts as well. The document and the establishment of a new leading group to carry out the reforms gave credence to Xi's claim to be a reformer and assuaged some of the anxieties about his dictatorial style.

In the eight years since, however, as Xi has taken command of every ligament in the system, he has not used his power to carry out these market reforms; most of the proposals remain on the drawing board.[25] Instead, he has thrown himself into reorganizing the military, building up the Party organization, cracking down on corruption, enhancing global influence through his signature Belt and Road Initiative, reducing rural poverty, and turning China into a technology superpower.

And he has done this by controlling all the levers of power in the Communist Party and the government, including the military and police. Xi's hands-on management extends further than that of any previous leader. He centralized decision-making and governs the country top-down according to his own "top-level design"[26] as the chair of eight powerful CCP interagency commissions. Instead of regular agency bureaucrats, he relies on trusted associates, whom he has appointed to head the commission offices, to advise him and carry out his orders. "Xi operates at the top of the hierarchy with tightly controlled groups of officials under him," according to a government minister. "He trusts these individuals and doesn't trust other officials in established departments."

Under Xi, the Party reclaimed the authority over economic policy that, starting in the 1980s, it had delegated to government agencies. The 2017 Party Congress report declared that "East-West North-South the Party is leading everything," harkening back to a slogan that Mao first proposed in 1962.[27] The Party's Commission on Comprehensively Deepening Reform, formed and chaired by Xi, has become a more powerful shadow State Council, meeting monthly and issuing specific policies on a wide range of issues, including but not limited to economic ones.[28] Xi also leads the Party Central Economic and Financial Affairs Commission and, with the support of his favorite technocrat, Liu He, who heads its office, has taken control over economic management in a manner atypical of Party general secretaries. The premier is usually the de facto manager of economic policy, but Xi has sidelined Premier Li Keqiang by making the Party commissions the decision-making bodies.[29]

Within the Party, collective leadership has not been formally renounced, but it is effectively nonexistent. The Politburo Standing Committee has been shrunk from nine to seven members. (As we'll remember, Hu had increased it to nine from seven.) Standing Committee members still have their own portfolios, but they are accountable to Xi and are required to submit annual written performance reports to him. As a result, these reviews prioritize, first, implementing Xi's instructions and, second, reflecting "Xi Jinping Thought on Socialism with Chinese Characteristics." As reported by Xinhua, what these members do in the fields over which they have responsibility comes in third.[30] According to one insider, at Standing Committee meetings, Xi discourages the airing of different viewpoints and insists that his colleagues express their opinions to him privately instead. And unlike Hu and other previous CCP general secretaries, Xi freely exercises power over the policy areas of the other Standing Committee members.[31]

Xi's hold on the People's Liberation Army is even more complete than his hold on the CCP and the government. As security scholar Tai Ming Cheung has observed, "No other Chinese Communist Party leader, not even Mao Zedong, controlled the military to the same extent as Xi does today. Mao had to share power with powerful revolutionary-era generals."[32] To show how hands-on he is, Xi has taken on the new post of commander-in-chief of the PLA Joint Battle Command and enjoys wearing his digital camouflage combat uniform. One officer told me that the military officers who are vice chairs of the Central Military Commission no longer administer the PLA. Now Xi runs it himself.

The Party Swallows the State

Under Xi Jinping, the Party has reclaimed the authority over all policy domains that after 1980 it had delegated to government agencies. Such delegation benefited from government officials' specialized knowledge and experience and facilitated policy implementation.[33] Today, Party control is the higher priority; the administrative lines between the Party and the government have been purposefully blurred. The heads of state institutions, including the National People's Congress, the State Council, government ministries, and the Supreme People's Court, must regularly report to the Politburo Standing Committee.[34] Government technocrats complain that many recent appointees to senior positions in government agencies and organizations are Party hacks with no experience in the field they are supposed to be managing. Private businesses, including foreign ones, as well as all public-sector organizations, including universities and social organizations, must set up Party committees and listen to the Party secretary; and pressure has been building to put at least one Party official on every corporate board of directors.

The primacy of the Party was clear for all to see in the August 2017 parade marking the ninetieth anniversary of the founding of the PLA: the Party flag came first, before the national flag and the PLA flag. Some Chinese netizens wryly noted that this placement violated the 1990 National Flag law that requires the national flag to always appear in front.[35]

The Party's political interests also drive foreign policy. In December 2016, the foreign minister, Wang Yi, declared that the number-one goal of China's foreign policy during the next year would be to "create a favorable external environment for the convening of the 19th CCP National Congress."[36] This is a truly remarkable statement—in what other country would the foreign minister openly state that the top foreign policy goal is to win the next election?

Xi's closest adviser (some might say his consigliere), Wang Qishan, who as chairman of the CCP Central Commission on Discipline Inspection (CCDI) between 2012 and 2017 led the anticorruption campaign, became a vocal advocate of merging Party and government as he climbed on the Xi Jinping bandwagon. Wang, like Xi, is a princeling; he is the son-in-law of Yao Yilin, a former Standing Committee member. The two young men became friends when they were both sent down as youths to work in Shaanxi province during the Cultural Revolution. Wang had devoted much of his career to reforming the financial system and practical problem-solving—as mayor of Beijing he had managed the SARS epidemic and prepared for the 2008 Olympics. He was respected by the public and was a favorite of Western bankers.[37] However, after 2012, Wang became Xi's henchman, devoting himself to the cause of his friend's absolute power. He spoke passionately about Party leadership being "the highest political principle in contemporary China" and the key to the "great rejuvenation of the Chinese nation." He criticized "unconditionally separating the party from the government,"[38] which had been Deng Xiaoping's goal in the 1980s. Wang argued that China's historical tradition was to define "government" broadly with "unlimited responsibilities," extending the concept to Party organs as well as state ones. He insisted that while there may be some "division of labor between the party and the government" (*dangzheng fengong*), there can be no "separation between party and government" (*dangzheng fenkai*).[39]

A Chinese scholar who gave a talk at the CCDI found himself debating Wang about the importance of separating Party and government. Wang said, "How can you say they are not the same? When I was a provincial Party secretary everyone regarded me as the head of the government." When the scholar referenced Deng's writings on separating Party and government, Wang dismissed them, "That was used by Zhao Ziyang," who was deposed because of the Tiananmen crisis and spent the rest of his life under house arrest. Wang also disparaged Deng's critique of the Kuomintang (KMT) government's fusing of Party and government in 1938 and 1939 as irrelevant because it had happened during the United Front period when the KMT and CCP were in a coalition.

During his second term Xi has carried out a reorganization that has melded the government and the Party. Nearly two million positions in thirty-one government ministries and related institutions were abolished when their government responsibilities were absorbed by Party bodies. The State Administration for Religious Affairs, State Ethnic Affairs Commission, and State Council Overseas Chinese Affairs Office were reorganized under the CCP United Front Department, which is responsible for relations with social groups outside the Party both at home and abroad. The Civil Servant Department was reorganized under the CCP Organization Department to prioritize political virtue in the appointment of civil servants.[40] The State Administration of Press, Publication, Radio, Film and Television was absorbed by the CCP Propaganda Department. The reorganization was designed to streamline administration, dissolve lingering bureaucratic resistance to Xi's ideas, and skew outcomes toward Xi's preferences.

Xi's expansion of the Party's authority was reflected in the new constitutionally mandated National Supervision Commission, which effectively extends the reach of the CCDI to non-Party state employees. Ostensibly a government institution, it is in fact a joint agency housed under the CCDI.[41] It has the power to investigate and punish professors, doctors, and executives of all state-led organizations except the military. It absorbed the Ministry of Supervision, in charge of civil servants, and the white-collar-crime division of the Procuratorate, the government prosecutor in criminal cases. Some legal scholars openly objected to the commission's encroachment on the courts' already very limited institutional autonomy and complained about the lack of lawyers and procedural protections for those detained by this body.[42]

Yet Xi claims to be committed to strengthening the legal system. By passing sweeping new laws governing NGOs, national security, and cybersecurity, he aims to augment his centralized power. The Party has always managed the courts, but now central or provincial CCP authorities — not local Party figures — appoint judges. In July 2015, about three hundred lawyers whose only crime was helping citizens to defend their rights under existing Chinese law were detained on charges of "subverting state power." This is not the adherence to the "rule of law" that Chinese reformers once envisioned. Instead, it is the Communist Party's central leadership using law to strengthen its rule.

Purging Rivals

Soon after assuming power, Xi launched a massive campaign against corrupt and disobedient officials, and part of its agenda, as we've seen, was to get rid of rivals. The campaign has continued during his second term. The main goal, said Xi, was to restore public respect for the Party. It was a matter of "survival or extinction."[43] Although the professed aim was to clean up the Party, the campaign, again, purged Xi's potential competitors, destroyed their factional networks, and enforced the absolute loyalty of the political elite through fear. The contrast between Xi and Hu Jintao in their willingness to share power with other Party leaders could not be more striking: Hu allowed the senior politicians in the CCP, as well as retired leader Jiang Zemin, to govern their own policy domains and build their own patronage networks. Xi set out to destroy the organizational bases for patronage networks controlled by others and to achieve unrivaled dominance over the Party. As one Chinese observer noted, "Xi has brought down the political oligarchy."

By June 2021, the CCDI had punished over 3.7 million officials since Xi came to office.[44] They included twenty-five full and eighteen alternate Central Committee members,[45] a pair of sitting Politburo members, an ex-member of the Politburo Standing Committee, and over two hundred officials at or above the provincial and ministerial levels.[46] When I asked a CCDI official why specific high-level officials were targeted for investigation, he told me that Xi, together with then-head Wang Qishan, had picked them. The results of the investigation were then passed on to the commission and the Politburo Standing Committee for final approval.[47] "Did the Standing Committee ever say no when someone was recommended for punishment?" I asked. "Never," he replied, "because Xi said that no one should be exempt."

One of the Commission's major targets was the Communist Youth League (CYL), the organizational base of Hu's following. In a 2015 speech,

Xi lambasted mass organizations like the CYL as being "bureaucratic, pro-cedurally minded, aristocratic (*guizuhua*), and entertainment oriented" and insufficiently selective because they admitted almost all middle-school students.[48] According to a Party official, the CYL, once a ladder of social mobility, had become dominated by people from high-level official family backgrounds, including the son of Zhao Leji (the Standing Committee member in charge of Party discipline) and Deng Xiaoping's grandson. By attacking the CYL and its leading alumni, Xi cleared openings for his own followers to take key positions at the 19th CCP Congress in 2017.

Xi Jinping accused the six most prominent "tigers" punished in the anti-corruption campaign of planning coups as well as bribery. Without giving details, he publicly charged them with plotting to seize power through "anti-Party activity." Xi's public revelation of these conspiracies lifted the curtain of secrecy to reveal the Party's backstage power struggles. On the one hand, it sent a warning to other ambitious politicians who might con-template challenging Xi. On the other, it raised questions about Xi's ma-nipulation of the political game to gain power for himself.

Among the broad public, Xi's anticorruption campaign boosted his pop-ularity. In 2022, television viewers were glued to their screens to watch *Zero Tolerance*, a five-part documentary series produced by the CCDI in which fallen officials confessed their misdeeds, highlighting their collusion with capitalists in the business world, who are increasingly being blamed for problems of inequality and corruption. Within Chinese officialdom, how-ever, the campaign created a climate of terror. Officials never know when they might be dragged off in the middle of the night because a disgruntled subordinate or bureaucratic rival had reported them. In January 2016, I re-ceived a phone call the night before my scheduled meeting with Gong Qinggai, a deputy director of the Taiwan Affairs Office with a reputation as a "clean-handed rising star," according to a Hong Kong newspaper,[49] informing me that the CCDI had just arrested him. Gong had served in Fujian province at the same time as Xi and may have gotten on the wrong side of a feud between Xi and the Party secretary.[50] Two years later, Gong was sentenced to fifteen years in prison for taking bribes of $7.78 million to help people get approvals for land acquisition, construction projects, and plan adjustment between 1996 and 2015.[51]

The terror is driving some officials to opt for a safe exit. According to one official, so many hundreds of people were quitting the Foreign Ministry and Commerce Ministry in a new wave of *xiahai* (quitting a state job to enter the business world) that both ministries had to enforce a rule that people would be investigated if they tried to quit. An economist explained to me that he had declined a government position that a few years ago he would have liked to accept because he didn't want to have to "be put in a position where I'd have to violate my own principles or become the target of other people." Moreover, he had a son who was studying abroad.

Xi's targeting of other politicians—even a few in his own faction—has made them feel dissatisfied and unsafe. Still, everyone I interviewed insisted that no focal point for elite resistance had yet emerged. Standing Committee politician Wang Yang, the former Guangdong CCP secretary with a reputation as a reformer who might be a potential challenger, has kept his head down because, as an official told me, he doesn't want to end up like Liu Shaoqi, Mao's chosen successor whom he destroyed during the Cultural Revolution.

Neither of Xi's predecessors tried to impede his efforts to consolidate power. Hu Jintao did him the favor of retiring completely and handing him all three of the top jobs. According to some political insiders, Hu continues to feel responsible for the leadership splits and rampant corruption that metastasized during his administration and has sought to make amends by supporting Xi in his drive to restore Party discipline. Jiang Zemin, ninety-four years old, appears to no longer be active. Another rumor is that Xi reached an agreement with Jiang to not touch his family or his close colleague Zeng Qinghong if Jiang doesn't challenge him. With no intergenerational bargain constraining Xi, elite politics are skewed in his favor.

Xi Jinping nevertheless is not taking anything for granted. As he seeks a controversial third term at the 20th CCP National Congress, he still seems worried about possible opposition from retired leaders. In May 2022, the CCP Organization Department issued a directive to "strengthen its political guidance over retired cadres" to make sure that they do "not spread politically negative remarks or participate in illegal social organization activities."[52]

He also has engineered a new power structure to safeguard himself from an elite coup. The head of the internal security apparatus no longer sits in the Politburo Standing Committee; the position has been demoted to the Politburo. Instead, Xi personally commands the entire country's police forces and can monitor all the communications of high-level politicians. This arrangement protects him against a conspiracy, such as the one the former internal security boss Zhou Yongkang was accused of plotting with Bo Xilai before they were purged in 2013.

Xi also seized command of the paramilitary People's Armed Police in January 2018 by removing it from joint civilian and military direction and placing it under him as commander in chief. The group got a new flag in

2020, one that features a big red stripe, signifying absolute loyalty to the Party and its leader.[53] Showing his unrelenting insecurity about pockets of resistance in the police forces, Xi ordered the CCDI to carry out a massive rectification campaign of the internal security apparatus in 2021.

People's Leader (*renmin lingxiu*)

Communist elites use ideological slogans and labels as an esoteric language with which to communicate with one another.[54] The top leader's designation speaks volumes about the distribution of power within the Party elite. Xi Jinping took on new titles as he consolidated power and built a cult of personality. In 2016, he started to be called the "leadership core" (*lingdao hexin*) of the Party, first, by sycophantic provincial politicians, and then by a meeting of the Central Committee. Deng Xiaoping had claimed the "leadership core" title for himself and then passed it down to Jiang Zemin to strengthen Jiang's authority after Tiananmen. Hu Jintao never achieved "core leader" status, however, and used only the more modest description, "the party center with Comrade Hu Jintao as General Secretary."

Since 2016, official Party documents have emphasized that it is the responsibility of every Chinese official to protect Xi's status as the leadership core, hinting that it may be in some jeopardy. The CCDI went so far as to declare, at its 2019 annual meeting, that its "fundamental mission" and top priority was to safeguard Xi Jinping's status as the "core" of the Party. In his speech, Zhao Leji, the CCDI chief, indicated that there remained threats to Xi's authority, singling out two senior politicians, Chongqing CCP secretary Sun Zhengcai and Internet boss Lu Wei, for being "disloyal, dishonest, and two-faced."[55]

Beginning in late 2017, politicians in Guizhou province began displaying their loyalty by calling Xi Jinping "great leader" (*weida lingxiu*) in local newspapers, a form of praise that only Chairman Mao (and before him, the Guomindang leader Chiang Kai-shek) had merited in the past. (Stalin, Hitler, and other foreign dictators also were called "supreme leader" or "führer.") The articles in the Guizhou newspapers lauding Xi as *lingxiu* were initially deleted for being excessive, but when the official flagship *People's Daily* and China Central Television called Xi the "people's leader" (*renmin lingxiu*) a few months later, the title stuck and started to be used frequently in combination with "leadership core."[56]

There are other titles Xi might covet. Mao Zedong held the title of chairman (*zhuxi*) of the CCP. Jiang Zemin and Hu Jintao never did; they had to settle for being just the CCP general secretary (*dangwei shuji*). I wouldn't be surprised if Xi became chairman at the 20th CCP Congress, in 2022, when he begins his third term. Having already made clear his intention to not retire in 2022 by not selecting a successor-in-training and eliminating the two-term constitutional limit for the presidency, he has little to lose by also claiming *zhuxi*. Xi might even pretend to follow the formalities of the regular turnover of power at the top by stepping down from the state presidency and the general secretaryship of the Party and handing those posts to two less powerful politicians, retaining the Party chairmanship and chairmanship of the Military Commission for himself.

Cult of Personality

I have focused on the cult of personality that Xi Jinping has developed because it is one of the central features of strongman rule. During the Mao era, of course, everyone carried the Little Red Book of *Quotations from Mao Zedong Thought* as a political bible, and posters of Mao surrounded by the worshipful masses were ubiquitous. Chinese propaganda has become slicker and more digital since then, but the focus is still very much on glorifying the leader. Xi's name is headlined on the front page of the *People's Daily* more often than Mao's ever was—even during the Cultural Revolution era.[57]

After Mao died, Party leaders relaxed their efforts to remold people's political thinking and focused instead on economic development. But Xi turned up the heat, intensifying ideological indoctrination because he believed that people's commitment to communist ideals had begun to waver. The theory behind this ideological effort, attributed by Xi's close comrade Wang Qishan to political philosopher Alexis de Tocqueville, is that the greatest risks of political upheaval come during a period of reform.[58]

Many of those I interviewed view the CCP Propaganda Department as the most powerful agency in China's political firmament and blame it for hijacking the policy process. One government minister accused the Propaganda Department of excess in its emphasis on ideological remolding and Xi's cult of personality. "It's due to 'over-implementation' by the Propaganda Department and other organizations," he said, and "not necessarily what Xi himself wants to see." For example, Xi talks about "positive energy," but the Propaganda Department, says the minister, "takes this to an extreme, stops the media from discussing problems, and only wants to see the good side. This approach isn't necessarily Xi's own idea and isn't actually good for him. After all, you can't forbid people to think."

The forced re-education of Uighur Muslims is the most extreme example of what used to be called "brainwashing." But the effort extends beyond Xinjiang. Today, every Chinese is subject to more ideological education, from kindergarten through adulthood, than they were a decade ago. The Propaganda Department has gone all-out to inculcate the population with an amalgam of Marxism-Leninism, nationalism, and a Xi cult. Since 2021, students from elementary school to graduate school are required to study "Xi Jinping Thought."[59]

Party members must devote many additional hours to the political study of Xi's wisdom. In January 2019, the Propaganda Department launched its first ideological education app, Xuexi Qiangguo, which all Party members must download on their devices. The name means "Study Strong Country," and "Xuexi" has the double meaning of "Study Xi" because its second character is the same as Xi Jinping's surname. The app prompts users multiple times during the day to watch videos of Xi's travels and meetings, read articles and share them with friends and family, and take tests about their political knowledge. They earn points for what they do on the app and the amount of time they spend on it. These points can be transferred to rewards for special discounts, and work supervisors use them to award employee bonuses and promotions. I was in Beijing when the app was introduced, and I saw it become as popular and addictive as a new video game. But before long, people started complaining that the app took too much time away from work and started hiring other people or paying for an automated software program to complete their tasks on the app.[60] Meanwhile, new social media technologies came on the scene. Nowadays the Propaganda Department worries less about enforcing time spent on Xuexi Qiangguo than competing for eyeballs to watch its short videos on TikTok and Bilibili.

Xi's signature contribution to the ideological canon, *Xi Jinping Thought on Socialism with Chinese Characteristics for a New Era*, has been written into the constitutions of both the state and the Party, an honor that neither Jiang Zemin nor Hu Jintao achieved until after they had retired from office; and even then, Jiang's "Three Represents" and Hu's "Scientific Development Concept" did not bear their names.[61] Xi appears on his way to shortening his signature term to the five-character

Xi Jinping Thought that sounds just like *Mao Zedong Thought*. Since 2017, high-level politicians have talked incessantly about the Cultural Revolution–style propaganda slogan "raising high the banner of 'Xi Jinping Thought on Socialism with Chinese Characteristics for a New Era.'"[62] Foreign minister Wang Yi ingratiates himself by speaking about "Xi Jinping Thought on Diplomacy," and generals do the same by talking about "Xi Jinping Thought on Military Affairs." Watch for the likely rollout of the omnibus slogan, "Xi Jinping Thought" at the 20th Party Congress in 2022.

Xi Jinping is a princeling and married to Peng Liyuan, a PLA folk singer and fashion icon, who was once more famous than her husband. Still, Xi's official hagiography portrays him as a man of the people. Liangjiahe, the small village in Shaanxi province where Xi lived in a cave dwelling for those seven years during the Cultural Revolution, has now became a political shrine, and a book about his experiences, *Xi Jinping's Seven Years as a Sent-Down Youth*, was published in 2017.[63]

Although Xi's cult of personality is not as over-the-top as Mao's was—no one gets up in the morning to bow down or shout "long live!" (*wansui*) before Xi's portrait—some object to it. My interviewees complain that whereas Mao earned his hero worship because of his great deeds as a revolutionary leader, Xi hasn't accomplished anything nearly as exceptional. His charisma is entirely manufactured by the Propaganda Department. This is precisely the kind of grumbling that makes Xi worry that no matter how much praise he hears from subordinates, opposition against him might be brewing under the surface.

Although Mao encouraged his personality cult, he recognized that the flattery wasn't a reliable indicator of true popularity. He advised Vietnamese leader Ho Chi Minh in 1966, "Not all of your subjects are loyal to you. Perhaps most of them are loyal but maybe a small number only verbally wish you 'long live,' while in reality they wish you a premature death. When they shout, 'long live,' you should beware and analyze [the situation]. The more they praise you, the less you can trust them. This is a very natural rule."[64]

Indeed, there is never a shortage of opportunism in expressions of loyalty.[65] Political chameleons such as Zhao Zhengyong, the former Party chief of Shaanxi province, who are accused of being "two faced" (*liang mian*)—that is, feigning loyalty while acting disloyally—abound in the system and are hard to screen out. At some point, Chinese netizens even coined catchy phrases—such as "high-level black" (*gaojihei*), referring to offering exaggerated praise to disguise an act of criticism, and "low-level red" (*dijihong*), meaning shameless and self-defeating displays of devotion to cloak internal opposition—to ridicule the hypocrisy.

For Xi, the popular caricature of the "fake reverence" has sounded the alarm. Knowing full well the danger of unwittingly promoting opportunists rather than sincere believers, Xi himself has criticized people who coast along "in the neutral gear" or hide "darkness under the light."[66] The Propaganda Department borrowed these phrases in its warnings against the Party cadres. As a *People's Daily* article observed in 2018, "to speak politics one must use discerning eyes to distinguish 'high-level black' and 'low-level red,' resolving the problem of 'fulsome expressions of loyalty with little real action.'"[67] A recent campaign to clean up the internal security and legal systems highlighted the danger of "two-faced cadres" and "wall-straddling factions," who could "undermine the authority and centralized unified leadership of the Party center."[68]

Despite all these verbal alarms, the Party has yet to find an effective way to identify the opportunists and put an end to this phenomenon once and for all. My UC San Diego colleague Victor Shih observed that even during the Hu Jintao era, a provincial politician who moved early to endorse his faction leader's latest favorite slogan would be disdained by his peers as a panderer. That willingness to pay a cost in one's social relations is what made these "nauseating displays of loyalty," credible signals of genuine loyalty.[69] Now that Xi Jinping has wiped out other faction leaders and turned China into a one-faction political system, he lacks a reliable loyalty test and cannot be certain that those who jump on the bandwagon behind him aren't plotting behind his back.

The political transformation Xi has brought about is not limited to the Party and the political system. It impacts all of Chinese society. For example, getting ahead at school and making a successful professional career now depend, at least in part, on your political behavior, just as it did when Mao ruled China.[70] Since 2013, the CCP has officially banned media and classroom discussion of seven topics associated with Western values and thus considered subversive: constitutional democracy, universal values, civil society, neoliberalism, freedom of the press, historical nihilism (naming past mistakes of the Party), and questioning reform and opening.[71] University professors who are Party members must defend the CCP in class if anyone criticizes it—silence isn't acceptable. Western textbooks have been banned and replaced with new indigenous textbooks that emphasize Marxism. At all education levels, more time is now devoted to mandatory politics courses. Schools of Marxism are enjoying a renaissance on campuses all over the country. Public intellectuals who have popular blogs have been arrested, and some of them forced to make humiliating televised confessions of malfeasance that call to mind the Cultural Revolution.

Xi, meanwhile, gives speeches promoting a rosy view of the Mao era that no one outside the hard-Left fringes had voiced in thirty years. He believes that what he calls "historical nihilism"—taking a critical perspective on the Great Leap Forward, the Cultural Revolution, and other historical episodes of the Mao era—could, as I've noted, undercut the legitimacy of Party rule and cause it to collapse "because," as was the case in the Soviet Union, "the ideals and beliefs were no longer there."[72] According to one Chinese journalist, by the time Xi became leader he had concluded that public opinion on the Internet was "out of control." He unified the Internet censors under the powerful, new Cyber Administration of China (CAC) and made himself the chair of the leading small group that oversees it. Now the censorship bureaucracies are more consolidated and centralized, as well as highly motivated to prove their loyalty to Xi.

During Xi's first term, several powerful barons of the propaganda system were still competing to win his approval: Liu Yunshan (who was in the Standing Committee), Liu Qibao (minister of propaganda and Politburo member), and Lu Wei, head of the Cyber Administration who reported directly to Xi. By the second term, Xi had consolidated control of the propaganda apparatus, with the relatively weak Standing Committee member Wang Huning assisting him. Liu Yunshan had retired, Liu Qibao had been demoted to a mere Central Committee member, and Lu Wei was in prison for corruption.

In 2016, Xi visited the three main official news organizations (Xinhua, *People's Daily*, and CCTV) to ask journalists to pledge loyalty to the Party and to him. He demanded that "official media make the Party their surname," and insisted that they "strictly adhere to the news viewpoint of Marxism" and "rebuild people's trust in the Party."[73] Editors of online news outlets report that official censorship has become more granular and efficient. Investments in censorship technologies to control social media have paid off. The censors have hounded critical voices off Sina Weibo (as noted, China's version of Twitter) and now are able to penetrate circles of friends who message one another on WeChat. Getting around the Great Firewall to access foreign media is now harder than ever. Tech and media companies also preemptively censor online postings to avoid trouble and get on the good side of the officials who regulate them, as in the case of Douyin (the Chinese version of TikTok) banning Peppa Pig videos.[74] This near-total control of information makes it extremely difficult not only to organize large-scale protests, but also for potential rivals to Xi to gather a mass following.

Culturally, Xi Jinping is turning China inward. Television entertainment is saturated with Chinese historical dramas and anti-Japanese war movies, and the broadcast of overseas content is restricted.[75] Western television shows cannot be legally shown in China until the censors clear the entire season of episodes. As a result, viewers rush to watch the low-quality pirated versions that are available immediately after the show is broadcast abroad. Regulations from 2021 have discouraged the learning of English by dropping it from the secondary school examination requirements and shuttering the after-school tutoring industry.

Efforts to promote the Party's propaganda messages have intensified outside China as well. Twitter may be banned in China, but Chinese officials and commentators are urged to tweet Beijing's version of events to the international audience. Under Xi, China's global drive to enhance its "discourse power"—which is aimed at the domestic audience as well as the global one—has gone beyond positive image-building to outright online information manipulation.[76]

By the end of his first five-year term, the Xi personality cult was in full sway as Xi sought, as historian Rana Mitter says, "to centralize as much authority and charisma under his own person" as he could.[77] The front page of the *People's Daily* the day after the 19th CCP Congress ended presented a visual contrast with the front page during the Hu Jintao era, when a photo of the collective leadership in the Politburo Standing Committee dominated. Now a large, air-brushed photo of Xi eclipsed a much smaller image of the new Standing Committee.[78]

Xi's Midterm That Wasn't

There is really nothing left to constrain Xi Jinping's leadership overreach. That 19th CCP Congress, coming as it did in 2017 at the midpoint of his allotted ten-year period in power, tested whether the Party's unwritten and written rules and precedents could constrain Xi. China's was the first communist system to achieve a regular turnover of power at the top, a singular accomplishment that improved the resilience of the regime by reassuring the elite that the leader was willing to share power with them and respect their career security. At each midterm Congress, one or two younger politicians would be identified as "successors-in-training" and promoted to the Standing Committee to prepare them to become CCP general secretary and premier five years hence.

The prudent move for Xi in 2017 would have been to name an heir apparent instead of signaling at this early stage that he intended to cling to power beyond the two-term limit. On the one hand, any leader would naturally prefer to avoid lame-duck status as their reign drew to a close. But on the other hand, if alerted too early about Xi's intentions to claim a third term, other politicians might try to block him. I myself had anticipated that the unwritten rules of succession established by Deng Xiaoping, Jiang Zemin, and Hu Jintao would be strong enough to induce Xi to abide by them or, at least, to wait until closer to the 20th Party Congress in 2022 to try to change them.[79]

I underestimated Xi's willingness to take political risks. When the Standing Committee nominations appeared, there was no one young enough to be a successor-in-training. Xi's audacious move sent shockwaves through Chinese politics. To engineer this outcome, Xi had had to change the nomination process to make it more centralized and dominated by the incumbent leader than it had been in 2007 and 2012. At those congresses, as I noted in chapter 3, members of the Central Committee had voted in a straw poll, a small step toward intra-Party democracy that helped avoid any surprises when the Central Committee formally elected the Party leadership. Xi reportedly won nomination as Hu Jintao's successor because he did so well in the 2007 straw poll.

In 2017, however, Xi scrapped elections because they would have diluted his personal control over the nomination process. Replacing the straw poll, Xi and other Standing Committee members interviewed and consulted with current and retired senior officials to choose the nominees. The elite, however, were unlikely to have been won over by the new method, seeing the rejection of elections as a sign of Xi's unwillingness to share power with them. To protect himself against a backlash, Xi provided some factional balance in the Standing Committee and followed precedent by elevating the most senior members of the Politburo to the Standing Committee, as had been done in all Party Congresses since 1997. Shanghai native and former mayor Han Zheng is linked to Jiang Zemin, and Li Keqiang and Wang Yang were associated with Hu Jintao and the Communist Youth League. Wang Huning, who had served as speech writer and ideological theorist for Jiang Zemin and Hu Jintao, has no power base of his own and was likely to toe the Xi Jinping line completely along with Xi's close allies Li Zhanshu and Zhao Leji.

The 2017 Politburo, however, was decisively packed with Xi followers who will support sustaining his rule in a third term. Of the fifteen new members, nine were widely identified as former coworkers or childhood and family friends of Xi, and a tenth, Wang Chen, had served with him as a sent-down youth in Yenan. Some of these close associates were ordinary Party members who were helicoptered into the Politburo, skipping the step of Central Committee membership.

One of the trickiest issues in the 19th Party Congress was what Xi would do about Wang Qishan, his longtime friend, whom he had put in charge of the anticorruption and Party discipline campaign. Wang had passed the normal retirement age of sixty-seven, but Xi likely wanted to keep Wang close by his side for several reasons—to continue to benefit from his advice, to protect him from the vengeance of politicians and their families whose careers he had destroyed in the purge, and to prevent Wang from turning against him. The compromise Xi adopted was to have Wang formally retire from the Party leadership but to make him state vice president (a powerless position) and have him attend CCP Standing Committee meetings informally.

The shock of Xi's decision not to appoint an heir apparent was amplified by the newly ambitious tone of his speech to the Congress, as well as by the incorporation of "Xi Jinping Thought on Socialism with Chinese Characteristics for the New Era" into the CCP Constitution and Xi's elevated status as the Party's Leader. In the speech, for the first time in recent history, a leader publicly declaimed that the Chinese system was a model for other countries to follow, not just one well suited to China. "Socialism with Chinese characteristics . . . is blazing a new trail for other developing countries to achieve modernization [and] offers a new option for other countries and nations who want to speed up their development while preserving their independence."[80] Xi also asserted that China is "moving closer to the center of the world stage" and a "global leader in terms of comprehensive national power and international influence."[81]

Following the 2017 Congress, I and a few other foreigners were invited to a conference at a southern regional university, where scholars at its School of Marxism parsed the meaning of Xi's speech. The Party center also sent propaganda preachers (*xuanjiang tuan*) to spread the message of the speech not just throughout the country, which was usual practice, but also to the capitals of some important foreign countries. To many Western ears, including those of Steve Bannon, President Trump's former chief strategist, Xi's speech proved that China "was the greatest existential threat ever faced by the United States."[82] Along with a few other China experts, I met with Steve Bannon a few days after the speech, and he compared it to *Mein Kampf*, Hitler's Nazi manifesto.

Leader for Life

In short, in his drive for permanent power, Xi Jinping went for broke by amending the state constitution to eliminate the two-term limit for the president. Although the presidency is the least powerful of his three positions, he was scrapping the only formal written limitation on his ability to rule China for life. The process was rushed through in secrecy; the public announcement was made on February 25, 2018, just four months after the Party Congress. (The previous revision of the constitution in 2002–2003 had taken a full year of meetings to complete.) Yet analysts of Chinese politics were unable to find any hard evidence of elite resistance—from retired leaders, provincial leaders, or anyone else—to this shattering of the protocols of regular turnover of top leadership.

Xi's surprisingly easy destruction of all institutional restraints on his ability to rule forever alarmed many Chinese businesspeople, academics, and professionals. In the past, they had counted on the provincial leaders, who are, as I've noted, the largest bloc in the Central Committee, to serve as a check on the dictatorial power of the Party center, in a kind of de facto federal balance of power.[83] But the provincial politicians went silent as Xi Jinping steamrolled over them and set himself up to be China's leader for life. Several private entrepreneurs told me that after the shock of the constitutional abolition of term limits, they felt that they no longer had any protection from various forms of expropriation by the center. (This was the lesson that some of them took away from the last-minute canceling of the Ant Financial IPO by central regulators in 2020.)

To many members of the urban middle class, the abolition of presidential term limits is a retrograde move, out of sync with China's modernization. Chinese urban public-opinion surveys conducted online since 2018 indicate that people are not happy about the constitutional revision.[84] But, as one academic explained about the surprising ease with which Xi accomplished it, "the middle class in China wasn't big enough [to stop it]." Still, once Xi revealed his intention to cling to power, he put a target on his back, risking pushback from disgruntled politicians. Chinese officials value term limits and retirement rules as protection against a leader who otherwise might wreck their careers at any time.

The political atmosphere in the lead-up to the 2022 20th Party Congress, where Xi is expected to claim a third term, has therefore been tense. As political scientist Milan Svolik has observed, "The ladder to ultimate power becomes more slippery as the dictator advances to the top."[85] The more repressive Xi's regime becomes, the more reluctant he will be to leave the throne because he has made too many enemies. His cult of personality could snap back against him. In 2012, the political elite was ready to embrace a stronger leader, but not one who aspired to make himself an object of worship.

No one dares any longer to talk publicly about Deng's warnings against "overconcentration of power." The latest official chronicle on the major events in Party history, published in 2021, is the same word for word as the one that preceded it in 2011, except that its summary of Deng's famous 1980 speech on the "Reform of the Leadership System" omits the key phrases about "excessive concentration of power, paternalism, and lifelong tenure" of leaders. This omission indicates an awareness that Deng's admonition could provide a focal point for elite opposition.[86] Still, no rival leader has emerged to lead the resistance, and the odds against a successful elite rebellion are high. Xi packed the Party bodies with his followers, directly controls all the instruments of coercion and surveillance of the elite, and remains popular with the public.

The COVID-19 Crisis

For years, Chinese political experts have told me that it would take a national crisis such as a financial crash or an epidemic like SARS to trigger a revolt against the increasingly dictatorial Xi Jinping. In January and February of 2020, at the beginnings of the COVID-19 pandemic, it looked as if that crisis moment had arrived. A tidal wave of anger against Xi and the regime surged in Wuhan, where the virus first appeared and then the anger inundated the nation on the Internet. The local authorities had suppressed information that could have prevented people from getting sick and dying from the disease. Eight whistle-blowers who tried to spread word about the virus to other health professionals were detained and forced to sign confessions of "rumor-mongering."[87] One of them, a thirty-five-year-old ophthalmologist named Dr. Li Wenliang, became a martyr to the cause of freedom of speech when he died of COVID in early February after police interrogation and admonition. Giving an interview to *Caixin* magazine from his hospital bed, he said, "I think there should be more than one voice in a healthy society, and I don't approve of using public power for excessive interference."[88] Outraged and grieving Wuhan citizens brought flowers to Dr. Li's hospital and banged pans out their windows, joined virtually by millions of netizens. The Internet was only very lightly censored during that early period when the system was in disarray.[89] As an excited Chinese businessman told me at the time, "It's an online version of Tiananmen."

Local officials evaded responsibility by suppressing information about the COVID-19 epidemic during its early phase, just as they had during the 2003 SARS epidemic. Information about the outbreak of the virus from an internally circulated notification was leaked on December 31, 2019, but officials played down the dangers for most of January. Hubei provincial leaders were intent on avoiding any disruption of the annual meetings of their People's Congress and Consultative Congress on January 11–16; Wuhan health authorities did not report a single new case between January 6 and January 16. On January 19, the Wuhan government went ahead with a massive holiday banquet for forty thousand families, despite the looming health disaster.

It wasn't until January 20, 2020, that people in Wuhan and elsewhere learned the crucial information that the virus could be transmitted between people and that it had already infected medical workers. Dr. Zhong Nanshan, the highly respected respiratory medicine expert who had dared to challenge official assurances seventeen years earlier during the SARS epidemic, made the revelation in a press briefing and televised interview. Dr. Zhong, who is eighty-four, still served as an adviser to national health authorities. Having traveled by train to inspect the situation in Wuhan personally, he advised people not to travel in or out of the city. Officials locked down the city and province two days later, but only after about five million of Wuhan's fourteen million people had left the city to return to their family homes for the Spring Festival holiday. In a television interview on January 27, the mayor of Wuhan, lambasted online by angry critics, offered to resign for not revealing information about the virus "in a timely manner." But he also tried to pass the buck to the central government, explaining that the country's infectious-disease-prevention law permitted local governments to publicly report information only after it had been approved by the State Council.[90] Soon after, the Party bosses of Hubei and Wuhan were fired and replaced by officials who were close to Xi; the Wuhan mayor also was moved to a less important post. But in contrast to the SARS crisis, when Hu Jintao fired the minister of health, no central official was held responsible for the spread of COVID-19.

China's central Party-state, including Xi Jinping himself, may have been complicit in the cover-up, which helps explain why they have been so extremely defensive in its aftermath. The findings of the scientists and national health officials about the human transmission of COVID-19 based on clinical data from Wuhan were available to the leadership after the first week in January 2020 (and were published in *The Lancet* on January 24), while the Chinese public remained in the dark.[91] The central authorities informed the World Health Organization (December 31) and the US Centers for Disease Control (January 3) about the virus. A secret meeting of health authorities on January 14 determined that the risk of transmission was high, but still no one warned the public.[92] Beijing's delay in providing crucial life-saving information to the public may have been caused by its decision to wait until after millions of migrants returned to their homes for the Spring Festival holiday and unburdened the coastal cities.[93] Another possible reason, suggested by a Chinese academic, was the leadership's priority on finalizing its trade deal with the United States.

The central authorities directed labs that were sequencing samples from Wuhan patients not to publish any information about the disease and to either destroy the samples or transfer them to specially designated institutions. However, the Fudan University scientist who was the first to sequence the new coronavirus defied Beijing and on January 10 authorized his Australian collaborator to post the data on the global virology website, a daring move that saved many lives throughout the world by greatly accelerating the international effort to develop tests, vaccines, and therapies for the virus.[94]

Immediately after Dr. Zhong's January 20 statements about the virulence of the virus, Xi spoke in public about it for the first time. Once he called on the Party to "use all resources to prevent and control the disease," the entire regime mobilized with impressive decisiveness to contain its spread, including initiating a complete lockdown of Wuhan and the rest of Hubei's sixty million people, banning interprovincial and international travel, and isolating those who contracted the disease.

The CCP provided the organizational backbone for the massive national effort, thereby vindicating Xi's efforts to strengthen Party discipline and extend the Party's tentacles to every facet of governance and society. Party members and cadres, along with employees of state companies and institutions, joined local residence committees to conduct in-person surveillance and contact tracing, enforce home quarantines, drive patients to the hospital, and deliver food and supplies to households. The heroic actions of Party members who exposed themselves to contagion to protect people inspired an uptick in applications to join the Party.[95] As the CCP was achieving complete control of the pandemic, America lost control of it, and the Trump administration scapegoated China for originating the virus and allowing it to spread throughout the world. The attacks from the United States and the contrast between the effectiveness of the two systems in preventing deaths from the disease boosted the Chinese public's trust in their government.[96]

Xi's own actions, however, were less than heroic. In an apparent effort to avoid being blamed for a catastrophe if the management of the epidemic failed, he put other leaders out in front and retreated into the background. Premier Li Keqiang was put in charge of the coronavirus leading small group established on January 26, with Wang Huning, the ideology and propaganda head, as vice chairman. Sun Chunlan, the vice premier for health, education, and culture, was the only public health official in the small group whose concerns were weighted toward propaganda, security, and foreign policy. Publicity videos and photographs of Politburo Standing Committee meetings emphasized its collective responsibility for managing the epidemic. Premier Li and Sun Chunlan visited Wuhan to see the situation on the ground.

During January 2020, Xi stepped out of the public eye and speculation about why continues. The likely reasons are that he had underestimated the severity of the health crisis or was seeking to reduce his exposure to blame. He traveled to neighboring Myanmar and Yunnan province. Li Keqiang, not Xi, was the first leader to visit Wuhan. When Xi re-emerged on January 21, emergency Standing Committee meetings began to be televised for the first time, emphasizing the collective responsibility of the leadership group. Xi made his first appearance on the front lines of the virus fight, visiting several Beijing communities on February 10, 2020.[97]

During this period, Xi may have been worried about criticism from the public and other political figures for abdicating his leadership during the public health crisis. On February 4, as the PRC ambassador, Cui Tiankai, was about to speak at the UC San Diego's Forum on US-China Relations, a young Chinese man in the audience stood up and shouted, "Xi Jinping, step down!" University security personnel escorted the man out of the auditorium. The ambassador proceeded to give his speech.

An unusual article published in *Qiushi*, the CCP ideological journal, on February 15 looked like an effort by Xi to present evidence that he had been completely in charge of managing the crisis from the beginning, but it also implicated him in the failure to provide life-saving information to the public.[98] The article consisted of a defensive speech Xi had supposedly given to the Politburo on February 3, in which he provided a timeline of his actions beginning with a forceful speech to a January 7 meeting of the Politburo Standing Committee. Of course, the question is, If he had by then recognized the severity of the health threat, why did he wait two weeks to warn Chinese citizens? A joint study by scientists in China, the United Kingdom, and the United States estimated that there would have been 86 percent fewer cases in China had the lockdown measures been enforced two weeks earlier.[99]

After mid-February, Xi made sure that no one could question whether he was in charge. On February 23, in a massive video conference, he gave direct orders to 170,000 officials and provided the official narrative for the pandemic: "The effectiveness of the prevention and control work has once again showed the significant advantages of the leadership of the Communist Party of China and the socialist system with Chinese characteristics."

By spring 2020, Xi's position looked stronger than ever. Chinese people rallied around their leader and the line that Xi's version of Leninist socialism had proved its superiority over market democracy. Paradoxically, the COVID crisis—and the Trump administration's blaming China for it—appeared to have smoothed Xi Jinping's path to a third term. But the political controversy over Xi Jinping's management of COVID flared up again during 2022 when the more contagious but less lethal Omicron strain overwhelmed the Zero-COVID system that was personally attributed to Xi.

8

Going to Extremes

WHEN XI JINPING TOOK command in 2012, some of us anticipated that he might turn foreign policy in a more conciliatory direction by centralizing the policy process and curbing the scrum of interest groups that had characterized Hu Jintao's oligarchy. Xi's personal authority was, and is, more than sufficient to restrain the various groups that had been promoting their own interests by overreaching under Hu's collective leadership.

But Xi Jinping is more ambitious for China's global power than Hu, and more willing to take risks to achieve it. Because he rules like a dictator, he is paranoid about challenges from rival politicians, wealthy private citizens, and social groups. And he appears to have concluded that he can boost domestic support for himself by mobilizing nationalism and demanding deference from other countries. Under Xi, China's "strategic prudence was significantly reduced," as a Chinese foreign policy expert has put it.[1] "Xi Jinping is proud of his hardline posture toward China's rivals, big and small, and is keenly aware of the domestic popular support for his stance."[2]

Xi aspires for China to be respected as a global leader—a "world class" power equal to or surpassing the United States. However, his domestic insecurities mix with his international ambitions and lead him to take bellicose actions that diminish China's global standing. In 2013, a year after assuming leadership, Xi dusted off plans that had been on the shelf for years for constructing those artificial islands on top of the reefs China claims in the Spratly Islands in the South China Sea and ordered them built immediately. Although Xi pledged to President Obama that he wouldn't militarize the artificial islands, the PLA proceeded to build runways and missile installations, and more, on the islands. The *Study Times*, an authoritative publication of the Communist Party, credited Xi for personally making the decision on "building islands, consolidating the reefs, and setting up the city of Sansha to govern the South China Sea." The publication also said Xi had personally decided to set up an air defense identification zone (ADIZ) over the East China Sea, where Beijing and Tokyo both claim the uninhabited Diaoyu/Senkaku Islands, a move that alarmed Japan and the United States.[3] Xi's eagerness to showcase Putin's support for him by issuing a joint statement before the Beijing 2022 Winter Olympics trapped China into tacitly endorsing the Russian invasion of Ukraine.

With the centralized power he has amassed, all the credit or the blame for these actions can be directly attributed to Xi's choices. Absolute power brings with it absolute responsibility, after all. And one of the main consequences of Xi's choices is that China's international behavior has triggered defensive reactions. Global opinion is more suspicious of China than ever before.[4] A loose American-led coalition of Asian and European countries is forming to counter China. And despite the magnetic attraction of China's giant market, foreign direct investment to China as a share of its GDP has declined over the past decade.[5] In 2022, as China sided with Russia in its war in Ukraine and persisted in its extreme approach to managing the COVID-19 epidemic, overseas investors showed their diminishing confidence in Xi's leadership by dumping Chinese equities and bonds.[6]

Some of Xi's most provocative steps have involved subduing the country's peripheral regions. Beijing imposed totalitarian controls over Xinjiang and extinguished Hong Kong's political freedoms, and then punished any foreign company or government that denounced these actions as human rights abuses. The forced re-education camps in Xinjiang and the National Security Law imposed on Hong Kong evoked comparisons to Germany in 1933 or Russia under Stalin. "A country that oppresses its own people rarely stops there," as vice president Mike Pence put it in a speech.[7]

Under Xi, the Chinese government's arm-twisting of foreign countries has reached new extremes. As mentioned, it cut off almost all imports from Australia after Canberra called for an international investigation into the origins of COVID-19. Merely questioning China's handling of the virus had become a diplomatic taboo. China's so-called wolf warrior diplomacy has become reflexive. Instead of moderating its actions and exploring practical steps to improve relations with the new Biden administration, China picked fights, not just with the US, but with India, Australia, and the Philippines; it ramped up military activities on the doorsteps of Japan and Taiwan; and it exchanged tit-for-tat sanctions over Xinjiang and Hong Kong with the United States and Europe.

By narrowing his circle of trusted advisers and darkening the veil of secrecy around his decision-making, Xi has made it hard to comprehend his true intent or predict his next moves.[8] His confronting of other countries, even when it harms China's reputation or economy, has cowed other politicians into not challenging him. As my graduate adviser Lucian Pye observed many years ago, policy debates in China serve a symbolic function, demonstrating the relative strength of different political factions.[9] Elites can infer from a policy, particularly if it doesn't clearly benefit the country, how dominant the faction promoting it is. A Chinese foreign policy expert observed this phenomenon in Xi's China: "Domestic politics determines foreign relations. The decisions aren't strategic. Foreign policy is a kind of performance by the leader."[10] One senior Chinese financial official speculated that Xi might be modeling his truculent behavior on former president Donald Trump, who acted unilaterally without heeding foreign reactions. "If an American president can do it, why can't I do it too?" Putin is another role model for Xi, he suggested. Xi sees that Western sanctions haven't inhibited Russia's aggression and expects the same will be true for China.

Yet Xi insists that he seeks cooperation. The government says that it seeks win-win outcomes, and it rejects the American notion of "competition" as a fig leaf for America's "unilateral bullying."[11] From the platform at the World Economic Forum in Davos and at other high-profile international gatherings, Xi defends globalization, open trade, and free markets,[12] contrasting Chinese policy with American protectionism. When the Biden administration activated the grouping of the so-called Quad (Japan, the United States, Australia, and India) as a counterweight to China, Xi contrasted China's "true multilateralism" with American attempts to "form small circles on geopolitical grounds."[13] Less than a day after the Australia, United Kingdom, and United States (AUKUS) partners announced a defense agreement to offset the China threat by providing nuclear-powered submarines to Australia, Beijing countered by showcasing its commitment to economic globalization by formally applying to join the Comprehensive and Progressive Agreement for Trans-Pacific Partnership, a regional trade agreement that requires high standards of intellectual property, labor rights, and market liberalization, from which the Trump administration had withdrawn.

Like previous Chinese leaders, Xi craves an international reputation as a responsible power and fears China's being ostracized as a rogue power like North Korea. But it is becoming increasingly awkward for him to sustain the straddle between his rhetoric and behavior.

Bandwagoning

Although many ascribe China's overreach to Xi Jinping's character, it is actually the structure of his dictatorial system that is responsible. Under his regime, loyalty to the leader and the Party has become the sine qua non of a successful official career. As I have noted, any hint of disloyalty could doom one's hopes for promotion and invite accusations of corruption and violation of Party discipline.

As they strive for advancement, officials at every level, from the Politburo Standing Committee to cities and counties, are incentivized to jump on the Xi bandwagon as early as possible to get an edge on other competitors. You earn recognition by lavishing praise on the leader and quoting his wisdom in your speeches and writings, as national security adviser Yang Jiechi did in an article on Xi's diplomatic innovations published early in Xi's first term.[14] You also win by staying alert to early cues of the leader's intentions, so as to move in that direction at the head of the pack. Subordinates overdo what they believe the leader wants, going overboard to show how keen they are to realize the leader's wishes. This can propel policy toward a more extreme version than what Xi himself may have wanted.

To avoid irritating Xi, no one dares tell him about the harmful consequences of his policies. There are no information feedback loops in the system. A Chinese general advised Americans against bringing up Xi's 2015 pledge not to militarize the artificial islands in the South China Sea. A group of Chinese policy advisers told me that they would be reluctant to report negative information—such as about the multinational firms that are frustrated about doing business with the Chinese—up the chain to the leadership because it might reflect badly on them. Foreign policy experts recently said that although they were aware of the international backlash against China's wolf warrior diplomacy, they were unwilling to criticize it internally. The best they can do is to call for China to exercise more restraint and "master the art of looking at itself from the rest of the world's perspective," as one of them put it, in English-language publications that attract less notice in Beijing.[15]

Xi's censorship further constricts the flow of accurate information to him. Behind the Great Firewall, decision-makers as well as public audiences are starved of objective information about external reactions to Chinese policies. Government agencies presumably still gather intelligence from abroad, but without the open reporting in public media that feeds honest information into the policy process in more pluralistic countries.

Xi Jinping Concentrates Power

The bandwagoning follows the way in which Xi Jinping has consolidated his power. International relations theorists have offered predictions about what behavior might result from various kinds of authoritarian regimes. Jack Snyder suggests that centralized leadership at the top, such as that in the Soviet Union for much of its history, can restrain interest groups from hijacking foreign policy in dangerous directions.[16] Yet he also argues that autocracies dominated by a single leader get themselves into fights because "everything hinges on a single, unpredictable personality" and "there is no political counterweight to correct whatever strategic myths the leader may happen to believe in."[17] Another scholar, Jessica Weeks, agrees that centralized regimes are more prone to fighting wars because they are less constrained by other politicians who weigh the costs and benefits of using force and can remove the top leader.[18] Deng Xiaoping made a similar argument about the mistakes that get made when there is an overconcentration of power at the top.

Xi started off his first term by disciplining the unruly bureaucracies that Hu had failed to rein in and taking personal control of the military and the internal security forces, to both protect himself from coups and strengthen his grip on foreign and domestic policy. He closed gaps and improved bureaucratic coordination by consolidating agencies, putting government agencies under CCP leading small groups and commissions, and drafting laws empowering central authority. In the early days, he was still surrounded by followers of former leaders Hu Jintao and Jiang Zemin in the Standing Committee and Politburo, and he sometimes used his enhanced control to moderate China's foreign policy to reassure the United States and China's Asian neighbors. According to Evan Medeiros, who managed Asia policy at the US National Security Council from 2009 to 2015, Xi initially came across as a more engaged and substantive leader than Hu, willing to cooperate with the Obama administration on climate change, North Korea, and Iran, although also potentially more of a risk taker.[19]

In a demonstration of his authority, as well as his appreciation of the value of solid relations with the United States, Xi told Obama at their first encounter in 2013 that he had ordered the PLA to stop canceling meetings with the US military to show its objections to US policies. At their 2015 summit in Washington, Xi publicly pledged not to "pursue militarization" of the Spratly Islands in the South China Sea and to stop cyberhacking American businesses to steal commercial and technical secrets. The first promise demonstrated his authority over the PLA, and the second helped him centralize control over the multitude of public and private hackers in China. Furthermore, in 2016, Xi overcame bureaucratic resistance to join with Obama to commit to slashing CO_2 and greenhouse-gas emissions and to join the UN Paris Climate Change Agreement.

As Xi has consolidated his power, however, he has increasingly used it to enact more extreme versions of policies begun under Hu. Domestically, media and Internet censorship and the controls over nongovernmental organizations and universities have tightened. The state is steering the economy and directing its high-tech import-substitution industrial policy more than ever before, frustrating foreign businesses and alarming governments. Propaganda to sell a positive China story to the outside world is crossing the line between public diplomacy and disinformation. China's "core interests" keep expanding.

Taking Command

Xi Jinping's consolidation started with establishing himself as commander in chief of the PLA—in sharp contrast to Hu Jintao's diffidence toward the military. Xi appeared in uniform to address PLA units.[20] And his message to them—that they must enhance their "real combat awareness" and "be able to fight and win battles"—played to their professional pride as soldiers.[21]

I've noted that Xi devoted much of his time and energy during his first term to the reform of the People's Liberation Army—purging corrupt officers, restoring its ideological commitment to the CCP, restructuring its organization, improving its warfighting abilities, and turning the PLA into an instrument of his personal will. He devoted more energy to military reform than to economic reform. A strong military was vital for Xi to realize his international ambitions. The more capable the military, the more difficult—and essential—for an autocrat to make himself coup-proof by guaranteeing its loyalty to him. Xi sought to thread the needle by doing both: beefing up the military's capabilities "to fight and win wars," as he put it, and at the same time deepening its commitment to the Party and the leader. In the speech in 2013 in which he drew lessons from the collapse of communism in the Soviet Union, he made clear his view that regime survival depends on the military's defense of the Party. "When Yeltsin stood on a tank and addressed the crowd, the army was completely indifferent and preserved its 'neutrality,'" as he put it.[22] The "neutrality" doomed the Soviet Union. To guarantee the military's absolute loyalty to him, Xi arrested and imprisoned for life Hu's generals, Xu Caihou and Guo Boxiong, and purged of over a hundred senior PLA officers, thereby creating openings in the upper ranks he could fill with his own supporters.[23]

Then in 2015, Xi initiated the most ambitious, wide-reaching, and important restructuring of the PLA since 1949.[24] The four general departments in charge of operations, political work, logistics, and armaments, whose leaders had often acted on their own and were prone to corruption, were eliminated, giving Xi direct control. To enhance the PLA's capability to conduct joint operations involving different services, essential for a modern military, the seven military regions were replaced by five theater commands. The army, air force, navy, and rocket forces are now operationally directed by the theater commanders, and administratively report to their service headquarters in Beijing.

By 2015, Xi was sufficiently confident of his control over the PLA to reduce the rate of the annual budget increases from a peak of 20 percent during the Hu Jintao era to less than 10 percent.[25] A large chunk of Hu's increased spending on defense had gone to improving officers' and soldiers' living conditions,[26] and some of it ended up in the pockets of corrupt officers in the responsible departments. As the new commander in chief, Xi called on the army to tighten its belts, embrace a frugal lifestyle, curb rampant corruption, and "spend money on the blade."[27]

Xi also is reviving the spirit of the early days of the Mao era when top political figures also served as military commanders. Xi often appears in the PLA's new green digital camouflage military uniform (without any rank insignia) and has assumed the operational title of commander in chief of the Joint Battle Command as well as chairman of the Central Military Commission. One American expert argues that Xi's battle-ready garb and title, in addition to signaling to the PLA his intention to exercise close control over the military, sends a "signal to the wider society and his rivals within the regime that he can and will use force to counter domestic challenges." Another US expert has a different take, viewing Xi's adoption of the uniform as a form of "overcompensation" that signifies "the weakness and dysfunction of the Chinese system."[28]

Xi's consolidation of operational control over the PLA was not without hiccups. Early in his first term, the PLA seems to have gotten out ahead of their commander in chief and spoiled his efforts to improve relations with China's Asian neighbors. At the "Peripheral Diplomatic Work Conference," held in October 2013, Xi had stressed that "the good neighbor policy must be the guiding star for China's behavior toward neighboring countries" if China were to achieve a peaceful rise.[29] Xi was looking forward to hosting the Asia-Pacific Economic Cooperation (APEC) Leaders' Summit in Beijing in November 2014. In May 2014, however, China moved a huge deep-sea oil rig, protected by a flotilla of a hundred fishing militia boats, as well as civil and naval vessels, into waters also claimed by Vietnam near the Paracel Islands. The PLA Navy South Sea Fleet had most likely coordinated the operation;[30] the China National Oil Company, which owned the platform, had originally declined to deploy it because its expectations of the oil reserves in the exploration area were low.[31]

Moving the oil rig so close to Vietnam led to clashes between ships of the two countries and three days of violent anti-Chinese protests in Vietnam. The Vietnamese minister of defense made repeated efforts to speak with his Chinese counterparts, but Beijing didn't respond.[32] The vice director of the Foreign Affairs Leading Small Group then called foreign policy experts together to discuss the situation. When they told him that the oil rig's presence had sparked anti-Chinese riots that might topple Vietnam's communist government, the official asked, "Was the decision a mistake then?" The participants agreed that it was. And shortly afterward, the rig was moved, a month ahead of schedule, as the CCP International Department led a process of diplomatic de-escalation with Hanoi.

The oil-rig fiasco produced multiple losses to China's national interests. The anti-Chinese riots had occurred during a Vietnamese Central Committee meeting that was debating a closer alignment with the United States. The clash also raised the possibility that Vietnam might take legal action against China through UN Commission of the Law of the Sea (UNCLOS) arbitration. The whole affair had evoked sharp criticism of China from the US and Europe, and a rare consensus statement by the ASEAN foreign ministers.[33]

The second PLA-led mistake involved Xi's fence-mending visit to India in September 2014, which was disrupted by the intrusion of a thousand PLA soldiers in Southern Ladakh, one of the contested regions along the Sino-Indian border. Xi and Prime Minister Modi were about to toast one another at the welcome banquet when the news reached the delegation. Modi asked Xi to call off his troops, which he did, but not before the incident had destroyed any possibility of a bilateral agreement; the two sides issued separate communiqués instead. Shortly after Xi had returned home, the PLA chiefs of staff were called to a Sunday meeting to address "inefficiencies" in the chain of command and ensure that "all PLA forces should follow the instructions of President Xi Jinping."[34]

Coast Guard Superpower

In addition to reforming the PLA according to his vision and purpose, Xi has unified China's civilian maritime agencies and built the largest Coast Guard in the world. The goal is to use the civil maritime forces in a way that is more controllable than the military and still use them as an instrument of national power.[35] The ultimate goal, of course, is to help China assert its sovereignty rights (*weiquan*).

In 2012 and 2013, I helped organize two US-China dialogues about maritime safety. Four of China's nine "dragons," so called because of their capabilities to enforce maritime claims—China Marine Surveillance (under the Ministry of Land's State Oceanic Administration), China Fisheries Law Enforcement (Ministry of Agriculture), the Border Defense Coast Guard (Ministry of Public Security), and the Anti-Smuggling Police of the General Administration of Customs—were unified into a centrally commanded China Coast Guard.[36] Before Xi, China's multiple maritime agencies had been administered by a patchwork of provincial and local governments and the central government. In addition to their traditional missions related to safety, border control, environmental protection, and law enforcement at sea, they were playing the leading role in China's "grey zone" operations to stake out and defend China's maritime sovereignty claims. As I've noted elsewhere, Beijing relied on the civilian cutters rather than the PLA Navy to patrol its claims in the East China and South China Seas to avoid escalating encounters with other countries into military incidents; their white hulls look tamer but still signal resolve. The agencies were enjoying bigger budgets and larger cutters, some of them hand-me-downs from the navy, and some new ships. The Chinese officers participating in our conferences were excited about the new equipment.

However, like all bureaucrats, these officers were jittery about the prospect of a merger, concerned about their status and career security. As they discussed their plans for a unified Coast Guard, it was obvious that they intended to model their organization on the US Coast Guard. They wanted to arm their ships, but as a PLA general had told me in a separate interview, the PLA Navy was jealously protective of its own privileges and opposed this.[37] The retired American Coast Guard generals at our meeting explained that their cutters were equipped with small arms mainly because the Coast Guard is the first line of defense against the gangs of drug smugglers operating at sea. China might not need them.

Today, a decade later, the Chinese Coast Guard is the largest in the world in terms of number of ships and tonnage. It has 130 ships, with a displacement of a thousand tons or more, twice what Japan has.[38] It also directs a large fishing militia. Previously under civilian command, the Coast Guard has become part of China's armed forces, and the Navy has abandoned its objections to arming it. In March 2018, it was transferred to the paramilitary People's Armed Police, which itself had been transferred only three months before from the joint command of the Ministry of Public Security and the Central Military Commission to be entirely under the Military Commission.

As of April 2021, a new Chinese Coast Guard Law authorizes China's fleets to use lethal force against foreign ships operating in "maritime areas under Chinese jurisdiction" and the airspace above them, including the disputed waters claimed by China and others.[39] This expansive assertion of Chinese domestic law over territory that may belong to other countries under the UN Convention on the Law of the Sea disturbs Japan and other Chinese neighbors.

National Security State

As his revamping of the military and Coast Guard shows, Xi Jinping has transformed China from a developmental state in which economic growth is the source of its popular support into a national security state.[40] Xi views the security environment China confronts today as much less benign than the "favorable conditions for overall stability" that Hu Jintao described in his valedictory to the Party Congress in 2012.[41] Xi's view is darker and more conspiratorial, emphasizing the linkages between internal and external threats and seeing "hostile foreign forces" lurking around every corner. His speeches repeat the refrain of "struggle" (*douzheng*), a notion with Cultural Revolution resonances. Every autocrat feels insecure because his legitimacy doesn't rest on a firm constitutional foundation. Xi's efforts to achieve his global ambitions and eliminate rivals at home have made him more enemies than other autocrats, which makes him even more insecure.

The centerpiece of Xi's drive to build a national security state is the National Security Commission (NSC), a Party coordinating body reporting directly to the Politburo Standing Committee and chaired by Xi. The Commission's composition is secret, but it is believed to include both military and civilian agencies. The NSC was established at the end of the Jiang Zemin administration but met only rarely. It played a role in helping Hu Jintao, then vice president, manage the collision, in 2001, of a PLA fighter jet and the US EP3 spy plane when Jiang Zemin was out of the country on a Latin America trip. At that time, however, it was just another sign outside the office of the Foreign Affairs Leading Small Group.

Xi's version of the NSC, according to Chinese policy advisers, focuses more on domestic security problems than international ones, a reflection of Xi's own priorities. Cai Qi, a politician who had worked with Xi in Zhejiang and Fujian and had no foreign affairs background, was made the deputy director of the NSC office and, a few years later, helicoptered into the Standing Committee as Party secretary of Beijing. The NSC meets infrequently—a meeting held in March–April 2020, shortly before the announcement of the new national security law in Hong Kong, was reportedly only the third since 2018.[42] The sprawling and competitive nature of the multiple bureaucracies in the Chinese security state makes it doubtful that the NSC operates as an effective platform for policy coordination. The NSC is more accurately serving, as one foreign scholar has put it, as "a personalistic symbol of Xi's command of the national security state."[43]

In Xi's national security state, the Foreign Ministry has lost power over foreign policy. Wang Yi, the foreign minister and state councilor, parrots Xi's views instead of saying what he actually believes, according to people who have known him for years. "The foreign ministry doesn't make policy, it only makes statements," one international relations expert said. "If they [were to] acknowledge problems in China's relations with other countries, they would have to decide who made the mistake."

Sovereignty Comes First

Xi Jinping has owned the maritime security portfolio ever since serving as vice president and vice chair of the Central Military Commission, hence before taking full power in 2012. To better prevent the "nine dragons" from "stirring up the sea," that is, working at cross-purposes, the CCP formed the Maritime Rights Protection Leading Small Group with Xi as chair in 2012; and as they improved coordination, they converged on a more aggressive strategy. As we've seen, Xi resuscitated two ideas for expanding China's sovereignty that the PLA had proposed but Hu Jintao rejected as destabilizing—an air defense identification zone over the space between China and Japan and construction of those artificial islands on top of the rocks in the part of the South China Sea controlled by China.

As I've argued, improving bureaucratic interaction from the top down could have helped Xi exercise restraint, precisely to avoid provoking China's Asian neighbors and the United States. Instead, Xi has used the new efficiency to take risks designed to bolster his domestic standing as a defender of China's nationalist honor. One PLA Navy officer explained that "the leaders have made a clear choice, an adjustment in their policy" related to maritime issues. He further explained the ultimate goals are, first, sovereignty and, second, stability. By stability, he means maintaining good relations with China's Asian neighbors and the United States. The officer had written an article in a Singapore newspaper advocating a balance between stability and sovereignty. "I couldn't advocate putting stability ahead of sovereignty," he admitted to me, "it would attract a lot of criticism." His point was that the leadership feels that to survive public pressure it must assert Chinese sovereignty. He recounted a joke: "We should start a war over the Diaoyu Islands; we will either win the islands or win a new China." More seriously, he added, "sovereignty is now the top priority over stability."[44] Stability was fine, to a point. But given that China is on the path to becoming a maritime power, as one Chinese academic put it, "we must consider both rights protection and stability maintenance."[45]

Some of China's most respected international relations experts disagree with Xi's high-profile pursuit of sovereignty over stability.[46] In their view, China's priority should be to maintain good relationships with regional neighbors and the United States to secure their support for China's rise. It would be a "strategic mistake," they argue, to attain sovereignty in the South China Sea but lose the whole of Southeast Asia. Starting in 2012, the annual report on the Asia-Pacific from the Chinese Academy of Social Sciences acknowledged that China's neighboring countries feel "uneasy" about China.[47] China has been losing soft power, particularly with Southeast Asians, because of its unyielding drive to enforce its narrowly self-interested sovereignty claims. The Asian Barometer Survey conducted from 2014 to 2016 shows a drop in positive perceptions of China's impact in the region compared to the wave it conducted from 2010 to 2012 in Malaysia, Singapore, the Philippines, Vietnam, Taiwan, Japan, and Mongolia.[48]

Diversionary Brinksmanship

Xi Jinping's first maritime crisis involved the Diaoyu-Senkaku Islands, and started in September 2012, before he formally assumed the posts of CCP general secretary and chairman of the Central Military Commission. As vice president and successor-in-waiting, Xi chaired the Maritime Rights Defense Leading Small Group and was in charge of China's response when the Japanese government took ownership of three of the islands, which Japan administers but China also claims.[49] The Japanese government bought the islands from a private owner to prevent Shintaro Ishihara, the right-wing populist governor of Tokyo, from purchasing them. Ishihara had raised the idea of buying the islands in a speech he gave in Washington, which suggested to some Chinese that the American government could be behind the move. To further complicate the situation, this was the moment of the Bo Xilai crisis and scandal. Bo and his wife had been arrested just weeks before the Party Congress that was expected to elevate Xi.

Xi Jinping diverted public attention from the Bo drama by dispatching, with a great flurry of publicity, civilian government ships and planes to challenge Japan's control of the islands. He also encouraged the large anti-Japanese protests that broke out in 320 Chinese cities.[50] Because the annual fishing ban around the islands had just ended, the television cameras were able to capture dramatic footage of a flotilla of one thousand fishing boats heading for the islands. In accordance with the UN Convention on the Law of the Sea, Beijing also announced its own baselines around the islands. The Chinese censors blocked publications that might have calmed the Chinese public by explaining that the Japanese government was trying to keep the islands out of the hands of Tokyo's nationalist governor.

Talk of war was in the air in September 2012. The *Beijing Evening News* made a callously flippant suggestion on its Weibo account that China drop a nuclear bomb on Japan.[51] Many believed that the Japanese government's action to change the status quo justified China's moves to break Japan's hold on the islands, a form of jujitsu that one foreign expert called "reactive assertiveness."[52] A senior foreign ministry official explained the Chinese tactics to me: "This is what we did with India and Vietnam, we hit them but then pulled back and didn't try to achieve the whole thing. It worked; the result was fifty years of peace along the borders of Vietnam and India."

Theories about the political motivations behind Beijing's extreme reactions were everywhere. One academic compared Xi's thinking to Deng Xiaoping's when he attacked Vietnam in 1979. It's "not so much diversionary war as trying to bolster authority," he said. Another floated the possibility that Hu Jintao might have created the crisis to stay on as head of the Central Military Commission after retiring from Party leadership, just as Jiang Zemin had done to manage the Taiwan crisis. Chinese artist Ai Weiwei tweeted that anti-Japan protests may have been orchestrated to save the seat of the internal security boss (Zhou Yongkang) on the Standing Committee."[53]

But the dominant theory was, and remains, that Xi Jinping was engaged in "diversionary brinksmanship" to navigate the power struggle that had erupted into the open on the eve of his leadership transition. Hu had been personally humiliated when Japan announced the purchase just two days after he had asked Prime Minister Noda not to do it.[54] Xi could show that he was a much stronger leader by forcing Japan to acknowledge that sovereignty over the islands was disputed, something that the Japanese had up till then refused to do.[55] As one Chinese expert on Japan noted, "Xi was a provincial leader who didn't know much about foreign policy. He became the leader during a crisis with Japan." This enabled him to gain control of the PLA. One foreign policy scholar compared Xi's "touchiness" toward Japan with that of Jiang Zemin: "Xi could be as anti-Japanese as Jiang, but not because of war memories like Jiang had but because he wants to use it to rally support."

The anti-Japanese protests, which were larger than any seen before—more than two million people on one weekend according to the vice foreign minister—had been engineered from above. The official media was very bellicose; censorship was light; and politicians, from the five top Standing Committee members on down, made tough public statements. Xi, meeting with US secretary of defense Leon Panetta at the time, called the Japanese purchase of the islands a "farce."[56] Even the outgoing premier, Wen Jiabao, not known for being an outspoken nationalist, vowed that China would "never yield an inch."[57] The Foreign Ministry, Defense Ministry, National People's Congress, national student union, women's association, and lawyers' association all issued belligerent statements. The vice minister of commerce held a press conference to praise the boycott of Japanese goods.

Though they wanted to show support for the staunch defense of China's "core interests," the PLA and the Foreign Ministry seemed confused about whether that loaded term should be applied to the Diaoyu Islands. When General Martin Dempsey, the chairman of the US Joint Chiefs of Staff, visited China in April 2013, he informed the press that Chinese officers had repeatedly told him that the Diaoyu-Senkakus were "one of China's core interests."[58] A few days later, the Foreign Ministry spokeswoman said from the podium, "The Diaoyu Islands are about sovereignty and territorial integrity. Of course, it's China's core interest."[59] This suggested that China was following the playbook that it had used in the lead-up to its short wars against India (1962) and Vietnam (1979).[60] However, the Foreign Ministry changed the written transcript of the spokeswoman's statement to something much less definitive. It quotes China's white paper on Peaceful

Development, which states that "China would resolutely safeguard the country's core interests, including national sovereignty, national security, and territorial integrity. The Diaoyu Islands issue involves China's territorial integrity."[61]

College students, who had dominated previous nationalist protests, were a minority in the 2012 ones. The students at Beijing University, Tsinghua, and Fudan whom I encountered in my visits to their universities at the time were not fired up over the Japanese government's acquisition of the islands; some of them understood that Tokyo's action was designed to keep the islands out of the hands of a firebrand mayor. A Beijing University professor explained that students didn't want to be used. When the Beijing University student union wrote a strong letter to Prime Minister Noda, some students objected. A PLA Navy officer offered another reason why students at the elite schools were calm: "Sixty percent of the students at these schools are from rich families, are not dissatisfied with the government, and are benefiting from current policies, so of course they weren't motivated to protest." Those who protested were blue-collar workers, he added. The white-collar people knew that Japan was not repeating its 1930s behavior. Some of the protestors held signs criticizing domestic policy failures such as inadequate protection of food safety and official corruption and land-grabbing.[62] Others were expressing their discontent on Weibo social media, saying that the *chengguan*, the despised city street patrols that local governments hired to enforce regulations, should be sent to Diaoyu. One Chinese journalist observed the police managing the protests and encouraging people to join in so long as they kept aiming their complaints at Japan, and not toward the Chinese government.[63]

Quite a few demonstrators carried portraits of Mao and placards with Maoist slogans. According to one professor, some were using the protest to further a Maoist agenda. Several believed that the organizers were promoting Bo Xilai's political salvation. Not all the people carrying Mao's picture were Leftists, according to a PLA Naval officer. "They wanted to make the point that China needs a strong leader, and today's leaders are too weak."

The protests and the extensive television coverage of the Chinese fishing boats and law enforcement cutters rushing to the islands may have boosted Xi's popularity as he started his reign, but they were a diplomatic disaster. Japan did not roll back its purchase of the islands or acknowledge that the administration of the islands was in dispute. Just as detrimental to China, the US government strengthened its commitment to defend the islands as part of its treaty with Japan, a pledge that President Obama restated when

he visited Japan two years later. The patrols by Chinese maritime law enforcement ships and planes into the islands' territorial (12 nautical miles)
and contiguous (up to 200 nautical miles) space continue to this day; there
was a slight drop in frequency in 2014 but another surge in 2020.[64] The
pressure of the incursions has motivated Japan to upgrade its Coast Guard
to narrow the gap with China's much larger Coast Guard; Japanese public
opinion of China has never recovered.

After the Diaoyu-Senkaku crisis, the risk of an unintended miscalculation or incident between China and Japan significantly increased.[65] The
crisis management talks between the two Coast Guards have been incon-
clusive. Neither side would back down. "China can't agree on the old
consensus of shelving the dispute, which would mean it would withdraw
from the islands," one expert explained, "and Japan can't accept having
both sides withdraw." When the Chinese Nobel Prize–winning novelist
Mo Yan suggested that both sides withdraw and turn the area into an environmental reserve, no one in China criticized him, noted the expert.
A cynical Chinese journalist explained why Xi might be glad not to settle
the controversy: "Diaoyu Islands is a long-term hot button for politicians,
and they want to keep it."

A Great Wall in the Sky

A little over a year later, on November 23, 2013, China's Defense Ministry
declared an air defense identification zone in the East China Sea, one
that overlapped with the zones the US military had drawn after World
War II and during the Korean War, which had been taken over by South
Korea, Japan, and Taiwan. Dai Bingguo, Hu Jintao's top foreign policy
adviser, who served until 2013, had tried to block the proposed ADIZ, but
Xi overruled him. Without conferring with any of its neighbors, China
unilaterally declared a large zone covering more than two-thirds of the
East China Sea, which included the Diaoyu-Senkaku Islands and areas
where the US Air Force trains with its Japanese allies. Rules that require
foreign aircraft to report their flight plans and identify themselves or else
face "defensive emergency measures" from China's armed forces went
into effect on the day they were announced.[66] The Foreign Ministry wasn't
even consulted.[67] The CCP Central Party School newspaper *Study Times*
later credited Xi with the decision.[68] The idea of a "Great Wall in the Sky"
had been proposed by the commander of the PLA Air Force in 2009, but
the Hu administration never picked it up.[69]

The Pentagon stated that the Chinese announcement wouldn't change how the United States conducted military operations and sent two B-52 bombers from Guam to put a point to the declaration. Japan and South Korea flew their own military jets through the zone without informing Beijing beforehand. The State Department advised US airlines to avoid danger by following the ADIZ rules, and Taiwan and Korea followed suit. Japan advised its two largest airline carriers not to file flight plans with China.[70]

The Chinese military did not enforce the ADIZ, and the US and its allies continue to fly military and civilian jets through the area without identifying themselves. The ADIZ was an act of bluster—tough sounding and vague—that increased public approval of the Xi government.[71] It also most likely won Xi fans within the PLA. But it was self-defeating diplomatically, further estranging the US and Asian countries.

Sitting Out the International Tribunal

In 2016, as governments awaited the judgment of the UNCLOS tribunal on China's claims in the South China Sea that the Philippines had initiated in 2013, the Obama administration fretted that Beijing might declare an ADIZ over the South China Sea if the tribunal decided against China. Secretary of State John Kerry warned the Chinese leadership that the US government would view a South China Sea ADIZ as "a provocative and destabilizing act."[72]

The Philippine government's move to arbitration had been prompted by its increasing frustration at its inability to deter Chinese attempts to push Filipinos off the coral shoals that they had previously controlled. China had pulled a fast one at Scarborough Shoal—blocking Filipino fishermen after promising to withdraw, as we've seen—and was harassing the Philippine vessels as they were provisioning another outpost (a wrecked warship that it hadn't towed away) at Second Thomas Shoal. Manila sought recourse through the mandatory arbitration process that UNCLOS had established. Although the court lacks the authority to rule on who owns the land features (reefs, atolls, and islands) in the South China Sea, it can determine what rights the features are entitled to. The Chinese government tried to convince Manila to suspend the arbitration case by promising to withdraw from Scarborough Shoal and to invest more money in the Philippines, but it had kept the pressure on by positioning its Coast Guard at the Second Thomas Shoal outpost. The

Philippine cabinet rejected Beijing's offer saying the deal was "not credible or 'enough'" and submitted its case to arbitration.[73]

One of the arguments the Chinese government made against recognizing the court's jurisdiction was that another process, related to the negotiation of an ASEAN-China Code of Conduct for the South China Sea, was already underway. The negotiating text of the Code of Conduct, however, didn't do much to reassure the Philippines or other Southeast Asians about China's intentions. China's draft attempted to limit the role of outside countries like the United States; it banned oil and gas prospecting by foreign companies from outside the region and allowed signatories to veto any joint military exercises with outside countries.[74] China and ASEAN have yet to agree on the code.

The Chinese government opted out of the arbitration process, a decision that no one but Xi Jinping himself could have made, according to those I interviewed. However, one person told me that the Politburo Standing Committee had deliberated as well. After listening to the recommendations of nineteen experts, a majority of whom favored nonparticipation, the Standing Committee voted 5 to 4 not to take part. Security chief Zhou Yongkang was strongly against participation, arguing that the public wouldn't condone it if the PRC government didn't do at least as much as Chiang Kai-shek's Republic of China to assert China's sovereignty over islands in the South China Sea.

By declining to participate, China gave up its chance to choose two of the five judges on the tribunal and to formally present its case. The decision to sit on the sidelines proved to have been a major error when, in 2016, the tribunal ruled decisively against China. The judges rejected China's historical rights to the entire sea inside the so-called nine-dash line and denied the legitimacy of the low-elevation land features it controlled, outlawing any exclusive economic zones around them. To defend Xi from criticism, Chinese propaganda maintained that the judges were biased because they had been chosen by the Japanese judge who was the president of the tribunal at the time. The Philippines "hired the judges," a PRC ambassador asserted.[75] The propaganda campaign in China discredited international law for years to come. The Chinese Foreign Ministry warned the Philippines and other claimants never to try to negotiate based on the ruling, or even to mention it.[76] Even now, Chinese diplomats refuse to discuss the ruling.

Island Building

As we've seen, under Xi, China has rapidly been building out those large artificial islands on seven small rocks it controlled in the Spratly area of the

South China Sea and constructing runways and other military facilities on them to fortify its territorial claims. Other claimants have built runways and military installations on their land features too. But no one else has built such massive islands in such record time.

The speed and scale of the reclamation effort raised international alarms about Beijing's intentions to control the entire South China Sea. Satellite photographs of the construction sites became front-page news.[77] The dramatic images had a greater effect than a newspaper article. US defense secretary Ashton Carter, in 2015, criticized China's actions and asserted that under international law, low-elevation features that have been artificially built out have no territorial waters or exclusive economic zones of their own; to reinforce the point, an American guided-missile destroyer sailed within 12 nautical miles of the islands, which, as noted, remains the conventional limit for territorial waters. However, the Obama White House, seeking to be nonprovocative, directed the Pentagon not to say anything publicly about the "freedom of navigation operations," as the Navy calls them.[78]

The actual military value of the installations on the new islands is debatable. Some defense experts argue that they expand China's ability to project force to Indonesia and beyond. The artificial island bases are "major gamechangers in any future Sino-US conflict," according to them.[79] Other experts see the bases on artificial islands as sitting ducks, easily targeted for attack during a conflict.[80]

In any case, though Xi's decisions to fortify China's presence may have been costly to China's international reputation, they appealed to the interest groups behind China's drive to solidify its control over the South China Sea. The PLA had long advocated extending its reach by building artificial islands and military bases on top of China's reefs, and state companies, such as the China Communications Construction Company, did the dredging and construction. Hainan province was the prime beneficiary of Xi's decision in July 2012 to set up Sansha, a prefecture-level city located on Woody Island, to strengthen China's administrative control of the more than 280 islands, shoals, reefs, and rocks and the surrounding seas in the entire South China Sea. Two district governments, one for the Paracels and one for the Spratlys, were created in April 2020.[81] Sansha is the largest city in the world, governing 800,000 square miles, most of it under salt water.

Punishing South Korea

All Xi Jinping's assertive decisions have taken a toll. Such was the case with his overreaction to South Korea's July 2016 decision to deploy the US

Army's THAAD (Terminal High-Altitude Area Defense) ballistic missile defense system against the growing North Korean threat. Xi may have felt misled by previous assurances from South Korean leaders that they did not intend to deploy the system anytime soon, or he may have been swayed by PLA analysts who told him that the US radars built into THAAD would give the United States a clear view of China's nuclear weapons. In any case, he immediately declared internally that THAAD must not happen, according to accounts from several Chinese defense specialists. The military, government agencies, and the nationalist media fell into line to carry out Xi's order. The Chinese military declined to accept a briefing on the system offered by the Americans. To strong-arm Seoul to reverse its decision, the Chinese government instead began an economic boycott of South Korean products and services.

But ordinary Chinese, who, by and large, are positively inclined toward South Korea, hadn't called for the boycott; it was imposed top-down, even if the government never officially acknowledged it. The construction of a new Lotte department store in Shenyang was halted, Korean video games and TV shows were banned, and trips to South Korea by Chinese tourist groups were canceled. Sales of Hyundai and Kia automobiles in China plummeted. By 2017, China's economic retaliation had cost the country $880 million, but it cost the Korean economy much more, $7.5 billion.[82]

The consequences went beyond economics. Chinese diplomats view good relations with Seoul as the linchpin for preventing two Cold War–style blocs in Northeast Asia. Nonetheless, Xi was determined to teach the South Koreans the lesson that they shouldn't integrate their defenses with the United States.

THAAD was, in the words of one former Korean diplomat, an "eye-opening event" that shattered South Korea's "naïve and romantic views" of China.[83] South Korea's newly inaugurated president, Moon Jae-in, who had opposed the THAAD system during his campaign, succumbed to Chinese economic pressure to a certain extent. The two foreign ministries negotiated a rapprochement based on Seoul's promise not to join the US missile defense system, participate in US-Japan-ROK trilateral military cooperation, or make additional THAAD deployments.[84]

Nevertheless, Korea remains bitter toward China. Economic pressure from Beijing—the boycott was formally ended but the effects linger—has made the Korean public increasingly anti-China. A 2021 survey shows that the Korean public feels more negative about China than it does about its historical enemy, Japan; South Korea is the only nation surveyed by the Pew Research Center in which young people have more unfavorable views toward China than the older generations.[85] Yoon Suk-yeol won the March 2022 presidential election by running on a "tough on China" platform.

Hedging on North Korea

Xi's feelings of fraternal solidarity with other communist countries make him more tolerant of North Korea. Under pressure from Washington to tighten economic sanctions on the Kim Jongun regime, Xi has carried out most of the UN sanctions but refuses to go beyond them. North Korea's economy depends on trade with China to stay afloat; China is the country's largest provider of oil.

Many Chinese have come to view North Korea as a serious threat to China, especially those living in Northeastern China, who are vulnerable to the seismic shocks and nuclear fallout from North Korean tests; they are ready to completely cut off the Kim regime. Kim has shown no solicitude for China; in 2017, he went so far as to assassinate his brother, who had been living in Macao, presumably under the protection of the Chinese government. The affront may have led Beijing to ban coal, iron, iron ore, and seafood imports from North Korea for the rest of that year, its strongest sanction against Pyongyang ever. Yet Xi seems reluctant to abandon his support of the Kim regime, perhaps because he considers the US military presence in the Western Pacific to be more threatening to China than any potential threat from North Korea. When President Trump was in the limelight for engaging in personal diplomacy with Kim Jong-un, Xi injected himself into the dynamic in a flurry of five visits with Kim in 2018 and 2019, staged to show that "any moves on North Korea must go through Xi," as the *Washington Post* reported.[86]

The North Korea issue is intertwined with China's domestic politics. Some say that Xi and other Party and PLA officials want to avoid squeezing North Korea so tightly that the Kim regime collapses because then there will be one less communist country in the world, making the CCP more vulnerable to domestic challenges. One leading Chinese foreign policy expert even suggested that the fall of the North Korean regime could bring Chinese people out on the street to celebrate and embolden them to rise up against the Chinese Communist Party.

One Belt One Road

In May 2017, with great fanfare, Beijing launched an international forum on the One Belt One Road (*yidai yilu*) strategy, a megaproject that aims to expand China's global sway by providing loans to countries in Asia, Europe, and Africa for building railroads, roads, ports, and energy infrastructure that links them with China. (The English but not the Chinese name was later changed to the Belt and Road Initiative to sound more innocuous.) Topiary in the shapes of camels and bridges, red banners displaying slogans about shared connectivity and shared prosperity, and big video screens with maps charting the history and future vision of the Silk Road were designed to excite the national pride of the Chinese public as it welcomed twenty-nine heads of state and government representatives from more than a hundred countries. Chinese taxpayers, much like American ones, were dubious, wondering why their government should spend so much money to help other countries when the needs at home remain so acute.

The Belt and Road Initiative, or BRI, already written into the Communist Party's constitution, is best seen as a projection of Xi's personal power. Like an imposing city hall or civic center in a Chinese city, it has become a prestige project that involves spending (and borrowing) extravagantly to elevate the influence of China and the reputation of its leader. As of 2021, 140 countries had signed memoranda of understanding to join the Initiative.[87]

The BRI exemplifies Xi's foreign policy style: a grand vision encapsulated in a grandiose slogan, and bureaucrats, regional officials, and company executives rallying behind it to prove their loyalty to the leader. The BRI is a "loose portfolio of disparate projects."[88] There are no official figures on the total amount of money China has loaned to other countries to finance these projects; for one thing, there is no clear definition of what distinguishes a BRI project from any other form of Chinese outbound investment or aid. Nor is there a central coordinating bureaucracy for the BRI; it is led by a small office in the National Development and Reform Commission, the agency that has broad responsibilities over the economy. Many of the projects are initiated by local authorities, a July 2020 article in the *South China Morning Post* reported, "to demonstrate their support for the central government and because Belt and Road projects open doors for new funding from banks."[89] Firms often rebrand their existing activities as BRI projects to signal the loyalty of the company's leaders—and to gain state funds. State-owned enterprises are the main investment partners behind the BRI; private firms lead state ones in total amount invested abroad but are more cautious about the commercial risks involved.[90] BRI projects, in short, have a stronger political rationale than a commercial one.

Ideas about reviving the trade and infrastructure links along the traditional Silk Road through Central Asia had been floated for years, including by Hu Jintao and American officials. In 2011, the United States proposed a New Silk Road initiative that would help Afghanistan integrate into the region by reviving traditional trading routes and reconstructing broken infrastructure links.[91] Hu, in his 2009 speech on China's grand strategy, had called on China to strengthen economic diplomacy with the Asian countries along its periphery.[92] Rising powers have historically pursued their ambitions through grand infrastructure projects: Germany's Berlin–Baghdad railway, Britain's Suez Canal, and the United States' Panama Canal.[93] As Ross Doshi notes, these projects not only facilitate trade and connectivity; they are a form of "economic power projection" designed to "reshape the strategic geography of great power competition.[94] Among other things, the BRI has helped turn China into the world's largest lender to developing countries.

The story behind Xi's determination to launch the BRI began as soon as he took power. In 2012, Chinese international relations scholar Wang Jisi wrote an article suggesting that China might avoid direct confrontation with the United States in maritime Asia by orienting its foreign policy westward toward Central Asia.[95] But when Xi, during a visit to Kazakhstan in September 2013, suddenly proposed the idea of an economic belt along the Silk Road,[96] Chinese Foreign Ministry diplomats had to scramble to figure out what the leader wanted and fill in the gaps between reality and his vision. Since then, the BRI has been promoted much as a mass campaign from the Mao era—with everyone rushing to link themselves to the leader's wishes and adopting a "one size fits all" (*yi dao qie*) approach. To those of us who remember the Potemkin-style models during Mao's rule, such as the Dazhai agricultural brigade and the Daqing Oil Field, the BRI campaign looks similarly impractical. But every region in China has rushed to get a piece of the action and show its devotion to the cause. Scholars at every think tank and university—including many in Europe and some in the United States—were generously funded to carry out research to laud BRI.

Although it became a useful platform for China to increase its international influence, the BRI has provoked a public backlash from many of the recipient countries and runs the risk of disappointing others, particularly should economic and financial pressures inside China make it impossible for Beijing to follow through on its extravagant promises. In recipient countries that hold elections, the incumbents' chummy relationship with China often becomes an election issue that challengers use to ride into office.

To a great degree, the Sinocentric nature of the BRI stands in contrast to efforts by the Asian Infrastructure Investment Bank, established by China in 2016, which governs itself as a multilateral financial institution. The United Kingdom was one of its first members. Its mission is to finance infrastructure "with sustainability at its core." Today it has 103 members and is capitalized at $100 billion. Bank head Jin Liqun told me that the bank has shown China's "sincerity for cooperation" by "getting the international community involved." In contrast, the BRI is a Chinese platform reflecting "China's exclusive interests."

A comparison between the Hu administration's "going out strategy" and Xi's BRI is emblematic of the differences between collective leadership and personalistic dictatorship. Hu's policies encouraged Chinese companies to invest abroad with a focus on supplying China's rapidly growing economy with energy resources and other minerals from Africa, Latin America, and Asia, which then expanded to investing in agriculture, manufacturing, and technology. What one Chinese historian has called the "haphazard and uncoordinated actions" of the mostly state firms that lacked knowledge about the world—their "bad behavior" included corruption, environmental harm, and mistreatment of labor—tarnished China's international image, but there was little the Foreign Ministry could do to improve it.[97]

Xi's Belt and Road Initiative is a far more ambitious version of Hu's plan to have Chinese development banks and other state banks provide loans to other countries to fund physical infrastructure construction. In effect, China is exporting its post–global financial crisis model of infrastructure-investment-led growth to other countries.

Beijing also promotes trade with the BRI countries via free trade zones and a commercial diaspora of Chinese migrants who are networked by Chinese cloud computing and other Internet services. For example, telecommunications infrastructure built by Huawei and other companies helps to spread Chinese technology standards. Indeed, telecommunications infrastructure is becoming a building block of Chinese influence that is arguably even more significant than that of physical infrastructure. People-to-people ties follow BRI linkages: the numbers of students from BRI countries increased eightfold between 2004 and 2016 and they now make up 61 percent of foreign students on Chinese government scholarships.[98] On the legal front, China has established two international commercial courts, in Xian and Shenzhen, to settle disputes between Chinese and foreign parties transacting as part of the BRI; the judges are all Chinese, however, raising questions about the impartiality of these courts.[99]

The BRI has become Xi Jinping's brand, a rubric that now includes the "Digital Silk Road," the "Belt and Road Space Information Corridor," the "Health Silk Road," and the "Green Belt and Road." BRI slogans stress the benevolence of China's vision of "build[ing] a community with a shared future for the betterment of all mankind." Non-Chinese skeptics wonder about the real motives behind what looks more like a Sinocentric project with strategic intent, reminiscent of the Qing dynasty relations between China and its surrounding tributary states or the Japanese Co-prosperity Sphere in the run-up to World War II. They point out China's self-interest in offloading overcapacity in polluting industries to overseas construction and in substituting BRI markets for American ones as a hedge against American sanctions. They view the BRI as Chinese neocolonialism aimed at pulling countries into China's orbit and away from America's.

These skeptics also suspect that Chinese investments in port construction are a step toward building overseas military bases, despite the PLA's claims that it has no such intentions. In particular, the BRI port projects that fail commercially (examples include Sri Lanka's Hambantota and Pakistan's Gwadar, neither of which has ever operated to capacity) are suspected to have dual civil-military use. China has so far established one overseas military facility, the Djibouti Logistic Support Facility, located at a trade chokepoint in the strait linking the Indian Ocean with the Suez Canal.

Predictably, China will want its military to be able to protect its overseas businesses and citizens. Approximately 40,000 Chinese firms have offices in foreign countries; China's overseas properties and investments are estimated to be $7 trillion; and the number of Chinese citizens living abroad has grown to more than 5.5 million.[100] China's overseas activities are also concentrated in countries that are vulnerable to terrorism and other dangers. Therefore, BRI projects are likely to adopt what two scholars have called a "first civilian, later military framework" that "seeks to lay the groundwork for military utilization without raising red flags or inviting resistance."[101]

One of the main targets of BRI's critics is the so-called debt trap by which China entices developing countries to borrow funds to build a port or a railroad, contingent on agreeing to sign away the property rights to China if they can't afford to repay the loan. Chinese loans forbid borrowers from revealing the terms and include informal collateral arrangements that benefit Chinese lenders over other creditors. The lack of transparency in China's overseas contracts, like its domestic secrecy, gives rise to suspicions that something untoward is being hidden. The AidData research lab at the College of William & Mary analyzed Chinese lending to overseas development projects implemented between 2000 and 2021 and found $385 billion of "hidden debt." This is "off the books" debt that the recipient government still owes to China; in forty-two of these countries such debt exceeds 10 percent of GDP.[102]

Xi's geopolitical ambition to expand Chinese influence Westward and the state banks and companies allied to that effort don't add up to good economic returns. Overland railroads to Europe through Central Asia can't compete with sea and air trade. The burden of sustaining the projects then falls on China.[103] The Chinese government often finds itself having to renegotiate the financial terms of its contracts to benefit the borrower as much as the lender;[104] China restructures the debt by extending the repayment period or changing the interest rate.[105] In 2018 the newly elected Malaysian prime minister, Mahathir Mohamad, who had campaigned against the "unfair" Chinese deal for construction of the East Coast Rail Link, was able to bargain down the cost to a third of the original price tag.

International controversies over the opaqueness and inequities of BRI contracts and China's own domestic belt-tightening have caused it in recent years to try to limit its overseas lending to more financially sustainable projects. Investment in BRI projects peaked in 2015 at $125 billion, and has leveled off since.[106] In response to international criticism, Xi has toned down the rhetoric to make China look less selfish and more benevolent, stressing "the principles of extensive consultation, joint contribution, and shared benefits," as well as green development.[107] In the aftermath of the COVID-19 pandemic, China also is participating in multilateral debt-relief negotiations for the first time, joining the G-20 countries in providing relief for African countries struggling with economic downturn.[108]

Influence Operations

Under Xi Jinping, the Chinese government and Communist Party are investing heavily to spread a positive narrative about the virtues of China's system throughout the world. As Xi put it at the start of his reign in 2012, the goal of external propaganda is to "tell China's story well."[109] But perversely, Xi's style of winning friends and influencing people has alienated many countries. The CCP's campaign to shore up its legitimacy at home by burnishing its image and winning approval for pursuing its "core interests" overseas has backfired.

Following Xi's lead, Party officials have overdone their efforts to influence public opinion in foreign countries, so that today China's "sharp power," as the US National Endowment for Democracy put it, referring to activities that "pierce, penetrate, or perforate the information and political environments in the targeted countries," has become one of the biggest irritants in relations with these countries.[110] China has gone far beyond what the West calls "public diplomacy"—the government communicating and influencing public audiences in other countries to further its soft power and foreign-policy objectives. It is no longer satisfied with just a government-run global television network, paid supplements in foreign newspapers, and patriotic demonstrations by Chinese students.[111] The CCP has become adept at using Twitter, Facebook, and other social media that are banned in China to spread praise of China and disparagement of the United States outside China's borders. The Internet propaganda officials in China enlist volunteers and paid young patriots, called the "50 cent army" or "little pinks," to attack foreign critics.

The incessant complaining by Chinese netizens that their feelings are being hurt by the words of people outside China has also backfired. Beijing comes across not as a confident rising power, but, as one writer has put it, as a "frowning, finger-pointing, never-erring crank."[112] "Fragile" (*boli xin*), written by a Malaysian songwriter and sung by a Chinese-Australian singer, satirizes these oversensitive netizens in a catchy rap song in which Taiwan apologizes for hurting the feelings of mainlanders. The video of the song went viral in Asia, garnering 30 million views, making it at the time the most viewed YouTube music video in Hong Kong and Taiwan.[113]

Beyond propagandizing, the Party's United Front organizations recruit an international corps of influencers—cheerleaders in politics, society, business, and education—targeting overseas Chinese in particular (as we'll see) and intruding into domestic politics in ways that other countries have found objectionable.

The goals of the Party's overseas propaganda and United Front work are largely defensive, and intended to shore up one-Party rule at home.[114] Without external legitimation, internal legitimation comes much harder. Beijing suppresses criticism of China's domestic practices, portrays its actions in a positive light, and twists the arms of foreign governments and organizations to take China's side on sensitive issues, such as Taiwan, Xinjiang, and Hong Kong. The primary purpose of the Party's influence operations is to improve its image rather than to subvert democracy, as Russia tries to do, or to spread authoritarianism to other countries. There is no evidence that China has illegally interfered in US elections.[115] Yet under Xi, China wants approval of its system from the outside.[116]

Australia and New Zealand were the test bed for Beijing's interference in domestic politics by making campaign contributions, creating front organizations, and intimidating media organizations and their advertisers.[117]

Australian prime minister Malcolm Turnbull was the first national leader to sound an alarm over Beijing's "covert, coercive, or corrupting" influence activities, and he introduced legislation that would ban foreign political contributions.[118] Controversies about these influence operations have made the Australian public deeply suspicious of China. In 2021, 94 percent of Australians saw foreign (Chinese) interference in its politics as a threat to the country's vital interests.[119]

What many people find most pernicious about China's influence operations is that Xi and his foot soldiers threaten and penalize those who speak out against its practices. As the PRC ambassador to Sweden put it bluntly, "We treat our friends with fine wine, but for our enemies we have shotguns."[120] By openly threatening governments and private actors who criticize its behavior China presents itself as a country that would rather be feared than loved. Offending China can be very costly for a government or a business if it means being frozen out of the Chinese market. Consumer-facing businesses such as sportswear, fashion brands, airlines, and hotels are the most vulnerable, caught in the dilemma of keeping quiet or losing sales in China or abroad, or both.

By expanding the redlines of China's "core interests" beyond Taiwan to include Tibet, Xinjiang, Hong Kong, and, most recently, the origins of COVID-19 and the virtues of China's political system, Xi has boxed himself into a corner. Beijing's insults and its treatment of Australia were particularly outrageous after Canberra proposed an international scientific investigation of the origins of COVID-19. In addition to banning most Australian exports, it publicized a list of fourteen areas in which Australia had harmed relations with China; and a Foreign Ministry spokesman tweeted a photoshopped image of an Australian soldier holding a bloody knife next to a child, meant to suggest that Australian soldiers were murdering civilians in Afghanistan. Australia-China relations sank to a nadir, and Australia moved to reinforce defense ties with the United States.

China's intimidation also has chilled the climate of academic freedom in universities. The Ministry of Education cut off fellowships and educational partnerships with universities that hosted the Dalai Lama to speak, denying that it had done so. At some schools, PRC students belonging to the Chinese Students Association are expected to report fellow Chinese students who express heterodox views about Hong Kong, Tibet, or Xinjiang in class to the PRC embassy; local police then threaten their parents in China.[121] Confucius Institutes teach the Mandarin language and Chinese culture but shy away from programs on politically sensitive topics that would embarrass their Ministry of Education sponsors. But when Confucius Institutes became a symbol of Chinese "sharp power," many of them were kicked off American campuses.[122]

Chinese bureaucrats signal loyalty by threatening foreign organizations that deviate from the Party orthodoxy in nomenclature and maps. China's Civil Aviation Administration threatened thirty-six international airlines that deviated from CCP protocols by listing Taiwan as a country on drop-down menus instead of as part of China; most of them complied. The Zara fashion chain apologized for making the same error. Marriott International also apologized after sending a letter to rewards club members asking customers their countries of residence and including Tibet, Hong Kong, Macau, and Taiwan among the options. The Gap clothing chain apologized to China for a selling a T-shirt featuring a map of China that left off Taiwan.[123] The Hong Kong Shanghai Banking Corporation (HSBC), Standard Chartered, and other banks that earn a large share of their revenue in Hong Kong complied when China threatened them with a consumer boycott if they didn't publicly endorse Beijing's new security law punishing "separatism, subversion, terrorism and foreign interference" in Hong Kong.[124]

Professional sports are also caught between a rock and a hard place. When the general manager of the Houston Rockets basketball team tweeted, "Fight for freedom, stand with Hong Kong," to support the protestors in 2019, China Central TV banned broadcasts of NBA games for one year, and the Rockets lost their streaming contract with Tencent. American fans then condemned the awkward attempts of NBA officials to smooth things.

Global clothing companies were put in a similarly untenable position over the Xinjiang cotton issue. They stopped using cotton grown there to comply with American sanctions over forced labor of Uighurs and other Muslims. Xinjiang produces more than 20 percent of the world's cotton and 85 percent of China's. Research by foreign NGOs indicated that the Chinese government gave mandatory work assignments to Uighurs and other Muslims who had graduated from the re-education camps to work in cotton fields and factories across China.[125] The large international garment companies H & M and Adidas pledged not to use Xinjiang cotton, and in January 2021, the Trump administration banned the import of Xinjiang cotton and products made with it. Then the Chinese government mobilized a national boycott of the global brands that were boycotting Xinjiang cotton (kicked off by a Weibo tweet from the Communist Youth League),[126] and a patriotic craze boosted the sales of Chinese brands such as Li-Ning and Anta.[127]

The long arm of the censors now reaches beyond China's borders. The General Administration of Press and Publication demanded that the *China Quarterly*, the premier journal in Chinese studies, remove three hundred articles related to the Tiananmen crackdown in 1989, Tibet and Xinjiang, Taiwan, and the Cultural Revolution or face the takedown of its entire website in China. After initially conceding, the publisher, Cambridge University Press, reversed itself after scholars rallied to defend the journal's academic freedom.[128]

Overseas Chinese

Xi Jinping wants the approximately sixty million ethnic Chinese living abroad in more than 180 countries to join the PRC's national team even though over 80 percent of them are citizens of the host countries. Xi is something of an expert on the overseas Chinese (*huaqiao*).[129] He spent seventeen years as an official in Fujian province, the coastal province opposite Taiwan, nicknamed "the hometown of overseas Chinese," because it was the origin of many early migrants. His father, Xi Zhongxun, had led Deng Xiaoping's 1980s drive to attract the capital and managerial expertise of the diaspora to assist the country's economic reforms.

But today, Beijing's approach to the overseas Chinese is very different; attitudes toward Chinese expatriates have changed in one generation, from father to son. Xi now values the ideological commitment of the overseas Chinese and their influence over their host country's policies toward China more than their financial investments. But by trying to turn them into agents of CCP influence, he has aroused suspicion of them in their countries of residence, exacerbating the anti-Chinese bigotry that has historically existed in the United States and other countries. Chinese students, scientists and engineers, and businesspeople who have one foot in each country are mistrusted; during the COVID-19 pandemic they were often harassed and assaulted.

As China moved forward from the mayhem of the Cultural Revolution, it was desperately in need of investment to reboot the economy. In a 1984 speech, Xi Zhongxun estimated that if China could absorb 10 percent of the estimated $200 billion in capital belonging to overseas Chinese, it would boost China's modernization.[130] Deng and Xi senior designed the Special Economic Zones in Guangdong and Fujian to "absorb large quantities of capital from *huaqiao* and other foreign investors."[131] The government also gave preferential treatment to investments on the mainland by Chinese citizens living in Hong Kong, Macao, and Taiwan.

Chinese law limited this preferential treatment to *huaqiao*, Chinese citizens living abroad and not to *huaren*, who had become citizens of other countries, because, as Xi Zhongxun explained, they didn't want to "put them in a dilemma, perplex and discompose their host countries, and create difficulties for their long-term survival there."[132] Since the 1950s, the Chinese government had encouraged ethnic Chinese living in Southeast Asia to be good citizens of the countries where they lived, and eliminated dual citizenship. Given how prosperous the ethnic Chinese communities were in Indonesia, Thailand, Malaysia, and other places, any hint of an ethnic Chinese fifth column would have antagonized those governments.[133]

Hu Jintao was the first leader who, instead of prioritizing the economic contributions of overseas Chinese, stressed their role in making friends overseas[134] and blurred the citizenship boundaries of the two groups by referring to all "Chinese sons and daughters at home and abroad" (*zhonghua er'nu*).[135] Hu also endorsed the *huaqiao* and *huaren* groups that volunteered or were organized by Chinese embassies to defend the overseas parts of the torch relay of the 2008 Beijing Olympics.[136] In enlisting the help of Chinese living abroad, regardless of their citizenship, Hu was also motivated by Beijing's competition with Taiwan. Taiwanese immigrants tended to emigrate to the United States, Canada, and Australia.[137] Hu cultivated relations with overseas Chinese to build, as he put it, a "patriotic united front of overseas compatriots and anti-independence and prounification organizations," focusing on Taiwan but also including Tibet and Xinjiang.[138]

Xi's approach to overseas Chinese is more politically proactive and Party-led than that of his predecessors. In 1995, when Xi was Party secretary of Fuzhou, he wrote an essay calling on overseas Chinese work to "become a major task for the Party."[139] He anticipated that the Party would want to reach out to the second and third generations of Chinese living abroad to strengthen their sense of identification with the PRC and win their hearts away from Taiwan.

Since ascending to power, Xi has been integrating overseas Chinese into his campaign to realize the China Dream: "Realizing the great rejuvenation of the Chinese nation is the common dream of Chinese sons and daughters at home and abroad."[140] To achieve unity he has called for "strengthen[ing] the ideological and political guidance to the overseas Chinese community."[141] The Ministry of Education tries to turn the more than 700,000 PRC students studying abroad into ambassadors for Chinese overseas propaganda.[142] As a result, some foreign governments have begun to see all ethnic Chinese as PRC agents, and it is now harder for Chinese to get visas to Canada and Australia. FBI head Christopher Wray called China a "whole of society threat," implying that ethnic Chinese were spying for Beijing or seeking to subvert America.

As the Party took over and politicized overseas Chinese work, the State Council Overseas Chinese Office, the responsible government organization, was dissolved and most of its responsibilities absorbed by the CCP United Front Department, the Party organization that traditionally focused on ties with non-Party groups inside China.[143] Some of the State Council Office's functions were moved to the Federation of Overseas Chinese, a mass organization for people who have returned from abroad to start companies and make other economic contributions to China. The Federation and the United Front Department are at odds bureaucratically and ideologically. As one official explained in 2018, the Federation's approach is that "overseas Chinese should support their local communities where they live first and promote friendship between their countries and China but not put loyalty to China first." While the United Front Department emphasizes the Sinocentric slogan, "China Dream," the Federation counters with another Xi slogan, aimed at sounding more universalistic, "community of shared destiny for all mankind."

Can China Restrain Itself?

Speaking at the United Nations General Assembly in 1974, Deng Xiaoping considered the possibility that one day China could become a superpower that bullies other countries.[144] It was a fate he wanted to avoid. In the eyes of many abroad, that day has arrived.

Xi Jinping is undoubtedly a far more ambitious leader than his immediate predecessors, Hu Jintao and Jiang Zemin, were. What's more, he is surrounded by yes-men who dare not contradict his vision. Now that Xi is no longer subject to the bureaucratic constraints that Hu and Jiang faced, Chinese foreign policy will be, by and large, whatever he wants it to be.

And what does he want it to be? The political and economic underpinnings of his policies suggest that Xi is taking China down a different path.

Much of Xi's publicly articulated vision of China's role in global affairs sounds positive and reassuring. From the global platform at Davos and at other high-profile international gatherings, he has spoken in defense of globalization, open trade, and free markets. He seeks a bigger role and more influence for China in global governance and has founded new institutions, such as the Asian Infrastructure Investment Bank, to supplement existing ones. He has embraced Western notions of global public goods and win-win relationships and made them the theme of the Belt and Road Initiative. Xi's rhetoric sets a high bar for evaluating Chinese actions.

The problem is that China's actions don't measure up. By strengthening the dictatorial features of the CCP regime, Xi is alienating China from what he disparagingly calls "universal values." And his economic policies are also increasingly divergent from global norms of fair market competition. China's industrial policy and foreign economic policies have become more mercantilistic, and it is using its huge economy to strengthen the power of the state at other countries' expense.

A few years ago, international business and private entrepreneurs had high hopes that Xi would revive the economic reforms and opening policies that had stalled under Hu. In 2013, at Xi's direction, the 3rd plenum of the 18th Central Committee issued an impressive document pledging that the market would play a "decisive role" in resource allocation and reduce the state's role. One of the most significant objectives was to reform the state-owned enterprises by turning them into mixed-ownership corporations in which the state would invest its capital through funds such as Temasek, the global investment company headquartered in Singapore.

Yet, notwithstanding his absolute hold on power, Xi has failed to take tangible steps to realize the 3rd plenum reforms; instead, he has tightened state control of the economy. He appears to believe that because state-owned enterprises are the economic foundation of Communist Party rule, they must be protected. To maintain a moderately high level of growth and avoid the risk of a financial or economic crisis in China's overleveraged system, the Chinese government has been intervening in financial markets instead of liberalizing them. The crashes in the Shanghai stock market and the foreign-currency market in 2015 shattered international confidence in the competence of Beijing's economic management. Private businesses in China are being buffeted by arbitrary government regulations as never before. When Chinese wealth started to flow out of the country, the government imposed strict capital controls.

Top-down, state-led industrial policies and a new commission for integrated military and civilian development (led personally by Xi, of course) reflect his determination to turn China into a high-tech power, a direction originally set by Premier Wen in 2006. China's outbound investment and inbound foreign investment today are governed by policies that reflect the state's priority of becoming the global leader in emerging technologies. Xi is quite comfortable using China's huge market power and deep pockets to suck up advanced technologies from abroad and into China. The aim of achieving self-reliance in semi-conductors, batteries, and other crucially important technologies has become increasingly overt. With the hands of the state so obviously orchestrating this massive effort, it is no wonder that China is provoking a backlash in the United States and Europe.

9

State of Paranoia

Despite the stark differences in the leadership of Xi Jinping and Hu Jintao, there is plenty of continuity in their domestic policies. Both leaders worried about the fragility of CCP rule in a rapidly changing Chinese society and sought to secure it by exerting greater control over social and economic life. Hu Jintao talked about "stability maintenance," and Xi Jinping talks about "comprehensive national security," but both saw the dangers as emanating mainly from domestic problems, though they also cast a suspicious eye on the "malign" international forces. As Xi often observes, the security threats confronting China come from the "increasingly complex" external and internal threats that "are interlocked and can be mutually activated."[1]

However, and this is key, Xi takes the paranoia that is endemic to Chinese politics to an extreme. China is stronger than ever. It has a hugely successful economy, a capable military, and growing global influence. The government enjoys a high level of social support. Yet Xi's fixation on security betrays his persistent feelings of vulnerability. Xi's "overall national security outlook" is more holistic than Hu's, more Party-centered, and more explicitly highlights external threats. Xi established the National Security Commission to focus on domestic security threats and turned the entire system into what one security scholar describes as a "national security state."[2] Another argues that Xi's grand strategy centers around the survival of CCP rule. Rather than being just a "constraint on foreign policy," internal security "is one of the chief ends of China's strategy.[3] No wonder the Xi Politburo has put political security first in its national security strategy for 2021–2025.[4] Security considerations inform every decision. Nearly every phrase in the communique of a Central Committee meeting in October 2020 included the word "security" (*anquan*); the document itself was an illustration of "integrating the development of security into every domain."[5]

Although China's concrete security environment had not drastically deteriorated when Xi came into office, he saw it as "darker and more menacing."[6] Xi sees himself as waging a life-or-death struggle for the survival of Party rule against subversive forces directed by hostile foreign governments and organizations. Xi may be less sanguine than Hu about China's international situation because by 2012, China's belligerent actions already were estranging other countries. And because his responsibility for policymaking is more concentrated than Hu Jintao's—and his decisions more arbitrary—his fears that his political critics are plotting his downfall are also greater.

Xi's moves to suppress domestic threats have often shocked the world in part because they have been so sudden. The revision of the constitution to allow Xi to remain leader for life; the incarceration of a million Muslims in Xinjiang; the imposition of the national security law that almost overnight destroyed Hong Kong's freedoms; the regulatory storm of 2021 against private Internet firms; and the two-month COVID lockdown of Shanghai—all of these actions exceeded the expectations of people inside and outside China. They came as proverbial bolts from the blue because Xi had decided on them with little broader debate or deliberation. Then the combination of Xi's unbridled power and the unquestioning loyalty of the officials behind him propelled policy toward overreach.

President for Life

I have amply discussed the first bolt from the blue—Xi Jinping's suddenly abolishing presidential term limits by revising the constitution in 2017, before the end of his first term. I have to say, however, that it remains one of the most stunningly unexpected events in my decades as a China watcher. I am not alone. His power grab sent shock waves throughout China and abroad.

One Chinese private businessman told me shortly afterward that he felt traumatized by Xi's move. If the provincial leaders, who constituted the largest bloc in the CCP Central Committee, had been unable to prevent Xi from destroying the regular turnover of top leadership, he said, neither would they be able to stop Xi from expropriating private wealth—his own and that of other private businesspeople. The 2021 regulatory storm against private Internet firms seemed a fulfillment of his darkest fears.

Overturning the hard-won rules of succession of power could backfire on Xi. A Leninist party leader who doesn't share power or patronage is bound to frustrate other politicians, especially if no end to the monopoly is in sight. And many of Xi's policy choices are controversial; critiques have appeared online before being erased by the censors.[7] Even after purging large numbers of officials during his first and second terms, Xi can't be fully confident he has the loyalty of the Party elites. As one foreign political scientist observes about Xi's China, "Elite discontent seems to be growing faster than social discontent."[8]

The inquisitors who had helped Xi get rid of potential enemies and consolidate his power in 2012 and 2018 are now themselves the targets of a third wave of purges to help Xi feel safer. As Zbigniew Brzezinski wrote in his classic study of the "permanent purge," after some officials fall "the vacuum thus created is rapidly filled by a realignment of power, and the internal struggle continues between new alliances, new leaders, new pretenders. The purge, in the meantime, has swallowed more victims."[9] It all came full circle when the former minister of justice Fu Zhenghua, a man sometimes called "Xi's muscle," who as Beijing police chief was called in by Xi Jinping to lead the investigation of Zhou Yongkang, was himself arrested for corruption and disciplinary infractions. Another former deputy head of public security, Sun Lijun, considered so reliable that he was sent by Xi to Wuhan after the COVID outbreak, was also arrested. Xi replaced Fu and Sun with two of his more trusted followers, Wang Xiaohong and Chen Yixin, who are likely to be elevated to the Politburo at the 20th Party Congress.

By fall 2021, nearly 180,000 officials working in China's judicial and law enforcement sector and its Party disciplinary departments had been reprimanded or punished for "violating party discipline and the law." Xi's campaign is modeled on the Yan'an rectification campaign of 1942, which was about achieving Mao's goal to "'drive the blade in' and 'scrape poison off the bone,' setting aside personal loyalties to expose wayward colleagues." Chen Yixin, who is heading up the campaign, called for officials within the political and legal system to "root out the harmful members of the herd."[10]

The Fengqiao Model

Xi Jinping's centralized version of social control is far more granular and pervasive—closer to a totalitarian state—than Hu Jintao's fragmented bureaucratic version. The regime has unprecedented capabilities to surveil people and collect and analyze their personal data. The security apparatus has grafted these surveillance technologies onto a system of mutual supervision by neighbors that is reminiscent of the Mao era.

"Pervasive" is the right word. Xi has consolidated all the internal security organizations, including the Central Political and Legal Commission that had been Zhou Yongkang's platform, and placed them under the CCP's Central National Security Commission, a body Xi chairs that holds higher rank than the other leading small groups. He holds in his hands both internal security, considered the "knife handle" of the entire system, and the military, its "gun." To fortify his authority in the security domain, Xi also had the legislature pass laws on national security, cybersecurity, counterterrorism, managing foreign NGOs, and national intelligence. These laws formalize the Party-state's long-standing broad powers over all Chinese citizens; everyone is required to assist in protecting the state's security. The Foreign NGO Law, for example, drove most international NGOs out of China because it required them to be supervised by the Public Security Ministry; as of December 2021, only 631 NGO offices were successfully registered.[11]

Like Hu Jintao, Xi wants to shift social management down to the grassroots to relieve the center's burden, and he has adopted the same slogan: "Small issues don't leave the village, big things don't leave the township, and no conflicts are passed on to higher authorities." Starting with when he became Party secretary of Zhejiang province, in 2002, Xi has been promoting a method developed in a Zhejiang township in 1963 during the Mao era. It is called the Fengqiao Experience, referring to the way this community involved the masses in the struggle against reactionaries, along with the Party and the police. According to Mao, pressure from one's neighbors is more effective than formal enforcement at bringing deviant thinking into line. It is what in CCP lingo is called a "mass line" approach to stability maintenance.

Xi has promoted the Fengqiao model of Party-led social control at the village, township, and community levels and combined it with grid management, which uses surveillance technology on a massive scale.[12] China leads the world in facial-recognition artificial intelligence.[13] The high-tech version of the Fengqiao Experience is supposed to be rolled out nationwide in the years to come. Many Chinese living in apartment communities throughout China welcomed this high-tech social policing system as a force for good during the early stages of the COVID epidemic, but they resented it during the enforced months-long lockdowns during the

Omicron surge. People outside of China also have become more afraid of China as a society in which artificial intelligence technology empowers an Orwellian totalitarian state.

Sinicization of Xinjiang

When Xi Jinping paid his first visit to the Xinjiang-Uighur Autonomous Region as China's leader in May 2014, he had a close brush with terrorism. As the trip was concluding, three people were killed and seventy-nine injured at the railway station in Urumqi by attackers using knives and detonating explosives.[14] The incident followed a March attack on the Kunming station in southern China in which twenty-nine people had died, and it preceded a May attack on the Urumqi vegetable market that killed thirty-one people. An earlier suicide attack in Tiananmen Square in 2013 had reportedly so alarmed Xi that he had focused his full attention on Xinjiang.[15]

Upon returning to Beijing in 2014, Xi addressed a leadership conference to set a new policy direction for Xinjiang and its Muslim population. His speech presaged the formation of massive re-education camps and mandatory labor assignments that have aroused such a strong international backlash. Xi said the CCP "must not hesitate" to deal a "crushing blow" against religious extremism; he also said that "unemployed people left to idle about are liable to provoke trouble," whereas work in enterprises is "conducive to ethnic interaction, exchanges and blending." Some of Xi's phrases were repeated later by other officials in Xinjiang, indicating his personal responsibility for the tough line.[16]

In February 2017, at a National Security Council meeting in Beijing that Xi attended the final decision was made to build the re-education camps.[17] Seemingly in the blink of an eye, Xinjiang was transformed into a huge gulag consisting of hundreds of camps. Leaked internal documents reveal that some local officials had doubts about using these draconian measures to make Uighur Muslims embrace Chinese communism.[18] But as one scholar has said about Xi's instructions, "It's an order. You can't resist or object."[19] Satellite images show that many of the camps almost tripled in size between April 2017 and August 2018, growing to a total area roughly the size of 140 soccer fields—a breakneck pace of construction.[20] Security expenditures in Xinjiang leapt from RMB 5.45 billion in 2007 to RMB 30.05 billion in 2016 to RMB 57.95 billion in 2017.[21] The region also built a panopticon of advanced surveillance technologies, including an "integrated joint operations platform" that uses facial recognition and machine learning to analyze data from video cameras, security checkpoints, and other graphic data.[22]

One objective of pacifying Xinjiang was to provide a stable corridor for China's Belt and Road Initiative to countries beset by terrorism.[23] Since the terrorist attacks of September 11, 2001, Chinese leaders have worried greatly about the threat from transnational jihadist networks. Uighur volunteers have fought with ISIS and other jihadist groups, and a few who had been trained by Bin Laden in Afghanistan were captured and sent to Guantanamo. Some believe that the threat from Uighur separatists who are members of international terrorist organizations is what drove Xi to move to collective detention.[24] Others believe that they pose no significant threat.[25]

A more compelling explanation is that Xi decided to overhaul ethnic policy to build "a nation for the state," as one expert has put it.[26] Xinjiang is nothing less than his laboratory for "assertive nation-building and ethnic re-engineering."[27] His goal is to thoroughly erase ethnic and religious identities and replace them with "a shared consciousness of the Chinese nation," a phrase that was written into the Party constitution in 2017.

To fulfill his vision of China's national rejuvenation and stability, Xi has decided to Sinicize ethnic and religious identities instead of tolerating their autonomy, as past Chinese leaders did to varying degrees. The ethnic autonomy model had been adopted from the Soviet Union where, Xi concluded, it helped bring about the USSR's disintegration.[28] He is striving to achieve more of a melting pot not just in Xinjiang but in other regions, including Hong Kong and Inner Mongolia, and with other ethnic and religious groups, as well. In 2018, the State Ethnic Affairs Commission and the State Administration for Religious Affairs, which favored the old-fashioned accommodationist approach to ethnic governance, were downgraded and put under the CCP's United Front Work Department.

In 2020, after parents, students, and regional officials in the Inner Mongolian Autonomous Region protested against Beijing's mandate to eliminate bilingual education and require all teaching to be in Mandarin (Putonghua) beginning in first grade, the central government, relying on the Central Discipline Inspection Commission as its muscle, purged local leaders and undertook an intensive ideological re-education campaign that resembles the one in Xinjiang, though without the incarceration into camps.[29]

Xi has been talking about the "Sinicization of religion" since 2015, when he announced that "religions in China must be Chinese in orientation," aligned with China's culture, political ideology, and Party rule.[30]

The Hui Muslim minority (roughly ten million in number, descendants of Persian traders who intermarried with Han Chinese and consider themselves Chinese) are also being targeted for Sinicization even though they have not received any backing from foreign groups the way the Uighurs and the Mongolians have. A few years ago, I visited Linxia, a Silk Road town in Gansu province famous for its religious toleration, and saw Hui boys studying Arabic in the mosques. Today, children under age eighteen are forbidden to enter the mosques, many of whose domes have been demolished and replaced with Chinese-style roofs.[31] Christians in other Chinese regions are also being Sinicized. Crosses on church steeples have been torn down. Bibles can no longer be sold online, and a project to "promote Chinese Christianity" is "retranslating and annotating" the Bible to find "commonalities with socialism and establish a correct understanding of the text."[32]

Indoctrination for Assimilation

The indoctrination of Muslims in Xinjiang takes a variety of forms. In the last few years, a total of more than one million Han Chinese, told to call themselves "relatives," have been assigned to stay for weeks or even months in the homes of Muslim families to have heart-to-heart talks, do patriotic education, and probe the loyalties of family members.[33]

Boarding schools also aim to instill feelings of loyalty to China and the Party. A Ministry of Education document in 2017 reported that almost 40 percent of all primary and secondary students in Xinjiang, about half a million children, were boarding in schools; many of them had parents in re-education camps. The parents worry that their children are being taught to view them as the enemy.[34]

After Chen Quanguo, the hardline Party secretary in Tibet, was transferred to Xinjiang and promoted to the Politburo in 2016, he led the building of the re-education camps. The facilities resembled prisons, featuring barbed-wire fences, armed guard towers, and locked cells.[35] As many as one million people have been detained in the camps. Local officials were given quotas and lists of the signs that could identify religious extremists who required re-education in the camps, including praying daily, owning a Quran, growing a beard, covering one's head with a headscarf, or abstaining from alcohol and smoking.[36] As a United Nations committee report notes, Muslims are being treated as "enemies of the state solely on the basis of their ethno-religious identity."[37]

Reports from the camps have evoked comparisons to Nazi concentration camps or Stalin's Gulag. US secretaries of state Mike Pompeo and Tony Blinken have both condemned the treatment of detainees in the camps as "genocide." But when twenty-two countries, including the United States, sent a letter to the UN Human Rights Council criticizing the arbitrary detention of Uighurs and other minorities in Xinjiang, China leveraged its economic and political influence to persuade a group of fifty countries, twenty-three of them Islamic-majority states, to back its Xinjiang policies.

Investigations by international human rights groups also found that Muslims imprisoned in the camps or after their release are being forced to work under a government labor-transfer program in Xinjiang and in other provinces. The human rights groups lobbied for international sanctions against Xinjiang officials responsible for the forced labor and mobilized consumers to pressure the companies sourcing cotton clothing in Xinjiang. The US House of Representatives passed into law a measure against forced labor and banning all imports from Xinjiang by a vote of 428 to 1.

China pays an economic price for the disruptions to supply chains caused by these sanctions. But censorship has left most Chinese ignorant of the details of their government's practices in Xinjiang. What they read instead are Beijing's claims that the US government has funded and trained both the Muslim terrorists in Xinjiang and the democracy activists in Hong Kong.[38] Islamophobic rhetoric is frequently expressed on Chinese social media and the censors allow it to stay up for people to read, a form of official approval. Most of the Chinese I've queried about the situation in Xinjiang reply that thanks to the government's detention of Muslim separatists, there haven't been any violent incidents there in years.

The Demise of Hong Kong Autonomy

In 1984, British prime minister Margaret Thatcher signed a joint declaration with Chinese prime minister Zhao Ziyang that transferred sovereignty over its colony of Hong Kong to China as of 1997. The Chinese government committed to a high degree of autonomy for Hong Kong under Deng Xiaoping's principle of "one country, two systems" for fifty years—until 2047. Hong Kong was allowed to retain its independent judiciary, rule of law, and civil and political rights in an unchanged social and economic system; Beijing would control only foreign affairs and defense.

After the 1997 turnover, Hong Kong enjoyed a partial democracy, with free elections for half of the legislative council and a chief executive chosen by a committee of 1,200 elites handpicked by Beijing. The Joint Declaration raised the prospect of direct election of the chief executive and other leaders by one person, one vote starting in 2007.[39]

Hong Kong's quasi-constitution, called the Basic Law, forbade the PRC central government or any unit under it from interfering in its affairs. Although thousands of Hong Kongers had obtained foreign residency in advance of the 1997 turnover because they were fearful of living under communist rule—many were refugees who had escaped from mainland China by swimming out to the colony—their freedoms remained untouched for almost half of the promised fifty years. Large gatherings in Victoria Park commemorated the anniversary of the Tiananmen massacre; and devotees of the Falun Gong spiritual movement, which is banned in mainland China, practiced their exercises in public parks. A required liberal studies course taught high school students critical thinking skills and values, such as rule of law. The professional civil service and the business elite governed capably, although economic inequality and youth unemployment bred some discontent.

As the years went by, Hong Kongers grew impatient to elect more of their representatives, and Chinese leaders became anxious about democratic ideas penetrating the mainland. Still the Hong Kong and the PRC governments tread carefully to accommodate local public opinion. They backed down in 2003, when an attempt to pass a Hong Kong national security act, envisioned by article 23 of the Basic Law, brought out over 350,000 demonstrators. In 2012, the Hong Kong government withdrew a proposed high school political education course because parents and students objected that it was too pro-CCP. The city's legal system was a bulwark against moves by Beijing to abridge its autonomy; in 1999 the Hong Kong Court of Final Appeal found that it had the power to declare "invalid" acts by China's National People's Congress or its Standing Committee that violated the Basic Law.[40]

Beijing kept delaying universal suffrage; in 2007, Hu Jintao put it off until 2017, passing the political hot potato to his successor. Nevertheless, under Beijing's "one country, two systems" guarantees, Hong Kong remained a free society with a semidemocratic political system.

Soon after taking power, Xi shook up the Hong Kong status quo. In a June 2014 white paper on Hong Kong, Beijing, for the first time, claimed "comprehensive jurisdiction" over Hong Kong and proposed political litmus tests for the city's judges. Many were taken aback.[41] According to a former president of the Hong Kong Legislative Council, the white paper was a turning point—from "high degree of autonomy" to "overall jurisdiction," a notion that did not appear in the Basic Law and had never been mentioned by Chinese officials.[42]

In reaction to the white paper, the Hong Kong democratic movement mobilized the public behind the demand to directly elect the chief executive by 2017. It held an unofficial vote on three options for choosing the chief executive, each of which would allow the public to nominate its own candidates (by endorsement from 1 percent of registered voters). The unofficial election gave its citizens the exhilarating experience of voting freely. Seven hundred and thirty thousand people, one-fifth of the registered electorate, voted. Following the informal poll, a large movement consisting of various generations of democracy activists, from older veterans to teenagers, organized a sit-in, calling it "Occupy Central for Love and Peace," that blocked the streets in downtown Hong Kong for two-and-a-half months, demanding direct election of the chief executive. The Beijing authorities condemned it as a "color revolution" instigated by Western governments and nongovernmental organizations. Beijing offered a last-minute compromise of direct election from a list of two to three nominees who would be selected by its handpicked nominating committee, but it was too little, too late, for the Hong Kong democrats.[43]

In 2017, Xi Jinping visited Hong Kong to celebrate the 20th anniversary of the handover. In his speech, he declared that any challenges to the central government's authority in Hong Kong "would cross a red line and will never be permitted." Xi's statement galvanized the city's policymakers to come up with ways to defend that "red line."[44]

Another round of massive protests erupted in 2019 in reaction to an extradition bill proposed by the Hong Kong government that would have allowed the handing over of individuals accused of crimes to face mainland Chinese justice. An estimated one million people marched on June 9, 2019, and continued marching every weekend against the bill that had become a symbol of the threat to Hong Kong autonomy. The demonstrators moved around to different neighborhoods, harassed people from the mainland, occupied several universities, and engaged in violent battles with the police. After Hong Kong's chief executive had conceded by suspending the bill, the protestors kept demonstrating for additional demands, including an inquiry into police brutality. Some of the more radical activists splattered black ink on the red and gold national emblem above the door of the Central Liaison Office, China's representative office in the city, a symbolic insult to the People's Republic that *People's Daily* said crossed the "red line." Some protestors also started calling for Hong Kong independence. The police made many arrests. Yet the November 2019 election of local district councils was won by the pro-democracy candidates in a landslide.

Xi was alarmed by the continuing massive protests and the electoral support for the democrats. He appeared to believe that Hong Kong had become a haven for Western-backed subversion of China. He may have quietly started to formulate a plan.

The Hong Kong Security Law

Democracy supporters in Hong Kong and pro-Beijing loyalists alike were caught by surprise by Xi's decision to bypass the Hong Kong government and enact a PRC law on Hong Kong security, the 2020 Hong Kong National Security Law. They had anticipated a long struggle with the Chinese central government rather than a legal blitzkrieg from it. Xi's 2014 white paper and his speech on "red lines" had been discounted as just "an intimidating political statement." The one Hong Kong member of the National People's Congress Standing Committee said about the Hong Kong Security Law, "I had never imagined that you could use this approach." There was no mainland academic discussion about the possibility of passing such a law, no discussion by officials in the bureaucratic agencies responsible for Hong Kong, and no consultation with Hong Kong elites, civil service, or elected officials.[45]

The National People's Congress Standing Committee passed the law unanimously on June 30, 2020, and it went into effect immediately, even before people were informed of its contents. Separatism, subversion, terrorism, and collusion with foreign powers, including what used to be considered legally protected speech, became crimes under the law with penalties of up to life imprisonment. Most remarkably, the law also applies to people who don't live in Hong Kong, so that, for example, an American scholar who criticizes the CCP's actions from abroad could be arrested when she visits Hong Kong. A new PRC security agency, the Office for Safeguarding National Security of the Central People's Government in the Hong Kong Special Administrative Region, was granted authority to investigate cases and try them on the mainland. The dean of the University of Hong Kong Law School said that not in his "wildest imagination" would he have thought there would be a PRC security agency in Hong Kong answering directly to the Party.[46] As one foreign legal expert has put it, "This is a takeover of Hong Kong, not as billed, a 'second handover.'"[47]

In the two years since the Hong Kong Security Law was passed, political life in Hong Kong has changed dramatically. Political parties and civic organizations have disbanded, some the day after the law went into effect, as many of their members headed into exile to escape imprisonment. Of the 10,500 people who have been arrested for their involvement in the 2019 protests, 2,944 had been prosecuted as of February 2022, and hundreds more remain in prison.[48] Fifty-three leading democratic activists and politicians were arrested on charges of "subversion of state power" under the new law because of their involvement, in July 2020, in an unofficial primary election to select a short list of candidates to avoid splitting the votes and improve the odds of electing a majority in the Legislative Council election; more than 600,000 people had taken part in the primary.

The re-engineering of electoral rules will henceforth prevent pro-democracy candidates from winning a legislative majority or the chief executive position. Of the ninety legislative slots, only twenty are directly elected, and all elected representatives must take a loyalty oath and be vetted for their patriotism; 72 percent of the local district council representatives and candidates either refused to take the required loyalty oath or their oaths were disqualified.[49]

Hong Kong's open society is rapidly closing as it becomes absorbed into the mainland's political culture. The government is deploying ideological indoctrination to erase Hong Kong's separate identity, just as it has been doing in Xinjiang and elsewhere on the mainland. Professional civil servants are being educated about the PRC's political system in mandatory short courses.[50] Students from kindergarten on up must take a new course that reinforces their national identity and teaches them about national security.[51] Academic freedom on university campuses is shrinking as students report faculty to the tip line and some administrators endorse the new law.[52] When the new contemporary art museum M+ opened, the Hong Kong official in charge of it said that all the works it shows must comply with the security law, and forbade some works, including a photograph by Ai Weiwei giving the middle finger in Tiananmen Square, from being displayed.[53] Books seen to violate the security law are being removed from libraries.

Media freedom is in free fall as journalists are prosecuted for colluding with foreigners to endanger national security, publishing a seditious publication, and other political offenses under the new law. The *Apple Daily*, one of Hong Kong's pro-democracy newspapers, was shuttered, its assets frozen, and its founder, Jimmy Lai, and several other of its journalists sent to jail; the police also raided the media outlet *Stand News* and arrested seven editors and former board members.

When the British Parliament complained that China was abrogating Hong Kong's civil rights, which the Joint Declaration had promised to protect for fifty years, the PRC official spokesmen replied that the Joint Declaration was a historical document and no longer in force.[54] Xi felt just as unconstrained by this international treaty as he did by the UN Law of the Sea arbitration decision.

The cost of China's breakneck destruction of freedoms in Hong Kong has been considerable, but Hong Kong has paid a much higher price than China. The White House declared that Hong Kong was no longer sufficiently autonomous to merit the preferential treatment that the United States had extended to it, so it will receive the same treatment, including export controls, tariffs, and visa restrictions, as any other Chinese city. The US also froze the assets of Chinese and Hong Kong officials involved in the Hong Kong crackdown and imposed other penalties, and the EU, UK, and Canada followed with their own sanctions. One of the most significant losses to Hong Kong has been the departure of skilled people; a number of countries are offering safe-haven visas to Hong Kong residents. London has offered Hong Kongers with British National (Overseas) passports (issued to Hong Kong natives who were adults at the time of the 1997 turn-over) and their dependents a six-year pathway to citizenship. Taiwan, Japan, Australia, Canada, and the United States are also considering special programs to take in Hong Kong political refugees.

The 2021 Regulatory Storm

The fourth bolt from the blue was the regulatory storm of 2021, when the state ambushed private companies in a slew of actions that wiped out billions of yuan of their value. Although Xi had appeared to appreciate the importance of the private economy when he was a provincial leader, after moving up to the center, he inclined more toward state control as his political objectives eclipsed his economic ones. "When Xi Jinping came into office," according to one political theorist, "he felt things were out of control. He had to make a fundamental judgment call: will the party have to adapt to the market economy or is the market economy damaging the fundamental interests of the Party? He decided to hold the line against more marketization."

Early in his first term, as I noted previously, Xi had presented an ambitious plan for market-oriented reforms to the Central Committee—it promised that the market would play the "decisive role" in the economy. Nonetheless, to this day most of its commitments haven't been fulfilled.[55] In 2019, I joined a group of foreign CEOs to meet with Premier Li

Keqiang, who tried to reassure these businesspeople that the government's commitment to market reforms and opening was genuine. But most sectors haven't opened to foreign businesses beyond China's original WTO pledges in 2001. The one exception is financial services. In 2019 and 2020 China started allowing foreign ownership of local banks, securities and mutual fund firms, and life insurers and futures-trading houses. The government aimed not just to deepen China's inadequate capital market but also to motivate Wall Street executives to lobby Washington for more friendly policies toward China.

According to one theory, Xi had been supportive of market reforms until 2015, when a stock market crash and an attempt to introduce a market-based mechanism to set the value of China's currency embarrassed him by creating chaos, leading him to conclude that the state needed to be more active in guiding the economy.[56] The central government tried to rebuild investor confidence and stabilize financial markets during that crash and a subsequent one in 2018 by deploying a "national team" consisting of a handful of state-backed financial institutions to make large purchases of Chinese shares (28.8 billion dollars' worth in 2015).[57] Xi prefers to rely on state companies and financial institutions because he can direct them to put a floor under financial markets as well as to support his pet projects like the Belt and Road Initiative, steer the economy, and achieve other non-economic objectives. He's also ordered the Party to penetrate private firms to bring them in line with his goals.

Instead of letting the market drive the economy, Xi has once again put the Chinese Communist Party right in the middle of it. He has strengthened the power of the government and the Party over businesses, with the Party in charge and the government implementing. By politicizing economic policymaking he is putting China's unprecedented economic success at risk. Xi's goals are political (winning a third term and ensuring longevity for the Party), ideological (demonstrating the wisdom of Xi Jinping Thought on Socialism with Chinese Characteristics for the New Era), and security (reducing vulnerability to Western sanctions by achieving technological self-reliance). To attain these goals, he appears willing to tolerate lagging productivity, declining private sector confidence and investment, and loss of stockholder value.

Under Xi the central state also is steering the economy and imposing new demands on private businesses related to data security, antimonopolistic practices, and advancing technological self-reliance and certain social objectives. In the name of what he calls "common prosperity," he demands that wealthy entrepreneurs make charitable contributions to redistribute wealth. He also expects businesspeople to lend their support to his pet projects, such as the new city of Xiong'An, which is being built to relieve overcrowding in Beijing, and the Guangdong–Hong Kong–Macao Greater Bay Area. No matter how often these entrepreneurs profess their political loyalty through their contributions, Xi doubts their sincerity, and he has shown that he is willing to cut them down to size even if that harms the economy.

The flurry of government actions in 2020 and 2021 directed at private tech firms shocked foreign and domestic investors alike. China's digital economy constitutes 38.6 percent of the country's GDP.[58] Xi's policy changes destroyed $1.1 trillion of market value from the stocks of China's six top tech companies alone.[59] The question was why the Xi regime would wound the homegrown Internet tech companies of which it was so proud.

The thunderclap was the decision, reportedly made by Xi himself, to block the $34 billion IPO of the Ant Group, Alibaba's financial affiliate, on the new STAR market in Shanghai and the Hong Kong market just two days before Ant was set to go public. Alibaba had been listed on the New York Stock Exchange since 2014, but Ant's listing inside China was supposed to win it brownie points by showing the company's patriotism.

Alibaba's founder and former CEO, Jack Ma, while addressing a financial forum, had criticized Chinese banking regulators for imposing overly tight controls and offered to help provide the government with innovative solutions to the country's financial problems. Ma's comments embarrassed vice president Wang Qishan and the top financial officials who were in the audience. The securities regulators had approved the IPO for the fintech firm, but the banking regulators had qualms about the risks Ant's microloans created for state-owned banks. After Xi ordered the IPO cancelled, the banking regulators imposed strict rules on Ant that require it to fund at least 30 percent of its loans, and forced Ant to turn itself into a financial holding company overseen by China's central bank.[60] Xi also may have been displeased that Ant's investors, who stood to make a killing from the IPO, included a number of children and grandchildren of retired leaders from other political factions.[61] All the current and potential investors lost money; Ant's dual listing had attracted orders totaling at least $3 trillion from individual investors,[62] and Alibaba lost more than half its market value in the year after Ant's IPO was scratched.[63]

Following this blow, the government hammered away at private Internet companies, both individually and as a class, almost weekly during 2021. The Chinese antimonopoly authority fined Alibaba $2.8 billion and the food-delivery company Mcituan $533 million for anticompetitive practices. The Ministry of Industry and Information Technology temporarily prohibited Tencent from upgrading its apps or launching new ones. Banking regulators zeroed out all the fintech peer-to-peer lending companies. The Cyberspace Administration of China (CAC) hauled individual firms onto the carpet to demand that they repair their data security problems. The CAC also cracked down on celebrity fan groups, which had become a big business because they viewed them as a potential collective-action threat, as well as a diversion from the fan worship of Xi Jinping.[64] After Xi condemned video games, the National Press and Publication Administration set rules to limit youth under age eighteen to playing only for an hour, between 8 o'clock and 9 o'clock at night, and only on weekends and holidays.[65] The central government made "capricious and abrupt"—as one American economist put it—interventions in the economy, forcing every business to "constantly look over its shoulder to comply with, or even to anticipate, the changing goals of the supreme authorities."[66]

Building on the 2017 Cybersecurity Law, two new laws, covering Data Security and Personal Information Protection, increased the government's sway over the data private companies collect. Data related to national security or public interests, broadly defined, must be shared with the government. In the name of security, the new rules forbid foreign firms like Apple or Tesla, as well as domestic firms, from transferring abroad information they collect in China about roads, shipping, coal use, or anything else that might fall into the ambiguous category of "sensitive information."

But beyond security concerns, Xi's underlying political objective is preventing big private companies from becoming alternative power centers. "Whoever controls data will have the initiative," he has said, according to reporting by the *Wall Street Journal*.[67] Just days after the ride-sharing company Didi, with 377 million annual active users and 13 million drivers, launched its IPO on the New York Stock Exchange, the CAC began an investigation into Didi's data practices, told the company to stop registering new users, and ordered all Chinese app stores to remove the Didi app. The CAC had earlier advised Didi that it had concerns about its data management. Didi went ahead with the IPO listing anyway, in the belief that the CAC could not prevent the overseas listing of a Chinese company.[68] Didi discovered that its assumption was wrong, and as a result, lost $40 billion in market value in the six months after the June IPO; its investors, including Uber, took a huge haircut. Meanwhile, the US Securities Exchange Commission had finalized a rule requiring Chinese companies to hand over more financial data to regulators within three years to conform with American accounting standards or be delisted on US exchanges. Didi's stockholders, caught between the two governments, voted to delist from the NYSE and move its IPO to Hong Kong.

In July 2021, a CAC opinion on data security required companies planning an overseas IPO and holding personal data from at least one million users (which is virtually all of them, because one million is a small number in China) to receive its prior approval and in addition to be approved by a new interagency group that includes propaganda, public security, court, justice, procuratorate, finance, and securities regulatory departments.[69]

Beijing also wiped out the entire after-school tutoring industry, a sector worth $120 billion that employed ten million people, by banning private educational firms from publicly listing and making profits. According to the *Wall Street Journal*, this draconian measure was the result of a brief instruction from Xi to the Education Ministry in which he indicated that he wanted to reform the industry and the ministry's desire to please him after he had rejected the first version of their policy as too soft.[70] His objective was to relieve parents of the financial burden of exam prep and encourage them to have more children. Although Chinese demographers have known for years that the country faced an aging population and labor shortages because of the one-child policy, Xi may have panicked when the census data showed that although the one-child restrictions had been eased, the 2020 fertility rate had still continued to decline to 1.3 children. He also claimed to be worried that the exam-prep rat race was unhealthy for children and that it disadvantaged low-income families, though online tutoring actually is a popular low-priced option such families can utilize.

Affluent Chinese parents will find workarounds to the ban by, for example, hiring household help who can teach English. (Parents in South Korea were able to evade a similar ban attempted in 1980.[71]) By discouraging the study of the English language, the tutoring ban will turn China inward; more than half of all tutoring is to teach English. Shanghai already has eliminated English final exams in primary school.[72]

Running through all the specific actions toward private tech firms that came in rapid progression during 2021 is a line of connection: that of expanding the power of the government and the party over the private sector[73] — what one foreign expert calls a "red thread."[74] Municipal and provincial governments, as well as central bureaucracies, have piled on with their own regulations, following behind Xi's drive to put the companies in a political cage. The authorities also are facilitating online nationalist broadsides against individual firms for selling out China's interests to foreign investors.

Xi's suspicion of capitalists is reflected in his Marxist-sounding catch-phrase "prevent the disorderly expansion of capital," which he raised in connection with what he called the "barbaric growth" of platform companies and their efforts to "get rich overnight."[75] It's handy for the government to deflect blame for its domestic problems by vilifying the rich capitalists.

The pressure on private firms in China has rarely been as intense as it is today. In addition to the difficult domestic situation, Beijing's clash with the United States and other of its trading partners has hurt the private firms, many of them foreign owned, that dominate exports. The share of private fixed-asset investment in manufacturing and infrastructure peaked in 2015 at more than half but has been shrinking since then.[76] A Chinese business school that tracks the business conditions for small- and medium-sized enterprises, most of which are private, found in 2018 that it had fallen to the lowest reading that had ever been recorded since the monthly survey began in 2011.[77] I've recently encountered quite a few CEOs of private companies who decided to sell them and move abroad with their families because after the 2021 storm, the pressure on them became intolerable.

In a rare dissent from the politically correct cheerleading for Xi's statist views, a retired Shenzhen Party secretary named Li Youwei argued for less state direction and equal protection for private business: "At this critical moment, the most important thing is to win the hearts of entrepreneurs, so that they feel that their personal safety and property rights are guaranteed by the government and laws and can hence be determined to work hard, invest, and develop in China."[78] Retired officials are practically the only voices daring to publicly question Xi's choices these days.

Winning the Tech Contest

Although Xi Jinping increasingly is focused on his political, ideological, and security goals, as one American economist observes, "they have not displaced the overarching goal to which China has been dedicated for a decade: building a world-beating high-tech industrial base."[79]

Made in China 2025 (MIC2025) is Xi's ambitious industrial policy, focused on putting China on the top rung of the global ladder in innovation-driven advanced manufacturing. The centralization of the economic decision-making process enables Xi to allocate all the resources he wants to further his grand scheme. The plan, which highlights ten sectors, was drawn up by the Ministry of Industry and Information Technology and experts from the China Academy of Engineering in 2015. The revolutionary technology that is its centerpiece is artificial intelligence (AI), which created a "Sputnik moment" for Chinese planners—at least in their minds—when DeepMind's AlphaGo Artificial Intelligence beat the world's best Go players.

The Innovation-Driven Development Strategy, which is the master plan for MIC2025 promulgated by the Party center and State Council in 2015, sees "revolutionary new technologies . . . reshaping the global competitive landscape and changing the relative strength of nations."[80] The explicitly competitive framing of the plan communicates clearly that China is playing to win what it sees as a zero-sum game. The plan's open ambition raised the hackles of American politicians, inspiring the Trump administration's Super 301 tariffs (which tracked the ten MIC2025 sectors) and the Entity List banning US technology sales to certain Chinese firms. The inclusion of the Military-Civilian Industry Fusion Program was another red flag for Americans, who worry about China's technological advances enhancing its military capabilities. And the huge sums of government money subsidizing Chinese firms to accelerate their innovations indicated that China was further diverging from the global norms of fair market competition.

The Chinese government has set explicit targets for the domestic content in the core components and materials it manufactures—40 percent by 2020, and 70 percent by 2025—and sectoral targets such as 80 percent by 2025 for electric vehicles and batteries, mobile devices, and high-performance computers. These goals all trumpet China's intention to cut its reliance on foreign technology, which means shoving out American producers as soon as China has domestic substitutes and ultimately supplanting the US and other advanced economies altogether. Xi openly acknowledges that while he wants China to be less dependent on inputs from other countries, he wants to keep other countries dependent on China "as a powerful countermeasure and deterrent," as he put it, "against them cutting off supply."[81]

American sanctions, especially the technology embargo of ZTE, Huawei, and other Chinese firms put on the Entity List, have strengthened Xi's determination to achieve the MIC2025 objectives and particularly to double-down on self-reliance in core technologies like advanced semiconductors and AI. However, recognizing that MIC2025 had become a symbol of China's ambition, Beijing stopped talking so much about it. Propaganda officials directed Chinese state media to avoid mentioning Made in China 2025 in their reports, and the number of mentions in the media plummeted.[82] Meanwhile, many Chinese see the plan itself as entirely legitimate, similar, for example, to the German plan for industrial upgrading. They believe the overreaction from America shows that its real motivation is to impede China's development.

The Innovation-Driven Development Strategy and MIC2025 are a more sophisticated version of state-led industrial policy than what was introduced during the Hu Jintao era. The Xi version throws even more money behind the innovation drive but also aims to take advantage of private firms and market dynamics instead of relying on clunky bureaucratic methods and hidebound state firms. By the time Xi entered office, there was a broad recognition that letting the state bureaucracy, the Chinese Academy of Sciences, and state-owned companies drive innovation translated into waste, corruption, and inefficiency. As a newspaper editor wryly observed to me, "Technological innovation is completely dominated by the state that is putting huge amounts of money into it. Whenever something is really important the state dominates it, which guarantees that it can't be achieved."

Xi's industrial policies are fueled largely by industrial guidance funds, unique financial instruments that bundle funds from central, provincial, and municipal governments and from state and private firms and international venture-capital firms and invests them in particular projects. Three-quarters of this funding comes from provinces and municipalities, and one-quarter from the central government. Economist Barry Naughton estimates that as of June 30, 2020, the total designated fundraising scope of all these funds was roughly $1.6 trillion. If actual fundraising amounts to about 60 percent of the registered scope, this still amounts to over 6 percent of GDP, "the greatest single commitment of government resources to an industrial policy objective in history," Naughton observes.[83]

In other words, the Chinese government has become a venture capitalist, putting its formidable resources behind its policies to steer China's economy. The industrial guidance funds may choose investments more wisely than government bureaucrats do, but their objectives are broader than the profits that any Silicon Valley venture capitalist would seek. Following Xi's obsession with security, the funds are doing government audits of supply chains and investing in some weak areas where China doesn't have a comparative advantage, such as semiconductor equipment. Then opportunistic companies raise funds to take advantage of the government's policy priorities. Some venture capitalists launched a "domestic replacement" fund that specializes in technologies in which Beijing is competing with Washington.[84] In 2020, more than 13,000 Chinese enterprises registered as semiconductor companies, though many of them come from sectors like seafood and auto parts.[85]

CCP Inc.

The complex funding arrangements underlying MIC2025 reflect how China's political economy has changed under Xi Jinping. As one China expert puts it, the paradigm has transmuted from "China Inc." to "CCP Inc." The line between what is a state enterprise and what is a private one has blurred because of Xi Jinping's concerted effort to expand the role of the CCP throughout the economy, both public and private.[86] Private companies, including foreign firms and joint ventures, are required to have CCP branches, the lowest level of Party organization—70 percent of them already did as of 2020—and the Party branches are expected to play significant roles in personnel decisions and social responsibility policies. Party branches also sometimes push to get involved in management decisions.[87] In state companies, the Party committee (the body above the branches) is supposed to steer the management as the "leadership core," much as it did during Mao Zedong's rule.

The financialization of industrial policy[88] means that private firms share both the benefits of state funding and the strictures of state guidance. State investment funds connected to powerful regulators like the Cyberspace Administration of China have become strategic investors in tech firms such as the social media giants Weibo and ByteDance, which owns TikTok. The funds' 1 percent discounted stake in these companies allows them to appoint board members and steer the company—it's as if the Federal Communications Commission were to take stakes in Facebook or Twitter. These strategic investors are focused more on the Party's social objectives and regulatory compliance than on profitability.[89]

Party-state capitalism is different from state capitalism, in which the government intervenes in the economy to achieve economic development goals, like growth and competitiveness in the globalized sectors of the economy. China, as one group of American scholars has put it, has a "sui generis form of political economy in which the party-state's political survival trumps developmental goals."[90]

Information Winter

Xi Jinping's paranoia about domestic threats to his power and to Party rule has spurred him to new extremes in manipulating the flow of information inside the country. Shortly after he became the Party leader, his determination to use his authority to control the media and Internet became clear in a case involving a special issue of *Southern Weekly*, an influential liberal-leaning newspaper published in the southern Chinese city of Guangzhou. After the provincial propaganda chief had chopped the special edition into ideological pulp, the journalists took to their personal Weibo microblog accounts to call for an investigation, and retired staff organized an online petition demanding that the propaganda chief be fired for overstepping the bounds of acceptable censorship.[91] The news of the incident spread rapidly over the Internet—a platform manager responsible for screening Weibo microblogs claimed that the site had helped the news spread by delaying deleting it for as long as they could.[92] Many people became aware for the first time of how much information the censors were screening out of the newspapers they read every day. Students, lawyers, and other intellectuals protested in open letters online. The actress Yao Chen, who had seventy-nine million followers on her microblog in 2015, posted a stirring defense of freedom of the press that quoted the late Soviet dissident author Aleksandr Solzhenitsyn: "One word of truth outweighs the whole world." Several hundred demonstrators and pro-government counterprotestors gathered outside the newspaper's offices in Guangzhou, and the journalists went out on strike. After the central Propaganda Department ordered publications throughout the country to reprint a harsh editorial from the loyal *Global Times* newspaper that blamed the *Southern Weekly* clash on irresponsible journalists and "hostile foreign forces," the publisher of the *Beijing News* resigned in protest.

The central propaganda officials in Beijing took the *Southern Weekly* journalists' activism and the nationwide online support it had evoked as a direct challenge to CCP rule and an argument for heightening Party control over the media.[93] Following an emergency high-level Party meeting, the Propaganda Department issued a national directive to remind everyone that "the Party control of the media is an unwavering basic principle." According to a newspaper editor, after the crisis "the propaganda and security bureaucracies exaggerated the threat to Xi Jinping and colluded with one another to show him how much they were needed."

Ideological Restoration

During his first year in office, Xi came at the media and Internet with an ideological militance that hadn't been felt in China since the Mao era. In an August 2013 speech to the national propaganda conference, he declared his intention to intensify the ideological cold war with the West. Xi's theory is that if people stop believing in communist ideology—including Marxism and Mao Zedong Thought—Party rule will not survive. The West, he said, is trying to destroy the regime through ideological subversion conducted largely through the media and on the Internet. Therefore, the Party must fight a "public opinion struggle" (*yunlun douzheng*, a phrase that evokes the Cultural Revolution) against hostile foreign forces, and social media is the main battlefield.[94] Following Xi's speech, the propaganda chiefs of China's thirty-one provinces, one after another, took a public stand (*biaotai*) endorsing Xi's ideas; at least sixteen used the phrase "public opinion struggle" or "ideological struggle" in their statements. After the popular tabloid *Beijing Daily* upped the tension in an article titled "In the Struggle in the Ideological Sphere We Must Have the Courage to Show Our Swords," the phrase "showing one's sword" started appearing everywhere.[95] Propaganda officials started talking about how to "purify" the online public sphere, classifying netizens into groups: a red group of patriotic CCP supporters, a black group of political critics, and a gray group of the silent majority, creating a framework with Cultural Revolution resonances that apparently came from Xi himself.[96]

Xi's top propagandist is Standing Committee member Wang Huning, the former Fudan University political scientist, who is a unique figure in that he has served as ideological adviser and speechwriter to Jiang Zemin, Hu Jintao, and now Xi Jinping. Xi is known to trust only those who were close to him before he was anointed China's leader, so Wang had to work extra hard to ingratiate himself. A policy adviser said that Wang tried to flatter Xi by promoting the stories of Liang Jiahe, the village Xi had been sent down to in 1968. However, said the adviser, Wang lost control of the propaganda, and "people everywhere started overdoing it." Like Mao, Xi claimed that he didn't want a personality cult and criticized Wang for creating one. Yet Wang kept his job, proving that you can't really go wrong by flattering a dictator.

The opening shot in Xi's ideological fight with the West was the CCP Central Office's Document No. 9 that warns against (somewhat confusingly) seven false Western values promoted by "Western forces hostile to China and dissidents within the country" to stir up popular discontent with the party and government: constitutionalism, universal values, civil society, neoliberal economics, freedom of the press, historical nihilism, and questioning the socialist nature of socialism with Chinese character-istics.[97] The document inspired a stream of critiques of universal values, constitutionalism, and the other forbidden topics by authors eager to show that they were on the right side of the ideological struggle. Television commentators followed the bans strictly, as I learned when I visited China Central Television for an interview show in 2013 and my fellow panelist reminded me not to use the term "civil society." "So many things we can't say," he complained.

During a 2016 visit to the three most authoritative CCP media outlets— Xinhua, China Central Television, and the *People's Daily*—Xi Jinping called on them to "have the surname of the Party," a phrase that immedi-ately became another buzzword. The journalists pledged their "absolute loyalty."[98] The Propaganda Department started requiring all journalists to undergo a refresher course on the Party line before renewing their press accreditation. The instructors taught that the US was trying to undermine China and that the West was using the so-called universal values of democ-racy and human rights to target the CCP.[99]

Consolidating the Hydra

Xi Jinping complains that the state's management of online media hasn't kept up with the rapid development of online media technologies, such as WeChat and Weibo, "which are rapid, influential, and have scale and so-cial mobilization capacity."[100] When Xi paid a call to Tencent in December 2012, he emphasized the need to utilize the information gleaned from on-line media to maintain stability: "In this sea of information, you possess the most comprehensive data and you can make the most objective and accurate analysis of it, which is of great value for recommendations to the government."[101] The mining of online public opinion has become a major part of China's propaganda operations and big business for universities and other contractors; in addition to domestic opinion, it now harvests opinion by foreigners and Chinese on social media outside the Great Firewall.[102]

The leaks in 2013 by US National Security Agency contractor Edward J. Snowden about the American government surveillance of China fo-cused Chinese attention on cybersecurity. Xi stressed that "without cybersecurity there is no national security."[103] The Snowden revelation also "discredited democracy in China," according to a magazine editor.

"The US is no longer in a morally superior category. China can fight back because we were victims of US surveillance."

Xi rejected his predecessor's fragmented management of the media and Internet, citing its "multi-head management, overlapping functions, different powers and responsibilities, and low efficiency."[104] He demanded better coordination of the agencies responsible for the Internet with a clear aim of unifying the message and tightening security. A journalist explained to me how central and local censors are now linked in a tight password-protected intranet network. The Ministry of State Security (China's CIA, essentially) and the Ministry of Public Security (China's FBI) have become increasingly active in policing the content of online communications. Using data mining, they can analyze who is following whom and identify dangerous individuals. Senior officials from the State Council Information Office and the Propaganda Department have been transferred to the Ministry of Public Security, and vice versa. Some journalists believe that the security bureaucracies are eavesdropping on the internal discussions of their magazines and newspapers and feeding intelligence to the propaganda agencies.

Consolidation of the propaganda Hydra has eliminated gaps and achieved more effective top-down control of the information landscape. Two administrative agencies, the State Administration of Radio, Film, and Television and the General Administration for Press and Publication, were merged to become the National Press and Publication Administration. As a magazine editor observed, "The propaganda watchdogs have become very experienced. There used to be a lot of loopholes, but not anymore. The whole system has become more mature and it's clear they have no intention to liberalize."

The Rise of the Cyberspace Administration of China

As I noted earlier, the State Internet Information Office was spun off from the State Council Information Office to become a separate entity, the Cyberspace Administration of China (CAC), which under Xi's sponsorship has become a powerful bureaucratic behemoth. It is responsible for monitoring all online content, as well as protecting the security of the critical information infrastructure, directing the technical censorship apparatus, and, as of 2021, approving or denying the overseas IPOs of Chinese Internet firms. The CAC is both a Party and a government agency; it serves as the office for the CCP Central Commission for Cybersecurity and

Informatization, founded as a leading group in 2014 and upgraded to a commission in 2018. Xi's chairmanship of the commission highlights the attention he places on cybersecurity.[105] According to an Internet company executive, the CAC has become even more powerful than the National Development and Reform Commission.

Xi recruited Lu Wei, the charismatic propaganda chief and vice mayor of Beijing, to be the founding director of the CAC in 2014. Although Lu Wei was only a vice-head of the CCP Propaganda Department, his informal influence exceeded that of the Politburo member who did head the department. Lu reported in person to Xi every Wednesday and sent reports three times a week. Lu was a workaholic, and under him, "the work tripled for the people in the office," according to an Internet executive.

Lu Wei's close relationship with Xi made him the man to see for Mark Zuckerberg and other American Internet moguls seeking access to China's huge market. With a group of Chinese Internet tycoons trailing behind him, Lu charmed the Americans at the US-China Internet Industry Forum in Washington in December 2014. As a prominent member of Xi's entourage during the leader's 2015 state visit to the US, Lu choreographed his Seattle encounter with tech company executives and his visit to Microsoft. Lu's personal star rose high before it crashed in 2016, when he was fired and subsequently sent to prison for fourteen years for taking bribes. The Discipline Inspection Commission made clear that his real crime was being a disloyal self-promoter, "a two-faced man in the Party."[106]

Nonetheless, Lu Wei had pursued a nationalist Internet agenda to give China a greater say in how the global Internet is governed, one that was in line with Xi's views. He also had implemented real name registration requiring Weibo users to reveal their identities and chilled the participation of influential microbloggers with a new legal guideline providing that Internet users who shared "false information that is defamatory or harms the national interest" faced up to three years in prison if their posts were viewed five thousand times or forwarded five hundred times.[107]

The public figures called "Big V" bloggers who could mobilize the public around their policy concerns had been his top targets. Lu Wei invited groups of them to dinners at fancy restaurants to warn them about the consequences of making trouble. Then he shut down their social media blogs, detained them on trumped-up charges, and forced them to make televised confessions.[108]

Those who didn't toe the line paid the price. After Xi Jinping said, "The media's surname is the Party," Ren Zhiqiang, an outspoken real-estate millionaire and blogger with more than 37 million followers, blogged that state media should serve the taxpayers and not the Party. His Weibo account was closed by the CAC and his Party membership put on probation. Then he wrote an essay criticizing Xi Jinping's speech of February 23, 2020, on the management of the COVID epidemic that called out the leader as not an emperor with new clothes but a clown trying to hide his nakedness—Xi's management of COVID is today the third rail in Chinese politics—which landed him in prison for eighteen years on charges of corruption.[109] Another well-known blogger, former *Caijing* editor Luo Changping, was detained in October 2021 for a new crime—that of defaming political martyrs—after questioning China's role in the Korean War in a critical review of the box-office-hit film *The Battle at Lake Changjin*.[110]

The CAC announced in December 2021 that it had shut down the microblog accounts of 20,000 top influencers, including those who had shared publicly their views on financial and economic issues.[111] The leadership's nervousness about the COVID epidemic and looming economic headwinds have triggered controls over information so expansive that they include the economic data and analysis essential for decision-making by businesses, investors, and consumers. Limiting the dissemination of economic information is bound to impede market efficiency and growth.

When Li Wenliang, the opthamologist who was investigated by the police for "spreading rumors" when he tried to warn fellow doctors about COVID-19, died from the disease, he became the focal point of a spontaneous national movement for openness and transparency. Even the Supreme People's Court posted a comment on social media saying that it would have been fortunate "if the public had believed the 'rumors' then and started to wear masks and carry out sanitization measures."[112] As we've seen, unlike during the SARS epidemic, when Hu Jintao changed laws and practices to increase information flow, the COVID crisis had the opposite effect. As an American expert observes, "The public demands for reform after Dr. Li's death appear to have alarmed Chinese leaders, prompting a crackdown on social media users and even more intense state censorship," including instructions not to report economic problems.[113]

Persistence Is Victory

Seeking to eliminate the threats he sees lurking in every corner, Xi Jinping has extended the powers of the Party-state over society and the economy to almost the totalitarian extent of Mao Zedong's regime. His domestic decisions and his foreign policy ones often are based on faulty information he has received from obsequious officials. The honest critics have been put out of action by Party discipline and anticorruption campaigns. The information feedback loops simply aren't functioning. Moreover, his defensiveness about his previous misjudgments leads him to rigidly stick to them in the name of revolutionary bravery—"persistence is victory"[114]—instead of pragmatically adjusting them to reduce costs. As a result, Xi keeps making choices that, though he may believe they benefit him in the short term, are jeopardizing the country's peaceful rise.

During 2022, Xi Jinping should have been cruising triumphantly toward a third term at the 20th Party Congress. But instead, he has tripped himself up by a series of decisions that increased domestic and foreign skepticism about his leadership, particularly the crackdown on private business, refusal to condemn Russia's war in Ukraine, and the continuation of the "dynamic zero-COVID" approach to epidemic control. In combination, these three decisions reinforced Xi's image as an autocrat who rigidly clings to self-defeating positions instead of adjusting them to benefit the country. Xi looked like a hero when China's strict management methods achieved miraculously low numbers of hospitalizations and deaths from COVID-19 while most other countries were struggling. Over time, however, life returned to normal more or less in the United States and many countries because they concentrated on vaccinating people.

China, in contrast, remained under a system of extreme control called "zero COVID" that was personally attributed to Xi Jinping. The universal testing, government surveillance, compulsory collective quarantines, travel bans, and lockdowns of whole cities required under zero COVID reinforced autocratic social control, devastated the economy, and frustrated the population.

When the more contagious but less lethal Omicron strain variant struck, Xi Jinping refused to budge, insisting that his way provided the best protection for people. He ordered Shanghai and other cities into strict lockdowns that drove the economy into recession and made it impossible to achieve the 2022 5.5 percent growth target.

Despite all the other mandatory features of zero COVID—such as multi-week quarantines in government facilities for anyone testing positive even if asymptomatic—the government had never required or encouraged vaccinations of its senior citizens. Instead it spread rumors about the risks of the foreign mRNA vaccines and banned them from the country even though they are actually more effective than the Chinese vaccine. One Chinese study estimated that 1.5 million people could die if China loosened up its restrictions, unless it was able to vaccinate more of its older population who were the most vulnerable to infection.[115]

Instead of transitioning to a more flexible approach by channeling resources into vaccination programs for senior citizens and other vulnerable groups, Xi opted to maximize social control by establishing permanent PCR testing sites and testing residents every 48 hours—at an estimated annual cost of 1.45 trillion yuan (1.27 percent of China's 2021 GDP).[116] The average number of third doses of vaccine administered per day among people age sixty and above in fact declined by almost half in late April 2022,[117] as local officials responded to Xi's preferences for lockdown measures and mass testing.

To silence criticism, Xi Jinping summoned the Politburo Standing Committee to a meeting on May 5, 2022. He insisted that the leaders stand behind him to endorse the zero-COVID strategy and "resolutely struggle against all words and deeds that distort, question, or dismiss" it. [118] The health experts and others who urged a change in approach were silenced by the censors. And China remained walled off from the rest of the world that was moving on from the pandemic.

Now speculation is spreading about an incipient split in the leadership between Xi and the leaders who are focused more economic-development, such as Premier Li Keqiang, Wang Yang, and Hu Chunhua.[119] To prevent middle-class professionals from heading to the exits, the government has restored Mao-era type restrictions on nonessential travel abroad.[120] What's more, college students are required to obtain a formal job offer before they are allowed to graduate, lest they become politically restive unemployed youths.[121] The costs of Xi's obstinacy are piling up. Xi's dilemma of how to adjust course without undermining his authority exemplifies Deng Xiaoping's warning about the dangers of arbitrary decision-making by personalistic leaders, a perspective that remains in the minds of at least some people in China. As the international community turns increasingly hostile toward China, Xi's stubbornness also proves to be costly for China globally as well.

10

Downward Spiral

ORLD HISTORY WAS CHANGED by the coincidence of the election of a personalistic autocratic American president, Donald Trump, with China's rule by Xi Jinping, its most personalistic autocrat since Mao Zedong. Trump Cabinet meetings eerily resembled high-level meetings in Beijing as, one by one, the senior officials praised the wisdom of their leader. Both Trump and Xi expected other officials to fall into line with them even when they acted erratically. Trump changed policy with his tweets; Xi didn't tweet, but his shifts could be just as sudden. The unpredictable interactions between the administrations of the two autocrats drove Sino-US relations into a downward spiral from which it has not yet recovered.

The Trump effect on Xi's China was unfortunate in two very different ways: First, Trump's unilateral "America first" strategy diminished American leadership as a constraint on Xi's international actions. America's abdication opened the way for Xi to step into its place, heightening his hubristic belief that China was already at the center of the world. Having a personalistic leader like Xi in Beijing operating without an effective American counterbalance was more dangerous than when China's previous leaders operated with a realistic respect for American hard and soft power.

The Trump administration reduced the US standing in Asia and its influence over China's foreign policy choices when it withdrew from the nascent Trans-Pacific Partnership (TPP), the Asia-Pacific regional trade agreement founded by Japan and other partners, and by picking trade fights with long-standing US allies Japan and South Korea.[1] Beyond Asia, the US pulled out of the Paris climate accord, hobbled the World Trade Organization by failing to appoint judges for its dispute resolution process, and alienated European leaders by disparaging NATO. By trashing US alliances, the Trump administration lost the most important multiplier of its influence over China. As the United States disengaged from the United Nations, UNESCO, and the World Health Organization, China's clout with them increased. Chinese diplomats now lead more than fifteen UN agencies, including the International Telecommunication Union and the UN Industrial Development Organization; inject Xi's favorite buzzwords into UN resolutions; and defend China in the UN Human Rights Council and other bodies from which the Trump administration withdrew. The UN secretary general praises the BRI as a model for economic development in speeches.[2] As the prestige of American democracy sunk to an all-time low around the world, advocates of political and economic reform inside China lost their inspiration and their voice. And during the time when Xi was using the formidable power of the Chinese Party-state to bring COVID-19 under control, Trump couldn't even protect himself from getting sick. Little wonder that Xi's triumphalism was in full flower during the Trump years.

Second, although Trump himself was fixated on the trade deficit with China and cared little about other issues, late in his term, when he was gearing up his re-election campaign, he unleashed the hawks in his administration, who were itching to push back against the overreaching of the Xi regime. The hawks weren't all high-level political appointees. Many career officials had been infuriated by the cybertheft, technological espionage, influence operations, and unfair treatment of American firms that they had observed for many years. Congress had also become more critical of China over time.

Although America was playing with a weakened hand, Trump greenlighted his administration to confront the China threat more broadly.[3] Trump and his campaign adviser Steve Bannon (who stepped down in the early days of the administration) believed that they had won the 2016 election by hammering on the Chinese economic threat in campaign speeches to blue-collar voters in key mid-Western states. Trump, having enjoyed economist Peter Navarro's documentary film *Death by China*, about the loss of US manufacturing jobs to China, recruited Navarro into his administration. Trump was keen to impose tariffs on Chinese products to narrow the trade deficit, even though almost no economist other than Navarro believed that the bilateral deficit mattered much for American prosperity, and the tariffs hurt American companies and consumers as much or more than they hurt China.[4] (The Trump tariffs remained in effect under the Biden administration which was reluctant to confront the domestic criticism that would inevitably ensue if they were removed.)

Although Trump didn't have any genuine animus toward China, or serious concerns about Chinese behavior beyond trade, he enabled harsh policies in the second half of his term, largely for his own political purposes. After the Republicans lost the 2018 midterm elections and Trump was consumed with worry about his own re-election, his administration took an increasingly antagonistic stance toward China. The Justice Department arrested and charged Chinese American scientists who hadn't reported their collaborations with researchers in China. The Navy increased its Freedom of Navigation operations and exercises in the South China and East China Seas. The State Department cut Chinese journalists' visas to ninety days. The Commerce and Treasury Departments sanctioned Chinese companies and officials for human rights abuses and various actions they deemed detrimental to US national security. Influential Chinese figures were denied visas to attend meetings in the United States. Prominent officials made coordinated hardline speeches to wake people up to the China threat.[5]

Getting to Know You

During Trump's early days in the White House, Xi and his foreign policy advisers had struggled to figure out the internal dynamics of his idiosyncratic administration—what motivated the president, who could speak for him, and where they might best exert their influence?—the kinds of questions that Americans typically ask about opaque Chinese politics. Some Chinese intellectuals and entrepreneurs told me they were positively inclined toward Trump, intrigued with his profile as a brash businessman–TV star, and hoped he would put pressure on Xi to undertake the reforms they believed were overdue in China.

Xi's government acted cautiously to avoid baiting the new president. Although Chinese elites were less awed by American power than they had been before the 2008 global financial crisis, Xi still seemed to believe it was too risky to go at the US head-on. Moreover, he was preoccupied with the preparations for his own transition to a second term, which would begin at the 19th Party Congress in fall 2017.

Even before Trump was sworn in, he showed both his lack of experience and his willingness to shake up the China relationship by taking a congratulatory phone call from Taiwan president Tsai Ing-wen, and then telling television interviewer Chris Wallace that whether he would continue the long-held "One China policy" depended on getting a deal with

China over "other things, including trade."[6] Xi sent his top envoy (Yang Jiechi) to Washington to make it clear that Trump would need to reaffirm the One China policy before the two leaders could meet. At the same time, Chinese diplomats cultivated a friendly relationship with the new president and his family—Trump's granddaughter was learning to sing Chinese songs, and his daughter Ivanka benefited from China's approvals of her fashion brand trademarks, made tactically before key interactions with the Trump administration.[7]

The two leaders then proceeded to flatter one another and themselves in an exchange of elaborately choreographed visits to Mar-a-Lago, Trump's Florida retreat, and to Beijing. They spoke frequently by phone. There was a positive vibe between the leaders that may have given both unrealistic expectations of what they could get from each other. Other than trade, Trump cared most about the North Korean nuclear problem and believed that Xi could help him solve it. Even after Xi explained to Trump at Mar-a-Lago that Kim Jong-un didn't listen to Chinese advice, Trump remained conciliatory toward his counterpart on everything other than trade. When the US banned American companies from selling to the Chinese telecom firm ZTE because it had violated American sanctions on Iran and other countries in April 2018, Xi took the unusual step of calling Trump to ask for his help, and Trump agreed to lift the ban, over the strong objections of members of Congress and some of his own advisers. Personalistic leaders sometimes like to do favors for one another.

The Trade and Technology War

In the trade negotiations, China had a hard time determining where Trump's bottom line was. When Beijing offered modest concessions—cutting steel output by closing antiquated steel mills, implementing an earlier promise to WTO to allow American credit-card companies to set up business in China, dropping the ban on US beef imports, and, later, the long-promised opening of financial services to foreign banks and companies—US trade representative Robert Lighthizer convinced the president that the deal wasn't good enough and that the administration should launch unilateral tariffs under Section 301 of the 1974 Trade Law instead. Section 301 permits tariffs against countries whose trade practices are "unjustifiable and burdens or restricts US commerce." The legal rationale was that China's statist system was diverging from market norms by pressuring foreign firms to transfer technology to China in exchange for access to the Chinese market, and then using cybertheft to make off with the proprietary technologies. The state was also subsidizing industries that it believed could transform China into a technology superpower. But as the Trump administration condemned Beijing for state interference in the market, it simultaneously forced the state to increase its control of the Chinese economy by demanding that Beijing guarantee purchases that would reduce the trade deficit by $200 billion in two years. The internal fights within the Trump White House and the president's affection for tariffs meant that the administration kept escalating its demands on China.

The Xi government's response to American unilateral tariffs was firm and commensurate. It imposed retaliatory tariffs that were equal in measure to but not more than the US tariffs, and sought a negotiated solution. Xi's favorite technocrat, Liu He, worked hard to forge internal agreement on many of the changes sought by the Americans, especially those related to market opening; many Chinese officials believed that they would benefit the Chinese economy. The Chinese also agreed to buy billions of dollars' worth of American soybeans, corn, coal, natural gas, and manufactured goods, a negotiating demand aimed to appease constituencies that Trump needed to win re-election, such as farmers.

The Chinese insisted, however, that any deal include dropping the tariffs and the Section 301 sanctions against unfair Chinese trade practices.[8] Still, the April 2019 draft agreement negotiated by Liu He and the Americans didn't include dropping the tariffs and gave Washington the right to enforce the agreement by imposing even more tariffs; it also tied China's hands by forcing it to agree not to retaliate with its own tariffs and further required sixty legal changes that the National People's Congress would have to enact. Because Xi wanted to avoid appearing to cave into American demands, he convened the Politburo Standing Committee to share the responsibility for reviewing the draft. When the Standing Committee rejected it, a furious Trump tweeted that China was reneging on the deal and threatened to raise tariffs on 200 billion dollars' worth of Chinese goods to 25 percent. To ramp up the pressure on Beijing, the president also agreed to the embargoing American technology from China's national champion telecommunications company, Huawei. At the same time, the administration, supported by Democrats and Republicans in Congress, was tightening the barriers to Chinese foreign direct investment, researchers in university labs, and telecom equipment that could threaten national security.

In May 2019, the Commerce Department put Huawei and sixty-eight of its affiliates on the US Entity List. This is a list of companies or other entities to which the sale of American technology or other items is forbidden without a special license because the US deems them to be engaged in activities that are contrary to American national security or foreign policy interests. It was a turning point in the relationship. American technology firms would lose one of their largest customers in China. The administration's willingness to accept the costs to American firms and consumers just to squeeze China was interpreted in China as a sign of extreme hostility. Chinese officials concluded that the American objectives were to slow China's development, and their propaganda convinced the public of this view.[9] As a former commerce vice minister put it, "The US is unwilling to accept China as a rising power."

Just weeks later, the Xi government hit back by announcing its own Unreliable Entity List of foreign firms and individuals that endanger China's sovereignty, security, or development interests or boycott or cut off supplies to Chinese companies for noncommercial purposes. These entities would be prohibited from trading and investing with China. A *Global Times* editorial heralded the decision as showing that "China will never give in to the pressure from the U.S." The public was now more supportive of tough countermeasures than it had been a year ago, it argued. The elites in Washington had hijacked China policy and were trying to hinder China's destiny.[10] Officials moved quickly to collect nominations of US firms to be blacklisted. But some senior officials, including Liu He, advised Xi to delay the list until after the US 2020 presidential election, and as of 2022, no specific names have been listed.[11]

The American sanctions, however, have convinced Xi to accelerate the pace of China's indigenous innovation, an effort initiated by the Hu administration. China's dependence on Western semiconductors and other technologies left it too vulnerable to American politics. It could no longer take access to an open market economy for granted. Preparing for the worst, China intensified industrial policies, such as the Made in China 2025 plan it had introduced in 2015, and invested massively to make the nation technologically self-reliant. The label "Made in China 2025" has since been dropped and its contents rebranded, however, because it became a negative symbol in the United States and other countries. Not surprisingly, given the amounts of money involved, there is no shortage of groups, including various tech and military industries, scientists and engineers, and universities, that are eager to jump on the opportunities it presents. In 2020 alone, more than 22,800 new semiconductor companies were established in China, up nearly 200 percent from the year before.[12]

In its efforts to challenge China, the Trump administration also took the unusual step of asking Canada to arrest Huawei's chief financial officer, Meng Wanzhou, the daughter of company founder Ren Zhengfei, when she landed in Canada in early December 2018. She remained under house arrest for almost three years. The US Justice Department sought Meng's extradition to face charges for defrauding Hong Kong Shanghai Bank Corporation to secretly do business in Iran. (The more usual legal approach would have been a civil action against the company.)[13] An embarrassed Xi heard about the arrest at a dinner with other world leaders, including President Trump (who had not been informed of the timing of the arrest), at the G-20 meeting in Buenos Aires. Xi nevertheless proceeded with the trade negotiations, having been encouraged by Trump's hint that he might trade away the Huawei indictment, as he had with ZTE, to get a good trade deal.[14] But Xi retaliated by arresting two Canadian men on trumped-up charges and not releasing them until just hours after Meng was released in September 2021, following a personal phone call by Xi to President Biden.

The hostage diplomacy damaged China's image. Foreign CEOs and scholars were afraid to travel to China.[15] Still, the Chinese government proclaimed Meng's release a victory of diplomacy and sign of its power. Guangdong province and Shenzhen city politicians gave her an extravagant patriotic homecoming, live-streamed by CCTV and broadcast across every media platform in China, including Weibo and the video-streaming site Bilibili. LED lights projected celebratory slogans across the exteriors of skyscrapers, and three hundred drones wrote slogans in the night sky over Shenzhen to welcome Meng home. Meng thanked Xi personally[16] and sang the patriotic song "Ode to the Motherland" along with the crowd.[17]

Contest of Systems

Competition between China and the United States has taken on a cold-war tenor since 2017, when Xi Jinping delivered his report to the 19th CCP Congress, in which he articulated China's global ambitions more openly than ever before. "This is an era that will see China move closer to the center of the world and make more contributions to humankind."[18]

What stands out even more than Xi's ambition was his touting a distinctive ideological model to legitimate his authority at home and abroad. Previous Chinese leaders have been more cautious about selling the China model as a competitive challenge to Western-style market democracy.

All the talk in the past about the superiority of the "China model" came from Westerners, not the Chinese. During the earlier cold war, the US and China were not engaged in a global contest for ideological hegemony. That is no longer the case. Xi's report called for "socialism with Chinese characteristics for a new era." He asserted that "socialist democratic politics" offered a viable model for other countries. As recently as in the November 2021 communiqué on Party history, the Party was proclaiming that it had "produced a profound influence on the course of world history" by offering a "uniquely Chinese path to modernization."[19]

As Xi campaigned for a third term at the 20th CCP Congress, in fall 2022, he emphasized the contrast between the death toll from COVID-19 in the United States (just over a million people) and China (fewer than 6,000) to claim that the Chinese socialist system performs better than Western democracy. Although this self-praise was targeted to the domestic audience, Xi also projected it internationally.[20]

History may judge Xi's open ideological challenge to the West as a strategic error. Ideological competition tends to turn into a Manichean struggle between good and evil. Once democratic publics perceive China as an existential threat to their way of life, they will demand that their politicians enact ever tougher policies to contain the threat.

These reactions are playing out now. American politicians, including President Biden, increasingly frame relations with China as an ideological contest between autocracy and democracy. Biden believes that he has a responsibility to prove that democracy can perform better than Chinese authoritarianism. In his first news conference as president, he depicted US-China relations as "a battle between the utility of democracies in the 21st century and autocracies. We've got to prove democracy works."[21] Biden also is making instrumental use of the Chinese threat to win bipartisan support in Congress for his large domestic-spending initiatives; competition with China is one of the only issues that unify Republicans and Democrats. The anti-autocratic fervor of the United States and other Western countries also has been fired up by the de facto alliance between Putin and Xi that came into focus after Russia's invasion of democratic Ukraine.

The Pandemic and US-China Relations

In the early days of the pandemic, relations between Xi and Trump appeared to be cooperative. After a call on February 6, 2020, Xi asked

Trump not to panic people about the outbreak in China, telling him that he had everything under control and that the virus was likely to abate when the weather turned warmer. Trump did what Xi requested, publicly praising Xi's leadership and China's discipline and predicting that it would be successful in eradicating the virus.[22] CNN identified thirty-seven separate instances where Trump praised China between January and April in 2020.[23] But as the chaotic American response to COVID became a vulnerability for Trump's re-election, he changed his tune, scapegoating China. The president and his Cabinet officers began calling COVID "the China virus" or "the Wuhan virus" in public; at campaign rallies, Trump aroused the crowd with the racist epithet "Kung Flu." Secretary of state Mike Pompeo refused to sign a G7 statement on the pandemic because it didn't call the disease the "Wuhan virus."

The Chinese Foreign Ministry spokesman, Zhao Lijian, had enraged Trump by tweeting that the US Army might have brought the virus to Wuhan from its bioresearch lab during the 2019 Military World Games. Zhao had acted on his own.[24] Although Cui Tiankai, the Chinese ambassador in Washington, publicly scoffed at Zhao's "harmful speculation," the government and official media soon embraced the line that COVID must have originated outside China. Before long, Trump and other American politicians fought back with the "lab-leak theory," accusing the Wuhan Institute of Virology of leaking the virus, as the result of a laboratory accident.[25]

Both sides exploited the issue of the origin of the virus to protect their leaders from criticism. The vilification of China as the source of the virus took a particularly heavy toll on Asian Americans, who became victims of hate attacks. Although we lack data about whether the Chinese people believe their government's claim that the COVID-19 virus originated outside China, Americans have concluded that China is guilty: According to surveys, 78 percent of Americans agree that the Chinese government's initial handling of the coronavirus outbreak in Wuhan was to blame for the global spread of the virus,[26] and 52 percent have accepted the lab-leak theory.[27]

As the pandemic worsened, Beijing sought to boost its global soft power by providing other countries with masks and other personal protective equipment and vaccines. Xi promised that Chinese vaccines would become a "global public good,"[28] and distributed them widely to more than a hundred countries, mainly in the developing world. Indeed, in this the Chinese have surpassed what the United States or any other nation has done, which has earned it the appreciation of many countries.[29]

But Chinese ambassadors, playing to their overlords in Beijing, went overboard to tie the Chinese donations to their propaganda campaigns. They scripted praise of China and Xi that local leaders in the recipient countries were obligated to parrot at handover ceremonies in front of the television cameras. These shows played poorly, particularly in Europe, which had access to other types of vaccines. The Chinese media reported that the government had distributed more than 1.7 billion vaccine doses — the largest number in the world — and recorded each and every expression of appreciation from recipient countries.[30] This publicity and other forms of propaganda and censorship have given Chinese people the mistaken impression that their country is popular internationally.[31] Most Chinese probably agree with the Party's November 2021 historical resolution that Chinese diplomacy has "resulted in a marked increase in China's international influence, appeal, and power to shape."[32]

Wolf Warrior Diplomacy

The truth is more complicated. Even before the COVID quarrels, some in the Chinese Ministry of Foreign Affairs were engaging in polemics against the United States and other foreign governments to further their careers by echoing Xi Jinping's assertiveness. Analysis of the Ministry's news conferences over the past twenty years shows that the proportion of speeches using combative language increased sharply under Xi. About 10 percent used hostile language before 2012. Between 2019 and 2020 more than 25 percent contained disparaging language.[33] Foreign minister Wang Yi had transformed, from bridge builder — he was the architect of China's successful Asia strategy in the 1990s and 2000s, negotiated the truce on Yasukuni Shrine visits with Japanese prime minister Shinto Abe, and carried out Hu Jintao's rapprochement with Taiwan — to Xi acolyte. The Foreign Ministry encouraged its representatives to take to overseas social media for public commentary, and in 2019, Xi himself reportedly sent the Ministry of Foreign Affairs a handwritten note calling on diplomats to show more "fighting spirit."[34] Diplomats posted abroad learned that they could attract positive notice back home by tweeting snarky comments against foreigners (though Twitter is blocked in China).

Zhao Lijian, posted to the Chinese Embassy in Pakistan, emerged as one of the most active diplomats on Twitter, with more than fifty thousand followers in 2019. His tweet about racial segregation in Washington provoked Susan Rice, who had been President Obama's national security advisor and is President Biden's director of the National Economic Council, to call him a racist, an epithet that Zhao tweeted back at her, followed by Chinese official journalists piling on to support Zhao. It was during this Twitter tiff that the BBC coined the term "wolf warrior diplomacy," referring to the patriotic Chinese action movie *Wolf Warrior 2* and its tagline, "Whoever attacks China will be killed no matter how far the target is."[35] The *Global Times* reported that Chinese diplomats were being maliciously attacked. "China will not stay silent in the face of groundless accusations from the US and the West," read an editorial in the newspaper in July 2019.[36] The Foreign Ministry defended the diplomats with a Mao slogan: "We will not attack unless we are attacked. But if we are attacked, we will certainly counterattack."[37]

Zhao's notoriety earned him a transfer back to Beijing and a promotion to Foreign Ministry spokesman. Ambassador to Canada Lu Shaye, who had also gained notice for criticizing the White supremacy of Canadians, was promoted to become the ambassador to France. The top spokesperson Hua Chunying, also known for her acerbic manner of poking the US from the podium, was promoted and named assistant foreign minister in October 2021. The message was clear.

But if wolf warrior diplomacy might be a successful career strategy for Chinese officials, it doesn't appear to gain China or Xi much affection from abroad. One experiment conducted with Indian citizens and real Twitter messages shows that positive messages emphasizing aid and friendship improved perceptions of China, but that wolf warrior messages backfired.[38] One scholar concluded that the Chinese system "is better at silencing critics than persuading others to share its point of view."[39]

A Fresh Start?

A new president in the White House presented Xi Jinping with a chance to restore a modicum of stability in China's relations with Washington. As noted earlier, Xi and Joe Biden formed a personal relationship when the two were the vice presidents of their countries. Xi hosted Biden during trips to China in 2011 and 2013 and spent time with him in Sichuan as well as Beijing; when Xi visited the United States in 2012, Biden hosted him in Los Angeles and Washington and dined with him at the vice president's residence. Biden estimates that they shared a total of twenty-four to twenty-five hours of private meetings.[40]

The senior foreign policy figures in the Biden administration served with President Obama and might be expected to be more receptive to friendly gestures from China than the Trump administration had been. During its first year, the administration devoted itself to putting the COVID-19 pandemic under control, getting Congress to pass its big domestic spending bills, mending ties with US allies, and reviving its active role in international institutions, before it turned to diplomatic engagements with China. But during this first phase of the administration, the Biden team watched for some reassuring signs from Xi, testing his pragmatic flexibility.

China's actions, however, were anything but reassuring. Beijing clashed with India and Australia, ramped up military and Coast Guard incursions of Japan and Taiwan, and got in hot water with Europe. It didn't pause in the steamrolling of civil liberties in Hong Kong and Xinjiang. And it showed no sign of trying to curtail the wolf warrior style of diplomacy. China's across-the-board belligerence deepened the skepticism within the Biden administration about the possibility of moderating China's behavior through diplomatic engagement and reinforced its inclination to push back instead.

To start with India, China clashed with India more violently than ever before along the two countries' unresolved boundary in the Himalayas. The June 2020 fighting between Chinese and Indian troops in multiple locations of the Galwan Valley of Ladakh resulted in the first deaths on the disputed boundary in forty-five years—twenty Indian soldiers and four Chinese soldiers were killed. In past skirmishes, the scuffles and stone throwing were more localized and ended without the loss of life. China sent in five thousand soldiers and began occupation of a terrain (40 to 60 square kilometers) that remains contested. India will have difficulty evicting them.

The Chinese incursion was, in part, a reaction to Prime Minister Modi's putting the Ladakh region under the direct governance of New Delhi, removing it as part of the autonomous state of Jammu and Kashmir.[41] The incursion was also an effort to signal resolve and strength after the international condemnation of China's allowing the pandemic to spread in its early stages—in line "with the new security law in Hong Kong, new administrative arrangements in the South China Sea, and increasing pressure on Taiwan."[42] Interestingly, even after India had retaliated by banning Chinese Internet mobile applications like WeChat and TikTok, Beijing downplayed the clashes in the media to avoid stirring up Chinese nationalist sentiment that might instigate escalation of the conflict; it also didn't disclose the death toll from the incidents until months later.

The 2020 boundary clashes marked a turning point in India's independent foreign policy toward the United States as well as China. As Indians' apprehensions about Chinese intentions deepened, they became more amenable to joining forces with the United States, Japan, and Australia in the informal grouping called The Quad. Still, India, like China, abstained in the UN Security Council vote to condemn Russia's invasion of Ukraine.

But if hostile rhetoric against the United States and the incursion into India undermined the fresh start, China's relationship with Japan offers mixed messages. Xi has tried to sustain the diplomatic thaw between China and Japan begun under Hu Jintao, despite the tense stand-off in the East China Sea that has existed since the 2012 Diaoyu/Senkaku Islands crisis. Xi established a modus vivendi with the late Prime Minister Abe that, while not warm—as can be seen from their awkward handshakes for the cameras when they met—was surprisingly respectful. Visits to the Yasukuni Shrine were no longer an issue. By 2019, the two leaders were agreeing to lift relations between their countries to a new level and exchange reciprocal visits. Their rapport was good enough that Xi consulted with Abe to get clues on how to handle Trump, and joked with him about which leader, Abe or Trump, was the better golfer.[43]

Yet at the same time, Xi has ordered the intensification of Chinese maritime and air pressure with the aim of shaking Japan's control of the Diaoyu/Senkaku Islands. The frequency and number of Chinese Coast Guard vessels entering the waters surrounding the islands, which, as mentioned earlier, spiked dramatically during the 2012 crisis, has never returned to the pre-crisis level.[44] The numbers were higher from 2019 to 2021 than they had been in the previous three years.[45] Chinese Navy ships conducting joint exercises with the Russians transversed the narrow strait between Japan's Honshu and Hokkaido Islands. The new Chinese law authorizing the Coast Guard to shoot weapons at foreign ships in the waters it claims created the possibility of a Coast Guard sea battle in the East China Sea. Chinese saber rattling toward Taiwan also unsettled the Japanese.

The Japanese government has reacted by strengthening defense ties with its American ally. The Biden administration's reaffirmation of its commitment to the defense of the Senkaku Islands led the Chinese foreign minister to issue a scathing statement denouncing Japan for acting as a "strategic vassal of the United States," and thereby "luring wolves into the room and betraying overall regional interests."[46]

Tokyo also signaled a new willingness to help defend Taiwan. In 2021, for the first time since 1969, the Japanese prime minister referred to

Taiwan in a joint statement with the American president; a deputy prime minister subsequently remarked that the possibility of a Chinese attack on Taiwan represented an existential risk to Japan. The Japanese Coast Guard started exercising its supply function with the US Coast Guard operating nearby, and the Japanese government explored legal mechanisms to enable its forces to provide even more active help to the American defense of Taiwan. A Japanese destroyer exercised with an American carrier group in the South China Sea. Japanese defense spending in fiscal 2021 rose to 773.8 billion yen, 1.09 percent of GDP, the highest percentage in a decade.[47] In June 2022, Prime Minister Fumio Kishida, along with his counterparts from South Korea, Australia, and New Zealand, took the unprecedented step of participating in a summit meeting of NATO leaders to dramatize their common security concerns about China as well as Russia.

For most of Philippines president Rodrigo Duterte's six-year term (which started in 2016 and ended in 2022), he had tilted toward Beijing and away from Washington. As we've seen, the UNCLOS tribunal confirmed the Philippines' maritime rights. Duterte stayed silent about the ruling, however, wagering that China would bankroll his infrastructure-building plans and strike a joint-exploration agreement in the waters both countries claimed. Duterte lost his bet. Not only has Beijing failed to deliver much financial help, but its bullying over the islands and reefs under Manila's control in the South China Sea has intensified. China's fishing militia — fishing trawlers that mainly engage in surveillance and harassment instead of catching fish — pressured Manila to cede the islands and reefs it controls, just as it had been forced to do at Scarborough Shoal. Hundreds of fishing militia boats surrounded Thitu Island for more than a year to prevent the upgrading of its runway and other buildings. In the spring of 2021, over two hundred fishing militia boats were lashed together and encircled the disputed Whitsun Reef in what looked like a prelude to an occupation. In November 2021, Chinese Coast Guard cutters used water cannons to block Philippine ships carrying supplies to the forces occupying Second Thomas Shoal, another disputed small island in the Philippines Exclusive Economic Zone.

China's aggression made it impossible for Duterte to defend his pro-China stance as the country headed into the next election. He pivoted toward Washington, restoring the US defense cooperation agreement that he had ended in 2016, which gives the US military access to Philippines bases. Manila also endorsed the AUKUS defense agreement by which the United States and the United Kingdom will give Australia the technology to build nuclear-powered submarines to help ASEAN countries to respond more rapidly to "regional threats" (read "China").[48] Additionally, after waiting four years, he finally took ownership of the UNCLOS tribunal's ruling in a speech to the UN General Assembly.[49]

Meanwhile, looming over China's deteriorating relationship with the United States is Taiwan, the greatest challenge to any fresh start. "The status quo in the Taiwan Strait is shaky," a PLA general told me with a worried frown in 2019, at a conference in Beijing. I assumed he was referring to actions by Taiwan's president, Tsai Ing-wen. Instead, it was that the PLA has denied the existence of the median line running down the center of the Strait. For decades, each side had tacitly agreed to avoid accidents by sticking to its half of the Strait. But in March 2019, two PLA Air Force J-11 fighters crossed the median line and flew 43 nautical miles toward Taiwan, forcing the Taiwan Air Force to scramble interceptors. More PLA flights across the median line or into Taiwan's Air Defense Identification Zone (a slightly less aggressive incursion) followed, and staged obvious upticks when senior American officials visited the island. During one such visit, in September 2019, eighteen PLA Air Force jets crossed the line on one day; and nineteen crossed it on the next. Three days later, the Foreign Ministry spokesman pronounced from the podium, "There is no so-called center line in the Taiwan Strait."[50] Beijing had vacated the stabilizer of the median line, risking a collision that could escalate into war. The message was directed at the United States and Taiwan; most of the 380 sorties into Taiwan's ADIZ that occurred over ninety-one days in 2020 followed some diplomatic exchange with the US.[51]

When President Biden entered the White House in January 2021, the pace of Chinese incursions increased, giving the impression that Beijing, instead of seeking rapprochement, was testing the new president.[52] PLA Air Force flights surged to even higher numbers and frequency, and the use of fighter jets and nuclear-capable bombers increased. On October 1, 2021, PRC National Day, a record fifty-six jets penetrated Taiwan's ADIZ. In the year after Taiwan began publishing information about the PRC air incursions, PRC military aircraft entered Taiwan's ADIZ on almost 250 days, usually after there had been a development related to US-Taiwan relations.[53]

Every Chinese leader would like to go down in its history books as having reunified Taiwan with the mainland. Hu Jintao, who had the benefit of having Guomindang president Ma Ying-jeou as his counterpart, drew Taiwan closer by deepening economic and social ties with it. He hoped that if he could win the hearts and minds (and pocketbooks) of the Taiwanese people, the island eventually would drop into the PRC's lap, like a ripe plum. Xi relies more on intimidation, especially now that the new Hong Kong Security Law has destroyed the credibility of the "one country, two systems" pledge to continue Taiwan's autonomy.

Xi's actions toward Taiwan have jangled nerves in Taiwan, America, and Japan—and even in China itself—with the threat of a possible war. Although Xi has not announced a deadline for reunification, he has raised expectations that it is in sight. Disagreements between the two sides must reach a final resolution and "cannot be passed on from generation to generation," he declared early in his administration.[54] In 2019, in an address on Taiwan, he said, "The country is growing strong, the nation is rejuvenating and unification between the two sides of the strait is the great trend of history."[55] Some Chinese believe that Xi plans to achieve reunification during his third term, which will begin in fall 2022 and continue to 2027.

If reunification happens, it won't be through dialogue. Xi has cut off talks because President Tsai Ing-wen, the Democratic Progressive Party leader elected in 2016, wouldn't accept the so-called 1992 consensus, an informal agreement between the two sides that there is one China, although each defines it differently (KMT president Ma Ying-jeou had accepted the consensus). Tsai tried unsuccessfully to wordsmith other formulations that might satisfy Xi, and she has been more restrained than former president Chen Shui-bian in making symbolic moves toward Taiwan independence. She would have been a good negotiating partner—had Xi given her half a chance.

Beijing's Taiwan Affairs Office (the Taiban) is bandwagoning in support of Xi's apparent desire to accelerate reunification and his proclivity for arm-twisting by ramping up various forms of pressure. It targets Taiwanese companies that are significant donors to the Democratic Progressive Party (even if they also donate to the Guomindang), fining them for minor infractions. The Taiban explained to the *Global Times* that "the financial backers of Taiwan independence must be punished."[56] The Taiban also imposed travel bans and other sanctions on three of the most senior politicians in the Taiwan government—the premier, head of the legislature, and foreign minister—whom it singled out as pro-independence "stubborn elements."[57]

Additionally, the Taiwan Affairs Office and the Customs Office have blocked imports of Taiwan fruit, claiming that it carries pests. Beijing once leveraged China's massive consumer appetite for fruit to ingratiate itself with the Taiwan fruit farmers. Now they are doing the opposite: punishing the farmers in the regions that vote for the Democratic Progressive Party by banning imports of their pineapples and apples.[58] Fruit exports to the mainland dropped by half, but the loss has mostly been absorbed by people in Japan and Hong Kong who stepped up to buy "freedom pineapples."[59] Nevertheless, the Taiwan government has taken the dispute to the World Trade Organization.

China's pressuring of Taiwan is snapping back against it. In the United States, politicians appear itching to engage in a contest of wills with Beijing and have proposed numerous new bills to prove that Beijing can't cow them. A former Republican US senator observed that Congress has never been as pro-Taiwan as it is today. The Biden administration is cautiously trying to strengthen deterrence against a Chinese military attack on Taiwan without provoking an actual fight.

Lastly, we can see the fresh start stalling in Europe, where the cumulative effects of the harsh repression in Xinjiang and Hong Kong, wolf warrior diplomacy related to COVID, and bullying in Asia have caused a chill—which became much colder after China refused to condemn Russia's war in Ukraine. Europeans have always been upset about China's human rights abuses, but their commercial interests—China is the EU's largest trading partner—usually eclipsed other concerns. Moreover, China's behavior once seemed irrelevant to the EU states' national security. Two-thirds of them have signed on as partners in BRI, and Greece, Portugal, Hungary, and a number of Eastern European countries have large port, energy, and railroad projects funded by Chinese loans.

Now, however, European governments are no longer biting their tongues to avoid antagonizing China. In December 2020, after seven years of on-again, off-again negotiations, Beijing put pressure on the EU to conclude the Comprehensive Agreement on Investment. Beijing wanted to finalize the agreement before Biden came into office, hoping to widen the wedge between America and Europe that had opened during the Trump era. The agreement promises a level playing field for European companies investing in China and Chinese ones investing in Europe and makes some aspirational environment and labor commitments. But shortly after the European Commission had agreed to the deal, members of the European Parliament, the body that has the authority to ratify the agreement, voted for a resolution criticizing Beijing's crackdown in Hong Kong, which also stated that by signing the agreement, the EU Commission "risks undermining its credibility as a global human rights actor."[60] In March 2021, the EU-China relationship unraveled when the EU joined with the United States, the United Kingdom, and Canada to sanction the Chinese government officials responsible for human rights abuses in Xinjiang. It was the first time since the 1989 Tiananmen crisis that Europe had leveled sanctions on China.

The countersanctions that China immediately slapped on European individuals and organizations from eight different countries, including Adrian Lenz, the German scholar who has done painstaking research on the detention camps in Xinjiang; MERICS, a large centrist think tank in Berlin; and several EU members of parliament and the parliament's sub-committee on human rights doomed the ratification of the China-EU investment agreement that the two sides had signed only five months before.

China's sanctioning of private researchers whose findings might cast the country in a negative light drew international condemnation as an attack on academic freedom and free speech. The European parliamentarians were outraged that China dared to tell them what they could and couldn't say about Xinjiang and considered the sanctions to be "part of a totalitarian threat."[61] China's punitive actions have so alarmed Europeans that their governments are increasingly willing to stand up to Beijing, including by engaging Taiwan diplomatically. The EU is also closely scrutinizing Chinese investments in tech industries. As one journalist has put it, they figure that "if most moves are likely to anger Beijing, why hold back from any of them."[62]

In short, the Xi regime has stimulated a sharp European backlash at the moment when the Biden administration and Russia's Ukraine war are reviving the traditional close European ties with the United States. Most people in European countries have turned negative about China and Xi.[63] Moreover, Chinese aggressiveness in Asia no longer seems as remote from the issue of Europe's security as it once did. In April 2021, the EU issued a statement that the tensions in the South China Sea threatened regional peace and stability, and France and Germany dispatched naval warships to show they had a direct stake in what happens there. An even more striking new development is that in recoiling from China's actions, Europe has drawn closer to Taiwan, standing on the side of the democratic David against the autocratic Goliath. The European Parliament overwhelmingly approved a resolution calling for upgrading its relations with its "key EU partner and democratically elected" Taiwan, though without abandoning the "One China" framework.[64] Legislators visited Taiwan and hosted Taiwan's foreign minister in Europe. Tiny Lithuania allowed Taiwan to open a representative office in Vilnius (while still adhering to its One China policy). In response, Chinese Customs wiped Lithuania from its list of origin countries so that cargoes from Lithuania couldn't be filed, effectively blocking all Lithuanian imports, an act that is incompatible with WTO membership and served to reinforce the European estrangement from China.

The Russian War in Ukraine

Much of the international animosity caused by China's actions during Xi Jinping's first decade in power could have been wiped clean had Xi chosen to condemn Russia's brutal invasion of Ukraine and helped end the war. Instead, China pretended to be neutral while siding with Russia by refusing to utter the word "invasion," propagandizing Russian positions (including blaming NATO and spreading disinformation about an America-run biological weapons lab in the Ukraine),[65] and abstaining from UN votes criticizing Russia. So far, at least, it has not provided tangible military or financial assistance to the Russian war effort.

Vladimir Putin may have tricked Xi into appearing to endorse the invasion in a five-thousand-word pre-Olympics joint statement pledging friendship "without limit" just weeks before the invasion started. The Americans had shared their intelligence about Putin's preparations for an invasion with high-level Chinese officials—a surprisingly hopeful gesture considering the growing mistrust between the two countries—but the Chinese did not believe them. After the Russians advanced an all-out invasion, Biden's national security adviser Jake Sullivan offered Xi an out by stating on television that Putin may have lied to him about what he was planning. But instead of taking advantage of these openings, Xi compounded the initial blunder of embracing his fellow-strongman Putin (with whom he had met thirty-eight times since 2012) by continuing to support Russia, even in the face of mounting civilian casualties. The bond between Xi and Putin, based on ideological affinity and their shared spite against the West, still held.

Yet Russia is a much weaker, declining power; its economy is less than one-tenth the size of China's and far less globally integrated. The two neighbors have a history of conflict and mistrust; there is no love lost between Chinese and Russians. I doubt that many of the other top Chinese leaders are enthusiastic about climbing out on a limb with Russia; policymakers in previous Chinese administrations have been reluctant to do so. On the other side, China had a friendly relationship with Ukraine; it is that country's largest trading partner.

Chinese critics of Beijing's stance on the war, if they had the freedom to express themselves on social media, would point out that it violates the 2013 treaty that Xi signed, pledging to defend Ukrainian sovereignty, as well as China's general principles of international relations.[66]

By aligning China with Russia during this war, Xi Jinping's policy will cost China dearly. The American and European imposition of secondary sanctions against Chinese assistance to Russia to evade financial sanctions could be almost as devastating as what they are imposing on Russia itself. And China's economy is already struggling because of the impact of the extreme zero-COVID policies and other self-inflicted wounds, coming on top of longer-term slowing growth. Finally, by joining Russia's camp, Xi is also hardening the determination of a newly unified and fortified coalition of America, Europe, and other democratic countries to counter Chinese autocracy. Relations with Europe and the United States may never recover.

Internal Fragility and Overreach

The Chinese Communist Party's hold on power remains more fragile than it might appear. Chinese leaders are constantly nervous that foreign threats could trigger a mass uprising.[67] This is mainly paranoia; China's leaders are more worried about it than they need to be. Far more likely is the possibility that the divisions within the Party leadership and the rise of a dictatorial leader threaten Party rule from within and, in the process, drive the rising power into conflicts caused by its international overreaching.

Comparing policymaking under Hu Jintao and Xi Jinping brings into sharp focus the two risks lurking in the highest reaches of power in the Chinese Communist Party and their consequences for international peace. During the Hu era, the biggest risk was open splits among the leaders. Bo Xilai campaigned publicly for the Politburo Standing Committee by staking out a position as a law-and-order populist and neo-Maoist because he was unlikely to succeed at playing the inside game.

To preserve elite unity and reduce the risks of open splits, the politicians in the Politburo and Politburo Standing Committee got along by log-rolling, which allowed each of them to rule his own policy domain and benefit from the patronage and corrupt spoils of office in that domain. No one listened to Hu or checked each other. As a result, bureaucratic interest groups, as well as the military, had license to aggrandize themselves by hyping foreign and domestic threats.

As I've tried to show, the flagrant failures of collective leadership help us understand why Xi Jinping was able to convince—or intimidate—other members of the Communist Party elite to go along with his return to a Mao-style personalistic dictatorship. Yet under the Xi regime, the risk of leadership splits hasn't entirely disappeared. Xi's power play could spark resistance from embittered politicians who have lost their patronage and chances for promotion. Even if no one dares to organize a challenge to him, Xi will continue to suspect everyone because he has no way to know who is truly loyal and who is just mouthing the words. Redistributing the spoils of power, as Xi has done, often leads to elite conflict. If Xi doesn't agree to restore some sharing of power with other leaders during his third term, a power struggle could very well occur—and lead to unpredictable international behavior by China.

The overreaching caused by Xi Jinping's overconcentration of power and the bandwagoning of officials behind him is also likely to become more acute during his third term. Xi's arbitrary and imprudent decisions during a crisis in the South China Sea, East China Sea, Korea, or Taiwan could escalate into war. He is unfettered domestically because he has grasped all the levers of power and is surrounded by sycophants who echo his judgments. Xi's overweening ambition for global leadership and his explicit ideological and mercantilistic challenge to market democracies could also provoke overreactions from the Western countries.

Leadership splits and the overconcentration of power therefore loom over China's future. To navigate between them in a peaceful manner China will need to find mechanisms to restrain itself. This problem has no obvious solution or simple answer. Democracies are generally less prone to use force, but transitions to democracy are less peaceful.[68] The growth of mass politics creates incentives for old and new elites to play the nationalist card. If Chinese politicians were to begin to compete openly for votes in a political environment without strong political institutions, they probably would appeal to popular nationalism by taking tough stands on issues like Japan, Taiwan, Tibet, Xinjiang, Hong Kong, and the South China Sea and thereby drive foreign policy toward dangerous risk-taking. The best hope for China's peaceful rise is gradual political reform that lays the foundation for an eventual democracy and builds international confidence by creating an independent legal system, a free press, and civil society. None of those exist today under Xi Jinping.

Conclusion

Overreach and Overreaction

CHINA'S AGGRESSIVE POSTURE IN world affairs and its relentlessly tight grip on domestic society are leading to what it most fears—a return to the politics of containment. Countries—those in Asia and globally—have grown leery of China's intentions and now fully doubt that it intends a peaceful rise to superpower status. They are defending themselves by various economic, diplomatic, and military measures. China's attention is welcomed by autocratic governments in Africa and the Middle East, places ignored or underserved by the rest of the developed world; they need its trade and investment. But its policies have become controversial in countries that hold free elections. Using intimidation and harassment to bolster its maritime and territorial claims in the South China Sea and East China Sea may play well inside China, but it violates international law and pits China against its neighbors and the United States. Threatening sovereign nations that criticize its policies toward Taiwan, Tibet, Xinjiang, Hong Kong, or COVID impels these nations to seek alternatives to their economic reliance—the main source of its power and influence—on China. Even some of China's most respected economists wonder whether they have, in fact, done the world a favor by strengthening the country through the market reforms they helped design.

After three decades of reassuring the world about its benign intentions, Chinese foreign policy began to lose its way under Hu Jintao's collective leadership, veering this way and that as leaders took different public positions and various bureaucratic and economic sectors pursued their own narrow interests. This both encouraged China to become reckless and overbearing and produced the corruption and power struggles that provided the justification for Xi Jinping's strongman rule. Under Hu's oligarchy, interest groups logrolled with one another, and produced an excess of *weiquan* (sovereignty rights defense) and *weiwen* (stability maintenance). Hu never mobilized the businesspeople, intellectuals, and urban middle class who might have helped sustain his first-term liberalizing reforms.

The beginnings of overreach can be traced back to 2006—the maritime agencies started using their ships for *weiquan*, and the central government deployed programs to turn state-owned companies into high-tech national champions. The control coalition clamped down on society and media to get ready for the Olympics and never relaxed even after. After the global financial crisis hit in 2008, China's stimulus, three times the size of the US effort, beefed up the state sector. China's rapid recovery stoked popular feelings of triumphalism and disillusionment with Western models.

I have argued that China's aggressiveness began during Hu's collective leadership and tried to show how it has accelerated dangerously since Xi Jinping took power in 2012. Xi has made himself chairman of everything, consolidating the agencies in every sector, from the coast guard to cybersecurity, and putting them under his personal command. Xi also promoted the loyalist officials who overcomplied with his edicts—until, that is, they fell out of his favor, and he replaced them with people he trusted more. Few officials now dare to give him honest feedback, such as that he might be harming China's interests by ordering the rapid construction of large and militarily fortified artificial islands in the South China Sea or the thought-reform camps in Xinjiang. By clinging to a zero-COVID model, he has set himself up for failure should he prove unable to negotiate the transition to a more flexible approach of living with the disease. Even if his support of Vladimir Putin's invasion of Ukraine is passive, it will likely isolate China further.

The costs to China of Xi's policies are piling up.[1] Its reputation as a responsible player on the world stage has been marred by its economic coercion, "wolf warrior" diplomacy, United Front influence operations, cyberhacking of private firms, intimidation against Taiwan and Japan, coast guard and fishing boat deployments in the exclusive economic zones of its neighbors in violation of international law, as well as by the Xinjiang internment camps and the Hong Kong Security Law. The global reactions come right out of the international relations textbooks: countries are forming balancing coalitions, like the Quad, AUKUS, and the US-EU Trade and Technology Council, to constrain China's aggressive actions and reduce their own economic dependence on China.

Economic costs also are mounting. Opportunities for overseas foreign direct investment, stock market listings, and scientific access are narrowing, as foreign governments grow increasingly suspicious of the Chinese government's intent. China's huge domestic market remains a powerful magnet for foreign investors, yet inbound FDI as a share of GDP declined between 2010 and 2020, reflecting concerns about political risk as well as economic factors like increased labor costs. Countries are moving their supply chains out of China or hedging them with alternative sources of supply. The United States and Europeans have imposed sanctions on hundreds of Chinese firms.

Xi Jinping's overconcentration of power, the bandwagoning of subordinates, and the echo-chamber problems that accompany it have had high domestic costs as well. His quest for security and social control clash as with other economic objectives. By blindly pursuing a model of self-sufficiency and industrial policy in its urgent pursuit of "whole of nation innovation" the state is wasting a tremendous amount of money. Some of Xi's measures that are reminiscent of Mao's rule—such as the turn against rich capitalists, more ideological courses and less English in schools, a clampdown on the entertainment industry, and extreme censorship that extends to economic information—are driving the middle class as well as the wealthy to consider moving their money and families out of China. The uncertainty about the 2022 power transition (or lack thereof) and how China will reopen to the world after years of a zero-COVID policy are weighing on private investment at home as well as abroad.

Policy Suggestions

No one expects Xi Jinping will change his style of leadership—or hand over power to a successor after the normal two terms at the Party Congress in fall 2022. However, there are things he might consider doing that are consistent with his domestic incentives and would help him reduce the risks to China. To avoid further escalation of the hostilities between China and the United States, he needs to find ways to reassure the outside world.

Xi wants China to be respected as a global power, as well it should be, by virtue of its large and talented population, geographic scale, centrality in Asia, and unique history. The question he faces is how best to achieve this ambition. He doesn't want China to be ostracized as a rogue state, an international spoiler trying to build a sphere of influence on intimidation or outright aggression. That's the Putin model, with which Xi Jinping sometimes flirts but hasn't, yet, fully adopted. Xi prefers other countries to be attracted to China, not afraid of it.

The country has formidable soft-power assets, including of course its huge market, but also its traditional culture, and its impressive contemporary accomplishments in poverty reduction, scientific discovery, space exploration, and many other realms. China is the top trading partner of 128 out of 190 countries in the world. And it is surrounded by neighbors who would provide it with a good security blanket were its relations with them friendly. Most of these neighbors—twenty in all—are electoral democracies, places where China's appeal needs to extend beyond their political leaders to their citizenry. China will achieve global leadership if it provides international public goods and if its presence is welcomed by other countries. The third essential factor is establishing a modus vivendi with the United States, "the one country that can make or break China," as one Chinese scholar has put it. A stable relationship with the United States should be considered a Chinese core interest.

In my earlier book *China: Fragile Superpower*, written before Xi came to power, I offered some policy suggestions to China that mainly involved counterweights to the domestic nationalism that I worried could drive the leadership into bellicose international actions. Young people in China today are even more nationalistic. However, I'm not sure that Xi is as interested in creating counterweights as previous leaders were. The system of concentrated personalistic rule he has put in place is designed to enhance his personal authority and freedom of action. Xi has accumulated more personal power than any Chinese leader since Mao. He therefore has the latitude to change his policies without jeopardizing his domestic standing; he might even enhance it with private business, intellectuals, and, indeed, the entire Chinese middle class. His formidable and highly efficient propaganda department can spin an explanation, such as "mission accomplished" or "circumstances changed," to justify any revision or reversal of previous policies.

In any case, what follows are my thoughts about how China's overreach might be moderated in the very places it has done the most self-inflicted damage.

Get Creative in the South China Sea

China's actions in the South China Sea have unsettled other countries because its sovereignty claims are inherently selfish and zero-sum; it's impossible to nurture friendships around them. By making territorial sovereignty its top priority "core interest," China inevitably generates friction with its neighbors. It also puts the nation in contravention to the UN Convention on the Law of the Sea, which grants coastal countries rights to the resources in their offshore exclusive economic zones, and the UNCLOS 2015 tribunal, which ruled that the "historical rights" asserted by China over the entire South China Sea had no legal basis. According to international law, almost the entire South China Sea is international waters that can be freely navigated, fished, and prospected by anyone.

It's unrealistic to expect China to modify its formal claims to conform to the UNCLOS ruling. But it should be possible for Xi Jinping to make some compromises. For example, if China dropped its objections to allowing claimants to drill with foreign energy companies or exercise with other militaries—objections aimed at keeping the United States out—it could get agreement on the ASEAN-China Code of Conduct. Another way would be to call for a freeze of all military installations on islands or undertake one unilaterally. After all, those installations are vulnerable to attack and not all that militarily useful.

If these moves look too much like backdowns to him, Xi might consider improving amity with the Southeast Asians by launching a high-profile initiative to preserve the South China Sea common resources. More than forty years ago, Deng Xiaoping argued that the best way to deal with maritime sovereignty disputes was to "pursue joint development while shelving disputes." Up to now, Chinese decision-makers have avoided collective arrangements and only introduced bilateral ones in which their leverage was greatest. Before Xi, China proposed bilateral joint energy development agreements with the Philippines and Vietnam, both in the other countries' EEZs, but they were never implemented. A regional fishing regime should be easier than joint development of energy because fish travel freely. Overfishing is depleting fish stocks, so everyone would benefit from a fishing management regime that regulated the catch. By founding the regime, Beijing would show how its leadership can serve the collective good.[2]

Close the Xinjiang Reeducation Camps

Of all China's actions since Xi Jinping took power, the most damaging to its international image involves the camps in Xinjiang, where more than a million Muslims are being confined while undergoing "thought reform." The Chinese government defends the camps as "vocational and educational training" for religious extremists whose "minds have been poisoned to the extent of losing reason."[3]

In the eyes of the world, however, the camps are reminiscent of the Nazi concentration camps and the Soviet Gulag. It took the Allied armies to liberate the Nazi concentration camps. Just days after Stalin died, Soviet officials released more than a million inmates from the labor camps; Khrushchev closed all of them down several years later because they cost more than they earned. If Xi doesn't want his historical legacy to be ruined by the camps in Xinjiang, he should close them down. They are expensive to build and maintain, and American sanctions against Xinjiang products and surveillance companies are dragging down the flagging Chinese economy. There is no way to defend or improve them.

Stop Economic Coercion

Xi Jinping's foreign-policy style involves using China's market power to threaten and punish countries, businesses, and universities to force them to adopt the CCP's line on domestic political issues. It's an obnoxious form of Chinese extraterritoriality to enforce political correctness against foreigners; the long aim of the propaganda censors is reaching overseas and forcing conformity. If you don't kowtow to Beijing's position on Taiwan, Xinjiang, Hong Kong, or COVID, you can be frozen out of the China market.

This coercive economic statecraft is backfiring. The uncertainty about when Beijing might punish you is driving the United States and other countries to find alternatives to dependence on trade with China by making tacit or formal agreements with one another to move supply chains outside of China. As a consequence, China faces greater economic and political isolation.

Showing greater tolerance of diverse opinions would be a sign of self-confidence and make good use of its huge market to expand China's network of friends instead of driving them away. There are other ways to win the support of the nationalist public than throwing economic weight around in fights over symbolic issues.

Revive Reform and Opening

Xi Jinping's obsession with security has eclipsed China's prior commitments to improve its market economy and open itself to foreign businesses. One of the latest slogans, "dual circulation," tries to reassure foreigners that China is still open for business even as its primary thrust is to reorient the economy toward domestic producers and consumers. Given how far the pendulum has swung toward Party-state capitalism, any recalibration toward market reform and opening would not only benefit the economy but win the enthusiastic support of international businesses and generate other reputational payoffs.

The old-fashioned way to stimulate China's flagging economy is to open the spigots on bank lending, government investment, and the real-estate market, but boosting market competition would reap greater gains. The government should publicly recommit to the Third Plenum (2013) blueprint that emphasized "the decisive role of the market," and do a detailed analysis of what remains undone and how it plans to do it. A consultation process, one that includes private entrepreneurs as well as economists, would help improve the practicality of the proposals as well as signify an appreciation for the vitality of the private sector. Xi needs to make amends for the way he battered private business in 2020 and 2021 if he hopes to restore its confidence. The private sector is crucially important especially for keeping unemployment low.

Opening sectors beyond financial services to foreign companies could revive their waning enthusiasm for China. US policy toward China has hardened, partly because there has been no business counterweight to the security hawks. Frustrated by an inhospitable climate in China, the business community went politically inert. If the climate in China improved, so would their lobbying in the US policy process.

China's application to become a member of the Comprehensive and Progressive Agreement for Trans-Pacific Partnership (CPTPP) helps symbolize its desire to reconverge with global market-oriented rules. The foreign cynics—who are in the majority—believe that China's interest in joining the agreement is purely tactical: by becoming a member before the United States or Taiwan, China could make it hard for either of them to join. To gain entry, however, China will have to prove its sincerity by doing more than just promise to make the required changes in its rules and practices; it will have to earn the trust of the CPTPP members by making some of these changes in advance. (Dropping sanctions against Australia as a signal that it is moving away from coercive use of trade would also be a good sign.) The bar for membership will be high because of China's disregard for other treaty commitments it has made in the past. The United States may quietly urge the members to exclude China. Because joining the agreement would pay such large dividends, China should bend over backward to make the changes necessary meet the membership requirements.

Operate the Belt and Road Initiative by International Standards

China's expansive global economic diplomacy would be more welcomed by other countries were it more inclusive and transparent, and less obviously a self-serving pet project of Xi Jinping. Engineering and construction companies from all countries should be able to compete for the jobs that are currently being monopolized by Chinese companies. Labor standards would improve too. The loan agreements and project contracts should be transparent and follow the standards of other international aid agencies.

Instead of being so Sinocentric, the BRI should emulate China's other international development initiative, the Asian Infrastructure Investment Bank (AIIB), which is governed by an international board of governors and board of directors, managed by an international staff, and operated according to international standards. For years, the AIIB leadership has watched the missteps of the BRI with frustration. Why doesn't the Chinese government explore a merger of the two development initiatives to make the BRI more of a multilateral institution? Or at least give the BRI a makeover and follow the example of the AIIB leadership and boards?

Open Dialogue with the Taiwan Government

Taiwan's democracy is strengthening the island's sense of a separate identity and, despite its economic ties with the mainland, driving its politics toward formal independence. The next Taiwan president (the election will be held in 2024) is almost certain to be a member of the Democratic Progressive Party (DPP) and likely to be more assertively pro-independence than the relatively accommodating current president, Tsai Ing-wen. The loss of political freedoms in Hong Kong under the new Hong Kong Security Law has destroyed any hope by the Taiwanese that they could retain their democracy under Beijing's "one country, two systems" formula for reunification. In the United States, support for Taiwan in Congress is higher than ever before, creating pressure on the White House to treat Taiwan as already a sovereign independent country.

Meanwhile, both China's military power vis-à-vis Taiwan and the United States, and the nationalist calls for China to use it, are growing. Although Xi Jinping says he remains committed to peaceful reunification, he has intensified the intimidation of Taiwan by means of economic sanctions and air patrols. Many Chinese believe that Xi is staying in office for a third term so he can go down in the history books as having achieved the reunification of the island.

Inside China, it is widely believed that the Communist Party would be overthrown if the country attacks Taiwan but loses the fight. Or if Taiwan declares independence and the mainland doesn't put up a fight. Xi's political fate hinges on the actions of the Taiwan and United States governments; although China's can't control either, its choice of approach to Taiwan — attraction or intimidation — could influence them.

Initiating direct talks with the Taiwan government without preconditions offers the only way for Xi to escape from this dilemma and take some of the air out of Taiwan's movement away from China. Xi has cut off all dialogue with the current government because President Tsai Ing-wen wouldn't utter the magic words "1992 consensus," meaning "one China," interpreted differently by the two sides. But there are precedents for Xi to put aside any preconditions for dialogue. For years China's leaders refused on principle to talk directly to the Taiwan government until its president said, "One China." Jiang Zemin ignored the "one China" precondition and invited Taiwan's cross-strait negotiator to get on an airplane to China in 1997. Then in 2008, when Taiwan elected a president from the KMT, Ma Ying-jeou, Hu Jintao and Ma were able to converge on a different compromise formula — the so-called 1992 consensus. Xi and Ma held a historic meeting in 2015 in Singapore under that formula. But when a president from the DPP was elected in 2016, Xi cut off all dialogue because her party was traditionally pro-independence and, while giving a nod to the 1992 consensus as a "historical fact," she was unwilling to appear like a supplicant. Xi also has ignored Tsai's calls for "meaningful dialogue."

Although Xi would receive some domestic criticism for dropping the "1992 consensus" precondition, it would be better to start dialogue with the current president than wait to see what her DPP successor has in store. The United States and the rest of the world could applaud Xi's statesmanship and put pressure on Taiwan to reciprocate with concessions of its own. Xi also might be surprised by the domestic reaction to his putting practicality ahead of a dogma. Some among the elite, the military, and passionate young nationalists would carp, but China's "silent majority" would greet the resumption of cross-strait talks with a sense of relief. They care more about not losing Taiwan than specific formulations about it. Xi would discover that he has more domestic latitude to handle Taiwan flexibly than he realized.

Make Some Domestic Governance Reforms

Even small steps in the direction of greater transparency and access to information would encourage people outside as well as inside China to see that Xi Jinping and the CCP are sufficiently confident in their popular support to relax secrecy and censorship. The information feedback would also help Xi better assess his standing with the public to reduce his legitimacy dilemma.

To respond to Western criticism of Chinese autocracy, the Party has been propagandizing outside China about its "Democracy That Works," laying out a Chinese version of democracy called "whole-process people's democracy" to compete with Western democracy.[4] Any reforms that strengthen the authority of China's legislatures (People's Congresses), legal system, or elections would reap dividends for China's international reputation as well as its good governance.

What Can Americans Do?

Those are my suggestions to China.[5] What about to the United States? Fifteen years of overreach by China's leaders has incited a forceful reaction from the US and many other countries. The impetus to push back against China now comes from every sector. No one has stepped forward to defend the value of good relations between China and the United States — not business leaders, not China scholars, and certainly no one in Congress. Indeed, the only issue that unites Democratic and Republican politicians is the "China threat." The Biden administration came into office intending to revise the Trump administration's confrontational strategy toward China, but it finds itself perpetuating it instead, using competition with China as a foil to try to win bipartisan support for an ambitious and expensive legislative agenda of self-renewal. Taking advantage of the rivalry with China, Biden is challenging the US Congress to prove that democracies can perform better than autocracies. Having heard both Democratic and Republican administrations inveighing against China, the public naturally has become more suspicious of it. Anti-China attitudes are therefore becoming the new bipartisan axis of American politics, making it difficult for policymakers to think sensibly about the cost-benefit trade-offs of their policies.

But China's overreach doesn't have to lead to overreaction by America. The next few years will tell whether the American body politic can respond to the Chinese government's actions in a proportionate and effective manner.

Xi Jinping's centralized personalistic regime has systemic features that make it prone to rash risk-taking, as we have seen. But we don't yet know if overreach is hard-baked into Xi's system of rule, or if other countries can influence Xi to exercise greater self-restraint. Nor do we know if Xi is aware of the growing international backlash to his actions or too insulated by the echo chamber produced by sycophancy and propaganda to hear the reactions. Some years ago, a Chinese academic told me that Xi was internally conflicted: "The greatest contradictions in Chinese politics are inside Xi Jinping's own mind," he said. "Inside he is hesitating [about] what to do." I believe that that may remain the case.

Don't Give Up on Diplomacy

After years of considering the matter, I'm agnostic about whether Xi Jinping's regime is influenceable. That is why I believe the United States needs to test the proposition by pursuing smart diplomacy that includes negotiations as well as pressure. Many Americans have concluded that China is bent on supplanting the United States as the world's number-one power and that to avert that dire outcome, we must trip China up. They believe that negotiating would be fruitless.

There are two reasons to reject that conventional wisdom. First, American primacy is the wrong goal for our China policy. It smacks of a playground fight instead of principled support for peace and order. The US aim should not be holding on to the top slot in a global pecking order. Instead, its overriding goal should be preventing a war by motivating China to behave constructively and not aggressively toward other countries, even if in some dimensions it outdoes the United States. China's cooperation on global climate and public health threats is also essential.

We have no choice but to coexist with a Communist Party–led China in the foreseeable future. Therefore, we need a strategy to influence its decision calculus, so that it acts in ways that are less detrimental to the US and other countries. "Intense competition," argues Biden's national security adviser Jake Sullivan, "depends on intense diplomacy."[6]

Americans have enjoyed the economic, political, and security benefits of being number one in a unipolar world ever since the fall of the Soviet Union ended the Cold War. They are having a hard time adjusting to the possibility of losing that status. The global financial crisis started them worrying that the nation is in decline; the latest dysfunctions of American democracy reflected in the Trump administration's mismanagement of the COVID pandemic and the insurrection on January 6, 2021, at the Capitol have added to their loss of confidence. Feeling the hot breath of China coming up behind them has thrown them into a panic. Yet concluding prematurely that China is their enemy could be a suicidal misperception, one that creates a self-fulfilling prophesy and leads to war.

Second, it's too soon to give up on diplomacy. Although Beijing is unlikely to make fundamental changes in its system and some issues, such as Hong Kong, may be intractable, greater moderation in China's international conduct would significantly reduce its threat. Chinese leaders have recalibrated their policies in the past. One encouraging sign is that Xi still appears motivated by a desire for international respect. Only after a serious diplomatic effort fails should Americans conclude that the only option is to degrade and defeat China. Moreover, China's domestic dynamics are unpredictable, and Xi won't be in charge forever. Dealing with China in a respectful manner that connotes goodwill toward the Chinese people will provide a foundation for a more stable relationship in the future.

My own government experience was more than twenty years ago, during what might in retrospect be considered a golden age of US-China engagement, when China stopped proliferating nuclear and missile technology to come into line with international rules and opened its economy to join the World Trade Organization. Yet some of the lessons I learned, I believe, remain applicable.

A successful diplomatic effort should involve clearly specifying our priority disputes where there's a realistic possibility of getting agreement, communicating our agenda to China, and negotiating the disputes in a businesslike manner at an appropriate level. Don't expect overnight miracles; be prepared to invest time and effort; and prepare for senior official and summit meetings to drive progress. Every agreement builds mutual confidence in the two sides' ability to work things out again. When it comes to carrots or sticks, choose ones that can be dialed up or dialed down to have the best effect. If considering sanctions, use them as leverage by first giving China a chance to avoid them by adjusting its conduct. We need to show that we are prepared to acknowledge China's willingness to make compromises to improve relations and reciprocate in positive ways. Every successful negotiation requires some goodwill, as well as a willingness to walk away if necessary.

Although large multiagency dialogues, such as the previously mentioned Strategic and Economic Dialogues, turned into bureaucratic circuses that accomplished little, some regular dialogues—such as between the assistant secretaries responsible for Asia policy in the State Department or between military commanders—can establish a familiarity that forms a foundation for practical problem-solving. General Mark Milley, the chairman of the Joint Chiefs, called his Chinese counterpart to reassure him that the Trump administration had no plans to attack China despite the chaos of its final days, precisely because he knew General Li Zuocheng well enough to sense that the Chinese general remained "unusually rattled," and needed a second call to ease his worries.[7]

China's recent efforts to modernize its nuclear weapons and develop new hypersonic missiles are destabilizing what is already a shaky strategic stability between the two nuclear powers. The United States has been pressing for strategic stability talks for years and should keep urging Xi to reduce the dangers of miscalculation by initiating such talks. Even if the talks do not achieve any breakthroughs, they could lead to exchanges on nuclear safety between the two countries and strengthen the cautious voices of the nuclear professionals inside China.

Freewheeling strategic dialogues for sharing perspectives on foreign policy hotspots throughout the world, with no scripted talking points, are invaluable for exploring areas of convergence and divergence; these strategic dialogues also connote respect, which is highly valued by China, by placing the two countries on an equal plane as they deal with world problems.

However, frustrating as they may be, negotiations test our assumptions about the Xi regime and provide vital information for updating our overall China strategy. The Biden administration has already learned, for example, that the Chinese government wants to restore the Iran nuclear deal; as an energy importer, instability in the Middle East is as little in Beijing's interests as it is in the United States'. China also agreed with other countries to release crude oil from its strategic reserves in February 2022 to reduce global prices, a collective move all the more needed to stabilize global energy markets after Russia's invasion of Ukraine. Will Beijing be willing to coordinate with Washington on its response to North Korea's resumption of missile tests? Can we induce the Chinese government to reconfirm Xi's previous commitments to President Obama not to militarize the artificial islands in the South China Sea, or to cease cyberhacking to steal technical and commercial secrets from private firms? Can we obtain Xi's agreement to hold talks on nuclear weapons? We can only assess Xi's pragmatic flexibility through negotiations.

Be Firm and Realistic on Human Rights

One of the secrets of effective diplomacy is to know what aspects of the other country's behavior you can change and what aspects you can't change. American diplomacy stands a better chance of inducing Beijing to moderate its foreign or economic policies than it does getting it to back off its harsh human rights abuses. China's human rights practices offend American values: China's police state repression of Xinjiang and Tibet; destruction of civil rights in Hong Kong; suppression of organized religion; Internet and media censorship; arrests of civil rights lawyers, feminists, and critical intellectuals; violations of LGBTQ rights; extrajudicial detention and torture—and the list goes on. Xi Jinping and the control coalition believe that heavy-handed repression is necessary to manage stability. There is little we can do that is going to persuade them otherwise. Although we must speak out against Chinese government abuses, join with other countries to name and shame them in international forums, and give moral support to their victims—to do otherwise would be antithetical to our identity as Americans—we should face up to the fact that we are unlikely to gain much traction on them.

Political reform in China will not be realized through outside pressure. Domestic demand, not foreign prodding, brings about political transformations. We inspire more progress on the ground by repairing our vibrant democracy than by preaching or threatening punishments that evoke a public backlash in China. My own experience in government taught me that Washington's typical approach to human rights in China—which involves public shaming and use of sanctions—wins points with American domestic audiences but can be counterproductive in China. Most Chinese, even those committed to democratization, resent American interference in the country's domestic affairs. The sanctions against companies whose products are manufactured with Xinjiang cotton have backfired, putting Chinese consumers on the side of the patriotic domestic companies that proudly use Xinjiang cotton and against the international companies that have purged Xinjiang cotton from their supply chains—as now required by US law. Nor is there sympathy inside China for the sanctions to condemn the Hong Kong Security Law.

What we need is a "smart" human rights approach—one that appeals to the Chinese public's sense of rights and justice, that leverages American leadership in international organizations, and finally, that is based on our self-recognition that we Americans need to constantly improve our own society.

Follow the Leader

In Xi Jinping's centralized system, the best way to get anything done is to bring the leader on board with it. Much of past progress in US-China relations has been accomplished before summit meetings, when both sides are keenest to show the achievements of their diplomacy. During their face-to-face encounters, the two leaders sometimes reach new understandings spontaneously, although usually their time together is too short and scripted to get to a deeper interpersonal level. To spend more time together in a relaxed setting conducive to candor President George W. Bush invited

Jiang Zemin to visit his ranch in Texas and President Obama invited Xi Jinping to the Sunnylands estate in Southern California. The Americans favor informality, while the Chinese side prefers the flourishes of a formal state visit to the White House, which play well on television back home.

President Trump may have overdone his effusive expressions of friendship toward Xi, but he had the right idea. Getting the Chinese president personally committed to a better relationship with the United States is the sine qua non for any accord on the difficult issues between the two countries. Because Xi is so busy micromanaging other issues, just getting him to pay attention to the United States is a challenge; he probably doesn't keep abreast of the latest developments in the US unless diplomatic events force him to. A scheduled encounter with the US president will entail briefings that may update his information and his reflexive assumptions that America is on the decline and ill-intentioned.[8]

Xi's reluctance to leave China during the COVID-19 pandemic has delayed a face-to-face meeting between Xi and Biden, but Zoom calls are a decent substitute if they occur frequently enough. Regularly checking in with each other can improve the leaders' interpersonal comfort level, jump-start lower-level negotiations, and lay the groundwork for managing future crises. Inviting Xi to pay a state visit to the United States as soon as COVID permits would signify both countries' high priority on stabilizing relations.

Race to the Top, Not to the Bottom

Science and technology have become the focal point of the competition between China and the United States, a competition that is colored by American fears about China's threat to their national security. Since the mid-2000s, the Chinese government has invested massively in science and technology as key to national power. China's share of global research and development is almost the same as the US share.

China's technology advances alarm Americans because of how the government achieved them and because it channels them into its military. Because China absorbs foreign technologies through illegal as well as legal methods, many people believe, incorrectly, that its technological advance has been achieved solely through unfair competition and pilfering of Western technologies. Xi Jinping's Military-Civilian Fusion program highlights the lack of clear boundaries between the defense and commercial sectors; China's technological progress is turning it into a more formidable military threat. The conventional wisdom in America today is that the United States is falling dangerously behind China in such frontier technologies as artificial intelligence, 5G broadband communications, electric-car batteries, and quantum computing. The only way to protect our national security, many believe, is to erect walls, blocking China from stealing the crown jewels of American technology from our university labs or tech start-ups.

I'd like to see competition between the United States and China become a race to the top: If both countries invest more, and achieve more, without closing their doors to collaboration with each other, it will be a boon to human progress. The secret of American success has always been its openness. Openness ensures a steady flow of global talents into the country and, combined with some targeted measures to manage the risks of openness, offers the best way to compete with China. When the Soviet Union launched the Sputnik satellite into orbit in 1957, the United States ramped up spending on higher education and research, as cross-fertilization between scientists continued. Soviet and US scientists collaborated on basic physics and other research. The Reagan administration determined in 1985 that federally funded, university-based research in science and engineering should remain unrestricted to the maximum extent possible, a rule that has been reconfirmed by several other presidents.

But the politicians who are panicking over what they see as a Chinese technological juggernaut favor a more exclusionary approach, which will do lasting damage to American society, higher education, and the economy. Security considerations have become so dominant that they are blinding us to the costs of the walls we are building. The United States is competing with China by becoming more like China — nationalist, fixated on security, and politicizing the market economy — instead of becoming a better version of itself.

We cripple the nation by operating under the illusion that we are the one place where innovation occurs. In today's global-knowledge economy much of the advanced work is being done in countries outside the United States and Europe, and the US government has little chance of stopping knowledge from spreading.[9] Yet Washington is engaging in an all-out attempt to prevent the leakage of knowledge to China, despite the high costs to our ability to attract and retain talented individuals from throughout the world. Attracting global talent to supplement our homegrown supply is America's asymmetric advantage. Our world-class universities are the magnet that draws the best foreign students to the United States. Many stay on after graduation, making new discoveries and starting companies. Those who return to China become the scientific collaborators of their American professors and classmates. The American and Chinese scientific research environments are already deeply enmeshed. For example, according to researchers at the UC San Diego China Data Lab, in the decade between 2010 and 2020, US scientists in the life sciences worked with more Chinese scientists than with scientists of any other country; and those who partnered with Chinese scientists were more productive than those who partnered with scientists from other countries. Their productivity declined after 2018 when federal agencies started their investigations.[10]

Washington's shortsighted policy places Chinese and Chinese American scientists and engineers under suspicion of being spies for China and hounds them out of America. In language that is redolent of the Red Scare during the Cold War, FBI director Christopher Wray proclaimed that the China Threat is "a whole of society threat on their end," one that would take "a whole of society response from us." It is a very small step from saying that China is mounting a "whole of society threat" to saying that anyone of Chinese nationality should be viewed with suspicion and a small step from that to generalizing to people of Chinese heritage. As a society America has made this sort of mistake more than once before, and always to its detriment.

University faculty who once were encouraged by the National Science Foundation and other federal agencies to undertake joint projects with their Chinese counterparts and to train Chinese graduate students were investigated by the Justice Department's China Initiative during the Trump administration for failing to declare their Chinese contacts on their grant proposals. None of the prosecutions were for espionage, or even intellectual property violations, and almost all of them have led to acquittals or dismissals. Under fire from civil rights critics, the Justice Department scrapped the China Initiative in February 2022 but promised to continue to "prioritize and aggressively counter" harmful actions by China.[11]

Chinese graduate students are denied visas purely based on the Chinese universities they attended. Those from military-affiliated institutions (which include some of China's best medical facilities, for example) or who joined the CCP as college students (there is no way to formally quit the Party) are turned down. Chinese graduate students in some specialties can only get one-year visas.

A cloud hangs over Chinese and Chinese American scientists and engineers. Some of them have made the agonizing decision to leave America and accept positions in China where they are offered lavish salaries, research funds, and laboratories. America's own innovation ecosystem is losing out by chasing talented people out of the United States and back to China, as we did to Qian Xuesen, the father of China's missile program, whom the United States deported from CalTech in 1955, during the McCarthy period.

The collateral damage is a rise in racial animus against all Asian Americans. Anyone walking on the sidewalk who looks Chinese has to fear racial slurs and even assault. It's disingenuous of US officials to speak out against anti–Asian American racial violence while ignoring the connection to their harsh rhetoric and actions against China.

The economic price of building walls to China's technological ambitions is also substantial. Chinese foreign direct investment in the United States has plummeted as the interagency Committee on Foreign Direct Investment to the US tightened its reviews of Chinese foreign investment in critical technology companies, critical infrastructure, or personal data companies. As export controls and the Entity List expand year after year, American technology companies are losing a large share of their sales, which also means fewer jobs for American employees. The technology embargos, moreover, have accelerated the Xi regime's already massive effort to achieve technological self-reliance; and companies based in third countries are reconsidering their plans to invest in the United States to avoid being caught in the crossfire between Washington and Beijing.

The barriers even extend to global financial markets, which would have been unimaginable several years ago. The Biden administration has continued the Trump-era ban on buying shares of publicly traded companies linked to the Chinese military; and a bill before Congress is proposing further limitations. The US-China Business Council has noted that "regulation of outbound capital flow is unprecedented in 250 years of American history."[12] By politicizing routine commercial dealings and turning them into matters of national security, we tell China's leaders and citizens that even when they follow the rules, we will fight dirty to keep our edge. This message not only inflames Chinese public reactions but robs China's leaders of any incentive to act responsibly. If Americans are going to keep them down no matter how they act, why bother to act as a responsible power?

Of course, American security and intelligence services need to prevent serious state-sponsored espionage and threats to US critical systems. There are discrete solutions to managing security risk.[13] But then we should let the natural immune system of a functioning, open, pluralistic society and market economy deal with a challenging China instead of panicking. As Francis Fukuyama wrote recently, "If Americans cease to believe in an open, tolerant and liberal society, our capacity to innovate and lead will also diminish."[14] The United States should unwind the self-defeating overreactions begun during the Trump administration that discourage

Chinese students and researchers and Chinese American collaborations. If we don't want to share knowledge in a handful of specific technologies related to the military, then we should classify the research and base it off the university campus. Other than that, university-based science shouldn't be restricted.

Work with Allies and Friends

One of the best multipliers of US influence over China's conduct is joint effort with allies and friends. President Trump tore up trade agreements with some of our closest allies in Europe and the Asia-Pacific. The Biden administration has moved quickly to repair those relationships and form coalitions among our allies to deal with the China challenge. The Quad, that informal grouping consisting of Japan, Australia, India, and the United States, has emerged as the most active such coalition. Its main function is to augment bilateral defense alliances as a security counterweight to China. Another headline-making small group effort is AUKUS, which will strengthen military defense and deterrence against China's growing military might (although the first submarines that are part of it aren't likely to be in the water until the late 2030s). America's Asian allies also are beginning to coordinate with its European ones in NATO.

In addition, the Biden administration is establishing strategic trade frameworks to reduce US interdependence with the Chinese economy and to provide alternatives to it. The US-EU Trade and Technology Council (TTC) aims to coordinate investment screening, export controls, technology standards, secure semiconductor supply chains, data governance, and clean technologies to protect against China's unfair trade practices and security threats while maintaining a global level playing field among market democracies.[15] If the United States acts alone to impose strict limitations against Chinese investments or trade while other countries continue their normal commercial relations with China it will accomplish nothing other than diverting business from American to foreign firms. The council presents a united front to China and moves supply chains out of China and into a large market of democracies whose technology regulations are more or less consistent.

Harmonizing regulations with our allies helps the United States avoid overly expansive self-defeating exclusions against Chinese technologies in the name of national security. Few other countries want to be forced into an either-or choice between China and America; they'd like to get along with and do business with both. Listening to our allies may help us make wiser and more effective policies.

What's striking, however, is that no one is inviting the PRC into any of these clubs; they are formed precisely to counter China or to reduce interdependence with its economy, not incentivize improvements in China's conduct. In line with my recommendation to test whether Xi Jinping's regime is influenceable, why not see whether China is willing to meet the high standards of membership in some other clubs? The moral sway and effective pressure a group of countries can bring to bear are greater than those of any one country, even the United States. The Chinese government is more likely to conform to international norms if the norms are established collectively by a group of its trading partners, and not just by the United States. The authority of multilateral agreements like the World Trade Organization or the Nuclear Nonproliferation Treaty is the strongest; Chinese leaders want to be respected and have a seat at the head table in such multilateral bodies. Even if leaders in China believe the United States is a declining power, the authority of multilateral institutions lives on.

Clubs that open membership to any country that can meet the stringent requirements for membership can test China's willingness to self-correct. Only a few years ago, economic reformers in China were sketching out a road map toward membership in the Trans-Pacific Partnership (TPP), the comprehensive regional trade agreement originally proposed by Japan and the Obama administration that sets a high bar of labor, intellectual property, anticorruption, and environmental standards in conjunction with lowered tariffs. In 2021, the Chinese government made a formal application to the new version of the TPP, the Comparative and Progressive Trans-Pacific Partnership (CPTPP). The members of the partnership should not reject China's application out of hand, as many in Washington would reflexively advise, and indeed, should negotiate China's entry in good faith. They can establish an objective standard by first negotiating the United Kingdom's application for membership. The Chinese government has burned a lot of bridges by failing to live up to its commitments, so it would be reasonable to require it to make a down payment by taking unilateral steps before it formally joins the partnership.

Unfortunately, the Trump administration pulled out of the Trans-Pacific Partnership and the Biden administration lacks the votes in Congress to re-enter the CPTPP, leaving the United States hobbled by its lack of an economic leg to stand on to anchor its presence in the region. The United States didn't deign to join the Regional Comprehensive Economic Partnership (RCEP), a more conventional Asia-Pacific regional free-trade agreement to which China and fourteen other Asian countries belong, and now it faces the prospect of a Chinese veto in the unlikely event that it applies to join.

Seeking an economic position in the region, the Biden administration has floated the idea of an Indo-Pacific Economic Framework that wouldn't require congressional approval and would involve several sectoral agreements, including one on digital trade that would be based on the digital-trade chapter of the US-Mexico-Canada Agreement (USMCA, the new version of NAFTA) and the US-Japan Digital Trade Agreement.

Why not make at least the digital trade agreement a club like the CPTPP, with an open door to any country that can meet its standards? China's motivation is strong; Huang Qifan, the former mayor of Chongqing, has said that China should join high-level economic and trade agreements like the CPTPP to "make more friends and fewer rivals" and "win the majority (on our side)," particularly given that the United States treats China as a threat.[16] China's reformist technocrats welcome the external pressure to make the changes they believe are necessary for China's own economic vitality. If Beijing meets the bar for membership, it could level the economic playing field for state, private, and foreign companies, and even if it doesn't, we'll get a good assessment of its economic system. By being inclusive, we also show that we don't want to divide the region into antagonistic blocs. Opening agreements to Chinese participation ultimately benefits the United States by enabling both countries to race to the top instead of to the bottom.

Keep a Strong US Military Presence but Avoid an Arms Race

US forces deployed in the Indo-Pacific, who exercise and train in close collaboration with their (increasingly capable) allies, remain essential for deterring adventurism by Xi Jinping. The hardening of China's authoritarian Party-state and its international aggressiveness have heightened the threat perceptions of Asian countries and increased their demand for the United States and its allies to defend them. We want China's commander in chief, when contemplating action, to look out to the Pacific and see forces with the will and capacity to defend Taiwan, Japan, South Korea, and Australia and our other friends. To incentivize Xi to forgo military actions that might make him a hero at home, we need to remind him of the likely humiliation of being defeated by our forces. The presence of US forces in the region also translates into leverage on nonmilitary issues.

Preserving strategic stability in the region is becoming increasingly difficult, however, as the two sides improve their military capabilities. Chinese leaders tolerated American alliances and forward deployment in the past, but to Xi they look like an imminent threat to his regime. The Quad and AUKUS no doubt contribute to his sense of being surrounded. The US should continue to try to engage Beijing in arms control and confidence-building before it's too late.

Stay Steady on Taiwan

Worries that Xi Jinping is preparing to attack Taiwan to compel reunification have created something of a war scare in the United States and China. The worries are all the sharper after Russia's invasion of Ukraine. The outgoing commander of the US Indo-Pacific Command, Admiral Phil Davidson, testified that the PRC was likely to attack Taiwan within six years. As I've noted, many Chinese are convinced that Xi sought a third term because that's when he intends to reunify the island. Meanwhile, although the people in Taiwan are well aware of Beijing's intimidation, only 30 percent of them are more worried about an attack than they were six months ago. Few Taiwanese believe that conflict in the Taiwan Strait is "imminent or inevitable."[17] Most of the leading American experts on Taiwan agree.

But members of Congress and the policy community are talking as if an attack is imminent and urgently proposing ways to deter Beijing and defend Taiwan. With support for Taiwan at an all-time high with the public and Congress, politicians are outdoing one another to show their affection for Taiwan. Some bills would elevate the US government's treatment of the island to more closely approximate formal statehood—for example, to require government agencies to treat the government of Taiwan the same way it treats other foreign states, create a partnership between Taiwan and the US National Guard, and give Taiwan the defense-related privileges of a major non-NATO ally. These symbolic gestures would inflame Beijing rather than provide any tangible improvements in Taiwan's security. Politicians should be cautious about scoring political points with measures that could endanger Taiwan instead of making it safer.

Leading foreign policy experts, including Richard Haass, the president of the Council on Foreign Relations, and a number of members of Congress propose reversing the strategic ambiguity toward the defense of Taiwan by which the United States announces that "any effort to determine the future of Taiwan by other than peaceful means" would be of "grave concern to the United States" and require it to consult with Congress to decide how to respond if Taiwan is attacked—a caveat designed to discourage Taiwan from declaring independence and provoking an attack from the mainland while also deterring the mainland from attacking Taiwan. The possibility of US intervention deters both sides from endangering the status quo while being assured that the other side will not unilaterally seek to change the status quo. Shifting to a policy of "strategic clarity" would not serve the US interest in sustaining a peaceful status quo in the Strait and maintaining working relationships with both China and Taiwan. It would confirm China's suspicion that the goal of US policy is to permanently detach Taiwan from the mainland and use it as a base for the US containment of China.[18]

The Biden administration has so far resisted the political pressure to make treatment of Taiwan more explicit or abandon strategic ambiguity, though Biden told an interviewer that the United States would defend Taiwan, heightening Beijing's suspicions that a change in US policy is afoot. What the Biden administration has done to make Taiwan more secure is encourage other countries to support it. Most significant from a strategic perspective is Japan's new position—that "the peace and stability of Taiwan is directly connected to that of Japan." The deputy prime minister stated that a major problem in Taiwan could "relate to a survival-threatening situation" for Japan, which, according to its constitution, would allow it to offer ballistic missile defense and combat operations alongside the United States.[19] Japan's new appreciation for how its own security is connected to Taiwan's, and its willingness to operationally assist in the defense of Taiwan with the United States, will certainly help deter Xi from launching an attack.

Another important new development is the interest European countries now have in strengthening their ties with Taiwan, something that in the past they would have been reluctant to do for fear of angering Beijing. The Taiwan foreign minister traveled on a charm offensive to Europe in 2021 and held unprecedented informal meetings with the European Union Parliament, which backed a resolution calling for stronger ties with Taiwan and sent a return delegation to the island.[20] Helping Taiwan weave a denser network of informal ties with other countries is a practical and effective route to making it more secure—Xi would pay a higher price for any attack on the island—and possibly open up new opportunities for it to negotiate trade agreements and participate in international organizations.

Avoid an Ideological Cold War

As I noted earlier, toward the end of his first term, Xi Jinping started to define the relationship between China and the West as an ideological contest. Party propaganda touted the superiority of China's system that follows "Xi Jinping Thought on Socialism with Chinese Characteristics for a New

Era" and contrasted it with the failures of American market democracy. The Trump administration pushed back by vilifying China's Communist Party autocracy and praising the virtues of Western democracy.

President Biden has perpetuated this ideological contest by anchoring his foreign policy to the defense of democratic values against authoritarianism. But it's an odd time to be playing a "values" game against China: The January 6 insurrection against Congress encouraged by President Trump looked like the start of an American civil war; and political polarization and congressional dysfunction have foiled efforts to protect the integrity of American elections. International respect for American democracy is not at a high point. A little humility might be called for.

Even if American democracy were in better shape, there are risks to over-emphasizing values differences if we want to coexist instead of dueling. As a Chinese academic said to me recently, "If we frame relations in ideological terms, we have 'less room to maneuver' which makes distrust and rivalry more likely." Ideological crusades inflame xenophobia and make it politically difficult for leaders to make the compromises necessary to stabilize relations. They also impede the United States from enlisting the cooperation of nondemocracies such as Vietnam, Thailand, and Singapore; those countries were not invited to President Biden's Democracy Summit.

Another reason not to target autocracies as a group is to prevent a comprehensive Russia-China alliance. If China and Russia coordinate their strategic moves against the United States in Europe and the Western Hemisphere, as well as in Asia, the dangers to US security would drastically increase.

By drawing cold-war lines between democracies and autocracies, the United States has helped send China into Vladimir Putin's open embrace, as we see in China's pro-Russian "neutrality" during the war in Ukraine. In the past, China and Russia had a self-limiting relationship because of a history of mistrust along their long border. Russia sold military equipment to China, and the two countries consulted and exercised together and had an informal agreement not to criticize each other.

But the two countries weren't close until Xi and Putin developed a personal affinity as strongman leaders who fear color revolutions and resent American pressure. In February 2022, on the eve of the war, their lengthy statement was filled with defensive language originating from China about the superiority of their version of democracy. A high priority in our China strategy coming out of the war in Ukraine should be to avoid the mistake we made in the 1960s—treating China and Russia as a unified ideological bloc instead of as countries with distinct interests.

Engage the Chinese People

In Xi Jinping's centralized system his voice and the choir of his acolytes drown out other voices, so that China comes across as frighteningly monolithic. But China's future will depend on its diverse and modernizing society, especially its growing middle class. Just as Americans are wondering if a rising China will threaten them, the Chinese are wondering about American intentions toward them. China's people, not just its leaders, are listening to what we say and watching what we do. We need to keep in mind how our words and actions resonate inside China, as well as how they sound to the American audience.

Until the COVID-19 pandemic and the sharp deterioration in US-China relations that coincided with it, the two societies were closely intertwined, and people-to-people contacts were a regular occurrence. Millions of businesspeople, academics, artists, and other professionals commuted back and forth across the Pacific and had residences, family members, and friends in both countries. About three million Chinese travelers visited America (and spent more per person than visitors from any other country) and 2.5 million Americans traveled to China. At the peak, more than 370,000 Chinese students were studying at American universities.[21] Nongovernmental organizations worked collaboratively in China for more than forty years until China's adoption of the NGO Law in 2017 drove many of them away.

These social interactions now are under severe strain. China is turning inward; draconian entry, visa, and quarantine rules designed to enforce zero-COVID have reduced international travel to a trickle. Governments in both countries are screening out people from the other as potential enemy agents.

American politicians have targeted Confucius Institutes on college campuses as "influence agents" of the Chinese Communist Party; their number has shrunk from 103 to 31.[22] Republican lawmakers have also targeted the 157 American sister-city partnerships with China for making communities "vulnerable to foreign espionage and ideological coercion."[23] A majority of Americans (55 percent) support limiting the number of Chinese students studying in the United States, even as a broad majority (80 percent) say it's good for US colleges to accept international students in general.[24]

In retaliation for the Hong Kong National Security Law, the Trump administration suspended the Fulbright program that allows American and Chinese academics to teach, research, and study in each other's countries. Under pressure from politicians who argued that "there's no reason we should prop up our adversaries with US tax dollars," the Peace Corps closed its program of teaching English in poor areas of Western China.[25]

Chinese universities also are increasingly resistant to foreign ideas and academics. Western textbooks even in the sciences must be replaced by Chinese textbooks that integrate Marxist and nationalist points of view.[26] Between 2013 and 2017, 109 Chinese universities modified their charters to delete language about academic freedom and to add a clause asserting that the university CCP committee was the core leadership of the school.[27] Getting permission from university administrations to hold a conference with American partners is now almost impossible. The Beijing University international relations expert Jia Qingguo proposed to the China People's Consultative Conference that universities remove unnecessary approval processes for exchanges with foreigners,[28] but so far, he has failed to make any headway. The political obstacles to archival and field research by foreign scholars—including the possibility of being detained by the police—are making many of them afraid to continue it.

From the US perspective, reviving people-to-people ties should be an urgent priority. Chinese nationalism has become virulently anti-American, and the more isolated we are from each other, the more bitter and resentful each side becomes toward the other. People-to-people interactions help temper the dangers of adversarial competition by humanizing relations.[29] They also are essential if we are to better understand the views of various types of people and factor them into our own policies and public diplomacy. People-to-people experiences also can help us penetrate the "one-sided information bubble" created by censorship and propaganda to portray America truthfully to the Chinese public.

Reaching Up

China's overreach has triggered an American overreaction that is almost as self-defeating. Based on an exaggerated view of China's threat to the United States and a lack of confidence in our own strengths, we have reverted to extreme measures against China that undercut our strengths and reinforce the hawkish elements in China. The interaction of overreach and overreaction could pull the two powers into a war. It has already put them into a cold war.

Our attempts to wound the other side could end up doing lasting damage to ourselves. We should think of our contest as a race instead of a boxing match—as one Chinese scholar puts it: "Each side doing its best to get ahead but neither has any intention of destroying or permanently changing the other."[30]

The United States should build on its assets instead of turning itself inside out trying to become more like China. We made the same mistake in the 1970s when we tried to compete with Japan's state-directed industrial policy; the flexible, market-driven US economy ended up proving more successful than the Japanese economy.

America's greatest asymmetric advantages are its open society, fair and law-based market economy, and our allure to talented people from throughout the world. Politicizing access to our market as China does may give us an edge in the short term, but it ultimately harms economic efficiency and innovativeness and tarnishes our credibility as the defender of open markets. Embargoing our technology to keep it out of the hands of Chinese firms will just align their incentives more closely to Beijing's security-driven pursuit of self-sufficiency. Every time we erect a new restriction against China to protect our security, we discourage businesses from locating in the United States, where they could get caught in the crossfire between the two countries.

I hope that by illuminating the domestic politics that caused China's overreaching—first under Hu Jintao's collective leadership and then under Xi Jinping's personalistic rule—this book can help us see China objectively, recognizing its fragility and its strengths, and avoid self-defeating overreactions.

Although collective leadership and personalistic rule function very differently, one constant is the persistent insecurity of China's leaders, who lack the legitimacy of having been chosen by popular elections. Paradoxically, greater prosperity and progress inside China make its leaders feel more vulnerable, not more secure. Xi has not merely purged his rivals in the Communist Party; he has decapitated and expropriated some of China's most successful private firms. Paranoia about threats to CCP rule strengthens the hand of the control coalition who promote excessive control of society and information in the name of *weiwen*. Until political reforms offer relief from the legitimacy dilemma of its leaders, China will remain domestically fragile, and prone to domestic and international overreach to overcompensate.

Xi Jinping is likely to hang on as China's top leader until his health fails or a power struggle deposes him. By dismantling the two-term rule that guaranteed a predictable, peaceful turnover of power at the top Xi injected more tension and uncertainty into Chinese politics. Were he to step down, he knows that his purge victims and their families would exact revenge. At the end of his fourth term, in 2032, Xi won't yet have reached eighty years of age. However, based on the experience of other countries in which leaders have clung to power for third and fourth terms, as the quality of his policymaking declines, his popularity will diminish, and he'll become increasingly vulnerable to a coup or political unrest.

This timeline is a reminder that, in addition to trying to influence Xi's short-term decision calculus, we should also keep broader long-term objectives in mind. Everything we say and do toward China reverberates through Chinese society and shapes public sentiment toward the United States. The festering resentment created by hostile US rhetoric and actions, which is then fueled by CCP propaganda, could become a liability for stabilizing the relationship. Looking toward the future, we should maintain a respectful posture toward the Chinese people by articulating a positive vision for the US-China relationship that includes welcoming Chinese students, tourists, and businesses, acknowledging what the Chinese people have accomplished, and showing a spirit of goodwill toward them. By means of smart and targeted management of security risks, as we do with cybersecurity, we can preserve the fabric of interdependence that for decades has benefited Americans, Chinese, and people throughout the world.

America's best response to China's overreach is to become a better version of its open-market democracy, and while that doesn't mean overreaching, it does mean reaching up.

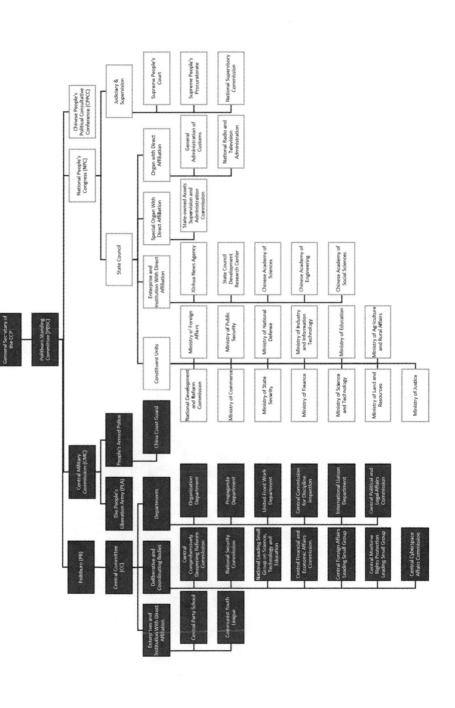

General Secretary of the CCP

Politburo Standing Committee (PBSC)

Politburo (PB)

Chinese People's Political Consultative Conference (CPPCC)

National People's Congress (NPC)

State Council

Judiciary & Supervision

Supreme People's Court

Supreme People's Procuratorate

National Supervisory Commission

Organ with Direct Affiliation

General Administration of Customs

National Radio and Television Administration

Special Organ With Direct Affiliation

State-owned Assets Supervision and Administration Commission

Enterprise and Institution With Direct Affiliation

Xinhua News Agency

State Council Development Research Center

Chinese Academy of Sciences

Chinese Academy of Engineering

Chinese Academy of Social Sciences

Constituent Units

Ministry of Foreign Affairs

Ministry of Public Security

Ministry of National Defense

Ministry of Industry and Information Technology

Ministry of Education

Ministry of Agriculture and Rural Affairs

National Development and Reform Commission

Ministry of Commerce

Ministry of State Security

Ministry of Finance

Ministry of Science and Technology

Ministry of Land and Resources

Ministry of Justice

Central Military Commission (CMC)

People's Armed Police

China Coast Guard

The People's Liberation Army (PLA)

Central Committee (CC)

Departments

Organization Department

Propaganda Department

United Front Work Department

Central Commission for Discipline Inspection

International Liaison Department

Central Political and Legal Affairs Commission

Deliberative and Coordinating Bodies

Central Comprehensively Deepening Reforms Commission

National Security Commission

National Leading Small Group on Science, Technology and Education

Central Financial and Economic Affairs Commission

Central Foreign Affairs Leading Small Group

Central Maritime Rights Protection Leading Small Group

Central Cyberspace Affairs Commission

Enterprises and Institution With Direct Affiliation

Central Party School

Communist Youth League

Organizations

Party

CCP Central Committee (中国共产党中央委员会): The CCP Central Committee is the top political body in China that is nominally empowered to perform various important political tasks, including electing the CCP general secretary and members of the Politburo and PSC and overseeing the work of the executive organs of the CCP. Historically, it has consisted of 100 to more than 200 formal members and roughly the same number of alternate members since the founding of the PRC.

CCP Central Commission for Discipline Inspection (中国共产党中央纪律检查委员会): The Central Commission for Discipline Inspection (CCDI) is the highest institution for enforcing rules and regulations and fighting corruption within the CCP. After merging with the Ministry of Supervision in 1993 under the Jiang Zemin administration, the CCDI became the most powerful institution for internal discipline within the CCP.

CCP Central Military Commission (中国共产党中央军事委员会): Founded in 1954, the CCP Central Military Commission (CMC) is the highest national defense organ in China. The CMC also shares an office with the CMC of the PRC, allowing the CCP to have direct control over the army. It is chaired by the general secretary of the CCP.

Central Party School (中共中央党校): The Central Party School was founded in 1955 as a higher education institution to train and cultivate cadres of the CCP.

Central Political and Legal Affairs Commission (中共中央政法委员会): Upgraded from the Central Political and Legal Affairs LSG founded in 1958, the Central Political and Legal Affairs Commission was established in 1980 to oversee all the law enforcement agencies in China, including the police force, prosecutors, and courts.

Communist Youth League of China (中国共产主义青年团): Established in 1921 along with the CCP itself, the Communist Youth League of China (CYL) is run by the CCP to recruit and manage young potential party members between fourteen and twenty-eight years old.

International Liaison Department of the CCP (中国共产党对外联络部): Founded in 1951, the International Liaison Department is responsible for tracking the development and change of major international issues, drafting responsive proposals to the CCP Central Committee, and coordinating exchanges with and gathering intelligence on foreign political parties and institutions of interest.

National Security Commission (国家安全委员会): The National Security Commission was established in 2013 to restructure the CCP security apparatus. Its main objectives include fighting terrorism, separatism, and religious extremism; dealing with national security strategy; crisis management; and interacting with foreign counterparts.

Organization Department of the CCP Central Committee (中共中央组织部): Formed in 1921, the Organization Department of the CCP Central Committee is responsible for staffing and personnel management within the CCP and the government.

People's Armed Police (中国人民武装警察部队): The modern form of the People's Armed Police (PAP) is a paramilitary force created in 1982 to professionalize the internal security units. It takes up a variety of responsibilities, including border defense, firefighting, and stability maintenance. Since January 1, 2018, the command of the PAP has been jointly held by the CCP Central Committee and the Central Military Commission.

Politburo (中国共产党中央政治局): The Politburo of the CCP is the highest body, overseeing the CCP and its decision-making process. Historically, it has had seventeen to twenty-five members since the founding of the PRC. PSC members are chosen from the Politburo.

Politburo Standing Committee (中国共产党中央政治局常务委员会). The Politburo Standing Committee (PSC) represents the supreme leadership of the Chinese Communist Party (CCP). The PSC historically consists of five to eleven members, and it presides over policy discussions and decides on major issues of supreme importance.

Propaganda Department of the CCP Central Committee (中共中央宣传部): Formed in 1924, the Propaganda Department of the CCP Central Committee is in charge of all types of ideology-related work, including guiding research on Marxism, guiding public opinion, and censorship of media and publications in China. It uses the English name Publicity Department.

United Front Work Department of the CCP Central Committee (中共中央统战部): Founded in 1946, the United Front Work Department of the CCP Central Committee is responsible for gathering intelligence on, managing relations with, and influencing individuals who are not CCP members but may be useful in furthering the CCP's cause. Those the department targets are usually elites of political, economic, or academic influence, living both inside and outside China.

Government

China Marine Surveillance (中国海监): Founded by the State Oceanic Administration in 1999, China Marine Surveillance (CMS) is primarily responsible for deploying patrols to areas in the South China Sea and East China Sea where China has territorial disputes with neighboring countries.

Chinese Academy of Social Sciences (中国社会科学院): The Chinese Academy of Social Sciences (CASS) was established in 1977 as a research institute and think tank with the objective of advancing research in the social sciences, philosophy, and policies. The academy is directly affiliated with the State Council.

Civil Aviation Administration of China (中国民用航空局): Established in 1949, the Civil Aviation Administration of China is responsible for overseeing civil aviation and investigates aviation accidents in China.

Cyberspace Administration of China (国家互联网信息办公室): Founded in 2014 under the Xi Jinping administration, the Cyberspace Administration of China (CAC) is the chief regulator and overseer of the Chinese Internet. Its main responsibilities include implementing policies related to cybercommunication, coordinating and supervising relevant organs to manage and censor Internet content, organizing Internet propaganda, and authorizing IPOs of Internet platform companies.

Department of Boundary and Ocean Affairs of the Ministry of Foreign Affairs (外交部边界与海洋事务司): Created in 2008, the Department of Boundary and Ocean Affairs of the Ministry of Foreign Affairs is responsible for developing policies concerning land and maritime boundaries; guiding and coordinating external work concerning oceans and seas; managing land boundary delimitation and demarcation and joint inspections with neighboring countries; handling external boundary matters and cases concerning territories, maps, and place names; and engaging in diplomatic negotiations on maritime delimitation and joint development.

Fisheries Bureau (渔业渔政管理局): The modern Fisheries Bureau was established in 2013 and placed under the Ministry of Agriculture and Rural Affairs. It is primarily responsible for drafting policies related to the development of Chinese fisheries, handling major fishing disputes involving foreign countries, and supervising and managing pelagic fishing.

General Administration of Customs (海关总署): The General Administration of Customs was established in 1949 to be responsible for the collection of custom duties and other indirect taxes and the management and inspection of the import and export of goods and services.

General Administration of Press and Publication (新闻出版总署): The General Administration of Press and Publication was established in 2001 to be in charge of regulating and distributing news, books, and Internet publications. It was merged with the State Administration of Radio, Film, and Television to form SAPPRFT in 2013 under the Xi Jinping administration.

Ministry of Agriculture (农业部): The Ministry of Agriculture was established in 1949 to be responsible for drafting policies related to the development of agriculture, overseeing the reform of the rural management system, and guiding major agricultural production. The Ministry was dissolved in 2018, and its primary functions were absorbed by the newly formed Ministry of Agriculture and Rural Affairs.

Ministry of Commerce (商务部): The Ministry of Commerce was created in 2003 under the Hu Jintao administration following a reorganization of several state agencies that shared overlapping functions related to trade. It is responsible for formulating policies for domestic and foreign trade and international economic cooperation, drafting trade-related laws and regulations, and devising relevant departmental rules and regulations.

Ministry of Education (教育部): The Ministry of Education was established in 1949 to oversee and regulate China's education system.

Ministry of Finance (财政部): The Ministry of Finance was founded in 1949 to be in charge of administering China's macroeconomic policies and the annual budget, drafting financial laws and regulations, managing government non-tax revenue, planning the treasury management system

Ministry of Foreign Affairs (外交部): The Ministry of Foreign Affairs (MoFA) was established in 1954 and has been responsible for China's foreign relations ever since.

Ministry of Health (卫生部): Established in 1949, the Ministry of Health was primarily responsible for researching and drafting health-related laws and regulations, formulating policies regarding maternity and childcare services, overseeing disease prevention, and ensuring the accessibility of health services and facilities nationwide.

The Ministry of Health was dissolved in 2013 under the Xi Jinping administration and most of its functions were integrated into the National Health and Family Planning Commission that was then reorganized and renamed as the National Health Commission.

Ministry of Industry and Information Technology (工业和信息化部): The Ministry of Industry and Information Technology (MIIT) was established in 2008 under Hu Jintao's administration to oversee the development of the Internet, broadcasting, communications, electronics production, information goods, and tobacco production.

Ministry of Land and Resources (国土资源部): The Ministry of Land and Resources was established in 1998 as a central authority to manage and regulate the preservation and exploitation of natural resources, including land, mines, and oceanic resources. It was dissolved under the Xi Jinping administration in 2018, and its main functions were taken over by the newly formed Ministry of Natural Resources.

Ministry of National Defense (国防部): Founded in 1954, the Ministry of National Defense is responsible for the management of the construction of the national armed forces, such as the recruitment and training of military personnel and the issuance of military ranks and salary. It manages the foreign relations of the military. It does not have actual command over the PLA.

Ministry of Public Security (公安部): Established in 1949, the Ministry of Public Security has been the overseer of China's police force. It is responsible for a wide range of activities, including regular policing, counterintelligence, and espionage.

Ministry of State Security (国家安全部): The Ministry of State Security was created in 1983 to take charge of work related to national security such as both espionage and counter-espionage domestically and abroad.

National Development and Reform Commission (国家发展和改革委员会): The National Development and Reform Commission (NDRC) is a comprehensive agency under the State Council that exercises broad administrative and planning authority over the economy including setting rules for foreign and private investment. It was founded in 1998 as part of the reorganization of the State Planning Commission.

State Administration of Press, Publication, Radio, Film and Television (国家广播电视总局): The State Administration of Press, Publication, Radio, Film and Television (SAPPRFT) was created after the merger of two agencies by the State Council in 2013 to oversee the work related to media operation in China. The SAPPRFT directly controlled major state-owned media organizations such as China Central Television, China National Radio, and China Radio International. Under the Xi Jinping administration, the SAPPRFT was dissolved in 2018, and many of its media-control functions were absorbed by the Propaganda Department of the CCP Central Committee.

State Administration for Religious Affairs (国家宗教事务局): The State Administration for Religious Affairs (SARA) was founded as the State Council Religious Affairs Bureau in 1998 to be responsible for managing religious affairs related to Buddhism, Taoism, Islamism, Catholicism, and Christianity, religious schools, and cults in China. It was dissolved in 2018 by the Xi Jinping administration, and most of its functions were assumed by the United Front Work Department.

State Bureau for Letters and Petitions (国家信访局): The State Bureau for Letters and Petitions, currently known as the National Public Complaints and Proposals Administration, was established in 2000 to be responsible for handling and receiving complaint and accusation letters and petitioners.

State Council (国务院): The State Council is China's highest administrative authority that oversees the work of both the central ministries and provincial governments. It is often described as the PRC Cabinet. It follows the instruction of the CCP and is headed by the premier and several vice premiers who are each responsible for certain areas of administration.

State Council Development Research Center (国务院发展研究中心): Founded in 1990, the State Council Development Research Center is a think tank and policy research institute affiliated with the State Council. Macroeconomy, social development, and reform and opening-up policies are the center's areas of research.

State Council Information Office (国务院新闻办公室): Formed in 1991, the State Council Information Office (SCIO) is an administrative office under the State Council that is responsible for explaining government policies to the foreign audience and supervising foreign journalists in China.

State Council Overseas Chinese Affairs Office (国务院侨务办公室): The State Council Overseas Chinese Affairs Office was established in 1978 to oversee the work related to liaising with overseas Chinese. The Office was absorbed into the United Front Work Department in 2018 under the Xi Jinping administration.

State Ethnic Affairs Commission (国家民族事务委员会): The State Ethnic Affairs Commission was founded in 1978 as a constituent unit of the State Council to supervise the implementation of policies related to nationality and ethnic minorities in China. The Commission was placed under the United Front Work Department in 2018 by the Xi Jinping administration.

State Oceanic Administration (国家海洋局): The State Oceanic Administration (SOA) was established in 1964 to be responsible for the supervision and management of China's oceanic area, including the protection of coastal environment and national maritime rights and the organization of scientific research. The SOA was dissolved in 2018 under the Xi Jinping administration, and its functions were taken over by the newly established Ministry of Natural Resources.

State-Owned Assets Supervision and Administration Commission (国务院国有资产监督管理委员会): Founded by the State Council in 2003 under the Hu Jintao administration, the State-Owned Assets Supervision and Administration Commission (SASAC) is responsible for managing state-owned enterprises (SOEs) in terms of appointing executives, approving mergers and sales of company stocks and assets, and drafting laws and regulations related to SOEs.

State Planning Commission (中华人民共和国国家计划委员会): The State Planning Commission was established in 1954 with the responsibility for national economic planning. It was reorganized into the National Development and Reform Commission (NDRC) in 1998 under the Jiang Zemin administration.

State Public Servant Bureau (国家公务员局): The State Public Servant Bureau was established in 2008 by the Hu Jintao administration and placed under the Ministry of Human Resources and Social Securities to be responsible for the recruitment, promotion, and training of the public servants in China. Under the Xi Jinping administration, the bureau was absorbed into the Organization Department of the CCP Central Committee in 2018.

Taiwan Affairs Office (国务院台湾事务办公室): Established by the State Council in 1988, the Taiwan Affairs Office is responsible for setting and implementing guidelines and polices related to Taiwan and preparing negotiations and agreements with its counterparts in Taiwan.

Xinhua News Agency (新华社): Founded in 1931, Xinhua News Agency is the official news agency of the Chinese government and the largest media organization in China. It is a ministry-level institution that is subordinate to the State Council.

Legislative/Judicial System

Chinese People's Political Consultative Conference (中国人民政治协商会议): Established in 1949, the Chinese People's Political Consultative Conference (CPPCC) is China's highest political advisory body and an important organ for the CCP's United Front work because it recruits non-CCP members who are prominent in their fields. The CPPCC meets annually in the same month as the NPC.

National People's Congress (中华人民共和国全国人民代表大会): Founded in 1954, the National People's Congress (NPC) is China's national legislature and nominally the highest state power. It has approximately 3,000 representatives who are elected indirectly by lower level legislators from nominees chosen by the CCP. The NPC convenes its full session annually to vote on important matters, including national legislation and personnel change. Its legislative authority is delegated to its Standing Committee that meets bi-monthly.

National Supervisory Commission (国家监察委员会): Founded in 2018 by the Xi Jinping administration, the National Supervisory Commission (NSC) is the highest state anticorruption organ in China. It has the authority to investigate all personnel exercising public power in China, not just CCP members, if they are suspected of violation of duties. In practice, the NSC's operation is merged with the CCDI.

Supreme People's Court (最高人民法院): The highest court in China's judicial system, the Supreme People's Court (SPC) was established in 1949 after the founding of the PRC. The SPC exercises appellate jurisdiction over cases from lower-level courts, original jurisdiction over cases of national importance, and it has the power to issue judicial interpretations on laws and court procedure.

Supreme People's Procuratorate (最高人民检察院): Founded in 1949, the Supreme People's Procuratorate is China's highest organ responsible for legal prosecution and investigation.

Leading Small Group/Central Commission

Central Cyberspace Affairs Commission (中央网络安全和信息化委员会): Formerly known as the Central Leading Group for Cybersecurity and Informatization, the Central Cyberspace Affairs Commission was established in 2018 to take charge of matters related to cybersecurity, informatization, and the implementation of policies regarding the development of China's cybersphere.

Central Financial and Economic Affairs Commission (中央财经委员会): Formerly known as the Central Leading Small Group for Financial and Economic Affairs, the Central Financial and Economic Affairs Commission was upgraded to lead and supervise the economic work of both the CCP Central Committee and the State Council in 2018 under the Xi Jinping administration.

Central Foreign Affairs Leading Small Group (中央外事工作领导小组): The Central Foreign Affairs Leading Small Group was established in 1981 to be in charge of guiding and coordinating work related to foreign affairs. It was reorganized into the Central Foreign Affairs Commission in 2018 under the Xi Jinping administration.

Central Maritime Rights Protection Leading Small Group (中央维护海洋权益工作领导小组): The Central Maritime Rights Protection Leading Small Group was established in 2012 to coordinate between departments regarding work on China's maritime rights protection. It was dissolved in 2018, and most of its functions were taken over by the Central Foreign Affairs Commission.

Leading Small Groups (领导小组): A leading small group (LSG) is an ad hoc body serving as either a central commander or a coordinator of decision-making on major functional areas that cut across the Party, the military, and the government. Such functional areas include foreign affairs, Party construction, Taiwan affairs, cybersecurity, military-civilian integration, etc. Over the past few years, some of the LSGs have been upgraded to commissions, as a more regular agency in the respective fields.

National Leading Small Group on Science, Technology, and Education (国家科技教育领导小组): The National Leading Small Group on Science, Technology, and Education was founded in 1998 to coordinate and instruct on work related to technology and education and the promotion of reform on science, technology, and the education system. It was transformed into the National Science and Technology Leading Small Group in 2018 under the Xi Jinping administration.

Notes

Prologue

1. Susan Shirk and Yanzhong Huang, "A Truce in the Trade War Will Save American Lives," *Think Global Health*, March 24, 2020, https://www.thinkglobalhealth.org/article/truce-trade-war-will-save-american-lives.

2. For a visual representation that shows global trading relations at a glance, see https://www.visualcapitalist.com/wp-content/uploads/2022/02/2020-trading-partners.html.

3. Data from 2010 to 2020. Ruixue Jia, Margaret E. Roberts, Ye Wang, and Eddie Yang, "The Impact of U.S.-China Tensions on U.S. Science," unpublished paper, https://www.nber.org/system/files/working_papers/w29941/w29941.pdf.

4. According to the search results on GovTrack.us, February 4, 2022, https://www.govtrack.us/congress/bills/subjects/taiwan/6787.

5. "Clinton: Senkakus Subject to Security Pact," *Japan Times*, September 25, 2010, https://www.japantimes.co.jp/news/2010/09/25/national/clinton-senkakus-subject-to-security-pact/

6. The White House, National Security Strategy of the United States, December 2017, chrome-extension://efaidnbmnnnibpcajpcglclefindmkaj/https://trumpwhitehouse.archives.gov/wp-content/uploads/2017/12/NSS-Final-12-18-2017-0905.pdf.

7. "Remarks by Vice President Pence on the Administration's Policy toward China," October 4, 2018, https://trumpwhitehouse.archives.gov/briefings-statements/remarks-vice-president-pence-administrations-policy-toward-china/.

8. Samuel Chamberlain, "Biden says China Believes It Will 'Own America' Within 15 Years," *New York Post*, May 28, 2021, https://nypost.com/2021/05/28/biden-china-believes-it-will-own-america-within-next-15-years/.

9. Kiran Stacey and Demetri Sevastopulo, "US Spy Chiefs Warn Tech Companies on China Dangers," *Financial Times*, May 19, 2019, https://www.ft.com/content/dde4f848-78ed-11e9-be7d-6d846537acab. The article says that these briefings are classified.

10. "NIH Probe of Foreign Ties Has Led to Undisclosed Firings—and Refunds from Institutions," *Science Magazine*, April 26, 2019, https://www.sciencemag.org/news/2019/06/nih-probe-foreign-ties-has-led-undisclosed-firings-and-refunds-institutions.

11. "US Energy Dept Blocks Participation in China's 'Thousand Talents' Program," Phys.org, June 13, 2019, https://phys.org/news/2019-06-energy-dept-blocks-china-thousand.html.

12. Fred Dews, "Watch: Sen. Mark Warner's Remarks on China's Growing Economic and Technology Power," Brookings, May 15, 2019, https://www.brookings.edu/blog/brooki ngs-now/2019/05/15/watch-sen-mark-warners-remarks-on-chinas-growing-economic-and-technology-power/.

13. Friedhoff Karl and Kafura Craig, "American Views toward US-Japan Relations and Asia-Pacific Security," Chicago Council on Global Affairs, April 17, 2018, https://www.thechicagocouncil.org/sites/default/files/2020-11/American%20Views%20toward%20US-Japan%20Relations%20and%20Asia-Pacific%20Security%20PDF%20Report.pdf .

14. Laura Silver, Kat Devlin, and Christine Huang, "U.S. Views of China Turn Sharply Negative amid Trade Tensions," Pew Research Center Report, August 13, 2019, https://www.pewresearch.org/global/2019/08/13/u-s-views-of-china-turn-sharply-negative-amid-trade-tensions/.

15. J. J. Moncus and Laura Silver, "Americans' Views of Asia-Pacific Nations Have Not Changed since 2018—with the Exception of China," Pew Research Center, April 12, 2021, https://www.pewresearch.org/fact-tank/2021/04/12/americans-views-of-asia-paci fic-nations-have-not-changed-since-2018-with-the-exception-of-china/.

16. Laura Silver, Christine Huang, and Laura Clancy, "Negative Views of China Tied to Critical Views of Its Policies on Human Rights," Pew Research Center, June 29, 2022, https://www.pewresearch.org/global/2022/06/29/negative-views-of-china-tied-to-critical-views-of-its-policies-on-human-rights/.By 2021, 67 percent of Americans believe that China wants to replace the United States as the dominant power in the world, and 78 percent and 67 percent, respectively, see China as a security threat and an economic threat. See Karl Friedhoff, "American Public Divided on Cooperating with, Confronting China," Chicago Council on Global Affairs, March 31, 2021, https://www.thechicagocouncil.org/research/public-opinion-survey/american-public-divided-coop erating-confronting-china. According to Gallup, favorability toward China plummeted from 53 percent in 2018 to 20 percent in 2021. See Mohamed Younis, "China, Russia Images in U.S. Hit Historic Lows," Gallup, March 1, 2021, https://news.gallup.com/poll/331082/china-russia-images-hit-historic-lows.aspx. A quarter of Americans view China as the greatest threat to America in the future (tied with Russia), twice as many as had this view in 2007, and the threat perceptions are now associated more with China's growing military power than its economic growth. See Silver, Devlin, and Huang, "U.S. Views of China Turn Sharply Negative." Even though Americans are concerned about China's military growth, half think China's growing economy is good for the United States, the same proportions as in 2005, when this question was first asked.

17. Laura Silver, Kat Devlin, and Christine Huang, "Most Americans Support Tough Stance toward China on Human Rights, Economic Issues," Pew Research Center, March 4, 2021, https://www.pewresearch.org/global/2021/03/04/most-americans-supp ort-tough-stance-toward-china-on-human-rights-economic-issues/; Silver, Devlin, and Huang, "U.S. Views of China Increasingly Negative amid Coronavirus Outbreak," Pew Research Center Report, April 21, 2020, https://www.pewresearch.org/global/2020/04/21/u-s-views-of-china-increasingly-negative-amid-coronavirus-outbreak/.

18. Surveys consistently find that Republicans are more critical toward China than Democrats and that older Americans' views are more unfavorable than those of younger ones.

19. Richard Q. Turcsanyi, Matej Simalcik, Kristina Kironska, Renata Sedlakova, et al., "European Public Opinion on China in the Age of Covid-19," 2021, https://web.archive.org/web/20211024211617/http://www.realinstitutoelcano.org/wps/wcm/connect/98d4c cd5-b504-4b2c-b53c-8411ef91a3f6/European-public-opinion-on-China-in-the-age-of-COVID-19.pdf?MOD=AJPERES&CACHEID=98d4ccd5-b504-4b2c-b53c-8411ef91a 3f6; Richard Wike, Bruce Stokes, Jacob Poushter, Laura Silver, Janell Fetterolf, and

Kat Devlin, "International Publics Divided on China," Pew Research Center Report, October 1, 2018, https://www.pewresearch.org/global/2018/10/01/international-publics-divided-on-china/. The Central European countries and Greece, where China has devoted a lot of attention and investment, are more positive toward Beijing.

20. Laura Silver, Kat Devlin, and Christine Huang, "Unfavorable Views of China Reach Historic Highs in Many Countries," Pew Research Center, October 6, 2020, https://www.pewresearch.org/global/2020/10/06/unfavorable-views-of-china-reach-historic-highs-in-many-countries/.

21. "China's Growing Presence in Africa Wins Largely Positive Positive Reviews," Afrobarometer Dispatch No. 122, October 24, 2016, http://afrobarometer.org/sites/default/files/publications/Dispatches/ab_r6_dispatchno122_perceptions_of_china_in_africa1.pdf; Wike et al., "International Publics Divided on China"; "Africans Regard China's Influence as Significant and Positive, but Slipping," Afrobarometer Dispatch No. 407, November 17, 2020, https://afrobarometer.org/sites/default/files/publications/Dispatches/ad407-chinas-perceived_influence_in_africa_decreases-afrobarometer_d ispatch-14nov20.pdf.

22. Laura Silver, Kat Devlin, and Christine Huang, "China's Economic Growth Mostly Welcomed in Emerging Markets, but Neighbors Wary of Its Influence," Pew Research Center, December 5, 2019, https://www.pewresearch.org/global/2019/12/05/chinas-economic-growth-mostly-welcomed-in-emerging-markets-but-neighbors-wary-of-its-influence/.

23. Laura Silver, "How People in Asia-Pacific View China," Pew Research Center, October 16, 2017, https://www.pewresearch.org/fact-tank/2017/10/16/how-people-in-asia-pacific-view-china/.

24. Silver, Huang, and Clancy, "Negative Views of China Tied to Critical Views of Its Policies on Human Rights"; Bruce Stokes, "How Asia-Pacific Publics See Each Other and Their National Leaders," Pew Research Center, September 2, 2015, https://www.pewresearch.org/global/2015/09/02/how-asia-pacific-publics-see-each-other-and-their-national-leaders/.

25. Tang Siew Mun, Moe Thuzar, Hoang Thi Ha, Termsak Chalermpalanupap, Pham Thi Phuong Thao, and Anuthida Saelaow Qian, "The State of Southeast Asia: 2019 Survey Report," January 29, 2019, ISEAS-Yusuf Ishak Institute, https://www.iseas.edu.sg/wp-content/uploads/pdfs/TheStateofSEASurveyReport_2019.pdf.

26. Sharon Seah, Hoang Thi Ha, Melinda Martinus, and Pham Thi Phuong Thao, "The State of Southeast Asia: 2021 Survey Report," ASEAN Studies Center, February 10, 2021, https://www.iseas.edu.sg/wp-content/uploads/2021/01/The-State-of-SEA-2021-v2.pdf.

27. Seah et al., "State of Southeast Asia: 2021 Survey Report."

28. Kelsey Munro, "Australian Attitudes to China Shift: 2019 Lowy Institute Poll," https://www.lowyinstitute.org/the-interpreter/australian-attitudes-china-shift-2019-lowy-poll.

29. Silver, Devlin, and Huang, "Unfavorable Views of China Reach Historic Highs."

30. "China's Might Prevents Muslim Nations from Criticizing It, Mahathir Says," Radio Free Asia, September 27, 2019, https://www.rfa.org/english/news/china/malaysia-china-09272019171146.html.

31. Liu Yanqing, "From Hiding Strength and Biding Time to Striving for Achievement, China's Rise Is Unstoppable," *China Economic Weekly,* November 11, 2013, http://www.ceweekly.cn/2013/1111/68562.shtml.

32. Ren Ping, "What Is the Nature of the US Initiating the Trade War?," *People's Daily,* August 9, 2018, http://world.people.com.cn/n1/2018/0809/c1002-30220096.html. Also see "60% Is the Red Line Drawn by the U.S. for Its Competitors," China Radio International, August 10, 2018, https://web.archive.org/web/20180811112331/http://www.xinhuanet.com/world/2018-08/10/c_1123254133.htm.

33. Graham Allison, *Destined for War: Can the United States and China Escape Thucydides's Trap?* (Boston: Houghton Mifflin Harcourt, 2017).
34. "Xi Jinping's Speech at the Joint Welcome Banquet of the Government of Washington State and American Friendship Groups," Xinhua, September 23, 2015, http://cpc.peo ple.com.cn/n/2015/0923/c64094-27625724.html.
35. Ren Ping, "What Is the True Intention of the U.S. Trying to Initiate the Trade War?," People.com, August 9, 2018, world.people.com.cn/n1/2018/0809/c1002-30220096.html. Also see Zhong Xuanli, "The Trade War Could Not Prevent China from Moving Forward," October 15, 2018, world.people.com.cn/n1/2018/1015/c1002-30340087.html.
36. Zhang Haichao, "The Trade War Has Become a Social Mobilization of a Comprehensive Strategic Containment of the United States toward China," Huanqiu. com, September 25, 2018, mil.huanqiu.com/strategysituation/2018-09/13104253. html?agt = 15422.
37. Avery Goldstein, *Rising to the Challenge: China's Grand Strategy and International Security* (Stanford, CA: Stanford University Press, 2005). Chinese military scholar Xu Qiyu wrote an excellent book on Germany's path to World War I to make the point to Chinese readers that Germany could have avoided war by sustaining Bismarck's good diplomacy. *Fragile Rise: Grand Strategy and the Fate of Imperial Germany, 1871–1914* (Cambridge, MA: MIT Press, 2017).

Chapter 1

1. Barry Naughton, *The Rise of China's Industrial Policy, 1978–2020* (Boulder: Lynne Riener, 2021), http://www.economia.unam.mx/cechimex/index.php/en/publications.
2. Andrew Chubb, "Xi Jinping and China's Maritime Policy," Brookings Institution, January 22, 2019, https://www.brookings.edu/articles/xi-jinping-and-chinas-maritime-policy/; Andrew Chubb, "PRC Assertiveness in the South China Sea: Measuring Continuity and Change, 1970–2015," *International Security* 45, no. 3 (2021): 79–121, https://direct.mit.edu/isec/article/45/3/79/95273/PRC-Assertiveness-in-the-South-China-Sea-Measuring.
3. Chubb, "Xi Jinping and China's Maritime Policy."
4. John Pomfret, "U.S. Takes a Tougher Tone with China," *Washington Post*, July 30, 2010, http://www.washingtonpost.com/wp-dyn/content/article/2010/07/29/AR201007 2906416.html. This was not the first time the US secretary of state had raised the South China Sea at the ASEAN Regional Forum. Madeleine Albright had spoken in favor of using the ASEAN Regional Forum as an appropriate mechanism for addressing the issue in 1999. See Secretary of State Madeleine K. Albright, Intervention at the Sixth ASEAN Regional Forum, Singapore, July 26, 1999, US Department of State Archive, https://1997-2001.state.gov/statements/1999/990726.html.
5. For example, Aaron L. Friedberg, *A Contest for Supremacy: China, America, and the Struggle for Mastery in Asia* (New York: W. W. Norton, 2011); Wu Xinbo, "U.S. Security Policy in Asia: Implications for China-U.S. Relations," *Contemporary Southeast Asia* 22, no. 3 (December 2000): 479–497, https://www.jstor.org/stable/25798508.
6. "Central Foreign Affairs Working Conference Held in Beijing; Hu Jintao Delivered an Important Speech," China News Service, August 23, 2006, https://webcache.google usercontent.com/search?q=cache:IE4A6COM05IJ:https://www.chinanews.com.cn/other/news/2006/08-23/778618.shtml+&cd=2&hl=en&ct=clnk&gl=us.
7. Aaron Friedberg, "The Sources of Chinese Conduct: Explaining Beijing's Assertiveness," *Washington Quarterly* (Winter 2015): 143.

8. Americans also increasingly viewed China as the world's leading economic power: 26% in 2008, 33% in 2009, and 41% in 2010. Pew Global Attitudes Project, June 17, 2010, http://assets.pewresearch.org/wp-content/uploads/sites/2/2010/06/Pew-Global-Attitu des-Spring-2010-Report-June-17-11AM-EDT.pdf.

9. Lu Feng, "Quantitative Estimation of Wages of Migrant Workers in China (1979– 2010)" (seminar presentation, National School of Development at Peking University, June 12, 2011), 6, http://www.nsd.pku.edu.cn/attachments/6548c6f9e6314a4fb2024 efdec5ff4a2.pdf. The number for 2018 is from the following report: "Monitoring and Investigation Report on Migrant Workers in 2018" (National Bureau of Statistics, April 29, 2019), http://www.stats.gov.cn/tjsj/zxfb/201904/t20190429_1662268.html.

10. This number was given by Ning Jizhe, the incumbent deputy director of the National Development and Reform Commission, on January 9, 2019. "China Has 140 Million Households with Annual Income over 100,000 to 500,000 RMB; Middle-Income Groups Exceed 400 million," China News, January 1, 2019, http://www.chinanews. com/cj/2019/01-21/8734806.shtml.

11. "Statistics of National College Entrance Examination and Admission Rate," Sina Education, June 18, 2015, http://edu.sina.com.cn/gaokao/2015-06-18/1435473862. shtml; "Total Number of Students Studying in Various Higher Education Institutes Nationwide Reached 38.33 Million," Xinhua, February 26, 2019, http://www.moe.gov. cn/fbh/live/2019/50340/mtbd/201902/t20190227_371430.html.

12. The 2003 number is from the "China Tourism Statistics Bulletin in 2003," July 12, 2004, compiled by the China National Tourism Bureau, http://www.gov.cn/test/2005-06/27/ content_10160.htm. The 2018 number is from "Chinese Citizens Traveled Nearly 150 Million Person-Times Abroad in 2018," Xinhua, February 13, 2019, http://www.xinhua net.com/politics/2019-02/13/c_1124110923.htm.

13. For more on these economic changes, see Barry Naughton, *The Chinese Economy: Adaptation and Growth* (Cambridge, MA: MIT Press, 2018).

14. Susan L. Shirk, *China: Fragile Superpower* (New York: Oxford University Press, 2007), 39.

15. A version of the series with English subtitles can be found on YouTube, https://www. youtube.com/watch?v=5fqxEiurovY.

16. Shirk, China: *Fragile Superpower*, 243.

17. Deng first used this phrase on April 28, 1992. Leng Rong and Wang Zuoling, *Deng Xiaoping's Chronicle*, vol. 2 (Beijing: Central Literature Publishing House, 2004), 1346.

18. Secretary of State Madeleine K. Albright, "Remarks at the State Department on the U.S.-China Summit," Washington, DC, October 28, 1997, US Department of State Archive, https://1997-2001.state.gov/statements/971028.html. President William J. Clinton, "Remarks by the President on Administration Efforts to Grant China Permanent Trade Relations Status," US Department of State Archive, January 10, 2000, https://1997-2001.state.gov/regions/eap/000110_clinton_china.html.

19. Robert L. Suettinger, "The Rise and Descent of Peaceful Rise," *China Leadership Monitor*, no. 12, October 30, 2004, https://www.hoover.org/sites/default/files/uploads/ documents/clm12_rs.pdf.

20. Robert B. Zoellick, "Whether China: From Membership to Responsibility?" (remarks to National Committee on US-China Relations, New York City, September 21, 2005), US Department of State Archive, 2001 to 2009, https://2001-2009.state.gov/s/d/former/ zoellick/rem/53682.htm.

21. Susan L. Shirk, "The Political Price of Reform Cycles: Elite Politics in Chinese-Style Economic Reforms," cited in Richard Baum, *Burying Mao: Chinese Politics in the Age of Deng Xiaoping* (Princeton, NJ: Princeton University Press, 1994), 6–7.

22. John M. Broder, "Clinton in China: The Overview; Clinton and Jiang Debate Views Live on TV, Clashing on Rights," *New York Times*, June 28, 1998, https://www.nytimes.com/1998/06/28/world/clinton-china-overview-clinton-jiang-debate-views-live-tv-clashing-rights.html.

23. "Clinton in China; Questions for the President: Give and Take with China's Students," *New York Times*, June 30, 1998, https://www.nytimes.com/1998/06/30/world/clinton-in-china-questions-for-the-president-give-and-take-with-china-s-students.html.

24. Barry Naughton, *Growing Out of the Plan: Chinese Economic Reform 1978–1993* (Cambridge, UK: Cambridge University Press, 1995).

25. Guoguang Wu, "Democracy and Rule of Law in Zhao Ziyang's Political Reform," in *Zhao Ziyang and China's Political Future*, ed. Guoguang Wu and Helen Lansdowne (London and New York: Routledge, 2008), 45.

26. Hongying Wang, "Zhao Ziyang's Visions: Victims of Political Turmoil or Seeds of a Democratic Future," in Wu and Lansdowne, *Zhao Ziyang and China's Political Future*, 18–19.

27. Chalmers Johnson, "Comparing Communist Nations," in *Change in Communist Systems*, ed. Chalmers Johnson (Stanford, CA: Stanford University Press, 1970), 1–32; and Richard Lowenthal, "Development and Utopia in Communist Policy," in Johnson, *Change in Communist Systems*, 33–116.

28. Bao Pu, epilogue to *Prisoner of the State: The Secret Journal of Premier Zhao Ziyang* (New York: Simon and Schuster, 2009), 278.

29. Wang Endong, chief scientist and executive president of the Inspur Group, an information technology company.

30. Susan L. Shirk, ed., *Changing Media, Changing China* (New York: Oxford University Press, 2011).

31. "General Office of the CCP Central and the State Council Issued Guidance on Strengthening and Improving Rural Governance," Xinhua, June 23, 2019, http://www.xinhuanet.com/politics/2019-06/23/c_1124660343.htm.

32. David Shambaugh, *China's Communist Party: Atrophy and Adaptation* (Washington, DC: Woodrow Wilson Press, 2008); Jonathan R. Stromseth, Edmund J. Malesky, and Dimitar D. Gueorguiev, *China's Governance Puzzle: Transparency and Participation in a Single-Party State* (Cambridge, UK: Cambridge University Press, 2017).

33. Deng Xiaoping, "On the Reform of the System of Party and State Leadership," August 18, 1980, *Selective Works of Deng Xiaoping*, 2: 322, https://www.marxists.org/reference/archive/deng-xiaoping/1980/220.htm.

34. "Full Text of Hu Jintao's Report at the 17th Party Congress," Xinhua, October 24, 2007, http://www.gov.cn/ldhd/2007-10/24/content_785431_12.htm.

35. Jack Snyder, *Myths of Empire: Domestic Politics and International Ambition* (Ithaca, NY: Cornell University Press, 1991), 44.

Chapter 2

1. Deng Pufang, "Speech at the Closing Ceremony of the Seventh National Congress of China's Disabled Persons' Federation," US-China Perception Monitor, September 16, 2018, http://www.uscnpm.com/model_item.html?action=view&table=article&id=17308.

2. "What Caught Xi's Eye at the Reform and Opening-Up Exhibition?," *China Daily*, November 26, 2018, http://www.chinadaily.com.cn/a/201811/26/WS5bfb41eca310eff30328af2b.html.

3. Amanda Lee, "What Does 'Opening Up' Exhibition Giving Credit to SOEs and Xi Jinping Say to China's Private Firms?," *South China Morning Post*, November 16, 2018, https://www.scmp.com/economy/china-economy/article/2173560/what-does-opening-exhibition-giving-credit-soes-and-xi-jinping.

4. Lee, "What Does 'Opening Up' Exhibition Giving Credit to SOEs and Xi Jinping Say to China's Private Firms?"

5. Frederick C. Teiwes, *Leadership, Legitimacy, and Conflict in China: From a Charismatic Mao to the Politics of Succession* (Armonk, NY: M. E. Sharpe, 1984), 69.

6. Andrew G. Walder, *China under Mao: A Revolution Derailed* (Cambridge, MA: Harvard University Press, 2015), 26, 28.

7. For Deng's account, see "Remarks on Successive Drafts of the 'Resolution on Certain Questions in the History of Our Party since the Founding of the People's Republic of China'" (excerpts from nine talks by Deng Xiaoping between March 1980 and the Sixth Plenary Session of the Party's Eleventh Central Committee in June 1981 on the drafting and revision of the resolution), en.people.cn/dengxp/vol2/text/b1420.html.

8. Walder, *China under Mao*, 54.

9. Susan L. Shirk, *Competitive Comrades: Career Incentives and Student Strategies in China* (Berkeley: University of California Press, 1981).

10. Shirk, *Competitive Comrades*, 123.

11. Deng Xiaoping, "Expand Political Democracy and Carry Out Economic Reform," April 15, 1985, in *Fundamental Issues in Present-Day China* (Beijing: Foreign Languages Press, 1987), 106.

12. Walder, *China under Mao*, 156, 178.

13. Frank Dikotter, *Mao's Great Famine: The History of China's Most Devastating Catastrophe, 1958–1962* (New York: Walker and Co., 2010), 324–325.

14. Andrew G. Walder and Yang Su, "The Cultural Revolution in the Countryside: Scope, Timing and Human Impact," *China Quarterly* 173 (March 2003): 74–99.

15. Ezra F. Vogel, *Deng Xiaoping and the Transformation of China* (Cambridge, MA: Belknap Press of Harvard University Press, 2011), 39.

16. Roderick MacFarquhar, *The Origins of the Cultural Revolution*, vol. 1, *Contradictions among the People 1956–1957* (New York: Columbia University Press, 1974), 44, 46.

17. "On the Historical Experience of the Dictatorship of the Proletariat," *Renmin Ribao*, April 5, 1956.

18. MacFarquhar, *Origins of the Cultural Revolution*, 1:10.

19. Avery Goldstein, *From Bandwagon to Balance of Power Politics: Structural Constraints and Politics in China, 1949–78* (Stanford, CA: Stanford University Press, 1991).

20. Frederick C. Teiwes, "The Establishment and Consolidation of the New Regime, 1949–1957," in *The Politics of China 1949–1989*, ed. Roderick MacFarquhar (Cambridge, UK: Cambridge University Press, 1993), 82.

21. Dikotter, *Mao's Great Famine*, x.

22. Kenneth Lieberthal, "The Great Leap Forward and the Split in the Yan'an Leadership, 1958–65," in MacFarquhar, *Politics of China*, 105.

23. Yang Jisheng, *Tombstone: The Great Chinese Famine 1958–1962*, trans. Stacy Mosher and Guo Jian (New York: Farrar, Straus and Giroux, 2008), 510.

24. Walder, *China under Mao*, 179.

25. Walder, 202.

26. Qiu Jin, *The Culture of Power: The Lin Biao Incident in the Cultural Revolution* (Stanford, CA: Stanford University Press, 1999).

27. Vogel, *Deng Xiaoping and the Transformation of China*, 218.

28. Deng Xiaoping, "Understand Mao Zedong Thought Completely and Accurately," July 21, 1977, *Selective Works of Deng Xiaoping* 2: 42–47; and Deng Xiaoping, "Rectification

Issues at the Frontlines of Education," September 19, 1977, *Selective Works of Deng Xiaoping* 2: 66–71.

29. "Resolution on Certain Questions in the History of Our Party since the Founding of the People's Republic of China" (adopted by the Sixth Plenary Session of the Eleventh Central Committee of the Communist Party of China on June 27, 1981).

30. "Resolution on Certain Questions in the History of Our Party."

31. Deng, "Remarks on Successive Drafts."

32. Deng, "Remarks on Successive Drafts."

33. "Deng Xiaoping Interviewed by Oriana Fallaci, August 21 and 23, 1980, in Oriana Fallaci, *Interviews with History and Conversations with Power* (New York: Universe Publishing, 2016).

34. Deng said that this suggestion originated with the veteran economic leader Chen Yun. See Deng, "Remarks on Successive Drafts."

35. "Resolution on Certain Questions in the History of Our Party."

36. "Resolution on Certain Questions in the History of Our Party."

37. Deng commented, "We hold that systems and institutions are the decisive factor and we all know what they were in those days. At the time, we used to credit everything to one person. It is true that there were certain things which we failed to oppose and for which we should be held partly responsible. Of course, in the circumstances, it was really difficult to express any opposition. However, we cannot evade our own responsibility." "Remarks on Successive Drafts."

38. "Xi Jinping: The Histories before and after the Reform and Opening Up Cannot Be Mutually Negated," Xinhua, January 5, 2013, https://web.archive.org/web/20140905220 838/http://news.ifeng.com/mainland/detail_2013_01/05/20823629_0.shtml.

39. "Xi Jinping: Speech at the Symposium Commemorating Comrade Mao Zedong's 120th Birthday," Xinhua, December 26, 2013, http://www.xinhuanet.com//politics/2013-12/26/c_118723453.htm.

40. Xi Jinping, "Uphold and Develop Socialism with Chinese Characteristics," *Qiushi*, April 1, 2019, originally given January 5, 2013, http://www.qstheory.cn/dukan/qs/2019-04/01/c_1124307480.htm.

41. The 1956 meeting upheld the correct line about "the need to uphold democratic centralism and collective leadership, oppose the personality cult, promote democracy within the Party and among the people and strengthen the Party's ties with the masses." See "Resolution on Certain Questions in the History of Our Party."

42. Samuel Huntington, *Political Order in Changing Societies* (New Haven, CT: Yale University Press, 2006), 12.

43. "On the Reform of the System of Party and State Leadership," *Selected Works of Deng Xiaoping*, August 18, 1980, https://dengxiaopingworks.wordpress.com/2013/02/25/on-the-reform-of-the-system-of-party-and-state-leadership/.

44. Joseph Torigian makes an interesting revisionist case that Hua Guofeng was the real proponent of collective leadership and that Deng, who operated unilaterally, gave the 1980 speech criticizing overconcentration of authority as a theoretical justification for getting rid of Hua. Joseph Torigian, "The Shadow of Deng Xiaoping on Chinese Elite Politics," War on the Rocks, January 30, 2017, https://warontherocks.com/2017/01/the-shadow-of-deng-xiaoping-on-chinese-elite-politics/.

45. Susan L. Shirk, *The Political Logic of Economic Reform in China* (Berkeley: University of California Press, 1993), 71.

46. Shirk, *Political Logic of Economic Reform*, 83.

47. There actually are two signs on the door of the Central Military Commission, one identifying it as a Party body, and one saying it belongs to the state. The 1982 Party and PRC constitutions created two formally delineated institutions. In reality, however, the

PLA and the commission are controlled by the CCP general secretary, who is also the head of the Central Military Commission.

48. Chen Yun had been on the Politburo twenty more years than Deng, and Peng Zhen had been on the Politburo nine more years than Deng.

49. China Photographers Association, *China's 30 Years* (New York: Oxford University Press, 2009), 116–117.

50. Liang Zhang, comp., and Andrew J. Nathan and Perry Link, eds., *The Tiananmen Papers* (New York: Public Affairs, 2001), 192–193. According to another account, the Standing Committee voted 3 to 2 to approve martial law, but the vote was then overruled by Deng Xiaoping. Hu Angang, *China's Collective Presidency* (Heidelberg: Springer-Verlag Berlin, 2014), 32.

51. Deng Xiaoping, "We Shall Speed Up Reform," June 12, 1987, in Deng, *Fundamental Issues in Present-Day China*, 192.

52. Susan L. Shirk, "The Political Price of Reform Cycles: Elite Politics in Chinese-Style Economic Reforms," unpublished paper. Also see Richard Baum, *Burying Mao: Chinese Politics in the Age of Deng Xiaoping* (Princeton, NJ: Princeton University Press, 1994), 7.

53. Deng Xiaoping, "Uphold the Four Cardinal Principles," March 30, 1979, http://en.peo ple.cn/dengxp/vol2/text/b1290.html.

54. Deng Xiaoping's speech to the Central Party Work Conference, December 13, 1978, quoted in Vogel, *Deng Xiaoping and the Transformation of China*, 243.

55. Deng Xiaoping, "Take a Clear-Cut Stand against Bourgeois Liberalization," December 30, 1986, in Deng, *Fundamental Issues in Present-Day China*, 165.

56. Suisheng Zhao, "Deng Xiaoping's Southern Tour: Elite Politics in Post-Tiananmen China," *Asian Survey* 33, no. 8 (August 1993): 739–756.

57. Shirk, *Political Logic of Economic Reform*.

58. Barry Naughton, *Growing Out of the Plan: Chinese Economic Reform, 1978–90* (Cambridge, UK: Cambridge University Press, 1995).

59. Shirk, *Political Logic of Economic Reform*.

60. Susan L. Shirk, *How China Opened Its Door: The Political Success of the PRC's Foreign Trade and Investment Reforms* (Washington, DC: Brookings Institution Press, 1994).

61. "How Much Do State-Owned Enterprises Contribute to China's GDP and Employment?," The World Bank, July 15, 2019, http://documents.worldbank.org/cura ted/en/449701565248091726/pdf/How-Much-Do-State-Owned-Enterprises-Contrib ute-to-China-s-GDP-and-Employment.pdf.

62. Nicholas R. Lardy, "State Sector Support in China Is Accelerating," Petersen Institute for International Economics, October 28, 2019, https://www.piie.com/blogs/china-economic-watch/state-sector-support-china-accelerating.

63. Julian Gewirtz, *Unlikely Partners: Chinese Reformers, Western Economists, and the Making of Global China* (Cambridge, MA: Harvard University Press, 2017), 149.

64. Janos Kornai, "Economists Share Blame for China's 'Monstrous' Turn," *Financial Times*, July 10, 2019, https://www.ft.com/content/f10ccb26-a16f-11e9-a282-2df48f366f7d.

65. Speech by Chairman of the Delegation of the People's Republic of China, Teng Hsiao-Ping, at the Special Session of the U.N. General Assembly, April 10, 1974, Deng Xiaoping Internet Archive, https://www.marxists.org/reference/archive/deng-xiaoping/1974/04/10.htm.

66. Memorandum of Conversation between Vice Premier Deng Xiaoping and President Jimmy Carter, January 30, 1979, 9:40 a.m., *Foreign Relations of the United States, 1977–1980*, vol. 13, China, https://history.state.gov/historicaldocuments/frus1977-80v13/d208.

67. Zbigniew Brzezinski, "America and the New Asia" (Michel Oksenberg Lecture, Asia-Pacific Research Center, Stanford Institute for International Studies, March 9, 2005),

https://fsi-live.s3.us-west-1.amazonaws.com/s3fs-public/evnts/media/Brzezinski_New_Asia_03_2005.pdf.

68. Evan Osnos, "The Cost of the Cultural Revolution, Fifty Years Later," *New Yorker*, May 6, 2016, https://www.newyorker.com/news/daily-comment/the-cost-of-the-cultural-revolution-fifty-years-later.

69. Vogel, *Deng Xiaoping and the Transformation of China*, 345.

70. Vogel, 298.

71. Vogel, 301.

72. John W. Garver, "China's Push through the South China Sea: The Interaction of Bureaucratic and National Interests," *China Quarterly*, no. 132 (December 1992), 1003.

73. Deng Xiaoping, "One Country, Two Systems, June 22–23, 1984," in Deng, *Fundamental Issues in Present-Day China*, 50.

74. Hu Wei, "How Did Deng Xiaoping Manage Both Domestic and International Situations?," *U.S.-China Perception Monitor*, February 21, 2022, http://cn3.uscnpm.org/model_item.html?action=view&table=article&id=27190.

75. Deng Xiaoping, "Be Good at Using Opportunities to Solve Development Problems," December 24, 1990, *Selected Works of Deng Xiaoping*, 3:363.

76. Leng Rong and Wang Zuoling, *Deng Xiaoping's Chronicle*, vol. 2 (Beijing: Central Literature Publishing House, 2004), 1346.

Chapter 3

1. This section draws on Susan Shirk, "What China's Lack of Transparency Means for U.S. Policy," ChinaFile, May 28, 2015, http://www.chinafile.com/reporting-opinion/two-way-street/what-chinas-lack-transparency-means-us-policy.

2. "Open Budget Survey 2017: China," International Budget Partnership, https://www.internationalbudget.org/wp-content/uploads/china-open-budget-survey-2017-summary.pdf.

3. Sui-Lee Wee and Li Yuan, "China Censors Bad Economic News amid Signs of Slower Growth," *New York Times*, September 28, 2018, https://www.nytimes.com/2018/09/28/business/china-censor-economic-news.html; Tom Hancock, "China Censorship Moves from Politics to Economics," *Financial Times*, November 13, 2018, https://www.ft.com/content/1daaaf52-e32c-11e8-a6e5-792428919cee; Josh Rudolph, "Minitrue Diary, February 2, 2020: Economic Optimism," *China Digital Times*, October 16, 2020, https://chinadigitaltimes.net/2020/10/minitrue-diary-february-2-2020-economic-optimism/.

4. Yu Keping, "Rule of Law Crucial to Good Governance," *China-U.S. Focus*, May 12, 2015, https://www.chinausfocus.com/political-social-development/rule-of-law-crucial-to-good-governance.

5. Yin, "China's Foreign Policy Isn't Transparent."

6. Milan W. Svolik, *The Politics of Authoritarian Rule* (Cambridge, UK: Cambridge University Press, 2012).

7. Barbara Geddes, Joseph Wright, and Erica Frantz, *How Dictatorships Work* (Cambridge, UK: Cambridge University Press, 2018), 179.

8. Douglas McAdam, *Political Process and the Development of Black Insurgency* (Chicago: University of Chicago Press, 1999).

9. Grace, "30 Years Ago: Zhao Ziyang: 'We Came Too Late'," *China Digital Times*, video of May 19, 1989, https://chinadigitaltimes.net/2019/05/30-years-ago-zhao-ziyang-we-came-too-late/.

10. Chu Yin, "China's Foreign Policy Isn't Transparent: You've Got to Be Kidding," ChinaFile, August 1, 2015, http://www.chinafile.com/reporting-opinion/two-way-street/chinas-foreign-policy-isnt-transparent-youve-got-be-kidding.
11. Geddes, Wright, and Frantz, *How Dictatorships Work*, 66.
12. Li Ling and Wenzhang Zhou, "Governing the 'Constitutional Vacuum': Federalism, Rule of Law and Politburo Politics in China," *China Law and Society Review* 4 (2019): 1–40.
13. Research by Dimitar Gueorguiev and Paul Schuler, "Keeping Your Head Down: Public Profiles and Promotion in One-Party Regimes," *Journal of East Asian Studies* 16, no. 1 (2016): 87–116, found that leaders whose public profiles were very large or very small were less likely to be promoted than other leaders.
14. Examples are Wen's 2008 speech at the World Economic Forum in Davos, http://transcripts.cnn.com/TRANSCRIPTS/0809/28/fzgps.01.html; his 2009 interview with the *Financial Times* in Davos, https://www.ft.com/content/795d2bca-f0fe-11dd-8790-00007 79fd2ac; his 2010 speech in Shenzhen on the thirtieth anniversary of the creation of the special economic zone, https://chinadigitaltimes.net/2019/05/30-years-ago-zhao-ziyang-we-came-too-late/; his 2010 interview with Fareed Zakaria on CNN, http://archives.cnn.com/TRANSCRIPTS/1010/03/fzgps.01.html; and his 2011 speech at the summer meeting of the World Economic Forum in Dalian, http://www.internationalviewpoint.org/spip.php?article2483.
15. David Barboza, "Billions in Hidden Riches for Family of Chinese Leader," *New York Times*, October 25, 2012, https://www.nytimes.com/2012/10/26/business/global/family-of-wen-jiabao-holds-a-hidden-fortune-in-china.html?auth=login-email.
16. An essay by Chinese political critic Wang Lixiong explains how the Mao-like charismatic leadership of Bo Xilai threatened the CCP leaders' political machine. See "Bo Xilai and the N-Series," *New Century News*, May 18, 2012, https://web.archive.org/web/20120630104140/http://www.newcenturynews.com/Article/gd/201205/20120518152414_3.html.
17. David Pilling, "Lunch with the FT: Han Han," *Financial Times*, April 21, 2012.
18. Bo Zhiyue (personal communication).
19. Max Fisher, "Clinton Reveals U.S. Role in High Level 2012 Incident with China," *Washington Post*, October 18, 2013, https://www.washingtonpost.com/news/worldviews/wp/2013/10/18/clinton-reveals-u-s-role-in-high-level-2012-incident-with-china/.
20. "Bo Xilai Responds to the Wang Lijun Incident, Claiming the Appointment Was an Oversight," *Caixin*, March 9, 2012, https://economy.caixin.com/2012-03-09/100366570.html.
21. "Premier Wen Jiabao Meets With Chinese and Foreign Reporters," Xinhua, March 14, 2012, http://www.news.cn/politics/2012lh/zhibo/zongli/wz.htm. For Caixin editor Hu Shuli'a reporting on Wen's press conference, see "Inside Lianghui: A Memorable Press Conference," Caixin Online, March 15, 2012, http://english.caixin.com/2012-03-15/100368871.html. See also Michael Wines, "Wen Calls for Political Reform but Sidesteps Details," *New York Times*, March 14, 2012, https://www.nytimes.com/2012/03/15/world/asia/china-wen-jiabao-calls-for-political-reform.html.
22. Zhou Yongkang, "Strengthen the Ranks of Secretaries of the Politics and Law Commissions in the New Situation and Strive to Create a New Situation in the Scientific Development of the Politics and Law Profession," *People's Daily*, April 24, 2012, https://web.archive.org/web/20150204204546/http://politics.people.com.cn/GB/1024/17727980.html.
23. Wen Jiabao, "Let Power Be Exercised under the Sunlight," *Qiushi*, April 16, 2012, https://china.caixin.com/2012-04-16/100380096.html.

24. Xi Jinping, *Selected Quotes from Xi Jinping on Making Clear the Party's Discipline and Regulations* (Beijing: Zhongguo fangzheng chubanshu, 2016), 28.
25. Zhou Li-An and Li Hongbin, "Political Turnover and Economic Performance: The Incentive Role of Personnel Control in China," *Journal of Public Economics* 89 (2005): 1743–1762.
26. Victor Shih, Christopher Adolph, and Mingxing Liu, "Getting Ahead in the Communist Party: Explaining the Advancement of Central Committee Members in China," *American Political Science Review* 106 (2012): 166–187.
27. Ruixue Jia, Masayuki Kudamatsu, and David Seim, "Political Selection in China: Complementary Roles of Connections and Performance," *Journal of the European Economic Association* 13 (2015): 631–668.
28. Pierre F. Landry, Xiaobo Lu, and Haiyan Duan, "Does Performance Matter? Evaluating Political Selection along the Chinese Administrative Ladder," *Comparative Political Studies* 51, no. 8 (2018): 1074–1105.
29. "The regime is quite successful at fostering meritocracy at the lower levels of the administrative hierarchy, where local leaders are several steps removed from the selectorate that is relevant to central leaders. However, the imperative of protection against potential competitors results in a weaker propensity to promote high-performing officials as they climb the political ladder." Landry, Lu, and Duan, "Does Performance Matter," 1076. Victor Shih similarly finds that because top leaders view high-performing officials as potential challengers they prefer to admit weaker figures into the topmost inner circle. See Victor Shih, *Coalitions of the Weak* (Cambridge: Cambridge University Press, 2022), 10–11.
30. "Xi Jinping's Speech at the National Organization Work Meeting," CCP Member Network, September 17, 2018, http://www.12371.cn/2018/09/17/ARTI1537150840597467.shtml.
31. "Insist on the Principle That the Organization Selects People," People's Daily Online, October 29, 2018, http://opinion.people.com.cn/n1/2018/1029/c1003-30367334.html.
32. Susan L. Shirk, *Competitive Comrades: Career Incentives and Student Strategies in China* (Berkeley: University of California Press, 1981).
33. Holly Snape, "A Shifting Balance between Political and Professional Responsibility: Paradigmatic Change in China's Civil Servant and Cadres Management Systems," *Mapping China Journal*, no. 3 (2019): 1–24, https://mappingchina.org/wp-content/uploads/2019/11/MCJ-2019_1_Holly-Snape.pdf.
34. Susan L. Shirk, "The Decline of Virtuocracy in China," in *Class and Social Stratification in Post-revolution China*, ed. James Watson (Cambridge, UK: Cambridge University Press, 1984), 63.
35. Geremie R. Barmé, "The Children of Yan'an: New Words of Warning to a Prosperous Age," *China Heritage Quarterly*, no. 26, June 2022, http://www.chinaheritagequarterly.org/features.php?searchterm=026_yanan.inc&issue=026.
36. David Kelly, "Chinese Political Transition: Split in the Princeling Camp?," East Asia Forum, March 21, 2011, https://www.eastasiaforum.org/2011/03/21/chinese-political-transition-split-in-the-princeling-camp/.
37. In 2006, two news outlets reported that 90% of China's wealthiest individuals are children of senior CCP cadres according to a research report. See Mo Ming, "90 Percent of China's Billionaires Are Children of Senior Officials," *China Digital Times*, November 2, 2006, https://chinadigitaltimes.net/2006/11/90-percent-of-chinas-billionaires-are-children-of-senior-officials/; and "Chinese Official Report Admits that 90 Percent of Billionaires Are Children of Senior Party Cadres," *Radio France Internationale*, August 3, 2008, http://www1.rfi.fr/actucn/articles/099/article_6365.asp. In 2009, People.cn, the news site of China's official newspaper People's Daily, published a report to debunk

the 90% figure. See Tang Weihong, Zhang Yuke, and Chang Hong, "The Investigation About the Story of '91% of Billionnaires Are Children of Senior Party Cadres'," People. cn, August 5, 2009, http://www.chinanews.com.cn/gn/news/2009/08-05/1805634.shtml.

38. Frederick C. Teiwes, *Leadership, Legitimacy, and Conflict in China: From a Charismatic Mao to the Politics of Succession* (Armonk, NY: M.E. Sharpe, 1984), 130.

39. Cheng Li, *Chinese Politics in the Xi Jinping Era* (Washington, DC: Brookings Institution Press, 2016), 268.

40. The Chinese do not use this term. I introduced it from British parliamentary politics in Susan L. Shirk, *The Political Logic of Economic Reform in China* (Berkeley: University of California Press, 1933). It was extended to theories of comparative politics by Bruce Bueno deMesquita, Alastair Smith, Randolph M. Siverson, and James D. Morrow, *The Logic of Political Survival* (Cambridge, MA: MIT Press, 2003).

41. Ruixue Jia and Yiqing Xu, "Rotating to the Top: How Elites and Commoners Rise in the Chinese Communist Party," unpublished paper.

42. Tibet and Xinjiang usually have one additional seat. And sometimes a province has only one seat because its leader lost the election by the Party Congress to the Central Committee.

43. The Central Committee also elects the Central Discipline Inspection Commission, the powerful body that investigates and penalizes Party members for corruption and abuses of power.

44. "Name List of the Presidum of the 19th CCP National Congress," Xinhua, October 15, 2007, https://www.mfa.gov.cn/ce/ceus//chn/zt/3456782/t372453.htm.

45. "Name List of the Presidum of the 19th CCP National Congress."

46. In 1957, Nikita Khrushchev defeated the effort by the Politburo Standing Committee to oust him by winning the support of the Central Committee. In 1964, however, the Central Committee removed Khrushchev from his leadership position.

47. Edmund Malesky, Regina Abrami, and Yu Zheng, "Institutions and Inequality in Single-Party Regimes: A Comparative Analysis of Vietnam and China," *Comparative Politics* 43, no. 4(2011): 401–419.

48. Liu Siyang, Sun Chengbin, and Liu Gang, "For the Prosperity and Development of the Party and the Country, Long-term Peace and Stability – Documenting the Emergence of the New Central Leadership," Xinhua, October 24, 2007, http://news.sohu.com/20071024/n252815676.shtml; Benjamin Kang Lim, "China Held Landmark Straw Poll to Choose Top Leaders: Xinhua," *Reuters*, November 16, 2012, https://www.reuters.com/article/us-china-congress-vote/china-held-landmark-straw-poll-to-choose-top-leaders-xinhua-idUSBRE8AF0FO20121116. The 2007 vote was for open Politburo seats; the 2012 vote was for the five open seats in the Politburo Standing Committee (Xi and Li held onto their seats without being subject to the straw poll).

49. See Yu Keping, *Democratic Governance and Political Reform in China* (Beijing: Zhongyang bianyi chubanshe, 2012).

50. "Name List of the Presidum of the 19th CCP National Congress."

51. Liu, Sun, and Liu, "For the Prosperity and Development of the Party and the Country, Long-term Peace and Stability."

52. "How a Son's Death in a High-Speed Car Crash Led to Powerful Chinese Official's Fall from Grace," *South China Morning Post*, December 23, 2014, https://www.scmp.com/news/china/article/1668151/how-sons-death-high-speed-car-crash-led-powerful-chinese-officials-fall.

53. "Pilots the Strong Leader in the New Era: A Record of the New Central Leadership of the Party," Xinhua News Agency, October 26, 2017, http://www.xinhuanet.com//politics/19cpcnc/2017-10/26/c_1121860147.htm.

54. Shirk, *Political Logic of Economic Reform*.

55. Gabriella Montinola, Yingyi Qian, and Barry R. Weingast, "Federalism, Chinese Style: The Political Basis for Economic Success in China," *World Politics* 48, no. 1 (October 1995): 50–81.

56. "China Braces for Next Act in Leadership Drama," Reuters, April 11, 2012.

57. Andrew J. Nathan, "Authoritarian Resilience," *Journal of Democracy* 14, no. 1 (2003): 6–17. Smooth, rule-bound leadership transitions have become a point of pride for the CCP. For example, see "China Completes Leadership Transition with Growing Maturity of Power Transfer Mechanism," Xinhua, March 16, 2013.

58. "Retreat in July Set Jiang's Exit in Motion," *Straits Times*, September 21, 2004, https://eresources.nlb.gov.sg/newspapers/Digitised/Issue/straitstimes20040921-1.

59. Liu Siyang and Sun Chengbin, "Hu Jintao and Jiang Zemin Meet With All Comrades Attending the Fourth Plenum and Deliver Important Speeches," Xinhua, September 20, 2004, http://news.sina.com.cn/c/2004-09-20/00553711841s.shtml.

60. Liu, Sun, and Liu, "For the Prosperity and Development of the Party and the Country, Long-term Peace and Stability."

61. "Xi Takes Charge: The Implications of the 19th Party Congress for China's Future" (briefing, UC San Diego 21st Century China Center, 2017), http://china.ucsd.edu/_files/2017_xi-briefing-web.pdf.

62. Milan W. Svolik, *The Politics of Authoritarian Rule* (Cambridge, UK: Cambridge University Press, 2012).

63. Cheng Li, *Chinese Politics in the Xi Jinping Era: Reassessing Collective Leadership* (Washington, DC: Brookings Institution Press, 2016), 53.

64. Central Committee, Politburo, and Politburo Standing Committee members concurrently holding government or military positions are governed by the written retirement rules associated with these positions.

65. Xiao Ma, "Term Limits and Authoritarian Power Sharing: Theory and Evidence from China," *Journal of East Asian Studies* 16 (March 2016): 62, https://www.cambridge.org/core/journals/journal-of-east-asian-studies/article/abs/term-limits-and-authoritarian-power-sharing-theory-and-evidence-from-china/8C0CBE5ED57367B1CF101966126D760A.

66. Ruixue Jia and Yiqing Xu, "Rotating to the Top: How Career Tracks Matter in the Chinese Communist Party," unpublished manuscript, August 31, 2018, SSRN, https://papers.ssrn.com/sol3/papers.cfm?abstract_id=3613276.

67. Deng Xiaoping, "On the Reform of the System of Party and State Leadership," August 18, 1980, *Selective Works of Deng Xiaoping*, 2: 322, https://www.marxists.org/reference/archive/deng-xiaoping/1980/220.htm.

Chapter 4

1. Yanzhong Huang, "The SARS Epidemic and Its Aftermath in China: A Political Perspective," in *Learning from SARS: Preparing for the Next Disease Outbreak: Workshop Summary*, ed. Stacey Knobler, Adel Mahmoud, Stanley Lemon, Alison Mack, Laura Sivitz, and Katherine Oberholtzer (Washington, DC: National Academies Press, 2004), 116–136, https://doi.org/10.17226/10915.

2. Lianhe zaobao online, 2003, http://www.zaobao.com/special/pneumonia/pages2/pneumonia250603.html, in Huang, "SARS Epidemic and Its Aftermath."

3. This was the beginning of a "government responsibility system" (*zhengfu wenze zhi*), the official said.

4. "China's Chernobyl?" *The Economist*, April 24, 2003, https://www.economist.com/leaders/2003/04/24/chinas-chernobyl.

5. Gary King, Jennifer Pan, and Margaret E. Roberts, "How Censorship in China Allows Government Criticism but Silences Collective Expression," *American Political Science Review* 107, no. 2 (May 2013): 1–18.

6. Susan L. Shirk, "Changing Media, Changing China," in *Changing Media, Changing China*, ed. Susan L. Shirk (New York: Oxford University Press, 2011), 1–37.

7. David Bandursky and Martin Hala, eds., *Investigative Journalism in China: Eight Cases in Chinese Watchdog Journalism* (Hong Kong: Hong Kong University Press, 2010).

8. Wu Qimin and Sun Chengbin, "Hu Jintao's Inspection at People's Daily: I am Very Happy to Communicate with Netizens," Xinhua, June 21, 2008, http://www.chinan ews.com.cn/gn/news/2008/06-21/1288574.shtml.

9. Huang, "SARS Epidemic and Its Aftermath."

10. "Scientific Outlook on Development," *China Daily*, September 8, 2010, https://web. archive.org/web/20210313061225/http://cpcchina.chinadaily.com.cn/2010-09/08/conte nt_13918103.htm.

11. Leonard Downie, Phil Bennett, John Pomfret, Philip P. Pan, and Peter S. Goodman, "Interview with Chinese Premier Wen Jiabao on Nov. 21, 2003," *Washington Post*, November 21, 2003, https://www.washingtonpost.com/archive/business/technology/ 2003/11/21/interview-with-chinese-premie/5a451649-e60d-429f-b550-9df77ca2a099/.

12. Huang, "SARS Epidemic and Its Aftermath."

13. D. Wilson and R. Dragusanu, "The Expanding Middle: The Exploding World Middle Class and Falling Global Inequality" (Goldman Sachs Global Economics Paper No. 170, July 2008), 10, cited in Jonathan R. Stromseth, Edmund J. Malesky, and Dimitar D. Gueorguiev, *China's Governance Puzzle: Enabling Transparency and Participation in a Single-Party State*, with Lai Hairong, Wang Xixin, and Carl Brinton (Cambridge, UK: Cambridge University Press, 2017), 2.

14. "Resolution on Enhancing the Governing Capacity of the Chinese Communist Party," passed at the Fourth Plenary session of the Sixteenth Central Committee of the Chinese Communist Party on September 19, 2004, *People's Daily*, September 26, 2004.

15. Zhai Wei, "Hu Jintao in the First Politburo Group Study: Strengthen Study and Improve the Ability of Governing and Rejuvenating the Country," Xinhua, December 26, 2002, http://43.250.236.3/GB/shizheng/16/20021226/896572.html, cited in Joseph Fewsmith, "Chinese Politics under Hu Jintao: *Riding the Tiger of Politics and Public Health*," *Problems of Post-Communism* 50, no. 5 (2003): 16.

16. Wen Jing and He Pei, "Voice from the World: 'China Model' Shows Value in Coping with Crisis," *Economic Reference*, March 6, 2009, http://jjckb.xinhuanet.com/gnyw/ 2009-03/06/content_147229.htm.

17. "Zhou Xiaochuan: Hopefully after Economic Recovery, We Can Overcome Past Problems," *Sohu*, April 18, 2009, http://business.sohu.com/20090418/n263468838. shtml.

18. "Why Must We Adhere to the Guiding Position of Marxism in the Field of Ideology and Not Diversify the Guiding Ideology?," *Qiushi*, April 15, 2009, http://news.cctv. com/china/20090415/108305.shtml.

19. "Report on the Work of the Standing Committee of the National People's Congress," Xinhua, March 16, 2009, http://www.gov.cn/2009lh/content_1260366.htm.

20. "Adhere to and Improve the People's Congress System," *Guangming Daily*, March 12, 2009, http://www.npc.gov.cn/npc/c12675/200903/06ff94a02a1b4b97828525080d71b042. shtml.

21. "Further Enhance the Self-Awareness and Resoluteness of Taking the Political Path of Socialism with Chinese Characteristics," *Magazine of National People's Congress*, September 19, 2011, http://www.npc.gov.cn/npc/c16115/201109/43fefadf8a474342ae7d2 15ad999afe2.shtml.

22. "Why Must We Adhere to the Guiding Position of Marxism in the Field of Ideology and Not Diversify the Guiding Ideology?"

23. Wang Zaibang, "The Three Strengths of 'Xi-plomacy'," *Globe*, March 28, 2013, http://news.sina.com.cn/c/sd/2013-03-28/112526668122_2.shtml.

24. Alice Miller, "Prospects for Solidarity in the Xi Jinping Leadership," *China Leadership Monitor*, no. 37, April 30, 2012, https://www.hoover.org/sites/default/files/uploads/documents/CLM37AM.pdf.

25. Tian Boqiang, "Revealing the Family Background of Former Chinese President Hu Jintao: Very Poor at the Beginning of Liberation," *Anhui News*, January 20, 2014, https://web.archive.org/web/20140120171336/http://news.ifeng.com/history/zhongguoxiandaishi/detail_2014_01/20/33162103_0.shtml.

26. Oliver August, "Emperor Who? China's New Ruler Keeps His Secrets," *The Times*, November 15, 2002, 17.

27. Deng Ke and Liu Jianping, "Hu Jintao in the Eyes of Relatives, Friends, and Classmates," *Southern Weekend*, November 16, 2002, http://news.sina.com.cn/c/2002-11-16/1159809070.html.

28. "Studying in Tsinghua, Harvests Politics: Hu Jintao's Way of Growth," *China Newsweek*, October 24, 2006, https://news.ifeng.com/history/200610/1024_25_23177.shtml. Hu sings a famous Chinese folk song called "In That Distant Place" and the Chinese version of a popular Soviet song called "Moscow Nights" in a quintet at the eighth national meeting of the China Federation of Literary and Art Circles, on November 10, 2006. It can be seen on YouTube, https://www.youtube.com/watch?v=AL6lgeDB2ZU&t=113s.

29. Su Jie, "Past of Tsinghua Dancing Team," *China Newsweek*, August 25, 2016, https://web.archive.org/web/20161107150918/http://www.tsinghua.org.cn/publish/alumni/4000382/11215876.html.

30. August, "Emperor Who?," 17.

31. Zhao Yi, "China's Knowledge-Based and Technocratic 'New Politicians' Debut," *Southern Window*, December 11, 2002, http://news.sina.com.cn/c/2002-12-11/1028836964.html.

32. Lin Xia, "Deng Xiaoping's Old Fellows: Three Have Passed Away This Year," *The Paper*, August 21, 2015, http://www.thepaper.cn/baidu.jsp?contid=1261834; "Six Events Song Ping—the Eldest Retired Standing Committee Members—Has Done since the 18th Party Congress," November 7, 2015, Beijing News, Political Matter account, http://news.ifeng.com/a/20151107/46153322_0.shtml.

33. Richard Daniel Ewing, "Hu Jintao: The Making of a Chinese General Secretary," *China Quarterly*, no. 173 (March 2003): 21.

34. A video of Hu Jintao hosting the CYL gala in 1984 is available on YouTube. See https://www.youtube.com/watch?v=Zur6ASgexGw.

35. Hu Jintao, "Deeply Study, Correctly Apprehend, Comprehensively Implement Jiang Zemin's Important 'July 1' Tal," Xuexi Shibao, September 10, 2001, cited in Joseph Fewsmith, "Rethinking the Role of the CCP: Explicating Jiang Zemin's Party Anniversary Speech," *China Leadership Monitor*, no. 1, pt. 2, December 2001.

36. Ewing, "Hu Jintao: The Making of a Chinese General Secretary," 27.

37. Hu Jintao, "Full Text of Hu Jintao's Speech on Constructing a Harmonious Socialist Society," Xinhua, June 27, 2005, http://www.gov.cn/ldhd/2005-06/27/content_9700.htm. The speech was delivered on February 19, 2005.

38. "Research Report on Contentious and Difficult Problems of Party Building in the New Period" (Beijing: Zhongyang bionyiju chubanshe, 2004), 80, cited in Joseph Fewsmith, "Inner-Party Democracy: Development and Limitations," *China Leadership Monitor*, no. 31, Winter 2010, 1.

39. "Hu Jintao's Report at the 18th National Congress of the Communist Party of China," Xinhua, November 17, 2012, http://www.xinhuanet.com//18cpcnc/2012-11/17/c_113711665_6.htm.

40. Hu Jintao, "The Speech at the Symposium Commemorating Comrade Mao Zedong's 110th Birthday," Xinhua, December 26, 2003, http://news.sina.com.cn/c/2003-12-26/22091440754s.shtml.

41. Summary of Special Report, CASS International Issues Forum, 2005. Party Building: Lessons from Abroad.

42. Summary of Special Report, CASS International Issues Forum, 2005. Party Building: Lessons from Abroad.

43. Stromseth, Malesky, and Gueorguiev, *China's Governance Puzzle*. The research found that increased transparency was closely associated with less corruption, and that higher rates of participation enhanced compliance and reduced disputes over environmental and labor issues.

44. Lai Hairong, *China's Rural Political Reform: A Study of Township Semi-competitive Elections* (Beijing: Yongyang bianyiju chubanshe, 2009), 86.

45. Willy Wo-Lap Lam, "China's Debate over Vietnam's Reforms," Jamestown Foundation China Brief, May 9, 2007, https://jamestown.org/program/chinas-debate-over-vietnams-reforms-3/.

46. "Latest Directives from the Ministry of Truth," *China Digital Times*, August 26, 30, 2010, https://chinadigitaltimes.net/2010/09/latest-directives-from-the-ministry-of-truth-august-26-august-30-2010/.

47. "Analysis on Jiangsu's Selection of City Party Committee Secretaries through 'Open Recommendation and Decision by Vote,'" *Liaowang*, no. 17 (April 25–May 1, 2011): 8–10.

48. "CPC Promotes Internal Democracy to Spearhead Reforms," Xinhua News Agency, September 15, 2009, http://www.china.org.cn/government/central_government/2009-09/15/content_18531872.htm.

49. "CPC Promotes Internal Democracy."

50. Richard McGregor, "China Opens Up to Redefine Democracy," *Financial Times*, June 13, 2007.

51. Zheng Qingyuan, "Actively and Steadily Push Forward the Political System Reform Along the Correct Political Direction," *People's Daily*, October 27, 2010, http://www.chinanews.com.cn/gn/2010/10-26/2614400.shtml.

52. Li Datong, "Wen Jiabao: The Verdict of History," Open Democracy, October 20, 2010, https://www.opendemocracy.net/en/wen-jiabaos-lonely-course/.

53. Wang Xiangwei, "Impromptu Remarks Reveal the Party's Pressure for Reforms," *South China Morning Post*, April 16, 2007, http://china.scmp.com/chimain/ZZZNNORUGoF.html.

54. "Retired Cadres Aim to Support Premier Wen through Political Reform Cable," US Embassy Beijing, March 24, 2009, http://wikileaks.org/plusd/cables/09BEIJING766_a.html.

55. Alice Miller, "Dilemmas of Globalisation and Governance," in *The Politics of China: Sixty Years of the People's Republic of China*, ed. Roderick MacFarquhar (Cambridge, UK: Cambridge University Press, 2011), 575.

56. Since 1997, the balance in the Politburo among the key bureaucratic constituencies in the Party, government, military, and provinces has remained consistent. According to Alice Miller, this system of institutional balancing within the Party's leadership bodies was also followed by the Soviet Union under Brezhnev and is intended "to reinforce collective leadership among the Politburo oligarchy by inhibiting any single sector from overwhelming the interests of the others and by inhibiting any single

leader—and especially the general secretary—from using any single group as a base of power to assert dominance over the rest of the leadership collective." Alice L. Miller, "The Politburo Standing Committee under Hu Jintao," *China Leadership Monitor*, September 21, 2011, no. 35, 5. https://www.hoover.org/research/politburo-standing-committee-under-hu-jintao.

57. Niu Lanchun, "Deng Xiaoping's Thinking on the Constraint of Power," *Study Times*, March 2007, https://kns.cnki.net/kcms/detail/detail.aspx?dbcode=CJFD&dbname=CJFD2005&filename=SLYT200501005&uniplatform=NZKPT&v=XvEjJmuDij381bCs2YnDlTasixj17npoj6cupLCJqJL2eu8mzct6jQOoajCjlh24.

58. "Full Text of Hu Jintao's Report at the 17th Party Congress," Xinhua, October 26, 2007, http://www.scio.gov.cn/37231/Document/1566887/1566887_11.htm.

59. "Several Principles on Political Life in the Party," February 29, 1980, CCP Member Network, http://news.12371.cn/2015/03/11/ARTI1426059362559711.shtml.

60. Hu Angang, *China's Collective Leadership* (Beijing: China Renmin University Press, 2015), 55, 77.

61. Hu Angang, "Insisting on Perfecting the Collective Leadership System of the CPC Central Committee: 'The Seven Mechanisms' and the Core" (Chia Study Reports, Institute for Contemporary China Studies, Tsinghua University, April 2017).

62. Milan W. Svolik, *The Politics of Authoritarian Rule* (Cambridge, UK: Cambridge University Press, 2012).

63. Charles Mitchell, Rebecca L. Ray, and Bart van Ark, "The Conference Board CEO Challenge® 2012: Risky Business—Focusing on Innovation and Talent in a Volatile World," The Conference Board, March 20, 2012, https://www.conference-board.org/publications/publicationdetail.cfm?publicationid=2152.

64. Hongyu Wang, "To Improve the Quality of Legislation, We Must Get Rid of Departmental Interests," *Beijing News*, September 15, 2004, http://news.sina.com.cn/c/2004-09-15/23384336080.shtml. The author is a researcher at the law committee of the National People's Congress. Chen Jieren, "Departmental Interest and Industry Interest: The Unbearable Weight for China's Legislation," Legal Person, March 16, 2005, http://news.sohu.com/20050316/n224714187.shtml .

65. Li Bin, "Chen Xunru: 'Forceful Interest Groups Influence Administration and Legislation," Xinhua, March 13, 2006, https://web.archive.org/web/20060618193438/http://opinion.people.com.cn/GB/8213/59285/59286/4195170.html .

66. Xu Jingsheng, "Administration and Legislation Must Not Be 'Kidnapped' by Forceful Interest Groups," Xinhua, March 14, 2006, http://news.sina.com.cn/c/2006-03-14/00009341301.shtml.

67. Pan Hongqi, "Xu Fangming's Case and the 'Intermediary Interest Group,'" *Beijing Youth Daily*, July 8, 2005, http://opinion.people.com.cn/GB/1034/3528922.html.

68. Joseph Kahn, "China's Leader, Ex-Rival at Side, Solidifies Power," *New York Times*, September 25, 2005, https://www.nytimes.com/2005/09/25/world/asia/chinas-leader-exrival-at-side-solidifies-power.html.

69. David Shambaugh, *China's Communist Party: Atrophy and Adaptation* (Berkeley: University of California Press, 2008), 157.

70. "Decision on the Enhancement of the Party's Governing Capacity," which David Shambaugh describes as "the most important party meeting and document to be published since the critical Third Plenum of 1978." *China's Communist Party: Atrophy and Adaptation* (Berkeley: University of California Press, 2008), 124.

71. Cheng Li, "Will China's 'Lost Generation' Find a Path to Democracy?," in *China's Changing Political Landscape: Prospects for Democracy*, ed. Cheng Li (Washington, DC: Brookings Institution Press, 2008), 108.

72. Zheng Yongnian, "The 18th CCP National Congress and Issues about China's Reform," *Lianhe Zaobao*, July 31, 2012, http://www.aisixiang.com/data/55976.html.

73. The propaganda czar was Li Changchun from 2002 to 2012; the internal security czar was Luo Gan from 2002 to 2007, followed by Zhou Yongkang from 2007 to 2012.

74. Zhaoguang Wang, Yang Yao, and Junni Zhang, "The Competence-Loyalty Tradeoff in China's Political Selection" (manuscript, National School of Development and China Center for Economic Research, Peking University).

75. Susan L. Shirk, *The Political Logic of Economic Reform* (Berkeley: University of California Press, 1993), 116.

76. Miller, "Prospects for Solidarity."

77. Mario Gilli, Yuan Li, and Jiwei Qian, "Logrolling under Fragmented Authoritarianism: Theory and Evidence from China," *Public Choice* 175, no. 1 (April 2018): 197–214..

78. Jack Snyder, *Myths of Empire: Domestic Politics and International Ambition* (Ithaca, NY: Cornell University Press, 1991), 17, describes this political process as "coalition logrolling," in which the coalitions are "trading favors so that each group gets what it wants most and costs are diffused to society through taxes imposed by the state." The term is adopted from the analysis of bargaining in democratic legislatures.

79. Pin Ho, "Why Is China Purging Its Former Top Security Chief, Zhou Yongkang?," ChinaFile, December 17, 2013, https://www.chinafile.com/conversation/why-china-purging-its-former-top-security-chief-zhou-yongkang.

80. Snyder, *Myths of Empire*, 17.

81. Xu Jilin, "Does China Need a Leviathan? Critique of Statist Trends in China in the Last Decade," Sina.com, September 30, 2011, http://old.21bcr.com/a/shiye/guancha/2012/0201/3262.html.

82. Wang Cungang, "Contemporary China's Diplomatic Policy: Who Is Making It? Who Influences It?," Waijiao Pinglun, March 5, 2012, 1–18, https://www.ixueshu.com/download/3750cf6b88dc8b12403d04cc7e13655b318947a18e7f9386.html.

83. The line on the map was intended to indicate which islands China claimed; Beijing raised the notion of "historic rights" to the entire sea only in the 1990s. Bill Hayton, "China's 'Historic Rights' in the South China Sea: Made in America?" *The Diplomat*, June 21, 2016, https://thediplomat.com/2016/06/chinas-historic-rights-in-the-south-china-sea-made-in-america/.

84. Stephen Van Evera, "Causes of War" (PhD diss., University of California, Berkeley, 1984); and Snyder, *Myths of Empire*, 41.

85. Andrew S. Erickson, "The Chinese Naval Shipbuilding Bookshelf," China Analysis from Original Sources website, February 11, 2021, https://www.andrewerickson.com/2021/02/the-chinese-naval-shipbuilding-bookshelf/.

86. Snyder, *Myths of Empire*, 67.

87. "Communique of the Sixth Plenum of the 16th Central Committee of the CCP," Xinhua, October 11, 2006, https://www.fmprc.gov.cn/ce/ceuk/chn/zyxw/t280114.htm.

88. Edward Cunningham, Tony Saich, and Jesse Turiel, "Understanding CCP Resilience: Surveying Chinese Public Opinion Through Time," July 2020, https://ash.harvard.edu/files/ash/files/final_policy_brief_7.6.2020.pdf.

89. Cheng Yuyang, "Hu Jintao Tried to Stop the Outbreak of the Color Revolution: The Communist Party of China Wanted to Fight a War without Smoke," *Open Magazine*, July 10, 2005, https://www.secretchina.com/news/gb/2005/07/10/120247.html; Joseph Khan, "China's Leader, Ex-Rival at Side, Solidifies Power," *New York Times*, September 25, 2005, https://www.nytimes.com/2005/09/25/world/asia/chinas-leader-exrival-at-side-solidifies-power.html; Hu Jintao, "Firmly Grasp the Leadership and Initiative of Ideological Work," *Selective Works of Hu Jintao*, October 11, 2006, 527–531; "Hu Jintao: Strengthen the Construction and Management of Internet Culture in the Spirit of Innovation," Xinhua, January 24, 2007, http://www.xinhuanet.com/zgjx/2007-01/24/content_5665025.htm.

90. Du Qiang and Ye Yuyang, "Renmin University of China Released the 2011 Public Opinion Report: Weibo Has Become the Biggest Information Source," *Southern Metropolis Daily*, April 14, 2012, http://news.sina.com.cn/c/2012-04-14/044024270692.shtml.

91. Man Kaiyan, "China in 140 Characters: Ten Biggest Events on Weibo in 2011," *Caijing*, December 7, 2011, http://finance.sina.com.cn/g/20111207/181610952482.shtml.

92. "Clinton's Words on China: Trade Is the Smart Thing," *New York Times*, March 9, 2000, https://www.nytimes.com/2000/03/09/world/clinton-s-words-on-china-trade-is-the-smart-thing.html.

93. Michael Wines, "China Creates New Agency for Patrolling the Internet," *New York Times*, May 4, 2011, https://www.nytimes.com/2011/05/05/world/asia/05china.html.

94. China attracted international media attention when its 2011 public security budget, at 624.4 billion yuan ($95 billion), became public. The budget exceeded China's defense budget ($92 billion), which was also experiencing stunning growth. Actually, China's public security spending had been increasing steadily and rapidly well before 2008 and already exceeded its defense budget in 2010. The 51% jump in paramilitary spending from 2006 to 2007 is especially noteworthy.

	National Defense		Public Security		Paramilitary Police	
	(Billion yuan)	Change from previous year	(Billion yuan)	Change from previous year	(Billion yuan)	Change from previous year
2005	247.5		218.0		32.7	
2006	297.9	20%	256.2	18%	38.8	19%
2007	355.5	19%	348.6	36%	58.5	51%
2008	417.9	18%	406.0	16%	66.4	13%
2009	495.1	18%	474.4	17%	86.6	30%
2010	533.3	8%	551.8	16%	87.2	1%

Source: Ministry of Finance.
Note: Public security spending reported includes paramilitary police spending. In 2005 and 2006, the ministry of finance did not publish a total public security budget. The numbers shown here add together spending on paramilitary police, public security, court, procuratorate, and justice and may be slightly underestimated.

95. Ching Kwan Lee and Yanghong Zhang, "The Power of Instability: Unraveling the Microfoundations of Bargained Authoritarianism in China," *American Journal of Sociology* 118, no. 6 (2013): 1475–1508.

96. "The Machinery of Stability Preservation," *Dui Hua*, June 8, 2011, https://www.duihuahrjournal.org/2011/06/translation-machinery-of-stability.html. The article by reporters Xu Kai and Li Weiao first appeared in *Caijing*, June 6, 2008.

97. "China's Top Paper Defends Grip of State Firms," Reuters, June 1, 2012, cited in James McGregor, *No Ancient Wisdom, No Followers* (Westport, CT: Prospecta Press, 2012), 12.

98. See the latest roster of the central SOEs, published on the SASAC website, on June 5, 2020, http://www.sasac.gov.cn/n2588035/n2641579/n2641645/index.html.

99. In the words of SASAC head Li Rongrong. See McGregor, *No Ancient Wisdom*, 21.

100. McGregor, *No Ancient Wisdom*, 8.

101. The "Guiding Opinion on Promoting and Adjustment of State-Owned Capital and the Reconstruction of State-Owned Enterprises," provides that "strategic industries" such as armaments, power generation and distribution, oil and petrochemicals, telecommunications, coal, aerospace, and air freight should be "state dominated," and

"pillar industries," including equipment manufacturing, automobiles, electronic communications, architecture, steel, nonferrous metals, chemicals, surveying and design, ad science and technology, should be majority state ownership. McGregor, *No Ancient Wisdom*, 17.

102. Tianlei Huang, "Chinese SOEs Should Help Fund China's Response to Pandemic," *Peterson Institute for International Economics*, April 2, 2020, https://www.piie.com/blogs/china-economic-watch/chinese-soes-should-help-fund-chinas-response-pande mic.

103. Tai Ming Cheung et al., "Planning for Innovation: Understanding China's Plans for Technological, Energy, Industrial and Defense Development" (report prepared for the U.S.-China Economic and Security Review Commission, September 2016), 33.

104. Erica Downs and Michal Meidan, "Business and Politics in China: The Oil Executive Reshuffle of 2011," *China Security*, no. 19, 5, February 8, 2012, https://www.brookings.edu/articles/business-and-politics-in-china-the-oil-executive-reshuffle-of-2011/.

105. McGregor, *No Ancient Wisdom*, 71.

106. Pin Ho, "Why Is China Purging Its Former Top Security Chief, Zhou Yongkang?," ChinaFile, December 17, 2013, https://www.chinafile.com/conversation/why-china-purging-its-former-top-security-chief-zhou-yongkang.

107. John Garnaut, "Princelings and Paupers," *Sydney Morning Herald*, May 26, 2012, https://www.smh.com.au/world/princelings-and-paupers-20120525-1za5n.html.

108. Peng Wang, "Military Corruption in China: The Role of Guanxi in the Buying and Selling of Military Positions," *China Quarterly*, no. 228 (December 2016), 970–991, https://www.cambridge.org/core/journals/china-quarterly/article/abs/military-cor ruption-in-china-the-role-of-guanxi-in-the-buying-and-selling-of-military-positions/970EC9E8D37441C1E03B4F055A39D42F.

109. Minxin Pei, *China's Crony Capitalism: The Dynamics of Regime Decay* (Cambridge, MA: Harvard University Press, 2016), 45.

110. Pei, *China's Crony Capitalism*, 134.

111. Xiao Hui, Yu Ning, and Li Rongde, "In Depth: The Mistress Who Ruled Chongqing," *Caixin*, February 6, 2018, https://www.caixinglobal.com/2018-02-06/the-mistress-who-ruled-chongqing-101208150.html.

112. Andrew Wedeman, "Flies into Tigers: The Dynamics of Corruption in China," *China Currents*, May 27, 2021, https://www.chinacenter.net/2021/china_currents/20-1/flies-into-tigers-the-dynamics-of-corruption-in-china/.

113. Benjamin Kang Lim, David Lague, and Charlie Zhu, "Special Report: The Power Struggle Behind China's Corruption Crackdown," *Reuters*, May 22, 2014, https://www.reuters.com/article/us-china-corruption-special-report/special-report-the-power-strug gle-behind-chinas-corruption-crackdown-idUSBREA4M00120140523.

114. Lily Kuo, "China Just Seized $14.5 Billion from Almost Everyone Close to Its Ex-security Chief," *Quartz*, March 31, 2014, https://qz.com/193646/china-just-seized-14-billion-from-almost-everyone-close-to-chinas-ex-security-chief/.

115. Michael Forsythe, Chris Buckley, and Jonathan Ansfield, "Investigating Family's Wealth, China's Leader Signals a Change," *New York Times*, April 19, 2014, https://www.nytimes.com/2014/04/20/world/asia/severing-a-familys-ties-chinas-president-sign als-a-change.html.

116. "Major General: Xu Caihou and Others Usurped the Then CMC Commander," *Caijing.com.cn*, 2015, March 9, 2015, https://web.archive.org/web/20150315004019/http://politics.caijing.com.cn/20150309/3835125.shtml.

117. "Insider Story of Raiding the Home of the National Thief Xu Caihou," *Phoenix Weekly*, no. 32, 2014, https://chinadigitaltimes.net/chinese/2014/11/%E5%87%A4%E5 %87%B0%E5%91%A8%E5%88%8A%EF%BD%9C%E5%9B%BD%E8%B4%BC

%E5%BE%90%E6%89%8D%E5%8E%9A%E6%9F%A5%E6%8A%84%E5%86%85
%E5%B9%95/. (The original link was quickly taken down after the story went out and
the link given here seems to be the online duplicate online.)

118. David Barboza, "Billions in Hidden Riches for Family of Chinese Leader," *New York Times*, October 25, 2012, https://www.nytimes.com/2012/10/26/business/global/family-of-wen-jiabao-holds-a-hidden-fortune-in-china.html.

119. "Xi Jinping Millionaire Relations Reveal Elite Chinese Fortunes," *Bloomberg*, June 29, 2012, https://www.bloomberg.com/news/articles/2012-06-29/xi-jinping-millionaire-relations-reveal-fortunes-of-elite?sref=I2I6qZII.

120. Garnaut, "Princelings and Paupers."

121. John Garnaut, "Rotting from Within: Investigating the Massive Corruption of the Chinese Military," *Foreign Policy*, April 16, 2012, https://foreignpolicy.com/2012/04/16/rotting-from-within/.

122. "Scores of PLA Officers Punished," *China Daily*, January 30, 2015, https://web.arch ive.org/web/20150703093317/http://english.chinamil.com.cn/news-channels/china-military-news/2015-01/30/content_6332591.htm.

123. Zhang Hui and Huang Chao, "The Army Has Filed More Than 4,000 Cases for Review and Investigation in Five Years and More Than 13,000 People Disciplined," *PLA Daily*, September 20, 2017, https://www.thepaper.cn/newsDetail_forw ard_1800542.

124. Dennis Blasko, "Corruption in China's Military: One of Many Problems," *War on the Rocks*, February 16, 2015, https://warontherocks.com/2015/02/corruption-in-chinas-military-one-of-many-problems/.

125. Stromseth, Malesky, and Gueorguiev, *China's Governance Puzzle*, 112.

126. Yawei Liu, "Bo Xilai's Campaign for the Standing Committee and the Future of Chinese Politicking," Jamestown Foundation China Brief 11, no. 21 (November 11, 2011), https://jamestown.org/program/bo-xilais-campaign-for-the-standing-committee-and-the-future-of-chinese-politicking/.

127. Ezra F. Vogel, *One Step Ahead in China: Guangdong under Reform* (Cambridge, MA: Harvard University Press, 1990).

128. Stromseth, Malesky, and Gueorguiev conducted field work in Chongqing and Guangdong to study transparency and corruption in both places. See "Comparing Approaches to Combating Corrupting: The Guangdong and Chongqing Models," in *China's Governance Puzzle*, 97–152.

129. Willy Wo-Lap Lam, "Wang Yang: The Future Torchbearer of Reform?," Jamestown Foundation China Brief, May 25, 2012, https://jamestown.org/program/wang-yang-the-future-torchbearer-of-reform/.

130. Dong Yu, "Wang Yang: It Is Necessary to Get Rid of the Misconception That People's Happiness Is a Gift from the Party and the Government," Xinhua, May 9, 2012, http://www.xinhuanet.com/politics/2012-05/09/c_123101245.htm.

131. Thomas L. Friedman, "Postcard from South China," Opinion, *New York Times*, August 31, 2008, https://www.nytimes.com/2008/08/31/opinion/31friedman.html.

132. For example, historian Zhang Lifan predicted that the regime would collapse in ten years if it hadn't reformed in five years. "Zhang Lifan's Remarks at the China Reform Forum," January 2, 2012, Radio France Internationale (RFI), https://www.rfi.fr/cn/%E9%A6%96%E9%A1%B5/20120201-%E7%AB%A0%E7%AB%8B%E5%87%A1%E5%9C%A8%E4%B8%AD%E5%9B%BD%E6%94%B9%E9%9D%A9%E8%AE%BA%E5%9D%9B%E7%9A%84%E5%8F%91%E8%A8%80. And sociologist Sun Liping said that if China reformed, it would be like Taiwan, but if it failed to reform, it would be like the Qing dynasty, "Sun Liping: A Silent Revolution Is Taking Place, Forcing China to Reform," *Caijing*, November 29, 2012, https://business.sohu.com/20121129/n359027586.shtml.

133. Wu Bangguo, "Work Report to the National People's Congress Standing Committee," Chinese Government's Official Web Portal, March 10, 2011, https://web.archive.org/web/20210501182546/http://english1.english.gov.cn/official/2011-03/18/content_1827 230.htm. Wu made the same points in his 2010 work report.

134. Fareed Zakaria, "Interview With Wen Jiabao," CNN, October 3, 2010, http://transcripts.cnn.com/TRANSCRIPTS/1010/03/fzgps.01.html.

135. Joseph Fewsmith, "Political Reform Was Never on the Agenda," *China Leadership Monitor*, no. 34, February 22, 2011, https://www.hoover.org/research/political-reform-was-never-agenda.

136. *Caixin* editor Hu Shuli emphasized that Premier Wen had mentioned the 1981 Resolution on Certain Questions in the History of Our Party since the Founding of the People's Republic of China twice in his remarks—the document that identified the features of China's political system that had to be reformed to prevent another Cultural Revolution in the future. She called for a "historical excavation" of the Cultural Revolution to make sure that younger generations of Chinese don't forget the lessons of this historical trauma. Hu Shuli, "Premier Wen Jiabao's Memorable Press Conference," Caixin Online, March 15, 2012, https://www.marketwatch.com/story/china-premier-wens-memorable-press-conference-2012-03-15.

137. Selected comments by Xi Jinping on Strictly and impartially (upholding) party discipline and rules, Central Literature Publishing House and China Lianzheng Press, 2015, 28–29. 18 Explanation of "some regulations concerning intra-party life under the new situation" and "regulations on intra-party supervision in the CCP", Xinhua, November 2, 2016, http://news.xinhuanet.com/politics/2016-11/02/c_1119838057.htm.

138. Jessica Chen Weiss, *Powerful Patriots: Nationalist Protest in China's Foreign Relations* (New York: Oxford University Press, 2014), 189–218.

139. Wang Heyan, "Closer Look: How a Protest in Beijing Stuck to the Script," *Caixin*, September 17, 2012, https://www.caixinglobal.com/2012-09-17/closer-look-how-a-protest-in-beijing-stuck-to-the-script-101015204.html.

140. Mimie Ouyang, "What Make China Accomplish A 'Glorious Decade'," *People's Daily Online*, July 4, 2012, http://en.people.cn/90883/7865436.html.

141. Deng Yuwen, "The Political Legacy of Hu-Wen," *Caijing*, September 2, 2012; "Profile of Deng Yuwen," *The China Story*, https://www.thechinastory.org/yearbooks/yearbook-2013/chapter-7-fitting-words/deng-yuwen/.

142. Sangkuk Lee, "An Institutional Analysis of Xi Jinping's Centralization of Power," *Journal of Contemporary China* 26, no. 105 (2017): 325–336.

143. "China 2030: Building a Modern, Harmonious, and Creative Society," World Bank, February 27, 2012, https://www.worldbank.org/en/news/feature/2012/02/27/china-2030-executive-summary.

144. Zheng Yongnian, "Strong Leadership Necessary to Avoid 'Middle Income' Trap," China.org.cn, December 12, 2012, http://www.china.org.cn/opinion/2012-12/12/content_27381597.htm.

145. "Report of Hu Jintao to the 18th CPC National Congress," China.org.cn, November 8, 2012, http://www.china.org.cn/china/18th_cpc_congress/2012-11/16/content_27137 540.htm.

146. David Cohen and Peter Martin, "A Mandate, Not a Putsch: The Secret of Xi's Success," Jamestown Foundation China Brief, February 4, 2015, https://jamestown.org/program/a-mandate-not-a-putsch-the-secret-of-xis-success/.

147. Chris Buckley, "Exclusive: China President-in-Waiting Signals Quicker Reform—Sources," Reuters, September 7, 2012, https://www.reuters.com/article/us-china-politics-xi/exclusive-china-president-in-waiting-signals-quicker-reform-sources-idUSBRE8860BI20120907.

Chapter 5

1. Rush Doshi, "Hu's to Blame for China's Foreign Assertiveness," Brookings Institution, January 22, 2019, https://www.brookings.edu/articles/hus-to-blame-for-chinas-foreign-assertiveness/; Dan Blumenthal, "China's Steps Backward Began under Hu Jintao," *Foreign Policy*, June 4, 2020, https://foreignpolicy.com/2020/06/04/china-xi-jingping-hu-jintao-aggression-ideology/.
2. Yuli Yang, "China Says U.S. Ship Violated International Law," CNN, March 10, 2009, http://edition.cnn.com/2009/WORLD/asiapcf/03/10/us.navy.china/index.html.
3. "Sino-US Sea Standoff Appears to Have Ended," *China Daily*, March 20, 2009, http://english.sina.com/china/2009/0319/227259.html.
4. Michael Green, Kathleen Hicks, Zack Cooper, John Schaus, and Jake Douglas, "Counter-Coercion Series: Harassment of the USNS *Impeccable*," Asia Maritime Transparency Initiative, Center for Strategic and International Studies, May 9, 2017, https://amti.csis.org/counter-co-harassment-usns-impeccable/.
5. "PRC 'Opposes' USNS *Victorious* Presence in China's EEZ," "Public Library of US Diplomacy," WikiLeaks, May 6, 2009, Beijing 001211, http://wikileaks.org/plusd/cab les/09BEIJING1211_a.html.
6. Susan L. Shirk, *China: Fragile Superpower* (New York: Oxford University Press, 2007).
7. Zheng Bijian, "A New Path for China's Peaceful Rise and the Future of Asia," November 3, 2003, http://history.boaoforum.org/English/E2003nh/dhwj/t20031103_184101.btk. The Chinese language version is available at https://web.archive.org/web/20040622001406/http://www.crf.org.cn/peacefulrise/zhengbijian.htm. The fact that the notion of a peaceful rise faced elite criticism and was revised to "peaceful development" illustrates the fractiousness of foreign policymaking under Hu. See Robert L. Suettinger, "The Rise and Descent of 'Peaceful Rise,'" *China Leadership Monitor*, 2004, no. 12, https://www.hoover.org/sites/default/files/uploads/documents/clm12_rs.pdf.
8. Wang Cungang, "Contemporary China's Diplomatic Policy: Who Is Making It? Who Influences It?," Waijiao Pinglun, March 5, 2012, 1–18.
9. Jing Sun, "Growing Diplomacy, Retreating Diplomate: How the Chinese Foreign Ministry Has Been Marginalized in Foreign Policymaking," *Journal of Contemporary China* 26, no. 5 (2017): 424.
10. Xue Li and Xu Yanzhuo, "The Problems with China's Foreign Policy Bureaucracy," *The Diplomat*, April 17, 2015, https://thediplomat.com/2015/04/the-problems-with-chi nas-foreign-policy-bureaucracy/.
11. Linda Jakobson and Dean Knox, "New Foreign Policy Actors in China" (SIPRI Policy Paper 26, Stockholm International Peace Research Institute, September 2010), https://lindajakobson.com/wp-content/uploads/2014/12/Jakobson-Knox-New-Foreign-Policy-Actors-in-China-SIPRIPP26.pdf.
12. John Pomfret, "In China, Officials in Tug of War to Shape Foreign Policy," *Washington Post*, September 24, 2010, https://www.washingtonpost.com/wp-dyn/content/article/2010/09/23/AR2010092306843.html.
13. Jack Snyder, *Myths of Empire: Domestic Politics and International Ambition* (Ithaca, NY: Cornell University Press, 1991).
14. Rush Doshi, *The Long Game: China's Grand Strategy to Displace American Order* (New York: Oxford University Press, 2021) compares the language of Hu Jintao's speeches at the 2006 Foreign Affairs Work Forum and the 2009 ambassadorial conference to highlight this increase in assertiveness.
15. A book from the Central Party School Press characterizes China's foreign policy during the pre-2008 period as one of both "self-constraint" (*ziwo yueshu*) and "accepting

constraint" (*jieshou yueshu*) from others in multilateral bodies aimed at reassuring neighbors. *Under the Banner of Peace, Development and Cooperation: A Longtitudinal Discussion on China's Foreign Strategy in the Period of Strategic Opportunity* 252, quoted in Suisheng Zhao, "China and East Asian Regional Cooperation: Institution-Building Efforts, Strategic Calculations, and Preference for Informal Approach," in *China and East Asian Strategic Dynamics: The Shaping of a New Regional Order*, ed. Mingjiang Li and Dongmin Lee (Lanham, MD: Rowman & Littlefield, 2011), 152.

16. Dai Bingguo, "Persisting with Taking the Path of Peaceful Development," Ministry of Foreign Affairs, December 6, 2010, http://www.gov.cn/ldhd/2010-12/06/content_1760 381.htm, and "The White Paper of China's Peaceful Development," The State Council Information Office of the People's Republic of China, September 6, 2011, http://www.scio.gov.cn/tt/Document/1011394/1011394.htm.

17. Andrew Chubb, "PRC Assertiveness in the South China Sea: Measuring Continuity and Change, 1970–2015," *International Security* 45, no. 3 (Winter 2020/2021): 103, https://muse.jhu.edu/article/781045/pdf/.

18. Zhang Yunling and Tang Shiping, "China's Regional Strategy," in *Power Shift: China and Asia's New Dynamics* (Berkeley: University of California Press, 2005), 50, cited in Doshi, *The Long Game*, 110.

19. Jiang Zemin, "Cultivate Good-Neighborly and Friendly Relations with Surrounding Countries," August 6, 2001, *Selective Works of Jiang Zemin*, 3, http://www.reformdata.org/2001/0806/5891.shtml.

20. John W. Garver, "China's Push through the South China Sea: The Interaction of Bureaucratic and National Interests," *China Quarterly* 132 (1992): 1021.

21. Doshi, *The Long Game*, 96.

22. Chubb, "PRC Assertiveness in the South China Sea," 110.

23. Chubb, "PRC Assertiveness in the South China Sea," 114.

24. Andrew Chubb, *Chinse Popular Nationalism and PRC Policy in the South China Sea* (Crawley: The University of Western Australia, 2016), 181–248.

25. Alastair Iain Johnston, "Is Chinese Nationalism Rising? Evidence from Beijing," *International Security* 41, no. 3 (Winter 2016/7): 9.

26. Andrew S. Erickson and Conor M. Kennedy, "China's Maritime Militia Report No. 1: China's Third Sea Force, The People's Armed Forces Maritime Militia: Tethered to the PLA," China Maritime Studies Institute, U.S. Naval War College, March 2017, 25, 27, https://www.cna.org/cna_files/pdf/chinas-maritime-militia.pdf.

27. Jakobson and Knox, "New Foreign Policy Actors in China," 19, 22.

28. The first-hand account from the National Security Council (NSC) official accompanying Secretary Clinton is from Jeffrey A. Bader, *Obama and China's Rise: An Insider's Account of America's Asia Strategy* (Washington, DC: Brookings Institution Press, 2012), 105.

29. For an excellent study of the deterrence signaling China used in the lead-up to its short wars against India (1962) and Vietnam (1979), see Paul Godwin and Alice Miller, *China's Forbearance Has Limits: Chinese Threat and Retaliation Signaling and Its Implications for a Sino-American Military Confrontation* (Washington, DC: National Defense University Press, 2013), https://ndupress.ndu.edu/Media/News/Article/717729/chinas-forbearance-has-limits-chinese-threat-and-retaliation-signaling-and-its/.

30. John Pomfret, "Obama's Meeting With the Dalai Lama Is Delayed," *Washington Post*, October 5, 2009, https://www.washingtonpost.com/wp-dyn/content/article/2009/10/04/AR2009100403262.html.

31. Bader, *Obama and China's Rise*, 55.

32. Josh Rogin, "The End of the Concept of 'Strategic Reassurance'?," *Foreign Policy*, November 6, 2009, https://foreignpolicy.com/2009/11/06/the-end-of-the-concept-of-strategic-reassurance/.

33. Michael D. Swaine, "China's Assertive Behavior—Part One: On 'Core Interests,'" *China Leadership Monitor*, no. 34, November 15, 2010, https://carnegieendowment.org/2010/11/15/china-s-assertive-behavior-part-one-on-core-interests-pub-41937.

34. Li Jing and Wu Qingcai, "The First Round of China-US Economic Dialogue: All Major Issues, Except for Going to the Moon, Have Been Discussed," China News Agency, July 28, 2009, http://www.chinanews.com/gn/news/2009/07-29/1794984.shtml.

35. Dai, "Persisting with Taking the Path of Peaceful Development"; "The White Paper of China's Peaceful Development."

36. Swaine, "China's Assertive Behavior—Part One: On 'Core Interests'"; Alastair Iain Johnston, "How New and Assertive Is China's New Assertiveness?," *International Security* 34, no. 4 (Spring 2013): 7–48.

37. Bader, *Obama and China's Rise*, 105–106.

38. "China-Philippines Cooperation Depends on Proper Settlement of Maritime Disputes," Xinhua, August 31, 2011, https://www.manilatimes.net/2011/09/01/opinion/analysis/china-philippines-cooperation-depends-on-proper-settlement-of-maritime-disputes/720108, quoted in David Pilling, "China's Spreading 'Core Interests',," *The Financial Times*, September 13, 2011, https://www.ft.com/content/7aadbf36-bdd2-373e-98f6-3d9e46547e7c.

39. "China's 'Core Interests' Should Not Be Expanded," *International Herald Leader*, January 11, 2011, https://www.guancha.cn/america/2011_01_11_53047.shtml?web.

40. "Foreign Ministry Spokesperson Hua Chunying's Regular Press Conference on April 26, 2013, Ministry of Foreign Affairs of the People's Republic of China, April 26, 2013, https://www.fmprc.gov.cn/ce/cejm/chn/wjbfyrth/t1035595.htm, quoted in "China's 'Core Interests' and the East China Sea" (staff background report, US-China Economic and Security Review Commission, May 10, 2013),https://www.uscc.gov/sites/default/files/Research/China%27s%20Core%20Interests%20and%20the%20East%20China%20Sea.pdf.

41. Edward Wong, "Security Law Suggests a Broadening of China's 'Core Interests,'" "Memo from China," *New York Times*, July 2, 2015, https://www.nytimes.com/2015/07/03/world/asia/security-law-suggests-a-broadening-of-chinas-core-interests.html.

42. Wong, "Security Law Suggests a Broadening"; National Security Law, July 1, 2015, China Law Translate, https://www.chinalawtranslate.com/en/2015nsl/.

43. Stephan Dziedzic, "Chinese Official Declares Beijing Has Targeted Australian Goods as Economic Punishment," ABC News, July 6, 2021, https://www.abc.net.au/news/2021-07-07/australia-china-trade-tensions-official-economic-punishment/100273964.

44. Jessica Chen Weiss and Allan Dafoe, "Authoritarian Audiences, Rhetoric, and Propaganda in International Crises: Evidence from China," *International Studies Quarterly* 63, no. 4 (2019): 966.

45. "President Bush and Premier Wen Jiabao Remarks to the Press," December 9, 2003, 11:05 a.m., The White House, https://georgewbush-whitehouse.archives.gov/news/releases/2003/12/20031209-2.html.

46. Sheryl Gay Stolberg, "Bush to Attend Opening Ceremonies of the Beijing Olympics," *New York Times*, July 4, 2008, https://www.nytimes.com/2008/07/04/world/americas/04iht-prexy.1.14235707.html.

47. "Dalai Lama and Bush Meet 'Like Old Friends,'" "World," CNN.com, May 23, 2001, http://edition.cnn.com/2001/WORLD/asiapcf/east/05/23/dalai.bush.02/index.html.

48. Bader, *Obama and China's Rise*, 59.

49. Bader, 59.

50. Bader, 66.

51. Bader, 166.

52. Bader, 121.

53. "Chinese President Urges Improved Social Management for Greater Harmony, Stability," Xinhua, February 19, 2011, http://news.xinhuanet.com/english2010/china/2011-02/19/c_13739874.htm.

54. Perry Link, "The Secret Politburo Meeting behind China's New Democracy Crackdown," *New York Review*, February 20, 2011, https://www.nybooks.com/daily/2011/02/20/secret-politburo-meeting-behind-chinas-crackdown/.

55. This section draws in part from Shirk, *China: Fragile Superpower*, 69–76.

56. Hu Jintao, "Renqing Xinshiji Xinjieduan Wojun Lishi Shiming" [See clearly our armed forces' historic missions in the new period of the new century], December 24, 2004, available on the official National Defense Education website of Jiangxi province, http://gfjy.jiangxi.gov.cn/yil.asp?id=11349.htm, cited in Daniel M. Hartnett, "Testimony before the US-China Economic and Security Review Commission," March 4, 2009, https://www.uscc.gov/sites/default/files/3.4.09Hartnett.pdf.

57. "China's National Defense in 2008," January 20, 2009, State Council Information Office, http://www.gov.cn/zwgk/2009-01/20/content_1210224.htm.

58. Office of the Secretary of Defense, "Military and Security Developments Involving the People's Republic of China 2011," Annual Report to Congress, US Department of Defense, 41, https://china.usc.edu/sites/default/files/article/attachments/2011_CMPR_Final.pdf.

59. Ministry of Finance, "Report on the 2012 Implementation of Central and Local Budgets and the 2013 Central and Local Budgets Draft," National Public Finance Expenditure Budget, 2013, Appendix 11.

60. "Spotlight: China's Defense Budget Increase 'Eclipsed' by U.S.," Xinhua, March 5, 2017, http://news.xinhuanet.com/english/2017-03/05/c_136104599.htm.

61. "What Does China Really Spend on ITS Military?," CSIS, China Power, https://chinapower.csis.org/military-spending/; Adam Taylor and Laris Karklis, "This Remarkable Chart Shows How the U.S. Defense Spending Dwarfs the Rest of the World," *Washington Post*, February 9, 2016, https://www.washingtonpost.com/news/worldviews/wp/2016/02/09/this-remarkable-chart-shows-how-u-s-defense-spending-dwarfs-the-rest-of-the-world/?utm_term=.71ddof062doa.

62. Mark Stokes, "China's Evolving Conventional Strategic Strike Capability," Project 2049 Institute, September 14, 2009, http://project2049.net/documents/chinese_anti_ship_ballistic_missile_asbm.pdf.

63. Lieutenant General Wang Zhiyuan, deputy director of the Science and Technology Commission of the PLA, told the Hong Kong newspaper *Wen Wei Po* (March 10, 2006, Foreign Broadcast Information Service (FBIS), CPP20060310508004), "As China is such a large country with such a long coastline and we want to protect our maritime interests, aircraft carriers are an absolute necessity." The story also reports that China has learned to make catapults for carrier-based aircraft, so it will be able to build horizontal deck carriers like the American ones.

64. Office of the Secretary of Defense, "Military and Security Developments Involving the People's Republic of China, 2021," Annual Report to Congress, US Department of Defense, 6, https://media.defense.gov/2021/Nov/03/2002885874/-1/-1/0/2021-CMPR-FINAL.PDF.

65. The 1991 Gulf War was the first impetus spurring China's military modernization, but the Taiwan issue is the strategic focus.

66. Andrew Scobell, "Show of Force: Chinese Soldiers, Statesmen, and the 1995–96 Taiwan Strait Crisis," *Political Science Quarterly* 115, no. 2 (Summer 2000): 227–246.

67. *China Daily*, May 9, 2006.

68. Jan van Tol, Mark Gunzinger, Andrew F. Krepinevich, and Jim Thomas, "AirSea Battle: A Point-of-Departure Operational Concept," Center for Strategic and

Budgetary Assessments, May 18, 2010, http://www.csbaonline.org/publications/2010/05/airsea-battle-concept/.

69. Van Tol et al., "AirSea Battle."

70. Chairman, Joint Chiefs of Staff, "Joint Operational Access Concept," January 17, 2012, https://web.archive.org/web/20120412201038/https://www.defense.gov/pubs/pdfs/JOAC_Jan%202012_Signed.pdf. Also see General Norton A. Schwartz and Admiral Jonathan W. Greenert, "Air-Sea Battle, Promoting Stability in an Era of Uncertainty," *American Interest*, February 20, 2012, http://www.the-american-interest.com/article.cfm?piece=1212; and "New US Military Concept Marks Pivot to Sea and Air," *Strategic Comments*, International Institute of Strategic Studies, May 2012, https://www.tandfonline.com/doi/pdf/10.1080/13567888.2012.698500?needAccess=true .

71. Thomas Pickering, Under Secretary of State, "Oral Presentation to the Chinese Government Regarding the Accidental Bombing of the P.R.C. Embassy in Belgrade, June 17, 1999," US Department of State Archive, https://1997-2001.state.gov/policy_remarks/1999/990617_pickering_emb.html.

72. Tai Ming Cheung, Thomas Mahnken, Deborah Seligsohn, Kevin Pollpeter, Eric Anderson, and Fan Yang, *Planning for Innovation: Understanding China's Plans for Technological, Energy, Industrial and Defense Development* (Report for the U.S.-China Economic and Security Review Commission, University of California Institute on Global Conflict and Cooperation, September 2016), 25–27.

73. James Mulvanon, "Chairman Hu and the PLA's 'New Historic Missions,'" *China Leadership Monitor*, no. 27, 2009.

74. "The State Military System," in *Zhonghua Gongheguo Zhengzhi Zhidu* [Political system of the People's Republic of China], ed. Pu Xingzu (Shanghai: Shanghai People's Publishing House, 2005); Andrew Scobell, "China's Evolving Civil-Military Relations," *Armed Forces & Society* 31, no. 2 (Winter 2005): 227–244, https://journals.sagepub.com/doi/pdf/10.1177/0095327X0503100204.

75. Of the 2,987 deputies in the 2013 National People's Congress, 268 were in the military. "2,987 Deputies Elected to New Nat'l Legislature," Xinhua, February 25, 2013, http://news.xinhuanet.com/english/china/2013-02/25/c_132191185.htm.

76. After Hu Jintao and Xi Jinping were selected as the heirs apparent and appointed vice presidents, each was also appointed a vice chairman of the Central Ministry Commission. The commission's current vice president, Li Yuanchao, is not a member of the Politburo Standing Committee and is unlikely to join the Military Commission.

77. Liu Huanmin, "The Military Newspaper Wrote that Leading Cadres Should Set an Example of Stressing Politics, Being Mindful of the Overall Situation and Abidinng By Discipline," *PLA Daily*, May 15, 2012, https://web.archive.org/web/20120518232447/http://politics.people.com.cn/GB/17889051.html.

78. Zhongdu Tongxun She (Hong Kong), October 23, 2005, FBIS, CPP20051023057019. The idea, first proposed by the US in 2003, was finally accepted by China in 2008. But the military hotline actually is the same telephone connection as the one between the two presidents, which also runs through the military connection.

79. James Mulvenon, "Rogue Warriors? A Puzzled Look at the Chinese ASAT Test," *China Leadership Monitor*, no. 20, Winter 2007.

80. The most detailed analysis of this case is provided by the WikiLeaks cable from the US Embassy Beijing. See "2007 Kitty Hawk Port Call Refusal Sheds Light on PRC Decision Making Process," Public Library of US Diplomacy, March 26, 2008, http://wikileaks.org/cable/2008/03/08BEIJING1145.html; also see Tim Johnson, "U.S. Ships, Barred From Hong Kong, Now Sail Under China's Nose," *McClatchy Newspapers*, December 1, 2007. https://web.archive.org/web/20170924045728/https://www.mcclatchydc.com/latest-news/article24472828.html.

81. Based on interviews with three Chinese experts who advise the government and the military.
82. Tai Ming Cheung, "Engineering Human Souls: The Development of Chinese Military Journalism and the Emerging Defense Media Market," in *Changing Media, Changing China*, ed. Susan L. Shirk (New York: Oxford University Press, 2011), 136.
83. Ananth Krishnan, "China Must Recover Territory 'Looted' By Neighbours, Said PLA General," *The Hindu*, December 21, 2010, https://web.archive.org/web/20101223105 534/http://www.hindu.com/2010/12/21/stories/2010122159491000.htm.
84. Chris Buckley, "China Top Military Paper Warns U.S. Aims to Contain Rise", January 9, 2012, *Reuters*, https://www.reuters.com/article/china-usa-defence/china-top-military-paper-warns-u-s-aims-to-contain-rise-idUKL3E8CA0EM20120110.
85. "Luo Yan on South China Sea: Do Not Push China beyond the Point of Tolerance," Xinhua News Agency, June 15, 2011, cited in International Crisis Group, "Stirring Up the South China Sea" (Asia Report No. 223, International Crisis Group, April 23, 2012).
86. Andrew Chubb, "Who Does Major General Luo Yuan Speak For?," *Southseaconversations* (blog), April 27, 2012, https://southseaconversations.wordpr ess.com/2012/04/27/who-does-major-general-luo-yuan-speak-for/.
87. Nectar Gan, "U.S. Can't Uproot China in South China Sea, Retired PLA General Says," *South China Morning Post*, April 7, 2016, http://www.scmp.com/news/china/ diplomacy-defence/article/1934183/us-cant-uproot-china-south-china-sea-retired-pla.
88. Chris Buckley, "China PLA Officers Urge Economic Punch Against U.S.," *Reuters*, February 9, 2010, https://www.reuters.com/article/us-china-usa-pla/china-pla-offic ers-urge-economic-punch-against-u-s-idUSTRE6183KG20100209.
89. Chubb, "Who Does Major General Luo Yuan Speak For?"
90. Andrew Chubb, "Propaganda, Not Policy: Explaining the PLA's 'Hawkish Faction' (Part One)," Jamestown Foundation China Brief 13, no. 15, July 25, 2013, https:// jamestown.org/program/propaganda-not-policy-explaining-the-plas-hawkish-faction-part-one/.
91. Liao Yi, "Taiwan Affairs Office of the State Council Called "Taiwan Independence" A War and "Referendum to Make A Constitution" Extremely Dangerous," Xinhua, November 18, 2003, https://news.sina.com.cn/c/2003-11-18/21502162041.shtml, quoted in Shirk, *China: Fragile Superpower*, 204.
92. Shirk, *China: Fragile Superpower*, 208–209.
93. The PRC had earlier rejected the notion of a "1992 consensus" that might serve as the basis for dialogue, and before Chen Shui-bian, Taiwan had embraced it. By 2001, however, positions of the two sides had flipped. Shirk, *China: Fragile Superpower*, 302.
94. US Embassy Beijing, "Taiwan: Hu Jintao's December 31 Speech Sets More 'Realistic' and 'Flexible' Policy, Contacts Say," January 16, 2009, https://wikileaks.org/plus/cab les/09BEIJING145_a.html.
95. Richard McGregor, *Asia's Reckoning: China, Japan, and the Fate of U.S. Power in the Pacific Century* (New York: Viking, 2017), 182.
96. Jessica Chen Weiss, *Powerful Patriots: Nationalist Protests in China's Foreign Relations* (New York: Oxford University Press, 2014), 131.
97. Weiss, *Powerful Patriots*, 154.
98. "Boycotting Japanese Goods Makes No Good," Xinhua, April 23, 2005, reposted on China Daily, http://www.chinadaily.com.cn/english/doc/2005-04/23/content_436 720.htm, quoted in Weiss, *Powerful Patriots*, 148.
99. James Reilly, *Strong Society, Smart State: The Rise of Public Opinion in China's Japan Policy* (New York: Columbia University Press, 2012).
100. Jakobson and Knox, "New Foreign Policy Actors in China," 39, https://www.sipri.org/ publications/2010/sipri-policy-papers/new-foreign-policy-actors-china.

101. McGregor, *Asia's Reckoning*, 219.

102. McGregor, 265.

103. Weiss and Dafoe, "Authoritarian Audiences, Rhetoric, and Propaganda," 963–973, https://academic.oup.com/isq/article-abstract/63/4/963/5559531.

104. Sam Suisheng Zhao, "Hu Jintao's Foreign Policy Legacy," E-International Relations, December 8, 2012, https://www.e-ir.info/2012/12/08/hu-jintaos-foreign-policy-legacy/ . "One of the loneliest powers in world history" is from John Lee, "Lonely Power, Staying Power: The Rise of China and the Resilience of U.S. Pre-eminence," Lowy Institute for International Policy, Strategic Snapshot 10, September 2011, 1, https://www.hudson.org/content/researchattachments/attachment/938/the_rise_of_china_and_the_resilience_of_us_preeminence.pdf .

Chapter 6

1. Murray Scot Tanner, "Unrest in China and the Chinese State's Institutional Responses," Testimony before the U.S.-China Economic and Security Review Commission, February 25, 2011, https://www.uscc.gov/sites/default/files/2.25.11Tanner.pdf. According to the police, the number of "mass incidents" (defined as more than one hundred people) surged from 8,700 in 1993 to approximately 10,000 in 1994 and then to 32,000 in 1999, 58,000 in 2003, and 74,000 in 2004. See Liu Neng, "Mass Incidents in Contemporary China: Change of Image and Reconstruction of Classification," *Sociology Research* 56, no. 2 (2011): 54, http://www.shehui.pku.edu.cn/upload/editor/file/20180309/20180309160207_4149.pdf.

   Citing the Regulations on Petitioning Work, sociologist Yu Jianrong argues that the definition of mass incidents should include any incidents that involve five people or more. See Yu Jianrong, "Main Types and Basic Characteristics of Mass Incidents in China," *Journal of China University of Political Science and Law*, no. 6 (November 10, 2009), 115, http://www.personpsy.org/uploadfiles/file/%E6%B3%84%E6%84%A4%E4%BA%8B%E4%BB%B6/%E5%BD%93%E5%89%8D%E6%88%91%E5%9B%BD%E7%BE%A4%E4%BD%93%E6%80%A7%E4%BA%8B%E4%BB%B6%E7%9A%84%E4%B8%BB%E8%A6%81%E7%B1%BB%E5%9E%8B%E5%8F%8A%E5%85%B6%E5%9F%BA%E6%9C%AC%E7%89%B9%E5%BE%81_%E4%BA%8E%E5%BB%BA%E5%B5%98.pdf, and "Party Central and State Council Issue Regulations on Petitioning Work," April 7, 2022, *Xinhua*, http://www.gov.cn/zhengce/2022-04/07/content_5683923.htm. This is the latest version of the Regulations.

2. Over this period of time, public interest in *weiwen* as a search term has not declined—see Baidu search trends for *weiwen* here: http://index.baidu.com/main/word.php?word=%CE%AC%CE%C8.

3. Liang Jing, "Snow Sweeps Away the Confidence of Those in Power in China," *China Digital Times*, February 18, 2008, translated by David Kelly, https://chinadigitaltimes.net/2008/02/snow-sweeps-away-the-confidence-of-those-in-power-in-china/.

4. Titus C. Chen, "China's Reaction to the Color Revolutions: Adaptive Authoritarianism in Full Swing," *Asian Perspective* 34, no. 2 (2010): 32.

5. Joseph Kahn, "China's Leader, Ex-Rival at Side, Solidifies Power," *New York Times*, September 25, 2005, https://www.nytimes.com/2005/09/25/world/asia/chinas-leader-exrival-at-side-solidifies-power.html.

6. Rowan Callick, "DVDs Tell Faithful How to Escape Russia's Fate," *The Australian*, December 11, 2006, http://chinesepolitics.blogspot.com/2006/12/; and Li Shenming,

Think of Danger in Times of Safety - Historical Lessons of the Demise of the Communist Party of Soviet Union (Beijing: Social Sciences Academic Press, 2011).

7. Susan L. Shirk, *China: Fragile Superpower* (New York: Oxford University Press, 2008), 84.
8. *Democracy and Law*, issue 16 (August 2005). The term "mass incidents" was publicly introduced at a news conference held by the CCP Organization Department on July 7, 2005. "Mass Incidents Challenge China," *Globe*, August 1, 2005.
9. "Former China Security Head Spied on Leaders, Probe Said to Find," Bloomberg News, April 19, 2015, https://www.bloomberg.com/news/articles/2015-04-19/former-china-security-head-spied-on-leaders-probe-said-to-find?sref=I2I6qZII.
10. Yuhua Wang, "Empowering the Police: How the Chinese Party Manages Its Coercive Leaders," *China Quarterly* 219 (September 2014): 625–648.
11. Wang, "Empowering the Police," 643.
12. Yuhua Wang and Carl Minzner, "The Rise of the Chinese Security State," *China Quarterly* 222 (June 2015): 352, https://www.cambridge.org/core/journals/china-quarterly/article/abs/rise-of-the-chinese-security-state/3C3D97C74C4D3AE07058A7FE6E61DACE.
13. Sun Liping, "The Third Stage in the Failure of Power," March 11, 2013, translated in David Bandurski, "Hu's Decade of Failed Power," China Media Project, March 27, 2013, https://web.archive.org/web/20130331004400/http://cmp.hku.hk/2013/03/27/32147/.
14. "Interview with Wang Anshun, Party Secretary of Beijing Political and Legal Committee: Peaceful Olympics Campaign in Combat," Xinhua, March 17, 2008, http://news.sohu.com/20080317/n255747170.shtml.
15. "Directive of State Administration for Industry and Commerce on Meticulously Handling the Petition Work during the Olympics," State Administration for Industry and Commerce, July 8, 2008, http://www.lsbar.com/law/44082.
16. "Beijing Olympics: Pride and Suspicion," *Deseret News*, August 5, 2008, https://www.deseret.com/2008/8/5/20267631/beijing-olympics-pride-and-suspicion.
17. "Olympic Disaster for Free Expression in China," Reporters without Borders, August 22, 2008, https://web.archive.org/web/20210206064902/https://rsf.org/en/news/olympic-disaster-free-expression-china.
18. "Summarize Successful Experience of Peaceful Olympics and Continuously Improve the Level of Peaceful Construction," Legal Daily, September 28, 2008, http://news.sina.com.cn/o/2008-09-28/081214512207s.shtml.
19. "Ministry of Public Security: The Number of Female Policemen in China Exceeds 280,000, Accounting for 14.3% of the Total Number of Policemen," Xinhua, March 8, 2021, https://news.cctv.com/2021/03/08/ARTIsZovpJvs2e88zfABIdcy210308.shtml.
20. The Political-Legal Commission also housed the Central Committee for Comprehensive Management of Public Security (*zong zhi wei*) and the Stability Maintenance Leading Small Group (*weiwen lingdao xiaozu*) until they were dissolved in 2018. Another special office focused entirely on suppressing religious cults, the Falun Gong, in particular; it also was dissolved in 2018. "Plan for Deepening the Reform on Party and State Institutions," Xinhua, March 21, 2018, http://www.gov.cn/zhengce/2018-03/21/content_5276191.htm#allContent.
21. The earliest stability maintenance leading group was established in Yunnan province in 2003 during the SARS epidemic, and the newest ones are barely a couple of years old. Hu Ben, "The Stability Maintenance Office Entered the Neighborhoods and Villages to Mediate Disputes Face-to-Face," *Southern Weekend*, August 18, 2010, http://www.infzm.com/content/49108.
22. Huirong Chen and Sheena Chesnut Greitens, "Information Capacity and Social Order: The Local Politics of Information Integration in China," *Governance*, April 1, 2021, https://onlinelibrary.wiley.com/doi/abs/10.1111/gove.12592.

23. Ching Kwan Lee and Yonghong Zhang, "The Power of Instability: Unraveling the Microfoundations of Bargained Authoritarianism in China," *American Journal of Sociology* 118, no. 6 (May 2013): 1483.

24. "Rethinking Weiwen," *Caijing*, June 7, 2011, https://web.archive.org/web/20140118121640/http://www.caijing.com.cn/2011-06-07/110738832_1.html.

25. Minxin Pei, "Grid Management: China's Latest Institutional Tool of Social Control," *China Leadership Monitor*, March 1, 2021, no. 67, https://www.prcleader.org/pei-grid-management.

26. Wu Qiang, "Urban Grid Management and Police State in China: A Brief Overview," China Change, August 8, 2013, http://chinachange.org/2013/08/08/the-urban-grid-management-and-police-state-in-china-a-brief-overview/. According to Wu, the grid management system was modeled on that of London. Its first local trial took place in Dongcheng district, Beijing, in 2004; the system was extended to fifty-one other cities over the next several years.

27. Wu Qiang, "Urban Grid Management."

28. Hu, "The Stability Maintenance Office Entered the Neighborhoods and Villages to Mediate Disputes Face-to-Face."

29. Charles Hutzler, "Watching Dissidents Is a Booming Business in China," Associated Press, May 27, 2012.

30. Deng Qifan, "Beijing Police Will Crack Down on Security Companies Illegally Intercepting Petitioners," Xinhua, December 3, 2011, https://www.chinanews.com.cn/fz/2011/12-03/3505465.shtml.

31. Zhang Guocheng, "Analysis on the Development Status and Market Size of China's Security Service Industry in 2022," Qianzhan Industry Research Institute, March 14, 2022, https://www.qianzhan.com/analyst/detail/220/220314-15bf0e9e.html.

32. "Several Tibetan Officials Dismissed for Unfullfilling Duties of Maintaining Stability," *Tibet Daily*, February 8, 2012, https://china.caixin.com/2012-02-09/100354845.html.

33. Lee and Zhang, "Power of Instability," 1486.

34. "ChinaAid: Chen Guangcheng's Newly Released 15 Minutes Video with English Caption," ChinaAid, April 28, 2012, http://www.chinaaid.org/2012/04/chinaaid-chen-guangchengs-newly.html.

35. Social Development Research Group, Tsinghua University Department of Sociology, "New Thinking on Stability Maintenance: Long-Term Social Stability via Institutionalized Expression of Interests," *Southern Weekend*, April 14, 2010, translated by David Kelly.

36. Ben Blanchard, "China Defense Budget to Stir Regional Disquiet," Reuters, March 3, 2011, https://www.reuters.com/article/us-china-defence/china-defense-budget-to-stir-regional-disquiet-idUSTRE7230ZN20110304.

37. Calculated using data from Ministry of Finance's annual budget and expenditure report at the annual plenary sessions of the National People's Congress.

38. Sun Liping et al., "Institutionalizing Expression of Interests to Achieve Long-Term Stability," *The Leaders*, no. 33, April 2010.

39. Yu Jianrong, "Holding Tight and Not Letting Go: The Mechanisms of 'Rigid Stability,'" *Global Asia* 5, no. 2 (Summer 2010): 28–39.

40. Hu Yinan and Lei Xiaoxun, "Urumqi Riot Handled 'Decisively, Properly,'" *China Daily*, July 18, 2009. Xinjiang University estimated the death toll to be four hundred, and the World Uyghur Congress estimated it to be eight hundred. "Repression in China: Roots and Repercussions of The Urumqi Unrest" (report by the Unrepresented Nations and Peoples Organization, The Hague, November 2009, https://unpo.org/images/reports/repression_in_china_roots_and_repercussions_of_the_urumqi_unrest_unpo_november_2009.pdf).

41. According to the 2020 census. "Main Data of Xinjiang Uygur Autonomous Region from the Seventh National Population Census," June 16, 2021, Statistics Bureau of Xinjiang uygur Autonomous Region, https://www.fmprc.gov.cn/ce/cgtrt/eng/news/t1884310.htm.

42. Chris Buckley, "China's Xinjiang Under Heavy Security as Stability Urged," Reuters, July 12, 2009, https://www.reuters.com/article/idUSPEK104744.

43. Lucy Hornby, "Needle Attacks and Rumours Spread in China's Xinjiang," Reuters, September 10, 2009, https://www.reuters.com/article/idUSSP440905.

44. For example, see Wu Yuanchun, "Zambia's Chinese-owned Coal Mine Shooting Incident, the President Warns Not to Always Blame the Chinese," *Global Times*, October 22, 2010, http://world.huanqiu.com/roll/2010-10/1190899.html; Huang Ye, "Dispute over Kelan Coal Mine in Zambia," *International Financial News*, August 7, 2012, https://web.archive.org/web/20120812102955/http://paper.people.com.cn/gjjrb/html/2012-08/07/content_1093191.htm?div=-1;; Han Na, "Ghanaian Military Police Kill 16-year-old Chinese Gold Prospector, Arrest More Than 100 Chinese," *Beijing Morning Post*, October 15, 2012, http://news.qq.com/a/20121015/000692.htm.

45. Wu Qimin and Sun Chengbin, "Hu Jintao's Inspection at People's Daily: I am Very Happy to Communicate with Netizens," Xinhua, June 21, 2008, http://www.chinanews.com.cn/gn/news/2008/06-21/1288574.shtml.

46. Qian Gang and David Bandurski, "China's Emerging Public Sphere: The Impact of Media Commercialization, Professionalism, and the Internet in an Era of Transition," in Susan L. Shirk, *Changing Media, Changing China* (New York: Oxford University Press, 2011), 56.

47. Shirk, *Changing Media, Changing China*, 18.

48. Ya-Wen Lei, *The Contentious Public Sphere: Law, Media and Authoritarian Rule in China* (Princeton, NJ: Princeton University Press, 2018).

49. According to the 2012 Government Microblog Evaluation Report, cited in Josh Rudolph, "Number of Government Weibo Accounts Soars," China Digital Times, March 28, 2013, http://chinadigitaltimes.net/2013/03/number-of-government-weibo-accounts-soars/.

50. To say that Sina Weibo's server is based in Beijing is a technical metaphor. It means that the servers are under the direct scrutiny of the Beijing Internet Office or that the user database can be accessed only by Beijing authorities rather than other local authorities. Tencent has put thousands of servers in every province to accelerate communication speed, but only the Shenzhen and Beijing Internet offices have the legal power to intervene in their content.

51. Tang Yiyuan, "Secretary of Beijing Municipal Party Committee: Firmly Grasp the Initiative of Public Opinion Online," *Beijing Youth Daily*, November 6, 2013, https://china.caixin.com/2013-11-06/100599856.html.

52. "Internet Public Opinion Analyst: What You Need to Do Is Not Deleting Posts," *Beijing News*, October 3, 2013, http://epaper.bjnews.com.cn/html/2013-10/03/content_469152.htm?div=-1.

53. Gary King, Jennifer Pan, and Margaret E. Roberts, "How Censorship in China Allows Government Criticism but Silences Collective Expression," *American Political Science Review* 107, no. 2 (May): 1–18.

54. Margaret E. Roberts, *Censored: Distraction and Diversion inside China's Great Firewall* (Princeton, NJ: Princeton University Press, 2018).

55. James T. Areddy, "China Releases Online Commentator Charles Xue," *Wall Street Journal*, April 17, 2014, https://www.wsj.com/articles/SB10001424052702304626304579506621788714390.

56. Wang Chen, Wang Shanshan, Ren Zhongyuan, Zhu Yishi, and Yuning, "The Business of Deleting Posts," *Caixin*, February 18, 2013, https://magazine.caixin.com/2013-02-08/100490897.html. Corruption is also a problem among journalists because businesses want to sully rival firms with negative stories or create positive stories about themselves. See the Caixin editorial on rent-seeking in journalism, Hu Shuli, "There Is No Room for Greed in Gathering News," *Caixin*, November 6, 2013, https://magazine.caixin.com/2013-11-01/100598439.html?sourceEntityId=100739563.

57. The percentages are from 2009 (industrial output and employment) and 2010 (exports). Barry Naughton, "China's Economic Policy Today: The New State Activism," *Eurasian Geography and Economics* 52, no. 3 (2011): 314, https://www.tandfonline.com/doi/abs/10.2747/1539-7216.52.3.313.

58. James McGregor, *No Ancient Wisdom, No Followers* (Westport, CT: Prospecta Press, 2012), 11, https://jamesmcgregor-inc.com/books/no-ancient-wisdom-no-followers-the-challenges-of-chinese-authoritarian-capitalism/.

59. Barry Naughton, "Inflation, Welfare, and the Political Business Cycle," *China Leadership Monitor*, no. 35, September 21, 2011, https://www.hoover.org/research/inflation-welfare-and-political-business-cycle.

60. McGregor, *No Ancient Wisdom*, 11.

61. State Council, "Guidelines for the Medium- and Long-Term National Science and Technology and Development Program (2006–2020)," February 9, 2006, quoted in Naughton, "Inflation, Welfare," 319.

62. Naughton, "Inflation, Welfare," 325.

63. Wen Jiabao, "Report on the Work of the Government," Third Session of the 11th National People's Congress, March 5, 2010, quoted in Naughton, "Inflation, Welfare," 320.

64. Barry Naughton, *The Rise of China's Industrial Policy, 1978 to 2020* (Mexico City: Universidad National Autonoma de Mexico, 2021), 62, https://dusselpeters.com/CECHIMEX/Naughton2021_Industrial_Policy_in_China_CECHIMEX.pdf.

65. Wendy Leutert, "Firm Control: Governing the State-Owned Economy under Xi Jinping," *China Perspectives* 2018/1-2, https://journals.openedition.org/chinaperspectives/7605.

66. McGregor, *No Ancient Wisdom*, 21.

Chapter 7

1. Alice Su, "Dreams of a Red Emperor: The Relentless Rise of Xi Jinping," *Los Angeles Times*, October 22, 2020, https://www.latimes.com/world-nation/story/2020-10-22/china-xi-jinping-mao-zedong-communist-party.

2. The vice president made this remark in his commencement speech, University of Pennsylvania, May 13, 2013. Xiaoying Zhou, "VP Biden's Penn Commencement Speech Inspires Viral Rant by 'Disappointed' Chinese Student," *Tea Leaf Nation*, May 19, 2013.

3. Hui Xiaoyong, He Yuxin, Jiang Zuoping, and Wu Guangyu, "To Build a Better Homeland—Documenting the Concern of the CCP Central Committee with Xi Jinping as the Core with the Recovery, Reconstruction, and Development in the Aftermath of the Wenchuan Earthquake," Xinhua, May 11, 2018, http://www.xinhuanet.com/politics/leaders/2018-05/11/c_129870199.htm.

4. Chinese Academy of Social Sciences World Socialism Research Center, *Sulian wang dang wang guo ershi nian ji—Eluosi ren zai sushuo* [The demise of the Soviet Union and the Soviet Communist Party, twenty years on—in the words of the Russian people] (Beijing: Zhongyang Jiwei Fangzheng Chubanshe, 2012).

5. "Xi Asks Officials to Remain Loyal Xi to Party 'at Any Time, and under Any Circumstance,'" Xinhua News Agency, January 11, 2018, www.xinhuanet.com/english/ 2018-01/11/c_136888644.htm.

6. "Xi Stresses Implementation of Major Policies, Integrity of Leading Officials," Xinhua News Agency, December 27, 2017, www.xinhuanet.com/english/2017-12/27/c_136853 671.htm.

7. Li Zhanshu, "Practicing the 'Five Persistences' Faithfully and Being a Central Executive with a Strong Party Spirit," *People's Daily*, September 29, 2014, cpc.people. com.cn/n/2014/0929/c164113-25759006.html.

8. David Bandurski, "Improper Readings of 'Improper Discussion,'" *China Media Project*, November 29, 2015, https://medium.com/china-media-project/improper-readi ngs-of-improper-discussion-80a99a0foeda.

9. An Baaijie, "Officials with Spouses Overseas Won't Be Promoted," *China Daily*, January 17, 2014, http://usa.chinadaily.com.cn/china/2014-01/17/content_17240367.htm.

10. Avery Goldstein, *From Bandwagon to Balance of Power Politics: Structural Constraints and Politics in China 1949–1978* (Stanford, CA: Stanford University Press, 1991), 47–48.

11. Alexandra Stevenson and Tariq Panja, "Inter Milan, a Storied Italian Soccer Club, Is Threatened by Shifting Prospects in China," *New York Times*, March 17, 2021, https:// www.nytimes.com/2021/03/16/business/china-football-inter-milan-suning.html.

12. Kurt Campbell and Mira Rapp-Hooper, "China Is Done Biding Its Time," *Foreign Affairs*, July 15, 2020, https://www.foreignaffairs.com/articles/china/2020-07-15/china- done-biding-its-time.

13. Jessica L. P. Weeks, *Dictators at War and Peace* (Ithaca, NY: Cornell University Press, 2014), 29–30.

14. Weeks, *Dictators at War and Peace*, 31.

15. Yang Yutao and He Wei, "Dialogue with Shi Yinhong—There Are Three Major Uncertainties in the Anti-China Alliance. Japan's Strategy Towards China 'Has Its Face Ripped Off,'" Motan Guoshi, April 6, 2021, https://mp.weixin.qq.com/s/QwHmuqQ kDzWBxsxdzIuczA.

16. Joseph Nye, "Only China Can Contain China," HuffPost, March 11, 2015, https://www. huffpost.com/entry/china-contain-china_b_6845588.

17. This chapter draws on Susan L. Shirk, "The Return to Personalistic Rule," *Journal of Democracy* 29, no. 2 (April 2018): 22–36.

18. Chalmers Johnson, ed., *Change in Communist Systems* (Stanford, CA: Stanford University Press, 1970).

19. "Xi Jinping: History Must Not Be Nihilistic"[习近平：历史不可虚无], *China Daily*, November 20, 2016, https://china.chinadaily.com.cn/2016-10/20/content_27123201. htm, cited in Sergey Radchenko, "Putin and Xi Eye the Soviet Collapse," Asan Forum, March 19, 2020, http://www.theasanforum.org/putin-and-xi-eye-the-soviet-collapse/.

20. Xi Jinping's view of the ideological collapse of the Soviet Party drew on a major pro- ject initiated in 2000 by Li Shenming, the well-known Maoist who was vice president of the China Academy of Social Science. Li argued that the beginning of the end of the CPSU was de-Stalinization: "The ideology of the CPSU was messed up. Stalin became a devil and Lenin became a scoundrel. The entire history of the CPSU and the Soviet Union was nothing but sins. The October Revolution and socialism brought nothing but cataclysm, while capitalism became the ideal paradise for freedom and prosperity in people's minds. Some people wanted to retreat even further, calling for rehabilitating the Russian monarchy." Li Shenming, *Be Vigilant of Danger in Times of Peace: Historical Lessons of the Death of the Communist Party of Soviet Union* (Social Sciences Academic Press, 2011), https://1lib.us/book/3650634/e9a344?regionChanged= &redirect=197145575.

21. Sophie Beach, "Leaked Speech Shows Xi Jinping's Opposition to Reform," *China Digital Times*, January 27, 2013, https://chinadigitaltimes.net/2013/01/leaked-speech-shows-xi-jinpings-opposition-to-reform/.

22. "Xi Jinping: We Can Not Separate the History before and after the Reform and Opening-Up and Negate One with the Other," Xinhua, January 5, 2013, http://www.chinanews.com/gn/2013/01-05/4460409.shtml.

23. For the English translation of the Qiushi version of the speech, see Tanner Greer, "Xi Jinping in Translation: China's Guiding Ideology," *Palladium*, May 31, 2019, https://palladiummag.com/2019/05/31/xi-jinping-in-translation-chinas-guiding-ideology/.

24. Christina Nelson, "The Third Plenum of the 18th Chinese Communist Party Congress: A Primer," *China Business Review*, September 16, 2013, https://www.chinabusinessreview.com/the-third-plenum-of-the-18th-chinese-communist-party-congress-a-primer/.

25. Asia Society Policy Institute and Rhodium Group, "Quarterly Net Assessment: Winter 2021, Final Quarter," China Dashboard, https://chinadashboard.gist.asiasociety.org/winter-2021/page/overview.

26. This concept was based on Chinese complex systems engineering theory. Sangkuk Lee, "An Institutional Analysis of Xi Jinping's Centralization of Power," *Journal of Contemporary China* 26, no. 105 (2017): 330.

27. The phrase was first used by the Xi administration at the PSC meeting on January 7, 2016. See "Xi Jinping Presides Over the Metting of the Standing Committee of the Politburo of the CCP Central," Xinhua, January 7, 2016, http://www.xinhuanet.com//politics/2016-01/07/c_1117705534.htm.

28. Christopher K. Johnson and Scott Kennedy, "Xi's Signature Governance Innovation: The Rise of Leading Small Groups," Center for Strategic and International Studies, October 17, 2017, http://csis.org/analysis/xis-signature-governance-innovation-rise-leading-small-groups.

29. "Piloting China's Economic Ships in the New Era: From the Central Financial and Economic Leading Group to the Party Central with Comrade Xi Jinping as the Core to Steer China's Economy," Xinhua, March 31, 2018, http://www.xinhuanet.com/2018-03/31/c_1122619515.htm; Zhou Xin and Frank Tang, "Why China's New Economic Commission Cements Xi Jinping's Grasp on Levers of Power," *South China Morning Post*, April 3, 2018, https://www.scmp.com/news/china/economy/article/2140125/why-chinas-new-economic-commission-cements-xi-jinpings-grasp.

30. "Xi Focus: Senior CPC Officials Report Work to CPC Central Committee, Xi," Xinhua, February 28, 2021, http://www.xinhuanet.com/english/2021-02/28/c_139773252.htm?bsh_bid=5591239234.

31. Sangkuk Lee, "Institutional Analysis of Xi Jinping's Centralization of Power," 336. The new model of centralized rule was spelled out clearly in the 2016 *Guidelines on Political Life within the Party*. A comparison with the 1980 Deng-era version of the *Guidelines* highlights the differences: in the Xi version, the section titled "Adhere to Collective Leadership and Oppose Individual Arbitrariness" was replaced with "Adhere to the Principle of Democratic Centralism." The Xi guidelines omit sentences and phrases such as "collective leadership is one of the highest principles of party leadership," "all major issues related to . . . shall not be arbitrarily decided by individuals," "forbid un-principled praising of achievements and virtues," and "forbid distorting history and fabricating facts in the promotion of a leader's record of accomplishments." The new version also includes a new section titled "Resolutely Safeguard the Authority of the Party Central" that highlights the party central's absolute authority. See "Several Principles on Political Life in the Party under New Situation," Xinhua News Agency,

November 2, 2016, http://www.xinhuanet.com//politics/2016-11/02/c_1119838382_3.htm.

32. Tai Ming Cheung, "Xi Jinping and the Remaking of Chinese Military Politics," in "Xi Takes Charge: Implications of the 19th Party Congress for China's Future" (21st Century China Center briefing, University of California, San Diego, October 2017), http://china.ucsd.edu/_files/2017_xi-briefing-web.pdf.
33. Susan L. Shirk, *The Political Logic of Economic Reform in China* (Berkeley: University of California Press, 1993), 62.
34. "China's Leadership Warns of National Security Risks," *China Daily*, January 23, 2015, http://www.chinadaily.com.cn/china/2015-01/23/content_19391741.htm.
35. Samuel Wade, "Party First, Country Second: Xi's Parade Breaks Flag Law," *China Digital Times*, August 1, 2017, https://chinadigitaltimes.net/2017/08/party-first-country-second-xis-parade-breaks-flag-law/.
36. Wang Yi, "China's Diplomacy in 2017 Should Fully Serve the Successful Convening of the 19th CPC National Congress," Ministry of Foreign Affairs of the People's Republic of China, December 3, 2016, http://www.fmprc.gov.cn/mfa_eng/zxxx_662805/t1421657.shtml.
37. Wang Qishan's smooth interview with US treasury secretary Tim Geithner on the *Charlie Rose* show, May 9, 2011, https://charlierose.com/videos/14139.
38. Wang Qishan, "Initiate the New Era, Set Foot on the New Journey," *People's Daily*, November 7, 2017, http://www.xinhuanet.com//politics/2017-11/07/c_1121915946.htm.
39. "Constructing the Anti-corruption System under the Unified Leadership of the Party, Improving the Ruling Ability and Perfecting the Governance System," Xinhua, March 5, 2017, http://www.xinhuanet.com//politics/2017lh/2017-03/05/c_1120572195.htm.
40. Holly Snape, "A Shifting Balance between Political and Professional Responsibility: Paradigmatic Change in China's Civil Servant and Cadres Management System," *Mapping China Journal*, no. 3 (2019), https://mappingchina.org/mcj-2019/.
41. Jamie P. Horsley, "What's So Controversial about China's New Anti-corruption Body," *The Diplomat*, May 30, 2018, https://www.brookings.edu/opinions/whats-so-controversial-about-chinas-new-anti-corruption-body/; Michael Laha, "The National Supervision Commission: From 'Punishing the Few' to 'Managing the Many,'" Center for Advanced China Research, July 15, 2019, https://www.ccpwatch.org/single-post/2019/07/15/The-National-Supervision-Commission-From-Punishing-the-Few-toward-Managing-the-Many.
42. Ma Huaide, "Supervision Commission Must Not Have Powers of Investigation, Arrest, and Prosecution," *Beijing News*, December 4, 2016, http://fzzfyjy.cupl.edu.cn/info/1138/6222.htm; Li Fenfei, "How Should Procuratorate Guides the Supervision Commission to Investigate Duty Crime," *Research on Comparative Law*, March 1, 2019, first issue of 2019, http://cacpl.chinalaw.org.cn/portal/article/index/id/4826.html; Chen Ruihua, "On the Attribute of National Supervisory Power," *Research on Comparative Law*, March 1, 2019, first issue of 2019, http://fzzfyjy.cupl.edu.cn/info/1331/10333.htm. The first issue of the *Research on Comparative Law* magazine in 2019 was on March 1.
43. Meng Na, "'Mass Line' Campaign Key to Consolidate CPC's Ruling Status," *People's Daily* (Beijing), June 19, 2013, http://english.peopledaily.com.cn/90785/8289769.html.
44. Xi Xiaodan, "CCDI: 4.089 Million People Investigated and Dealt with since 18th Party Congress," *Jiemian*, June 28, 2021, https://finance.sina.com.cn/tech/2021-06-28/doc-ikqcfnca3716443.shtml.

45. "List of Disgraced Full and Alternate Members of the Central Committee since 18th Party Congress," *Economic Daily*, May 20, 2019, http://district.ce.cn/newarea/sddy/201 412/19/t20141219_4160824.shtml.

46. "List of Senior Officials at or above Provincial and Ministerial Level," *Economic Daily*, February 3, 2021, http://district.ce.cn/newarea/sddy/201403/03/t20140303_2403198. shtml.

47. It wasn't clear if the Politburo had to give its approval as well.

48. "Excerpts from Xi Jinping's Discussion on Socialist Political Construction," 189, Literature Research Office of CCP Central Committee, July 2017. In April 2016, when a CCDI team investigated the Youth League, they used the four adjectives "bureaucratic, procedurally-minded, aristocratic and entertainment-oriented" to describe the Youth League. Tengfei Xu and Qiang He, "How Can the CYL Central Correct Mistakes When Accused of Being 'Aristocratic' and Having Other Problems?," *Beijing News*, April 25, 2016, http://www.bjnews.com.cn/news/2016/04/25/401267.html.

49. "Taiwan-Based 'Clean-Handed Rising Star' Suddenly Falls under China's Anti-graft Probe after Being Tipped for Higher Office," *South China Morning Post*, January 19, 2016, https://www.scmp.com/news/china/policies-politics/article/1903294/taiwan-based-clean-handed-rising-star-suddenly-falls.

50. "Taiwan-Based 'Clean-Handed Rising Star' Suddenly Falls."

51. "Former Senior Taiwan Affairs Official Sentenced to 15 Years for Graft," *China Daily*, April 20, 2017, https://www.chinadaily.com.cn/china/2017-04/20/content_29016 724.htm.

52. "Head of the Central Organization Department Answering Reporters' Questions on the 'Opinions on Strengthening the Party Building Work for Retired Cadres in the New Era," *People's Daily*, May 16, 2022, http://dangjian.people.com.cn/n1/2022/0516/ c117092-32422125.html.

53. Xiong Feng, "Chinese People's Police Flag Pattern Announced," Xinhua, August 26, 2020, http://www.xinhuanet.com/2020-08/26/c_1126416290.htm.

54. The classic work on esoteric communication in Soviet politics is Nathan Leites, *The Operational Code of the Politburo* (New York: RAND Corporation, 1951), https://www.rand.org/pubs/commercial_books/CB104-1.html.

55. "Zhao Leji's Work Report at the Third Plenum of the 19th Central Commission for Discipline Inspection," Xinhua, February 20, 2019, http://www.ccdi.gov.cn/toutiao/201 902/t20190220_188859.html.

56. "Declarations for Xi Jinping," *China Media Project*, January 20, 2018, https://chinam ediaproject.org/2018/01/20/declarations-for-chinas-new-lingxiu/; Bill Bishop, "'人民 领袖'—The People's 'Leader' Xi Jinping Gets a New Propaganda Title," *Sinocism*, February 11, 2018, https://sinocism.com/p/-the-peoples-leader-xi-jinping.

57. See Christian Goebel's tweet on January 5, 2022, https://twitter.com/ChristianGoebel/ status/1478872576831152137.

58. Joseph Fewsmith, "De Tocqueville in Beijing," *China Leadership Monitor*, no. 39, Fall 2012, https://www.hoover.org/sites/default/files/uploads/documents/CLM39JF.pdf.

59. State Textbook Commission, "Guide to Incorporate into Textbooks Xi Jinping Thought on Socialism with Chinese Characteristics for a New Era," Ministry of Education, July 23, 2021, http://www.moe.gov.cn/srcsite/A26/s8001/202107/t20210723_546307.html.

60. The software program Fuck Xuexi Qiangguo (FXQ) was available on Gihub for two years, 2019–2021. China Digital Times, March 15, 2021, https://chinadigitaltimes.net/ 2021/03/translation-developer-discontinues-support-for-ideological-app-automation-tool/.

61. Jiang's "'Three Represents" was not incorporated in either the CCP or state constitutions until he had retired. Hu's "Scientific Development Outlook" was included in the CCP

constitution between his first and second terms but was not added to the state constitution until his retirement.

62. "Raising Up the General Secretary," *China Media Project*, October 14, 2020, https://chinamediaproject.org/2020/10/14/raising-up-the-general-secretary/.

63. Chris Buckley, "Chinese Village Where Xi Jinping Fled Is Now a Monument to His Power," *New York Times*, October 8, 2017, https://www.nytimes.com/2017/10/08/world/asia/xi-jinping-china-propaganda-village.html.

64. Daniel Leese, *Mao Cult: Rhetoric and Ritual in China's Cultural Revolution* (Cambridge, UK: Cambridge University Press, 2011), 168.

65. Susan L. Shirk, *Competitive Comrades: Career Incentives and Student Strategies in China* (Berkeley: University of California Press, 1982).

66. "Xi Jinping on the Force of Political and Legal Affairs: We Must Not Have (Cadres) Coasting Along in the Neutral Gear," *People.cn*, May 19, 2015, http://star.news.sohu.com/20150519/n413310452.shtml; "Strictly Prohibit 'Darkness Under Light', Says Xi Jinping," Party Construction, October 9, 2021, http://xitheory.china.com.cn/2021-10/09/content_77797263.html.

67. Guang Hai and Wei Lu, "'Low-Level Red' and Other Concerns," *China Media Project*, March 11, 2019, https://chinamediaproject.org/2019/03/11/low-level-red-and-other-concerns/.

68. Wang Xiaohong, "Resolutely Eliminate the 'Two-Faced' Cadres and 'Wall-Riding Factions' and Struggle against Any Acts That Undermine the Party's Central Authority and Unified Leadership," *People's Police Daily*, August 28, 2020, https://www.sohu.com/a/415659932_203783.

69. Victor Chung-Hon Shih, "'Nauseating' Displays of Loyalty: Monitoring the Factional Bargain through Ideological Campaigns in China," *Journal of Politics* 70, no. 4 (October 2008): 1177–1192, https://www.journals.uchicago.edu/doi/10.1017/S0022381608081139.

70. Shirk, *Competitive Comrades*.

71. These were set out in "Communique of the Current State of the Ideological Sphere" of April 22, 2013. For an English translation online, see "Document no. 9: China File Translation: How Much Is a Hardline Party Directive Shaping China's Current Political Climate?," ChinaFile, November 8, 2013, www.chinafile.com/document-9-chinafile-translation.

72. Xi Jinping, "The Efforts to Promote the New Great Project of Party Building Must Be Consistent" [推进党的建设新的伟大工程要一以贯之], *Qiushi* no. 19, http://www.qstheory.cn/dukan/qs/2019-10/02/c_1125068596.htm, cited in Radchenko, "Putin and Xi Eye the Soviet Collapse."

73. Zhuang Pinghui, "China's Top Party Mouthpieces Pledge 'Absolute Loyalty' as President Makes Rare Visits to Newsrooms," *South China Morning Post*, February 19, 2016, http://www.scmp.com/news/china/policies-politics/article/1914136/chinas-top-party-mouthpieces-pledge-absolute-loyalty.

74. Amy Qin, "Peppa Pig, Unlikely Rebel Icon, Faces Purge in China," *The New York Times*, May 1, 2018, https://www.nytimes.com/2018/05/01/world/asia/peppa-pig-china-censors.html.

75. "Full Text of Regulation on the Introduction and Dissemination of Overseas Audio-Visual Programs (Draft for Comments)," *The Paper*, September 20, 2018, https://www.thepaper.cn/newsDetail_forward_2461137.

76. Atlantic Council, "Chinese Discourse Power: China's Use of Information Manipulation in Regional and Global Competition," December 2020, https://www.atlanticcouncil.org/wp-content/uploads/2020/12/China-Discouse-Power-FINAL.pdf.

77. Ben Blanchard, Philip Wen, and Benjamin Kang Lim, "Xi's Power on Parade as China Party Congress Looms," Reuters, September 1, 2017, https://www.reuters.com/article/us-china-congress-xi/xis-power-on-parade-as-china-party-congress-looms-idUSKCN1BC4SY.

78. "Pointing to the Future, Parroting the Past," *China Media Project*, October 26, 2017, https://chinamediaproject.org/2017/10/26/pointing-to-the-future-parroting-the-past/.

79. "Xi Takes Charge: Implications of the 19th Party Congress for China's Future" (21st Century China Center briefing, School of Global Policy and Strategy, UC San Diego, 2017), https://china.ucsd.edu/_files/2017_xi-briefing-web.pdf.

80. "19th CCP National Congress Work Report," Xinhua, November 3, 2017, http://www.xinhuanet.com/english/special/2017-11/03/c_136725942.htm.

81. "19th CCP National Congress Work Report."

82. Steve Bannon, "We're in an Economic War with China, It's Futile to Compromise," *Washington Post*, May 6, 2019, https://www.washingtonpost.com/opinions/steve-bannon-were-in-an-economic-war-with-china-its-futile-to-compromise/2019/05/06/0055af36-7014-11e9-9eb4-0828f5389013_story.html.

83. Gabriella Montinola, Yingyi Qian, and Barry Weingast, "Federalism China Style: The Political Basis for Economic Success," *World Politics* 48, no. 1 (1996): 50–81; Shirk, *Political Logic of Economic Reform*.

84. Shane Xuan, Jennifer Pan, and Yiqing Xu, "Political Preference in the Shadow of Institutional Backsliding" (Working Paper, University of California, San Diego, and Stanford University, 2022).

85. Milan W. Svolik, *The Politics of Authoritarian Rule* (Cambridge, UK: Cambridge University Press, 2012), 62.

86. Party History Research Institute of the CCP Central Committee, "Memorabilia of CCP History (July 1921–June 2011) Part 3," Xinhua, July 22, 2011, http://www.ce.cn/xwzx/gnsz/szyw/201107/22/t20110722_22558829_1.shtml; Party History and Literature Research Institute of the CCP Central Committee, "Memorabilia of the Communist Party of China in 100 Years (July 1921–June 2021)," Xinhua, June 28, 2021, http://www.xinhuanet.com/2021-06/28/c_1127603399.htm.

87. At the end of January, the Supreme People's Court chastised the local police and reversed their ruling on the whistle-blowers, but it failed to defuse the crisis.

88. Qin Jianhang and Timmy Shen, "Whistleblower Li Wenliang: There Should Be More Than One Voice in a Healthy Society," *Caixin Global*, February 6, 2020, https://www.caixinglobal.com/2020-02-06/after-being-punished-by-local-police-coronavirus-whistleblower-vindicated-by-top-court-101509986.html.

89. Researchers have found that there was very little censorship of the Internet before March 2020, when the United States began accusing China of originating the virus and allowing it to spread. During that early period, positive posts on the social media site Weibo spiked at the same time critical ones did—for example, on the day Dr. Li died—but from December 1, 2019, to the end of February 2020, criticism of the central government significantly increased. Yingdan Lu, Jennifer Pan, and Yiqing Xu, "Public Sentiment on Chinese Social Media during the Emergence of COVID-19" (21st Century China Center Research Paper #2021-04); Yixin Dai, Yuejiang Li, Chao-Yo Cheng, Hong Zhao, and Tianguang Meng, "Government-Led or Public-Led? Chinese Policy Agenda Setting during the COVID-19 Pandemic" (21st Century China Center Research Paper No. 2021-03).

90. Lu Zhenhua, "Wuhan Mayor Offers to Resign Over Coronavirus Response," *Caixin Global*, January 28, 2020, https://www.caixinglobal.com/2020-01-28/wuhan-mayor-offers-resignation-over-coronavirus-response-101508899.html.

91. Huang Chaolin, Wang Yeming, Li Xingwang, Ren Lili, Zhao Jianping, and Hu Yi, "Clinical Features of Patients Infected with 2019 Novel Coronavirus in Wuhan,

China," *Lancet* 395 (2020): 497–506; and Victor Shih, "China's Leninist Response to COVID-19: From Information Suppression to Total Mobilization," in *Coronavirus Politics*, ed. Scott Greer, Elizabeth J. King, Elize Massard da Fonseca, and André Peralta-Santos (Ann Arbor: University of Michigan Press, forthcoming).

92. Tom Mitchell, "What Xi Knew: Pressure Builds on China's Leader," *Financial Times*, May 20, 2020, https://www.ft.com/content/3a294233-6983-428c-b74b-3cc58c713 eb8?desktop=true&segmentId=7c8f09b9-9b61-4fbb-9430-9208a9e233c8#myft:notif ication:daily-email:content.

93. Victor Shih, "China's Leninist Response to COVID-19: From Information Suppression to Total Mobilization" (21st Century China Center Paper, 2021-02), SSRN, https://pap ers.ssrn.com/sol3/papers.cfm?abstract_id=3756580.

94. "Novel 2019 Coronavirus Genome," January 2020, https://virological.org/t/novel-2019-coronavirus-genome/319.

95. Zesen Yang and Tianguang Meng, "Unveiling Party Recruitment Dynamics in Contemporary China: Evidence from New Materials" (annual meeting paper, American Political Science Association, 2021).

96. Lei Guang, Molly Roberts, Yiqing Xu, and Jiannan Zhao, "Pandemic Sees Increase in Chinese Support for the Regime and Decrease in Views towards the U.S.," China Data Lab, http://chinadatalab.ucsd.edu/viz-blog/pandemic-sees-increase-in-chinese-support-for-regime-decrease-in-views-towards-us/.

97. Mitchell, "What Xi Knew: Pressure Builds on China's Leader."

98. Xi Jinping, "Speech at the Meeting of the Standing Committee of the Politburo to Study the Response to the Novel Coronavirus Epidemic," *Qiushi*, February 15, 2020, http://www.qstheory.cn/dukan/qs/2020-02/15/c_1125572832.htm.

99. Charlie Campbell, "Exclusive: The Chinese Scientist Who Sequenced the First COVID-19 Genome Speaks Out about the Controversies Surrounding His Work," *Time*, August 24, 2020, https://time.com/5882918/zhang-yongzhen-interview-china-coronavirus-genome/.

Chapter 8

1. Shi Yinhong, "What a Trump Presidency Means to the World and China," *China-US Focus*, November 18, 2016, https://www.chinausfocus.com/foreign-policy/what-a-trump-presidency-means-to-the-world-and-china.

2. Shi Yinhong, "China's Complicated Foreign Policy," European Council on Foreign Relations, March 31, 2015, https://ecfr.eu/article/commentary_chinas_complicated_f oreign_policy311562/.

3. Jun Mai and Sarah Zheng, "Xi Personally Behind Island-Building in the South China Sea," *South China Morning Post*, July 28, 2017, https://www.scmp.com/news/china/policies-politics/article/2104547/xi-personally-behind-island-building-south-china-sea.

4. Laura Silver, Christine Huang, and Laura Clancy, "Negative Views of China Tied to Critical Views of Its Policies on Human Rights," Pew Research Center, June 29, 2022, https://www.pewresearch.org/global/2022/06/29/negative-views-of-china-tied-to-criti cal-views-of-its-policies-on-human-rights/

5. IMF, China Pathfinder Data.

6. "Chinese Markets Continue to See Foreign Investment Outflows in April," Reuters, April 22, 2022, https://www.reuters.com/world/china/chinese-markets-continue-see-foreign-investment-outflows-april-2022-04-22/.

7. "Remarks by Vice President Pence on the Administration's Policy toward China," Hudson Institute, October 4, 2018, https://www.hudson.org/events/1610-vice-president-mike-pence-s-remarks-on-the-administration-s-policy-towards-china102018.

8. "China Is Evading U.S. Spies—and the White House Is Worried," Bloomberg, November 9, 2021, https://www.bloomberg.com/news/articles/2021-11-10/china-under-xi-is-tough-target-for-cia-spies-hurting-biden-s-beijing-policy.

9. Lucian W. Pye, *The Dynamics of Chinese Politics* (Cambridge: Oelgeschlager, Gunn, and Hain, 1981).

10. *Financial Times*, "China's Long March to National Rejuvenation," editorial, September 30, 2019, https://www.ft.com/content/d45119de-e11f-11e9-b112-9624ec9edc59.

11. Han Bing, "Xinhua's International Commentary: The US Fair Competition Is Not Fair," Xinhua, October 27, 2021, http://www.news.cn/world/2021-10/27/c_1128000 834.htm.

12. CGTN, "Full Text of Xi Jinping Keynote at the World Economic Forum," January 17, 2017, CGTN America, https://america.cgtn.com/2017/01/17/full-text-of-xi-jinping-keyn ote-at-the-world-economic-forum.

13. Xi Jinping, "Pursuing Sustainable Development in a Concerted Effort to Build an Asia-Pacific Community with a Shared Future," APEC CEO Summit, November 11, 2021, Ministry of Foreign Affairs, https://www.fmprc.gov.cn/mfa_eng/zxxx_662805/t1919060. shtml.

14. Yang Jiechi, "Innovations in China's Diplomatic Theory and Practice under New Conditions," August 16, 2013, http://www.fmprc.gov.cn/eng/zxxx/t1066869.shtml; in Chinese, see http://www.fmprc.gov.cn/mfa_chn/zyxw_602251/t1066866.shtml.

15. For example, Zhang Baijia, "If History Is Any Guide," *China-US Focus*, April 11, 2019, https://www.chinausfocus.com/foreign-policy/historical-lessons-and-future-implicati ons-for-evolving-china-us-relations.

16. Jack Snyder, *Myths of Empire: Domestic Politics and International Ambition* (Ithaca, NY: Cornell University Press, 1991), 214.

17. Snyder, *Myths of Empire*, 18.

18. Jessica L. P. Weeks, *Dictators at War and Peace* (Ithaca, NY: Cornell University Press, 2014), 19.

19. Bonnie Glaser, "Obama's Legacy in U.S.-China Relations: A Conversation with Evan Medeiros," China Power Podcast, Center for Strategic and International Studies, September 29, 2016, https://www.csis.org/podcasts/chinapower/obama's-legacy-us-china-relations-conversation-evan-medeiros.

20. For example, "Xi Jinping Visits Army at Shenyang Military Region," CCTV, August 30, 2013, http://tv.cctv.com/2013/08/30/VIDE1377861846506982.shtml; "Xi Jinping Visits Navy Force Stationed at Sanya," *People's Daily*, April 12, 2013, http://cpc.people. com.cn/n/2013/0412/c64094-21107967.html. In these visits in 2013 Xi wore the teal military office uniform.

21. "Xi Jinping: Do a Good Job in Preparing for Military Struggle at a New Starting Point and Resolutely Complete the Mission Entrusted by the Party and the People," Xinhua, January 4, 2019, http://www.xinhuanet.com/politics/leaders/2019-01/04/c_1123949 395.htm.

22. Sophie Beach, "Leaked Speech Shows Xi Jinping's Opposition to Reform," *China Digital Times*, January 27, 2013, https://chinadigitaltimes.net/2013/01/leaked-speech-shows-xi-jinpings-opposition-to-reform/.

23. Joseph Fewsmith, *Rethinking Chinese Politics* (Cambridge, UK: Cambridge University Press, 2021). Fewsmith notes that the 19th Central Committee brought in the largest turnover of military members in the history of post-Mao China—76 percent of the full members and 83 percent of the alternates were new.

24. Dean Cheng, "Xi Jinping and His Generals: Curiouser and Curiouser," *War on the Rocks*, January 18, 2018, https://warontherocks.com/2018/01/xi-jinping-generals-curiou ser-curiouser/.

25. Data calculated using official data from the annual report of defense budget during the plenary sessions of the National People's Congress.

26. "China's National Defense in 2008," State Council Information Office, January 20, 2009, http://www.gov.cn/zwgk/2009-01/20/content_1210224.htm.

27. Li Xueyong, Li Xuanliang, and Mei Shixiong, "Xi Jinping Attends Plenary Meeting With PLA and Armed Police Force Delegations," Xinhua, March 12, 2019, http://www.xinhuanet.com/politics/leaders/2019-03/12/c_1124227000.htm.

28. James Mulvenon, "Xi Jinping Has a Cool New Nickname: 'Commander-in-Chief,'" *China Leadership Monitor*, no. 51, Fall 2016, https://www.hoover.org/sites/default/files/research/docs/clm51jm.pdf.

29. Shi, "China's Complicated Foreign Policy."

30. Yingxian Long, "China's Decision to Deploy HYSY-981 in the South China Sea: Bureaucratic Politics with Chinese Characteristics," *Asian Security* 12, no. 3 (2016), https://www.tandfonline.com/doi/abs/10.1080/14799855.2016.1227322.

31. Carl Thayer, "4 Reasons China Removed Oil Rig HYSY-981 Sooner Than Planned," *The Diplomat*, July 22, 2014, https://thediplomat.com/2014/07/4-reasons-china-removed-oil-rig-hysy-981-sooner-than-planned/.

32. Thayer, "4 Reasons."

33. ASEAN Foreign Ministers' Statement on the Current Developments in the South China Sea, May 10, 2014, https://asean.org/wp-content/uploads/2012/05/24th-AFMs-Statement-on-SCS.pdf.

34. "China's Military Told 'to Follow Xi Jinping's Instructions,'" *India Today*, September 21, 2014, https://www.indiatoday.in/world/story/china-military-told-to-follow-xi-jinping-instructions-293684-2014-09-21; "Who Sabotaged Chinese President Xi Jinping's India Visit?," *Forbes*, September 23, 2014, https://www.forbes.com/sites/ericrmeyer/2014/09/23/who-sabotaged-xi-jinpings-india-visit/?sh=74eb18od70fa.

35. Andrew Erickson and Gabe Collins, "New Fleet on the Block: China's Coast Guard Comes Together," *Wall Street Journal*, March 11, 2013, https://www.wsj.com/articles/BL-CJB-17380.

36. The Maritime Safety Administration under the Ministry of Transport remained separate.

37. Some of the ships of the Fisheries Law Enforcement, Maritime Anti-Smuggling Police, and Border Defense Coast Guard were already equipped with desk-mounted guns and water cannons. Ryan D. Martinson, "From Words to Actions: The Creation of the China Coast Guard" (paper, China as a "Maritime Power" Conference, July 28–29, 2015, Center for Naval Analysis, Arlington, Virginia), https://www.cna.org/cna_files/pdf/creation-china-coast-guard.pdf.

38. "The Coast Guard Law of the People's Republic of China," according to the Ministry of Defense, 2020, https://www.mod.go.jp/en/d_act/sec_env/ch_ocn/index.html.

39. Nguyen Thanh Trung, "How China's Coast Guard Law Has Changed the Regional Security Structure," CSIS Asia Maritime Transparency Initiative, April 12, 2021, https://amti.csis.org/how-chinas-coast-guard-law-has-changed-the-regional-security-structure/.

40. Tai Ming Cheung, "The Chinese National Security State Emerges from the Shadows to Center Stage," *China Leadership Monitor*, September 1, 2020, https://www.prclea der.org/cheung.

41. Hu Jintao, "Unswervingly Advance along the Path of Chinese Characteristics, Struggle to Complete the Building of a Well-Off Society in an All-Round Way" (Report to the Eighteenth Chinese Communist Party National Congress, November 8, 2012), *People's Daily*, November 9, 2012, http://politics.people.com.cn/n/2012/1109/

c1001-19529890.html, quoted in Cheung, "Chinese National Security State Emerges from the Shadows."

42. Matt Ho, Holly Chik, and Echo Xie, "China's National Security Commission Met in Secret Amid Coronavirus Pandemic," *South China Morning Post*, June 29, 2020, https://www.scmp.com/news/china/politics/article/3091101/chinas-national-security-commission-met-secret-amid-coronavirus.

43. Cheung, "Chinese National Security State Emerges."

44. Chinese Academy of Social Science researcher Zhang Jie describes three phases in Chinese dispute strategy as a function of how policymakers balance the two desires for sovereignty and stability. She says that during first period, prior to 2009, China "self-consciously strived not to let its claims harm relations with other states." During 2010 and 2011, the policy "oscillated" between assertive action and restraint. And a third phase, in 2012, began a period of "proactivity." Zhang Jie, "The Huangyan Island Model and the Shift of China's Maritime Protection Policy," *Southeast Asian Studies*, no. 4 (2013), https://edu.wanfangdata.com.cn/Periodical/Detail/dnyyj201304003, quoted in Ryan Martinson, "China's Great Balancing Act Unfolds: Enforcing Maritime Rights vs. Stability," *National Interest*, September 11, 2015, https://nationalinterest.org/feature/chinas-great-balancing-act-unfolds-enforcing-maritime-rights-13821.

45. *People's Daily*, July 2014, quoted in Martinson, "China's Great Balancing Act Unfolds."

46. Feng Zhang, "Chinese Thinking on the South China Sea and the Future of Regional Security," *Political Science Quarterly* 132, no. 3 (2017): 435–466, http://bellschool.anu.edu.au/sites/default/files/uploads/2017-09/feng_zhang-2017-political_science_quarterly.pdf.

47. Liu Linlin, "Asia-Pacific Geopolitics in Transition, Says CASS Report," *Global Times*, December 27, 2012, https://www.globaltimes.cn/content/752551.shtml.

48. Yun-han Chu and Yu-tzung Chang, "Xi's Foreign-Policy Turn and Asian Perceptions of a Rising China," *Global Asia* 12, no. 1 (Spring 2017), https://www.globalasia.org/v12no1/focus/xis-foreign-policy-turn-and-asian-perceptions-of-a-rising-china_yun-han-chuyu-tzung-chang.

49. According to Linda Jakobson, "Xi Jinping was reportedly made head of a new 'Office to Respond to the Diaoyu Crisis' soon after the Japanese government's announcement. State counsellor Dai Binguo, China's top diplomat for the past five years, as well as several senior military officers were assigned to this task force." See Linda Jakobson, "How Involved Is Xi Jinping in the Diaoyu Crisis?," *The Diplomat*, February 8, 2013, https://thediplomat.com/2013/02/how-involved-is-xi-jinping-in-the-diaoyu-crisis-3/. This office was probably part of the working group that Xi chaired.

50. Jeremy Wallace and Jessica Chen Weiss, "The Political Geography of Nationalist Protest in China: Cities and the 2012 Anti-Japanese Demonstrations," *China Quarterly* 222 (June 2015): 403–429.

51. "Beijing Evening News Says 'Nuke Japan,'" *China Digital Times*, September 12, 2012, https://chinadigitaltimes.net/2012/09/beijing-evening-news-says-nuke-japan/.

52. Stephanie Kleine-Ahlbrandt, "Choppy Weather in the China Seas," *Le Monde Diplomatique*, December 2012, https://mondediplo.com/2012/12/08chinaseas.

53. Ai Weiwei, September 15, 2012, https://twitter.com/aiww/status/247122153756041216.

54. "Hu Jintao States China's Position on Relations with Japan, Diaoyu Islands," September 9, 2012, Ministry of Foreign Affairs of the People's Republic of China, https://www.fmprc.gov.cn/mfa_eng/topics_665678/diaodao_665718/t969863.shtml.

55. Jakobson, "How Involved Is Xi Jinping?" The Diaoyu Islands small group may be the same as the Maritime Rights Protection leading small group that Xi Jinping was put in charge of.

56. "Xi Slams 'Purchase' of Dialyu Islands," China.orgncn, September 19, 2012, http://www.china.org.cn/china/2012-09/19/content_26574964.htm.

57. "Dangerous Waters: China-Japan Relations on the Rocks," International Crisis Group, April 8, 2013, https://www.refworld.org/pdfid/51b830571.pdf.

58. "China Officially Labels Senkakus a 'Core Interest'," *Japan Times*, April 27, 2013, https://www.japantimes.co.jp/news/2013/04/27/national/china-officially-labels-senka kus-a-core-interest/.

59. Michael D. Swaine, "Chinese Views regarding the Senkaku/Diaoyu Islands Dispute," *China Leadership Monitor*, no. 41, Spring 2013, June 4, 2013, https://carnegieendowm ent.org/files/CLM41MS.pdf.

60. "What's Really at the Core of China's 'Core Interests'?," ChinaFile, April 30, 2013, https://www.chinafile.com/conversation/whats-really-core-chinas-core-interests.

61. "On April 26, 2013, Foreign Ministry Spokesperson Hua Chunying Presided Over Regular Press Conference," Ministry of Foreign Affairs of the People's Republic of China, https://www.fmprc.gov.cn/ce/cejm/chn/wjbfyrth/t1035595.htm, quoted in Michael Swaine, "Chinese Views on the South China Sea Arbitration Case between the People's Republic of China and the Philippines," *China Leadership Monitor*, no. 51 (Fall 2016); also see "White Paper on China's Peaceful Development," The State Council Information Office of the People's Republic of China, September 6, 2011, http://www.scio.gov.cn/tt/Document/1011394/1011394.htm.

62. "Dangerous Waters: China-Japan Relations on the Rocks."

63. Caixin, September 17, 2012, quoted in Jessica Chen Weiss, *Powerful Patriots: Nationalist Protest in China's Foreign Relations* (New York: Oxford University Press, 2014), 214.

64. Alessio Patalano, "What Is China's Strategy in the Senkaku Islands?," *War on the Rocks*, September 10, 2020, https://warontherocks.com/2020/09/what-is-chinas-strat egy-in-the-senkaku-islands/. The patrols into the territorial waters of the Senkakus had begun on an occasional basis in December 2008.

65. Adam P. Liff and Andrew S. Erickson, "From Management Crisis to Crisis Management? Japan's Post-2012 Institutional Reforms and Sino-Japanese Crisis (In) stability," *Journal of Strategic Studies* 40, no. 5 (2017): 604, https://doi.org/10.1080/01402 390.2017.1293530.

66. "Announcement of the Aircraft Identification Rules for the East China Sea Air Defense Identification Zone of the People's Republic of China," *China Daily*, November 23, 2013, https://www.chinadaily.com.cn/china/2013-11/23/content_17126618.htm.

67. Bonnie Glaser, "China's Maritime Rights Protection Leading Small Group — Shrouded in Secrecy," Asia Maritime Security Initiative, Center for Security and International Studies, September 11, 2015, https://amti.csis.org/chinas-maritime-rights-protection-leading-small-group-shrouded-in-secrecy/.

68. "General Secretary Xi Jinping's Road to Growth," *Study Times*, July 28, 2017, http://news.sina.com.cn/o/2017-07-28/doc-ifyinryq6629735.shtml, quoted in Mai and Zheng, "Xi Personally Behind Island-Building in the South China Sea."

69. Feng Chunmei, Sun Maoqing, Li Xuanliang, and Li Guowen, "Take the Road of Scientific Development and Build the Great Wall of Steel In The Sky," Xinhua, November 1, 2009, quoted in Jun Osawa, "China's ADIZ over the East China Sea: A 'Great Wall in the Sky'?," Brookings Institution, December 17, 2013, https://www.brooki ngs.edu/opinions/chinas-adiz-over-the-east-china-sea-a-great-wall-in-the-sky/.

70. Sydney J. Freedberg Jr., "U.S. Japan, Korea Defy New China Air Defense Zone, Biden to Rebuke Beijing; PRC Move Drives Korea, Japan Together," *Breaking Defense*, November 26, 2013, https://breakingdefense.com/2013/11/chinas-new-defense-zone-dri ves-korea-japan-together/.

71. Jessica Chen Weiss and Allan Dafoe, "Authoritarian Audiences, Rhetoric, and Propaganda in International Crises: Evidence from China," *International Studies Quarterly* 63, no. 4 (2019): 963–973, https://academic.oup.com/isq/article-abstract/63/4/963/5559531?redirectedFrom=fulltext.

72. "Kerry Warns Beijing over Air Defense Zone for South China Sea," Reuters, June 4, 2016, https://www.reuters.com/article/us-southchinasea-usa-china/kerry-warns-beijing-over-air-defense-zone-for-south-china-sea-idUSKCN0YR01D.

73. Michael Green, Kathleen Hicks, Zack Cooper, John Schaus, and Jake Douglas, "Counter-coercion Series: Second Thomas Shoal Incident," Asia Maritime Transparency Initiative, CSIS, June 9, 2017, https://amti.csis.org/counter-co-2nd-thomas-shoal/.

74. Carl Thayer, "A Closer Look at the ASEAN-China Single Draft South China Sea Code of Conduct," *The Diplomat*, August 3, 2018, https://thediplomat.com/2018/08/a-closer-look-at-the-asean-china-single-draft-south-china-sea-code-of-conduct/.

75. Swaine, "Chinese Views regarding the Senkaku/Diaoyu Islands Dispute."

76. PRC Ministry of Foreign Affairs, "China's Sovereignty and Maritime Rights and Interests in the South China Sea Shall Not Be Affected by Arbitration Award," July 16, 2016, http://www.fmprc.gov.cn/nanhai/eng/wjbxw_1/t1382766.htm.

77. "What China Has Been Building in the South China Sea," *New York Times*, October 27, 2015, https://www.nytimes.com/interactive/2015/07/30/world/asia/what-china-has-been-building-in-the-south-china-sea.html.

78. Helene Cooper and Jane Perlez, "White House Moves to Reassure Allies With South China Sea Patrol, but Quietly," *New York Times*, October 28, 2015, https://www.nytimes.com/2015/10/28/world/asia/south-china-sea-uss-lassen-spratly-islands.html.

79. Gregory B. Poling, "The Conventional Wisdom on China's Island Bases Is Dangerously Wrong," *War on the Rocks*, January 10, 2020, https://warontherocks.com/2020/01/the-conventional-wisdom-on-chinas-island-bases-is-dangerously-wrong/.

80. Lyle J. Goldstein, "The South China Sea Showdown: 5 Dangerous Myths," National Interest, September 29, 2015, https://nationalinterest.org/feature/the-south-china-sea-showdown-5-dangerous-myths-13970.

81. "Sansha and the Expansion of China's South China Sea Administration," Asia Maritime Transparency Initiative, CSIS, May 12, 2020, https://amti.csis.org/sansha-and-the-expansion-of-chinas-south-china-sea-administration/.

82. Bonnie S. Glaser and Lisa Collins, "China's Rapprochement with South Korea: Who Won the THAAD Dispute?," *Foreign Affairs*, November 7, 2017, https://www.foreignaffairs.com/articles/china/2017-11-07/chinas-rapprochement-south-korea.

83. Victoria Kim, "When China and U.S. Spar, It's South Korea That Gets Punched," *Los Angeles Times*, November 19, 2020, https://www.latimes.com/world-nation/story/2020-11-19/south-korea-china-beijing-economy-thaad-missile-interceptor.

84. The Chinese side made the most of these promises by publicizing them as "Three Noes," but the Moon government insisted that it had just affirmed South Korea's long-standing position. South Korea's foreign minister had offered the same three assurances in response to a parliamentary question the same day the compromise with China was announced. "China's foreign ministry appears to have co-opted her statement, implying that it had been part of the bilateral agreement." Glaser and Collins, "China's Rapprochement with South Korea."

85. Choe Sang-Hun, "South Koreans Now Dislike China More Than They Dislike Japan," *New York Times*, August 20, 2021, https://www.nytimes.com/2021/08/20/world/asia/korea-china-election-young-voters.html; and Laura Silver, Christine Huang, and Laura Clancy, "Across 19 Countries, More People See the U.S. Than China Favorably—But More See China's Influence Growing," Pew Research Center, June

29, 2022, https://www.pewresearch.org/fact-tank/2022/06/29/across-19-countries-more-people-see-the-u-s-than-china-favorably-but-more-see-chinas-influence-growing/.

86. Emily Rauhala and Anna Fifield, "Kim-Xi Meeting Presents a New Challenge for Trump on North Korea," *Washington Post*, March 28, 2018, https://www.washingtonpost.com/world/asia_pacific/kim-xi-meeting-presents-a-new-challenge-for-trump-on-north-korea/2018/03/28/55e7e8a6-31f9-11e8-b6bd-0084a1666987_story.html.

87. "Chinese President Calls for Building Closer Belt and Road Partnership," Xinhua, June 23, 2021, http://www.xinhuanet.com/english/2021-06/23/c_1310024161.htm.

88. Daniel R. Russel and Blake H. Berger, "Weaponizing the Belt and Road Initiative," Asia Society Policy Institute, September 2020, 7, https://asiasociety.org/sites/default/files/2020-09/Weaponizing%20the%20Belt%20and%20Road%20Initiative_0.pdf.

89. Amanda Lee, "Belt and Road Initiative Debt: How Big Is It and What's Next?," *South China Morning Post*, July 19, 2020, https://www.scmp.com/economy/china-economy/article/3093218/belt-and-road-initiative-debt-how-big-it-and-whats-next.

90. State Council of China, "ODI Led for First Time by Private Firms," September 23, 2016, http://english.www.gov.cn/state_council/ministries/2016/09/23/content_281475449151124.htm.

91. "U.S. Support for the New Silk Road," US Department of State Archived Content, January 20, 2009, to January 20, 2017, https://2009-2017.state.gov/p/sca/ci/af/newsilkroad/index.htm.

92. Hu Jintao, *Hu Jintao Selected Works*, 3:241, quoted in Rush Doshi, *The Long Game: China's Grand Strategy to Displace American Order* (New York: Oxford University Press, 2021), 235.

93. Doshi, *Long Game*, 236.

94. Doshi, 240–241.

95. Wang Jisi, "'Marching Westwards': The Rebalancing of China's Geostrategy," *Global Times*, October 17, 2012.

96. Wu Jiao and Zhang Yunbi, "Xi Proposes a 'New Silk Road' with Central Asia," *China Daily*, September 8, 2013, http://www.chinadaily.com.cn/china/2013xivisitcenterasia/2013-09/08/content_16952228.htm.

97. Weiyi Shi and Brigitte Seim, "A Reputation Deficit? The Myths and Reality of Chinese Investment in Zambia." *Journal of East Asian Studies* 21, no. 2 (2021): 259–282. Bonnie S. Glaser, "Ensuring the 'Go Abroad' Policy Serves China's Domestic Priorities," Jamestown Foundation China Brief 7, no. 5, May 9, 2007, https://jamestown.org/program/ensuring-the-go-abroad-policy-serves-chinas-domestic-priorities-3/.

98. "Why China Is Lavishing Money on Foreign Students," *The Economist*, January 26, 2019, https://www.economist.com/china/2019/01/26/why-china-is-lavishing-money-on-foreign-students..

99. Yang Sheng, "China to Set Up International Courts to Settle Belt and Road Disputes," *Global Times*, January 25, 2018, https://web.archive.org/web/20180628160650/https://www.globaltimes.cn/content/1108794.shtml.

100. Zhou Bo, "The Future of the PLA," *Foreign Policy*, August 6, 2019, https://foreignpolicy.com/2019/08/06/the-future-of-the-pla/; and Christopher D. Yung, and Ross Rustici, "'Not an Idea We Have to Shun'. Chinese Overseas Basing Requirements in the 21st Century," with Scott Devary and Jenny Lin (China Strategic Perspectives No. 7, Center for the Study of Chinese Military Affairs, Institute for National Strategic Studies, National Defense University, October 2014), https://ndupress.ndu.edu/Portals/68/Documents/stratperspective/china/ChinaPerspectives-7.pdf, cited in Daniel R. Russel and Blake H. Berger, "Weaponizing the Belt and Road Initiative," Asia Society Policy Institute, September 2020, 7, 16, https://asiasociety.org/sites/default/files/2020-09/Weaponizing%20the%20Belt%20and%20Road%20Initiative_0.pdf.

101. Russel and Berger, "Weaponizing the Belt and Road Initiative," 19.
102. AidData's new dataset of 13,427 Chinese development projects worth $843 billion reveals a major increase in "hidden debt" and BRI implementation problems. See Ammar A. Malik, Bradley Parks, Brooke Russell, Joyce Jiahui Lin, Katherine Walsh, Kyra Solomon, et al., "Banking on the Belt and Road: Insights from a New Global Dataset of 13,427 Chinese Development Projects" (policy report by AidData at the College of William & Mary, Williamsburg, VA, September 2021), https://www.aidd ata.org/publications/banking-on-the-belt-and-road.
103. David Fickling, "Soviet Collapse Echoes in China's Belt and Road," Bloomberg, August 11, 2018, https://www.bloomberg.com/opinion/articles/2018-08-12/soviet-colla pse-echoes-in-china-s-belt-and-road-investment?sref=I2I6qZII.
104. "New Data on the 'Debt Trap Question," Rhodium Group, April 29, 2019, https://rhg. com/research/new-data-on-the-debt-trap-question/.
105. Kevin Acker, Deborah Brautigan, and Yufan Huang, "The Pandemic Has Worsened Africa's Debt Crisis. China and Other Countries Are Stepping In," *Washington Post*, February 26, 2021, https://www.washingtonpost.com/politics/2021/02/26/pandemic-has-worsened-africas-debt-crisis-china-other-countries-are-stepping/.
106. "China's Investments in the Belt and Road Initiative (BRI) in 2020," International Institute of Green Finance, China University of Finance and Economics, January 2021, https://greenfdc.org/wp-content/uploads/2021/01/China-BRI-Investment-Rep ort-2020.pdf.
107. Xinhua, June 23, 2021, http://www.xinhuanet.com/english/2021-06/23/c_1310024161.htm.
108. Business Daily Africa, "Kenya Seeks IMF Aid to Repay China Loans," The Citizen, September 21, 2021, https://www.thecitizen.co.tz/tanzania/news/africa/kenya-seeks-imf-aid-to-repay-china-loans-3558074. Acker, Brautigan, and Huang, "The Pandemic Has Worsened Africa's Debt Crisis."
109. "Telling China's Story Well," *China Media Project*, April 16, 2021, https://chinamedia project.org/the_ccp_dictionary/telling-chinas-story-well/.
110. Christopher Walker and Jessica Ludwig, "From 'Soft Power' to 'Sharp Power': Rising Authoritarian Influence in the Developing World," National Endowment for Democracy, December 5, 2017, https://www.ned.org/wp-content/uploads/2017/12/ Introduction-Sharp-Power-Rising-Authoritarian-Influence.pdf.
111. During the Olympic Torch Relay in 2008, Chinese security police were dispatched abroad to work with PRC embassies to orchestrate pro-China protests to counter pro-Tibet demonstrations. Bethany Allen-Ebrahimian and Zach Dorfman, "China Has Been Running Global Influence Campaigns for Years," *The Atlantic*, May 13, 2019, https://www.theatlantic.com/international/archive/2019/05/beijing-olympics-china-influence-campaigns/589186/.
112. Chris Horton, "The World Is Fed Up With China's Belligerenc," *The Atlantic*, November 9, 2021, https://www.theatlantic.com/international/archive/2021/11/china-taiwan-democracy/620647/.
113. Namewee, "Fragile," music video, YouTube, https://www.youtube.com/watch?v=-Rp7UPbhErE; "'Came From Heart': Rapper Defends China Satire as Views Hit 30 Million," NDTV, November 15, 2021, https://www.ndtv.com/world-news/china-news-fragile-by-malaysian-rapper-namewee-came-from-the-heart-rapper-defends-pop-sat ire-as-views-hit-30-million-2611607.
114. Rosemary Foot, "A World Unsafe for Democracy? China and the Shaping of Global Order," *Journal of the British Academy*, no. 9, July 16, 2021, https://www.thebritishacad emy.ac.uk/documents/3377/JBA-9-p213-Foot.pdf.
115. Jessica Chen Weiss, "A World Safe for Autocracy? China's Rise and the Future of Global Politics," *Foreign Affairs*, July/August 2019, https://www.foreignaffairs.com/ articles/china/2019-06-11/world-safe-autocracy.

116. Foot, "World Unsafe for Democracy?"

117. John Garnaut, "How China Interferes in Australia and How Democracies Can Push Back," *Foreign Affairs*, March 9, 2018, https://www.foreignaffairs.com/articles/china/2018-03-09/how-china-interferes-australia.

118. Malcolm Turnbull, "Speech Introducing the National Security Legislation Amendment (Espionage and Foreign Interference) Bill 2017," December 7, 2017, https://www.malcolmturnbull.com.au/media/speech-introducing-the-national-security-legislation-amendment-espionage-an.

119. See "Threats to Australia's Vital Interests," Security and Defence, Lowy Institute Poll 2021, https://poll.lowyinstitute.org/charts/threats-australias-vital-interests.

120. "How Sweden Copes With Chinese Bullying," *The Economist*, February 20, 2020, https://www.economist.com/europe/2020/02/20/how-sweden-copes-with-chinese-bullying.

121. "They Don't Understand the Fear We Have," Human Rights Watch, June 30, 2021, https://www.hrw.org/report/2021/06/30/they-dont-understand-fear-we-have/how-chinas-long-reach-repression-undermines.

122. "Confucius Institutes in the United States," newsletter, USC US-China Institute, November 18, 2021, https://china.usc.edu/confucius-institutes-united-states.

123. Simon Denyer, "Gap Apologizes to China over Map on T-Shirt That Omits Taiwan, South China Sea," *Washington Post*, May 15, 2018, https://www.washingtonpost.com/news/worldviews/wp/2018/05/15/u-s-retailer-gap-apologizes-to-china-over-map-on-t-shirt-that-omits-taiwan-south-china-sea/.

124. Narayanan Somasundaram and Michelle Chan, "HSBC's Bow to China Stirs Up Internal Anxiety and Patience," *Nikkei Asian Review*, June 15, 2020, https://asia.nikkei.com/Business/Companies/HSBC-s-bow-to-China-stirs-up-internal-anxiety-and-patience.

125. Helen Davidson, "Xinjiang: More Than Half a Million Forced to Pick Cotton, Report Suggests," *The Guardian*, December 15, 2020, https://www.theguardian.com/world/2020/dec/15/xinjiang-china-more-than-half-a-million-forced-to-pick-cotton-report-finds.

126. Angeli Datt, "The CCP Hand Behind China's Xinjiang Cotton Backlash," *The Diplomat*, April 29, 2021, https://thediplomat.com/2021/04/the-ccp-hand-behind-chinas-xinjiang-cotton-backlash/.

127. "Chinese Sportswear Brands Report Sweeping Business Performance in H1 of 2021," *Global Times*, September 6, 2021, https://www.globaltimes.cn/page/202109/1233408.shtml?id=11.

128. Simon Denyer, "In Reversal, Cambridge University Press Faces Backlash After Bowing to China's Censorship Pressure," *Washington Post*, August 21, 2017, https://www.washingtonpost.com/news/worldviews/wp/2017/08/21/cambridge-university-press-faces-backlash-after-bowing-to-china-censorship-pressure/.

129. China categorizes the overseas Chinese population in three groups. For the first two groups, there are three names that are frequently used in official documents and media reports in reference to them—that is, *huaqiao*, *huaren*, and *huayi*. According to the CCP's regulation on managing overseas Chinese affairs, *huaqiao* refers to Chinese nationals who have been living overseas for at least two consecutive years and have permission for long-term or permanent residence in the host country, or to Chinese nationals who have legally lived in the host country for five consecutive years, albeit without permission for long-term or permanent residence. *Huaren* and *huayi* (used interchangeably), on the other hand, refer to either Chinese nationals who have obtained naturalized foreign citizenship of the host country or their offspring (foreign citizens of Chinese descent). See "What Are the Definitions of *Huaqiao* and *Huaren*?," Overseas Chinese Affairs Office of the State Council, November 25, 2015, http://www.gqb.gov.cn/news/2015/1125/37146.shtml.

There is a third group of Chinese living or sojourning overseas that is legally and technically distinct from the previous two categories. Unlike the *huaqiao* and *huaren/ huayi*, the third group doesn't have a uniform name, and it mostly includes Chinese students studying overseas, Chinese nationals working overseas for official purposes (*gongwu chuguo*), and Chinese nationals contracted by Chinese companies to work overseas (*waipai laowu*). The same CCP regulation, in fact, stipulates that Chinese nationals who fit into any of the three subcategories shall not be considered *huaqiao* and that children born overseas to Chinese students are not *huaren*—that is, foreign citizens of Chinese descent.

130. "Comrade Xi Zhongxun's Speech at the Meeting with Directors of Overseas Chinese Affairs Office at the Provincial Level, Autonomous Region Level, and the Level of the Municipalities under the Jurisdiction of the Central Government," included in the internal document *Compilation of Regulations on Overseas Chinese Affairs* compiled by the Overseas Chinese Affairs Office of the State Council, 1997, pp. 23–24, cited in Zhuang Guotu, "Chinese Government Policy towards Overseas Chinese since 1979," *Southeast Asian Affairs* (Xiamen University), 103, no. 3 (2000): 8.

131. Deng Xiaoping, "Develop Special Economic Zones Well and Increase the Number of Cities Open to the Outside World," February 24, 1984, in *Selective Works of Deng Xiaoping*, 3:52.

132. "Comrade Xi Zhongxun's Speech at the Meeting with Directors . . . ," cited in Zhuang, "Chinese Government Policy towards Overseas Chinese since 1979," 5.

133. Leo Suryadinata, "Blurring the Distinction between *Huaqiao* and *Huaren*: China's Changing Policy towards the Chinese Overseas," *Southeast Asian Affairs* 2017 (2017): 102, https://muse.jhu.edu/article/658015/pdf.

134. Hu Jintao, "International Situations and Works on Foreign Affairs," August 21, 2006, *Selective Works of Hu Jintao*, 2: 518.

135. "The Origin of the Term *Zhonghua Er'nv*," Propaganda Office of the Central United Front Work Department, May 4, 2014, http://tyzx.people.cn/n/2014/0504/c372202-24972647.html.

136. Hu Jintao, "Speech at the Summary and Commendation Conference for Beijing Olympics and Paralympics," Xinhua, September 29, 2008, http://www.gov.cn/ldhd/2008-09/29/content_1109754.htm; "Hu Jintao Thanks Chinese Students in Japan for Defending the Torch," Xinhua, May 9, 2008, http://news.cctv.com/china/20080509/100464_1.shtml.

137. Zhuang Guotu, "Historical Changes in the Number and Distribution of *Huaqiao* and *Huaren* in the World," *World History*, May 2011, 10, http://www.ims.sdu.edu.cn/_local/9/99/95/A19FE7592B133012032B8879B2A_2A396900_696AF.pdf; "Research Results: There Are About 50 Million Overseas *Huaqiao and Huaren* in the World," Overseas Chinese Affairs Office of the State Council, December 1, 2011, http://www.gqb.gov.cn/news/2011/1201/24945.shtml; "The Origin of the Term *Zhonghua Er'nv*."

138. Hu Jintao, "Initiate Special Legislation Directed towards Taiwan and Grasp the Initiative of Cross-Strait Relations," *Selective Works of Hu Jintao*, 2: 251. This is a summary of two speeches given respectively on December 14, 2004, and March 3, 2005.

139. Xi Jinping, "The Establishment of the Concept of 'Big Overseas Chinese Affairs'," February 1995, *Strategy and Management*, Second Issue, 111.

140. "Build the Bridge with *Huaqiao*: This Is How Xi Jinping Talks about Works on Overseas Chinese Affairs," CCTV, May 29, 2019, http://news.cctv.com/2019/05/29/ARTI9uVgvrYLub6XLtIXWiW8190529.shtml.

141. "General Office of the Party Central Issue the Reform Plan for All-China Federation of Returned Overseas Chinese," Xinhua, December 4, 2016, http://www.gov.cn/xin wen/2016-12/04/content_5142958.htm.

142. Christine Han and Yaobin Tong, "Students at the Nexus between the Chinese Diaspora and Internationalisation of Higher Education: The Role of Overseas Students in China's Strategy of Soft Power," *British Journal of Educational Studies* 69, no. 5 (2021): 579–598.

143. "Plan for Deepening the Reform on the Party and State Institutions," Xinhua, March 21, 2018, http://www.xinhuanet.com/2018-03/21/c_1122570517.htm.

144. Jose Ma. Montelibano, "China Defies Deng Xiaoping Warning," April 4, 2014, https://webcache.googleusercontent.com/search?q=cache:UtrC2WoH2HwJ:https://opinion.inquirer.net/73236/china-defies-deng-xiaoping-warning+&cd=1&hl=en&ct=clnk&gl=us.

Chapter 9

1. "Xi Jinping: Explanation of the 'Decision of the Central Committee of the Communist Party of China on Several Major Issues of Comprehensively Deepening Reform,'" Xinhua, November 15, 2013, http://www.xinhuanet.com/politics/2013-11/15/c_118164294.htm; Xi Jinping, "Safeguard National Security and Social Stability," April 25, 2014, in Xi Jinping, "Adhere to the Overall View of National Security and Follow the Path of National Security with Chinese Characteristics," April 15, 2014, Xinhua, http://www.xinhuanet.com//politics/2014-04/15/c_1110253910.htm.

2. Tai Ming Cheung, *Innovate to Dominate: The Rise of the Chinese Techno-Security State* (Ithaca, NY: Cornell University Press, 2022).

3. Sheena Chestnut Greitens, "Internal Security and Grand Strategy: China's Approach to National Security under Xi Jinping" (Statement before the U.S.-China Economic and Security Review Commission, hearing on "U.S.-China Relations at the Chinese Communist Party's Centennial" Panel on "Trends in China's Politics, Economics, and Security Policy," January 28, 2021), https://www.uscc.gov/sites/default/files/2021-01/Sheena_Chestnut_Greitens_Testimony.pdf.

4. "The Politburo of the Party Center Reviews 'National Security Strategy 2021–2025,'" Xinhua, November 11, 2021, http://www.gov.cn/xinwen/2021-11/18/content_5651753.htm.

5. "The CCP Central Committee-Formulated Proposal for the 14th Five-Year National Economic and Social Development Plan, and 2035 Long-Term Goals, Xinhua, http://www.xinhuanet.com/2020-10/29/c_1126674147.htm, quoted in Greitens, "Internal Security and Grand Strategy," 1.

6. Cheung, *Innovate to Dominate*, 56.

7. Bing Ye, "Urging CCP Leadership to Hold Expanded Session, Anonymous Post about Taking Down Xi Jinping Circulates Online," Voice of America, March 23, 2020, https://www.voachinese.com/amp/anonymous-letter-demanding-xi-removal-is-widely-spread-online/5340451.html.

8. Guoguang Wu, "Continuous Purges: Xi's Control of the Public Security Apparatus and the Changing Dynamics of CCP Elite Politics," *China Leadership Monitor*, December 1, 2020, https://www.prcleader.org/wu.

9. Zbigniew K. Brzezinski, *The Permanent Purge: Politics in Soviet Totalitarianism* (Cambridge, MA: Harvard University Press, 1956), 23.

10. Ling Li, "Xi's 2021 Political-Legal Rectification Campaign," *China Story* (blog), August 18, 2020, https://www.thechinastory.org/xis-2021-political-legal-rectification-campaign/; Chris Buckley, "Drive the Blade In: Xi Shakes Up China's Law-and-Order Forces," *New York Times*, August 20, 2020, https://www.nytimes.com/2020/08/20/world/asia/china-xi-jinping-communist-party.html.

11. "The Foreign NGO Law and its implementation—LEGAL Path for Foreign NGOs in China," Dentons, March 4, 2021, https://www.dentons.com/en/insights/articles/2021/march/4/the-foreign-ngo-law-and-its-implementation.

12. "Forge the Urban Version of Fengqiao Experience in the New Era," Xinhua, September 24, 2021, http://www.news.cn/mrdx/2021-09/24/c_1310206968.htm; "Promote All-Discipline Grid Construction—Lishi District Constructs Upgraded Version of Fengqiao Experience," *People's Daily*, June 3, 2020, http://sx.people.com.cn/n2/2020/0603/c189133-34061583.html; "Luqiao District in Zhejiang Comprehensively Promotes All Discipline Grid Construction with Significant Achievements," Xinhua, September 20, 2017, http://www.xinhuanet.com/info/2017-09/20/c_136624160.htm.

13. The Working Group on Science and Technology in US-China Relations, "Meeting the China Challenge: A New American Strategy for Technology Competition," UC San Diego 21st Century China Center and Asia Society Center on U.S.-China Relations, November 16, 2020, 41, https://china.ucsd.edu/_files/meeting-the-china-challenge_2020_report.pdf;

14. Michael Forsythe, "Assailants Attack Train Station in Restive Western China," *New York Times*, April 30, 2014, https://www.nytimes.com/2014/05/01/world/asia/blast-hits-railway-station-in-restive-western-china.html.

15. James Leibold, "The Spectre of Insecurity: The CCP's Mass Internment Strategy in Xinjiang," *China Leadership Monitor*, March 1, 2019, https://www.prcleader.org/leibold.

16. Josh Chin, "Leaked Documents Detail Xi Jinping's Extensive Role in Xinjiang Crackdown," *Wall Street Journal*, November 30, 2021, https://www.wsj.com/articles/leaked-documents-detail-xi-jinpings-extensive-role-in-xinjiang-crackdown-11638284709.

17. Leibold, "Spectre of Insecurity."

18. Austin Ramzy and Chris Buckley, "'Absolutely No Mercy': Leaked Files Expose How China Organized Mass Detentions of Muslims," *New York Times*, November 16, 2019, https://www.nytimes.com/interactive/2019/11/16/world/asia/china-xinjiang-documents.html.

19. Chin, "Leaked Documents Detail Xi Jinping's Extensive Role."

20. Lindsay Maizland, "China's Repression of Uyghurs in Xinjiang" (Backgrounder report, Council on Foreign Relations, March 1, 2021), https://www.cfr.org/backgrounder/chinas-repression-uyghurs-xinjiang.

21. Adrian Zenz, "China's Domestic Security Spending: An Analysis of Available Data," Jamestown Foundation China Brief, March 12, 2018, https://jamestown.org/program/chinas-domestic-security-spending-analysis-available-data/.

22. Sheena Chestnut Greitens, "Domestic Security in China under Xi Jinping," *China Leadership Monitor*, no. 59, March 2019, 8, https://www.prcleader.org/greitens.

23. Dru C. Gladney, "Xinjiang: Bridge or Barrier to Xi Jinping's Belt and Road Initiative?," *The Caravan*, no. 1819, September 27, 2018, https://www.hoover.org/research/xinjiang-bridge-or-barrier-xi-jinpings-belt-and-road-initiative.

24. Sheena Chestnut Greitens, Myunghee Lee, and Emir Yazici, "Counterterrorism and Preventive Repression, China's Changing Strategy in Xinjiang," *International Security* 44, no. 3 (Winter 2019/20): 9–47.

25. Gladney, "Xinjiang: Bridge or Barrier."

26. Uradyn E. Bulag, "Minority Nationalities as Frankenstein's Monsters? Reshaping 'the Chinese Nation' and China's Quest to Become a 'Normal Country,'" *China Journal* 86, no. 1 (2021): 46–67, https://doi.org/10.1086/714737.

27. Leibold, "Spectre of Insecurity." https://www.prcleader.org/leibold.

28. In 2011, Tsinghua academic Hu Angang and counterterrorist expert Hu Lianhe called for a "second generation of ethnic policies," that would scale back various preferences

for minority groups while increasing interethnic contacts and mingling. Leibold, "Spectre of Insecurity."

29. James Leibold, "The Not-So-Model Minority: Xi Jinping's Mongolian Crackdown," *China Leadership Monitor*, December 1, 2021, https://www.prcleader.org/leibold-1.

30. Sanskriti Falor, "Explained: What Is the Chinese Govt's 'Sinicization of Religion' Push?'," *The Indian Express*, December 9, 2021, https://indianexpress.com/article/explained/explained-chinese-govt-sinicization-of-religion-7660980/.

31. Gerry Shih, "'Boiling Us Like Frogs': China's Clampdown on Muslims Creeps into the Heartland, Finds New Targets," *Washington Post*, September 20, 2019, https://www.washingtonpost.com/world/asia_pacific/boiling-us-like-frogs-chinas-clampdown-on-muslims-creeps-into-the-heartland-finds-new-targets/2019/09/20/25c8bb08-ba94-11e9-aeb2-a1o1a1fb27a7_story.html.

32. Lily Kuo, "In China, They're Closing Churches, Jailing Pastors – and Even Rewriting Scripture," *The Guardian*, January 13, 2019, https://www.theguardian.com/world/2019/jan/13/china-christians-religious-persecution-translation-bible.

33. Darren Byler, "China's Government Has Ordered a Million Citizens to Occupy Uighur Homes. Here's What They Think They're Doing," "Postcard," ChinaFile, October 24, 2018, https://www.chinafile.com/reporting-opinion/postcard/million-citizens-occupy-uighur-homes-xinjiang.

34. Amy Qin, "In China's Crackdown on Muslims, Children Have Not Been Spared," *New York Times*, December 28, 2019, https://www.nytimes.com/2019/12/28/world/asia/china-xinjiang-children-boarding-schools.html.

35. Leibold, "Spectre of Insecurity."

36. Leibold, "Spectre of Insecurity."

37. Greitens, "Committee on the Elimination of Racial Discrimination Reviews the Report of China."

38. Catherine Wong, "US-China Ties: Washington Funded Terrorists in Xinjiang, Beijing Says," *South China Morning Post*, April 14, 2021, https://www.scmp.com/news/china/diplomacy/article/3129545/us-china-ties-washington-funded-terrorists-xinjiang-beijing.

39. "The Joint Declaration of the Government of the United Kingdom of Great Britain and Northern Island and the Government of the People's Republic of China on the Question of Hong Kong," Constitutional and Mainland Affairs Bureau, Government of the Hong Kong Special Administrative Region of the People's Republic of China, December 19, 1984, https://www.cmab.gov.hk/en/issues/jd2.htm.

40. The decision was from the court's ruling in *Ng Ka Ling and Another v. The Director of Immigration (January 29, 1999)*. See Hong Kong Legal Information Institute, https://www.hklii.hk/cgi-bin/sinodisp/eng/hk/cases/hkcfa/1999/72.html?stem=&synonyms=&query=title(ng%20ka%20ling)&nocontext=1.

41. Alan Wong, "Beijing's 'White Paper' Sets Off a Firestore in Hong Kong," *New York Times*, June 11, 2014, https://web.archive.org/web/20140618000943/http://mobile.nytimes.com/blogs/sinosphere/2014/06/11/beijings-white-paper-sets-off-a-firestorm-in-hong-kong/.

42. Karen Cheung, "Ex-LegCo Head: 2014 White Paper Was Turning Point of Beijing Exercising 'Overall Jurisdiction' in Hong Kong," *Hong Kong Free Press*, November 20, 2017, https://hongkongfp.com/2017/11/20/ex-legco-head-2014-white-paper-turning-point-beijing-exercising-overall-jurisdiction-hong-kong/.

43. Richard Bush considers the rejection of the Beijing proposal to be a "tactical mistake" by the pro-democracy movement. Richard C. Bush, *Hong Kong in the Shadow of China: Living with the Leviathan* (Washington, DC: Brookings Institution Press, 2016).

44. Chris Buckley, Vivian Wang, and Austin Ramzy, "Crossing the Red Line: Behind China's Takeover of Hong Kong," *New York Times*, June 28, 2021, https://www.nytimes.com/2021/06/28/world/asia/china-hong-kong-security-law.html.

45. Buckley, Wang, and Ramzy, "Crossing the Red Line."

46. Buckley, Wang, and Ramzy.

47. Jerome Cohen, personal communication.

48. Kong Tsung-gan, "Arrests and Trials of Hong Kong Protesters and Opposition Leaders," Kong Tsung-gan/Medium (blog), February 16, 2022, https://kongtsunggan.medium.com/arrests-and-trials-of-hong-kong-protesters-and-opposition-leaders-2144f 5d6895b.

49. Kari Soo Lindberg, "China Loyalty Oath Drives 72% of Hong Kong Councilors From Ceats," *Bloomberg*, October 21, 2021, https://www.bloomberg.com/news/articles/2021-10-22/china-loyalty-oath-drives-72-of-hong-kong-councilors-from-seats?sref=I2I6qZII.

50. "Completion of the Seminar for Hong Kong Civil Servants Studying National Conditions Helps Deepen Understanding of 'Patriots Governing Hong Kong,'" China News Service, November 22, 2021, http://www.news.cn/gangao/2021-11/22/c_1211456 480.htm.

51. "Young People from All Walks of Life in Hong Kong Talk about Strengthening Patriotic Education and Integrating into the Overall Situation of National Development," Xinhua, April 27, 2021, http://www.xinhuanet.com/2021-04/27/c_1127384022.htm.

52. Timothy McLaughlin, "How Academic Freedom Ends," *The Atlantic*, June 5, 2021, https://www.theatlantic.com/international/archive/2021/06/china-hong-kong-free dom/619088/June%205,%202021.

53. James Pomfret, "Hong Kong Opens New Modern Art Museum Under National Security Cloud," Reuters, November 11, 2021, https://www.theguardian.com/world/2021/nov/11/hong-kong-opens-modern-art-museum-security-law-casts-pall.

54. "UK Parliament Foreign Affairs Committee (Hong Kong Visit)" (Hansard report 589, UK Parliament, debated December 2, 2014), https://hansard.parliament.uk/Comm ons/2014-12-02/debates/14120247000001/ForeignAffairsCommittee(HongKongVi sit)#contribution-14120262000116; *New York Times*, July 1, 2017, https://www.nytimes.com/2017/07/01/world/asia/hong-kong-china-xi-jinping.html.

55. An Asia Society Policy Institute–Rhodium Group analysis of the sixty-part reform program concluded that of the ten main baskets, there had been either zero progress or actual policy regression in most of them by 2021. Kevin Rudd, "Xi Jinping's Pivot to the State," Asia Society, September 8, 2021, https://asiasociety.org/policy-institute/xi-jinpi ngs-pivot-state.

56. Lingling Wei, "A Rare Look Inside China's Central Bank Shows Slackening Resolve to Revamp Yuan," *Wall Street Journal*, May 23, 2016, https://www.wsj.com/articles/china-preferring-stability-to-free-markets-loses-resolve-to-revamp-currency-1464022 378?mod=article_inline.

57. Charlotte Yang, "Caixin Explains: How a Stock Market Crash Created China's 'National Team'," *Caixin*, October 19, 2018, https://www.caixinglobal.com/2018-10-19/caixin-explains-how-a-stock-market-crash-created-chinas-national-team-101337 087.html.

58. David Wertime and the China team, "The Butterfly Effect Comes For Global Tech," *Protocol*, September 29, 2021, https://www.protocol.com/newsletters/protocol-china/china-tech-butterfly-effect?rebelltitem=1#rebelltitem1.

59. Jing Yang, Keith Zhai, and Quentin Webb, "China's Corporate Crackdown Is Just Getting Started. Signs Point to More Tumult Ahead," *Wall Street Journal*, August 5, 2021, https://www.wsj.com/articles/china-corporate-crackdown-tech-markets-investors-11628182971?mod=article_inline.

60. Jing Yang and Lingling Wei, "China's President Xi Jinping Personally Scuttled Jack Ma's Ant IPO," *Wall Street Journal*, November 12, 2020, https://www.wsj.com/articles/china-president-xi-jinping-halted-jack-ma-ant-ipo-11605203556.

61. Lingling Wei, "China Blocked Jack Ma's Ant IPO After Investigation Revealed Likely Beneficiaries," *Wall Street Journal*, February 16, 2021, https://www.wsj.com/articles/china-blocked-jack-mas-ant-ipo-after-an-investigation-revealed-who-stood-to-gain-11613491292.

62. Jeanny Yu and Emily Cadman, "A $3 Trillion Investor Craze Implodes After Ant's IPO Bust," *Bloomberg*, November 4, 2020, https://www.bloomberg.com/news/articles/2020-11-04/a-3-trillion-investor-craze-comes-undone-after-ant-s-busted-ipo?sref=I2I6qZII.

63. Naoki Matsuda, "Alibaba Market Cap Sinks by Half in a Year Since Ant IPO Shelved," *Nikkei Asia*, November 30, 2021, https://asia.nikkei.com/Business/China-tech/Alibaba-market-cap-sinks-by-half-in-a-year-since-Ant-IPO-shelved.

64. David Bandurski, "Why China Is Cracking Down on Its Online Fandom Obsessed Youth," *Brookings*, November 2, 2021, https://www.brookings.edu/techstream/why-china-is-cracking-down-on-its-online-fandom-obsessed-youth/.

65. Josh Ye, "China Limits Gaming Time for Under-18s to One Hour a Day On Fridays, Saturdays, Sundays and Public Holidays," *South China Morning Post*, August 30, 2021, https://www.scmp.com/tech/policy/article/3146918/china-limits-gaming-time-under-18s-one-hour-day-fridays-saturdays?module=inline&pgtype=article.

66. Barry Naughton, "What's behind China's Regulatory Storm?," *Wall Street Journal*, December 12, 2021, https://www.wsj.com/articles/what-is-behind-china-regulatory-storm-11638372662.

67. Lingling Wei, "China's New Power Play: More Control of Tech Companies' Troves of Data," *Wall Street Journal*, June 12, 2021, https://www.wsj.com/articles/chinas-new-power-play-more-control-of-tech-companies-troves-of-data-11623470478?mod=article_inline.

68. Clay Chandler, Grady McGregor, and Eamon Barrett, "How Didi's Data Debacle Doomed China's Love Affairs with Wall Street," Fortune, July 9, 2021, https://fortune.com/2021/07/09/didi-ipo-stock-data-crackdown-china-wall-street-investors/.

69. "The Opinions on Strictly Cracking Down on Illegal Securities-Related Activity in Accordance with Law," Wilmer Hale, July 12, 2021, https://webcache.googleusercontent.com/search?q=cache:d9eICLjMVdEJ:https://www.wilmerhale.com/en/insights/client-alerts/20210712-china-tightens-control-over-overseas-securities-listings-in-name-of-data-security+&cd=3&hl=en&ct=clnk&gl=us.

70. Josh Chin, "Xi Jinping's Leadership Style: Micromanagement That Leaves Underlings Scrambling," *Wall Street Journal*, December 15, 2021, https://www.wsj.com/articles/xi-jinpings-leadership-style-micromanagement-that-leaves-underlings-scrambling-11639582426.

71. James Palmer, "Why China Is Cracking Down on Private Tutoring," *Foreign Policy*, July 28, 2021, https://foreignpolicy.com/2021/07/28/china-private-tutoring-education-regulation-crackdown/.

72. Chingman Yitong Wu and Gigi Lee, "Shanghai Bans English Exams Amid Calls for Less English Teaching," Radio Free Asia, August 12, 2021, https://www.rfa.org/english/news/china/exams-08122021132625.html.

73. Naughton, "What's behind China's Regulatory Storm?"

74. Kevin Rudd, "Xi Jinping's Pivot to the State," Asia Society, September 8, 2021, https://asiasociety.org/policy-institute/xi-jinpings-pivot-state.

75. "What Xi Means by 'Disorderly Capital' Is $1.5 Trillion Question," *Bloomberg*, September 9, 2021, https://www.bloomberg.com/news/articles/2021-09-09/what-xi-means-by-disorderly-capital-is-1-5-trillion-question?sref=I2I6qZII.

76. Lingling Wei, "China's Xi Ramps Up Control of Private Sector. 'We Have No Choice But to Follow the Party'," *Wall Street Journal*, December 10, 2020, https://www.wsj.com/articles/china-xi-clampdown-private-sector-communist-party-11607612531.

77. Colin Peebles Christensen, "State Advances, Private Retreats," Cheung Kong Graduate School of Business, March 25, 2019, https://english.ckgsb.edu.cn/knowled ges/soes-versus-private-firms-in-china-retreat/.

78. Li Youwei, "Which Way to Go (Part 1)," *Wen Wei Pao*, September 21, 2020, http://www.personpsy.org/uploadfiles/file/paper/%E5%8E%89%E6%9C%89%E4%B8%BA%EF%BC%9A%E8%B7%AF%E5%9C%A8%E4%BD%95%E6%96%B9.pdf. Li Youwei, "Which Way to Go (Part 2)," *Wen Wei Pao*, September 22, 2020, http://www.personpsy.org/uploadfiles/file/paper/%E5%8E%89%E6%9C%89%E4%B8%BA%EF%BC%9A%E8%B7%AF%E5%9C%A8%E4%BD%95%E6%96%B9.pdf.

79. Naughton, "What's behind China's Regulatory Storm?"

80. Barry Naughton, *The Rise of China's Industrial Policy, 1978 to 2020* (Mexico City, Universidad National Autonoma de Mexico, 2021), 72, https://dusselpeters.com/CECHIMEX/Naughton2021_Industrial_Policy_in_China_CECHIMEX.pdf.

81. Xi Jinping, "Several Major Issues in the National Medium and Long-Term Economic and Social Development Strategy," *Qiushi*, October 31, 2020, http://www.qstheory.cn/dukan/qs/2020-10/31/c_1126680390.htm.

82. Sidney Leng and Zheng Yangpeng, "Beijing Tries to Play Down 'Made in China 2025' as Donald Trump Escalates Trade Hostilities," *Politico*, June 26, 2018, https://www.politico.com/story/2018/06/26/beijing-made-in-china-2025-trump-trade-651852.

83. Naughton, *Rise of China's Industrial Policy*, 80–82.

84. Samuel Shen and Josh Horwitz, "China Tech Veterans to Launch 'Domestic Replacement' Fund Amid U.S. Sanctions," Reuters, September 8, 2020, https://www.reuters.com/article/china-tech-fund/china-tech-veterans-to-launch-domestic-repl acement-fund-amid-u-s-sanctions-idUSKBN25Z1R9.

85. Kathrin Hille and Sun Yu, "Chinese Groups Go From Fish to Chips in New 'Great Leap Forward'," *Financial Times*, October 12, 2020, https://www.ft.com/content/46edd 2b2-1734-47da-8e77-21854ca5b212.

86. Jude Blanchette, "From 'China Inc.' to 'CCP Inc.': A New Paradigm for Chinese State Capitalism," *China Leadership Monitor*, December 1, 2020, https://www.prcleader.org/blanchette.

87. Michael Martina, "Exclusive: In China, the Party's Push for Influence Inside Foreign Firms Stirs Fears," Reuters, August 24, 2017, https://www.reuters.com/article/us-china-congress-companies/exclusive-in-china-the-partys-push-for-influence-inside-foreign-firms-stirs-fears-idUSKCN1B40JU.

88. Barry Naughton, "The Financialization of China's State-Owned Enterprises," in *China's Economic Modernization and Structural Changes: Essays in Honor of John Wong*, ed. Yongnian Zheng and Sarah Y. Tong (Singapore: World Scientific, 2019).

89. "China's Communist Authorities Are Tightening Their Grip on the Private Sector," *The Economist*, November 18, 2021, https://www.economist.com/business/chinas-communist-authorities-reinvent-state-capitalism/21806311.

90. Margaret Pearson, Meg Rithmire, and Kellee S. Tsai, "Party-State Capitalism in China," *Current History* 120, no. 827 (September 2021): 207–213, https://online.ucpress.edu/currenthistory/article/120/827/207/118341/Party-State-Capitalism-in-China.

91. David Bandurski, "Open Letter Ups the Ante in the Southern Weekly Incident," China Media Project, Hong Kong University, January 4, 2013, http://cmp.hku.hk/2013/01/04/30311/.

92. The Weibo manager's micro-blog post explaining the situation was translated by Oiwan Lam, "China: Sina Weibo Manager Discloses Internal Censorship Practices," *Global Voices Advocacy*, January 7, 2013, http://advocacy.globalvoicesonline.org/2013/01/07/china-sina-weibo-manager-discloses-internal-censorship-practices/.

93. Over the next several years, the newspaper's reputation and its readership was decimated by the departure of many editors and journalists and the fusion of censorship and market pressures. Maria Repnikova and Kecheng Fang, "Behind the Fall of
China's Greatest Newspaper," *Foreign Policy*, January 29, 2015, https://foreignpolicy.
com/2015/01/29/southern-weekly-china-media-censorship/.

94. An internal version of Xi Jinping's speech on August 19, 2013, was published by
China Digital Times, November 9, 2013, http://chinadigitaltimes.net/chinese/2013/
11/%E7%BD%91%E4%BC%A0%E4%B9%A0%E8%BF%91%E5%B9%B38%E2%80
%A219%E8%AE%B2%E8%AF%9D%E5%85%A8%E6%96%87%EF%BC%9A%E8
%A8%80%E8%AE%BA%E6%96%B9%E9%9D%A2%E8%A6%81%E6%95%A2%E
6%8A%93%E6%95%A2%E7%AE%A1%E6%95%A2/. Interestingly, the initial reporting on the speech by *Xinhua* and *People's Daily* was quite mild and didn't mention a "public opinion struggle," but the PLA Central Political Office issued a more
hard-line interpretation, highlighting Xi's call for a "public opinion struggle" with
Western ideas. One brave commentator wrote in the *China Youth Journal* that the
concept of "public opinion struggle" made many people uneasy because it harkened
back to the bad old days of the Cultural Revolution. Nevertheless, *Xinhua, People's
Daily, Global Times*, and many provincial leaders publicly endorsed the PLA's tough
line, which they must have assumed reflected the true intentions of Xi Jinping, its
commander in chief. See Qian Gang's exegesis of the reporting on Xi's speech,
"Parsing the 'Public Opinion Struggle,'" in China Media Project, September 24,
2013, http://cmp.hku.hk/2013/09/24/34085/.

95. Qian Gang, "Parsing the 'Public Opinion Struggle,'" *China Media Project*,
September 24, 2013, https://chinamediaproject.org/2013/09/24/parsing-chinas-public-
opinion-struggle/.

96. Ya-Wen Lei, *The Contentious Public Sphere: Law, Media and Authoritarian Rule in
China* (Princeton, NJ: Princeton University Press, 2018), 174.

97. "Document 9: A ChinaFile Translation," ChinaFile, November 8, 2013, https://www.
chinafile.com/document-9-chinafile-translation.

98. Zhuang Pinghui, "China's Top Party Mouthpieces Pledge 'Absolute Loyalty' as
President Makes Rare Visits to Newsrooms," *South China Morning Post*, February
19, 2016, https://www.scmp.com/news/china/policies-politics/article/1914136/chinas-
top-party-mouthpieces-pledge-absolute-loyalty. https://www.japantimes.co.jp/news/
2013/10/20/national/all-chinese-journalists-ordered-to-censor-supportive-stances-tow
ard-japan/.

99. "All Chinese Journalists Ordered to Censor Supportive Stances Toward Japan,"
Japan Times, October 20, 2013, https://www.japantimes.co.jp/news/2013/10/20/natio
nal/all-chinese-journalists-ordered-to-censor-supportive-stances-toward-japan/.

100. Xi Jinping, "Explanation of Decision of the CCP Central Committee on Several
Issues in Perfecting the Socialist Market Economy," *People.cn*, November 15, 2013,
http://cpc.people.com.cn/xuexi/n/2015/0720/c397563-27331312.html.

101. Guo Jing, "Xi Jinping Inspects Tencent, Asking Pony Ma How Many Followers He
Has on Weibo," Chinanews.com, December 14, 2012, http://goo.gl/Bc2p4.

102. Cate Cadell, "China Harvests Masses of Data on Western Targets, Documents
Show," *Washington Post*, December 31, 2021, https://www.washingtonpost.com/natio
nal-security/china-harvests-masses-of-data-on-western-targets-documents-show/2021/
12/31/3981ce9c-538e-11ec-8927-c396fa861a71_story.html.

103. Rogier Creemers, Paul Triolo, and Graham Webster, "Xi Jinping's April 20 Speech
at the National Cybersecurity and Informatization Work Conference," New America
Foundation (blog post), April 30, 2018, https://www.newamerica.org/cybersecurity-ini

tiative/digichina/blog/translation-xi-jinpings-april-20-speech-national-cybersecurity-and-informatization-work-conference/.

104. "Xi Jinping: Explanation of the 'Decision of the Central Committee of the Communist Party of China on Several Major Issues of Comprehensively Deepening Reform,'" Xinhua, November 15, 2013, http://www.xinhuanet.com/politics/2013-11/15/c_118164294.htm.

105. Rogier Creemers, Paul Triolo, Samm Sacks, Xiaomeng Lu, and Graham Webster, "China's Cyberspace Authorities Set to Gain Clout in Reorganization," New America Foundation (blog post), March 26, 2018, https://www.newamerica.org/cybersecurity-initiative/digichina/blog/chinas-cyberspace-authorities-set-gain-clout-reorganizat ion/.

106. Charlotte Gao, "'Double-Faced' Lu Wei Jailed for 14 Years for Bribery: China's Former Internet Czar Accepted the Judgment in Court and Said He Would Not Appeal," *The Diplomat*, March 27, 2019, https://thediplomat.com/2019/03/double-faced-lu-wei-jailed-for-14-years-for-bribery/.

107. "Fighting Online Rumors Will Protect Free Speech," Xinhua, *China Daily*, September 10, 2013, https://www.chinadaily.com.cn/china/2013-09/13/content_16969 273.htm.

108. Didi Tang, "China's Latest Tactic: Confessions on State TV," *South China Morning Post*, November 6, 2013, https://www.yahoo.com/news/chinas-latest-tactic-confessi ons-state-152812863.html.

109. Josh Rudolph, "Translation: Essay by Missing Property Tycoon Ren Zhiqiang," *China Digital Times*, March 13, 2020, https://chinadigitaltimes.net/2020/03/translat ion-essay-by-missing-property-tycoon-ren-zhiqiang/.

110. Steven Lee Myers and Amy Chang Chien, "Chinese Journalist Detained after Criticizing Government-Sponsored Blockbuster," *New York Times*, October 8, 2021, https://www.nytimes.com/2021/10/08/world/asia/luo-changping-china-battle-at-lake-changjin.html.

111. Iris Deng and Tracy Qu, "China's Internet Censors Are Taking Down Top Influencers for Not Being Good Enough Socialists," *South China Morning Post*, December 16, 2021, https://www.scmp.com/tech/policy/article/3159947/chinas-internet-censors-are-taking-down-top-influencers-not-being-good.

112. Gao Yu, Ding Gang, Dave Yin, Qin Jianhang, and Timmy Shen, "Coronavirus Whistleblower Li Wenliang Dies of the Disease," *Caixin*, February 7, 2020, https://www.caixinglobal.com/2020-02-07/coronavirus-whistleblower-dies-101512456.html.

113. Yanzhong Huang, "Xi Jinping Won the Coronavirus Crisis: How China Made the Most of the Pandemic It Unleashed," *Foreign Affairs*, April 13, 2020, https://www.for eignaffairs.com/articles/china/2020-04-13/xi-jinping-won-coronavirus-crisis.

114. "Persistence Is Victory," China Media Project, May 5, 2022, https://chinamediaproj ect.org/2022/05/05/persistence-is-victory/.

115. David Stanway and Jennifer Rigby, "Dropping zero-COVID Policy in China without Safeguards Risks 1.5m Lives – Study," Reuters, May 10, 2022, https://www.reuters. com/business/healthcare-pharmaceuticals/china-medical-experts-say-zero-covid-strategy-buys-time-vaccinate-more-people-2022-05-10/.

116. Xu Wen, Cui Xiaotian, Dong Hui, Zhang Yukun and Li Leyan, "Five Things to Know about China's Plans for Regular Mass Covid Testing," *Caixin Global*, June 3, 2022, https://www.caixinglobal.com/2022-06-03/five-things-to-know-about-chinas-plans-for-regular-mass-covid-testing-101894513.html.

117. Arjun Neil Alim, Edward White, and Andy Lin, "China Digs In for Permanent Zero-Covid," *Financial Times*, June 8, 2022, https://www.ft.com/content/d3f3b52c-e4bb-40c2-b2e9-afc2b22f0c19.

118. "China will Surely win Anti-COVID War in Shanghai, With Time-Tested Epidemic Control Policy: Top Leadership" Xinhua, May 6, 2022, https://english.www.gov.cn/news/topnews/202205/06/content_WS62747913c6d02e533532a4de.html.

119. Lingling Wei, "China's Forgotten Premier Steps Out of Xi's Shadow as Economic Fixer," *Wall Street Journal*, May 11, 2022, https://www.wsj.com/articles/china-premier-li-keqiang-xi-jinping-11652277107.

120. Phoebe Zhang and Guo Rui, "China Tightens Curbs on Overseas Travel as Part of Covid-19 Battle," *South China Morning Post*, May 13, 2022, https://www.scmp.com/news/china/politics/article/3177536/china-tightens-curbs-overseas-travel-part-covid-battle.

121. Chen Pengduo, Fan Qiaojia, and Wang Xintong, "Some Chinese Colleges Won't Let Students Graduate without Proof of Employment," Caixin Global, June 8, 2022, https://www.caixinglobal.com/2022-06-08/some-chinese-colleges-wont-let-students-graduate-without-proof-of-employment-101896541.html.

Chapter 10

1. Susan Shirk, "Giving Away Advantage: Donald Trump and Beijing," Global Asia, December 27, 2017, https://www.globalasia.org/login_guide.php?url=https%3A%2F%2Fwww.globalasia.org%3A443%2Fbbs%2Fboard.php%3Fbo_table%3Darticles%26amp%3Bwr_id%3D9242.

2. "In the UN, China Uses Threats and Cajolery to Promote Its Worldview," *The Economist*, December 7, 2019, https://www.economist.com/china/2019/12/07/in-the-un-china-uses-threats-and-cajolery-to-promote-its-worldview.

3. According to Bob Davis and Lingling Wei, *Superpower Showdown: How the Battle between Trump and Xi Threatens a New Cold War* (New York: HarperCollins, 2020), 167, the China strategy was laid out in a ten-page memo drafted for the Trump transition by Matt Pottinger, a former journalist who joined the Trump National Security Council and eventually became the deputy national security adviser.

4. Mary Amiti, Stephen J. Redding, and David E. Weinstein, "Who's Paying for the US Tariffs? A Longer-Term Perspective," AEA *Papers and Proceedings* 110 (2020): 541–546.

5. Josh Rogin, *Chaos under Heaven: Trump, Xi, and the Battle for the Twenty-First Century* (New York: HarperCollins, 2021), 358.

6. Davis and Wei, *Superpower Showdown*, 164.

7. Davis and Wei, 164.

8. Davis and Wei, 164.

9. Davis and Wei, 24–27.

10. "Editorial: The Establishment of An Unreliable Entity List System Sends Two Major Signals," *Global Times*, May 31, 2019, https://opinion.huanqiu.com/article/9CaKrnKkMDG.

11. Lingling Wei, "Chinese Leaders Split over Releasing Blacklist of U.S. Companies," *Wall Street Journal*, September 21, 2020, https://www.wsj.com/articles/chinese-leaders-split-over-releasing-blacklist-of-u-s-companies-11600708688.

12. Semiconductor Industry Association, "Taking Stock of China's Semiconductor Industry" (SIA white paper, July 13, 2021), https://www.semiconductors.org/taking-stock-of-chinas-semiconductor-industry/.

13. Scott Kennedy, "Beijing Suffers Major Loss from Its Hostage Diplomacy," Center for Strategic and International Studies, September 29, 2021, https://www.csis.org/analysis/beijing-suffers-major-loss-its-hostage-diplomacy.

14. Davis and Wei, *Superpower Showdown*, 307.

15. Kennedy, "Beijing Suffers Major Loss."

16. "In a Red Dress, Meng Wanzhou Landed and Delivered a Moving Speech," *Guancha*, September 26, 2021, https://www.163.com/news/article/GKQBGAQ100018990.html.

17. See the footage of Meng singing Ode to the Motherland with the welcoming crowd at the airport, https://www.youtube.com/watch?v=owm5ptbM2NA&ab_channel=CCTV%E4%B8%AD%E6%96%87%E5%9B%BD%E9%99%85.

18. Xi Jinping, "Secure a Decisive Victory in Building a Moderately Prosperous Society in All Respects and Strive for the Great Success of Socialism with Chinese Characteristics for a New Era" (speech delivered at the 19th National Congress of the Communist Party of China, October 18, 2017), http://www.xinhuanet.com/english/download/Xi_Jinping's_report_at_19th_CPC_National_Congress.pdf.

19. "Communiqué of the 6th Plenary Session of the 19th CPC Central Committee," Xinhua, November 11, 2021, https://peoplesdaily.pdnews.cn/china/full-text-communique-of-6th-plenary-session-of-19th-cpc-central-committee-236004.html.

20. "Put People's Life Safety and Health First (Key Choices in the New Era)," *People's Daily*, November 2, 2021, https://wap.peopleapp.com/article/6348610/6238053?mc_cid=0e9e722c33&mc_eid=7b33e85a9e.

21. Davis E. Sanger, "Biden Defines His Underlying Challenge with China: 'Prove Democracy Works,'" *New York Times*, March 27, 2021, https://www.nytimes.com/2021/03/26/us/politics/biden-china-democracy.html.

22. Rogin, *Chaos under Heaven*, 338.

23. "The Many Times Trump Has Praised China's Handling of the Coronavirus Pandemic," CNN, May 19, 2020, https://www.cnn.com/2020/04/21/politics/trump-china-praise-coronavirus-timeline/index.html.

24. Peter Martin, *China's Civilian Army: The Making of Wolf Warrior Diplomacy* (New York: Oxford University Press, 2021), 220.

25. Carolyn Kormann, "The Mysterious Case of the COVID-19 Lab-Leak Theory," *New Yorker*, October 12, 2021, https://www.newyorker.com/science/elements/the-mysterious-case-of-the-covid-19-lab-leak-theory.

26. "Most Americans See China as Having Dealt Poorly with Covid-19," Pew Research Center, July 30, 2020, https://www.pewresearch.org/global/2020/07/30/americans-fault-china-for-its-role-in-the-spread-of-covid-19/pg_20-07-30_u-s-views-china_0-02/.

27. Alice Miranda Ollstein, "Politico-Harvard Poll: Most Americans Believe Covid Leaker from Lab," Politico, July 9, 2021, https://www.politico.com/news/2021/07/09/poll-covid-wuhan-lab-leak-498847.

28. Sarah Wheaton, "Chinese Vaccine Would Be 'Global Public Good,' Xi Says," Politico, May 18, 2020, https://www.politico.com/news/2020/05/18/chinese-vaccine-would-be-global-public-good-xi-says-265039.

29. Yanzhong Huang, "Vaccine Diplomacy Is Paying Off for China," *Foreign Affairs*, March 11, 2021, https://www.foreignaffairs.com/articles/china/2021-03-11/vaccine-diplomacy-paying-china.

30. "China Shows Its Image as a Responsible Country Promoting International Cooperation in the Fight against the Epidemic," *People's Daily*, November 12, 2021, http://paper.people.com.cn/rmrb/html/2021-11/12/nw.D110000renmrb_20211112_4-02.htm.

31. In a 2021 survey by the Carter Center, 77 percent of respondents believed that China is viewed favorably internationally. See "The Pulse: Chinese Public Opinion," *U.S.-China Perception Monitor*, https://uscnpm.org/the-pulse/. Surveys by Haifeng Huang from 2020 and 2021 show that the Chinese public overwhelmingly overestimates China's soft power and global popularity, and that correcting such misperceptions with additional information "moderates Chinese citizens' evaluations of China and

its governing system and lowers their expectations for the country's external success." Haifeng Huang, "Triumphalism and the Inconvenient Truth: Correcting Inflated National Self-Images in a Rising Power" (unpublished paper).

32. Xi Jinping, "Communiqué of 6th Plenary Session of the 19th CPC Central Committee," Xinhua, November 11, 2021, http://www.news.cn/english/2021-11/11/c_131 0305166.htm.

33. Yaoyao Dai and Luwei Rose Luqiu, "China's 'Wolf Warrior' Diplomats Like to Talk Tough," *Washington Post*, May 12, 2021, https://www.washingtonpost.com/politics/2021/05/12/chinas-wolf-warrior-diplomats-like-talk-tough/.

34. Keith Zhai and Yew Lun Tian, "In China, a Young Diplomat Rises as Aggressive Foreign Policy Takes Root," Reuters, March 30, 2020, https://www.reuters.com/article/us-china-diplomacy-insight/in-china-a-young-diplomat-rises-as-aggressive-foreign-pol icy-takes-root-idUSKBN21I0F8.

35. "Sino-US Diplomats' Twitter Scolding War Resumes, and China's Diplomacy Becomes More 'Wolf-Warrior'-like," BBC, July 17, 2019, https://www.bbc.com/zhong wcn/simp/world-49012321.

36. "Western Pride and Prejudice Must Stop," *Global Times*, editorial, July 17, 2019, https://www.globaltimes.cn/content/1158237.shtml.

37. Zhai and Tian, "In China, a Young Diplomat Rises."

38. Daniel C. Mattingly and James Sundquist, "When Does Online Public Diplomacy Succeed? Evidence from China's 'Wolf Warrior' Diplomats," unpublished paper, July 29, 2021, https://static1.squarespace.com/static/51cdc7e5e4b0d7474642bcb0/t/61030 573b20c603771a1282ec/1627587958755/China_Public_Diplomacy_v4.pdf.

39. Martin, *China's Civilian Army*, 9.

40. Glenn Kessler, "Biden's Repeated Claim He Is 'Traveled 17,000 Miles with' Xi Jinping," *Washington Post*, February 19, 2021, https://www.washingtonpost.com/politics/2021/02/19/bidens-repeated-claim-hes-traveled-17000-miles-with-xi-jinping/.

41. Ashley J. Tellis, "Hustling in the Himalayas: The Sino-Indian Border Confrontation," Carnegie Endowment for International Peace, June 4, 2020, https://carnegieen dowment.org/2020/06/04/hustling-in-himalayas-sino-indian-border-confrontat ion-pub-81979.

42. Tellis, "Hustling in the Himalayas." Also see M. Taylor Fravel, "China's Sovereignty Obsession, Beijing's Need to Project Strength Explains the Border Clash with India," *Foreign Affairs*, June 26, 2020, https://www.foreignaffairs.com/articles/china/2020-06-26/chinas-sovereignty-obsession.

43. Davis and Wei, *Superpower Showdown*, 302.

44. Matthew M. Burke and Aya Ichihashi, "Tokyo Again Protests to Beijing about Incursions Near Senkaku Islands in East China Sea," *Stars and Stripes*, January 21, 2021, https://www.stripes.com/news/pacific/tokyo-again-protests-to-beijing-about-inc ursions-near-senkaku-islands-in-east-china-sea-1.659294.

45. See the graph compiled by Japan's Ministry of Foreign Affairs, as of October 31, 2021, https://web.archive.org/web/20190929161826/https://www.mofa.go.jp/files/000465 486.pdf.

46. "On March 17, 2021, Foreign Ministry Spokesperson Zhao Lijian Held Regular Press Conference," Ministry of Foreign Affairs, March 17, 2021, https://www.fmprc.gov.cn/web/fyrbt_673021/t1861952.shtml.

47. Junnosuke Kobara, "Japan Defense Spending Tops 1% of GDP for Fiscal Year," *Nikkei Asia*, November 27, 2021, https://asia.nikkei.com/Politics/Japan-defense-spending-tops-1-of-GDP-for-fiscal-year.

48. "Philippines Throws Support Behind AUKUS Pact," *Radio Free Asia*, September 21, 2021, https://www.rfa.org/english/news/china/pact-09212021152655.html.

49. Derek Grossman, "Duterte's Dalliance with China Is Over," *The Rand Blog*, November 2, 2021, https://www.rand.org/blog/2021/11/dutertes-dalliance-with-china-is-over.html.

50. J. Michael Cole, "China Ends 'Median Line' in the Taiwan Strait: The Start of a Crisis?," National Interest, September 22, 2020, https://nationalinterest.org/feature/china-ends-%E2%80%98median-line%E2%80%99-taiwan-strait-start-crisis-169402.

51. William Langley, "PLA Warplanes Made a Record 380 Incursions into Taiwan's Airspace in 2020, Report Says," *South China Morning Post*, January 6, 2021, https://www.scmp.com/news/china/military/article/3116557/pla-warplanes-made-record-380-incursions-taiwans-airspace-2020.

52. This pattern occurred during leadership transitions during the US–Soviet Union Cold War, according to Li Chen and Odd Arne Westad, "Can Cold War History Prevent U.S.-Chinese Calamity?," *Foreign Affairs*, November 29, 2021, https://www.foreignaffairs.com/articles/china/2021-11-29/can-cold-war-history-prevent-us-china-calamity.

53. Thomas J. Shattuck, "Assessing One Year of PLA Air Incursions into Taiwan's ADIZ," *Global Taiwan Brief* 6, no. 20, October 20, 2021, https://globaltaiwan.org/2021/10/vol-6-issue-20/?mc_cid=f3c668ee20&mc_eid=39b0511b94#ThomasShattuck10202021.

54. James Pomfret and Ben Blanchard, "China's Xi Says Political Solution for Taiwan Can't Wait Forever," Reuters, October 6, 2013, https://www.reuters.com/article/us-asia-apec-china-taiwan/chinas-xi-says-political-solution-for-taiwan-cant-wait-forever-idUSBRE99503Q20131006.

55. Chris Buckley and Chris Horton, "Xi Jinping Warns Taiwan That Unification Is the Goal and Force Is an Option," *New York Times*, January 1, 2019, https://www.nytimes.com/2019/01/01/world/asia/xi-jinping-taiwan-china.html.

56. Yang Sheng, Wang Qi, and Chi Jingyi, "Chinese Mainland Punishes Pro-Secessionist Taiwan Companies 'For Better Cross-Straits Economic Ties, to Push Reunification,'" *Global Times*, November 23, 2021, https://www.globaltimes.cn/page/202111/1239752.shtml; also see "Taiwan Affairs Office of the State Council: Those Who Support 'Taiwan Independence' and Undermine Cross-Strait Relations Will Never Be Allowed to Make Money in the Mainland," Xinhua, November 22, 2021, http://www.gwytb.gov.cn/xwdt/xwfb/wyly/202111/t20211122_12392201.htm.

57. "Taiwan Affairs Office of the State Council: Su Zhenchang, You Xikun, Joseph Wu and a Very Small Number of 'Taiwan Independence' Diehards Are Punished according to Law," Xinhua, November 5, 2021, http://www.gwytb.gov.cn/xwdt/xwfb/wyly/202111/t20211105_12389168.htm.

58. Matthew Strong, "Taiwan Fresh Fruit Exports to China Have Dropped by Half," *Taiwan News*, October 10, 2020, https://www.taiwannews.com.tw/en/news/4320384.

59. Strong, "Taiwan Fresh Fruit Exports to China Have Dropped by Half."

60. "EU Parliament Condemns China Deal Over Hong Kong Crackdown," *Agence France-Presse*, January 22, 2021, https://www.scmp.com/news/world/europe/article/3118743/eu-parliament-condemns-china-deal-over-hong-kong-crackdown.

61. Jorge Liboreiro, "MEPs Vote to Freeze Controversial EU-China Investment Deal," Euronews, June 24, 2021, https://www.euronews.com/2021/05/20/european-parliament-votes-to-freeze-controversial-eu-china-investment-deal.

62. Chris Horton, "The World Is Fed Up with China's Belligerence," *The Atlantic*, November 9, 2021, https://www.theatlantic.com/international/archive/2021/11/china-taiwan-democracy/620647/.

63. Laura Silver, Christine Huang, and Laura Clancy, "Negative Views of China Tied to Critical Views of Its Policies on Human Rights," Pew Research Center, June 29, 2022,

https://www.pewresearch.org/global/2022/06/29/negative-views-of-china-tied-to-criti
cal-views-of-its-policies-on-human-rights/.

64. "EU-Taiwan Relations: MEPs Push for Stronger Partnership," press release, European
Parliament, October 21, 2021, https://www.europarl.europa.eu/news/en/press-room/
20211014IPR14926/eu-taiwan-relations-meps-push-for-stronger-partnership.

65. Wang Haoyu and Tang Qingyuan, "The Strategy of the US: Lie to Everyone,"
Guangming Daily, March 25, 2022, http://world.people.com.cn/n1/2022/0325/c1002-
32384343.html; Yang Chenxi, "The United States Is the "Initiator" of the Russia-
Ukraine Conflict," *Guangming Daily*, March 25, 2022, http://world.people.com.cn/n1/
2022/0325/c1002-32384342.html; Ye Zhu, "International Observation: 'The Empire of
Lies' Is Trying to Deceive the World," People.cn, March 25, 2022, international section,
http://world.people.com.cn/n1/2022/0325/c1002-32384282.html.

66. "2013 PRC-Ukraine Treaty of Friendship and Cooperation/Joint Communiqué: Signed
by Xi, But What's It Worth?," China Analysis from Original Sources, Andrew
S. Erickson website, March 13, 2022, https:/www.andrewerickson.com/2022/03/2013-
prc-ukraine-treaty-of-friendship-cooperation-joint-communique-signed-by-xi-but-
whats-it-worth/.

67. Wang Jisi also makes the point that "a unique feature of Chinese leaders' understanding of their country's history is their persistent sensitivity to domestic disorder
caused by foreign threats." See "China's Search for a Grand Strategy," *Foreign Affairs*,
March–April 2011.

68. Edward D. Mansfield and Jack Snyder, *Electing to Fight: Why Emerging Democracies
Go to War* (Cambridge, MA: MIT Press, 2005).

Conclusion

1. Jia Qingguo, "Thoughts on the Characteristics of National Security and Governance
Principles," *Journal of International Security Studies* 1 (2022): 4–25; also Zhang Jiadong,
"How to Decode America's Three Cards to Contain China?," *Global Times*, January
20, 2022, https://opinion.huanqiu.com/article/46TMTFuOgbL.

2. The Center for China's Relations with Neighboring Countries at Fudan University
convened a group that proposed a concrete plan for a Spratly Resources Management
Authority. See Qi Huaigao, Xue Song, Jolene H. Y. Liew, Evi Fitriani, Ngeow Chow
Bing, Aaron Jed Rambena, and Bui Thi Thus Hien, "Cooperative Research Report
on Joint Development in the South China Sea: Incentives, Policies & Ways Forward,"
Center for China's Relations with Neighboring Countries of Fudan University, Fudan
Development Institute, Network of ASEAN-China Academic Institutes, May 27, 2019,
http://www.iis.fudan.edu.cn/_upload/article/files/9f/21/992faf20465fae26c23ccce1e
cc6/f003a68f-eb6a-4b09-a506-3c00897b0862.pdf.

3. The State Council Information Office of the PRC, August 2019, "White Paper on
Vocational Education and Training in Xinjiang," August 16, 2021, http://www.scio.gov.
cn/ztk/dtzt/39912/41373/41375/Document/1662035/1662035.htm.

4. "China: Democracy That Works," State Council Information Office, December 4,
2021, http://www.china-embassy.org/eng/zgyw/202112/t20211204_10462468.htm.

5. Some of this section reprises what I advised in *China: Fragile Superpower* and what
I continue to believe.

6. "The U.S. and China Must Manage 'Intense Competition,' Top Biden Advisor Says,"
CNBC, October 7, 2021, https://www.cnbc.com/2021/10/08/us-china-must-manage-
intense-competition-top-biden-advisor-says.html.

7. Michael S. Schmidt, "Fears That Trump Might Launch a Strike Prompted General to Reassure China, Book Says," *New York Times*, September 14, 2021, https://www.nyti mes.com/2021/09/14/us/politics/peril-woodward-book-trump.html.

8. Victor Chung Shih, "CCP Decision-Making and the 20th Party Congress," testimony before the U.S.-China Economic and Security Commission, January 27, 2021, https://www.uscc.gov/sites/default/files/2022-01/Victor_Shih_Testimony.pdf.

9. Working Group on Science and Technology in U.S.-China Relations, "Meeting the China Challenge: A New American Strategy for Technology Competition," 21st Century China Center, University of California, San Diego, November 16, 2020, https://china.ucsd.edu/_files/meeting-the-china-challenge_2020_report.pdf.

10. Ruixue Jia, Margaret E. Roberts, Ye Wang, and Eddie Yang, "The Impact of U.S.-China Tensions on U.S. Science," unpublished paper, UC San Diego, 2022, https://www.nber.org/papers/w29941. Also see Sujata Gupta, "Partnerships between US and Chinese Scientists Surge," Nature Index, November 18, 2016, https://www.natureindex.com/news-blog/partnerships-between-us-and-chinese-scientists-surge.

11. Ryan Lucas, "The Justice Department Is Ending Its Controversial China Initiative," National Public Radio, February 23, 2022, https://www.npr.org/2022/02/23/1082593735/justice-department-china-initiative.

12. Kate O'Keeffe, "U.S. Should Restrict Investment in China Due to Security Concerns, Panel Says," *Wall Street Journal*, November 17, 2021, https://www.wsj.com/articles/panel-urges-restricting-u-s-investment-in-china-over-security-concerns-11637163001.

13. Working Group on Science and Technology in U.S.-China Relations, "Meeting the China Challenge."

14. Francis Fukuyama, "One Single Day. That's All It Took for the World to Look Away from Us," *New York Times*, January 5, 2022, https://www.nytimes.com/2022/01/05/opin ion/jan-6-global-democracy.html.

15. "U.S.-EU Trade and Technology Council Inaugural Joint Statement," The White House, September 29, 2021, https://www.whitehouse.gov/briefing-room/statements-releases/2021/09/29/u-s-eu-trade-and-technology-council-inaugural-joint-statement/.

16. Huang Qifan, "Joining CPTPP Is an Important Strategy to Deal with the New Changes," *Caixin*, October 13, 2020, http://opinion.caixin.com/2020-10-13/101614 088.html.

17. Shelley Rigger, Lev Nachman, Chit Wai John Mok, and Nathan Kar Ming Chan, "How Are People Feeling in the 'Most Dangerous Place on Earth'?," Brookings Institution, October 13, 2021, https://www.brookings.edu/blog/order-from-chaos/2021/10/13/how-are-people-feeling-in-the-most-dangerous-place-on-earth/.

18. Steven M. Goldstein, "In Defense of Strategic Ambiguity in the Taiwan Strait," National Bureau of Asian Research, October 15, 2021, https://www.nbr.org/publication/in-defense-of-strategic-ambiguity-in-the-taiwan-strait/.

19. David Sacks, "The United States and Japan Should Prepare for Chinese Aggression against Taiwan," Council on Foreign Relations, January 18, 2022, https://www.cfr.org/blog/united-states-and-japan-should-prepare-chinese-aggression-against-taiwan.

20. Amy Qin and Steven Erlanger, "As Distrust of China Grows, Europe May Inch Closer to Taiwan," *New York Times*, November 10, 2021, https://www.nytimes.com/2021/11/10/world/asia/taiwan-europe-china.html.

21. After COVID the number declined to 317,000 in 2020–2021. Laura Silver, "Amid Pandemic, International Student Enrollment at U.S. Universities Fell 15% in the 2020–21 School Year," Pew Research Center, December 6, 2021, https://www.pewresearch.org/fact-tank/2021/12/06/amid-pandemic-international-student-enrollment-at-u-s-unive rsities-fell-15-in-the-2020-21-school-year/.

22. "Confucius Institutes in the United States: Selected Issues," Congressional Research Service, December 2, 2021, chrome-extension://efaidnbmnnnibpcajpcglclefind mkaj/viewer.html?pdfurl = https%3A%2F%2Fcrsreports.congress.gov%2Fprod uct%2Fpdf%2FIF%2FIF11180.

23. Audrey Conklin, "Republican Lawmakers Warn China Using U.S. 'Sister Cities' to Spy, Gain Influence," Fox Business, March 11, 2021, https://www.foxbusiness.com/polit ics/blackburn-china-us-sister-cities-spy-gain-influence.

24. Silver, "Amid Pandemic, International Student Enrollment at U.S. Universities Fell 15% in the 2020–21 School Year."

25. Rob Schmitz, "Peace Corps to End China Program," National Public Radio, January 24, 2020, https://www.npr.org/2020/01/24/799358578/peace-corps-to-end-china-program.

26. Tom Phillips, "China Universities Must Become Communist Party 'Strongholds', Says Xi Jinping," *The Guardian*, December 9, 2016, https://www.theguardian.com/world/ 2016/dec/09/china-universities-must-become-communist-party-strongholds-says-xi-jinping.

27. Emily Feng and Amy Cheng, "Chinese Universities Are Enshrining Communist Party Control in Their Charters," National Public Radio, January 20, 2020, https://www.npr. org/2020/01/20/796377204/chinese-universities-are-enshrining-communist-party-cont rol-in-their-charters.

28. Teddy Ng, "China's Restrictions on Overseas Academic Exchanges 'Could Harm Policy'," *South China Morning Post*, March 6, 2021, https://www.scmp.com/news/ china/diplomacy/article/3124362/chinas-restrictions-overseas-academic-exchan ges-could-harm.

29. Sichen Li and Weiyi Shi, "Interpersonal Expression of Anti-foreign Sentiment: Evidence from a Parallel Survey in the US and China" (Working Paper, University of California, San Diego).

30. Yan Xuetong, "Becoming Strong, The New Chinese Foreign Policy," *Foreign Affairs*, July/August 2021, https://www.forcignaffairs.com/articles/united-states/2021-06-22/becoming-strong.

Index

For the benefit of digital users, indexed terms that span two pages (e.g., 52–53) may, on occasion, appear on only one of those pages.